"This book is outstanding in so m[any ways... comprehensive] treatment of the turnover topic. T[he reader is exposed to] the literature and constructs being tested, as well as the complex methods being used to study this phenomenon over time, contexts and samples, and the practical implications of these findings. It will serve as the 'go-to' book for years to come."

Terence Mitchell, University of Washington

EMPLOYEE RETENTION AND TURNOVER

This exploration of what employee turnover is, why it happens, and what it means for companies and employees draws together contemporary and classic theories and research to present a well-rounded perspective on employee retention and turnover. The book uses models such as job embeddedness theory, proximal withdrawal states, and context-emergent turnover theory, as well as highlighting cultural differences affecting global differences in turnover.

Employee Retention and Turnover contextualizes the issue of turnover, its causes, and its consequences, before discussing underrepresented antecedents of turnover, key aspects of retention and methods for regulating turnover, and future research directions.

Ideal for both academics and advanced students of industrial/organizational psychology, *Employee Retention and Turnover* is essential for understanding the past, present, and future of turnover and related research.

Peter W. Hom is a Management Professor at the WP Carey School of Business, Arizona State University, USA. He has investigated why people quit, how managers react when their subordinates are being poached, and why employees trapped in jobs misbehave.

David G. Allen is Professor in the Neeley School of Business at Texas Christian University, USA. His teaching, research, and consulting on people and work focus on the flow of human capital into and out of organizations.

Rodger W. Griffeth is a Professor Emeritus in the Psychology Department at Ohio University. He has authored many seminal top-tier journal articles on employee turnover while authoring three books on this topic.

SERIES IN APPLIED PSYCHOLOGY

Bridging both academic and applied interests, the Applied Psychology Series offers publications that emphasize state-of-the-art research and its application to important issues of human behavior in a variety of societal settings. To date, more than 50 books in various fields of applied psychology have been published in this series.

Jeanette N. Cleveland, Colorado State University
Donald Truxillo, Portland State University
Edwin A. Fleishman, Founding Series Editor (1987–2010)
Kevin R. Murphy, Emeritus Series Editor (2010–2018)

Patterns of Life History
The Ecology of Human Individuality
Michael D. Mumford, Garnett Stokes, and William A. Owens

Work Motivation
Uwe E. Kleinbeck, Hans-Henning Quast, Henk Thierry, and Hartmut Häcker

Teamwork and the Bottom Line
Groups Make a Difference
Ned Rosen

Aging and Work in the 21st Century
Edited by Kenneth S. Schultz and Gary A. Adams

Employee Retention and Turnover
Peter W. Hom, David G. Allen, and Rodger W. Griffeth

EMPLOYEE RETENTION AND TURNOVER

Why Employees Stay or Leave

Peter W. Hom, David G. Allen, and Rodger W. Griffeth

Routledge
Taylor & Francis Group
NEW YORK AND LONDON

First edition published 2020
by Routledge
52 Vanderbilt Avenue, New York, NY 10017

and by Routledge
2 Park Square, Milton Park, Abingdon, Oxon, OX14 4RN

Routledge is an imprint of the Taylor & Francis Group, an informa business

© 2020 Taylor & Francis

The right of Peter W. Hom, David G. Allen and Rodger W. Griffeth to be identified as authors of this work has been asserted by them in accordance with sections 77 and 78 of the Copyright, Designs and Patents Act 1988.

All rights reserved. No part of this book may be reprinted or reproduced or utilized in any form or by any electronic, mechanical, or other means, now known or hereafter invented, including photocopying and recording, or in any information storage or retrieval system, without permission in writing from the publishers.

Trademark notice: Product or corporate names may be trademarks or registered trademarks, and are used only for identification and explanation without intent to infringe.

Library of Congress Cataloging-in-Publication Data
A catalog record has been requested for this book

ISBN: 978-1-138-50379-3 (hbk)
ISBN: 978-1-138-50381-6 (pbk)
ISBN: 978-1-315-14558-7 (ebk)

Typeset in Bembo
by Swales & Willis, Exeter, Devon, UK

For Tom Lee, Terry Mitchell, and Bob Vecchio, who provided invaluable inspiration and mentorship for my twilight years as a turnover and embeddedness scholar. For my family (Cheree, Dexter, Theodora, and Sophie) for tolerating my long absences working on this book.

—PWH

I am incredibly grateful for the mentoring, role modeling, and support that Rodger Griffeth and Peter Hom have provided me throughout my career. It was an honor for them to ask me to collaborate on an update of their classic turnover book. Thanks also to my always supportive family, who are not allowed to turn over: Heather, Dawson, and Hadley.

—DGA

For my soulmate Jacqui, my four-legged children, and my grandkids.
—RWG

CONTENTS

List of Figures — xv
List of Tables — xvii
Author Biographies — xviii
Series Foreword — xx
Preface — xxii

1 What is Employee Turnover, Why is it Important, and How is it Measured? The Practical and Academic Significance of Turnover — 1

Definitions of Employee Turnover 3
   Voluntary vs. Involuntary Turnover 3
   Functional and Dysfunctional Turnover 6
   Avoidable and Unavoidable Turnover 7
   Withdrawal Behavioral Construct 8
   Turnover Destinations 9
Collective Turnover 10

2 Turnover Consequences — 17

Consequences for Leavers 18
   Positive Consequences for the Leaver 18
   Negative Consequences for the Leaver 18
   Forfeiture of Seniority and Fringe Benefits 19
   Transition Stress in New Employment 19
   Relocation Costs 20
   Disruption of Spouses' Careers and Marital Discord 21

How Leavers Leave and Where They Go   21
Consequences for Stayers   22
   Opportunities in Promotion and Empowerment for Stayers   22
   Employee Demoralization   22
   Social Network Disruption   23
Consequences for Organizations   24
   Costs and Benefits for Organizations   24
   Negative Consequences for the Organization   25
   Productivity Losses   26
   Impaired Quality of Service   27
   Lost Business Opportunities   29
   Positive Consequences for the Organization   29
      Functional Turnover and Displacement of Poor Performers   29
   Infusion of New Knowledge and Technology   30
   New Business Ventures   31
   Labor Cost Savings   31
   Theories of the Consequences of Turnover Rates and Collective Turnover   31
   Empirical Evidence of the Consequences of Turnover Rates and Collective Turnover   32
   Is There an Optimal Turnover Rate? The Search for Curvilinearity   34
   Executive Post-Acquisition Turnover   37
Future Directions for Research   38
   Study the Processes Linking Collective Turnover to Unit Performance   38
   Track Types of Turnover, Turnover Destinations, and Interactions of Types and Levels of Turnover   38

3   Causes and Correlates of Turnover   47
Demographic and Personal Characteristics   48
Job Satisfaction and Organizational and Work Environment   50
   Commitment   50
   Other Commitment   53
   Met Expectations   53
   Compensation-Related Predictors   53
   Leadership and Supervision   54
   Peer-Group Relations   54
   Role States   55
   Company Climate   55
   Promotions   56
Job Content, Intrinsic Motivation, and Miscellaneous New Constructs   56
   Job Scope   58
   Routinization   58

Work Satisfaction   58
   Job Stress/Exhaustion   58
   Intrinsic or Internal Motivation   58
   Job Involvement   58
   Professionalism   59
   Managerial Motivation   59
 A Variety of New Constructs   59
   New Predictors Weakly Related to Turnover   59
   New Predictors Moderately Related to Turnover   60
   A New Predictor Strongly Related to Turnover   60
   Overall Conclusions for New Variables   60
 External Environment   60
   Alternative Employment   60
   Comparison of Alternatives to Present Job   62
 Probability of Finding Another Alternative   63
   Expected Utility of Alternatives   63
   Withdrawal Cognitions and SEU Beliefs about Withdrawal Acts   63
   Withdrawal Cognitions   63
   Expected Utilities of the Present Job, Searching, and Quitting   63
 Other Withdrawal Behaviors   65
 Concluding Remarks   67

4 Theories of Employee Turnover   72
 March and Simon: Theory of Organizational Equilibrium   72
   Perceived Desirability of Movement   73
   Perceived Ease of Movement   73
   Review   74
 Porter and Steers: Met-Expectation Model   74
   Review   75
 Mobley: Turnover Process Model   76
   Review   77
 Hom and Griffeth: Revised Intermediate Processes Model   78
   Price: Structural Model   81
   Review   82
 Mobley, Griffeth, Hand, and Meglino: Expanded Model   83
   Requisites for Intentions   84
   Job Satisfactio   84
   Expected Utility of the Present Role   84
   Expected Utility of Alternative Roles   84
   Moderators and Distal Determinants   85
   Review   85
 Muchinsky and Morrow: Multidisciplinary Model   86
   Review   86

Farrell and Rusbult: Investment Model 87
  Review 89
Steers and Mowday: Multi-Route Model 90
  Origins of Job Expectations and Attitudes 90
  Affective Responses to the Job 91
  How Job Attitudes Affect Intent to Leave 91
  The Process by Which Job Search Leads to Turnover 91
  Review 92
Sheridan and Abelson: Cusp Catastrophe Model 94
  Review 95
Hulin, Roznowski, and Hachiya: Model of Labor Market Effects 97
  Different Economies Produce Different Workforces 98
  Job Opportunities Directly Influence Job Satisfaction 98
  Job Opportunities Directly Affect Turnover 99
  Review 100
Lee and Mitchell: Unfolding Model 101
  Decision as a Response to Shock 102
  Review 105
Turnover Events and Shocks Scale (TESS) 107
Emerging Theories of Collective Turnover 113

5 The Psychology of Staying: Job Embeddedness 122
Additional Embedding Forces 123
Embeddedness Forms 125
Other Direct and Moderating Effects by Job Embeddedness 126
Multifocal Model of Job Embeddedness 127
Proximal Withdrawal State Theory (PWST) 130
  Reluctant Staying 132
  Reluctant Leaving 132
  Enthusiastic Staying 133
  Enthusiastic Leaving 133
Antecedents of Staying/Leaving Preferences 134
Antecedents of Perceived Volitional Control 136
PWS Subtypes 137
  Enthusiastic Staying Subtypes 137
  Reluctant Staying Subtypes 141
  Enthusiastic Leaving Subtypes 141
  Reluctant Leaving Subtypes 142
The Dark Side of Job Embeddedness 143

6 New Perspectives on Classic Turnover Antecedents   150
Organizational Commitment: Commitment Profiles   150
Job Satisfaction: Satisfaction Trajectories   155
Job Performance: Complex Relationships   160
Movement Ease: Does It Explain Quits?   167

7 Research Streams on Understudied Turnover Antecedents   181
Job Search Mechanism   182
Evolutionary Job Search   183
Leadership Influences   186
     Leader Affect and Relationship Quality   186
     Leader Motivational Behaviors   187
     Leader Humility   188
     Leader Attempts to Predict and Prevent Turnover   190
     Leader Departures   191
Social Networks   194
Personality Influences   197
Cognitive-Affective Processing System Theory   198

8 Methodological Approaches in Turnover Research   206
Standard Research Practice (SRP)   206
Dominant Analytical Mindset (DAM)   207
Statistical Methods of Turnover Prediction   208
     Logistic Regression   208
     Survival Analysis   208
     Cox Regression Model   215
     Random Coefficient Modeling for Assessing Predictor Change   217
Testing Causal Models of the Turnover Process   221
     Structural Equation Modeling (SEM)   222
     SEM Panel Analysis   224
     Latent Growth Modeling (LGM)   227
     Second-Order Factor (SOF) Latent Growth Modeling   230
Applying Other Research Methods   235

9 Controlling Turnover   240
Realistic Job Previews (RJPs)   240
     Theoretical Explanations   242
     Comprehensive Assessments of Mechanisms   244

Practical Design and Implementation 245
Job Complexity as a Moderator of RJP Efficacy 246
Recruitment Source: Employee Referrals 247
Biographical Predictors: Biodata 248
Personality 250
Fit 251
Socializing Newcomers 252
Work Design 255
Compensation and Reward Practices 256
Promising Avenues for Future Research 264

10 Diversity and Global Research on Turnover   276
Domestic Workforce Diversity and Turnover 276
Voluntary Turnover among Women in Male-Dominated Fields 276
Racial Minority Turnover 279
Double Jeopardy: Minority Female Flight 282
International Diversity and Turnover 286
Expatriate Withdrawal 286
Employee Turnover in Other Cultures or Societies 288

11 Future Research Directions   300
Methodological Recommendations for Turnover Research 300
Investigating Change Trajectories 300
Person-Centered Analyses 301
Construct Validation 302
Expanded Research on Shocks, Link Defections, and Turnover Destinations 302
Shocks 302
Link Defections 303
Turnover Destinations 304
Generalization vs. Contextualization 305
Collective Turnover 306
Empirical Research on Turnover Control or Prediction 306

Index   312

FIGURES

4.1	Mobley's (1977) Intermediate Linkages Model	77
4.2	Hom and Griffeth's (1991) Intermediate Linkages Model	79
4.3	Mobley, Griffeth, Hand, and Meglino's (1979) Expanded Turnover Model	83
4.4	Steers and Mowday's (1981) Theory of Employee Turnover	90
4.5	Sheridan and Abelson's (1983) Cusp Catastrophe Model of Turnover	95
4.6	Hulin, Rosznowski, and Hachiya's (1985) Model of Labor Economic Effects	98
4.7	Unfolding Model Paths 1, 2, and 4	103
4.8	Unfolding Model Path 3	104
5.1	Conservation of Resources Multi-Foci Theory of Job Embeddedness	128
5.2	Prime Proximal Withdrawal States	131
5.3	Proximal Withdrawal States Theory	131
5.4	Antecedents of Proximal Withdrawal States	135
5.5	Proximal Withdrawal Substates	137
7.1	Steel's (2002) Evolutionary Search Model of Employee Turnover	184
7.2	A 360-Degree Relational Perspective on Leader Departure Effects	192
7.3	Zimmerman, Swider, Woo, and Allen's (2016) Theory of How Psychological Individual Differences Affect Withdrawal via Cognitive-Affective Units	199
8.1	Standard Research Practice	207
8.2	Computing Hazard Rates for New Nurses	211
8.3	Survival Analysis: Hazard and Survival Functions	212
8.4	Life Table for Computing Survival Probabilities	213

8.5	Hazard and Survival Functions between Treatment and Control Groups (New Nurses Receiving Job Previews or No Previews)	214
8.6	Discrete-Hazard Survival Analysis Demonstrating RJP Effect on Nursing Turnover	215
8.7	Estimated Continuous Hazard Functions for RJP and Control Nurses	216
8.8	Individual Variability in Regression Equations	218
8.9	Average Trajectory and Between-Person Variance in Trajectory	219
8.10	Trajectory of Change for Organizational Commitment between Stayers and Leavers	221
8.11	Hom and Kinicki's (2001) Latent Variables Structural Model	223
8.12	Cross-Lagged Latent Variables Structural Model	225
8.13	Nested Models Specifying Different Causal Directions	226
8.14	Cross-Lagged LV Structural Model for Multiple Waves	227
8.15	First-Order Factor Latent Growth Model	228
8.16	Using FOF LGM to Test Dynamic Relationships in Ajzen's (1991) Theory of Planned Behavior	229
8.17	Longitudinal Measurement Model for Indicators Assessing the Same Construct	231
8.18	Second-Order Factor Latent Growth Model	232
8.19	Second-Order Factor Latent Growth Model for Withdrawal Cognitions	233
8.20	Second-Order Factor LGM Model Predicting Time-4 Withdrawal Cognitions	234
9.1	Hom and Griffeth's (1995) Model of How Pay Satisfaction and Its Antecedents May Affect Turnover	259
10.1	Fitzgerald, Drasgow, Hulin, Gelfand, and Magley's (1997) Model of Sexual Harassment	278
10.2	Theory of Repatriation by Self-Initiated Expatriates	287

TABLES

2.1	Voluntary Turnover Costs and Benefits	24
2.2	Meta-Analysis of Direct Relationships between Employee Turnover and Types of Organizational Performance	33
2.3	Meta-Analysis of Employee Turnover and Overall Organizational Performance Moderators	35
3.1	Individual Demographic and Personal Characteristics	49
3.2	Job Satisfaction and Organizational and Work Environment Factors	51
3.3	Job Content, Intrinsic Motivation, and Miscellaneous New Constructs	57
3.4	Alternative Employment	61
3.5	Withdrawal Cognitions	64
3.6	Other Withdrawal Behaviors	66
4.1	TESS Item Correlations with Intentions to Quit (BIQ) and Means, Standard Deviations, Independent T-Test Values, and Probability Levels for Staying and Quitting Social Workers	110
5.1	Theoretical Summary and Integration	138
6.1	Employment Opportunity Index (EOI)	172
9.1	Evidence-Based HR Management Strategies for Reducing Turnover	241

AUTHOR BIOGRAPHIES

Peter W. Hom is a Professor of Management at the WP Carey School of Business, Arizona State University. He has investigated why people quit, how managers react when subordinates are being poached by other employers, and why employees trapped in jobs may misbehave. Currently, he studies how different mindsets arise from different reasons for staying, how human resource management practices affect collective turnover in Brazil, and how leader departures undermine followers' attachment to organizations. He and Rodger Griffeth won the 1992 Scholarly Achievement Award from the Human Resource Management Division of the Academy of Management. He has authored three books on turnover and serves on the editorial boards for the *Journal of Applied Psychology*, *Academy of Management Journal*, and *Journal of Management*.

David G. Allen, Ph.D., is Associate Dean for Graduate Programs and Professor of Management and Leadership at the Neeley School of Business at Texas Christian University; Distinguished Research Environment Professor at Warwick Business School; and Editor-in-Chief of the *Journal of Management*. His teaching, research, and consulting cover a wide range of topics related to people and work, with a particular focus on the flow of human capital into and out of organizations. His award-winning research has been regularly published in the field's top journals, and he is the author of the book *Managing Employee Turnover: Dispelling Myths and Fostering Evidence-Based Retention Strategies*. Professor Allen is a Fellow of the American Psychological Association, the Society for Industrial and Organizational Psychology, and the Southern Management Association.

Rodger W. Griffeth is a Professor Emeritus in the Psychology Department at Ohio University. He first advanced the turnover literature by developing a comprehensive and integrative theory of turnover causes with Bill Mobley (*Psychological Bulletin*, 1979), which later dominated turnover perspectives for decades. He next extended referents cognition theory to clarify how organizational injustice impacts turnover (*Academy of Management Journal*, 1997). Later, he teamed up with Carl Maertz to develop a motive-based theoretical synthesis to explain turnover and attachment behavior (*Journal of Management*, 2004). Further, he proposed "proximal withdrawal states theory" with Tom Lee and Terry Mitchell (*Psychological Bulletin*, 2012) to elucidate how different participation or withdrawal mindsets drive different attitudes and behaviors. Besides theoretical contributions, he and Peter Hom tested Mobley's (1977) theory about the process which dissatisfaction impels quits. Structural equations modeling and meta-analytic tests supported an alternative "intermediate linkage" model (*Journal of Applied Psychology*, 1991, 1992). With Robert Steel, he demonstrated the shortcomings of prevailing operationalizations of employees' perceptions of job alternatives, while introducing a more comprehensive assessment of employee views of the labor market that better explain turnover (*Journal of Applied Psychology*, 1989, 1995). Finally, he and David Allen showed that performance visibility and reward contingency moderate performance–turnover relationships, identifying conditions when dysfunctional turnover arises (*Journal of Applied Psychology*, 2001).

SERIES FOREWORD

The goal of the Applied Psychology series is to create books that exemplify the use of scientific research, theory, and findings to help solve real problems in organizations and society. Hom, Allen, and Griffeth's *Employee Retention and Turnover: Why Employees Stay or Leave* exemplifies this approach. We believe that this book will quickly become the go-to reference for research and practice on virtually every aspect of employee attachment. Within this exciting book, three leading experts in this field of study adeptly introduce new ways of viewing classic turnover antecedents and consequences, reflecting a more wholistic view of employee experiences of organizational life.

This authored book includes 11 chapters dealing with a wide range of current as well as emerging theories of turnover. This includes traditional issues such as the diverse definitions of the turnover construct, its causes, consequences, and correlates. This is followed by a review of classic models of turnover and enriched by the description and introduction of more complex and emerging theories. Consistent with the wholistic view, Hom and colleagues address not only what organizations want to avoid—turnover—but also what organization want to achieve—job embeddedness. We know of no other book that examines both turnover and job embeddedness together.

In addition, several chapters take a forward-looking and novel approach to turnover and job embeddedness. For example, Chapter 7 examines a number of relevant yet understudied turnover antecedents, including the role of job search, leadership, social networks, and personality in relation to turnover. In Chapter 8, the authors address methodological issues, including needed research designs for understanding turnover and the use of new statistical methods for predicting it. Chapter 9 includes a number of practical suggestions for interventions that organizations can use to control turnover, including realistic job previews, recruitment strategies, selection, socialization, and work design. Importantly, in Chapter 10, the authors address emerging issues in relation to turnover, such as the changing nature of our society and workplaces, diversity, and global issues.

The chapters in this volume are thorough and thought-provoking, and they cover a broad range of important, current, and emerging workplace issues. We are confident that *Employee Retention and Turnover: Why Employees Stay or Leave* will become an essential resource for both researchers and practitioners, impacting both future research questions as well as science-based practice.

We are thrilled to add *Employee Retention and Turnover: Why Employees Stay or Leave* to the Applied Psychology series. This book accomplishes the goals that exemplify the challenge of balancing the science and practice goals of this series, bringing together the best scholarship and new and emerging ideas to address problems that are becoming increasingly important in the workplace.

Jeanette N. Cleveland
Donald Truxillo

PREFACE

We began our book *Employee Turnover* (1995) to summarize the emerging theorizing and research in employee turnover began by Chuck Hulin, Lyman Porter, Bill Mobley, and Jim Price in the late 1960s and 1970s. Their seminal works initiated the then-modern era of developing and testing turnover theories. While other books (including those by these pioneers) on turnover were published in the 1980s, they readily became dated given the plethora of new theories and empirical findings. Twenty-five years later, we find our 1995 book to be extremely dated in the wake of a continued avalanche of new theorizing and empirical discoveries occurring since its publication. Indeed, a paradigm shift (such as started by Tom Lee and Terry Mitchell's unfolding model, and other less momentous tremors) began since our "first" edition.

Our current edition strives to review the key highlights in theory and research since the 1995 edition. While much of the research transpiring since then has been incremental (e.g., recent meta-analyses about effect sizes of various turnover predictors replicate earlier meta-analytical findings), there have been major developments theoretically and empirically. As we later note, Tom Lee and Terry Mitchell have formulated novel and insightful theories about staying and leaving (aka job embeddedness and the unfolding model) that have changed our understanding and research undertakings. Most contemporary scholarly inquiries since the advent of the twentieth century had been inspired by their thinking and how they tested their conceptual innovations (e.g., pioneering qualitative methodology). They have become central figures in the annals of turnover research, much like March and Simon (1958). Not surprisingly, our latest book devotes entire sections—if not a whole chapter—to their prodigious scholarly achievements.

Since 1995, withdrawal scholars have also forged new and productive research trends in other ways. In particular, they have begun investigating collective turnover (moving beyond individual-level turnover) and identifying its distinct causes and consequences. Other investigators are applying new statistical methods for analyzing longitudinal repeated-measures data to assess the trajectory of change of turnover causes, identifying their potential for predicting turnover and verifying dynamic relationships implicit in most process-oriented models. Moreover, emerging research is revisiting potential antecedents long neglected in prevailing formulations about staying or leaving, such as personality traits (moderating relationships between quit intentions and quits) and leadership influences (e.g., certain leader personality traits can deter leaving, while leader defections may induce leaving). In keeping with our original suggestions in 1995, international research on domestic frameworks across different nationalities and cultures has proliferated in recent years, affirming their generality as well as identifying their theoretical shortcomings abroad.

Originally, we credit Chuck Hulin and Bill Mobley for starting our early journey on turnover research and Jim Price for keeping us on this path. Now we express gratitude to Terry Mitchell and Tom Lee for maintaining our journey during our mature years by reinvigorating our passion and igniting creative thoughts about "future" turnover research. After all, even senior citizens like Peter and Rodger can still benefit from mentors. We thank Bob Vecchio, who was our beloved friend and inspirational role model, for publishing one of our most-cited turnover meta-analyses while he was the editor of the *Journal of Management*. For David, it was Rodger Griffeth who mentored him into turnover research and this scholarly career and Peter Hom who serves as an ongoing mentor. The opportunity to collaborate on updating the classic Hom–Griffeth 1995 book is a career highlight. We also acknowledge the contributions of Jamila Maxie for organizing the extensive references provided in this book. Further, we thank the countless Ph.D. students and colleagues who made the journey fun and worthwhile, such as Min Carter, Julie Gaffney, Tim Gardner, Brooks Holtom, Ralph Katerberg, Angelo Kinicki, Kiazad Kohyar, Amy Ou, Jamie Seo, Debra Shapiro, Anne Tsui, James Vardaman, and Jason Wu. Finally, we owe a tremendous debt to our families for their patience and understanding. Because some are illiterate (aka our dogs), they will never read our book, but we thank them nonetheless for keeping us happy and entertained all these years.

1

WHAT IS EMPLOYEE TURNOVER, WHY IS IT IMPORTANT, AND HOW IS IT MEASURED?

The Practical and Academic Significance of Turnover

Employee turnover—or voluntary termination of employees from employing organizations (Mobley, 1982)—has attracted interest from employers and scholars alike for a century (Hom, Lee, Shaw, & Hausknecht, 2017). As early as 1917, management consultants and academicians have written about turnover's costs, its amelioration, and its causes (Hom et al., 2017). Managers have long focused on employee turnover because of the personnel costs incurred when employees quit, such as those for hiring and training replacements (Cascio, 2000). To illustrate, turnover costs can range from 90% to 200% of annual pay (Allen, Bryant, & Vardaman, 2010). Though difficult to compute for some occupational fields, turnover can impair productivity because short-staffed workforces may underproduce, while inexperienced replacements may produce inefficiently during early employment (Hom & Griffeth, 1995).

Beyond such familiar tangible expenses, other ramifications of high turnover may prove costly or worrisome (Hom & Griffeth, 1995). In particular, corporate America frets about excessive attrition among minority and female incumbents that can impede its progress toward a diversified staffing in executive posts or occupational fields where these demographic subgroups are underrepresented (Hom, Roberson, & Ellis, 2008). What is more, human capital loss can stymie how firms deliver products or services or even enter new markets. Thus, talent recruiters at Fortune 1000 firms report that unfilled STEM (science, technology, engineering, and mathematics) jobs resulted in "lower productivity" (56%) and "limits to business growth" (47%; Bayer Corporation, 2014). While the existence of a STEM shortage is widely debated, STEM attrition surely worsens the dysfunctional effects of insufficient STEM supply in firms (Mervis, 2014). Further, such talent losses most harm source firms when leavers join competing (destination) firms (and thus supply proprietary knowledge or former clients to them), or becoming new competitors (as start-ups; Campbell, Ganco, Franco, & Agarwal, 2012; Somaya, Williamson, & Lorinkova, 2008; Wezel, Cattani, & Pennings, 2006). Finally, turnover can endanger entire industries, such as manufacturing in export-oriented processing zones in developing countries (notably, China and Mexico). There, 60% to 100% turnover rates among Chinese and Mexican assemblers (Miller, Hom, & Gomez-Mejia, 2001; Qin, Hom, & Xu, 2019; West, 2004) can boost labor costs, product defects, and production shortfalls, and thus hamper global supply chains (dependent on finished goods) and export-driven growth of emerging economies (Jiang, Baker, & Frazier, 2009).

Although turnover remains a perennial concern for employers, it continues to be a lively and enduring fascination for scholarly inquiry. Though such investigations began 100 years ago (Hom et al., 2017), March and Simon (1958) legitimize this scholarly focus by theorizing that effective organizational functioning hinges on employee decisions to perform as well as their decisions to *participate* (vs. withdraw from organizations, aka turnover). Over 1,000 articles have appeared on this topic alone (Steers & Mowday, 1981). Employee turnover is a popular criterion for validating or extending general theories of motivation, such as expectancy theory (Hom, 1980), equity theory (Dittrich & Carrell, 1979), the theory of reasoned action (Hom & Hulin, 1981; Westaby, 2005), and the theory of planned behavior (Van Breukelen, Van der Vlist, & Steensma, 2004). Moreover, theories of organizational behavior often regard turnover as one among many outcomes of their motivational processes. To illustrate, models about job characteristics (Grant, 2007; Hackman & Oldham, 1980), leadership (Graen & Ginsburgh, 1977; Nishii & Mayer, 2009), influence tactics (Reina, Rogers, Peterson, Bryon, & Hom, 2018), and network closure (Hom & Xiao, 2011) explicate how turnover may arise from their central explanatory constructs.

Of course, employee turnover is a significant motivated behavior in its own right, inspiring theoretical formulations explicating its occurrence. Pioneering the first formal theory of turnover, March and Simon (1958) theorized that leaving hinges on movement desirability and ease. Drawing from this model, Price (1977; Price & Mueller, 1981) and Mobley (1977; Mobley, Griffeth, Hand, & Meglino, 1979) derived models that represent movement desire and ease with job satisfaction and job alternatives, respectively. Early—and successful—validations of the Price–Mobley models (Mobley, Horner, & Hollingsworth, 1978; Price & Mueller, 1981) inspired widespread empirical and theoretical critiques of these models (Hom, Caranikis-Walker, Prussia, & Griffeth, 1992; Price & Mueller, 1986). Over the next 15 years, other theorists began revising the first-generation Price–Mobley models by reconfiguring structural pathways (Hom & Kinicki, 2001) or elaborating subsystems (e.g., job search → quit path or dissatisfaction → quit path; Hulin, Roznowski, & Hachiya, 1985; Steel, 2002), expanding the array of causal determinants (Steers & Mowday, 1981), or reconceptualizing the turnover process (e.g., invoking turnover drivers besides job attitudes and specifying additional turnover paths; Lee & Mitchell, 1994). Breaking away from the March–Simon legacy, other scholars adapted turnover models from other research traditions, such as Rusbult and Farrell's (1983) investment model (based on Kelley and Thibaut's interdependence theory) and Sheridan and Abelson's (1983) cusp catastrophe model. In a radical departure from historic focus on why people quit, Mitchell, Holtom, Lee, Sablynski, and Erez (2001) envisioned the forces on why people stay, introducing job embeddedness. Embeddedness scholarship has since dominated modern turnover research, demonstrating that this construct explains additional variance in turnover beyond that by standard turnover antecedents, but also other workplace behaviors (Lee, Burch, & Mitchell, 2014; Li, Lee, Mitchell, Hom, & Griffeth, 2016).

Rather than testing comprehensive or complex theories about turnover (the dominant concern of turnover scholarship) per se, other scholars scrutinize special turnover phenomena, such as the relationship between individual (or firm) performance and turnover (Shaw, 2011; Sturman, Shao, & Katz, 2012), turnover contagion (Felps et al., 2009; Shapiro, Hom, Shen, & Agarwal, 2016), the impact of job-satisfaction trajectories (Liu, Mitchell, Lee, Holtom, & Hinkin, 2012), the honeymoon-hangover effect (Wang, Hom, & Allen, 2017), commitment mindsets (Hom, Mitchell, Lee, & Griffeth, 2012; Xu & Payne, 2018), high-performance work practices (Hom et al., 2009), social network effects (Ballinger, Cross, & Holtom, 2016; Feeley & Barnett, 1997), employee guarding (Gardner, Munyon, Hom, & Griffeth, 2018), and resignation styles (Klotz & Bolino, 2016). In summary, employee turnover is a crucial organizational phenomenon that has commanded longstanding and pervasive attention from managers and scholars for over a century. While organizations worry about turnover's varied dysfunctional effects, academicians regard turnover as a striking expression of employee malaise or organizational malfunction.

Definitions of Employee Turnover

Voluntary vs. Involuntary Turnover

Employee turnover is classically defined as an employee's "voluntary" severance of his or her current employment ties (Mobley, 1982; Price, 1977). Scholars have focused on employees' self-initiated leaving because such behavior represents the most appropriate criterion for validating theories of "individual motivated choice behavior" (Campion, 1991, p. 199), while employers are most concerned because they have less control over this form of leaving than involuntary terminations. To illustrate, prevailing theories of turnover presume that employees autonomously decide to terminate their employment because they find the job disagreeable or find other jobs more appealing (Hom & Griffeth, 1995). This standard definition construes voluntary quits as separations from employing organizations and excludes promotions, job transfers, or other internal job movements. Further, this notion typically excludes cessation of membership in organizations where members receive no payment, such as volunteers, interns, and parishioners (though turnover models have been generalized to explain their departures).

Given its intuitive appeal, many researchers and practitioners operationally measure voluntary turnover as a dichotomy, differentiating *employee-initiated* terminations from *employer-initiated* (e.g., dismissals, layoffs). Despite their simplicity, the types of leaving that constitute voluntary self-determined quits often vary across employers and scholars (Mobley et al., 1979), making determination of whether turnover is voluntary or not difficult. To illustrate, some researchers regard pregnancy as a form of voluntary exit (Lee, Mitchell, Wise, & Fireman, 1996; Marsh & Mannari, 1977), though others say otherwise (Mirvis & Lawler, 1977; Waters, Roach, & Waters, 1976). Moreover, changing laws and human resource management practices may prompt redefinition of turnover voluntariness. While traditionally construed as a form of involuntary turnover (Hanisch & Hulin, 1990), retirement increasingly resembles voluntary turnover as mandatory retirement is now outlawed and employees increasingly receive defined contribution (e.g., 401K) instead of defined benefits plans (enabling them to retire on their own timetable when they have accumulated enough pension funds; Hom, 2011).

Besides inconsistent classification, the measurement of the causes or reasons for leaving is also subject to various errors. Turnover research often relies on personnel files from employers who determine via exit interviews or supervisory observations to ascertain turnover motives. Yet exiting employees may not reveal truthfully their reasons for leaving to avoid "burning their bridges" (thus underreporting negative job events; Griffeth & Hom, 2001; Hom, 2011). Employers or supervisors too may distort official records, such as classifying firings as voluntary quits to safeguard leavers' reputation (and avoid defamation lawsuits) or recording voluntary quits as layoffs to enable leavers to qualify for unemployment compensation (Hom & Griffeth, 1995). Indeed, Mobley et al. (1979) had long recognized that "personnel practitioners readily admit that a variety of factors influence the administratively recorded reason for attrition" (p. 515). Further, existing classification schemes may be deficient by failing to capture all exit reasons or recording only one reason when multiple ones underlie leaving (Campion, 1991).

Given that accurate determination of turnover voluntariness is crucial for its prediction and control, it behooves scholars and firms to give more attention to criterion measurement. Conceivably, the simplistic remedy is to classify all turnover cases as voluntary (regardless of reason, and thus obviating the need to assess leavers' motives) if they are *not* officially initiated by employers. Such an approach fits with Maertz and Campion's (1998) definition of voluntary turnover as "instances wherein management agrees that the employee had the physical opportunity to continue employment with the company, at the time of termination" (p. 50). Thus, "voluntariness means that there was no impediment to continued employment from physical disability or from company management" (p. 50). Under this system, all reasons other than dismissals, layoffs, or retirement would represent voluntary quits (e.g., quitting due to pregnancy or spousal relocation) as they imply "individual choice, even though the employee may feel as though the choice to stay is extremely costly" (p. 51).

All the same, scholars and employers often prefer fine-grained assessment of turnover voluntariness that includes assessment of quit motives to enable more effective turnover management and prediction (Hom & Griffeth, 1995; Mobley et al., 1979). To illustrate, determination that so-called "voluntary" quits are often driven by family reasons (e.g., leaving to care for dependents or follow a relocating spouse) than job dissatisfaction or perceived alternatives (standard turnover causes; Hom et al., 2017) suggests that prevailing turnover models can be enhanced by including predictors reflecting external influences (Price & Mueller, 1986) that can forecast such exits (such as work–family conflicts, anticipated spousal relocations, or family pressures to quit; Hom & Kinicki, 2001; Lee et al., 1996; Maertz & Campion, 2004). While exit interviews are common ways to assess quit motives (Griffeth & Hom, 2001), turnover scholars since Mobley et al. (1979) have long prescribed additional assessments for triangulation (Hom & Griffeth, 1995), such as delayed or third-party *confidential* surveys or interviews with leavers (Hom, 2011), given that leavers often misrepresent their motives to firm representatives at departure time (Campion, 1991; Hom et al., 2012). Attesting to the value of assessing employees' perception over volitional control over leaving, Li et al. (2016) demonstrated that job attitudes and job embeddedness more accurately predict turnover among *enthusiastic* stayers and leavers (people who either want to—and can—stay or leave). By contrast, those antecedents poorly predicted turnover among *reluctant* stayers and leavers (employees perceiving little control over their decisions to stay or leave). These findings dispute the classic definition of voluntary quits as employee-initiated exits (or turnover *not* mandated by employers), revealing that such quits still vary in perceived or experienced voluntariness.

Although more valid and thorough assessment of turnover reasons may increase accuracy of classifying whether or not a turnover case is voluntary, Campion (1991) and Maertz and Campion (1998) noted that "mutual separations" (where both employees and employers agree to end their relationships), quitting to avoid expected dismissals, or leaving to follow a relocating spouse include both voluntary and involuntary aspects. Maertz and Campion (1998) thus recommend measuring turnover voluntariness as a *continuous* rather than dichotomous variable, perhaps via employee self-reports as they do not closely match supervisory perceptions of turnover voluntariness (Campion, 1991). In support, Batt and Colvin (2011) found that some HR practices similarly affected voluntary and involuntary turnover (as classically defined) in call centers. Specifically, "performance-enhancing HR" practices (commission pay, monitoring intensity) boost voluntary quits (as such conditions induce more job stress) as well as involuntary quits (as consistently low or few commissions signal that poor performers will likely face dismissal).

Functional and Dysfunctional Turnover

While voluntary turnover was historically prescribed as the best (or most appropriate) criterion for validating models of motivated choice (Mobley et al., 1979; Price, 1977), Dalton and colleagues (Dalton, Krackhardt, & Porter, 1981; Dalton & Todor, 1979) also suggested "turnover functionality"—or voluntary turnover that has functional (rather than dysfunctional) effects for organizations, such as the loss of poor-performing or "overpaid" employees. This categorization scheme emerged when scholars began disputing the conventional view that turnover is inherently bad for organizations, arguing that functional turnover can prevent stagnation, enhance promotional opportunities for lower-level employees, and displace marginal performers (Mobley, 1982; Staw, 1980). By comparison, dysfunctional turnover represents turnover among high performers or those that have difficult-to-replace skills or competencies.

More formally, Hollenbeck and Williams (1986) operationally defined turnover functionality as $T_{funct} = T_{freq} \times Z$, where T_{freq} represents whether or not the employee voluntarily resigned (coding stayers as +1 and leavers as −1) and Z is a standardized performance measure. T_{funct} is thus a continuous variable with positive scores representing functional turnover, which includes a higher performer staying (positive Z-score multiplied by +1) or a poor performer leaving (negative Z-score multiplied by −1). Negative scores, however, represent dysfunctional turnover as either a top performer quits (positive Z-score multiplied by −1) or a low performer stays (negative Z-score multiplied by +1). While the Hollenbeck–Williams index is rarely used in turnover research (to our knowledge), the notion of dysfunctional turnover has profoundly influenced turnover research and management. Thus, a long and independent research stream has investigated the relationship between job performance and turnover (Allen & Griffeth, 2001; Salamin & Hom, 2005; Williams & Livingstone, 1994) as its sign suggests whether turnover is generally functional (negative; low performers quit more than high performers) or dysfunctional (positive; high performers quit more than low performers). Corporate America now routinely tracks (and benchmarks) various forms of dysfunctional turnover, such as quits among high performers, incumbents in critical occupational fields (e.g., STEM, executives), or racial minorities (Hom, 2011; Hom et al., 2008). Although the loss of women or underrepresented minorities may not necessarily affect organizational effectiveness, their higher attrition will surely prevent firms from achieving a more diversified workforce.

Avoidable and Unavoidable Turnover

Abelson (1987) further differentiated between organizationally "unavoidable" and "avoidable" turnover. The former includes employee separations that employers *cannot* control, such as quits due to full-time dependent care, family moves, medical disability, or death, whereas the latter includes dissatisfying workplace features (or inferior conditions relative to other workplaces), such as supervisory abuse or better pay elsewhere. By focusing on avoidable turnover, organizations can more precisely gauge the severity of turnover (which is overestimated when including unavoidable turnover; cf. Griffeth & Hom, 2001). Turnover researchers can more accurately forecast avoidable turnover with conventional predictors such as job attitudes and perceived alternatives (Barrick & Zimmerman, 2005; Price & Mueller, 1981).

Despite its intuitive appeal, determining whether turnover is avoidable or unavoidable may prove difficult as employees may misrepresent why they are leaving during exit interviews (Dalton et al., 1981). They likely overstate unavoidable reasons, such as leaving to follow relocating spouses or to care for dependents full-time, rather than cite poor working conditions or abusive bosses (Hom, 2011). Even supervisors may overstate unavoidable causes in official records as high avoidable turnover may reflect poorly on their leadership (Hom et al., 2012). Moreover, many firms realize that they can more effectively reduce turnover—especially among women, baby boomers, and millennials—if they tackle unavoidable quits, such as providing various family- and lifestyle-friendly programs (e.g., telecommuting, flexible work schedules, phased retirement) that help employees resolve work–family or work–lifestyle conflicts (Griffeth & Hom, 2001). Further, contemporary theories since March and Simon (1958) increasingly incorporate theorized antecedents of unavoidable turnover, such as work–family conflict (Hom & Kinicki, 2001), preexisting plans to quit (e.g., planned pregnancy; Lee & Mitchell, 1994) or family pressures to leave (Maertz & Griffeth, 2004). Unlike traditional theories (March & Simon, 1958) that seem well suited for predicting avoidable turnover, these expanded formulations have the potential to enhance the predictability of *overall* voluntary turnover.

Over the years, turnover scholars have long recommended that organizations apply these three classification schemes (voluntariness, functionality, and avoidability) to more accurately diagnose the rate of "undesirable" turnover (Allen et al., 2010; Campion, 1991). They suggest that employers focus on discouraging high performers or valued contributors from voluntarily leaving for avoidable reasons (such as abusive bosses, uncompetitive wages, or stunted career progress). Instead of the gross turnover rate, employers should thus monitor the rate of turnover that is voluntary, dysfunctional, and avoidable. Griffeth and Hom (2001) illustrated how computing this turnover rate can materially change an apparent turnover crisis. For example, they learned that the rate of overall turnover among new nursing graduates in a hospital was 14.6%. Although 87% of all quits were voluntary, only 58% of voluntary quits were truly dysfunctional (as such leavers received positive performance reviews). Exit interviews further revealed that 72% of dysfunctional quits were unavoidable—beyond hospital control as these nurses quit due to marriage and spousal relocation. Once involuntary, functional, and unavoidable exits were removed, the actual extent of unwanted turnover that can be controlled by management was only 1.3%!

Withdrawal Behavioral Construct

Instead of being treated as an isolated act, a few scholars prefer to treat turnover as a member of a family of "withdrawal behaviors" that "physically distance employees from unpleasant work settings," such as absences and tardiness (Hom & Griffeth, 1995, p. 121). All withdrawal acts presumably serve the same psychological function (reduce time spent in aversive workplaces and thus lower dissatisfaction). Yet theorists disagree about how they are interrelated, positing five alternative structural models (Hom & Griffeth, 1995). The "independence-form" model posits that withdrawal acts are unrelated as their antecedents and consequences differ (Hulin, 1991; Porter & Steers, 1973). By contrast, an "alternative-forms" model suggests that withdrawal acts are substitutable as certain acts are displayed when others are foreclosed, while a "compensatory" model assumes that enactment of any response makes other responses unnecessary as they all represent a relief valve for escaping noxious working conditions (Rosse & Miller, 1984). Finally, a "spillover" model specifies positive covariation among withdrawal acts because dissatisfying jobs elicit a general avoidance tendency that expresses itself in manifold ways (Hulin, 1991), while a "progression-of-withdrawal" model posits a progression from mild (e.g., tardiness) to extreme (e.g., quitting) withdrawal over time.

Available empirical evidence (primarily bivariate correlations) generally supports the latter two models, positing positive covariation among withdrawal acts and sharing dissatisfaction as a root cause (Hanisch, Hulin, & Roznowski, 1998; Harrison, Newman, & Roth, 2006; Hom & Griffeth, 1995). Even so, Hulin (1991) cautioned that "empirical correlations among ... infrequent withdrawal behaviors with badly skewed distributions provide little information about the underlying relations" (p. 474). Indeed, even zero or negative cross-sectional correlations may reflect a withdrawal progression if they are based on response data aggregated over short periods (Rosse, 1988). After all, one cannot simultaneously attend work late, miss a day's work, and quit all in the same day. Generally speaking, withdrawal scholars have identified two withdrawal families, namely: (a) job withdrawal (withdrawing from workplaces, such as quitting or retiring early); and (b) work withdrawal (withdrawing from tasks, such as absences and leaving work early) based on composites of different withdrawal acts. Harrison et al. (2006) further posited a latent factor underlying withdrawal, organizational citizenship, and job performance (termed "individual effectiveness") and highly predicted by job attitudes.

Hulin and colleagues (Hanisch et al., 1998; Hulin, 1991) offer compelling reasons for focusing on defining and operationalizing a broad behavioral construct manifested in varied withdrawal behaviors, such as leaving, seeking other employment, and early retirement. For one, they contend that a behavioral aggregate based on multiple withdrawal acts is more predictable because a single-item (dichotomous) measure of a behavior is less reliable and often exhibits a badly skewed distribution if its occurrence (base rate) is low. Single-act indicators of organizational withdrawal (aka turnover) also have considerable unique variance relative to construct-relevant variance. To overcome such limitations, Hanisch et al. (1998) suggest forming a composite comprising multiple withdrawal acts because the "proportion of construct-related variance can be increased by aggregating across measures of behaviors that share common construct-related variance" (p. 467). This behavioral aggregate is less poorly skewed, more reliable, and comprises a higher proportion of construct-relevant—and predictable—variance.

By scrutinizing a behavioral construct instead of a turnover index, researchers and employers can more accurately predict this criterion—especially with measures of general attitudes (cf. Hanisch et al., 1998; Harrison et al., 2006). Indeed, employers can more efficiently attack a syndrome of withdrawal responses by improving job satisfaction levels instead of developing special remedies for each problem behavior. Apart from practical advantages, Hulin and colleagues claim that a withdrawal-behavior aggregate is best suited for validating general and parsimonious theories of withdrawal or participation. Rather than formulating and testing separate models to explain each withdrawal behavior (cf. Ajzen & Fishbein, 1980), scholars can identify broader explanatory constructs (e.g., job attitudes) that underlie a syndrome of withdrawal acts.

Turnover Destinations

More recently, Hom et al. (2012) proposed tracking and predicting "turnover destinations"—where leavers end up after leaving. No doubt, many employers routinely do this from exit interviews to learn why their employees quit and may use destination data to determine if employees have joined competitors (and thus perhaps violated non-compete clauses). Indeed, employers may feel most threatened when their employees join competing firms (or become their competitors as new start-ups; Gardner et al., 2018), a fear not unfounded according to strategic management scholars who determined that loss of human and social capital to industry competitors can harm source firms (Phillips, 2002; Somaya et al., 2008; Wezel et al., 2006). When destinations are unknown, employers may underestimate the severity of dysfunctional turnover as former employees joining their competitors may provide proprietary knowledge or take away clients.

Traditional theories (Mobley et al., 1979; Rusbult & Farrell, 1983; Steers & Mowday, 1981) posit that employees often leave for they perceive (and receive) more attractive employment elsewhere, often using a rational calculation of expected utilities for different alternatives (aka destinations; Griffeth & Hom, 1988). Based on these SEU models, Griffeth and Hom (2001) suggest that employers solicit employees' SEU perceptions of major employers in the local labor market (e.g., likelihood ratings of each firm's instrumentality for supplying valued job outcomes) to identify potential competitors for their talent. Despite historical focus on employment destinations, turnover theory (cf. Hulin et al., 1985) and research began recognizing that many leavers opt for extra work or unpaid roles. Thus, some research studies assessed those destinations (often as "nonemployment"; Lee, Gerhart, Weller, & Trevor, 2008; Lee, Mitchell, Holtom, McDaniel, & Hill, 1999; Royalty, 1998), whereas others examined root causes for such alternatives, such as demonstrating that work–family conflict or a perceived glass ceiling can induce employees to quit (presumably to assume full-time parental duties; Hom & Kinicki, 2001; Stroh, Brett, & Reilly, 1996).

Newer perspectives (Griffeth, Lee, Mitchell, & Hom, 2012; Hom et al., 2012; Lee & Mitchell, 1994) more formally recognized turnover destinations besides other employment. Specifically, the unfolding model proposed that employees following turnover path 1 (triggered by a matching script) often pursue destinations outside paid employment. To illustrate, an employee may plan to quit once she or he receives notification of law school admission or becomes pregnant (Lee et al., 1999). More recently, Hom et al.'s (2012) theory about proximal withdrawal states introduced "destination preferences" to recognize not only desirable employment alternatives, but also unpaid alternatives (such as relocations to desirable geographic locales, retirement, or full-time dependent care). Despite formal recognition of extra-work destinations, contemporary scholars have not systematically identified why employees possess certain matching scripts (Lee & Mitchell, 1994) or why they prefer particular turnover destinations (Hom et al., 2012). The etiology of such destination plans or preferences awaits further theorizing and research.

Collective Turnover

Collective turnover represents the aggregate employee departures that occur within collectives, such as teams, work units, or organizations (Hausknecht & Holwerda, 2013). Commonly, collective turnover is operationalized as a turnover rate where the numerator represents all voluntary quits during a certain time span (e.g., monthly, quarterly, yearly) divided by a denominator representing the total workforce within a collective (N at the beginning of the measurement window or average N during this time period; Mobley, 1982; Price, 1977). Different forms of collective turnover can be computed for voluntary and involuntary turnover (Batt & Colvin, 2011). Quit rates can exceed 100% if the numerator includes not only the original employees leaving, but also their replacements who joined but then quit during this time span (Hausknecht & Holwerda, 2013). Using this index to capture collective, growing research increasingly identifies its antecedents, correlates, and consequences (Heavey, Holwerda, & Hausknecht, 2013).

Hausknecht and Holwerda (2013) criticize prevailing measures of collective turnover because they focus only on quantity, not the qualities of departures. What is more, they neglect departure sequence and timing, as well as the quality of the replacements. Instead, they propose a "capacity" index that more fully captures how collective turnover adversely affects the functioning of a team, business unit, or organization by weighing more: (a) the loss of a proficient member of a collective than a novice (*leaver proficiencies*); (b) when multiple quits occur all at once rather than sporadically over time (*time dispersion*); (c) when turnover afflicts numerous different positions rather than a few positions (*positional distribution*); (d) when members in a collective who remain are mostly novices rather than proficient performers (*remaining member proficiencies*); and (e) when incoming replacements possess less general human capital than the leavers (*newcomer proficiencies*). They explain how each property can impair collective performance.

The capacity index has practical value for it may diagnose more precisely the damage incurred by collective turnover for organizations. According to Hausknecht and Holwerda (2013), this index does not require extensive effort for its computation as necessary data are often available in personnel records, such as hiring and separation dates. Managers, however, must generate defensible estimates of the time required for newcomers to become proficient in a given job. Moreover, the capacity index can advance the rapidly emerging scholarship in collective turnover on turnover–consequence relationships (Hancock, Allen, Bosco, McDaniel, & Pierce, 2013; Heavey et al., 2013; Park & Shaw, 2013). Hausknecht and Holwerda (2013) thus contend their index may help explain the variability in observed relationships between turnover rates and varied outcomes (e.g., customer satisfaction, financial performance). They further prescribe scholarly explorations of potential antecedents of this capacity index, which can explicate why turnover is distributed across different positions or different time periods.

References

Abelson, M. A. (1987). Examination of avoidable and unavoidable turnover. *Journal of Applied Psychology*, 72, 382–386.

Ajzen, I., & Fishbein, M. (1980). *Understanding Attitudes and Predicting Social Behavior*. Englewood Cliffs, NJ: Prentice Hall.

Allen, D. G., Bryant, P., & Vardaman, J. (2010). Retaining talent: Replacing misconceptions with evidence-based strategies. *Academy of Management Perspective*, 24, 48–64.

Allen, D. G., & Griffeth, R. W. (2001). Test of a mediated performance–turnover relationship highlighting the moderating roles of visibility and reward contingency. *Journal of Applied Psychology*, 86(5), 1014–1021.

Ballinger, G. A., Cross, R., & Holtom, B. C. (2016). The right friends in the right places: Understanding network structure as a predictor of voluntary turnover. *Journal of Applied Psychology*, 101(4), 535–548.

Barrick, M. R., & Zimmerman, R. D. (2005). Reducing voluntary, avoidable turnover through selection. *Journal of Applied Psychology*, 90(1), 159–166.

Batt, R., & Colvin, A. (2011). An employment systems approach to turnover: Human resources practices, quits, dismissals, and performance. *The Academy of Management Journal*, 54(4), 695–717.

Bayer Corporation (2014). The Bayer facts of science education XVI: US STEM workforce shortage—myth or reality? Fortune 1000 talent recruiters on the debate. *Journal of Science Education & Technology*, 23(5), 617–623.

Campbell, B. A., Ganco, M., Franco, A. M., & Agarwal, R. (2012). Who leaves, where to, and why worry employee mobility, entrepreneurship and effects on source firm performance. *Strategic Management Journal*, 33(1), 65–87.

Campion, M. A. (1991). Meaning and measurement of turnover: Comparison of alternative measures and recommendations for research. *Journal of Applied Psychology*, 76, 199–212.

Cascio, W. F. (2000). Managing a virtual workplace. *Academy of Management Perspectives*, 14(3), 81–90.

Dalton, D. R., Krackhardt, D. M., & Porter, L. W. (1981). Functional turnover: An empirical assessment. *Journal of Applied Psychology*, 66, 716–721.

Dalton, D. R., & Todor, W. D. (1979). Turnover turned over: An expanded and positive perspective. *Academy of Management Review*, 4, 225–235.

Dittrich, J. E., & Carrell, M. R. (1979). Organizational equity perceptions, employee job satisfaction, and departmental absence and turnover rates. *Organizational Behavior and Human Performance*, 24, 29–40.

Feeley, T. H., & Barnett, G. A. (1997). Predicting employee turnover from communication networks. *Human Communication Research*, 23, 370–387.

Felps, W., Mitchell, T. R., Hekman, D., Lee, T. W., Holtom, B. C., & Harman, W. S. (2009). Turnover contagion: How coworkers' job embeddedness and coworkers' job search behaviors influence quitting. *Academy of Management Journal*, 52, 545–561.

Gardner, T. M., Munyon, T. P., Hom, P. W., & Griffeth, R. W. (2018). When territoriality meets agency: An examination of employee guarding as a territorial strategy. *Journal of Management*, 44(7), 2580–2610.

Graen, G. B., & Ginsburgh, S. (1977). Job resignation as a function of role orientation and leader acceptance: A longitudinal investigation of organizational assimilation. *Organizational Behavior and Human Performance*, 19, 1–17.

Grant, A. M. (2007). Relational job design and the motivation to make a prosocial difference. *Academy of Management Review*, 32, 393–417.

Griffeth, R. W., & Hom, P. W. (1988). A comparison of different conceptualizations of perceived alternatives in turnover research. *Journal of Organizational Behavior*, 9, 103–111.

Griffeth, R. W., & Hom, P. W. (2001). *Retaining Valued Employees*. Thousand Oaks, CA: Sage.

Griffeth, R. W., Lee, T. W., Mitchell, T. R., & Hom, P. W. (2012). Further clarification on the Hom, Mitchell, Lee, and Griffeth (2012) model: Reply to Bergman, Payne, and Boswell (2012) and Maertz (2012). *Psychological Bulletin*, 138(5), 871–875.

Hackman, J. R., & Oldham, G. R. (1980). *Work Redesign*. Reading, MA: Addison-Wesley.

Hancock, J. I., Allen, D. G., Bosco, F. A., McDaniel, K. R., & Pierce, C. A. (2013). Meta-analytic review of employee turnover as a predictor of firm performance. *Journal of Management*, 39, 573–603.

Hanisch, K. A., & Hulin, C. L. (1990). Job attitudes and organizational withdrawal: An examination of retirement and other voluntary withdrawal behaviors. *Journal of Vocational Behavior*, 37(1), 60–78.

Hanisch, K. A., Hulin, C. L., & Roznowski, M. (1998). The importance of individuals' repertoires of behaviors: The scientific appropriateness of studying multiple behaviors and general attitudes. *Journal of Organizational Behavior*, 19, 463–480.

Harrison, D. A., Newman, D. A., & Roth, P. L. (2006). How important are job attitudes? Meta-analytic comparisons of integrative behavioral outcomes and time sequences. *Academy of Management Journal*, 49, 305–325.

Hausknecht, J. P., & Holwerda, J. A. (2013). When does employee turnover matter? Dynamic member configurations, productive capacity, and collective performance. *Organization Science*, 24(1), 210–225.

Heavey, A. L., Holwerda, J. A., & Hausknecht, J. P. (2013). Causes and consequences of collective turnover: A meta-analytic review. *Journal of Applied Psychology*, 98(3), 412–453.

Hollenbeck, J. R., & Williams, C. R. (1986). Turnover functionality versus turnover frequency: A note on work attitudes and organizational effectiveness. *Journal of Applied Psychology*, 71, 606–611.

Hom, P. W. (1980). Expectancy predictions of reenlistment in the National Guard. *Journal of Vocational Behavior*, 16, 235–248.

Hom, P. W. (2011). Organizational exit. In S. Zedeck (Ed.), *APA Handbooks in Psychology: APA Handbook of Industrial and Organizational Psychology. Vol. 2: Selecting and Developing Members for the Organization* (pp. 325–375). Washington, DC: American Psychological Association.

Hom, P. W., Caranikas-Walker, F., Prussia, G. E., & Griffeth, R. W. (1992). A meta-analytical structural equations analysis of a model of employee turnover. *Journal of Applied Psychology*, 77, 890–909.

Hom, P. W., & Griffeth, R. W. (1995). *Employee Turnover*. Cincinnati, OH: South/Western.

Hom, P. W., & Hulin, C. L. (1981). A competitive test of the prediction of reenlistment by several models. *Journal of Applied Psychology*, 66(1), 23–39.

Hom, P. W., & Kinicki, A. J. (2001). Toward a greater understanding of how dissatisfaction drives employee turnover. *Academy of Management Journal*, 44, 975–987.

Hom, P. W., Lee, T. W., Shaw, J. D., & Hausknecht, J. P. (2017). One hundred years of employee turnover theory and research. *Journal of Applied Psychology*, 102(3), 530–545.

Hom, P. W., Mitchell, T. R., Lee, T. W., & Griffeth, R. W. (2012). Reviewing employee turnover: Focusing on proximal withdrawal states and an expanded criterion. *Psychological Bulletin*, 138, 831–858.

Hom, P. W., Roberson, L., & Ellis, A. (2008). Challenging conventional wisdom about who quits: Revelations from corporate America. *Journal of Applied Psychology*, 93, 1–34.

Hom, P. W., Tsui, A. S., Wu, J. B., Lee, T. W., Zhang, A. Y., Fu, P. P., & Li, L. (2009). Explaining employment relationships with social exchange and job embeddedness. *Journal of Applied Psychology*, 94(2), 277–297.

Hom, P. W., & Xiao, Z. (2011). Embedding social capital: How guanxi ties reinforce Chinese employees' retention. *Organizational Behavior and Human Decision Processes*, 116, 188–202.

Hulin, C. L. (1991). Adaptation, persistence, and commitment in organizations. In M. D. Dunnette & L. M. Hough (Eds.), *Handbook of Industrial and Organizational Psychology* (2nd ed., pp. 445–505). Palo Alto, CA: Consulting Psychologists Press.

Hulin, C. L., Roznowski, M., & Hachiya, D. (1985). Alternative opportunities and withdrawal decisions: Empirical and theoretical discrepancies and an integration. *Psychological Bulletin*, 97(2), 233–250.

Jiang, B., Baker, R. C., & Frazier, G. V. (2009). An analysis of job dissatisfaction and turnover to reduce global supply chain risk: Evidence from China. *Journal of Operations Management*, 27(2), 169–184.

Klotz, A. C., & Bolino, M. C. (2016). Saying goodbye: The nature, causes, and consequences of employee resignation styles. *Journal of Applied Psychology*, 101(10), 1386–1404.

Lee, T. H., Gerhart, B., Weller, I., & Trevor, C. O. (2008). Understanding voluntary turnover: Path-specific job satisfaction effects and the importance of unsolicited job offers. *Academy of Management Journal*, 51(4), 651–671.

Lee, T. W., Burch, T. C., & Mitchell, T. R. (2014). The story of why we stay: A review of job embeddedness. *Annual Review of Organizational Psychology and Organizational Behavior*, 1, 199–216.

Lee, T. W., & Mitchell, T. R. (1994). An alternative approach: The unfolding model of voluntary employee turnover. *The Academy of Management Review*, 19(1), 51–89.

Lee, T. W., Mitchell, T. R., Holtom, B. C., McDaniel, L. S., & Hill, J. W. (1999). The unfolding model of voluntary turnover: A replication and extension. *Academy of Management Journal*, 42, 450–462.

Lee, T. W., Mitchell, T. R., Wise, L., & Fireman, S. (1996). An unfolding model of voluntary employee turnover. *Academy of Management Journal*, 39, 5–36.

Li, J., Lee, T. W., Mitchell, T. R., Hom, P. W., & Griffeth, R. W. (2016). The effects of proximal withdrawal states on job attitudes, job searching, intent to leave, and employee turnover. *Journal of Applied Psychology*, 101(10), 1436–1456.

Liu, D., Mitchell, T. R., Lee, T. W., Holtom, B. C., & Hinkin, T. (2012). When employees are out of step with coworkers: How job satisfaction trajectory and dispersion influence individual- and unit-level voluntary turnover. *Academy of Management Journal*, 55, 1360–1380.

Maertz, C. P., & Campion, M. A. (1998). 25 years of voluntary turnover research: A review and critique. In C. L. Cooper & I. T. Robertson (Eds.), *International Review of Industrial and Organizational Psychology* (vol. 13, pp. 49–81). New York: Wiley.

Maertz, C. P., & Campion, M. A. (2004). Profiles in quitting: Integrating process and content turnover theory. *Academy of Management Journal*, 47, 566–582.

Maertz, C. P., & Griffeth, R. W. (2004). Eight motivational forces and voluntary turnover: A theoretical synthesis with implications for research. *Journal of Management*, 30(5), 667–683.

March, J. G., & Simon, H. A. (1958). *Organizations*. New York: Wiley.

Marsh, R. M., & Mannari, H. (1977). Organizational commitment and turnover: A prediction study. *Administrative Science Quarterly*, 22, 57–75.

Mervis, J. (2014). Studies suggest two-way street for science majors. *Science*, 343, 125–126.

Miller, J. S., Hom, P. W., & Gomez-Mejia, L. (2001). The high cost of low wages: Does maquiladora compensation reduce turnover? *Journal of International Business Studies*, 32(3), 585–595.

Mirvis, P. H., & Lawler, E. E. (1977). Measuring the financial impact of employee attitudes. *Journal of Applied Psychology*, 62(1), 1–8.

Mitchell, T. R., Holtom, B. C., Lee, T. W., Sablynski, C. J., & Erez, M. (2001). Why people stay: Using job embeddedness to predict voluntary turnover. *Academy of Management Journal*, 44, 1102–1121.

Mobley, W. H. (1977). Intermediate linkages in the relationship between job satisfaction and employee turnover. *Journal of Applied Psychology*, 62(2), 237–240.

Mobley, W. H. (1982). *Employee Turnover: Causes, Consequences, and Control*. Reading, MA: Addison-Wesley.

Mobley, W. H., Griffeth, R. W., Hand, H. H., & Meglino, B. M. (1979). Review and conceptual analysis of the employee turnover process. *Psychological Bulletin*, 86, 493–522.

Mobley, W. H., Horner, S. O., & Hollingsworth, A. T. (1978). An evaluation of precursors of hospital employee turnover. *Journal of Applied Psychology*, 63, 408–414.

Nishii, L., & Mayer, D. (2009). Do inclusive leaders help to reduce turnover in diverse groups? The moderating role of leader–member exchange in the diversity to turnover relationship. *Journal of Applied Psychology*, 94, 1412–1426.

Park, T.-Y., & Shaw, J. D. (2013). Turnover rates and organizational performance: A meta-analysis. *Journal of Applied Psychology*, 98(2), 268–309.

Phillips, D. (2002). A genealogical approach to organizational life chances: The parent–progeny transfer among silicon valley law firms, 1946–1996. *Administrative Science Quarterly*, 47(3), 474–506.

Porter, L. W., & Steers, R. M. (1973). Organizational, work, and personal factors in employee turnover and absenteeism. *Psychological Bulletin*, 80, 151–176.

Price, J. L. (1977). *The Study of Turnover*. Ames, IA: Iowa State University Press.

Price, J. L., & Mueller, C. W. (1981). A causal model of turnover for nurses. *Academy of Management Journal*, 24, 543–565.

Price, J. L., & Mueller, C. W. (1986). *Absenteeism and Turnover of Hospital Employees*. Greenwich, CT: JAI Press.

Qin, X., Hom, P. W., & Xu, M. (2019). Am I a peasant or a worker? An identity strain perspective on turnover among developing-world migrants. *Human Relations*, 72(4), 801–833.

Reina, C., Rogers, K., Peterson, S., Byron, K., & Hom, P. W. (2018). Quitting the boss? The role of manager influence tactics and employee emotional engagement in voluntary turnover. *Journal of Leadership and Organizational Studies*, 25(1), 5–18.

Rosse, J. G. (1988). Relations among lateness, absence, and turnover: Is there a progression of withdrawal? *Human Relations*, 41, 517–531.

Rosse, J. G., & Miller, H. E. (1984). Relationship between absenteeism and other employee behaviors. In P. S. Goodman & R. S. Atkin (Eds.), *Absenteeism: New Approaches to Understanding, Measuring, and Managing Employee Absence (pp. 194–228)*. San Francisco, CA: Jossey-Bass.

Royalty, A. B. (1998). Job-to-job and job-to-nonemployment turnover by gender and educational level. *Journal of Labor Economics*, 16, 392–443.

Rusbult, C. E., & Farrell, D. (1983). A longitudinal test of the investment model: The impact of job satisfaction, job commitment, and turnover of variations in rewards, costs, alternatives, and investments. *Journal of Applied Psychology*, 68, 429–438.

Salamin, A., & Hom, P. W. (2005). In search of the elusive U-shaped performance–turnover relationship: Are high performing Swiss bankers more liable to quit? *Journal of Applied Psychology*, 90, 1204–1216.

Shapiro, D. L., Hom, P. W., Shen, W., & Agarwal, R. (2016). How do leader departures affect subordinates' organizational attachment? A 360-degree relational perspective. *The Academy of Management Review*, 41(3), 479–502.

Shaw, J. D. (2011). Turnover rates and organizational performance: Review, critique, and research agenda. *Organizational Psychology Review*, 1, 187–213.

Sheridan, J. E., & Abelson, M. A. (1983). Cusp catastrophe model of employee turnover. *Academy of Management Journal*, 26, 418–436.

Somaya, D., Williamson, I., & Lorinkova, N. (2008). Gone but not lost: The different performance impacts of employee mobility between cooperators versus competitors. *Academy of Management Journal*, 51, 936–953.

Staw, B. M. (1980). The consequences of turnover. *Journal of Occupational Behavior*, 1, 253–273.

Steel, R. P. (2002). Turnover theory at the empirical interface: Problems of fit and function. *Academy of Management Review*, 27, 346–360.

Steers, R. M., & Mowday, R. T. (1981). Employee turnover and postdecision accommodation processes. In L. L. Cummings & B. M. Staw (Eds.), *Research in Organizational Behavior* (vol. 3, pp. 235–282). Greenwich, CT: JAI Press.

Stroh, L. K., Brett, J. M., & Reilly, A. H. (1996). Family structure, glass ceiling, and traditional explanations for the differential rates of turnover of female and male managers. *Journal of Vocational Behavior*, 49, 99–118.

Sturman, M. C., Shao, L., & Katz, J. (2012). The effect of culture on the curvilinear relationship between performance and turnover. *Journal of Applied Psychology*, 97, 46–62.

Van Breukelen, W., Van der Vlist, R., & Steensma, H. (2004). Voluntary employee turnover: Combining variables from the "traditional" turnover literature with the theory of planned behavior. *Journal of Organizational Behavior*, 25, 893–914.

Wang, D., Hom, P. W., & Allen, D. G. (2017). Coping with newcomer hangover: How socialization tactics affect declining job satisfaction during early employment. *Journal of Vocational Behavior*, 100, 196–210.

Waters, L. K., Roach, D., & Waters, C. W. (1976). Estimates of future tenure, satisfaction, and biographical variables as predictors of termination. *Personnel Psychology*, 29(1), 57–60.

West, M. (2004). Investigating turnover in the international context. In R. W. Griffeth & P. W. Hom (Eds.), *Innovative Theory and Empirical Research on Employee Turnover* (pp. 231–256). Greenwich, CT: Information Age Publishing.

Westaby, J. D. (2005). Behavioral reasoning theory: Identifying new linkages underlying intentions and behavior. *Organizational Behavior and Human Decision Processes*, 98, 97–120.

Wezel, F. C., Cattani, G., & Pennings, J. M. (2006). Competitive implications of interfirm mobility. *Organization Science*, 17(6), 691–709.

Williams, C. R., & Livingstone, L. P. (1994). A second look at the relationship between performance and voluntary turnover. *Academy of Management Journal*, 37, 269–298.

Xu, X., & Payne, S. C. (2018). Predicting retention duration from organizational commitment profile transitions. *Journal of Management*, 44(5), 2142–2168.

2
TURNOVER CONSEQUENCES

The bulk of the attention and research on employee turnover focuses on understanding the antecedents and processes that lead to turnover. This emphasis is understandable given the substantial impact that turnover has on organizations, on leavers, and on those who remain in the organization. In this chapter, we address the now substantial and accelerating body of research on the consequences of turnover. Although the general assumption may be that turnover, especially voluntary turnover, is costly and disruptive for firms, there is substantial research that these effects are complex. Dalton, Todor, and Krackhardt (1982) first distinguished between dysfunctional and functional turnover, a distinction that remains useful. As Allen, Bryant, and Vardaman (2010) summarize:

> Dysfunctional turnover is harmful to the organization, such as the exit of high performers or of employees who have difficult-to-replace skill sets. Functional turnover, although disruptive, may not be harmful, such as the exit of employees who are easy to replace, and may even be beneficial, such as the exit of poor performers.
>
> *(pp. 50–51)*

Indeed, Allen et al. (2010) called the idea that turnover is bad one of the key misconceptions about employee turnover.

Similarly, although voluntary leavers might be expected to benefit from their decision, transitioning out of a job has complex relationships with work and life well-being. In this regard, Mobley's (1982) framework remains useful. This framework classifies the consequences of turnover along two dimensions: consequences for the organization and for leavers, and whether consequences are positive or negative. In this vein, we will discuss positive and negative consequences for the organization and for leavers; to this perspective, we will also add discussion of turnover consequences for those who remain, and of more complex relationships beyond simply positive or negative, such as curvilinear relationships. We begin by considering turnover consequences for leavers followed by a brief discussion of emerging considerations of the impact of turnover on those who remain. We then discuss the rapidly growing literature on turnover consequences for organizations.

Consequences for Leavers

Positive Consequences for the Leaver

Naturally, leavers, at least those who depart voluntarily, would be expected to be leaving for something better in some way. For example, leavers may assume a better position—one that better matches their talents and interests—or escape a stressful job (Mowday, Porter, & Steers, 1982). In a national sample of young men, Antel (1991) found that job quitters often obtain higher wages in their new employment, especially if they underwent an intervening period of joblessness. Indeed, a new position may rejuvenate leavers, instilling a greater commitment to work (Mobley, 1982). Moreover, leavers—assuming new (or no) employment that offers a more convenient work schedule—can devote more time to other endeavors, such as family or avocations (Hom & Griffeth, 1991; Hulin, Roznowski, & Hachiya, 1985). Exit surveys reveal that young female nurses and teachers, for example, often resign to bear or raise children (Cavanagh, 1989; Murnane, Singer, & Willet, 1988). A sociological study found that young adults often opt out of full-time employment to attend school (Kandel & Yamaguchi, 1987). Relocation may provide leavers and their families with better schools, safer communities, or more attractive climates and recreational opportunities (Cascio, 1991; Mowday et al., 1982; Turban, Campion, & Eyring, 1992).

Leavers abandoning current positions to trail spouses who are accepting better career assignments elsewhere may willingly and gladly assume this sacrifice if they had already fulfilled their career ambitions or if they welcome the opportunity to switch careers, to open a business, or to return to school (Lublin, 1993). Such "sacrifice" is not uncommon: exit surveys show that many nurses quit when their spouses relocate (Donovan, 1980). Members of dual-career couples may preserve their marriage by quitting firms that request them to transfer. For example, female managers at Mobil Corporation often resigned for fear that their husbands would not go along with the move (Lublin, 1993), while military officers often left the armed services to appease spouses who rejected the harsh military life (Hunter, 1983).

Negative Consequences for the Leaver

Even for voluntary leavers, though, turnover can be associated with negative consequences. This section considers the adverse repercussions to employees who quit their jobs. Traditionally, managers and scholars have worried about how turnover harms organizations. Yet attention to negative consequences for leavers may pay dividends for companies. They can forewarn prospective leavers about the full ramifications of their decisions to exit the firm—namely, loss of seniority benefits, transition stress in a new job, relocation costs and family dislocation, and disruption to spouses' careers. Such warnings can help prospective quitters to make wiser decisions about changing jobs as well as deter their exits.

Forfeiture of Seniority and Fringe Benefits

Research and anecdotal evidence identify sundry personal disadvantages for leavers, notably the surrender of various rewards of organizational membership (Mobley, 1982; Staw, 1980). Theorists on turnover have long insisted that the expectancy of forfeiting job seniority, unvested pensions, and other fringe benefits deters turnover (Hom & Griffeth, 1991; Mobley, 1977; Rusbult & Farrell, 1983). Research suggests that individuals tend to become embedded in their organization and acquire resources associated with such membership, and that relinquishing these resources upon leaving is viewed as a sacrifice (Kiazad, Holtom, Hom, & Newman, 2015; Mitchell, Holtom, Lee, Sablynski, & Erez, 2001). For example, the loss of healthcare benefits could be quite costly. Research by labor economists has long confirmed that pension and healthcare coverage deter job turnover (Ippolito, 1991; Mitchell, 1983). A recent survey showed that 56% of U.S. adults believe their health coverage is a key factor in deciding whether to stay at their current job (Miller, 2018).

Transition Stress in New Employment

Researchers into socialization and turnover further contend that quitters encounter stress during their transition into a new job (Allen, 2006; Feldman & Brett, 1983; Mobley, 1982). Their new employment may disappoint the leavers, failing to confirm their expectations, and therefore eliciting dissatisfaction and turnover (Wanous, 1980; Wanous, Poland, Premack, & Davis, 1992). Leavers entering new work roles must repeat basic tasks of socialization, such as learning work practices and winning acceptance form new colleagues (Feldman, 1976, 1988). Acknowledging this consequence of leaving, Feldman and Brett (1983) documented various strategies for coping with transition stress (such as working longer hours and delegating more responsibilities) used by employees who simply changed jobs within the same company.

Following this line of research, scholars have identified a *honeymoon-hangover effect* associated with changing organizations (Boswell, Boudreau, & Tichy, 2005). Leavers do, in fact, tend to experience increased job satisfaction immediately following job change—a honeymoon. However, once confronted with new organizational realities and the challenges of adjusting to a new work environment, many leavers subsequently experience a marked decline in job satisfaction—the hangover (Boswell, Shipp, Payne, & Culbertson, 2009).

In a related vein, scholars are recognizing the phenomenon of *boomerang* employees: those who voluntarily leave the organization, only to return and be rehired at a subsequent time (Shipp, Furst-Holloway, Harris, & Rosen, 2014). For this reason, companies are increasingly proactively managing relationships with alumni, not only as brand and employment ambassadors, but also as potential pools of future talent (Carnahan & Somaya, 2015). Thus, one longer-term consequence associated with leaving an organization is to return as a rehire at some future point in time.

Relocation Costs

Leavers may face additional losses if they move to new geographic regions (Mobley, 1982; Mowday et al., 1982; Rusbult & Farrell, 1983). Obviously, leavers bear the financial costs of moving, especially if they do not receive full reimbursement from their new employer or if they move to a region where the living costs are higher (Mowday et al., 1982). Apart from moving expenses, relocating leavers may sever their social support networks (Allen, 2006; Zedeck & Mosier, 1990). Various empirical studies implicate this potential exit cost, showing that extensive friendships with coworkers and relatives within a community reinforce the likelihood of remaining in a job (Blegen, Mueller, & Price, 1988; Mitchell et al., 2001; Rusbult & Farrell, 1983).

Unfortunately, writers on turnover have neglected to consider the cost of family separation when married leavers relocate but leave their families behind, perhaps because of a spouse's employment or the children's education. The armed services have long known that protracted and repeated family separations caused by military assignments abroad produce not only marital strain, but also attrition among soldiers seeking to preserve their marriages (Brown, Carr, & Orthner, 1983; Hunter, 1983). Researchers on turnover must acknowledge the effects of quitting and relocating on child custody arrangements among divorced leavers. That is, parents who move and do not have custody of their children may find their ties to their children severed; parents who do have custody and relocate may face lawsuits from former spouses trying to preserve visitation rights (Lublin, 1992). Theorists on turnover have also overlooked the ways in which relocation can dissolve the social network of a leaver's family, who must adapt to a new community without support from friends or extended family. Research on expatriate managers attests to such family dislocations in adjusting to new cultural milieus (Caliguri, Hyland, Joshi, & Bross, 1998). Indeed, the failure of a family to adapt culturally has prematurely terminated overseas assignments (Dowling & Schuler, 1990; Hechanova, Beehr, & Christiansen, 2003).

Consistent with the job embeddedness perspective, (Mitchell et al., 2001), relocating leavers and their families may lose valued community services, such as those of the family physician and good schools (Abelson & Baysinger, 1984; Rusbult & Farrell, 1983). Indicative of these costs, Turban et al. (1992) found that long-term tenure in a community discourages people from moving to new jobs elsewhere, while Hunter (1983) observed that many navy personnel chose to leave the U.S. Navy because they disliked the frequent moves imposed on their families.

Disruption of Spouses' Careers and Marital Discord

The geographic relocation of leavers who are married to working spouses may disrupt their spouses' careers (Mobley, 1982; Zedeck & Mosier, 1990). Attesting to its impact, Turban et al. (1992) found that more married employees refused offers by employers to relocate than did single employees. Milliken, Dutton, and Beyer (1990) reported that between 25% and 30% of employees declined promotions that required relocation, mainly to avoid threatening the careers of their spouses. Conversely, members of dual-career couples who resign to follow their relocating spouses may not obtain comparable employment in the new community (Lublin, 1993). In particular, trailing husbands adhering to traditional sex roles may feel psychological distress if they cannot find work or become underemployed (Staines, Pottick, & Fudge, 1986). Indeed, their wives' employment status would threaten their cherished status as primary breadwinners, and this sex-role reversal would produce marital strain (Lublin, 1993; Mirowsky, 1987).

How Leavers Leave and Where They Go

Two recent research trends extend our understanding of the consequences of leaving by considering how individuals approach exiting the organization and the destinations to which they are leaving. For example, Kulik, Rae, Sardeshmukh, and Perera (2015) drew from research on relationship dissolution to examine how employees engaged in exit communication strategies. Employees who left for largely external reasons engaged in direct communication strategies, resulting in more positive evaluations from managers and higher potential for maintaining positive post-exit relationships, compared to those who left for largely internal reasons (e.g., dissatisfaction) who engaged in more indirect communication strategies. Similarly, Klotz and Bolino (2016) found that managers had the most positive reactions to resignation styles characterized as keeping the manager "in the loop" as opposed to more avoidant or indirect resignation styles. Hom, Mitchell, Lee, and Griffeth (2012) emphasized "turnover destinations": what people do after they exit. Examples include: a new job, a new venture, full-time parenting, retirement, disability, unpaid work, no work, and bridge or gig employment. It is likely that turnover destinations interact with reasons for leaving, resignation strategies, post-exit relationships, honeymoon-hangover effects, and the likelihood of boomerang employment to affect the consequences of turnover on leavers.

Consequences for Stayers

As social network and turnover contagion theorists have noted (e.g., Krackhardt & Porter, 1986), even though individuals make turnover decisions, each individual is embedded in a network of colleagues, some of whom leave and some of whom remain with the organization. When individuals leave, it disrupts the relationships, workflows, and communication networks of those who remain (Methot, Rosado-Solomon, & Allen, 2018). Thus, we also turn attention to the research literature considering the effects of turnover on those who stay.

Opportunities in Promotion and Empowerment for Stayers

Writers on turnover suggest that there are various advantages for the remaining employees, although empirical findings are sparse (Price, 1977, 1989; Staw, 1980). Exits may expand opportunities for promotion among continuing members by opening up the jobs vacated by the leavers and lessening competition for promotions (Mobley, 1982; Staw, 1980). Still, Mueller and Price (1989) did *not* find turnover rates in hospital units to increase prospects for advancement. In a similar vein, managerial turnover may empower subordinates (Price, 1977, 1989). Conceivably, incoming managers feel uncertain about their authority because they are unfamiliar with the position. They may thus initially consult subordinates for background information and advice. Sustaining this view, Price (1977) interpreted several empirical studies as implying that managerial exits and succession decentralize power. Lastly, the departure of participants in divisive interpersonal disputes will alleviate tension and conflict among coworkers (Staw, 1980).

Employee Demoralization

Alternatively, turnover may erode the morale and stability of those who remain employed (Mowday et al., 1982). Their morale suffers because they lose friends (O'Reilly, Caldwell, & Barnett, 1989; Price, 1977) and may interpret motives for quitting as social criticisms about the job (Mowday et al., 1982). Awareness that a leaver has a better job elsewhere may change employees' perception of jobs (Steel, 2002). As a result, the stayers may denigrate their present position in the light of superior alternatives (Hulin et al., 1985) and begin contemplating other employment (Mobley, 1982). In line with these hypothesized effects, research into small groups finds that personnel instability weakens the cohesion of the group (Sundstrom, De Meuse, & Futrell, 1990). Work group conflicts and dissatisfaction with coworkers breed dissatisfaction about the job, and subsequently turnover (Mobley, 1982; Mowday et al., 1982; O'Reilly et al., 1989; Pfeffer, 1983; Price & Mueller, 1981, 1986). Collectively, these findings imply that colleagues' resignations may undermine the employees' social integration and in turn stimulate more turnover (Price, 1989). More revealing, Mueller and Price (1989) reported that rising quit rates in hospital units foreshadowed an inability to keep staff, although quit rates did not affect the units' morale or integration. Still, turnover may increase job demands for remaining employees who may thus experience motivation and performance challenges (Reilly, Nyberg, Maltarich, & Weller, 2014).

All the same, the exodus of their colleagues may not invariably demoralize the remaining members of organizations. Krackhardt and Porter (1985) argued that employees may form more positive attitudes toward the job to rationalize their remaining employed while their friends quit. Sustaining this claim, the researchers found that the departure of friends reinforced the stayers' satisfaction and commitment. These provocative findings deserve replication. Krackhardt and Porter (1985) sampled adolescents who worked for extra spending money, rather than economic survival, in fast-food restaurants whose turnover ran to 200% annually.

Staw (1980) speculated that imputed motives for leaving may dictate whether or not turnover demoralizes stayers. That is, if it is believed that leavers quit for reasons that have nothing to do with the organization (to meet family obligations or relocate to a different community), employees may not be induced to rethink their own motives for staying. Besides this, job mobility is a traditional avenue for career advancement in some professions (e.g., public accounting; Sheridan, 1992). In such occupations, regular departures may not necessarily undermine the stayers' allegiance to the organization.

Social Network Disruption

Given that employees are embedded in webs of relationships at the workplace, turnover necessarily reshapes and reforms individuals' social networks. Krackhardt and Porter (1985) long ago observed a "snowball effect" in which occupants of similar structural positions in communication networks may quit in clusters. Krackhardt and Porter (1986) also demonstrated that employees whose close network contacts quit tend to form positive job attitudes, presumably to rationalize why they stay when their friends exit. More recent research describes how "turnover contagion" (Felps et al., 2009) can result in stayers becoming more likely to leave. Most recently, Methot et al. (2018) describe how leavers can disrupt stayers' relational identities: how individuals enact their roles in relation to others in the workplace (e.g., manager, coworker, subordinate, friend). Departures necessarily disrupt these relational identities; for example, the loss of a mentor may reduce access to social capital, but may also shift one's sense of purpose, allow development of a unique identity, or enable one to recover from an over-identified relationship (Methot et al., 2018).

Consequences for Organizations

Costs and Benefits for Organizations

Turnover incurs significant costs for organizations, with estimates for some job types approaching 200% of annual salary (Cascio, 2006). Allen et al. (2010) summarize some of the primary costs associated with turnover. When someone leaves the organization, there are both tangible and intangible costs associated with their departure. Tangible costs tend to be more apparent and easier to calculate; for example, HR staff and manager time to conduct exit interviews, accrued benefits to be paid out, and temporary coverage or overtime to minimize work disruptions. Often the intangible costs are more difficult to calculate, but can be more harmful; for example, loss of customers or clients, teamwork disruptions, decreased performance or quality, loss of organizational memory, diminished diversity, contagion to other employees, and even direct competition from leavers.

Allen et al. (2010) also summarize additional costs associated with replacing leavers, including HR and manager time spent on recruitment, selection, and orientation, recruitment costs, referral bonuses, selection costs, onboarding and training costs, and potential productivity losses associated with newcomer learning curves. There are a variety of sources for formulae for calculating turnover costs (cf. Cascio, 2006; Griffeth & Hom, 2001), something beyond the scope of this book. As Allen et al. (2010) note, more important than the specific formula is consensus among decision-makers concerning the appropriateness of the metrics.

As noted above, however, there can be organizational benefits associated with turnover. Table 2.1 also illustrates potential benefits; for example, savings from

TABLE 2.1 Voluntary Turnover Costs and Benefits

Separation Costs

Tangible

HR staff time (e.g., salary, benefits, exit interview)
Manager's time (e.g., salary, benefits, retention attempts, exit interview)
Accrued paid time off (e.g., vacation, sick pay)
Temporary coverage (e.g., temporary employee, overtime for current employees)

Intangible

Loss of workforce diversity
Diminished quality while job is unfilled
Loss of organizational memory
Loss of clients
Competition from quitter if he or she opens a new venture
Contagion—other employees decide to leave
Teamwork disruptions
Loss of seasoned mentors

(*Continued*)

TABLE 2.1 (Cont.)

Replacement Costs

General Costs

HR staff time (e.g., benefits enrollment, recruitment, selection, orientation)
Hiring manager time (e.g., input on new hire decision, orientation, training)

Recruitment

Advertising
Employment agency fees
Hiring inducements (e.g., bonus, relocation, perks)
Referral bonuses

Selection

Selection measure expenses (e.g., costs of RJP, work samples, selection tests)
Application expenses

Orientation and Training

Orientation program time and resources
Formal and informal training (e.g., time, materials, equipment, mentoring)
Socialization (e.g., time of other employees, travel)
Productivity loss (e.g., loss of production until replacement is fully proficient)

Turnover Benefits

Savings may be achieved by not replacing leaver
Infusion of new skills or creativity into the organization
Vacancy creates transfer or promotion opportunity for others
Cost savings may be achieved by hiring a replacement with less experience or seniority
Replacement could be a better performer and organization citizen
Replacement could enhance workplace diversity
Departure may offer the opportunity to reorganize the work unit

Adapted from Allen, Bryant, and Vardaman (2010), Fitz-enz (2002) and Heneman and Judge (2006)

lower-cost replacements, opportunities to hire better performers, new skills and perspectives, the creation of new opportunities for remaining employees, enhanced workplace diversity, opportunities to reorganize, and sometimes cost savings achieved by not replacing leavers. Below, we elaborate on some of the most important organizational consequences.

Negative Consequences for the Organization

This section describes the various adverse repercussions for organizations engendered by employee turnover. In addition to the economic costs described above, there are less direct costs such as potential productivity losses and impairments to delivery of customer service. In particular, departure of employees—especially experienced or talented ones—may threaten overall firm productivity or client retention. Furthermore, personnel losses may endanger firms' future opportunities in the marketplace or the morale of their remaining workforces. We subsequently return to recent efforts to estimate the financial ramifications of turnover for the organization.

Productivity Losses

Some writers on turnover contend that voluntary quits impair organization productivity, which is the ratio of company goods and services to inputs (Price, 1977, 1989). Many schools of thought and indirect evidence (besides cost data; Price, 1977) implicate productivity losses as potential exit outcomes. Specifically, leavers often miss work or are tardy before they depart (Rosse, 1988); missing employees obviously produce nothing (Rhodes & Steers, 1990). The productivity of leavers may deteriorate before they depart, according to progression-of-withdrawal models (Hulin, 1991; Rosse, 1988).

New replacements may produce fewer goods or services than the veteran employees who left did (Price, 1977), a result that is consistent with positive age–productivity relationships (Waldman & Avolio, 1986). In line with this contention, Sheridan (1992) documented that public accounting firms lose $47,000 in profits whenever a new accountant replaces a third-year veteran who leaves. Furthermore, resignations may disrupt other employees' work if their work depends on the leavers or they must assume the leavers' duties (Mobley, 1982; Schlesinger & Heskett, 1991; Staw, 1980). Remaining employees must also adjust to the replacements' work style and habits and interrupt work to train them (Louis, Posner, & Powell, 1983; Mowday et al., 1982). In summary, turnover may decrease productivity because of the leaver's declining productivity, the replacement's inexperience, and disruptions of the workflow.

Ulrich, Halbrook, Meder, Stuchlik, and Thorpe (1991) provided direct evidence that turnover may yield productivity losses. They found that the financially successful Ryder Truck Rental districts had lower termination rates than did the less successful districts. Although it is a noteworthy finding, this preliminary assessment did not statistically control other determinants of firm performance that might underlie the relationship between performance and quitting.

Hom's (1992) research on turnover among mental health professionals showed how certain opportunity costs for turnover—namely, the productivity losses long theorized about by human resources accounting scholars—can be estimated (Boudreau & Berger, 1985). Leavers may produce fewer goods or services before exiting, and new replacements may perform less efficiently while learning new job skills (Mobley, 1982). Yet turnover costing studies typically omit productivity losses because they are difficult to measure (Cascio, 1991). Hom (1992) operationalized these opportunity costs as losses of client revenue. Fewer clients are served while a position is vacant (because of staff shortages) and new replacements are less productive (because they serve fewer clients as they master their jobs). Thus, the costs of "foregone client revenues" may be more amenable to quantification, especially when service personnel leave (Darmon, 1990; Sheridan, 1992; Whiting, 1989).

Thus, performance differentials between leavers and replacements may influence whether or not turnover generates economic losses for organizations. According to Call, Nyberg, Ployhart, and Weekley (2015), turnover research has only recently begun addressing the relative quality of leavers and replacements over time. In their sample of retail chain units, they found that units in which higher-quality employees were leaving suffered significantly larger performance losses. Several circumstances may, however, determine the relative effectiveness of these types of employees and thus whether turnover does yield productivity losses. For one, the presence of merit-pay schemes widens the performance differential by distributing fewer incentives to marginal performers who then become dissatisfied and quit (Staw, 1980; Williams & Livingstone, 1994; Zenger, 1992). More valid selection procedures or aggressive recruitment may enhance the quality of new replacements who may out-produce leavers. A shrinking demand for labor may allow companies to hire more qualified replacements for a particular occupation and may also inhibit marginal performers from quitting.

The organizational climate may also influence relationships between performance and quitting. For example, Sheridan (1992) found that ineffective accountants quit more than did effective accountants in public accounting firms that value task achievements. In contrast, varying quit rates were not apparent in firms that endorsed interpersonal relationships, a climate that encouraged both high and low performers to stay on the job longer. By extension, voluntary resignations may thus enhance productivity in firms with task-oriented cultures (assuming that replacements are better performers) more than they might in firms with interpersonal-relationship cultures.

Staw (1980) proposed that departures of employees in pivotal rather than peripheral positions interrupt work flows most, given the greater dependency of other employees' work on crucial jobs. Organizations such as public accounting firms (Sheridan, 1992) may anticipate regular exit occurrences and prepare contingency plans to offset personnel shortages by maintaining a pool of temporary employees or training employees to assume multiple jobs (Turbin & Rosse, 1990).

Impaired Quality of Service

Turnover may also hinder the delivery of service and retention of customers, additional dimensions of organizational effectiveness (Price, 1977; Reichheld, 1993). This potential repercussion of turnover increasingly attracts academic and managerial interest as service jobs account for more than 80% of private sector employment and service occupations continue to account for the bulk of job growth. According to Call et al. (2015), service contexts require interactions with customers with diverse expectations, teamwork, and coordination, leading turnover to be particularly disruptive.

Presumably, attrition among service personnel impairs customer service because understaffed offices or stores delay or withhold service (Darmon, 1990). Unlike experienced leavers, new employees may also provide less competent or less personalized service because they do not know the clients. Customers may also switch firms if their loyalties depend on an affinity with former sales employees (Darmon, 1990; Schlesinger & Heskett, 1991). Recognizing such loyalty bonds, State Farm recruits new insurance agents who have stable community ties, and thus long-term relationships with prospective customers, and Olive Garden restaurants hire local managers known and trusted in the community (Reichheld, 1993). If satisfied employees make customers feel well treated, disgruntled employees may provide careless service before they leave (Schneider & Bowen, 1992). Turnover also interrupts the transmission of service values and norms, which are essential underpinnings of high-quality service, to successive generations of employees (Bowen & Schneider, 1988). In sum, turnover may cumulatively affect wait times, quality, satisfaction, and loyalty (Kacmar, Andrews, Van Rooy, Steilberg, & Cerrone, 2006), resulting in negative word of mouth and lower purchasing (Schneider, Ehrhart, Mayer, Saltz, & Niles-Jolly, 2005).

Consistent with this perception, internal research at Automatic Data Processing discerned a strong association between retaining service employees and retaining clients (Shellenbarger, 1992). Marriott Corporation projected that a 10% turnover reduction would reduce the incidence of customers not returning by between 1% and 3% and raise revenues by between $50 million and $150 million (Schlesinger & Heskett, 1991).

The type of client service—namely, consumer service, as provided by department stores and restaurants, distinguished from professional service, as provided by doctors and lawyers—may influence the degree to which turnover impairs client service. In particular, the departure of deliverers of professional services may most undermine the quality of the customer's experience. Because they are less tangible than consumer services, which offer goods, professional services, which are *simultaneously* produced for and consumed by each consumer, depend more on the presence and actions of the service personnel (Bowen & Schneider, 1988).

Several studies have established, consistently with this reasoning, that departures of health or mental health providers diminish the care given to patients (Price, 1977). For example, Coser (1976) found that the departure of a psychiatrist or senior resident—who oversees and trains residents in a mental hospital—preceded every wave of suicide among patients. Presumably, the departure of their superiors impaired the preparation and social support available to psychiatric trainees, and thus their capacity to recognize suicidal clues. Spector and Takada (1991) predicted that the quality of care in 80 nursing homes varied with the turnover among the staff. Their regression disclosed that low turnover among registered nurses enhances residents' functional skills (their competence in bathing and eating by themselves) more noticeably than other predictors of patient care do. Murnane,

Singer, and Willett (1988, 1989) presented evidence to suggest that attrition among teachers detracts from the students' achievements. The researchers' survival analysis determined that teachers with high aptitude scores left the profession earlier than those with low aptitude scores. The briefer careers of brighter teachers might erode the quality of education as teachers' aptitude scores covary positively with students' achievement scores. Equally alarming, the researchers found that science teachers in particular abandoned education more readily, a tendency that compounds the acute shortage of science teachers and limits the availability of science instruction.

Lost Business Opportunities

Besides affecting the current success of a firm, personnel turnover may hamper the future survival of the organization. Anecdotal evidence abounds about business opportunities lost because key contributors left (Mobley, 1982). For example, the flight of scientists and engineers can delay or prevent the introduction of new products and threaten future profitability in new markets (Gomez-Mejia, Balkin, & Milkovich, 1990; Turbin & Rosse, 1990). Equally important, expatriates from existing firms may form competing businesses, such as the Silicon Valley firms Solectron and Lam (Mandel & Farrell, 1992).

Positive Consequences for the Organization

Functional Turnover and Displacement of Poor Performers

Human resources accounting formulas may overstate exit costs because they ignore the identity of the leavers (Dalton, Krackhardt, & Porter, 1981). The exit of marginal performers, which may be termed "functional turnover," benefits employers, who may replace them with superior performers (presuming that productivity gains offset replacement and training expenses; Darmon, 1990). Importantly, several meta-analyses concluded that poor performers are more likely to quit than are good performers, in which case productivity is more likely to improve from turnover (McEvoy & Cascio, 1987; Williams & Livingstone, 1994). Thus, as Dalton et al. (1981) documented, gross quit rates are misleading. Their inspection of who left banks revealed that high performers constituted only 58% of all quits, a finding that made the overall 32% quit rate seem less alarming. A computation of *net* performance gains (or losses) that result from hiring replacements who outperform leavers may correct estimates by human resources accounting formulas of the true costs of turnover (Boudreau & Berger, 1985).

This section reviews the positive contributions of personnel attrition for organizations, underappreciated effects. Just as it can lower productivity, incur financial costs, and undermine stayers' morale, turnover can have the opposite ramifications under certain circumstances for certain firms. That is, exits of marginal performers may improve overall firm productivity, while new replacements for leavers can infuse companies with new ideas and technology. Though turnover is obviously costly, personnel shrinkage—especially among administrative staff—can nonetheless reduce overhead costs. Further, resignations may create more job and empowerment opportunities for employees who remain in firms.

In fact, some meta-analyses concluded that turnover generally promotes productivity because functional turnover is more common than dysfunctional turnover (i.e., the loss of valued personnel; McEvoy & Cascio, 1987; Williams & Livingstone, 1994). Besides this, low performers who remain on the payroll because they cannot find other employment may engage in other forms of withdrawal, such as absenteeism and sabotage (Martin & Schermerhorn, 1983; Mobley, 1982). Clearly, the absence of such disruptive employees would enhance the organization's effectiveness (Price, 1989).

Even among adequate performers, turnover in high-stress jobs susceptible to burnout may bring positive consequences. The relationship between job tenure and performance in stressful work, that of traffic controllers, physically demanding work, that of miners or construction workers, technologically changing work, that of electrical engineers, and public service work, that of social workers, may be modeled by an inverted-U curve (Staw, 1980). While lacking experience, new entrants to these stressful occupations are highly motivated or have more current skills, enabling them to outperform seasoned employees. As newcomers accumulate more job seniority, they may also lose their effectiveness; they become sluggish or burn out and their skills atrophy. Resignations by experienced personnel may not invariably yield productivity losses because the conventional J-shaped performance curve—holding that newcomers perform less effectively than veterans do—may not hold in stressful occupations.

Infusion of New Knowledge and Technology

Beyond performance improvements, turnover may benefit firms through the infusion of new knowledge and technology from the newcomers (Price, 1977), as well as new social capital (Shaw, Duffy, Johnson, & Lockhart, 2005a), a contention that a review of the literature affirms (Mobley, 1982; Mowday et al., 1982; Price, 1989; Staw, 1980). For example, research on R&D teams indicates that in groups that are excessively long-lived or stable, R&D performance decreases (Katz, 1980, 1982; Price, 1977). Notwithstanding the importance of external technical knowledge and new ideas, long-lived R&D teams become ineffective because increasingly they rely on customary work patterns and insulate themselves from outside information that might threaten their comfortable, predictable work habits.

Similarly, exits from top management may lay the groundwork for necessary changes in entrenched but maladaptive company policies (Staw, 1980). Finkelstein and Hambrick (1990) found that long-tenured executive teams followed more persistently company strategies that mirrored industry norms, whereas short-tenured teams adopted novel strategies that departed from industry patterns. Such policy changes may occur only if outsiders, rather than insiders, fill vacant executive posts (Staw, 1980). The business press has chronicled revolutionary transformations in IBM, Allied-Signal, and other Fortune 500 companies wrought by chief executive officers recruited from other firms (Bremner, 1991; Steward, 1993).

New Business Ventures

Exiting employees may provide new business to their former employers. For example, staff accountants leaving public accounting often initiate or continue audit work for their former accounting firms with their current business. Similarly, U.S.-trained Chinese returning to Taiwan to develop its high-tech industry often maintained ties to their former companies (Barnathan, Einhorn, & Nakarmi, 1992).

Labor Cost Savings

Voluntary turnover may help corporations control or lower labor costs by reducing the workforce as they face stiffer global competition (Balkin, 1992; Henkoff, 1990; Jacob, 1992; Nussbaum, 1991). Voluntary quits represent a less costly way of downsizing than do layoffs, early retirement inducements, or job buyouts (Balkin, 1992; Faltermeyer, 1992).

Theories of the Consequences of Turnover Rates and Collective Turnover

Given the range of potential costs and benefits, are there useful frameworks and empirical evidence for thinking about the consequences of turnover? While the loss of any one individual can be harmful (e.g., a particularly high-performing salesperson, scientist, or executive), much of the attention has focused on the consequences of high turnover rates. A growing body of research links turnover rates with organizational performance. For example, research shows that reducing turnover rates is associated with sales growth, improved employee morale, and increased firm profitability and market value (Batt, 2002; Huselid, 1995). Therefore, we turn now to consider major frameworks and theories that describe these relationships, followed by a summary of empirical evidence.

Hausknecht and Trevor (2011) defined collective turnover as "the aggregate levels of employee departures that occur within groups, work units, or organizations" (p. 353). They proposed a model of collective turnover that posits direct effects on firm financial and market performance, as well as indirect effects through the impact of collective turnover on productivity and customer outcomes. Their review of research up to that point concludes that there is widespread evidence of a negative relationship between collective turnover and performance, although these relationships are more consistent with more proximal outcomes such as productivity and customer outcomes and there are moderators that may exacerbate or mitigate these effects, particularly in situations where the importance of human capital to organizational functioning varies. This review also suggests that existing evidence is more consistent with the causal ordering that turnover rates affect performance, rather than the reverse.

Hausknecht and Trevor (2011) conclude their review by calling for theory explicitly focused on collective turnover. In response, Nyberg and Ployhart (2013) describe context-emergent turnover (CET) theory. They shift the definition of collective turnover to consider the depletion of human capital resources from the unit (i.e., the aggregate quantity and quality of employee knowledge, skills, and abilities that exit). Their formulation explicitly focuses on the dynamic flow of human capital and the emergence of collective turnover in context. In essence, their framework suggests that collective turnover directly influences unit performance and human capital and moderates the strength of the relationship between unit human capital and performance. They further propose that the consequences of turnover are magnified in more complex environments and when workflow is more interdependent.

As Lee, Hom, Eberly, and Li (2017) describe, CET advances more nuanced calculations of turnover rates that incorporate quality as well as quantity, accounts for coordination and efficiency losses beyond individual turnover events, and highlights the need to consider context and time. Initial tests of CET propositions demonstrate the relationship between turnover rate changes and unit performance change is indeed moderated by the quality of leavers, the quantity and quality of replacements, and turnover dispersion across time (Call et al., 2015), and that employee or manager turnover results in a greater decrement in bank branch performance and a slower recovery rate when branches are highly interdependent (Hale, Ployhart, & Shepherd, 2016).

Empirical Evidence of the Consequences of Turnover Rates and Collective Turnover

A growing body of research concerns the relationship between collective turnover and various indicators of performance or unit-level performance, such as customer service (e.g., Koys, 2001), financial performance (e.g., Batt, 2002; Huselid, 1995; Kacmar et al., 2006), and labor productivity (e.g., Guthrie, 2001; Siebert & Zubanov, 2009). In 2013 alone, three meta-analyses empirically summarized this literature (Hancock, Allen, Bosco, McDaniel, & Pierce, 2013; Heavey, Holwerda, & Hausknecht, 2013; Park & Shaw, 2013). Theoretically, these meta-analyses emphasized human capital theory (e.g., Osterman, 1987; Shaw, Gupta, & Delery, 2005b), a cost-based perspective (e.g., Dalton & Todor, 1979), social capital theory (e.g., Leana & Van Buren, 1999), and operational disruption (e.g., Staw, 1980) in explaining the likely effects of collective turnover on performance. Most recently, Hancock, Allen, and Soelberg (2017) updated and expanded these meta-analyses summarizing 2,149 effect sizes from 159 studies across 150 articles (see Table 2.2).

TABLE 2.2 Meta-Analysis of Direct Relationships between Employee Turnover and Types of Organizational Performance

	k	N	avg $r_{(uw)}$	$\bar{r}$	S_r^2	σ_e^2	σ_p^2	σ_p	%σ_e^2	95% ConfHI	95% ConfLO	80% CredHI	80% CredLO	Q	$I2$
Linear Turnover–Overall Performance	121	87898.5	−.091	−.039*	.010	.001	.008	.091	14.361	−.021	−.056	.077	−.155	842.53*	85.757
Curvilinear Turnover–Performance Relationship[a]	35	31449.1	.021	.006*	.000	.001	−.001	.000	727.193	.010	.002	.006	.006	4.81	−606.416
Performance Variables															
Overall Productivity	68	58587.3	−.042	−.031*	.010	.001	.009	.092	11.972	−.008	−.055	.087	−.150	567.99*	88.204
Sales/Output	47	49346.3	−.056	−.021	.009	.001	.009	.092	10.034	.006	−.049	.097	−.140	468.42*	90.18
Efficiency	20	6701.8	−.097	−.111*	.009	.003	.006	.075	34.205	−.071	−.152	−.015	−.207	58.47*	67.505
Costs	12	7803	−.025	−.038	.007	.002	.005	.073	22.485	.009	−.084	.056	−.131	53.37*	79.389
Innovation	4	525	−.157	−.232*	.010	.007	.003	.054	70.472	−.135	−.328	−.163	−.300	5.676	47.146
Overall Firm Performance	72	42803.9	−.076	−.047*	.009	.002	.008	.088	17.659	−.024	−.069	.066	−.160	407.71*	82.586
Financial Performance	68	64951.6	−.076	−.033*	.007	.001	.006	.075	15.561	−.013	−.052	.064	−.129	436.978	84.667
Market Performance	4	811	−.098	−.086	.002	.005	−.002	.000	197.086	−.038	−.135	−.086	−.086	2.030	−47.814
Customer Outcomes	30	8327	−.260	−.144*	.029	.003	.026	.160	11.971	−.083	−.205	.061	−.348	250.61*	88.428
Wait Time	5	2935	.236	.081	.010	.002	.008	.089	17.582	.167	−.005	.195	−.033	28.44*	85.934
Customer Satisfaction	16	4220	−.247	−.145*	.025	.004	.021	.146	14.548	−.067	−.222	.043	−.332	109.978	86.361
Service Quality	9	1033	−.260	−.215*	.029	.008	.021	.144	27.954	−.105	−.326	−.031	−.399	32.195	75.152

Note: k = number of samples; N = number of observations; avg $r(uw)$ = unweighted mean; $\bar{r}$ = sample size-weighted mean effect size; 95% CI = 95% confidence interval; 80% CR = 80% credibility interval; Q-statistic = chi-square test for homogeneity of effect sizes; I2 = % of variance across studies due to heterogeneity (Higgins, Thompson, Deeks, & Altman, 2003).

* $p < .05$

[a] Results of a semi-partial correlation analysis as described by Cohen and Cohen (1983) and Williams and Livingstone (1994).

The consequences of collective turnover were grouped into three clusters: productivity (sales/output, efficiency, costs, innovation), firm performance (financial performance, market performance), and customer outcomes (wait time, customer satisfaction, service quality). As expected, the overall relationship between collective turnover and unit-level performance is negative and significant ($r = -.04$, $p < .05$, 95% CI = $-.06$ to $-.02$). This relationship is strongest with respect to customer outcomes ($r = -.14$, $p < .05$, 95% CI = $-.21$ to $-.08$), followed by firm performance ($r = -.05$, $p < .05$, 95% CI = $-.07$ to $-.02$), and productivity ($r = -.03$, $p < .05$, 95% CI = $-.06$ to $-.008$). Hancock et al. (2013) conducted a meta-analytic path analysis suggesting that turnover rates are most directly related to customer service, quality, and safety, and that decrements in quality and safety are the primary mediating mechanisms by which turnover affects financial performance. Although the overall observed relationship may appear modest, the practical impact can be substantial. Hancock et al. (2013), using a similar effect size, estimated that the financial impact of a one standard deviation reduction in collective turnover could range from approximately $40,000 for a sample of chain restaurants to more than $150 million for the world's largest Fortune 1000 companies. Similarly, Call et al. (2015) estimated that a one standard deviation increase in a retail store's collective turnover reduces yearly profit by nearly 9%.

Additionally, moderators likely play an important role (Hausknecht & Trevor, 2011). Combining perspectives from prior meta-analyses, Hancock et al. (2017) examined turnover type (voluntary, involuntary, or total), geographic location (North America, Europe, or Asia), type of economy (market or coordinated), culture (individualistic or collectivistic), industry, organization size, and types of employees (managers or non-supervisory) as potential moderators. Findings include that location moderated ($Qb = 64.652$, $p < .05$) the turnover–performance relationship, with North America exhibiting a stronger negative relationship ($r = -.10$, $p < .05$, 95% CI = $-.08$ to $-.04$) than either Europe or Asia; industry was a significant moderator ($Qb = 46.784$, $p < .05$) such that studies in hospital/healthcare samples ($r = -.09$, $p < .05$, 95% CI = $-.18$ to $-.01$) or samples across multiple industries ($r = -.09$, $p < .05$, 95% CI = $-.15$ to $-.03$) had the strongest relationships, followed by oil/manufacturing/transportation ($r = -.06$, $p < .05$, 95% CI = $-.09$ to $-.03$); and samples with only managers ($r = -.14$, $p < .05$, 95% CI = $-.19$ to $-.09$) demonstrated stronger relationships than those with non-supervisory employees ($r = -.05$, $p < .05$, 95% CI = $-.09$ to $-.02$) (see Table 2.3).

Is There an Optimal Turnover Rate? The Search for Curvilinearity

Allen et al. (2010) emphasize that even if the organization were to invest heavily in retention, some turnover is likely unavoidable (Abelson, 1987). In most cases, it is neither feasible nor desirable for the turnover rate to be zero. At the same time, excessive turnover that is far greater than competitors or simply creating too much human capital churn is almost certainly disruptive and harmful for organizational

TABLE 2.3 Meta-Analysis of Employee Turnover and Overall Organizational Performance Moderators

	k	N	$avg\ r_{iwy}$	$\bar{r}$	S_r^2	σ_e^2	σ_p^2	σ_p	$\%\sigma_e^2$	95% ConfHI	95% ConfLO	80% CredHI	80% CredLO	Q	$I2$	Qb
Moderator Variables																
Turnover Type																6.093
Total	69	6,3648.5	−.097	−.034*	.008	.001	.007	.086	12.890	−.012	−.056	.076	−.144	535.28*	87.296	
Voluntary	34	18,289	−.090	−.049*	.011	.002	.009	.097	16.540	−.013	−.084	.075	−.173	205.56*	83.947	
Involuntary	10	2,150	−.108	−.046	.031	.005	.027	.163	14.872	.063	−.156	.163	−.255	67.24*	86.615	
Reduction in Force	8	3,811	−.028	−.065*	.007	.002	.005	.073	28.168	−.005	−.124	.029	−.158	28.40*	75.353	
Location																64.652*
North America	71	3,4685.7	−.102	−.070*	.009	.002	.007	.085	22.041	−.048	−.093	.038	−.179	322.13*	78.270	
Europe	16	38,601	−.023	−.011	.005	.000	.005	.069	7.982	.024	−.046	.078	−.100	200.44*	92.516	
Asia	16	3,524	−.058	−.031	.028	.005	.023	.152	16.484	.050	−.113	.163	−.226	97.06*	84.546	
Location (Economy)																75.108*
LME	77	3,7817.7	−.112	−.073*	.012	.002	.010	.099	17.005	−.049	−.098	.054	−.200	452.81*	83.216	
CME	16	37,039	−.092	−.010	.003	.000	.002	.046	16.740	.015	−.035	.050	−.069	95.58*	84.307	
Location (Culture)																.031
Individualistic	86	73,346.7	−.106	−.042*	.008	.001	.007	.085	13.976	−.022	−.061	.067	−.150	615.32*	86.186	
Collectivistic	15	3,145	−.072	−.045	.030	.005	.025	.158	16.075	.042	−.132	.157	−.247	93.31*	84.997	
Industry																46.784*
Oil, Manufacturing, Transportation	22	15,667.5	−.099	−.058*	.004	.001	.003	.055	31.579	−.030	−.085	.013	−.128	69.67*	69.857	

(Continued)

Table 2.3 (Cont.)

	k	N	avg r_(uw)	r̄	S²_r	σ²_e	σ²_p	σ_p	%σ²_e	95%	95%	80%	80%	Q	I2	Qb
										ConfHI	ConfLO	CredHI	CredLO			
Retail, Restaurant, Service	25	9,896.5	−.049	−.029	.019	.003	.017	.130	13.075	.026	−.083	.137	−.195	191.20*	87.448	
Banking and Technology	38	5,2063.7	−.094	−.025	.006	.001	.006	.076	11.288	.001	−.050	.073	−.122	336.64*	89.009	
Education	6	546.8	−.082	−.039	.022	.011	.010	.102	51.352	.079	−.156	.092	−.170	11.68*	57.207	
Hospital, Healthcare	9	2,471	−.203	−.094*	.018	.004	.014	.120	20.044	−.006	−.181	.060	−.247	44.90*	82.183	
Cross-Industry	21	7,253	−.081	−.094*	.019	.003	.017	.129	14.655	−.034	−.154	.071	−.259	143.30*	86.043	

Note: k = number of samples; N = number of observations; avg r(uw) = unweighted mean; r̄ = sample size-weighted mean effect size; 95% CI = 95% confidence interval; 80% CR = 80% credibility interval; Q-statistic = chi-square test for homogeneity of effect sizes; I2 = % of variance across studies due to heterogeneity (Higgins et al., 2003); Qb = between-group test of homogeneity

* p < .05

functioning. This implies that there may be an optimal level of turnover that allows for new human and social capital and for some inevitable mobility, but not so high as to cripple effectiveness. As Hancock et al. (2017) note, there are studies that have demonstrated a positive relationship between turnover rates and unit performance (e.g., Seleim, Ashour, & Bontis, 2007), and evidence of curvilinearity that would be consistent with an optimal level (e.g., Glebbeek & Bax, 2004; Meier & Hicklin, 2008; Shaw et al., 2005a, 2005b). Hancock et al. (2017) derived semi-partial correlations (Williams & Livingstone, 1994) for 35 effect sizes resulting in a significant positive mean quadratic semi-partial correlation. This finding suggests a curvilinear relationship resembling an inverted U-shape.

Executive Post-Acquisition Turnover

One special case of turnover that warrants attention is executive turnover following a merger or acquisition. Although popular strategies, many if not most acquisitions fail to create value for the acquiring firm (King, Dalton, Daily, & Covin, 2004). One reason may be that a quarter of acquired firms' top executives leave within a year, and nearly 60% within five years (Krug, 2009; Krug, Wright, & Kroll, 2014). Conflicting theoretical accounts suggest the likelihood of positive and negative effects of executive turnover on post-acquisition performance; for example, agency theory suggests post-acquisition executive turnover is a rational outcome of market processes driving acquisitions, while a resource-based view suggests value in retaining acquired executives firm-specific knowledge and capabilities (Krug, 2009).

Bilgili, Calderon, Allen, and Kedia (2017) conducted a meta-analysis and a meta-analytic structural equation model (MASEM) to address the consequences of post-acquisition CEO and top-management team (TMT) turnover. They summarized data from 112 studies and 399 observed effect sizes, and base their analyses in the theory of relative standing (Frank, 1985): certain firm and acquisition deal characteristics affect the relative standing of acquired and acquiring executives that influence executive turnover and subsequent firm performance (Hambrick & Cannella, 1993). Interestingly, their results showed a negative association between TMT turnover and post-acquisition performance (corrected effect size = −.17) and a positive association between CEO turnover and post-acquisition performance (corrected effect size = .13), and that both types of executive turnover explained (via full or partial mediation) the role of firm and acquisition deal antecedents on post-acquisition performance (Bilgili et al., 2017).

The negative association between TMT turnover and post-acquisition performance supports the idea TMT members possess valuable social capital, firm-specific knowledge, and boundary-spanning capabilities such that too much TMT turnover, following what is already a disruptive event, is more disruptive than adaptive. Conversely, Bilgili et al. (2017) concluded that the positive association between CEO turnover and post-acquisition performance may represent symbolic and signaling functions regarding the reasons for the acquisition and the future direction of the firm.

Future Directions for Research

In summary, turnover introduces various contradictory and complex consequences for leavers and organizations. Some are advantageous for organizations or individuals; others are not. Such contradictory outcomes make it difficult, however, to forecast the *net* impact (Nyberg & Ployhart, 2013; Staw, 1980). Toward this end, we must develop and test more complex conceptualizations of the impact of turnover that acknowledge these complexities. For example, turnover among personnel may impair a department's productivity by disrupting production, but enhance the corporation's productivity by reducing the workforce; turnover may increase job satisfaction when disagreeable colleagues leave or opportunities for promotion expand, but decrease satisfaction by prompting employees to question their motivation for staying. Thus, we identify several key avenues for future research on turnover consequences.

Study the Processes Linking Collective Turnover to Unit Performance

Meta-analytic summaries suggest that proximal performance indicators mediate relationships with more distal ones (Hancock et al., 2013), and CET-based models suggest that timing and environmental complexity likely moderate how collective turnover affects unit performance (Call et al., 2015; Nyberg & Ployhart, 2013). Hausknecht and Trevor (2011) note that scholars have speculated about multiple potential mediating mechanisms that are rarely addressed, including lowered morale, shifting roles, socializing new hires, and communication challenges, among others. Lee et al. (2017) suggest efforts to integrate interactive processes among individual, group, and collective turnover events and processes. This may especially be the case because the types and strengths of moderators may vary across organizational levels. For example, the moderating role of structural independence may be stronger at the team as opposed to broader unit levels because of greater awareness of interdependencies (Lee et al., 2017).

Track Types of Turnover, Turnover Destinations, and Interactions of Types and Levels of Turnover

For example, turnover destinations may interact with reasons for leaving, resignation strategies, post-exit relationships, honeymoon-hangover effects, and the likelihood of boomerang employment to affect the consequences of turnover on leavers. As one illustration, knowing which competing firms hire away employees may enable a more fine-grained analysis of turnover dysfunctionality. As Hausknecht and Trevor (2011) note, the expected functional consequences of involuntary turnover are not typically found empirically at the collective level, perhaps because of important conceptual differences between individual and collective exits. Additionally, meta-analyses often find that researchers routinely fail to differentiate the type of turnover being investigated, making such progress difficult (e.g., Hancock et al., 2013). Bilgili et al. (2017) emphasize that future research on post-acquisition performance following executive turnover should model CEO and TMT turnover as different types of turnover, and differentiate between voluntary and involuntary executive turnover. And research on stayers may find that whether quitting demoralizes remaining employees may depend on whether they believed that the leavers departed voluntarily or involuntarily (Staw, 1980). It may matter a great deal who leaves, yet leaver characteristics are often not available (Hausknecht & Trevor, 2011). Another way of thinking about who leaves would be to study whether the departure of generic or specific human capital resources affect collective turnover differently (Nyberg & Ployhart, 2013).

Future research needs to consider turnover effects longitudinally to trace their distribution over time (Price, 1989) to reveal that some effects are short term, while others are long term.

Beyond this, a particular consequence may manifest *different* effects over time. Thus, some outcomes may appear harmful in the short term but yield long-term benefits. For instance, the departure of top executives from troubled companies may prove temporarily disruptive but pave the way to new strategic initiatives that will revitalize these companies. Hausknecht and Trevor (2011) emphasize that although there are numerous calls for truly longitudinal investigations, the majority of studies relate a one-year aggregate turnover rate with concurrent or time-lagged performance indicators, consistent with the dominant turnover analytical mindset identified by Allen, Hancock, Vardaman, and McKee (2014). Such research, like Call et al.'s (2015) study, may reveal novel insights such as their distinction between turnover rates and turnover rate change. Additionally, Nyberg and Ployhart (2013) suggest focusing on the relative importance of quality vs. quantity in explaining collective turnover effects, and whether relative importance changes based on context or temporal dynamics.

More research on various moderators that shape the effects of turnover will advance the understanding of its consequences, as will examinations of nonlinear effects (Staw, 1980). Potential moderators include industry, job types, complexity, and climate. Hausknecht and Trevor (2011) note there is a rich history of collective turnover research in some industries (e.g., healthcare, hospitality, restaurants), but research should extend into other domains where there is variance in the extent to which turnover is more or less likely to be destabilizing. They also encourage the study of a broad array of job types, as collective turnover dynamics may differ considerably even within the same organization. For example, Nyberg and Ployhart (2013) note that bundling multiple types of jobs together may be problematic if jobs vary in complexity. They also suggest studying the extent to which climate may act as a buffer or magnifier of collective turnover's effects on unit performance. There is also value in continuing to assess the existence of nonlinear relationships. Various patterns have implications that differ in important ways, and Hausknecht and Trevor (2011) lament that we might know more about these patterns if scholars in the area would routinely report tests for curvilinearity.

Consider the role of organizational interventions in influencing the consequences of turnover. For example, Lee et al. (2017) posit effective replacement hiring and strong knowledge management systems as mechanisms for mitigating the impact of turnover on organizations. Effective alumni networks may influence consequences for leavers by providing continued social support and potential destinations for future employment. As Hausknecht and Trevor (2011) note, we know organizations take steps to retain talent; however, the efficacy of interventions at the collective level is understudied. Doing so may also lead scholars to identify conditions under which positive consequences of turnover emerge for organizations. Ignoring positive effects may lead to offsetting negative effects, resulting in more difficult to detect relationships of any kind (Hausknecht & Trevor, 2011). More empirical work on turnover consequences may improve managers' projections of the costs and benefits of turnover interventions and alert them to potential side effects. To illustrate, some programs may reduce departures but evoke counterproductive effects, such as retention of marginal employees (Sheridan, 1992). Thus, research documenting side effects would help managers make more informed decisions about choosing turnover interventions that yield *net* positive effects for their organizations apart from reducing quits.

References

Abelson, M. A. (1987). Examination of avoidable and unavoidable turnover. *Journal of Applied Psychology*, 72, 382–386.

Abelson, M. A., & Baysinger, B. D. (1984). Optimal and dysfunctional turnover: Toward an organizational level model. *Academy of Management Review*, 9, 331–341.

Allen, D. G. (2006). Do organizational socialization tactics influence new-comer embeddedness and turnover? *Journal of Management*, 32, 237–256.

Allen, D. G., Bryant, P., & Vardaman, J. (2010). Retaining talent: Replacing misconceptions with evidence-based strategies. *Academy of Management Perspective*, 24, 48–64.

Allen, D. G., Hancock, J. I., Vardaman, J. M., & McKee, D. N. (2014). Analytical mindsets in turnover research. *Journal of Organizational Behavior*, 35, 61–68.

Antel, J. J. (1991). The wage effects of voluntary labor mobility with and without intervening unemployment. *Industrial and Labor Relations Review*, 44, 299–306.

Balkin, D. B. (1992). Managing employee separations with the reward system. *The Executive*, 6, 64–71.

Barnathan, J., Einhorn, B., & Nakarmi, L. (1992, December 7). Bringing it all back home. *Businessweek*, 7, 133.

Batt, R. (2002). Managing customer services: Human resource practices, quit rates, and sales growth. *Academy of Management Journal*, 45, 587–597.
Bilgili, T. V., Calderon, C. J., Allen, D. G., & Kedia, B. L. (2017). Gone with the wind: A meta-analytic review of executive turnover, its antecedents, and postacquisition performance. *Journal of Management*, 43(6), 1966–1997.
Blegen, M. A., Mueller, C. W., & Price, J. L. (1988). Measurement of kinship responsibility for organizational research. *Journal of Applied Psychology*, 73, 402–409.
Boswell, W. R., Boudreau, J. W., & Tichy, J. (2005). The relationship between employee job change and job satisfaction: The honeymoon-hangover effect. *Journal of Applied Psychology*, 90, 882–892.
Boswell, W. R., Shipp, A. J., Payne, S. C., & Culbertson, S. S. (2009). Changes in newcomer job satisfaction over time: Examining the pattern of honeymoons and hangovers. *Journal of Applied Psychology*, 94, 844–858.
Boudreau, J. W., & Berger, C. J. (1985). Decision-theoretical utility analysis applied to employee separations and acquisitions. *Journal of Applied Psychology*, 70(3), 581–612.
Bowen, D. E., & Schneider, B. (1988). Services marketing and management: Implications for organizational behavior. In B. M. Staw & L. L. Cummings (Eds.), *Research in Organizational Behavior* (vol. 10, pp. 43–80). Greenwich, CT: JAI Press.
Bremner, B. (1991, November 25). Tough times, tough bosses. *Businessweek*, 174–179.
Brown, R. J., Carr, R., & Orthner, D. K. (1983). Family life patterns in the air force. In F. Margiotta, J. Brown, & M. Collins (Eds.), *Changing U.S. Military Manpower Realities* (pp. 207–220). Boulder, CO: Westview Press.
Caliguri, P. M., Hyland, M. M., Joshi, A., & Bross, A. S. (1998). Testing a theoretical model for examining the relationship between family adjustment and expatriates' work adjustment. *Journal of Applied Psychology*, 83, 598–614.
Call, M. L., Nyberg, A. J., Ployhart, R. E., & Weekley, J. (2015). The dynamic nature of collective turnover and unit performance: The impact of time, quality, and replacement. *Academy of Management Journal*, 58, 1208–1232.
Carnahan, S., & Somaya, D. (2015). The other talent war: Competing through alumni. *MIT Sloan Management Review*, 56(3), 14–16.
Cascio, W. F. (1991). *Costing Human Resources: The Financial Impact of Behavior in Organizations*, 3rd ed. Boston, MA: Kent Publishing Company.
Cascio, W. F. (2006). The economic impact of employee behaviors on organizational performance. *California Management Review*, 48, 41–59.
Cavanagh, S. J. (1989). Nursing turnover: Literature review and methodological critique. *Journal of Advanced Nursing*, 14, 587–596.
Cohen, J., & Cohen, P. (1983). *Applied Multiple Regression/Correlation Analysis for the Behavioural Sciences* (2nd ed.). Hillsdale, NJ: Erlbaum.
Coser, R. L. (1976). Suicide and the relational system: A case study in a mental hospital. *Journal of Health and Social Behavior*, 17, 318–327.
Dalton, D. R., Krackhardt, D. M., & Porter, L. W. (1981). Functional turnover: An empirical assessment. *Journal of Applied Psychology*, 66, 716–721.
Dalton, D. R., & Todor, W. D. (1979). Turnover turned over: An expanded and positive perspective. *Academy of Management Review*, 4, 225–235.
Dalton, D. R., Todor, W. D., & Krackhardt, D. M. (1982). Turnover overstated: A functional taxonomy. *Academy of Management Review*, 7, 117–123.
Darmon, R. Y. (1990). Identifying sources of turnover costs: A segmental approach. *Journal of Marketing*, 54, 46–56.

Donovan, L. (1980). What nurses want. *RN*, 43, 22–30.
Dowling, P. J., & Schuler, R. S. (1990). *International Dimensions of Human Resource Management*. Boston, MA: PWS-Kent.
Faltermeyer, E. (1992, June 1). Is this layoff necessary? *Fortune*, 71–86.
Feldman, D. C. (1976). A contingency theory of socialization. *Administrative Science Quarterly*, 21(3), 433–452.
Feldman, D. C. (1988). *Managing Careers in Organizations*. Glenview, IL: Scott, Foresman.
Feldman, D. C., & Brett, J. M. (1983). Coping with new jobs: A comparative study of new hires and job changers. *Academy of Management Journal*, 26, 258–272.
Felps, W., Mitchell, T. R., Hekman, D., Lee, T. W., Holtom, B. C., & Harman, W. S. (2009). Turnover contagion: How coworkers' job embeddedness and coworkers' job search behaviors influence quitting. *Academy of Management Journal*, 52, 545–561.
Finkelstein, S., & Hambrick, D. C. (1990). Top-management-team tenure and organizational outcomes: The moderating role of managerial discretion. *Administrative Science Quarterly*, 35, 484–503.
Fitz-enz, J. (2002). *How to Measure Human Resources Management* (3rd ed.). New York: McGraw-Hill.
Frank, R. H. (1985). *Choosing the Right Pond*. New York: Oxford Univeristy Press.
Glebbeek, A. C., & Bax, E. H. (2004). Is high employee turnover really harmful? An empirical test using company records. *Academy of Management Journal*, 47, 277–286.
Gomez-Mejia, L. R., Balkin, D. B., & Milkovich, G. T. (1990). Rethinking your rewards for technical employees. *Organizational Dynamics*, 18, 62–75.
Griffeth, R. W., & Hom, P. W. (2001). *Retaining Valued Employees*. Thousand Oaks, CA: Sage.
Guthrie, J. P. (2001). High-involvement work practices, turnover, and productivity: Evidence from New Zealand. *Academy of Management Journal*, 44(1), 180–190.
Hale, D. Jr., Ployhart, R. E., & Shepherd, W. (2016). A two-phase longitudinal model of a turnover event: Disruption, recovery rates, and moderators of collective performance. *Academy of Management Journal*, 59, 906–929.
Hambrick, D. C., & Cannella, A. A. (1993). Relative standing: A framework for understanding departures of acquired executives. *Academy of Management Journal*, 36(4), 733–762.
Hancock, J. I., Allen, D. G., Bosco, F. A., McDaniel, K. R., & Pierce, C. A. (2013). Meta-analytic review of employee turnover as a predictor of firm performance. *Journal of Management*, 39, 573–603.
Hancock, J. I., Allen, D. G., & Soelberg, C. (2017). Collective turnover: An expanded meta-analytic exploration and comparison. *Human Resource Management Review*, 27(1), 61–86.
Hausknecht, J. P., & Trevor, C. O. (2011). Collective turnover at the group, unit, and organizational levels: Evidence, issues, and implications. *Journal of Management*, 37, 352–388.
Heavey, A. L., Holwerda, J. A., & Hausknecht, J. P. (2013). Causes and consequences of collective turnover: A meta-analytic review. *Journal of Applied Psychology*, 98(3), 412–453.
Hechanova, R., Beehr, T. A., & Christiansen, N. D. (2003). Antecedents and consequences of employees' adjustment to overseas assignment: A meta-analytic review. *Applied Psychology*, 52, 213–236.
Heneman III, H. G., & Judge, T. A. (2006). *Staffing Organizations* (5th ed.). Middleton, WI: Mendota House.
Henkoff, R. (1990, April 9). Cost cutting: How to do it right. *Fortune*, 40.
Higgins, J. P., Thompson, S. G., Deeks, J. J., & Altman, D. G. (2003). Measuring inconsistency in meta-analyses. *British Medical Journal*, 327, 557–560.

Hom, P. W. (1992). *Turnover Costs among Mental Health Professionals*. Tempe, AZ: College of Business, Arizona State University.

Hom, P. W., & Griffeth, R. W. (1991). Structural equations modeling test of a turnover theory: Cross-sectional and longitudinal analyses. *Journal of Applied Psychology*, 76, 350–366.

Hom, P. W., Mitchell, T. R., Lee, T. W., & Griffeth, R. W. (2012). Reviewing employee turnover: Focusing on proximal withdrawal states and an expanded criterion. *Psychological Bulletin*, 138, 831–858.

Hulin, C. L. (1991). Adaptation, persistence, and commitment in organizations. In M. D. Dunnette & L. M. Hough (Eds.), *Handbook of Industrial and Organizational Psychology* (2nd ed., pp. 445–505). Palo Alto, CA: Consulting Psychologists Press.

Hulin, C. L., Roznowski, M., & Hachiya, D. (1985). Alternative opportunities and withdrawal decisions: Empirical and theoretical discrepancies and an integration. *Psychological Bulletin*, 97(2), 233–250.

Hunter, E. J. (1983). Family power: An issue in military manpower management. In F. Margiotta, J. Brown, & M. Collins (Eds.), *Changing U.S. Military Manpower Realities* (pp. 195–206). Boulder, CO: Westview Press.

Huselid, M. A. (1995). The impact of human resource management practices on turnover, productivity, and corporate financial performance. *Academy of Management Journal*, 38, 635–672.

Ippolito, R. A. (1991). Encouraging long-term tenure: Wage tilt or pension? *Industrial and Labor Relations Review*, 44, 520–535.

Jacob, R. (1992). The search for the organization of tomorrow. *Fortune*, 125(10), 92–98.

Kacmar, K. M., Andrews, M. C., Van Rooy, D. L., Steilberg, R. C., & Cerrone, S. (2006). Sure everyone can be replaced ... but at what cost? Turnover as a predictor of unit-level performance. *Academy of Management Journal*, 49, 133–144.

Kandel, D. B., & Yamaguchi, K. (1987). Job mobility and drug use: An event history analysis. *American Journal of Sociology*, 92 (4), 836–878.

Katz, R. (1980). Time and work: Toward an integrative perspective. In B. M. Staw & L. L. Cummings (Eds.), *Research in Organizational Behavior* (vol. 2, pp. 81–127). Greenwich, CT: JAI Press.

Katz, R. (1982). The effects of group longevity on project communication and performance. *Administrative Science Quarterly*, 27(1), 81–104.

Kiazad, K., Holtom, B. C., Hom, P. W., & Newman, A. (2015). Job embeddedness: A multifoci theoretical extension. *Journal of Applied Psychology*, 100, 641–659.

King, D. R., Dalton, D. R., Daily, C. M., & Covin, J. G. (2004). Meta-analyses of post acquisition performance: Indications of unidentified moderators. *Strategic Management Journal*, 25(2), 187–200.

Klotz, A. C., & Bolino, M. C. (2016). Saying goodbye: The nature, causes, and consequences of employee resignation styles. *Journal of Applied Psychology*, 101(10), 1386–1404.

Koys, D. J. (2001). The effects of employee satisfaction, organizational citizenship behavior, and turnover on organizational effectiveness: A unit-level, longitudinal study. *Personnel Psychology*, 54, 101–114.

Krackhardt, D., & Porter, L. W. (1985). When friends leave: A structural analysis of the relationship between turnover and stayers' attitudes. *Administrative Science Quarterly*, 30, 242–261.

Krackhardt, D., & Porter, L. W. (1986). The snowball effect: Turnover embedded in communication networks. *Applied Psychology*, 71, 50–55.

Krug, J. A. (2009). Brain drain: Why top management bolts after M&As. *Journal of Business Strategy*, 30(6), 4–14.

Krug, J. A., Wright, P., & Kroll, M. (2014). Top management turnover following mergers and acquisitions: Solid research to date but much still to be learned. *Academy of Management Perspectives*, 28(2), 147–163.

Kulik, C., Rae, B., Sardeshmukh, S. R., & Perera, S. (2015). Can we still be friends? The role of exit conversations in facilitating post-exit relationships. *Human Resource Management*, 54(6), 893–912.

Leana, C. R., & Van Buren, III. H. J. (1999). Organizational social capital and employment practices. *Academy of Management Review*, 24, 538–555.

Lee, T. W., Hom, P. W., Eberly, M. B., & Li, J. (2017). On the next decade of research in voluntary employee turnover. *Academy of Management Perspectives*, 31(3), 201–221.

Louis, M. R., Posner, B. Z., & Powell, G. N. (1983). The availability and helpfulness of socialization practices. *Personnel Psychology*, 36, 857–866.

Lublin, J. S. (1992, November 20). After couples divorce, long-distance moves are often wrenching. *Wall Street Journal*, 1.

Lublin, J. S. (1993, April 13). As more men become "trailing spouses," firms help them cope. *Wall Street Journal*, 1.

Mandel, M. J., & Farrell, C. (1992, July 13). The immigrants. *Businessweek*, 114.

Martin, T. N., & Schermerhorn, J. R. (1983). Work and nonwork influences on health: A research agenda using inability to leave as a critical variable. *Academy of Management Review*, 8(4), 650–659.

McEvoy, G. M., & Cascio, W. F. (1987). Do good or poor performers leave? A meta-analysis of the relationship between performance and turnover. *Academy of Management Journal*, 30, 744–762.

Meier, K. J., & Hicklin, A. (2008). Employee turnover and organizational performance: A theoretical extension and test with public sector data. *Journal of Public Administration Research and Theory*, 18, 573–590.

Methot, J. R., Rosado-Solomon, E. H., & Allen, D. G. (2018). The network architecture of human capital: A relational identity perspective. *Academy of Management Review*, 43(4), 723–748.

Miller, S. (2018, February 14). Employees are more likely to stay if they like their health plan. *SHRM*. Retrieved from www.shrm.org/resourcesandtools/hr-topics/benefits/pages/health-benefits-foster-retention.aspx

Milliken, F., Dutton, J. E., & Beyer, J. M. (1990). Understanding organizational adaptation to change: The case of work–family issues. *Human Resource Planning*, 13, 91–107.

Mirowsky, J. (1987). The psycho-economics of feeling underpaid: Distributive justice and the earnings of husbands and wives. *American Journal of Sociology*, 92(6), 1404–1434.

Mitchell, O. S. (1983). Fringe benefits and the cost of changing jobs. *Industrial and Labor Relations Review*, 37, 70–78.

Mitchell, T. R., Holtom, B. C., Lee, T. W., Sablynski, C. J., & Erez, M. (2001). Why people stay: Using job embeddedness to predict voluntary turnover. *Academy of Management Journal*, 44, 1102–1121.

Mobley, W. H. (1977). Intermediate linkages in the relationship between job satisfaction and employee turnover. *Journal of Applied Psychology*, 62(2), 237–240.

Mobley, W. H. (1982). *Employee Turnover: Causes, Consequences, and Control*. Reading, MA: Addison-Wesley.

Mowday, R. T., Porter, L. W., & Steers, R. M. (1982). *Employee–Organization Linkages*. New York: Academic Press.

Mueller, C. W., & Price, J. L. (1989). Some consequences of turnover: A work unit analysis. *Human Relations*, 42, 389–402.

Murnane, R. J., Singer, J. D., & Willett, J. B. (1988). The career paths of teachers. *Educational Researcher*, 17, 22–30.

Murnane, R. J., Singer, J. D., & Willett, J. B. (1989). The influences of salaries and "opportunity costs" on teachers' career choices: Evidence from North Carolina. *Harvard Educational Review*, 59, 325–346.

Nussbaum, B. (1991, October 7). I'm worried about my job! *Business Week*, 94.

Nyberg, A. J. & Ployhart, R. E. (2013). Context-emergent turnover (CET) theory: A theory of collective turnover. *Academy of Management Review*, 38, 109–131.

O'Reilly, C. A., Caldwell, D. F., & Barnett, W. P. (1989). Work group demography, social integration, and turnover. *Administrative Science Quarterly*, 34, 21–37.

Osterman, P. (1987). Choice of employment systems in internal labor markets. *Industrial Relations*, 26, 46–57.

Park, T. Y., & Shaw, J. D. (2013). Turnover rates and organizational performance: A meta-analysis. *Journal of Applied Psychology*, 98, 268–309.

Pfeffer, J. (1983). Organizational demography. In L. L. Cummings & B. M. Staw (Eds.), *Research in Organizational Behavior* (vol. 5, pp. 299–357). Greenwich, CT: JAI Press.

Price, J. L. (1977). *The Study of Turnover*. Ames, IA: Iowa State University Press.

Price, J. L. (1989). The impact of turnover on the organization. *Work and Occupations*, 16, 461–473.

Price, J. L., & Mueller, C. W. (1981). A causal model of turnover for nurses. *Academy of Management Journal*, 24, 543–565.

Price, J. L., & Mueller, C. W. (1986). *Absenteeism and Turnover of Hospital Employees*. Greenwich, CT: JAI Press.

Reichheld, F. F. (1993). Loyalty-based management. *Harvard Business Review*, 71, 64–73.

Reilly, G., Nyberg, A. J., Maltarich, M., & Weller, I. (2014). Human capital flows: Using context-emergent turnover (CET) theory to explore the process by which turnover, hiring, and job demands affect patient satisfaction. *Academy of Management Journal*, 57(3), 766–790.

Rhodes, S. R., & Steers, R. M. (1990). *Managing Employee Absenteeism*. Reading, MA: Addison-Wesley.

Rosse, J. G. (1988). Relations among lateness, absence, and turnover: Is there a progression of withdrawal? *Human Relations*, 41, 517–531.

Rusbult, C. E., & Farrell, D. (1983). A longitudinal test of the investment model: The impact of job satisfaction, job commitment, and turnover of variations in rewards, costs, alternatives, and investments. *Journal of Applied Psychology*, 68, 429–438.

Schlesinger, L. A., & Heskett, J. L. (1991). The service-driven service company. *Harvard Business Review*, 69, 71–81.

Schneider, B., & Bowen, D. E. (1992). Personnel/human resources management in the service sector. In G. Ferris & K. Rowland (Eds.), *Research in Personnel and Human Resources Management* (vol. 10, pp. 1–30). Greenwich, CT: JAI Press.

Schneider, B., Ehrhart, M. G., Mayer, D. M., Saltz, J. L., & Niles-Jolly, K. (2005). Understanding organization–customer links in service settings. *Academy of Management Journal*, 48, 1017–1032.

Seleim, A., Ashour, A., & Bontis, N. (2007). Human capital and organizational performance: A study of Egyptian software companies. *Management Decision*, 45(4), 789–901.

Shaw, J. D., Duffy, M. K., Johnson, J. L., & Lockhart, D. E. (2005a). Turnover, social capital losses, and performance. *Academy of Management Journal*, 48(4), 594–606.

Shaw, J. D., Gupta, N., & Delery, J. E. (2005b). Alternative conceptualizations of the relationship between voluntary turnover and organizational performance. *Academy of Management Journal*, 48(1), 50–68.

Shellenbarger, S. (1992). Lessons from the workplace: How corporate policies and attitudes lag behind workers' changing needs. *Human Resource Management*, 31(3), 157–169.

Sheridan, J. E. (1992). Organizational culture and employee retention. *Academy of Management Journal*, 35, 1036–1056.

Shipp, A. J., Furst-Holloway, S., Harris, T. B., & Rosen, B. (2014). Gone today but here tomorrow: Extending the unfolding model of turnover to consider boomerang employees. *Personnel Psychology*, 67, 421–462.

Siebert, W. S., & Zubanov, N. (2009). Searching for the optimal level of employee turnover: A study of a large U.K. retail organization. *Academy of Management Journal*, 52(2), 294–313.

Spector, W. D., & Takada, H. A. (1991). Characteristics of nursing homes that affect resident outcomes. *Journal of Aging and Health*, 3, 427–454.

Staines, G. L., Pottick, K. J., & Fudge, D. A. (1986). Wives' employment and husbands' attitudes toward work and life. *Journal of Applied Psychology*, 71(1), 118–128.

Staw, B. M. (1980). The consequences of turnover. *Journal of Occupational Behavior*, 1, 253–273.

Steel, R. P. (2002). Turnover theory at the empirical interface: Problems of fit and function. *Academy of Management Review*, 27, 346–360.

Steward, T. A. (1993, January 11). The king is dead. *Fortune*, 34.

Sundstrom, E., De Meuse, K. P., & Futrell, D. (1990). Work teams: Applications and effectiveness. *American Psychologist*, 45(2), 120–133.

Turban, D. B., Campion, J. E., & Eyring, A. R. (1992). Factors relating to relocation decisions of research and development employees. *Journal of Vocational Behavior*, 41, 183–199.

Turbin, M. S., & Rosse, J. G. (1990). Staffing issues in the high technology industry. In L. Gomez-Mejia & M. Lawless (Eds.), *Organizational Issues in High Technology Management* (pp. 227–241). Greenwich, CT: JAI Press.

Ulrich, D., Halbrook, R., Meder, D., Stuchlik, M., & Thorpe, S. (1991). Employee and customer attachment: Synergies for competitive advantage. *Human Resource Planning*, 14, 89–103.

Waldman, D. A., & Avolio, B. J. (1986). A meta-analysis of age differences in job performance. *Journal of Applied Psychology*, 71, 33–38.

Wanous, J. P. (1980). *Organizational Entry: Recruitment, Selection and Socialization of Newcomers*. Reading, MA: Addison-Wesley.

Wanous, J. P., Poland, T. D., Premack, S. L., & Davis, K. S. (1992). The effects of met expectations on newcomer attitudes and behaviors: A review and meta-analysis. *Journal of Applied Psychology*, 77, 288–297.

Whiting, L. (1989). *Turnover Costs: A Case Example*. Columbus, OH: Ohio Department of Mental Health.

Williams, C. R., & Livingstone, L. P. (1994). A second look at the relationship between performance and voluntary turnover. *Academy of Management Journal*, 37, 269–298.

Zedeck, S., & Mosier, K. L. (1990). Work in the family and employing organization. *American Psychologist*, 45, 240–251.

Zenger, T. R. (1992). Why do employers only reward extreme performance? Examining the relationships among performance, pay, and turnover. *Administrative Science Quarterly*, 37, 198–219.

3
CAUSES AND CORRELATES OF TURNOVER

Many reviews of the antecedents and correlates of turnover have appeared over the years (Brayfield & Crockett, 1955; Hulin, Roznowski, & Hachiya, 1985; Mobley, 1982; Mobley, Griffeth, Hand, & Meglino, 1979; Muchinsky & Tuttle, 1979; Porter & Steers, 1973; Price, 1977; Steers & Mowday, 1981). In the earlier edition of this book (Hom & Griffeth, 1995), we presented the first meta-analyses of individual-level relationship magnitudes with employee turnover. (*Note*: Cotton and Tuttle (1986) earlier published a comprehensive review of multiple turnover correlates; however, they assessed only the *significance* of their relationships to turnover.) Since our 1995 analyses, Griffeth, Hom, and Gaertner (2000) published an update in 2000. More recently, Rubenstein, Eberly, Lee, and Mitchell (2018) updated the two previous meta-analyses and examined many new predictors of turnover they found. As there is no need to conduct still another meta-analysis so soon on the heels of that one, we decided on a different approach for this chapter. We decided to tabularize the results of *all* three meta-analyses. Thus, interested researchers could see the results of all three analyses in one place. Our focus will be on examining new and old constructs to document changes in the interests of researchers with an eye on the needs for future research.

All three previous meta-analyses published their methodologies, so there is little need to rehash them here. Suffice it to say that all three meta-analyses were comprehensive for the time and as inclusive as possible. For the most part, we classified the antecedents of turnover using the taxonomy developed by Mobley et al. (1979). Thus, the chapter is organized into discussion of: (1) individual and personal predictors; (2) overall satisfaction and organizational and work environment factors; (3) job content factors, intrinsic motivation, and miscellaneous new constructs related to this category; and (4) alternative employment predictors. To this taxonomy, we added: (5) withdrawal cognitions; and (6) other withdrawal behaviors. Although Rubenstein et al. (2018) used a different taxonomy, the two were similar enough to allow them to be combined without any loss of information.

In Tables 3.1 through 3.6 (we thank Michael Hanna for his assistance in developing these tables), we show population (corrected mean r) correlations between predictors and voluntary quits, reporting the number of samples and overall sample size on which they were based for each of the three meta-analyses. The population correlation represents the best measure of the relationship between turnover and a determinant because this index was derived from double corrections for measurement and sampling errors.

Demographic and Personal Characteristics

Individual demographic and personal characteristics are shown in Table 3.1. Many of the personal attributes such as cognitive ability, education, training, marital status, kinship responsibilities (a complex measure of family obligations based on number of children, their ages, and marital status; Blegen, Mueller, & Price, 1988), ethnicity (race), and gender are weakly related to turnover. However, relatives (r = .22; number of relatives in the community) and weighted application blanks (r = .33) are moderately related, although these constructs do not seem to have been studied relative to turnover after Hom and Griffeth (1995). When not included in the complex calculations of kinship responsibilities, children were moderately related to turnover (−.14, −.16, −.20), indicating that the number of children at home were likely to encourage an employee to stay. A number of new explanatory constructs were reported by the Rubenstein et al. (2018) meta-analysis, including several personality constructs. Agreeableness (−.08), extraversion (.02), and locus of control (.10) were weakly related to turnover, while conscientiousness (−.16), emotional stability (−.19), internal motivation (−.16), and openness to experience (.14) were moderately related to turnover.

Also contrary to popular stereotypes, women did not quit their jobs more readily than did men; rather, they were more loyal employees (r = −.07, −.11):

> This result conforms to a labor economic finding that educated women actually resemble men in turnover rate and pattern (leaving to assume another job rather than to abandon the labor force—a route generally taken by less educated female leavers; Royalty, 1998).
>
> *(Griffeth et al., 2000, p. 479)*

Neither did minority employees (−.02, .02) quit more often than White employees as the race–turnover relationship was negligible in two of the meta-analyses:

> However, racial effects on turnover may depend on type of racial minority (minorities might vary in their quit propensity) and demographic composition of the work group (racial minorities are prone to exit when they are underrepresented in work groups; Williams & O'Reilly, 1998).
>
> *(Griffeth et al., 2000, p. 479)*

TABLE 3.1 Individual Demographic and Personal Characteristics

Predictors	From Hom and Griffeth (1995)		From Griffeth et al. (2000)			From Rubenstein et al. (2018)		
	k	N	Corrected Mean r (r_{cor})[1]	k	N	Corrected Mean r (r_{cor})[2]	k	N	Corrected Mean r (r_{cor})[3]
Cognitive ability	2	1,879	−.09	7	6,062	.02	15	17,651	−.06
Education	29	8,915	.07	35	11,708	.06	51	59,574	.04
Training	4	3,394	−.08	6	3,815	−.08	nr	nr	nr
Marital status (0 = unmarried, 1 = married)	23	7,599	.01	28	16,684	−.05	27	134,505	−.10
Kinship responsibilities	9	5,354	−.10	11	8,220	−.10	nr	nr	nr
Relatives	2	440	.22	nr	nr	nr	nr	nr	nr
Children	4	727	−.14	8	9,043	−.16	25	40,201	−.20
Weighted application blanks	6	1,329	.33	nr	nr	nr	nr	nr	nr
Age	29	12,356	−.12	22	17,301	−.03	121	209,588	−.21
Gender (0 = female, 1 = male)	15	6,748	−.07	45	21,656	−.11	89	602,689	.00
Tenure	36	12,106	−.17	53	29,313	−.23	118	669,753	−.20
Agreeableness	nr	nr	nr	nr	nr	nr	6	2,449	−.08
Conscientiousness	nr	nr	nr	nr	nr	nr	8	3,409	−.16
Emotional stability	nr	nr	nr	nr	nr	nr	16	7,593	−.19
Ethnicity/race (0 = White, 1 = non-White)	nr	nr	nr	7	10,683	−.02	29	457,562	.02
Extraversion	nr	nr	nr	nr	nr	nr	13	6,795	.02
Internal motivation	nr	nr	nr	nr	nr	nr	17	5,960	−.16
Locus of control (higher = external)	nr	nr	nr	nr	nr	nr	13	3,187	.10
Openness to experience	nr	nr	nr	nr	nr	nr	5	1,009	.14

Note: k = the number of samples; N = the number of employees; nr = not recorded.
[1] Corrected mean r = average correlations across all studies that have been corrected for measurement errors.
[2] Average r that corrects for measurement error in the predictors, sampling error, and variations in the turnover base rates across studies.
[3] Corrects for measurement error and turnover base rates.

Thus, such findings may not be conclusive.

As expected, older (−.12, −.03, −.21) and long-tenure employees (−.17, −.23, −.20) generally quit less often than did younger and short-tenure employees. This finding possibly reflects a greater long-term job investment by older, more senior personnel (Rusbult & Farrell, 1983). Benefits may accrue with time on the job and many employees are not willing to lose them. Younger and lower-tenured employees more likely leave because they are neither strongly invested in the job nor receive sizeable benefits. The weighted application blank (WAB) correctly identified mobile personnel. Like an employment test, this procedure scores a job applicant's responses to questions on an application blank based on a scoring key that empirically differentiates between short- and long-term employees (Cascio, 1976). As noted above, WAB is no longer a popular topic of scholarly inquiry as its predictive efficacy had been well documented by past studies ($r = .33$).

Job Satisfaction and Organizational and Work Environment

Table 3.2 shows a large number of predictors, many of which were not examined in the first two meta-analyses (Griffeth et al., 2000; Hom & Griffeth, 1995), while others were omitted or combined with other predictors in the third meta-analysis (Rubenstein et al., 2018). Generally, most of these constructs serve as distal predictors of turnover, and as such are mediated by more proximal predictors such as job satisfaction, organizational commitment, and withdrawal cognitions (e.g., intentions to quit and search, thoughts of quitting), perceived probability of finding a better alternative, and search behaviors. Consistent with most theoretical perspectives (Mobley, 1977; Porter & Steers, 1973; Price & Mueller, 1986; Steers & Mowday, 1981), job dissatisfaction was moderately related ($r = -.19, -.22, -.28$) to resignations across all three meta-analyses. That is, dissatisfied employees (presumably reacting to poor working conditions; see Mobley et al., 1979; Price & Mueller, 1986) more readily abandoned their present employment.

Commitment

Similarly, commitment to the organization, whose early measures routinely tapped propensity to withdraw from the job, foreshadowed employment changes (see Mathieu & Zajac, 1990; Mowday, Porter, & Steers, 1982). Across all three meta-analyses, commitment was consistently and moderately related to turnover (−.18, −.27, −.29). As shown in Table 3.2, commitment is also one of the most widely studied predictors. Unfortunately, the Rubenstein et al. (2018) study combined all commitment indices, masking differential effects by different measures (cf. Porter, Steers, Mowday, & Boulian, 1974) or commitment dimensions (Meyer & Allen, 1991).

TABLE 3.2 Job Satisfaction and Organizational and Work Environment Factors

Predictors	From Hom and Griffeth (1995)			From Griffeth et al. (2000)			From Rubenstein et al. (2018)		
	k	N	Corrected Mean $r\,(r_{cor})^1$	k	N	Corrected Mean $r\,(r_{cor})^2$	k	N	Corrected Mean $r\,(r_{cor})^3$
Job satisfaction	78	27,543	−.19	67	24,566	−.22	174	107,625	−.28
Organizational commitment	36	13,085	−.18	67	27,540	−.27	129	71,862	−.29
Other commitment	nr	nr	nr	nr	nr	nr	12	3,601	−.34
Met expectations	8	1,435	−.13	8	1,486	−.18	11	3,236	−.12
Salary	7	3,763	−.06	nr	nr	nr	55	177,634	−.17
Pay satisfaction	16	4,094	−.04	18	4,425	−.08	nr	nr	nr
Distributive justice/pay equity	9	4,110	−.07	11	4,871	−.11	nr	nr	nr
Reward contingency	nr	nr	nr	nr	nr	nr	4	678	−.20
Rewards offered	nr	nr	nr	nr	nr	nr	25	30,743	−.28
Leader–member exchange/leadership	3	161	−.23	3	161	−.25	42	28,637	−.24
Supervisory satisfaction	14	3,002	−.10	16	3,333	−.13	nr	nr	nr
Leader communication	8	5,185	−.11	nr	nr	nr	nr	nr	nr
Participation	5	1,584	−.08	10	4,825	−.13	5	1,895	−.13
Instrumental communications	nr	nr	nr	nr	nr	nr	8	5,185	−.14
Cohesion	3	412	−.14	9	4,558	−.13	24	11,104	−.14
Integration	4	3,394	−.10	nr	nr	nr	nr	nr	nr
Coworker satisfaction	11	1,313	−.10	13	1,606	−.13	nr	nr	nr
Role clarity	3	391	−.24	5	795	−.24	nr	nr	nr
Role ambiguity	nr	nr	nr	nr	nr	nr	8	5,765	.15
Role overload	3	2,627	.11	5	3,419	.12	nr	nr	nr
Role conflict	2	244	.16	5	780	.22	10	10,903	.15

(*Continued*)

TABLE 3.2 (Cont.)

Predictors	From Hom and Griffeth (1995)		From Griffeth et al. (2000)			From Rubenstein et al. (2018)		
	k	N	Corrected Mean r (r_{cor})[1]	k	N	Corrected Mean r (r_{cor})[2]	k	N	Corrected Mean r (r_{cor})[3]
Climate	nr	nr	nr	nr	nr	nr	8	2,711	-.24
Centralization	4	2,506	.09	nr	nr	nr	6	4,128	-.06
Supportiveness	2	256	.02	nr	nr	nr	nr	nr	nr
Promotions	24	8,999	-.15	nr	nr	nr	nr	nr	nr
Promotion satisfaction	13	3,276	-.14	nr	nr	nr	nr	nr	nr
Promotional opportunity	8	4,878	-.10	10	5,752	-.16	nr	nr	nr
Actual promotions	3	845	-.45	nr	nr	nr	nr	nr	nr
Actual promotions without outlier	2	657	-.35	nr	nr	nr	nr	nr	nr

Note: k = the number of samples; N = the number of employees; nr = not recorded.
[1] Corrected mean r = average correlations across all studies that have been corrected for measurement errors.
[2] Average r that corrects for measurement error in the predictors, sampling error, and variations in the turnover base rates across studies.
[3] Corrects for measurement error and turnover base rates.

Other Commitment

A relatively new construct examined in the Rubenstein et al. (2018) meta-analysis was other commitment, which is the loyalty one reports toward one's career or occupation. Clearly, with its sizeable adjusted r ($-.34$), it is a useful turnover predictor.

Met Expectations

A leading source of job satisfaction according to longstanding research (Porter & Steers, 1973; Wanous, 1980; Wanous, Poland, Premack, & Davis, 1992), met expectations moderately predicts turnover across all three meta-analyses ($r = -.13$, $-.18$, $-.12$). Thus, employees quit jobs if their work experiences disconfirm the expectations they had about their jobs before taking them up; they remain employed if their experiences confirm their initial expectations. The correlations between expectation and quitting fell below that between job satisfaction and quitting, which suggests that job satisfaction mediates the impact of met expectations on turnover (Porter & Steers, 1973; Wanous et al., 1992).

Compensation-Related Predictors

Although compensation authors commonly believe that pay dissatisfaction strongly underlies turnover (Gomez-Mejia & Balkin, 1992; Milkovich & Newman, 1999), we find very little direct support for this view. The routine omission of other forms of compensation, notably fringe benefits and incentive pay (Heneman, 1985), surely understated the effect of compensation. In marked contrast, the popular press and labor economic studies have underscored the ways in which pension and health coverage and profit-sharing significantly improve workforce retention (Ippolito, 1991; Peel & Wilson, 1990). More than this, most turnover scholars have examined pay levels in a single company or occupation (limiting pay variance), while labor economists, for example, study compensation factors at the company level across a wide range of organizations. Quite likely, scrutinizing base pay alone in one firm or job possibly underestimated how compensation influences turnover (Steel & Griffeth, 1989). For example, salary, pay satisfaction, and distributive justice/pay equity were weakly related to turnover in the first two meta-analyses, and salary was moderately ($r = -.17$) related to turnover in the third meta-analysis:

> Interestingly, effect sizes for pay and pay related variables are modest in light of their significance to compensation theorists and practitioners (Milkovich & Newman, 1999). Continued exclusion of other compensation forms (e.g., fringe benefits) and restricted pay variance surely underestimated how financial inducements deter quits (Miller, Hom, & Gomez-Mejia, 2001).
> *(Griffeth et al., 2000, p. 479)*

According to Rubenstein et al. (2018), rewards contingently paid and offered predict turnover ($r = -.20$ and $-.28$, respectively) somewhat better than do pay level or satisfaction. Yet reward contingency was examined in only four studies with relatively modest samples ($n = 678$; mean study size = 169.5).

From Table 3.2, it is apparent that existing turnover studies, with the exception of Aquino, Griffeth, Allen, and Hom (1997), neglected procedural fairness of organizational rules and procedures for allocating rewards (Greenberg, 1990). Conceivably, procedures that are perceived fair may do more to encourage employees to stay than do just pay distributions. For instance, Folger and Konovsky (1989) showed that satisfaction with the fairness of a merit-pay distribution (procedures) promotes higher commitment to the organization than does satisfaction with the amount distributed. It could be argued, however, that fair treatment would create a desirable work environment that would encourage high performers to stay and low performers to leave (e.g., Mobley et al., 1979).

Leadership and Supervision

Leader–member exchange/leadership style predicts turnover more strongly (−.23, −.25, −.23) than do participative management (−.08, −.13, −.13), satisfaction with the supervisor (−.10, −.13, nr), and the leader's communication skills ($r = -.11$). The latter measures focus on a particular action by a leader or an attitude toward the leader, whereas leader–member exchange is a more general construct summarizing these and other actions (e.g., supportiveness) on the part of supervisors. Specifically, leader–member exchange represents the interdependence between superiors and subordinates and reflects a host of benefits—including influence on decision-making, information, and social support—given to subordinates who develop high-quality exchanges with their superiors (Dansereau, Graen, & Haga, 1975; Graen & Scandura, 1986). However, general or instrumental communication by organizations was moderately related to turnover ($r = -.14$).

Notwithstanding current findings, future research (and meta-analyses) may disclose that new forms of participative management may become pivotal deterrents to turnover (Manz & Sims, 1989). Organizations are increasingly flattening the management structure and delegating more authority that was formerly held by supervisors to front-line employees (Jacob, 1992). Modern developments in employee empowerment and self-management greatly enlarge the workers' sphere of influence beyond that of conventional participative management, in which workers are given control only over work methods or time schedules (Hackman & Oldham, 1980).

Peer-Group Relations

Good peer-group relations, consisting of cohesion among the work group (−.14, −.13, −.14), integration (degree to which an individual has close friends at work; Price & Mueller, 1981; −.10), and satisfaction with coworkers (−.10, −.13, nr), modestly decreased turnover. Such modest correlations suggest that peer-group relations are remotely related to turnover and are one source of job satisfaction

(Price & Mueller, 1986). Nonetheless, few studies of turnover have investigated the formation of cohesion in work groups and integration. Work in organizational demography, although it overlooks the underlying mechanisms of value conflict and miscommunication among heterogeneous members, has shown that group heterogeneity induces decisions to leave (Jackson et al., 1991; O'Reilly, Caldwell, & Barnett, 1989; Pfeffer, 1983). Whether this translates to lower turnover remains to be seen. Thus, more inquiry into the integration of a group's members may identify more potent influences exerted by coworkers on job separations.

Role States

Table 3.2 also shows that role clarity (clear perceptions about one's role in the organization) was moderately related to turnover ($r = -.24$ in the first two meta-analyses) as well as or slightly better than other predictors in this table (e.g., leadership $r = -.23$; reward contingency $r = -.20$). Table 3.2 also reports that role overload, role conflict, and role ambiguity increase turnover. This is not too surprising as they are typically stressors. The magnitudes of these relationships are consistent with correlations for job stress and exhaustion presented in Table 3.3. Even though these results support theoretical expectations (Katz & Kahn, 1978), they are based on only a few studies across all three meta-analyses and so should be interpreted cautiously. All the same, their modest effects, particularly role clarity ($r = -.24$ in two meta-analyses), affirm certain perspectives on commitment and turnover that regard role states as remote influences mediated by cognitions about terminating work and job attitudes (Mathieu & Zajac, 1990; Netemeyer, Johnston, & Burton, 1990). Thus, clarifying roles can help reduce turnover.

Company Climate

Characteristics of an organization moderately affected quits, possibly because they are distal causes (Mobley et al., 1979; Price & Mueller, 1981, 1986). That is, centralization (or the degree to which power is concentrated in the higher echelons of management; .09, nr, −.06) and supportiveness barely predicted turnover (see Table 3.2; .02, nr, nr). Though barely affecting departures of individuals, attributes of a company may still considerably influence aggregate turnover rates (see Alexander, 1988; Heavey, Holwerda, & Hausknecht, 2013; Price, 1977; Terborg & Lee, 1984). As noted earlier, causal determinants may affect aggregate and individual quits in different ways because the turnover construct may shift in meaning across different levels of aggregation (Price & Mueller, 1986; Rousseau, 1985). Interestingly, the single predictor climate better predicted turnover than the two aforementioned dimensions of the construct (nr, nr, −.24).

Given the complexity of the organizational climate, our consideration of only two dimensions probably underestimated the impact of climate (see James & James, 1989). For instance, Sheridan (1992) considered other attributes of climate and found that new accountants working in firms that valued interpersonal relationships stayed in the jobs there for much longer than did those working in firms that emphasized accomplishment of tasks, the median survival time being 45 months and 31 months, respectively. Most of all, the *fit* between dimensions of climate and personal values may shape loyalty to a company more than effects of the climate itself. In keeping with this view, Chatman (1991) and O'Reilly, Chatman, and Caldwell (1991) found that new accountants whose personal values matched those of their employers exhibited higher inclinations to stay.

Promotions

Table 3.2 reveals that promotions ($r = -.15$, nr, nr), satisfaction with promotions ($r = -.14$, nr, nr), and promotional opportunity ($r = -.10$, $-.16$, nr) modestly predicted turnover. Perhaps dissimilar constructs assessed by promotion indices may underpin such between-study variation (Hunter & Schmidt, 1990). That is, current scales might assess different, though related, aspects of job promotions, among them satisfaction with promotion, opportunities for promotion, or actual promotions. As Carson, Carson, Griffeth, and Steel (1994) observed, these operationalizations differ as to whether they measure affect (satisfaction with promotion), beliefs (perceived opportunities for promotion), or events (actual promotion). Moreover, equivalency in measurement cannot be assumed because employees may be dissatisfied with their current rate of promotion but still perceive ample prospects for advancement. Conversely, promoted employees may feel satisfied with their *current rates* of advancement but expect limited promotional *opportunities* beyond their current position.

Actual promotions, by contrast, strongly predicted turnover ($r = -.45$). This sizeable correlation was derived from three studies; one sample may represent an outlier as its correlation is $-.81$ (Stumpf & Dawley, 1981; second sample). After removing this aberrant element, the corrected correlation between actual promotion and turnover shrank from $-.45$ to $-.35$, which still indicates that actual promotions appreciably promote retention. It should be noted that this relationship is only based on two or three studies with sample sizes of 657 or 845. Considerably more research is needed to verify whether this relationship is actually this strong. Unfortunately, interest in promotions has waned since 2000 as no promotion-related constructs appear in the Rubenstein et al. (2018) review.

Job Content, Intrinsic Motivation, and Miscellaneous New Constructs

Correlations for job content, intrinsic motivation, and a host of new turnover predictors are shown in Table 3.3.

TABLE 3.3 Job Content, Intrinsic Motivation, and Miscellaneous New Constructs

Predictors	From Hom and Griffeth (1995)			From Griffeth et al. (2000)			From Rubenstein et al. (2018)		
	k	N	Corrected Mean r (r_{cw})[1]	k	N	Corrected Mean r (r_{cw})[2]	k	N	Corrected Mean r (r_{cw})[3]
Job scope	7	1,604	−.13	15	4,285	−.14	nr	nr	nr
Routinization	6	3,707	.09	6	3,707	.11	6	4,106	−.12
Work satisfaction	25	7,632	−.19	32	9,859	−.19	nr	nr	nr
Job stress/exhaustion	5	779	.19	8	1,716	.16	32	18,740	.21
Intrinsic/internal motivation	2	1,681	−.13	nr	nr	nr	17	5,960	−.16
Job involvement	8	2,816	−.17	16	7,666	−.12	19	5,158	−.19
Professionalism	4	3,390	−.02	nr	nr	nr	nr	nr	nr
Managerial motivation	2	753	−.15	nr	nr	nr	nr	nr	nr
Organizational prestige	nr	nr	nr	nr	nr	nr	5	2,433	−.06
Organizational size	nr	nr	nr	nr	nr	nr	15	30,422	.03
Fit	nr	nr	nr	nr	nr	nr	17	4,146	−.29
Influence	nr	nr	nr	nr	nr	nr	7	24,331	−.09
Job embeddedness	nr	nr	nr	nr	nr	nr	29	31,158	−.26
Met expectations	nr	nr	nr	nr	nr	nr	11	3,236	−.12
Peer/group relations	nr	nr	nr	nr	nr	nr	24	11,104	−.14
Psychological contract breach	nr	nr	nr	nr	nr	nr	7	8,083	.18
Coping	nr	nr	nr	nr	nr	nr	7	880	−.39
Engagement	nr	nr	nr	nr	nr	nr	4	1,408	−.20

Note: k = the number of samples; N = the number of employees; nr = not recorded.

[1] Corrected mean r = average correlations across all studies that have been corrected for measurement errors.

[2] Average r that corrects for measurement error in the predictors, sampling error, and variations in the turnover base rates across studies.

[3] Corrects for measurement error and turnover base rates.

Job Scope

Job scope, the overall complexity and challenge of work duties, sustained job incumbency, although this effect may depend on moderators. A likely moderator is the strength of individuals' growth needs. Hackman and Oldham (1980) conceptualized that job complexity most enhances satisfaction with work and commitment to the organization for employees having strong growth needs. Loher, Noe, Moeller, and Fitzgerald's (1985) meta-analysis found that job complexity and job satisfaction correlated .57 for employees with high growth needs but correlated only .32 for those with weak growth needs.

Routinization

Routinization, or the degree to which a job is repetitive (Price & Mueller, 1981), has been examined in a few studies. Predictably, employees doing routine work more likely quit according to earlier meta-analyses, but this relationship was not replicated by Rubenstein et al. (2018): $r = .09$, $r = .11$, and $r = -.12$.

Work Satisfaction

Work satisfaction—reflecting experienced affect to a job's intrinsic content—moderately predicted terminations ($r = -.19$), which is similar to the predictive validity ($r = -.18$) of job characteristics (based on skill variety, task significance, task identity, autonomy, and feedback; Hackman and Oldham, 1980, estimated by Rubenstein et al., 2018).

Job Stress/Exhaustion

Job stress/exhaustion moderately, positively, and consistently predicts turnover ($r = .19, .16, .21$), a finding shown in Table 3.3. Stressful work over time takes a toll on employees.

Intrinsic or Internal Motivation

Theories of job characteristics hold that internal motivation—or self-esteem based on job accomplishments—is derived from performing complex, enriched work (Hackman & Oldham, 1980). Because complex jobs bind employees to firms, it is not surprising that internal motivation ($-.13$, nr, $-.16$)—which complex jobs induce—also diminishes withdrawal from an organization.

Job Involvement

Logically, employees who feel involved in their jobs, and thus psychologically identified with their jobs, may feel bound to their jobs (Kanungo, 1982). This hypothesis is supported by data shown in Table 3.3 indicating that involvement with a job ($r = -.17, -.12, -.19$) moderately predicts lower turnover.

Professionalism

Many sociologists contend that norms of efficiency and bureaucratic control in the workplace clash with professional standards and ethical codes, weakening people's commitment to an organization (Abbott, 1988; Kramer, 1974; Raelin, 1986). Despite those persuasive arguments and observations, our meta-analysis found that professionalism (adherence to professional values and standards) was unrelated to withdrawal ($r = -.02$, nr, nr). Quite likely, unrepresentative sampling accounts for this null finding, and absence of moderators. All the studies ($k = 4$, $n = 3,390$) on the relationship between professionalism and turnover were carried out in hospital settings. Because hospitals, especially teaching hospitals affiliated with medical schools, are devoted to patient care, the personnel may face little conflict between their professional standards and hospital practices. In other organizations that value efficiency and bureaucratic control over professional norms, professionalism may influence turnover. The extent to which employers adhere to employees' professional values and standards may in part determine whether or not professionalism induces them to seek jobs elsewhere.

Managerial Motivation

Managerial orientation—or a drive to manage people—slowed the exodus from organizations ($r = -.15$, nr, nr; see Butler, Lardent, & Miner, 1983). The subjects ($n = 753$) of investigations ($k = 2$) of how managerial orientation deters exits have been military officers. Managerial motivation appears to persuade people in leadership positions to stay; this personality trait may not similarly affect those in other jobs.

A Variety of New Constructs

Table 3.3 reports a variety of new predictors that were studied after the first two meta-analyses. We will summarize these predictors in terms of their relative strength predicting turnover.

New Predictors Weakly Related to Turnover

Table 3.3 shows that several of these new constructs were only weakly related to turnover: organizational prestige ($-.06$), size ($.03$), and influence ($-.09$; the impact an employee can have on others). Thus, the greater the prestige, the smaller the organization, and the more impact an employee has, the lower the turnover. These relationships suggest that these constructs may serve as distal predictors of turnover.

New Predictors Moderately Related to Turnover

Table 3.3 shows that several new constructs were moderately related to turnover. Fit (−.29; the compatibility of the person with the job and/or the organization), job embeddedness (−.26; this construct is reviewed in considerable detail in Chapter 5), met expectations (−.12), peer-group relations (−.14), and engagement (−.20) were all moderately related to turnover. Thus, the higher the compatibility of a person to the job and/or organization, the more embedded in the job, organization, or community a person is, the more closely initial job expectations to reality are, the better the intergroup relations, and the more a person is emotionally engaged in their work role, the lower is turnover. While not as distal to turnover as the previous set of constructs, these constructs should have mid-level status in the prediction of turnover.

A New Predictor Strongly Related to Turnover

Table 3.3 shows that only coping was strongly (−.39) related to turnover. Thus, the better able one is to manage the demands of the job, the lower turnover. Coping has long been suggested as a mechanism by which RJPs adapt to new work roles (Hom & Griffeth, 1995; Ilgen & Dugoni, 1977; Wanous & Colella, 1989). Coping in life is no doubt an important feature in today's complex world. It is encouraging that coping on the job is related to lower turnover. One can hope that these results hold up in future research as it is hard to generalize with relatively few studies based on modest samples ($k = 7$; $n = 880$; mean sample size = 125).

Overall Conclusions for New Variables

Although we are encouraged by the relatively large number of new predictors in this table, most of which moderately predict turnover, it is clear that several of them (e.g., organizational prestige and engagement) have relatively few studies examining their relationships with turnover, causing us to doubt their stability. Clearly, more research is needed for many of these predictors.

External Environment

Alternative Employment

Organizational scientists and labor economists universally proclaim that employment opportunities stimulate job changes (Forrest, Cummings, & Johnson, 1977; Gerhart, 1990; Mobley, 1977; Mobley et al., 1979; Price & Mueller, 1986). Table 3.4 shows that the perceived attraction and availability of other jobs modestly encouraged individuals to quit ($r = .11$) in the Hom and Griffeth (1995)

TABLE 3.4 Alternative Employment

Predictors	From Hom and Griffeth (1995)			From Griffeth et al. (2000)			From Rubenstein et al. (2018)		
	k	N	Corrected Mean r (r_{cor})[1]	k	N	Corrected Mean r (r_{cor})[2]	k	N	Corrected Mean r (r_{cor})[3]
Attraction and availability of alternatives	27	10,447	.11	23	18,189	.15	79	58,512	.23
Comparison of alternatives to present job	7	1,635	.26	6	826	.19	nr	nr	nr
Probability of finding another alternative	17	5,007	.14	nr	nr	nr	nr	nr	nr
Expected utility of alternative	4	2,276	−.01	nr	nr	nr	nr	nr	nr

Note: k = the number of samples; N = the number of employees; nr = not recorded.
[1] Corrected mean r = average correlations across all studies that have been corrected for measurement errors.
[2] Average r that corrects for measurement error in the predictors, sampling error, and variations in the turnover base rates across studies.
[3] Corrects for measurement error and turnover base rates.

meta-analysis, a finding that approximates Steel and Griffeth's (1989) earlier .13 estimate. These correlations increase in more recent meta-analyses involving more samples (.15, .23), although they still fail to match the strong relations between unemployment rates and quit rates observed by labor economic studies (Hulin et al., 1985; Mobley, 1982).

In a major critique of the literature on employee perceptions of alternatives, Steel and Griffeth (1989) speculated that several methodological factors may explain why perceived alternatives (PA) modestly predict resignations. For one, most PA studies drew samples from one organization, one industry, one region, one occupation, and one time period. Such homogeneous sampling may restrict the variance of the PA measures, attenuating their effects on turnover. By contrast, studies by labor economists sample broadly across various occupational and geographic lines, contributing variance to aggregate indices of employment opportunity (aka unemployment rates).

In a similar vein, extreme turnover base rates (ordinarily low quit rates) in most studies possibly constrained turnover variance, weakening relationships between PA and turnover. Although pervading most research, extreme turnover rates may be most problematic in the PA literature where homogeneous occupational sampling *and* low quit base rates restrict the range of both predictor and criterion. In such circumstances, the attenuation bias on correlations is multiplicative rather than additive. What is more, poor PA instrumentation further attenuates correlations between PA and quits (Steel & Griffeth, 1989). That is, most investigations used global, one-item PA ratings to assess a complex multifaceted construct (see Mobley et al., 1979). Quite possibly, deficient and unreliable PA scales additionally underestimate the observed effects of perceived employment alternatives on quits.

Acting on this latter critique of PA literature (e.g., poor instrumentation), Griffeth, Steel, Allen, and Bryan (2005) developed a psychometric sound and multidimensional PA measure that appreciably enhances its incremental validity for predicting turnover (beyond other turnover predictors). This finding revealed that some employees quit jobs simply because they perceive more attractive or ample jobs in the labor market, *not* because they necessarily have job offers in hand before leaving (Hulin et al., 1985). Anecdotally, two of the book authors learned from interviews with nurses that some nurses planned to quit their job, take whatever sick or vacation pay they had coming, and then go on a vacation. They were confident that they could find other employment after their vacation. These nurses thus quit jobs merely on the basis of favorable job market perceptions.

Comparison of Alternatives to Present Job

The above statements are further supported when one examines this variable in Table 3.4. Two of three meta-analyses found this predictor to be moderately related to turnover (.26, .19, nr). Thus, when employees directly compare their current job to a concrete alternative and find the latter superior, they more likely quit.

Probability of Finding Another Alternative

Expected Utility of Alternatives

Basically, the subjective expected utility (SEU) of an alternative (Mobley et al., 1979) was unrelated (−.01, nr, nr) to turnover.

Withdrawal Cognitions and SEU Beliefs about Withdrawal Acts

Table 3.5 reports predictive validities for withdrawal cognitions and beliefs about the subjective expected utilities (SEUs) of the present job (aka "future job attraction"; Mobley, 1982) and withdrawal acts (e.g., perceived costs and benefits of leaving; Mobley, 1977).

Withdrawal Cognitions

A fundamental tenet of modern thought on turnover based on historic roots in social psychology (Fishbein, 1967) is that decisions to withdraw from the workplace best portend subsequent withdrawal (Hulin et al., 1985; Mobley et al., 1979; Price & Mueller, 1986; Rusbult & Farrell, 1983; Steers & Mowday, 1981). This supposition is corroborated by findings in Table 3.5, which reveal that one's intentions to search, quit, thoughts of quitting, and especially the combination of these three constructs (aka "withdrawal cognitions") best predicted actual departures. Although Steel and Ovalle (1984) first verified the predictive superiority of cognitions about job withdrawal with meta-analysis, our 1995 and 2000 meta-analyses reported somewhat weaker predictive validities by including studies assessing quits long after such cognitions were surveyed or studies comprising few leavers (Hom, Caranikas-Walker, Prussia, & Griffeth, 1992). Encouragingly, Rubenstein et al.'s (2018) meta-analysis, with its massive collection of studies ($k = 211$), reported much higher predictive efficacy for withdrawal cognitions (.56). This finding is remarkable because their meta-analysis included not only studies with relatively long time-lags between predictor and criterion assessments, but also studies whose turnover rates fall below 50% (thereby attenuating turnover variance; Carsten & Spector, 1987; Steel & Griffeth, 1989; Steel & Ovalle, 1984).

Expected Utilities of the Present Job, Searching, and Quitting

Consistent with longstanding social psychological models (Ajzen, 1991; Bagozzi & Warshaw, 1990; Fishbein & Ajzen, 1975; Triandis, 1979), meta-analyses showed that terminations emerge from conscious calculations of perceived costs and benefits of enacting withdrawal acts (e.g., job search, quitting) as well as remaining (aka work-role SEU; Mobley et al., 1979). Rather than quitting impulsively over poor work conditions, many employees formulate decisions to withdraw after considering the possible results. Therefore, they would desert their workplace if

TABLE 3.5 Withdrawal Cognitions

Predictors	From Hom and Griffeth (1995)		From Griffeth et al. (2000)			From Rubenstein et al. (2018)		
	k	N	Corrected Mean r (r_{cor})[1]	k	N	Corrected Mean r (r_{cor})[2]	k	N	Corrected Mean r (r_{cor})[3]

Predictors	k	N	Corrected Mean r (r_{cor})[1]	k	N	Corrected Mean r (r_{cor})[2]	k	N	Corrected Mean r (r_{cor})[3]
Search intentions	24	6,601	.27	19	4,308	.34	27	18,685	.40
Quit intentions	70	78,078	.35	71	63,232	.45	nr	nr	nr
Thoughts of quitting	17	5,007	.27	10	1,964	.29	nr	nr	nr
Withdrawal cognitions	4	486	.30	7	1,209	.36	211	73,405	.56
Expected utility of present job	4	2,276	.25	nr	nr	nr	nr	nr	nr
Expected utility of search	6	1,175	.22	nr	nr	nr	nr	nr	nr
Expected utility of quitting	7	1,349	.25	7	1,303	.28	nr	nr	nr

Note: k = the number of samples; N = the number of employees; nr = not recorded.
[1] Corrected mean r = average correlations across all studies that have been corrected for measurement errors.
[2] Average r that corrects for measurement error in the predictors, sampling error, and variations in the turnover base rates across studies.
[3] Corrects for measurement error and turnover base rates.

they believe that job-seeking or quitting will be beneficial (if, for instance, they could obtain a better job elsewhere), and if they believe that they can avoid or minimize negative repercussions, such as losing a sizeable investment in the job (e.g., giving up non-portable benefits; Mobley, 1977).

Other Withdrawal Behaviors

Table 3.6 shows that other (milder) forms of workplace withdrawal—notably, absenteeism ($r = .33$) and lateness ($r = .15$)—can forecast later turnover. The size of the positive relationship between absence and quitting accords with Mitra, Jenkins, and Gupta's (1992) meta-analysis. These same researchers found that the duration of a study moderates the correlation between absence and turnover. There is a stronger covariation in short-term studies that last 12 months or less. They also reported that this relationship is moderated by the type of industry: stronger associations are to be found in manufacturing settings than in non-manufacturing settings.

Such positive covariation between milder forms of work avoidance and quitting—the most extreme and irrevocable form of withdrawal—is consistent with a progression-of-withdrawal model (Hulin, 1991; Rosse & Miller, 1984) that posits dissatisfied employees progressively enact more extreme manifestations of job withdrawal over time (lateness, absenteeism, and ultimately turnover; see Rosse, 1988). We can see this trend in Table 3.6 to a certain extent if one extrapolates from the data. Across all three meta-analyses, one can see that lateness—a mild withdrawal response—predicts turnover (.15, .06, .14) less accurately than does absenteeism (.33, .21, .23), a more extreme withdrawal response.

We include performance as an act of withdrawal because classic theorists submit that poor performance may reflect dissatisfaction and thus foreshadow quitting (Brayfield & Crockett, 1955; Hulin, 1991; Mobley, 1977; Steers & Mowday, 1981; Vroom, 1964). Two of the three meta-analyses reveal a modest negative relationship between job performance and turnover ($r = -.19, -.17$), which accords with Williams and Livingstone's (1994) meta-analysis. The more recent meta-analysis records a weak relationship ($-.08$). This inverse correlation between performance and departure contradicts conventional views that more capable personnel resign more readily—presumably because they have more employment options (see Jackofsky, 1984). However, this thinking assumes that one's performance is visible to other employers, which is unlikely for most occupations. For example, McEvoy and Cascio's (1987) meta-analysis suggests that positive performance–turnover correlations sometimes emerge. In occupations where accomplishments are visible, Allison (1974) and Schwab (1991) did find that productive scholars leave research universities more often than do less productive academicians.

Rewards that are contingent on job effectiveness may also strengthen negative relationships between job performance and quitting (Williams & Livingstone, 1994). Conceivably, in organizations where rewards were contingent on

TABLE 3.6 Other Withdrawal Behaviors

Predictors	From Hom and Griffeth (1995)			From Griffeth et al. (2000)			From Rubenstein et al. (2018)		
	k	N	Corrected Mean r (r_{cor})[1]	k	N	Corrected Mean r (r_{cor})[2]	k	N	Corrected Mean r (r_{cor})[3]
Lateness	2	413	.15	6	2,283	.06	5	1,431	.14
Absenteeism	28	4,371	.33	28	5,364	.21	36	44,405	.23
Performance	56	15,318	−.19	72	25,234	−.17	86	473,624	−.08
Organizational citizenship behaviors (OCB)	nr	nr	nr	nr	nr	nr	9	6,047	−.10
Selection process performance	nr	nr	nr	nr	nr	nr	4	3,016	−.11

Note: k = the number of samples; N = the number of employees; nr = not recorded.

[1] Corrected mean r = average correlations across all studies that have been corrected for measurement errors.
[2] Average r that corrects for measurement error in the predictors, sampling error, and variations in the turnover base rates across studies.
[3] Corrects for measurement error and turnover base rates.

performance, better performers (who receive more rewards) would be more satisfied with their job and less likely quit. Conversely, marginal performers in these organizations would receive fewer incentives or recognition, become less satisfied with their jobs, and therefore more likely quit. Williams and Livingstone's (1994) meta-analysis did, in fact, find that contingent reward systems increase negative performance–turnover correlations. Table 3.6 also reports two new behavioral predictors of turnover—namely, organizational citizenship behaviors (OCBs) and selection process performance, both of which show fairly weak correlations with turnover (−.10 and −.11, respectively). Reflecting withdrawal progression, the *absence* of OCBs (failure to perform behaviors that fall outside one's formal job duties but nonetheless benefit the organization) may predict turnover, as it too—like absences and tardiness—may represent an early (milder) form of withdrawal that culminates in subsequent turnover. By comparison, job applicants who are hired despite subpar or poor performance during hiring interviews or selection testing may later perform jobs less effectively (assuming selection procedures are valid). Thus, poor selection process performance may translate into higher turnover because weaker job applicants end up as worse performers.

Concluding Remarks

These meta-analytical findings carry significant theoretical and practical implications. First, the findings suggest which managerial interventions may likely control voluntary quits, a subject addressed in Chapter 9. They provide a stronger empirical foundation for prescriptions than do anecdotal evidence or speculation, the prime basis for popular advice. These results also identify robust causal antecedents that any viable model of turnover must incorporate. Lastly, even though meta-analysis is, we contend, a significant methodological breakthrough in the organizational sciences, we must bear in mind the familiar adage, "garbage in, garbage out." After all, it is the quality of empirical studies that determines the validity of conclusions drawn from meta-analysis.

References

Abbott, A. D. (1988). *The System of Professions*. Chicago, IL: University of Chicago Press.

Ajzen, I. (1991). The theory of planned behavior. *Organizational Behavior and Human Decision Processes*, 50, 179–211.

Alexander, J. A. (1988). The effects of patient care unit organization on nursing turnover. *Health Care Management Review*, 13(2), 61–72.

Allison, P. D. (1974). *Inter-Organizational Mobility of Academic Scientists*. Paper presented at Annual Meeting of the American Sociological Association, Montreal, Canada.

Aquino, K., Griffeth, R. W., Allen, D. G., & Hom, P. W. (1997). Integrating justice constructs into the turnover process: A test of a referent cognitions model. *Academy of Management Journal*, 40, 1208–1227.

Bagozzi, R. P., & Warshaw, P. R. (1990). Trying to consume. *Journal of Consumer Research*, 17, 127–140.

Blegen, M. A., Mueller, C. W., & Price, J. L. (1988). Measurement of kinship responsibility for organizational research. *Journal of Applied Psychology*, 73, 402–409.

Brayfield, A. H., & Crockett, W. H. (1955). Employee attitudes and employee performance. *Psychological Bulletin*, 52, 396–424.

Butler, R. P., Lardent, C. L., & Miner, J. B. (1983). A motivational basis for turnover in military officer education and training. *Journal of Applied Psychology*, 68, 496–506.

Carson, P. P., Carson, K. D., Griffeth, R. W., & Steel, R. P. (1994). Promotion and employee turnover: Critique, meta-analysis, and implications. *Journal of Business and Psychology*, 8(4), 455–466.

Carsten, J. M., & Spector, P. E. (1987). Unemployment, job satisfaction, and employee turnover: A meta-analytic test of the Muchinsky model. *Journal of Applied Psychology*, 72, 374–381.

Cascio, W. F. (1976). Turnover, biographical data, and fair employment practice. *Journal of Applied Psychology*, 61, 576–580.

Chatman, J. A. (1991). Matching people and organizations: Selection and socialization in public accounting firms. *Administrative Science Quarterly*, 36, 459–484.

Cotton, J. L., & Tuttle, J. M. (1986). Employee turnover: A meta-analysis and review with implications for research. *Academy of Management Review*, 11, 55–70.

Dansereau, F., Graen, G., & Haga, W. J. (1975). A vertical dyad linkage approach to leadership within formal organizations. *Organizational Behavior and Human Performance*, 13, 46–78.

Fishbein, M. (1967). Attitude and the prediction of behavior. In M. Fishbein (Ed.), *Readings in Attitude Theory and Measurement* (pp. 477–492). New York: Wiley.

Fishbein, M., & Ajzen, I. (1975). *Belief, Attitude, Intention and Behavior: An Introduction to Theory and Research*. Reading, MA: Addison-Wesley.

Folger, R., & Konovsky, M. A. (1989). Effects of procedural and distributive justice on reactions to pay-raise decisions. *Academy of Management Journal*, 32, 115–130.

Forrest, C. R., Cummings, L. L., & Johnson, A. C. (1977). Organizational participation: A critique and model. *Academy of Management Review*, 2, 586–601.

Gerhart, B. (1990). Voluntary turnover and alternative job opportunities. *Journal of Applied Psychology*, 75, 467–476.

Gomez-Mejia, L. R., & Balkin, D. B. (1992). *Compensation, Organizational Strategy, and Firm Performance*. Cincinnati, OH: South/Western.

Graen, G. B., & Scandura, T. A. (1986). A theory of dyadic career reality. In K. Rowland & G. Ferris (Eds.), *Research in Personnel and Human Resources Management* (vol. 4, pp. 147–181). Greenwich, CT: JAI Press.

Greenberg, J. (1990). Employee theft as a reaction to underpayment inequity: The hidden cost of pay cuts. *Journal of Applied Psychology*, 75(5), 561–568.

Griffeth, R. W., Hom, P. W., & Gaertner, S. (2000). A meta-analysis of antecedents and correlates of employee turnover: Update, moderator tests, and research implications for the next millennium. *Journal of Management*, 26, 463–488.

Griffeth, R. W., Steel, R. P., Allen, D. G., & Bryan, N. (2005). The development of a multidimensional measure of job market cognitions: The employment opportunity index (EOI). *Journal of Applied Psychology*, 90, 335–349.

Hackman, J. R., & Oldham, G. R. (1980). *Work Redesign*. Reading, MA: Addison-Wesley.

Heavey, A. L., Holwerda, J. A., & Hausknecht, J. P. (2013). Causes and consequences of collective turnover: A meta-analytic review. *Journal of Applied Psychology*, 98(3), 412–453.

Heneman, H. G. (1985). Pay satisfaction. In K. M. Rowland & G. R. Ferris (Eds.), *Research in Personnel and Human Resources Management* (vol. 3, pp. 115–140). Greenwich, CT: JAI Press.

Hom, P. W., Caranikas-Walker, F., Prussia, G. E., & Griffeth, R. W. (1992). A meta-analytical structural equations analysis of a model of employee turnover. *Journal of Applied Psychology*, 77, 890–909.

Hom, P. W., & Griffeth, R. W. (1995). *Employee Turnover*. Cincinnati, OH: South/Western.

Hulin, C. L. (1991). Adaptation, persistence, and commitment in organizations. In M. D. Dunnette & L. M. Hough (Eds.), *Handbook of Industrial and Organizational Psychology* (2nd ed., pp. 445–505). Palo Alto, CA: Consulting Psychologists Press.

Hulin, C. L., Roznowski, M., & Hachiya, D. (1985). Alternative opportunities and withdrawal decisions: Empirical and theoretical discrepancies and an integration. *Psychological Bulletin*, 97(2), 233–250.

Hunter, J. E., & Schmidt, F. L. (1990). *Methods of Meta-Analysis*. Newbury Park, CA: Sage.

Ilgen, D. R., & Dugoni, B. L. (1977). *Initial Orientation to the Organization*. Paper presented at the Annual Meeting of the Academy of Management, Kissimmee, Florida (August).

Ippolito, R. A. (1991). Encouraging long-term tenure: Wage tilt or pension? *Industrial and Labor Relations Review*, 44, 520–535.

Jackofsky, E. F. (1984). Turnover and job performance: An integrated process model. *Academy of Management Review*, 9, 74–83.

Jackson, S. E., Brett, J. F., Sessa, V. I., Cooper, D. M., Julin, J. A., & Peyronnin, K. (1991). Some differences make a difference: Individual dissimilarity and group heterogeneity as correlates of recruitment, promotions, and turnover. *Journal of Applied Psychology*, 76, 675–689.

Jacob, R. (1992). The search for the organization of tomorrow. *Fortune*, 125(10), 92–98.

James, L. A., & James, L. R. (1989). Integrating work environment perceptions: Explorations into the measurement of meaning. *Journal of Applied Psychology*, 74, 739–751.

Kanungo, R. N. (1982). Measurement of job and work involvement. *Journal of Applied Psychology*, 67, 341–349.

Katz, D., & Kahn, R. L. (1978). *The Social Psychology of Organizations* (2nd ed.). New York: Wiley.

Kramer, M. (1974). *Reality Shock: Why Nurses Leave Nursing*. St. Louis, MO: Mosley.

Loher, B. T., Noe, R. A., Moeller, N. L., & Fitzgerald, M. P. (1985). A meta-analysis of the relation of job characteristics to job satisfaction. *Journal of Applied Psychology*, 70, 280–289.

Manz, C. C., & Sims, H. P. (1989). *Super Leadership*. New York: Prentice Hall Press.

Mathieu, J. E., & Zajac, D. (1990). A review and meta-analysis of the antecedents, correlates, and consequences of organizational commitment. *Psychological Bulletin*, 108, 171–194.

McEvoy, G. M., & Cascio, W. F. (1987). Do good or poor performers leave? A meta-analysis of the relationship between performance and turnover. *Academy of Management Journal*, 30(4), 744–762.

Meyer, J. P., & Allen, N. J. (1991). A three-component conceptualization of organizational commitment. *Human Resource Management Review*, 1, 61–89.

Milkovich, G. T., & Newman, J. M. (1999). *Compensation* (6th ed.). Burr Ridge, IL: Irwin.

Miller, J. S., Hom, P. W., & Gomez-Mejia, L. (2001). The high cost of low wages: Does maquiladora compensation reduce turnover? *Journal of International Business Studies*, 32(3), 585–595.

Mitra, A., Jenkins, G. D., & Gupta, N. (1992). A meta-analytic review of the relationship between absence and turnover. *Journal of Applied Psychology*, 77, 879–889.

Mobley, W. H. (1977). Intermediate linkages in the relationship between job satisfaction and employee turnover. *Journal of Applied Psychology*, 62(2), 237–240.

Mobley, W. H. (1982). *Employee Turnover: Causes, Consequences, and Control*. Reading, MA: Addison-Wesley.

Mobley, W. H., Griffeth, R. W., Hand, H. H., & Meglino, B. M. (1979). Review and conceptual analysis of the employee turnover process. *Psychological Bulletin*, 86, 493–522.

Mowday, R. T., Porter, L. W., & Steers, R. M. (1982). *Employee–Organization Linkages*. New York: Academic Press.

Muchinsky, P. M., & Tuttle, M. L. (1979). Employee turnover: An empirical and methodological assessment. *Journal of Vocational Behavior*, 14, 43–77.

Netemeyer, R. G., Johnston, M. W., & Burton, S. (1990). An analysis of role conflict and role ambiguity in a structural equations framework. *Journal of Applied Psychology*, 75, 148–157.

O'Reilly, C. A., Caldwell, D. F., & Barnett, W. P. (1989). Work group demography, social integration, and turnover. *Administrative Science Quarterly*, 34, 21–37.

O'Reilly, C. A., Chatman, J., & Caldwell, D. F. (1991). People and organizational culture: A profile comparison approach to assessing person–organization fit. *Academy of Management Journal*, 34(3), 487–516.

Peel, M. J., & Wilson, N. (1990). Labor absenteeism: The impact of profit sharing, voice and participation. *International Journal of Manpower*, 11, 17–24.

Pfeffer, J. (1983). Organizational demography. In L. L. Cummings & B. M. Staw (Eds.), *Research in Organizational Behavior* (vol. 5, pp. 299–357). Greenwich, CT: JAI Press.

Porter, L. W., & Steers, R. M. (1973). Organizational, work, and personal factors in employee turnover and absenteeism. *Psychological Bulletin*, 80, 151–176.

Porter, L. W., Steers, R. M., Mowday, R. T., & Boulian, P. V. (1974). Organizational commitment, job satisfaction, and turnover among psychiatric technicians. *Journal of Applied Psychology*, 59(5), 603–609.

Price, J. L. (1977). *The Study of Turnover*. Ames, IA: Iowa State University Press.

Price, J. L., & Mueller, C. W. (1981). A causal model of turnover for nurses. *Academy of Management Journal*, 24, 543–565.

Price, J. L., & Mueller, C. W. (1986). *Absenteeism and Turnover of Hospital Employees*. Greenwich, CT: JAI Press.

Raelin, J. A. (1986). *The Clash of Cultures*. Boston, MA: Harvard Business School Press.

Rosse, J. G. (1988). Relations among lateness, absence, and turnover: Is there a progression of withdrawal? *Human Relations*, 41, 517–531.

Rosse, J. G., & Miller, H. E. (1984). Relationship between absenteeism and other employee behaviors. In P. S. Goodman & R. S. Atkin (Eds.), *Absenteeism: New Approaches to Understanding, Measuring, and Managing Employee Absence* (pp. 194–228). San Francisco, CA: Jossey-Bass.

Rousseau, D. (1985). Issues in level in organizational research: Multi-level and cross-level perspectives. In L. L. Cummings & B. M. Staw (Eds.), *Research in Organizational Behavior* (vol. 7, pp. 1–37). Greenwich, CT: JAI Press.

Royalty, A. B. (1998). Job-to-job and job-to-nonemployment turnover by gender and educational level. *Journal of Labor Economics*, 16, 392–443.

Rubenstein, A. L., Eberly, M. B., Lee, T. W., & Mitchell, T. R. (2018). Surveying the forest: A meta-analysis, moderator investigation, and future-oriented discussion of the antecedents of voluntary employee turnover. *Personnel Psychology*, 71(1), 23–65.

Rusbult, C. E., & Farrell, D. (1983). A longitudinal test of the investment model: The impact of job satisfaction, job commitment, and turnover of variations in rewards, costs, alternatives, and investments. *Journal of Applied Psychology*, 68, 429–438.

Schwab, D. P. (1991). Contextual variables in employee performance–turnover relationships. *Academy of Management Journal*, 34, 966–975.

Sheridan, J. E. (1992). Organizational culture and employee retention. *Academy of Management Journal*, 35, 1036–1056.

Steel, R. P., & Griffeth, R. W. (1989). The elusive relationship between perceived employment opportunity and turnover behavior: A methodological or conceptual artifact? *Journal of Applied Psychology*, 74, 846–854.

Steel, R. P., & Ovalle, II, N. K. (1984). A review and meta-analysis of research on the relationship between behavioral intentions and employee turnover. *Journal of Applied Psychology*, 69, 673–686.

Steers, R. M., & Mowday, R. T. (1981). Employee turnover and postdecision accommodation processes. In L. L. Cummings & B. M. Staw (Eds.), *Research in Organizational Behavior* (vol. 3, pp. 235–282). Greenwich, CT: JAI Press.

Stumpf, S. A., & Dawley, P. K. (1981). Predicting voluntary and involuntary turnover using absenteeism and performance indices. *Academy of Management Journal*, 24, 148–163.

Terborg, J. R., & Lee, T. W. (1984). A predictive study of organizational turnover rates. *Academy of Management Journal*, 27, 793–810.

Triandis, H. C. (1979). Values, attitudes, and interpersonal behavior. In H. E. Howe, Jr. (Ed.), *Nebraska Symposium on Motivation* (pp. 159–259)</ed>. Lincoln, NE: University of Nebraska Press.

Vroom, V. H. (1964). *Work and Motivation*. New York: Wiley.

Wanous, J. P. (1980). *Organizational Entry: Recruitment, Selection and Socialization of Newcomers*. Reading, MA: Addison-Wesley.

Wanous, J. P., & Colella, A. (1989). Organizational entry research: Current status and future directions. In G. Ferris & K. Rowland (Eds.), *Research in Personnel and Human Resources Management* (pp. 59–120). Greenwich, CT: JAI Press.

Wanous, J. P., Poland, T. D., Premack, S. L., & Davis, K. S. (1992). The effects of met expectations on newcomer attitudes and behaviors: A review and meta-analysis. *Journal of Applied Psychology*, 77, 288–297.

Williams, C. R., & Livingstone, L. P. (1994). A second look at the relationship between performance and voluntary turnover. *Academy of Management Journal*, 37, 269–298.

Williams, K. Y., & O'Reilly, III, C. A. (1998). Demography and diversity in organizations: A review of 40 years of research. In B. M. Staw & L. L. Cummings (Eds.), *Research in Organizational Behavior* (pp. 77–140). Greenwich, CT: JAI Press.

4

THEORIES OF EMPLOYEE TURNOVER

During the past 50 years, turnover researchers have devoted considerable attention to the reasons why employees quit jobs. The low turnover predictions by traditional empirical work partly inspired this contemporary theoretical orientation (Locke, 1976; Mobley, 1977). In this chapter, we review classic and modern conceptual developments, describing and evaluating various theoretical frameworks for understanding turnover. Although turnover has been researched since the turn of the twentieth century, March and Simon (1958) pioneered the first formal theory, proposing an *explicit, formal*, and *systematic* conceptual analysis of the withdrawal process.

March and Simon: Theory of Organizational Equilibrium

In *Organizations*, March and Simon (1958) introduced a general theory of motivation called *organizational equilibrium* (Barnard, 1938; Simon, 1947), which describes the organization's ability to pay members to motivate them to continue their participation. Each member participates so long as the inducements, such as pay, that are offered match or exceed (measured in terms of the member's values and available alternatives) the member's contributions. Each individual receives a set of inducements from an organization, with each inducement having a separate utility value. In return, the member contributes work, called "contributions," to the organization. Each contribution has its own utility, which is the value of the alternative that an individual forgoes to make the contribution. Both the individual and organization strive for an equilibrium state between inducements and contributions. The ensuing equilibrium assures survival of an organization.

Increases in the balance of inducement utilities over contribution utilities reduce the propensity of the member to leave the organization; decreases in that balance enhance the propensity. The balance between inducements and contributions is a function of two distinct but interdependent motivational components: the perceived desirability and the perceived ease of leaving the organization.

Perceived Desirability of Movement

The primary influencing factor is the individual's satisfaction with the job. That is, job satisfaction reduces perceived desirability of movement. March and Simon (1958) identified three sources of job satisfaction. First, conformity of job characteristics to self-image enhances job satisfaction: "Dissatisfaction arises from a disparity between reality and the ego-ideal held by the individual. The greater the disparity, the more pronounced the desire to escape from the situation" (March & Simon, 1958, p. 94). Relevant dimensions of self-image—namely, self-evaluations of independence, worth, and competencies or interests—are then satisfied (or frustrated) by supervisory practices, wages, participation in job assignment, and educational level. Besides a fit between person and job, predictability in instrumental relationships on the job and compatibility of work requirements with other role requirements promotes job satisfaction. Inter-role compatibility in turn depends on congruency of work time patterns with those of other roles and work group size.

Apart from job satisfaction, organizational size shapes the desirability of moving. The "larger the organization, the greater the perceived possibility or organizational transfer, and therefore, the less the perceived desirability of leaving the organization" (March and Simon, 1958, p. 99). Paradoxically, organizational size may *increase* desirability of movement because organizational and other roles become less compatible in larger firms (creating more dissatisfaction).

Perceived Ease of Movement

Drawing from the well-established tenet that "under nearly all conditions the most accurate single predictor of labor turnover is the state of the economy," March and Simon (1958, p. 100) specified antecedents of perceived ease of movement. They proposed that plentiful extra-organizational alternatives enhance perceived ease of movement. In turn, business activity and personal attributes determine an individual's available extra-organizational alternatives. In particular, young, male, high-status, or short-tenure employees perceive that they have greater ease of movement.

March and Simon (1958) further conceptualized that the number of visible firms increases the number of perceived extra-organizational alternatives. In turn, the company's prestige, the size of the organization, the production of a well-known product, the number of high-status occupations and employees, and rapid growth determine the visibility of the firm. In addition, the individual's residence and number of outside organizations to which she belongs increase her personal contacts, which expand the number of visible firms.

Because companies also scan people, an individual's visibility increases the number of visible organizations (who would seek to employ her). Such visibility among individuals may depend on the heterogeneity of personal contacts, high social status, and individual uniqueness. March and Simon (1958) posited that the individual's propensity to search them out boosts the number of visible companies. Job satisfaction and habituation in turn shape the propensity to search: "Dissatisfaction makes movement more desirable and also (by stimulating search) makes it appear more feasible" (March & Simon, 1958, p.105). By contrast, habituation to a particular job, which mounts with age and job tenure, diminishes the propensity to search.

Review

Although few studies *directly* tested March and Simon's (1958) model (cf. Mobley, 1982), their conceptualization nonetheless influenced successive generations of theorists. Their seminal work shaped much prevailing contemporary thinking about turnover, including that of Hulin, Roznowski, and Hachiya (1985), Lee and Mitchell (1994), Mitchell, Holtom, Lee, Sablynski, and Erez (2001), Mobley (1977), and Steers and Mowday (1981). More directly, Jackofsky and her colleagues (Jackofsky, 1984; Jackofsky & Slocum, 1987) incorporated March and Simon's constructs of desirability and ease of movement into a model relating job performance to turnover. Pettman (1973) reviewed research related to the March and Simon model, and found many of the hypotheses to be valid. But because of a number of methodological issues, it was difficult to identify the principal factors affecting turnover. Nonetheless, March and Simon's persistent influence over the decades illustrates the durability of their explanatory scheme.

Porter and Steers: Met-Expectations Model

Many years elapsed before a new theory emerged. In 1973, Porter and Steers posited that met expectations were the central determinant of decisions about turnover. They argued that although most employees value pay, promotions, supervisory relations, and peer-group interactions, individuals have distinctive sets of expectations. If an organization fails to meet an individual's set of expectations, dissatisfaction will result and the probability of withdrawal increases. They view this "as a process of balancing perceived or potential rewards with desired expectations" (Porter & Steers, 1973, p. 171).

More specifically, Porter and Steers suggested that expectations of work rewards are fluid from the beginning of employment to some later period when the individual decides to stay or leave. Two new employees holding similar job expectations at the outset may later find their expectations fulfilled in different ways. One employee's expected rewards may be met or exceeded by the job, resulting in satisfaction and participation; the other may discover that the job does not confirm her expectations, inducing dissatisfaction and withdrawal. To summarize, Porter and Steers posited a causal sequence, wherein unmet expectations → job dissatisfaction → turnover.

Review

Porter and Steers' model represents a pivotal theoretical advancement in turnover research. They introduced a parsimonious, integrative construct—namely, met expectations—that summarizes the effects of myriad work-related determinants on turnover (via reward experiences) and acknowledges the existence of personal attributes, which underpin expectation levels. In line with their view, a meta-analysis (Wanous, Poland, Premack, & Davis, 1992) found that met expectations correlated most closely with job attitudes than with intentions to quit and, last, with turnover. What is more, their model became the dominant explanation for why realistic job previews (RJPs) work (Datel & Lifrak, 1969; Earnest, Allen, & Landis, 2011; Wanous, 1973; Youngberg, 1963). RJPs communicate positive and negative features of a job to new employees, and such communication bolsters tenure in the job (Premack & Wanous, 1985; Wanous, 1992). Supporting the Porter–Steers formulation, various studies have confirmed that RJPs reduce turnover by deflating initial expectations, leading to higher actualization of expectations on the job (Hom, Griffeth, Palich, & Bracker, 1993; Premack & Wanous, 1985). Yet a recent meta-analysis supported an alternative mechanism in which RJPs improve retention by signaling organizational honesty (Earnest et al., 2011).

Some issues continue, however, to elude scholarly scrutiny. One involves the met-expectations concept itself. In its present form, this concept may be too simplistic (Ilgen & Dugoni, 1977). According to Festinger (1947), cognitive dissonance occurs when initial expectations are not consistent with later experience. Dissatisfaction will result. Dissonance is aroused regardless of whether the disconfirming experience is positive or negative. Dissonance theory predicts dissatisfaction when expectations are unmet or are exceeded and satisfaction when expectations are met. Thus, dissonance theory predicts a quadratic relationship between met expectations and job satisfaction. In contrast, Porter and Steers (1973) hypothesized that most dissatisfaction would arise when expectations are unmet and would decline (linearly or monotonically) as expectations are met or exceeded. Griffeth (1981) tested these two competing predictions and found stronger support for a curvilinear relationship between dissatisfaction and met expectations.

Louis (1980) further argued that the Porter–Steers notion fails to differentiate between initial expectations that are not fulfilled by the job ("unmet") and those that are surpassed ("over-met"). She reasoned that over-met expectations produce surprise rather than dissatisfaction. She also criticized the Porter–Steers viewpoint as simplistically presuming that all pre-entry expectations are conscious, clearly defined, and refer to qualities of the job. To overcome the concept's limitations, she introduced a comprehensive taxonomy of different types of unmet expectations based on three levels of awareness: emergent, tacit, and conscious. Besides the mismatch between expectation and reality, she suggested that expectations have a focus (initial expectations can refer to the self or job) and that there is a level of awareness about expectation (expectations may be conscious or preconscious).

To illustrate awareness in expectation, she discussed possible disconfirmation of unconscious job expectations, such as unexpected features of the job, and quoted a newcomer who said, "I had no idea how important windows were to me until I'd spent a week in a staff room without any" (Louis, 1980, p. 238). To illustrate expectation focus, Louis mentioned that newcomers may harbor mistaken assumptions about their proficiency ("I'm less competent on this job than I expected to be") or attitudes ("I knew I would put in lots of overtime but I did not expect that 65-hour weeks would be so grueling"). Louis's taxonomy holds great promise for understanding how unmet expectations affect turnover and awaits future validation. Her conceptualization may clarify how RJPs improve job survival because RJPs may also establish entry expectations for the job and the worker, besides promoting met expectations (see Meglino, DeNisi, Youngblood, & Williams, 1988).

Though Porter and Steers (1973) acknowledged that unmet expectations do not invariably evoke quits, they did not state why this occurs. Conceivably, some disappointed newcomers do not withdraw only because they lack viable alternatives to the present job (Wanous, 1973). Thus, Porter and Steers omitted a key moderator of the unmet expectations → turnover pathway, perceived alternatives, which played such a key role in March and Simon's (1958) model. Thus, without a mention of a role for alternatives, the Porter and Steers (1973) model is focused on intra-organizational factors. Further, they prescribed use of RJPs to deflate newcomers' expectations so that the existing job might more easily fulfill their expectations and improve the chances of their staying on the job. An *increase* in initial job expectations may, however, benefit new entrants to certain occupations. Meglino et al. (1988) showed that an "enhancement" RJP promotes recruits' survival in the army by reversing overly pessimistic expectations about their ability to complete basic training. Porter and Steers (1973) nevertheless recognized that more theoretical work must examine the psychology of the decisional processes underlying turnover. This call was soon answered by Mobley.

Mobley: Turnover Process Model

In response to Locke's (1976) observation that the relationship between satisfaction and turnover has rarely exceeded .40, Mobley (1977) envisioned a series of intermediate linkages between evaluation of the present job—the result of which is satisfaction or dissatisfaction—and turnover. This decisional sequence is illustrated in Figure 4.1. Individuals evaluate their existing job via any number of models (e.g., equity theory; Griffeth & Gaertner, 2001), possibly resulting in job dissatisfaction. Job dissatisfaction stimulates thoughts of quitting, which elicit assessments of the utility of seeking other employment (for instance, the chances of finding comparable work) and turnover costs (among them the loss of unvested pension benefits). If the exit will not be costly, the expectation that it would be beneficial to seek another job will induce intentions of making a search and, thereafter, searching. After finding alternatives, dissatisfied employees will evaluate them and compare them with the present job. When the alternatives are found to be the more attractive, the disparity motivates the employee to quit.

Review

In the annals of turnover work, Mobley's theory has most furthered understanding of the withdrawal process and has drawn the most empirical scrutiny. Though March and Simon (1958) provided impetus for modern theory and research,

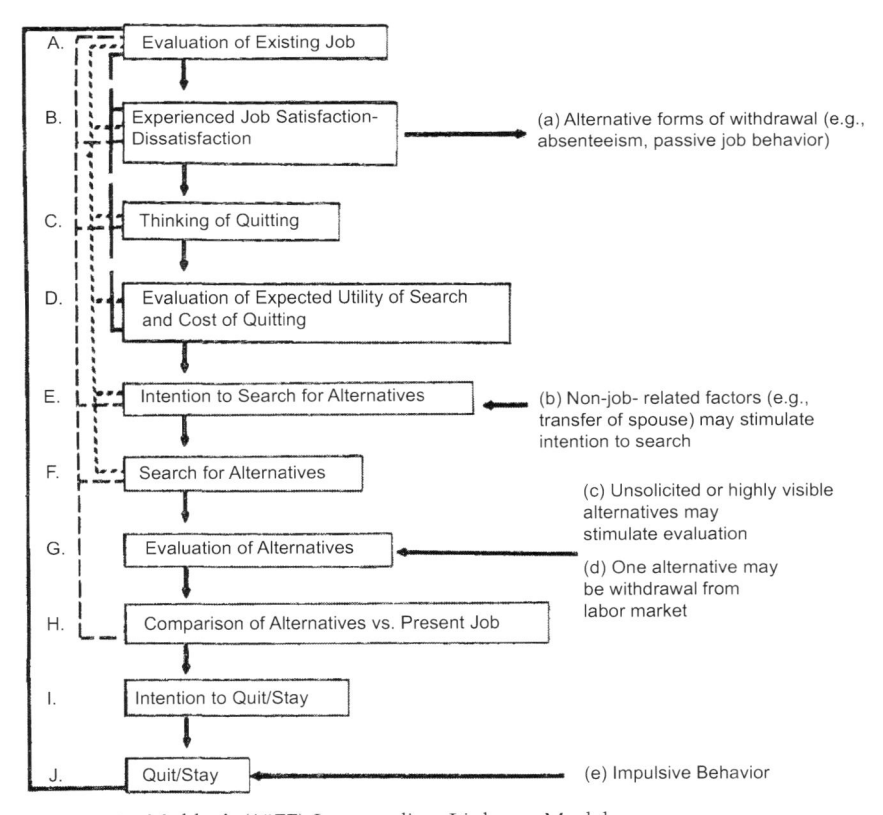

FIGURE 4.1 Mobley's (1977) Intermediate Linkages Model

Mobley's (1977) model dominates all later work on psychological approaches to turnover. This model stimulated substantial investigations on its validity and inspired subsequent theoretical elaborations or refinements. Some theorists (such as Mobley, Griffeth, Hand, & Meglino, 1979) expanded Mobley's model by introducing more distal determinants of the process from satisfaction to quitting. Others have restated or clarified this termination process (Steers & Mowday, 1981). Still, other scholars have refined this model by reconfiguring intervening mechanisms that translate dissatisfaction (Hom & Griffeth, 1991), or by construing Mobley's withdrawal sequence as only one of multiple routes to turnover (Lee & Mitchell, 1994). If they have not adopted the model in its entirety, other turnover theorists have nonetheless adopted one or more of the theoretical constructs Mobley pioneered—notably, withdrawal intentions (Price & Mueller, 1986) and perceived alternatives (Hulin et al., 1985; Rusbult & Farrell, 1983). In one form or another, Mobley's conceptualization of the turnover process continues to infuse present-day thinking about organizational withdrawal (e.g., Allen, Hancock, Vardaman, & McKee, 2014; Hom, Mitchell, Lee, & Griffeth, 2012; Lee & Mitchell, 1994). All told, Mobley's theory is unmatched in its far-reaching and enduring influence.

Early investigations tested an abbreviated version of Mobley's model that Mobley, Horner, and Hollingsworth (1978) had proposed (Coverdale & Terborg, 1980; Miller, Katerberg, & Hulin, 1979; Mowday, Koberg, & McArthur, 1984; Peters, Jackofsky, & Salter, 1981; Spencer, Steers, & Mowday, 1983). While generally supported (Hom, Caranikas-Walker, Prussia, & Griffeth, 1992), tests of the abbreviated 1978 model do not directly substantiate the earlier more elaborate model (Hom, Griffeth, & Sellaro, 1984). Though surprisingly scant, the few complete tests of the original 1977 formulation have consistently disputed several model pathways, although upholding most pathways (Hom et al., 1984; Laker, 1991; Lee, 1988; Steel, Lounsbury, & Horst, 1981). These mixed findings prompted the development of a growing number of alternative structural networks linking Mobley's constructs that secured stronger corroboration than Mobley's original structure (Blau, 1993; Hom et al., 1992; Hom & Griffeth, 1991; Hom et al., 1984; Jaros, Jermier, Koehler, & Sincich, 1993; Sager, Griffeth, & Hom, 1992).

Hom and Griffeth: Revised Intermediate Processes Model

Responding to growing challenges to Mobley's structural relations (Hom et al., 1984; Lee, 1988; Steel et al., 1981), Hom et al. (1984) proposed an alternative network. They suggested that dissatisfaction evokes thoughts of quitting, which in turn stimulate decisions to quit and an evaluation of the expected costs and benefits of search and quitting. At this juncture, employees follow one of two paths. Some employees who perceive that alternatives are available undertake a job search. They then compare the alternatives with their present job and, when the alternatives are better, they quit. Other employees, who may expect to find another job easily or who may pursue alternatives other than work, simply resign after deciding to quit. The path analytical test by Hom et al. (1984) supported this causal structure better than Mobley's original model. Nonetheless, several model pathways were empirically derived rather than theorized a priori (James, Mulaik, & Brett, 1982), and Hom, Griffeth and Sellaro measured employees' generalized impressions of alternative work rather than their perceptions of specific jobs.

Afterward, Hom and Griffeth (1991) cross-validated the structural alternative proposed by Hom et al. (1984) in two nursing samples, using structural equation modeling (SEM) and more precise measures of specific job offers. Figure 4.2 depicts their model. In study 1, they investigated the dimensionality of model constructs.

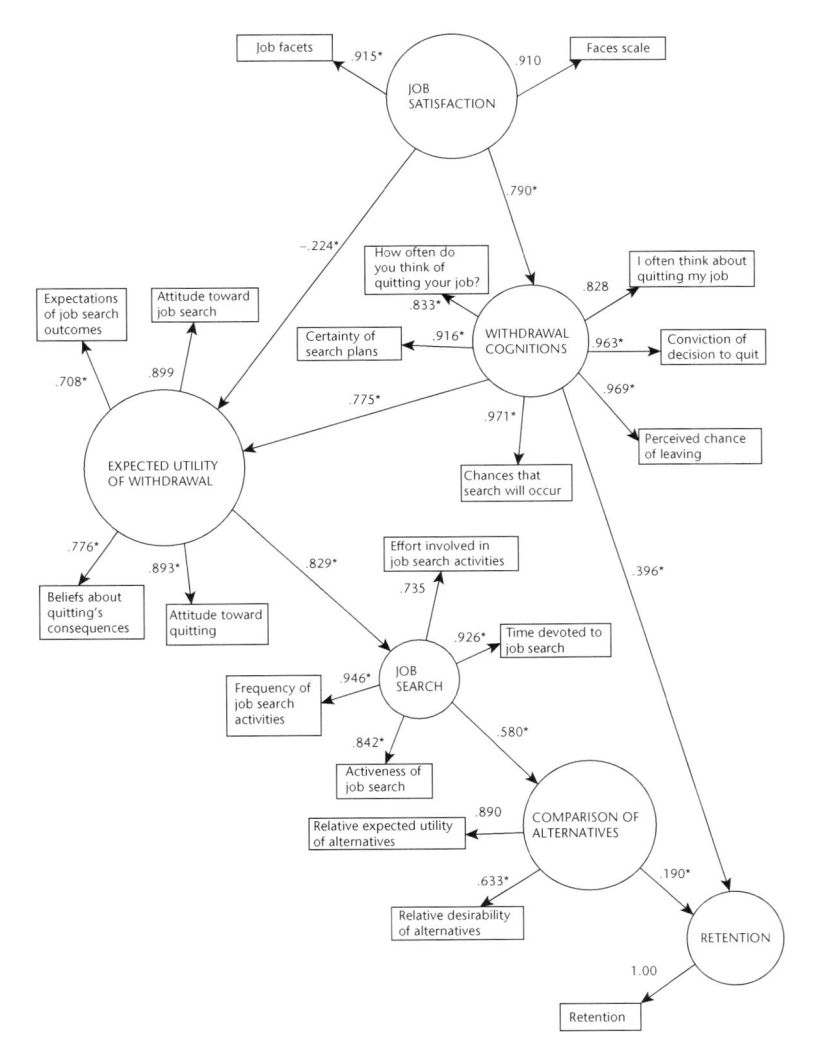

FIGURE 4.2 Hom and Griffeth's (1991) Intermediate Linkages Model

Discriminating most constructs, SEM analysis, however, identified a global construct underlying thoughts of quitting, search intentions, and quit decisions. After reconceptualizing withdrawal intentions as different facets of the same construct, Hom and Griffeth supported the structural model. In study 2, surveying new nurses on three occasions, the researchers tested causal priorities among model variables more rigorously. By and large, this SEM analysis supported the theorized causal directions and demonstrated that some causal effects occur instantaneously and others transpire over time. Moreover, causal effects systematically changed during the assimilation of newcomers into the organization.

Though their validation is encouraging, Hom and Griffeth's revision of Mobley's withdrawal stages requires further corroboration. Jaros et al. (1993) similarly verified a global withdrawal cognition, but Sager et al. (1992) upheld a multidimensional conceptualization. The theoretical model merits substantiation in samples of other workers, who may withdraw from organizations for different reasons than nurses do (Hom et al., 1992). More contemporary formulations suggest that Mobley's—and Hom and Griffeth's (1991)—depiction of intervening mechanisms between dissatisfaction and turnover is incomplete. Indeed, Mobley et al. (1979) later theorized that the attraction of the job—or future improvements in the work role or future attainment of other desirable work roles within the company—may interrupt the translation of dissatisfaction into departure. That is, dissatisfied employees may decide *not* to leave if they foresee workplace improvements. Similarly, Hulin et al. (1985) and Steers and Mowday (1981) argued that an alternative reaction to dissatisfaction besides (or before) departure is to improve the workplace—either by directly eliminating job frustrations or by moving to other positions in the organization. Later investigators started to elaborate the Hom–Griffeth model by introducing other variables mediating the impact of dissatisfaction on exits.

Extending the Hom–Griffeth 1991 model, Hom and Kinicki (2001) reasoned that in today's fast-paced and complex work environments, inter-role conflict arising from the struggle between work and non-work role demands might initiate job dissatisfaction and thus withdrawal cognitions. From Hulin et al. (1985), they also introduced job avoidance, representing actions employees may take to distance themselves from frustrating work environments, as mediating between job dissatisfaction and withdrawal cognitions. They tested this expanded Hom–Griffeth model with employees from a national automotive retail store chain, using SEM and survival analyses. SEM results for the expanded model showed excellent fit to the data, with inter-role conflict inversely related to job dissatisfaction and positively related to withdrawal cognitions. Job satisfaction was negatively related to job avoidance, while job avoidance was marginally and positively ($p < .10$) related to withdrawal cognitions. As theorized, withdrawal cognitions were positively related to turnover. Affirming the Hom–Griffeth model (its 1991 and 2001 variants), survival analyses further established that *both* withdrawal cognitions *and* job comparisons increase turnover. Moreover, job avoidance (i.e., taking more sick leave, missing work, or reducing effort and quality when frustrated) raised the risk of turnover, as predicted. Encouragingly, this study more firmly supported Hom and Griffeth's (1991) turnover theory, using both latent variables SEM and survival analysis with a nationwide workforce other than nursing samples, while corroborating its theoretical refinement (incorporation of job avoidance and inter-role conflict).

Price: Structural Model

In a comprehensive review of the literature, the sociologist James Price (1977) developed a model that integrated past findings about turnover. He theorized that pay, integration, instrumental communication, formal communication, and centralization shape job satisfaction, which influences turnover. Further, opportunity—or the availability of alternative employment—moderates the relationship between satisfaction and turnover. Trial evaluations of this early model subsequently inspired a more comprehensive theory (Bluedorn, 1982; Martin, 1979; Price & Bluedorn, 1979).

Expanding Price's (1977) model, Price and Mueller (1981) proposed that repetitive work (e.g., routinization) reduces satisfaction and that workers who are participating in job-related decisions, receiving work-related information, forming close friends with others at work, earning good and fair compensation, and enjoying opportunities for promotion are more likely to be satisfied. Job satisfaction, in turn, increases intentions of staying, whereas professionalism, generalized training, and minimal kinship responsibility weaken these intentions. Together, intentions to stay and opportunities for employment elsewhere determine turnover.

Subsequently, Price and Mueller published in 1986 a version of their 1981 version. They introduced two antecedents to satisfaction, role overload and family pay, and another determinant of decisions to quit (and thus of commitment to the organization), the size of the company and work groups. They renamed participation to reflect centralization (the concentration of power) and interposed commitment to the organization between job satisfaction and intentions to quit. Gaertner (1999) later conducted a meta-analytical SEM test of the Price–Mueller structural determinants of job satisfaction and organizational commitment using nine empirical studies. He found that three structural determinants (distributive justice, promotional chances, and supervisory support) directly related to organizational commitment over and above their impact on job satisfaction. He also found that the structural determinants of job satisfaction were directly related to their criterion. The notable exception was amount of pay, which was not related to job satisfaction or organizational commitment. Regarding this latter finding, the author suggests that while pay is not unimportant, pay *fairness* may be the more important issue, as distributive justice *was* related to both job satisfaction and organizational commitment.

Review

Price's theorizing and research represent landmark contributions to research into turnover. Unlike more speculative theorists, he identified in 1977 a comprehensive set of determinants of turnover based on a systematic and broad review of the research in labor economics, sociology, and psychology. Thus, his causal determinants are empirically well grounded (based on consistent empirical findings) and include explanatory constructs historically overlooked by organizational researchers. In particular, Price introduced the notions of kinship responsibilities, professionalism, and economic opportunity, which eventually entered the mainstream of modern thought about withdrawal (see Gerhart, 1990; Hulin et al., 1985; Rusbult & Farrell, 1983; Steers & Mowday, 1981). Moreover, Price and Mueller's (1981, 1986) empirical investigations of their models became hallmarks of methodological rigor. They pioneered causal modeling techniques to assess structural networks, evaluating the nomological validity of a theory as well as its predictive validity, the customary preoccupation. They carefully constructed scales to assess model constructs validly and reliably. For example, they factor-analyzed items reflecting the same construct and created reliable factor-based scales of items with high factor loadings (average .75 reliability). Such painstaking validation stands in marked contrast to traditional ad hoc operationalizations and provided psychometrically sound scales for investigations into turnover.

Notwithstanding their rigorous methodology, Price and Mueller found that all the components of the 1981 model together explained only 18% of turnover's variance. Importantly, they partially verified theorized causal pathways. Although finding significant estimates for nearly 70% of predicted causal effects, their research failed to sustain other expected linkages in the model. Surprisingly, they uncovered significance for 20% of the pathways theorized to be absent. To improve predictions about turnover, they recommended that intentions to quit be replaced with commitment to the organization and they reconceptualized the meaning of distributive justice, professionalism, and integration. Even so, the revised (and expanded) 1986 model explained only 13% of turnover's variance. Here again, Price and Mueller (1986) partially supported their a priori causal structure. They obtained significant estimates for roughly 75% of theorized causal pathways, but rejected the remaining pathways. Importantly, approximately 40% of supposedly null pathways were estimated as statistically significant, which contradicted their theoretical predictions.

In summary, the few research studies of the Price–Mueller models partly affirmed their nomological networks. Besides this, a competitive two-sample test by Griffeth and Hom (1990) found that the Price–Mueller models provide less parsimonious explanations of turnover compared with Hom et al.'s (1984) variant of Mobley's (1977) model. Still, a joint model synthesizing promising concepts from Mobley's and Price and Mueller's models yielded excellent model fit and parsimony. Future inquiry might attempt integration between Price and Mueller's structural formulation and process-oriented models, such as those of Hom and Griffeth (1991), Lee and Mitchell (1994), and Steers and Mowday (1981), that explicate the translation of dissatisfaction into terminations (cf. Griffeth & Hom, 1995). Future validations of the Price–Mueller theories (or their variants) should be performed on samples of workers other than nurses or hospital personnel, who comprise the validation samples for the original models and may follow a different process of withdrawal than would other members of the workforce.

Mobley, Griffeth, Hand, and Meglino: Expanded Model

Since proposing the 1977 model, Mobley et al. (1979) reviewed the literature on turnover and organized its potential causes into a heuristic model using an expectancy theory approach reflecting many indirect and direct influences on the phenomenon. Figure 4.3 depicts this expanded model.

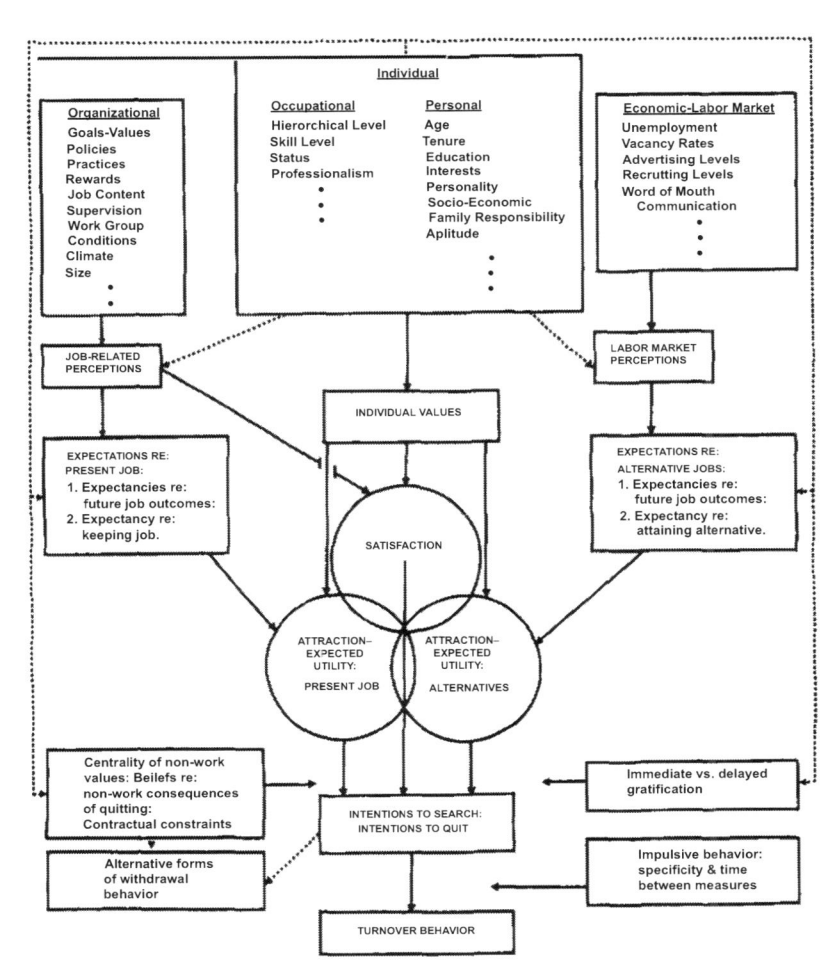

FIGURE 4.3 Mobley, Griffeth, Hand, and Meglino's (1979) Expanded Turnover Model

Requisites for Intentions

As in the earlier model, the researchers proposed quit intentions as the immediate precursor to turnover. They further conceived intentions (and turnover) as a function of: (1) job satisfaction; (2) expected utility of the present work role; and (3) expected utility of alternative work roles.

Job Satisfaction

They defined satisfaction as an affective response resulting from evaluation of the job. Drawing from Locke's theory (1969, 1976), they conceptualized that personal values and job-related perceptions shape job evaluation. Basically, job satisfaction derives from the extent to which an employee's important values are attained in the job (Mobley, 1982). Mobley et al. further theorized that satisfaction is present-oriented and generates an approach or avoidance orientation toward the job. However, job dissatisfaction imperfectly foreshadows turnover, which also derives from the employee's expectations of conditions in the organization (Mobley 1982).

Expected Utility of the Present Role

Besides satisfaction, the "expected utility of the present role," which is an individual's "expectancies that the job will lead to the attainment of various positively or negatively valued outcomes" and expectancy of retaining the current job also underpins decisions about turnover (Mobley et al., 1979, p. 518). Thus, an employee may not quit a dissatisfying job if she or he expects the job to lead to future better things, such as a transfer to a better job, a promotion, or an improvement in conditions in the organization (Mobley, 1982). The expected utility of the present job thus explains why job satisfaction imperfectly predicts terminations: optimistic expectations about the job may prevent some dissatisfied employees from leaving; pessimistic expectations about career prospects within the company may induce even satisfied employees to quit.

Expected Utility of Alternative Roles

Building on the work of Forrest, Cummings, and Johnson (1977), March and Simon (1958), and Schneider (1976), Mobley et al. posited the expected utility of external alternatives as a third determinant of intentions to withdraw. The expectancy that the alternatives will be better (and the expectancy of attaining those alternatives) also explains why job satisfaction imperfectly predicts turnover. The absence of attractive alternatives may discourage dissatisfied employees from resigning, whereas the availability of desirable employment elsewhere may motivate even satisfied employees to exit (Mobley, 1982; Mobley et al., 1979).

Moderators and Distal Determinants

Impulsive quitting, the centrality of non-work values, and a need for immediate gratification moderate the effects of job satisfaction and expected utilities on turnover. Mobley et al. (1979) suggested that employees who cannot secure attractive alternatives may engage in alternative forms of withdrawal, such as low performance, absences, accidents, and even sabotage. Further, job satisfaction and expected role utilities in turn emanate from various determinants such as organizational (e.g., policies and practices), occupational (e.g., skill level and status), personal (e.g., tenure and education), and economic and labor market (e.g., unemployment and vacancy rates) factors.

Review

By emphasizing values, expectancies, job-related and external perceptions, and moderators, Mobley et al.'s (1979) conceptualization introduced a welcome multivariate explanation of the turnover process. Unlike Mobley's (1977) process-oriented formulation, the later perspective sought to identify a comprehensive set of determinants of turnover and has been hailed by Muchinsky and Morrow (1980) as "well developed and highly articulated" (p. 265). Borrowing from expectancy theory, Mobley et al. further popularized notions of the expected utility of the present role and the expected utility of alternatives, which explain why dissatisfied employees do not invariably quit their jobs: the possibility of attractive work roles in the future in their present job and/or the undesirability of external alternatives may discourage dissatisfied employees from severing their employment. Moreover, Mobley et al. emphasized the role of non-work influences on withdrawal decisions, a concept that now pervades turnover perspectives (see Hom & Kinicki, 2001; Hulin et al., 1985; Steers & Mowday, 1981). Notwithstanding these contributions, this comprehensive framework left unspecified the relative impact of the three classes of distal antecedents on job-related perceptions, individual values, and perceptions of the labor market, as well as overlooking causal interactions within and between classes of antecedents.

Two research streams have tested the 1979 theory. Although the tests were not exhaustive, many researchers investigated portions of the theory: Griffeth and Hom (1988), Michaels and Spector (1982), Motowidlo and Lawton (1984), and Youngblood, Mobley, and Meglino (1983). Other researchers, among them Arnold and Feldman (1982) and Hom et al. (1984), borrowed components of the model to validate a different theory. Both approaches affirmed that expected utilities of a work role can improve predictions of turnover decisions and behavior better than measures of job satisfaction alone can, although the results are not consistent (see Griffeth & Hom 1988; Youngblood et al., 1983). Nevertheless, most investigations inadequately operationalized the expected utility of the present work role, emphasizing the present attainment rather than the *future* attainment of role outcomes (Hom & Kinicki, 2001). In a similar vein, existing studies imprecisely represented the expected utility of alternative jobs, typically measuring the attractiveness of some general alternative rather than considering specific job offers (Griffeth & Hom, 1988). Conceivably, better representations of the original notions of Mobley et al. may enhance the predictive power of the expected utilities of current and other work roles.

Beyond this, many of the model's propositions remain untested. For example, does failure to find attractive alternatives lead to alternative forms of withdrawal as Mobley et al. (1979) hypothesized? Or after failing to find an alternative, do employees re-evaluate their present jobs more favorably? No study has attempted to operationalize the model completely. Admittedly, Mobley et al., in providing illustrative components rather than an exhaustive taxonomy, did not specify fully *all* the components of the three sets of distal organizational, individual, and labor market causes.

Muchinsky and Morrow: Multidisciplinary Model

Muchinsky and Morrow (1980) conceived economic determinants, such as employment rates and opportunity to obtain work, as immediate precursors of turnover. The rationale for direct employment effects is that most employees will not leave their present job unless alternative opportunities for employment exist. Individual and work-related factors then "flow" through economic opportunity, which acts as a valve to regulate their influence on turnover. That is, when jobs are plentiful, individual and work-related determinants affect turnover more than they do when few jobs exist. As a result, the relationship between job dissatisfaction and quits is stronger for employees that have alternative jobs than for those who do not. Without alternatives, dissatisfied employees are more likely to endure their present situation. Muchinsky and Morrow also acknowledged the likelihood of alternative forms of withdrawal, such as absenteeism or depressed productivity, if employees cannot find more attractive alternatives, and argued that individual and work-related factors interact.

Review

Though Muchinsky and Morrow's (1980) model has rarely been tested, Carsten and Spector (1987) examined the thesis that employment moderates relationships between individual and work-related variables. Using meta-analysis, Carsten and Spector considered two correlates of turnover, satisfaction and intentions to quit, during periods of low and high unemployment. Muchinsky and Morrow hypothesized that the relationship would be strong during low unemployment and weak during high unemployment. Generally, the results supported their prediction, although correlations between job satisfaction and turnover ranged from −.18 to −.52, depending upon whether unemployment rates were calculated at state or occupational levels. Relationships between intention and turnover were somewhat lower (−.28 to −.36).

Generalizing from these findings, other scholars substantiated the moderating effects of unemployment on relationships between perceived alternatives and quitting and on structural networks of causes of turnover (Gerhart, 1990; Steel & Griffeth, 1989; Hom et al., 1992). These compelling results persuaded organizational psychologists to begin modeling the effects of unemployment rates on turnover among individuals (see Hom et al., 1992; Hulin et al., 1985). Yet theoretical consideration of unemployment rates challenges the prevailing psychological models of turnover, which overlook macro-level determinants (Hom & Hulin, 1981; Rousseau, 1985).

Conceivably, the unemployment rate affects an individual's turnover because it is a crude proxy for various psychological forces, such as the crystallization of alternatives and the visibility of alternatives (Griffeth, Steel, Allen, & Bryan, 2005; Steel & Griffeth, 1989). Also, watching coworkers leave for presumably better jobs may increase turnover among stayers (Felps et al., 2009). Additionally, rates of joblessness may indirectly ("spuriously") affect the withdrawal process by impacting the quit base rate (Hom & Hulin, 1981). Essentially, high unemployment depresses turnover rates, thereby attenuating relationships between turnover and its antecedents (Steel & Griffeth, 1989). Furthermore, high employment may encourage marginal drifters, whose decisions about changing jobs may not be regulated by the same process as those of regular, full-time workers, to join the workforce (Hulin et al., 1985). Once they accumulate sufficient funds, many may simply resign, drop out of the labor market, or pursue more "fulfilling" avocations. Therefore, the familiar bases of turnover, which underlie the quit decisions of regular employees, may scarcely determine those of peripheral workers who forsake even satisfying jobs.

Lastly, scant evidence supports other relationships among the variables, especially interactions, which were depicted in Muchinsky and Morrow's (1980) theory. By de-emphasizing the process underlying turnover, the Muchinsky and Morrow model represents a "content" model that catalogues factors of turnover, but omitted many essential determinants—most notably, withdrawal cognitions. Obviously, more research is warranted to validate this model.

Farrell and Rusbult: Investment Model

Farrell and Rusbult (1981) derived a model from exchange (Homans, 1961) and interdependence (Kelley & Thibaut, 1978; Thibaut & Kelley, 1959) theories. From these conceptualizations, they attempted to explain organizational commitment, which is "the binding of the individual to behavioral acts" (Kiesler & Sakumura, 1966, p. 349):

> Thus, job commitment is related to the probability that an employee will leave his job, and involves feelings of attachment, independent of affect. Job commitment reflects behavioral intention, primarily (but not solely) [the] degree of intention to stay with a job.
>
> (Farrell & Rusbult, 1981, p. 79)

They proposed various antecedents of commitment—notably, job satisfaction (SAT_x)—which they defined as: $SAT_x = (R_x - C_x) - CL$, where R_x is the reward value of an association, defined by:

$$R_x = E(w_i r_i),$$

where r_i is the individual's subjective estimate of the reward value of attribute i available from association X and w_i represents its subjective importance, and:

$$C_x = E(w_j c_j),$$

where c_j is the magnitude of the subjective costs of association X regarding attribute j and w_j is the importance of the attribute in the association.

CL is the comparison level (Thibaut & Kelley, 1959), or internal standard, that the employee has come to expect from associations. Presumably, job satisfaction arises from a comparison between the CL and the difference between job rewards and costs—called the association outcome value (O_x).

Alternatives also influence commitment. This alternative value (A_y), or the quality of the best available alternative, is defined as:

$$A_y = (R_y - C_y) - CL_{alt},$$

where A_y corresponds to the CL_{alt} construct of interdependence theory, which is the standard by which individuals decide whether or not they will remain in an association. That is, CL_{alt} is "the lowest level of outcomes a member will accept in the light of available alternative opportunities" (Thibaut & Kelley, 1959, p. 21).

Lastly, job investments (I_x) reinforce job commitment. These investments comprise resources that are intrinsic to the job, including unvested retirement benefits and non-portable training, and extrinsic resources inextricably tied to the job, such as community services and friends at work, that are relinquished if employees quit their jobs. More formally:

$$I_x = E(w_k i_k),$$

where i_k refers to the size of the investment of resource k in relationship X, and w_k refers to the importance of resource k.

To summarize, job commitment (COM_x) is a function of job satisfaction, quality of job alternatives, and size of job investments. In other words:

$$COM_x = SAT_x + I_x - A_y.$$

Review

The investment model is a rich interdisciplinary model predicated on sociological and psychological constructs. Although widely cited, it is surprising that it has not attracted more research since its inception. To our knowledge, only Farrell and Rusbult have directly tested their model. Their first study (Farrell & Rusbult, 1981) with a laboratory work simulation and a cross-sectional survey of industrial workers sustained the major relationships among model variables. That is, they found that job rewards and job costs strongly predicted job satisfaction. In combination, job rewards and costs, value of other alternatives, and job investments also strongly predicted job commitment. Further, job commitment predicted turnover more accurately than did job satisfaction.

Surveying 88 new nurses and accountants, Rusbult and Farrell (1983) next conducted a longitudinal test and found that job satisfaction rose over time as job rewards increased and job costs decreased. Meanwhile, escalating job rewards and investments boosted commitment over time, as did declining costs and quality of alternatives. Importantly, they found that temporal changes in model variables rather than their absolute levels best differentiated between stayers and leavers. For example, job costs and job investments scarcely affected the commitment of newcomers during the initial period of employment. But as time passed, job costs grew more apparent and investments began accumulating, thereby increasingly shaping the newcomers' commitment. Consequently, temporal *changes* in costs and investments predicted commitment more than did initial job cost and investment values. Most of all, *changes* in job commitment powerfully forecast resignations.

Although their evidence is encouraging, Rusbult and Farrell narrowly construed their commitment construct as primarily withdrawal cognitions. This conceptualization conflicts, however, with more popular, multidimensional commitment constructs, which embody not only withdrawal cognitions, but also identification with organizational values and willingness to go beyond formal work-role definitions (Mowday, Porter, & Steers, 1982; O'Reilly & Chatman, 1986). Whether or not the same model determinants would predict an expanded notion of organizational commitment awaits future research. Rusbult and Farrell's operationalization of job commitment includes both decisions about termination and about search, which other researchers theoretically and empirically distinguish as separate constructs (Blau, 1993; Mobley, 1977; Steers & Mowday, 1981). The theory oversimplifies perceived alternatives, considering only the *attractiveness* of other employment opportunities. Yet turnover scholars envision increasingly more complex, multifaceted conceptualizations of the employment market, taking into account specific job offers (Griffeth & Hom, 1988), attainability of alternatives (Mobley et al., 1979), and crystallization of alternatives (Griffeth et al., 2005). Lastly, one of the main strengths of investment theory—its parsimony—nonetheless constitute a weakness. In light of more comprehensive formulations (Lee & Mitchell, 1994; Mobley et al., 1979; Steers &

Mowday, 1981), the omission from this model of many determinants, such as job search and efforts to improve working conditions, weakens its predictive efficacy (Blau, 1993; Hulin et al., 1985).

Steers and Mowday: Multi-Route Model

Steers and Mowday (1981) advanced another comprehensive turnover model that integrates earlier theories while overcoming their conceptual shortcomings. To clarify its dynamics, they presented this framework in three segments, shown in Figure 4.4.

Origins of Job Expectations and Attitudes

Steers and Mowday theorized that an individual's value system influences his or her expectations about various aspects of a job, such as the nature of the job and rewards for satisfactory performance. Besides values, personal characteristics—such as age, tenure, and family responsibilities—underpin the expectations of employees by determining "what they expect from a job: what they feel they must have, what they would like to have, and what they can do without" (Steers & Mowday, 1981, p. 243). The accuracy of prior information about the job and the company will make the initial expectations more realistic and thereby lower turnover. The alternatives that are available modify expectations about the job because employees who have many attractive options may set higher expectations for their current jobs.

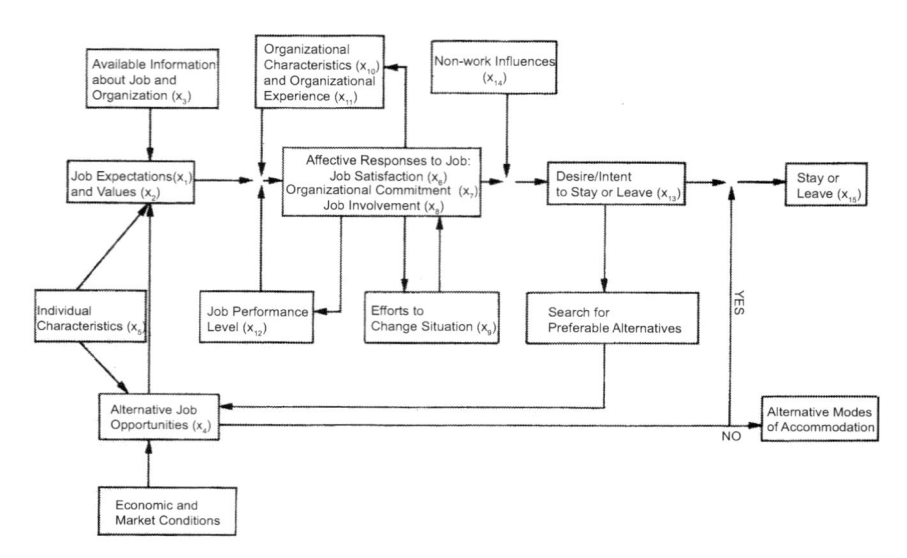

FIGURE 4.4 Steers and Mowday's (1981) Theory of Employee Turnover

Affective Responses to the Job

Steers and Mowday conceived affective responses to the job as embodying job satisfaction, organizational commitment, and job involvement. They further hypothesized that job expectations and values would interact with organizational characteristics and experiences, and that job performance would influence affective responses. Extrapolating from met-expectations theory (Porter & Steers, 1973), they contended that the more closely pre-entry expectations align with the work experience, the greater the employee's job satisfaction and propensity to remain in the organization. Job performance also influences affective responses because high performers receive more merit pay (see Lawler, 1981) and expect more job security.

Steers and Mowday further suggested a reciprocal causation between job performance and organizational experiences and affective responses. As previously described, job performance and organizational experiences shape job attitudes, but job attitudes may themselves impact performance and organizational experiences. That is, poor attitudes may prompt employees to change the work environment or transfer to other jobs before they decide to leave. If the workplace becomes more tolerable, attitudes toward their workplace may become positive. A failure to improve the environment would strengthen the employee's resolve to abandon the job and, in the meantime, worsen the attitude toward the job.

How Job Attitudes Affect Intent to Leave

Steers and Mowday further envisioned that job attitudes influence intentions to leave, although outside influences may condition the effect. That is, some employees remain employed in unpleasant jobs due to a constellation of "non-work" influences. To illustrate, they may tolerate dissatisfying jobs to avoid sacrificing spousal careers by relocating elsewhere for work or anticipate future promotions into higher-paid and prestigious positions (e.g., advancing from apprenticeships to master craftsmen).

The Process by Which Job Search Leads to Turnover

The third segment of the framework specifies the ways in which intentions to withdraw induce turnover. Following March and Simon (1958), Steers and Mowday posited that intentions to quit multiplicatively combine with the availability of alternatives. In essence, intentions to quit affect turnover via two causal routes. The formation of a decision to quit may directly trigger the resignation or may indirectly influence turnover by prompting employees to seek alternative jobs. Alternative opportunities partly depend on individual traits, such as age, sex, and occupation, which affect the likelihood of the person's attaining other employment. Failing to find an alternative, a job-seeking employee may revert to other forms of withdrawal, such as absenteeism, sabotage, and alcohol abuse. Dissatisfied individuals, unable to find better alternatives, may accommodate an unpleasant job by rationalizing their reasons for remaining.

Steers and Mowday also noted that employees may be presented with attractive alternatives, which will boost their expectations of their present job. Inflated expectations may, however, translate into frustration (for these expectations are less likely to be realized by the current job), worsening job attitudes and increasing the desire to leave.

Review

The Steers and Mowday (1981) model is a complex representation of the turnover process that pioneered many innovative constructs, including the long-neglected notion that efforts to change the work environment may interrupt the process by which job dissatisfaction develops into departure. Efforts to change the job may also directly affect other determinants of turnover. For instance, Hulin et al. (1985) implied that efforts to change the job may reduce withdrawal cognitions because dissatisfied employees who manage to improve their working conditions would not quit. Moreover, Steers and Mowday introduced job performance as a determinant of turnover, influencing later writers to give special heed to withdrawal by superior performers whose loss produces sizeable costs for the organization (see Jackofsky, 1984). Furthermore, their "non-work influences" construct persuaded other scholars to acknowledge that factors outside organizational boundaries may impel people to quit (Hom & Kinicki, 2001; Mitchell et al., 2001). Lastly, Steers and Mowday rejected Mobley's (1977) prevailing view that dissatisfied employees follow only one course to departure, holding that they actually pursue one of several possible routes. Some dissatisfied employees quit immediately; others undertake the search process described by Mobley (1977). Later portrayals of the translation of dissatisfaction into quitting increasingly included Steers and Mowday's perspective (see Hom & Griffeth, 1991; Hom et al., 1984; Sager et al., 1992), and, in other models, researchers sought to explain why employees simply quit without first seeking alternative jobs (Hulin et al., 1985; Lee & Mitchell, 1994).

Although Steers and Mowday's introduction of job performance and non-work influences extend prior formulations, their conceptualization still demands additional refinement. They proposed that job performance interacts with organizational characteristics and experiences and with job expectations and values, but they left unspecified the form of those interactions. Moreover, their definition of non-work influences is vague, although Lee and Mowday's (1987) operationalization considered perceptions by employees of how various external factors (such as unemployment, personal lifestyle, and time left for the family) influence job affect. This operationalization does not directly reflect attachments to outside pursuits (see Mobley et al., 1979; Price & Mueller, 1981, 1986) or work conflicts with outside interests (Hom & Kinicki, 2001; Mobley, 1982); both are more specific and promising constructs of extraneous influences. The determinant job expectation originated by Porter and Steers (1973) suffers the same conceptual shortcomings as the original. Indeed, new employees may most respond to unmet expectations by quitting than any other group of employees (Wanous, 1980).

Despite its process orientation, Steers and Mowday's theory imprecisely describes several structural connections among theoretical constructs. In the wake of modern views on varied reactions to dissatisfaction, their formulation explains only incompletely how job affect influences job performance or efforts to change the job, omitting essential behavioral antecedents such as perceived consequences to those responses (Rosse & Miller, 1984; Withey & Cooper, 1989). Nor did Steers and Mowday specify how outside influences moderate the effects of job attitudes on decisions to quit or how performance interacts with attributes of the firm and job expectations to determine job affect (Lee & Mowday, 1987). Besides this, this model did not specify the particular variables embodying its key distal causal determinants: job expectations and values, individual attributes, and organizational characteristics and experiences. Are they referring to work values (as Hulin & Blood, 1968) or a general structure of values (as Rokeach, 1973)? Steers and Mowday describe processes that *mediated* components of their model, but schematically they represent these processes as *moderators* in their illustration.

Several studies (including Arnold & Feldman, 1982; Hom & Griffeth, 1991; Hom et al., 1984; Sager et al., 1992) have sustained the prediction by Steers and Mowday that termination cognitions can directly stimulate resignations and predate search decisions. Only Lee and Mowday (1987) fully tested this model, surveying 445 employees of a financial institution. A regression equation comprising information about the job and organization, alternative job opportunities, and personal traits significantly predicted met expectations and job values. However, only available job and firm information explained extra variance in met expectations; alternative job opportunities and personal characteristics did not. Likewise, available information and individual attributes made independent contributions to the prediction of job values; work alternatives did not.

From regression analyses testing the hypothesized multiplicative effect of performance, met expectations, job values, company attributes, and work experiences, the researchers found that the complete model (comprising predictors and interaction terms) significantly predicted each job attitude. Yet these analyses did not estimate additional predictive contributions for the interaction terms, beyond that explained by the main effects (Cohen & Cohen, 1983), and did not describe how predictors interacted (though Steers and Mowday never specified their form). Similarly, a full regression equation containing job satisfaction, organizational commitment, job involvement, and nonwork influences—and their interaction terms—significantly predicted decisions to quit. Here again, this analysis did not determine whether interaction terms added any independent predictive variance and did not describe the nature of interactions, although the original theoretical statements are ambiguous in depicting those multiplicative effects. Last, a regression of turnover onto intentions to quit and work alternatives found that only intentions make a significant independent contribution to prediction, and that both predictors accounted for only 5% of the variance in turnover.

In summary, the one complete test of the Steers–Mowday model yielded mixed or incomplete support for its validity (Lee & Mowday, 1987). Regression analyses found that each model variable was significantly predicted by its theorized *set* of antecedents. Yet several determinants did not explain independent criterion variance (notably, influences outside work, alternatives, and efforts to change the job). Hypotheses about moderators received incomplete support because the regression analyses did not estimate the special contributions interaction terms make to prediction beyond that predicted by main effects nor described the exact form of their effects. Moreover, this empirical test neglected "omitted parameters" tests, determining whether pathways omitted from the Steers–Mowday model are truly nonexistent (James et al., 1982). That is, model tests must validate not only pathways explicitly posited by theorists, but also pathways they implied as absent (Motowidlo & Lawton, 1984). Further, intentions to quit and alternative jobs explained only 5% of the turnover variance. Additional research is thus warranted to validate the Steers–Mowday model—notably, refining operationalizations of non-work influences, efforts to change the job, and job alternatives—as their substantive validity can be enhanced when they are assessed with more psychometrically sound scales.

Sheridan and Abelson: Cusp Catastrophe Model

Deviating from conventional thinking, Sheridan and Abelson (1983) developed a cusp catastrophe model based on two determinants. In their model, organizational commitment and job tension define a two-dimensional control surface, with withdrawal behavior projected as a third, vertical axis (see Figure 4.5). The conceptualization has three characteristics. First, withdrawal behavior is a discontinuous variable with abrupt changes observed between different states of withdrawal. Presumably, employees try to maintain their current employment as long as possible. Once dissatisfaction accumulates (from declining commitment to the company or work stress), employees abruptly shift states from being determined to stay to being determined to leave. Second, the theory represents a hysteresis zone of behavior as a fold in the behavior surface. Projected as a bifurcation plane on the control surface, this fold reflects the state of transition from retention to termination. Third, divergent behaviors occur on opposite ends of the bifurcation plane. That is, "as an employee approaches the fold region, even small changes in the control variables can result in discontinuous changes from retention to termination" (Sheridan & Abelson, 1983, p. 422). Thus, two employees may have minimally different commitment and stress. Yet if they reside on opposite sides of the bifurcation plane, one may quit, while the other stays. Conversely, two

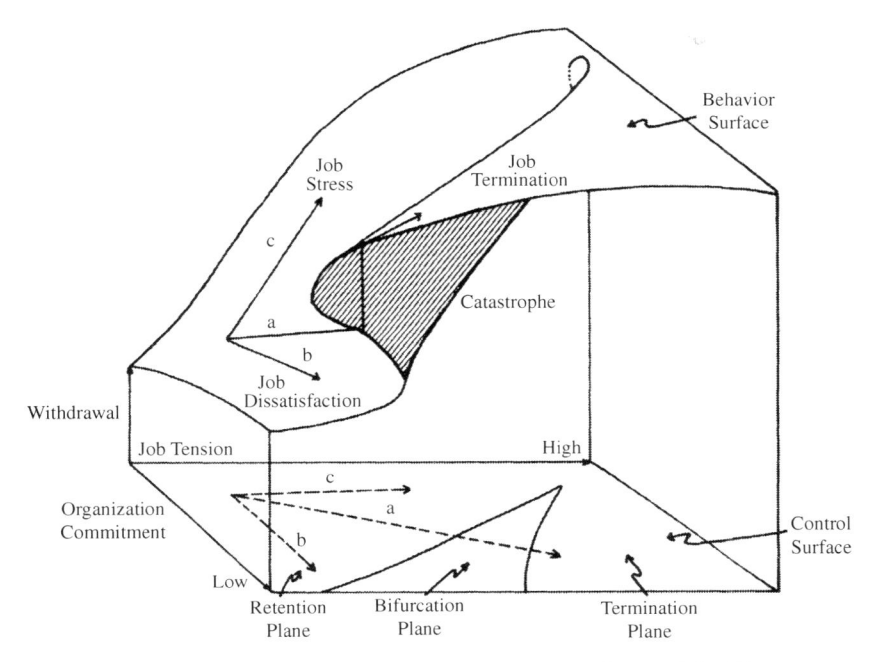

FIGURE 4.5 Sheridan and Abelson's (1983) Cusp Catastrophe Model of Turnover

employees expressing quite dissimilar commitment and stress may still exhibit the same withdrawal behavior if they fall on the same side of the bifurcation plane.

Review

To our knowledge, two studies have tested the cusp catastrophe model sampling nurses. In the first study, Sheridan and Abelson (1983) assessed job tension and organizational commitment to define the control surface. To test the existence of a bifurcation plane, they compared quit rates on both sides of the bifurcation plane to the total quit rate. The turnover rate in the bifurcation plane was 22% (compared to a 17% overall quit rate), 4% in the retention plane, and 41% in the termination plane. The total quit rate varied significantly from quit rates in the retention and termination planes, but not the bifurcation plane. Sheridan and Abelson also estimated this model's accuracy in classifying the nurses' employment status in the retention and termination planes. In line with the model, the bifurcation plane accurately differentiated most quitters from stayers in the retention plane, misclassifying merely 4% of the quitters as stayers. Still, the bifurcation plane misclassified 59% of the stayers as quitters in the termination plane.

Using a panel survey, Sheridan and Abelson further tracked temporal changes in job tension and commitment for stayers and leavers. In general, these tests upheld the cusp catastrophe model, showing that leavers were positioned closer to (or in) the bifurcation plane than were stayers. Over time, the leavers moved into the bifurcation or termination plane, while the stayers barely changed. Regression analyses disclosed that the cusp catastrophe model more correctly classified turnover status (84%) than did a linear model (49%), although hit rates did not significantly differ. In a study of new nurses, Sheridan (1985) replaced commitment to the company with group cohesion as a control surface variable, deeming it a more relevant "attractor" for newcomers than commitment is. From cusp catastrophe theory, he derived a topological equation describing the cusp catastrophe surface. This equation predicts withdrawal changes from Time-1 withdrawal actions (declining performance or absenteeism) to Time-2 turnover as a function of the following:

$$B_0 + B_1 W_1^3 + B_2 W_1^2 + B_3(T \times W_1) + B_4 C + B_5 T,$$

where W_1 = current Time-1 withdrawal behavior (either poor job performance or absenteeism), T = job tension, and C = group cohesion.

Using regression analysis, he estimated this equation, running separate analyses for different Time-1 withdrawal acts. The regression equation including poor performance as the Time-1 withdrawal act did *not* significantly predict terminations (R = .129). However, the equation specifying absenteeism as the Time-1 withdrawal behavior significantly predicted turnover (R = .207, $p < .05$). In this equation, quadratic and cubic components for past absences explained additional turnover variance, suggesting discontinuous transition as withdrawal becomes progressively more extreme. As he did in his 1983 study, Sheridan next examined observations of turnover on the control surface defined by cohesion and job tension. Using cusp catastrophe criteria, he identified boundaries for retention, termination, and bifurcation regions on the control surface and found that quit rates for these planes were 18%, 89%, and 33%, respectively. Regional location on the control surface accurately forecast turnover status, correctly classifying 86% of the participants in the study.

The cusp catastrophe model is a major breakthrough in thinking about turnover. Departing from prevailing linear assumptions, this model depicts quits as a discontinuous function of turnover determinants. As confirmed by two tests, the consideration of nonlinear effects of the antecedents of turnover may enhance predictions of terminations (Sheridan, 1985; Sheridan & Abelson, 1983). Counteracting modern theoretical developments, this model explains turnover with a parsimonious set of antecedents while retaining predictive power. All too often, in successive generations of theories, explanatory constructs proliferate and how parsimonious a model accounts for turnover is neglected (Hom & Griffeth, 1991, 1995). This model considers a broader pattern of withdrawal responses than have previous theories that focus narrowly on turnover. That is, in this theory, resignations are seen as one manifestation of job avoidance and turnover is considered to evolve from less extreme forms, such as absenteeism and poor performance. This model may also explain transitions among the less extreme forms of withdrawal (see Sheridan, 1985).

All the same, the cusp catastrophe model merits more empirical and theoretical work. For example, its two determinants (job tension and commitment/cohesion) insufficiently capture the sundry reasons why employees quit, because the vast literature on motives for turnover (Mobley, 1982; Mobley et al., 1979) has been overlooked. Moreover, Sheridan and Abelson suggested that differences among individuals be taken into account in the model but provided little theoretical guidance. Future tests should include the Time-1 linear term of withdrawal in addition to its quadratic and cubic terms in the *same* regression equation. Though quadratic and cubic terms are posited by cusp catastrophe theory, true nonlinear effects are revealed after statistically controlling the linear effects (Cohen & Cohen, 1983). Indeed, Sheridan's (1985) estimated linear interaction models, comprising the Time-1 linear term of withdrawal and job tension and group cohesion (and their interaction), consistently uncovered linear effects for Time-1 withdrawal behaviors on quits.

This preliminary work possibly overestimated the accuracy of classification in the cusp catastrophe model. The researchers identified the boundaries of the bifurcation plane by inspecting the distribution observations on turnover in the two-dimensional control space and used the various combinations of threshold scores on the control variables to predict whether or not employees quit. Such *empirical* identification of cutoff scores must be cross-validated on another sample because threshold scores uncovered empirically improve the accuracy of prediction by capitalizing on chance (Wiggins, 1973).

Despite these shortcomings, the cusp catastrophe model is a provocative divergence from traditional linear thinking. More research is needed to test the theory in general and with samples of employees who are not nurses. Though many scholars (Mobley et al., 1979; Steers & Mowday, 1981) have suggested that turnover is a dynamic process, the cusp catastrophe theory formally models this process and thus becomes a significant theoretical milestone advancing understanding of the turnover process.

Hulin, Roznowski, and Hachiya: Model of Labor Market Effects

Reviewing empirical tests on job alternatives, Hulin et al. (1985) concluded that perceptual estimates of labor market prospects have predicted turnover poorly, whereas aggregate labor market statistics, such as unemployment rates, predicted turnover consistently (and strongly). To account for such discrepant findings, they proposed that work alternatives can directly affect job satisfaction, a reversal of the contention that it is satisfaction that influences alternatives (see Mobley, 1977). They also hold that job opportunities may directly induce turnover because employees quit when they are assured of an actual job, not because they surmise from local unemployment data that there is a *probability* of a job. The reconceptualization envisioned a different role in the turnover process for job opportunities (see March & Simon, 1958; Mobley, 1977). They hypothesized that there were three mechanisms to explain why perceived alternatives minimally affect individual turnover. In the following sections, we review those mechanisms, which are portrayed in Figure 4.6.

Different Economies Produce Different Workforces

Hulin et al. (1985) argued that economic expansion attracts casual or marginal workers into the labor force. They do not normally work regularly, but prosperous times lure them into full-time employment because the job surplus drives up wages. Nevertheless, marginal employees do not plan to stay employed for very long. After accumulating enough funds, they will quit to pursue more pleasurable or less stressful avocations. Given their weak orientation toward work, these workers are unlikely when quitting to engage in the complex cognitive processes theorized by turnover scholars (such as Mobley, 1977).

Job Opportunities Directly Influence Job Satisfaction

Drawing from several models (March & Simon, 1958; Salancik & Pfeffer, 1978; Smith, Kendall, & Hulin, 1969; Thibaut & Kelley, 1959), the researchers maintained that economic activities, such as employment levels, directly influence job satisfaction. High unemployment in decreasing adaptation and comparison levels for alternatives bolsters job satisfaction. Low unemployment and plentiful alternatives

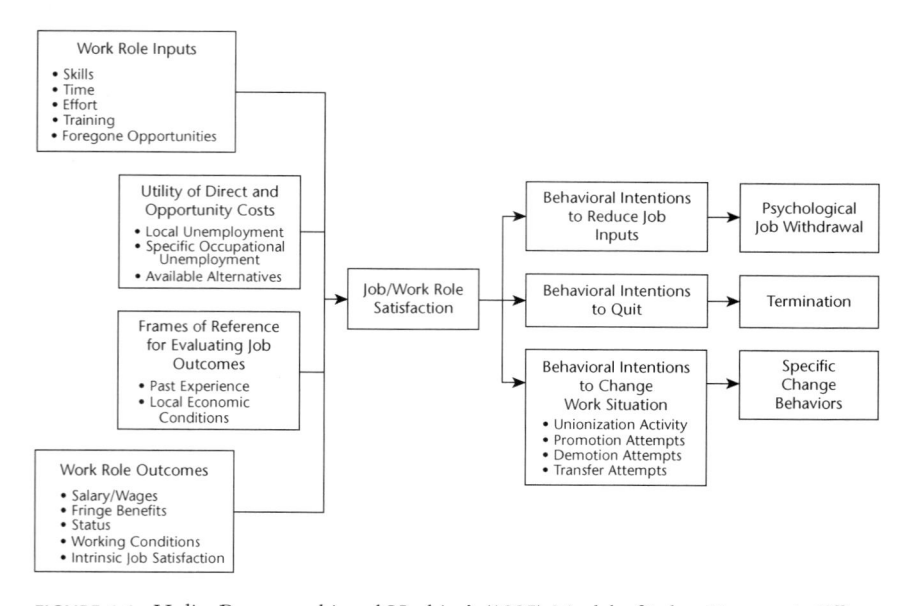

FIGURE 4.6 Hulin, Rosznowski, and Hachiya's (1985) Model of Labor Economic Effects

promote dissatisfaction and intentions to quit. More precisely, Hulin et al. (1985) conceptualized that foregone alternatives are "opportunity costs" employees incur to maintain membership in their present organization. During good economic times when jobs are abundant, the utilities of foregone alternatives increase, thereby reducing satisfaction with the present job. During economic stagnation, the expected utility of alternatives declines and satisfaction with the present job increases.

Job Opportunities Directly Affect Turnover

Extrapolating from Michaels and Spector's (1982) work, Hulin et al. (1985) further contended that job opportunities affect turnover directly and not necessarily through intentions to quit. Presumably, most employees do not quit merely on the chance of finding an alternative (i.e., because they perceive that alternatives are available), but when they actually secure job offers. Thus, they reasoned, alternative work and dissatisfaction about the job interact in affecting quitting. The more jobs there are available, the more likely it is that dissatisfied employees can find and obtain other jobs and thus can leave their unsatisfactory positions. Job dissatisfaction and job offers must both exist for withdrawal to occur. In passing, the researchers also observed that present-day models of turnover implicitly assume that dissatisfied employees only consider alternative work, failing to recognize that many leavers pursue alternatives other than work, which may also explain why perceptions of alternative work do not readily translate into departures.

Combining these explanations, Hulin et al. (1985) designed a model that clarifies the influence of labor market factors on decisions to quit. Their specification that the availability of alternatives directly influences satisfaction in two ways is consistent with an economic utility theory (e.g., March & Simon, 1958). Economic conditions affect the value of an employee's contribution of skills, time, and effort to the firm. Low unemployment increases the value of an individual's contributions and the utility of foregone opportunities, making continued membership in a company costly. As a result, job satisfaction declines unless the benefits of membership are equivalently increased. At the same time, the good economic conditions bolster an employee's frame of reference for evaluating the quality of the job. Therefore, the employee devalues the current job and becomes more dissatisfied. Unemployment, by comparison, decreases the utilities of direct and opportunity costs *and* lowers the frame of reference for judging the job, thereby boosting job satisfaction.

For many people, job dissatisfaction translates directly into decisions to quit. Once dissatisfied, some employees simply form intentions to quit without considering alternatives; others secure alternative offers before quitting. For the latter, the attractiveness of *certain* job offers, rather than the mere probability of a job estimated from local unemployment data, dominates their decision to quit. Still other workers in intolerable jobs may simply decide to quit, assuming that anything would be better than what they are currently doing.

Some dissatisfied employees never make the decision to quit because of various lures or obstacles (perhaps inertia, low self-esteem, "golden handcuffs," or the perceptions that advancement is eminent). Such trapped employees may reduce their dissatisfaction by enacting other withdrawal behaviors, thereby decreasing their job inputs. Given the same level of job outcomes, their satisfaction should grow with declining inputs. Moreover, they may successively enact different withdrawal behaviors over time until they can successfully lower their dissatisfaction. Some employees who cope with dissatisfaction by performing other withdrawal acts may be implicitly forming decisions to quit in that their excessive withdrawal behaviors may lead to their dismissal.

Marginal drifters—drawn into regular work by job surpluses—also quit because they are dissatisfied. Yet these individuals would be dissatisfied with any full-time, regular job. They quit, not to take a better job, but because they became bored with their present job and assume that any new position will be superior—at least in the short run. Casual workers translate dissatisfaction into decisions to quit because of a general dislike of regular, full-time work.

Review

Hulin et al. (1985), offering a perceptive re-examination of the role of work alternatives in the withdrawal process, resolved a longstanding controversy in the study of turnover. They provided an invaluable taxonomy of the different types of quitters, including marginal drifters and leavers seeking alternatives other than work. These leavers follow a different route to departure from the conventional pathway of job dissatisfaction → job search → quit decisions → quit (Mobley, 1977). Their theory explains why job dissatisfaction does not invariably lead to quitting: employees may respond to dissatisfaction not by quitting, but by reducing their job inputs or by changing the current job by way of transfers or unionization. For them, presumably, psychological withdrawal or a change of job would substitute for departure. The formulation reconceptualizes turnover as one among many behavioral reactions to dissatisfaction, thereby going beyond the traditional preoccupation with surface behaviors (Hulin, 1991).

Although explaining the different effects of unemployment rates and perceived alternatives on turnover, Hulin and his fellow researchers provided no direct evidence. While we did not uncover direct empirical tests of their formulation in its entirety, their propositions nevertheless influenced subsequent theorizing (Hom & Kinicki, 2001; Hom et al., 2012; Lee & Mitchell, 1994). In particular, theoretical perspectives that followed incorporated Hulin et al.'s notions about impulsive quits (depicted as another turnover path; Maertz & Campion, 2004), job to non-job turnover (Lee & Mitchell, 1994), psychological withdrawal (occurring when dissatisfied employees cannot leave; Hom et al., 2012), other behavioral reactions to dissatisfaction besides leaving (e.g., job avoidance; Hom & Kinicki,

2001), and direct job opportunity effects on turnover (unfolding model path 3; Lee & Mitchell, 1994; as Hulin et al. (1985, p. 244) claim that employees "quit on the basis of certainties represented by alternative jobs already offered"). Moreover, several scholars (Farrell, 1983; Rosse & Hulin, 1985; Withey & Cooper, 1989) developed and validated scales to assess behavioral responses to dissatisfaction. Hulin and his colleagues later differentiated work withdrawal (avoiding specific tasks associated with work role, such as taking long work breaks or doing poor-quality work) from job withdrawal (partial or full withdrawal from a job in a specific organization, such as quit intentions) and how the former may substitute for the latter (Fitzgerald, Drasgow, Hulin, Gelfand, & Magley, 1997; Glomb, Munson, Hulin, Bergman, & Drasgow, 1999; Hanisch & Hulin, 1990).

Though not striving for a comprehensive model, Hulin et al. (1985) nonetheless excluded many fundamental explanatory constructs, such as organizational commitment, outside influences, and job search, that have been widely affirmed as turnover underpinnings (Blau, 1993; Hom & Griffeth, 1991; Lee & Mowday, 1987; Price & Mueller, 1986). Moreover, Griffeth et al. (2005), in developing a multidimensional measure of perceived alternatives, did find that perceptions of alternatives directly predicted employee turnover, contrary to Hulin et al.'s assertion that employees only quit when they have secured another job. Hom et al. (1984) also speculated that employees may quit without conducting a search when they perceive a favorable job market. (Anecdotally, when two of the authors of this book interviewed nurses for a turnover study, they learned that several exiting nurses had received a check for accumulated vacation/sick leave days and went on vacation, knowing that they could easily find another job afterwards. They thus had not obtained job offers before exiting for they believed that they could readily find nursing work upon re-entering the labor market.)

Lee and Mitchell: Unfolding Model

Lee and Mitchell (1994) generalized Beach's (1990) image theory to advance understanding of termination decisions. Image theory disputes prevailing turnover theories that assume an economic rational basis for turnover decision-making (Hulin et al., 1985; Mobley et al., 1979). Rather, this theory presumes that people make decisions by comparing the fit of the options in the decision to various internal images rather than by maximizing subjective expected utility. Image theory posits that people filter the constant bombardment of information to select suitable options. This screening is rapid, requires little cognitive effort, and compares the characteristics of options to one of three internal images: value (set of general values and standards that define the self); trajectory (set of goals that energizes and directs individual behavior); or strategic (set of behavioral tactics and strategies for attaining personal goals). This test of compatibility is non-compensatory and requires that the options fit one or more images. If a behavioral option meets the test, the individual compares the alternative to the status quo. Usually, the individual continues with the status quo; sometimes she or he chooses to behave differently. If numerous options survive the screening, a person runs a "profitability" test, choosing the best alternative according to a cost–benefit analysis.

Decision as a Response to Shock

Extending image theory, Lee and Mitchell (1994) further proposed that the entire process of screening and decision-making begins with a "shock to the system," a specific event that jars the employee to make deliberate judgments about his or her job and perhaps to consider quitting the job. Lee and Mitchell theorized that the social and cognitive context that surrounds the experienced shock provides a "decision frame"—or frame of reference—with which to interpret the shock along dimensions such as novelty, favorability, or threat. Then, according to their theory, employees will take one of four ways, "decision paths," to leave their jobs. Figures 4.7 and 4.8 depict those turnover paths.

Decision Path 1

In the first path, a shock jars an employee to construct a decision frame for interpreting the shock and prompts the employee to search his or her memory for decisions, rules, or learned responses to similar shocks. For example, a shock might be IBM's acquisition of one's smaller company; a rule might be "I will never fit the IBM mold." This probe of memory also brings forth recollections of whether one's previous staying or quitting was appropriate. If the decision frame of the current experience is identical to prior frames and quitting was the appropriate response, then a match occurs. Quitting is thus automatically enacted with little mental deliberation ("I have previously quit large corporations"). If a match does not occur, another decision path is initiated. In summary, decision path 1 is basically a script-driven response (involving a match with past decisions) to an experienced shock.

Decision Path 2

In the second decision path, the employee experiencing a system shock cannot recall an identical shock that has an appropriate response associated with it or a rule of action. Therefore, no match occurs. Rather, the employee considers the situation and frames the shock as a choice, without specific job alternatives in mind, between staying with or quitting the present firm. Next, the employee relies on the value, trajectory, or strategic images to reassess his or her basic commitment to the company. If the shock violates these images, the employee changes the image or leaves. If the shock fits, the employee stays. To illustrate, a woman may unexpectedly

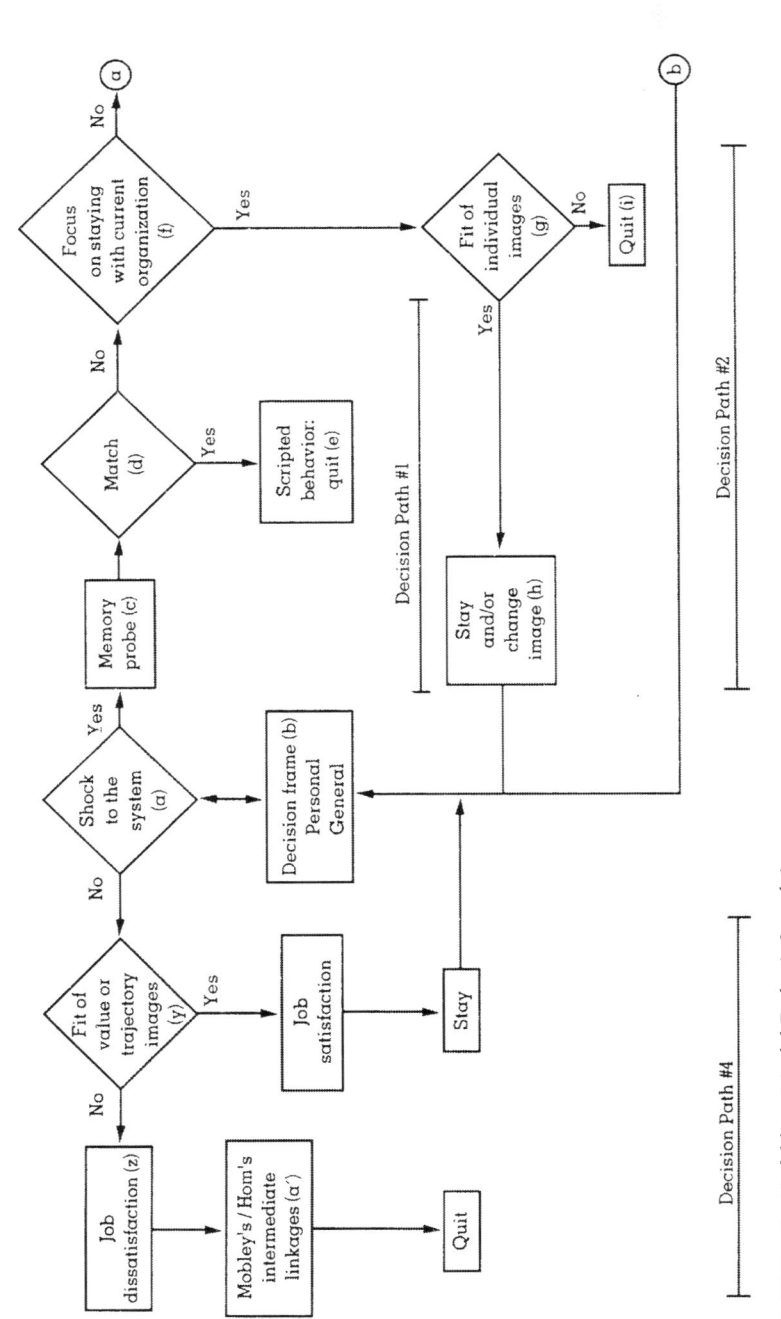

FIGURE 4.7 Unfolding Model Paths 1, 2, and 4

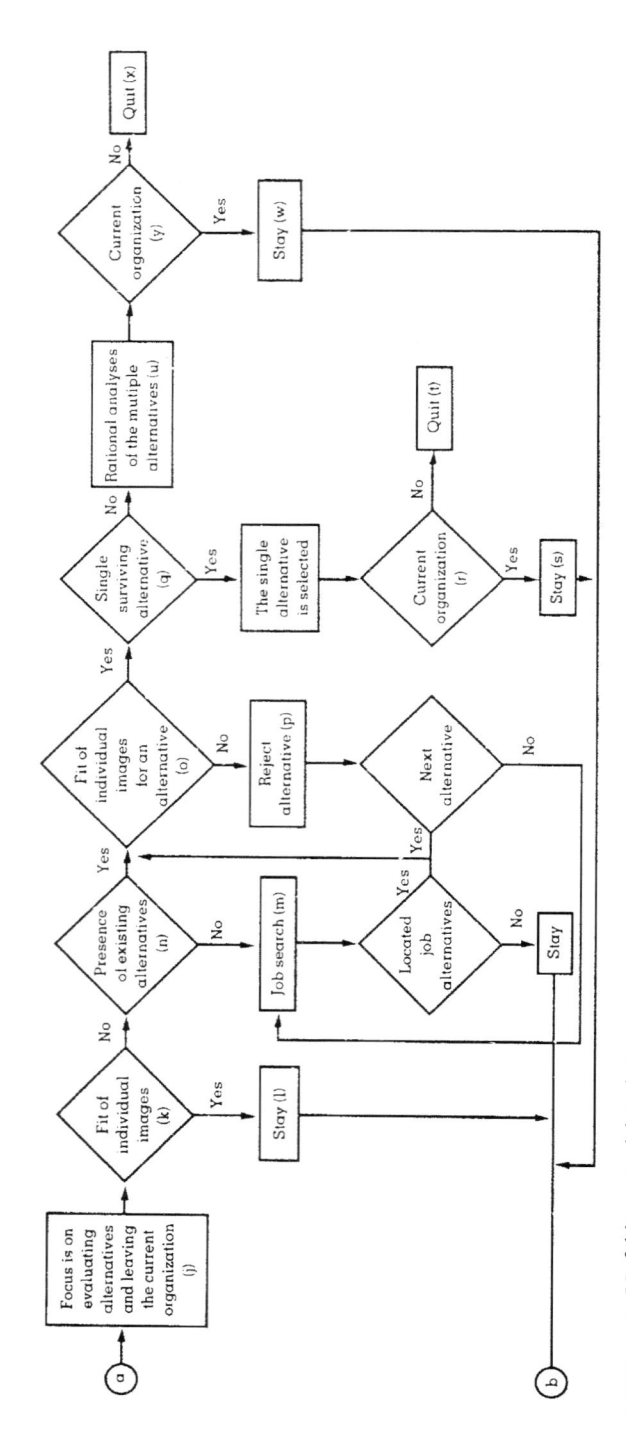

FIGURE 4.8 Unfolding Model Path 3

become pregnant and must decide whether working fits with her images of being a competent mother (value), having a career (trajectory), or continuing in her sales job (strategy). If the shock violates any image, she will resign her job.

Decision Path 3

Here, a shock elicits a memory probe, but a match between the shock currently being experienced and the recall of a similar shock or an easily accessible rule does not occur. The employee frames the shock as a choice between staying with the company or quitting for one or more specific job alternatives. The shock is next judged for image compatibility. The employee stays if the shock fits but considers and seeks alternatives if it does not. Should the shock violate images, he or she then compares other alternatives to value, trajectory, or strategic images and deletes those failing the compatibility test. If only one alternative fits, the employee contrasts this alternative to the benefits of remaining employed. The employee stays if the current job provides more benefits but leaves if the alternative is superior. If numerous alternatives survive the compatibility test, the employee conducts a profitability test, comparing their subjective expected utilities against that of the present job. If the current job surpasses all alternatives, the employee remains; if an alternative is superior, the employee quits.

Decision Path 4

According to the fourth path, some employees will occasionally reassess their commitment to the company. Their reassessment does not emanate from shock, but occurs more routinely or casually. Over time, the employee or company may change and the job may no longer fit the employee's value or trajectory images. The resulting dissatisfaction triggers the withdrawal process described by Mobley (1977) or Hom and Griffeth (1991), wherein employees evaluate their prospects of alternative employment, seek other jobs, compare them to the present job, and form decisions about quitting. This fourth path thus complies with traditional depictions of the translation of dissatisfaction into quitting. In a 1999 follow-up study, Lee, Mitchell, Holtom, McDaniel, and Hill (1999) modified the unfolding model by adding non-work alternatives and separating search behavior and evaluation of alternatives. Using this revised classification procedure, they improved their classification of quitters (Hom, 2011).

Review

Deviating from conventional wisdom, Lee and Mitchell's (1994) theory contributes many invaluable theoretical insights and provides a refreshing new perspective to what is, no doubt, a very complex process: the decision to stay or leave one's job. Their generalization of image theory may depict the procedure of decisions to quit more accurately and comprehensively than does rational expectancy theory, which may best apply to decision paths 3 and 4 where prospective leavers are comparing jobs. Lee and Mitchell introduced the notion of scripted (routinized, non-analytical) turnover behavior, which may underlie impulsive quitting (Maertz & Campion, 2004; Mobley, 1977) and departures by members of the secondary labor market (Hulin et al., 1985). Their notion of system shocks—external, unexpected, or random events—accords greater theoretical attention to the origin of the turnover process, an aspect that prevailing formulations have long neglected (see Baysinger & Mobley, 1983). Lastly, this theory specifies various sequences of withdrawal, broadening the generalizability of the model to more segments of the labor force (Hom & Griffeth, 1991; Hulin et al., 1985).

Pioneering qualitative methodology, Lee and his colleagues (Lee, Mitchell, Wise, & Fireman, 1996; Lee et al., 1999) interviewed exiting employees, collecting retrospective self-reports about their reasons and manner for leaving. Proliferating qualitative tests are substantiating this theoretical framework, finding that the *majority* of former employees follow one of the four turnover routes (Donnelly & Quinn, 2006; Holtom, Mitchell, Lee, & Eberly, 2008; Lee, Hom, Eberly, Li, J., & Mitchell, 2017; Lee et al., 1996, 1999; Maertz & Campion, 2004). Summarizing results from 1,200 leavers in various fields (i.e., nurses, accountants, bank personnel, prison guards, GMAT takers), Holtom, Mitchell, Lee, and Inderrieden (2005) further estimated that shocks (60% citing a precipitating event) initiate quits more than do job dissatisfaction, and that more leavers take shock-driven paths to withdrawal. Assessing cross-cultural validity, international researchers have further validated this model with British nurses (Morrell, Loan-Clarke, Arnold, & Wilkinson, 2008), finding that 44.3% of nurses attribute their decisions to resign to shocks (Morrell, Loan-Clarke, & Wilkinson, 2004).

While encouraging, empirical verifications of the unfolding model thus far are predominantly based on *leavers' recollections* about how shocks drove them to quit (Lee et al., 1996, 1999; Maertz & Campion, 2004). Asking only leavers why they quit *reverses* the causal order of the shock as one leading to turnover. Exit interviews thus rely on leavers' retrospective explanations for why they performed this past behavior. In a traditional turnover study, the presumed causal factor (e.g., pay inequity) is measured some time *before* (e.g., 6 or 12 months; Allen et al., 2014) turnover occurrence so that the presumed cause *precedes* the effect in time (a criterion for causal evidence; Shadish, Cook, & Campbell, 2002). Then, if pay inequity "predicts" subsequent turnover, turnover researchers can infer that pay inequity possibly caused turnover. Moreover, this qualitative approach interviews only leavers, excluding stayers—thus, "sampling on the dependent variable" (Berk, 1983; Winship & Mare, 1992). Yet comparing leavers' and stayers' experiences would enhance estimates of the impact of turnover causes. For example, stayers may have experienced the same shock (e.g., unfair pay raise) as did leavers but decided *not* to leave. Given retrospective biases and demand effects, self-reported explanations about past withdrawal decisions may overstate support for the unfolding model and shocks' causal influence (for a description of biases associated with exit interviews, see Griffeth & Hom, 2001).

Further, the confluences of circumstances that lead individuals to quit are likely to vary in practically every case. (Anecdotally, one of the authors of this book voluntarily quit multiple times for different reasons, e.g., pay, promotion, organizational culture, superior alternative, family reasons, and only once quit because of a shock—a hurricane threatened job security. Every other departure was a result of an accumulation of experiences and resulting dissatisfaction.) Although Lee and Mitchell (1994) emphasize four prime turnover paths, such parsimony may overlook idiosyncratic paths to turnover for different individuals or mask distinctive paths within the four major turnover paths. To illustrate, the unfolding model classifies an employee leaving to care for a terminally ill parent and another leaving to attend law school as turnover path 1 induced by matching scripts. Yet the shocks differ in disruptiveness, positivity, and perceived control (Morgeson, Mitchell, & Liu, 2015), which may result in dissimilar manners of leaving.

In contrast to retrospective qualitative evidence, Kammeyer-Mueller, Wanberg, Glomb, and Ahlburg (2005) used a predictive research design, assessing personal or work events *before*—rather than after—the date of exit. Their "discontinuation event" scale, in which respondents judge how much recent significant events induced them to discontinue working, predicted turnover beyond that accounted by job satisfaction and joblessness statistics. All the same, survival analyses did not clearly establish that shocks predict quits more accurately than do job attitudes (Kammeyer-Mueller et al., 2005, p. 652, Table 3) as only 26.5% of leavers encountered discontinuation events before exiting. Their findings imply that qualitative retrospective research may have inflated shocks' impact on actual quits.

Turnover Events and Shocks Scale (TESS)

Griffeth, Hom, Allen, Morse, and Weinhardt (2008) extend Kammeyer-Mueller et al.'s (2005) work to develop a comprehensive psychometrically valid measure of shocks, the "prime mover" for most turnover paths in the unfolding model, using critical incidents methodology (Bhagat, McQuaid, Lindholm & Segovis, 1985). Their approach also extends the conceptualization of how events drive turnover decisions by drawing from research on how to predict other phenomena that are relatively infrequent, intertwined with many facets of an individual's life, and where unique profiles of antecedents can lead to the same probability level of an event occurring (e.g., stressors and major stress-related outcomes). Though the Kammeyer-Mueller et al. (2005) test is promising, study participants only described "significant" recent events, omitting minor stressors whose frequency or volume may incite more stressful reactions. After all, life stress research reveals that the accumulation of small, everyday life events elevates psychological distress—sometimes more so than major life events (Tein, Sandler, & Zautra, 2000; Wagner, Compas, & Howell, 1988). The cumulative effects of such events may precipitously instigate individual turnover propensity. For example, research using the stressful life events scale (SRE; Holmes & Rahe, 1967) suggests that at some point, the accumulation of antecedent events dramatically increases the risk of major illness.

In an ambitious attempt to alleviate the problems of shock measurements noted above using three different samples, Griffeth et al. (2008) focused squarely on events that induce people to think about quitting—a defining attribute of shocks—rather than significant (Kammeyer-Mueller et al., 2005) or stressful (Bhagat et al., 1985; Tein et al., 2000) events. The objective for creating this measure was to produce a list of shocks that could be used predictively and in most organizations, thus providing a diagnostic tool that meets at least two of the three conditions for inferring causality: (1) the cause must precede the effect; and (2) the cause must be related to the effect. A third criterion, which is the absence of an alternative explanation for the causal effect (Shadish et al., 2002), is more difficult to show in applied organizational research. All the same, we address such competing explanations by taking into account other prime turnover antecedents to establish the *incremental* predictive validity for shocks.

Lee and Mitchell (1994) noted that not all events are shocks, and argued that a shock is an event that "*jars* employees toward deliberate judgments about their jobs and ... to voluntarily quit their job" (p. 60, emphasis in original). Griffeth et al. (2008) thus began by developing a list of common workplace events that have theoretical and practical grounds to be considered turnover-related shocks. The Kammeyer-Mueller et al. (2005) study generated a few salient and idiosyncratic events, which could yield a less reliable predictor instrument, as well as less useful data that are difficult to summarize and quantify for evidence-based remedies. Indeed, Holtom et al. (2005) prescribe surveys of current employees to help managers anticipate when employee expectations might be violated.

Two of the three studies presented in Griffeth et al. (2008) were published in Purl, Hall, and Griffeth (2016). The third study we present here in Table 4.1. This was a sample of approximately 300 social workers working in a large southeastern metropolitan city. The turnover criterion was measured about one year after the predictors were collected from the social workers on organizational time. Following Purl et al. (2016), the 55 items of the TESS, measured as a part of a larger survey, were conceptually organized into three major categories: (1) personal; (2) work-related, which were further categorized into mistrust, conflict, opportunity lost, and missing rewards; and (3) opportunity.

Table 4.1 presents the abbreviated shocks or events with the original numbering of the item in the survey, the correlation between the item and an intention to quit measure (alpha = .92), means and standard deviations of the items for stayers and quitters, an independent t-test value, and the t-tests' probability level. The results of these analyses show that only the item "desire for a career change" were the means significantly different ($p < .01$) between stayers ($m = 1.87$) and quitters ($m = 2.69$). This shock suggests a type of disillusionment with one's career choice that the organization may be unable to change, unlike other shocks, such as the item directly below it in Table 4.1: inadequate training. If this item had significantly differentiated between stayers and quitters, managers could create focus groups among social workers to explore what kind(s) of training may be needed, and then develop or identify training programs for the workers that could improve their performance. As it is, desire for a career change suggests that education and/or training of these social workers may not provide enough realistic content to enable people to self-select out of the education/training *before* committing to a career in the field. Thus, eventually their disillusionment with the field grows, and they desire a career change.

An interesting side benefit found in Table 4.1 underscores the importance of using *actual* turnover as the criterion rather than intention to quit. From this table, a count of the events that are significantly related to intention to quit resulted in 44 items ($p < .05$). Thus, by definition, these 44 items could be considered a shock because they stimulated employees to think about quitting (e.g., Lee & Mitchell, 1994). If a researcher stopped at this point and presented the results to the management, the researcher would have to advocate widespread changes to the organization and management. Thus, the researcher would be suggesting work-related changes such as encouraging supervisors to be less critical, make sure managers are making better decisions, improving the workers' autonomy on the job, etc. Other personal events that were significantly related to intention to quit are more difficult for managers to address, such as allowing social workers to work from home or shortening work commutes.

Similar findings were reported by Purl et al. (2016) in their two samples. First, the cross-sectional results for department store personnel found that 38 out of the 55 TESS items were significantly related to intention to quit. But when the results were examined predictively, only 12 of the items significantly differentiated between actual quitters and stayers. For example, one item that was significantly different between the two groups was the item "uncomfortable work environment." While an important finding, it is too general to be of much use. One would have to wonder *what specifically* about the work environment was making some employees uncomfortable enough to quit. We would suggest, as we did above, that management would want to conduct a series of focus groups among employees to attempt to clarify this finding.

TABLE 4.1 TESS Item Correlations with Intentions to Quit (BIQ) and Means, Standard Deviations, Independent T-Test Values, and Probability Levels for Staying and Quitting Social Workers

Item #[1]	Item Description[2]	Correlation with BIQ	Stayers Mean (SD)	Quitters Mean (SD)	T-Test Statistic	p
Personal						
13	Little interaction with people	.16	.37 (.83)	.35 (.89)	.13	ns
14	Health concerns	−.04	.97 (1.38)	1.04 (1.43)	−.24	ns
15	Undesirable transfer	.07	.11 (.51)	.04 (.20)	.71	ns
19	Opportunity to work from home	.23**	1.12 (1.52)	1.38 (1.53)	−.85	ns
34	Makes a difference	.19**	2.03 (1.33)	2.42 (1.10)	−1.44	ns
39	Desire for shortened commute	.21**	.64 (1.29)	1.00 (1.47)	−1.31	ns
49	Demands against personal ethics	.20**	.49 (.91)	.62 (1.17)	−.65	ns
54	Unfriendly co-workers	.46**	2.49 (1.50)	2.58 (1.63)	.28	ns
Work-related Mistrust						
1	Critical supervisor	.14**	1.19 (1.32)	1.46 (1.58)	−.98	ns
2	Bad decisions by management	.30**	1.96 (1.43)	2.08 (1.32)	−.38	ns
3	Low autonomy	.25**	1.12 (1.26)	1.27 (1.22)	−.58	ns
4	Uncomfortable work environment	.37**	1.51 (1.39)	1.88 (1.63)	−1.27	ns
5	Unsafe environment	.16**	1.09 (1.20)	1.15 (1.32)	−.27	ns
6	Low confidence in management	.32**	1.75 (1.46)	2.12 (1.45)	−1.21	ns
9	Sexual harassment	.032	.08 (.415)	.12 (.431)	−.456	ns
12	Promises not kept	.30**	.95 (1.24)	.96 (1.18)	−.047	ns
17	Petty rules and policies	.26**	1.36 (1.35)	1.73 (1.60)	−1.27	ns
22	Felt undervalued	.34**	1.38 (1.44)	1.54 (1.56)	−.52	ns
24	Difficult coworkers	.25**	1.54 (1.38)	1.92 (1.57)	−1.30	ns
25	Poor communication	.33**	1.86 (1.45)	1.96 (1.59)	−.32	ns
27	Little feedback from supervisor	.091	.91 (1.21)	1.16 (1.11)	−.989	ns

(Continued)

TABLE 4.1 (Cont.)

Item #[1]	Item Description[2]	Correlation with BIQ	Stayers Mean (SD)	Quitters Mean (SD)	T-Test Statistic	p
28	Unrealistic organization goals	.33**	1.66 (1.49)	1.96 (1.54)	−.98	ns
33	Weak management support	.35**	1.57 (1.49)	1.69 (1.54)	−.41	ns
35	Arbitrary change in rules	.22**	1.61 (1.42)	2.08 (1.38)	−1.57	ns
37	Unfair management practices	.18**	.91 (1.33)	.96 (1.46)	−.19	ns
48	Negative organizational culture	.28**	1.38 (1.45)	1.69 (1.49)	−1.04	ns
51	Major reorganization	.20**	1.12 (1.49)	1.04 (1.34)	.27	ns
53	Lack of recognition	.27**	1.60 (1.47)	1.92 (1.57)	−1.06	ns
55	Low organizational morale	.33**	2.49 (1.50)	2.58 (1.63)	−.26	ns
Conflict						
10	Loss of respect by work team	.12*	.70 (1.17)	1.04 (1.51)	−1.34	ns
16	Poor appraisal	.05	.26 (.76)	.19 (.63)	.41	ns
40	Feared demotion	−.03	.32 (.85)	.19 (.49)	.75	ns
42	Abuse of authority	.26**	1.04 (1.37)	1.12 (1.56)	−.26	ns
45	Public criticism	.09	.40 (.89)	.50 (1.11)	−.54	ns
47	Conflict with supervisor	.24**	.74 (1.12)	1.00 (1.47)	−1.06	ns
Opportunity lost						
18	Job monotony	.31**	1.28 (1.43)	1.50 (1.48)	−.73	ns
32	No growth opportunity	.35**	1.97 (1.53)	2.15 (1.74)	−.57	ns
41	Passed over for promotion	.17**	.94 (1.37)	1.00 (1.39)	−.21	ns
43	Lack of challenge	.42**	.88 (1.18)	1.15 (1.19)	−1.01	ns
44	Little involvement in decisions	.30**	1.61 (1.50)	1.54 (1.48)	.23	ns
46	Little advancement opportunities	.34**	2.02 (1.67)	2.27 (1.78)	−.72	ns
Missing rewards						
20	Workload increase without benefit increase	.27**	2.17 (1.62)	2.19 (1.60)	−.08	ns
23	Inflexible work schedule	.20**	.89 (1.33)	.65 (1.29)	.87	ns

(Continued)

TABLE 4.1 (Cont.)

Item #[1]	Item Description[2]	Correlation with BIQ	Stayers Mean (SD)	Quitters Mean (SD)	T-Test Statistic	p
26	Unstable finances of the company	.19**	.94 (1.26)	.96 (1.46)	-.08	ns
29	Work or time pressures	.30**	2.38 (1.54)	2.19 (1.60)	.58	ns
30	Frequent policy changes	.26**	2.45 (1.48)	3.00 (1.17)	-1.83	ns
36	Shift or work schedule change	.12*	.58 (1.12)	.62 (.98)	-.16	ns
38	Inadequate benefits	.069	.58 (1.12)	.44 (1.0)	.61	ns
50	Inadequate pay	.21**	.82 (1.42)	.54 (1.24)	.95	ns
Opportunity						
7	Opportunity to go into own business	.14*	.36 (.92)	.42 (1.03)	-.35	ns
8	Uncertain future	.19**	.81 (1.14)	1.00 (1.30)	-.79	ns
11	Job alternative opportunity	.09	.73 (1.51)	.84 (1.25)	-.44	ns
21	Better external opportunity	.16**	.58 (.97)	.77 (1.11)	-.93	ns
31	Desire for career change	.62**	1.87 (1.55)	2.69 (1.52)	-2.54	.01
52	Inadequate training	.21**	.96 (1.32)	1.27 (1.51)	-1.11	ns

Note: ** $p < .01$ and * $p < .05$ denotes significance at the corresponding level (two-tailed) for Pearson correlations.
[1] Original item number.
[2] Items have been abbreviated from the original wording. We thank Makenna Tipple for her assistance in compiling this table.

In Purl et al.'s (2016) second sample of nurses, the results were very similar, but even more problematical: *all* 55 items in the cross-sectional analyses were related to intention to quit! Thus, to quote Purl et al. (2016):

> HR managers who relied only on the relationships between turnover events and turnover intentions to help improve the work situation, would be faced with myriad of issues and conclude that "We have to change everything." Clearly this would be a frustrating and daunting series of tasks that would result in huge costs in financial and HR resources. On the other hand, a more prudent HR manager would say, "Let's wait and collect actual turnover data BEFORE we undertake these sweeping changes."
>
> *(p. 236)*

And this manager would be correct as only 13 shocks actually differentiated significantly between stayers and leavers. Thus, by collecting turnover data one year later, this hospital would have a much more reasonable list of shocks to deal with and be able to prioritize the most important ones.

In conclusion, research (Griffeth et al., 2008; Purl et al., 2016) showed that when the TESS is used predictively: (1) shocks may be used to distinguish between stayers and quitters; and (2) a useful starting point for diagnosing organizational problems related to turnover.

Emerging Theories of Collective Turnover

Thus far, we have been discussing individual-level turnover theories. However, there is a long history of research on discovering group, work unit, or organizational causes and consequences of turnover (Heavey, Holwerda, & Hausknecht, 2013). This work looks for systems or the absences of systems that may be related to turnover, and as such represents content theories of collective turnover. Recently, there were several major reviews and meta-analyses of this literature that examine in detail the relationships between human resource management systems and collective turnover, as well as relationships between turnover rates and organizational performance (Heavey et al., 2013; Hom, Lee, Shaw, & Hausknecht, 2017; Jiang, Liu, McKay, Lee, & Mitchell, 2012; Park & Shaw, 2013), so we will summarize these valuable reviews. More specifically, we will examine the more consequential variables related to turnover rate (based on effect sizes) and the authors' conclusions of the relationships reported.

One might ask: How did three meta-analyses come to be published on the single topic of collective turnover? The answer is that each focused on different issues. Two of the studies were very broadly based. One examined the influence of human resource management systems on voluntary turnover (Jiang et al., 2012). These authors also examine operational (e.g., product quality) and financial outcomes (e.g., sales growth) as criteria, but given the focus of the current book, we will only examine the results for turnover. Heavey et al. (2013) examined both antecedents and consequences of collective turnover. Park and Shaw (2013) focused on the relationship between turnover rates and organizational performance.

Regarding the relationship between turnover and firm performance, these meta-analyses find that the higher the turnover rate, the lower organizational performance ($p = -.15$; Park & Shaw, 2013). Similar results were reported by Jiang et al. (2012) for operational and financial outcomes. Moreover, Jiang et al.'s results further suggest that the higher skill-, motivation-, and opportunity-enhancing practices an organization has, the lower the turnover rates, which supports the ability-motivation-opportunity (AMO) model of HRM. These authors also found support for both the human capital model (employee KSAs are central drivers of organizational performance) and the behavioral model (organizations use HR practices to motivate higher productivity from employees, which in turn results in improved operational and financial objectives). Jiang et al. (2012) also tested a structural equation model (SEM) integrating the human capital model, employee motivation, voluntary turnover, and operational outcomes as mediating the effects of skill-, motivation-, and opportunity-enhancing practices on financial outcomes, their final criterion. Both direct and indirect effects of the three HRM practices were observed.

Heavey et al. (2013) organized the many antecedents of collective turnover into six categories: (1) HRM inducements and investments; (2) HRM expectation-enhancing practices; (3) shared attitudes toward the job and organization; (4) quality of work group and supervisory relations; (5) job alternative signals; and 6) job embeddedness signals. They hypothesized that: (1) HRM inducements and investments (e.g., pay and benefits) would be negatively related to collective turnover; while (2) HRM expectations-enhancing practices (e.g., employee monitoring and routinization practices) would be positively relative to turnover rates. Depending on the variable in the remaining four categories, the relationships would be either positive or negative with collective turnover. Heavey et al. (2013) also proposed several moderators of antecedents and consequences of turnover rates.

The results not only supported most of the hypotheses; they were also consistent with previous meta-analyses showing that HRM practices and systems were negatively related to total and voluntary collective turnover (e.g., benefits $-.16$, high commitment HR systems $-.24$, commitment $-.13$, etc.). As noted above, there were also positive relationships predicted and found (e.g., electronic monitoring .19, routinization .34, workforce diversity in age .19, workforce diversity in tenure .15, alternative availability .26). *Note*: we have only presented a few of the extraordinarily large number of effects reported in this and the previously described meta-analyses, mainly for illustrations. Also, the authors of these papers provide avenues for needed research (such as development of process models) and practical implications (such as providing for internal mobility). Interested readers are encouraged to review these papers for many of the other effects and conclusions they found.

In conclusion, the research on collective turnover has really "taken off" since the first edition of this book (Hom & Griffeth, 1995). At that point, we made a conscious decision not to include research on collective turnover because there seemed to be so little of it. Indeed, Heavey et al. (2013) noted that of the 100 studies published on the topic, nearly two-thirds were published in the last decade. Regarding the theoretical development in the area, the theory is predominantly of the content variety, with much more research needed on the processes underlying the many and varied constructs that influence collective turnover. For example, take the construct electronic monitoring and its negative relationship to collective turnover (−.19), suggesting that the more monitoring present, the higher the turnover rate. What are the psychological processes mediating this relationship? For example, do employees who receive monitoring experience high levels of distrust of management or fear of retaliation by management or both, triggering a decisional process leading to the decision to quit? None of the individual-level meta-analyses reported in Chapter 3 examined this construct. This would seem to suggest that individual-level turnover research can benefit from collective-level turnover results. Is the opposite true as well? It seems it is when one looks at the categories of constructs both areas are studying. For example, both investigate HRM inducements and expectation-enhancing practices, work attitudes, work group and supervisory relationships, job alternatives, and job embeddedness. Influence can go both ways.

References

Allen, D. G., Hancock, J. I., Vardaman, J. M., & McKee, D. N. (2014). Analytical mindsets in turnover research. *Journal of Organizational Behavior*, 35, 61–68.

Arnold, H. J., & Feldman, D. C. (1982). A multivariate analysis of the determinants of job turnover. *Journal of Applied Psychology*, 67, 350–360.

Barnard, C. I. (1938). *The Functions of the Executive*. Cambridge, MA: Harvard University Press.

Baysinger, B., & Mobley, W. (1983). Employee turnover: Individual and organizational analysis. In K. Rowland & G. Ferris (Eds.), *Research in Personnel and Human Resources Management* (vol. 1, pp. 269–319). Greenwich, CT: JAI Press.

Beach, L. R. (1990). *Image Theory: Decision Making in Personal and Organizational Contexts*. Chichester: Wiley.

Berk, R. A. (1983). An introduction to sample selection bias in sociological data. *American Sociological Review*, 48, 386–398.

Bhagat, R. S., McQuaid, S. J., Lindholm, H., & Segovis, J. (1985). Total life stress: A multimethod validation of the construct and its effects on organizationally valued outcomes and withdrawal behaviors. *Journal of Applied Psychology*, 70(1), 202–214.

Blau, G. (1993). Further exploring the relationship between job search and voluntary individual turnover. *Personnel Psychology*, 46, 313–330.

Bluedorn, A. C. (1982). A unified model of turnover from organizations. *Human Relations*, 35, 135–153.

Carsten, J. M., & Spector, P. E. (1987). Unemployment, job satisfaction, and employee turnover: A meta-analytic test of the Muchinsky model. *Journal of Applied Psychology*, 72, 374–381.

Cohen, J., & Cohen, P. (1983). *Applied Multiple Regression/Correlation Analysis for Behavioral Sciences* (2nd ed.). Hillsdale, NJ: Erlbaum.

Coverdale, S., & Terborg, J. (1980). *A Re-Examination of the Mobley, Horner, and Hollingsworth Model of Turnover: A Useful Replication.* Paper presented at the Annual Meeting of the Academy of Management, Detroit, Michigan.

Datel, W. E., & Lifrak, S. T. (1969). Expectations, affect change, and military performance in the army recruit. *Psychological Reports*, 24, 855–879.

Donnelly, D. P., & Quinn, J. J. (2006). An extension of Lee and Mitchell's unfolding model of voluntary turnover. *Journal of Organizational Behavior*, 27, 59–77.

Earnest, D. R., Allen, D. G., & Landis, R. S. (2011). Mechanisms linking realistic job previews with turnover: A meta-analytic path analysis. *Personnel Psychology*, 64(4), 865–897.

Farrell, D. (1983). Exit, voice, loyalty, and neglect as responses to job dissatisfaction: A multidimensional scaling study. *Academy of Management Journal*, 26, 596–607.

Farrell, D., & Rusbult, C. E. (1981). Exchange variables as predictors of job satisfaction, job commitment, and turnover: The impact of rewards, costs, alternatives, and investments. *Organizational Behavior and Human Performance*, 28, 78–95.

Felps, W., Mitchell, T. R., Hekman, D. R., Lee, T. W., Holtom, B. C., & Harman, W. S. (2009). Turnover contagion: How coworkers' job embeddedness and job search behaviors influence quitting. *Academy of Management Journal*, 52(3), 545–561.

Festinger, L. (1947). The treatment of qualitative data by "scale analysis." *Psychological Bulletin*, 44(2), 149–161.

Fitzgerald, L. F., Drasgow, F., Hulin, C. L., Gelfand, M. J., & Magley, V. J. (1997). Antecedents and consequences of sexual harassment in organizations: A test of an integrated model. *Journal of Applied Psychology*, 82(4), 578–589.

Forrest, C. R., Cummings, L. L., & Johnson, A. C. (1977). Organizational participation: A critique and model. *Academy of Management Review*, 2, 586–601.

Gaertner, S. (1999). Structural determinants of job satisfaction and organizational commitment in turnover models. *Human Resource Management Review*, 9(4), 479–493.

Gerhart, B. (1990). Voluntary turnover and alternative job opportunities. *Journal of Applied Psychology*, 75, 467–476.

Glomb, T. M., Munson, L. J., Hulin, C. L., Bergman, M. E., & Drasgow, F. (1999). Structural equation models of sexual harassment: Longitudinal explorations and cross-sectional generalizations. *Journal of Applied Psychology*, 84(1), 14–28.

Griffeth, R. W. (1981). *An Information Processing Model of Employee Turnover Behavior.* Unpublished doctoral dissertation, University of South Carolina, Columbia.

Griffeth, R. W., & Gaertner, S. (2001). A role for equity theory in the turnover process: An empirical test. *Journal of Applied Social Psychology*, 31, 1017–1037.

Griffeth, R. W., & Hom, P. W. (1988). A comparison of different conceptualizations of perceived alternatives in turnover research. *Journal of Organizational Behavior*, 9, 103–111.

Griffeth, R. W., & Hom, P. W. (1990). *Competitive Examination of Two Turnover Theories: A Two-Sample Test.* Paper presented at the Annual Convention of the Academy of Management, San Francisco, California (August).

Griffeth, R. W., & Hom, P. W. (1995). The employee turnover process. *Research in Personnel and Human Resources Management*, 13, 245–293.

Griffeth, R. W., & Hom, P. W. (2001). *Retaining Valued Employees.* Thousand Oaks, CA: Sage.

Griffeth, R. W., Hom, P. W., Allen, D. G., Morse, B., & Weinhardt, J. (2008). *Shock-Driven Turnover: Development and Validation of a Multidimensional Measure of the Turnover Events and Shocks Scale (TESS)*. Paper presented at the Annual Meeting of the Academy of Management, Anaheim, California.

Griffeth, R. W., Steel, R. P., Allen, D. G., & Bryan, N. (2005). The development of a multidimensional measure of job market cognitions: The employment opportunity index (EOI). *Journal of Applied Psychology*, 90, 335–349.

Hanisch, K. A., & Hulin, C. L. (1990). Job attitudes and organizational withdrawal: An examination of retirement and other voluntary withdrawal behaviors. *Journal of Vocational Behavior*, 37(1), 60–78.

Heavey, A. L., Holwerda, J. A., & Hausknecht, J. P. (2013). Causes and consequences of collective turnover: A meta-analytic review. *Journal of Applied Psychology*, 98, 412–453.

Holmes, T. H., & Rahe, R. H. (1967). The social readjustment rating scale. *Journal of Psychosomatic Research*, 11, 213–218.

Holtom, B. C., Mitchell, T. R., Lee, T. W., & Eberly, M. B. (2008). Turnover and retention research: A glance at the past, a closer review of the present, and a venture into the future. *Academy of Management Annals*, 2, 231–274.

Holtom, B. C., Mitchell, T. R., Lee, T. W., & Inderrieden, E. J. (2005). Shocks as causes of turnover: What they are and how organizations can manage them. *Human Resource Management*, 44(3), 337–352.

Hom, P. W. (2011). Organizational exit. In S. Zedeck (Ed.), *Handbook of Industrial and Organizational Psychology* (vol. 2, pp. 67–117). Washington, DC: American Psychological Association.

Hom, P. W., Caranikas-Walker, F., Prussia, G. E., & Griffeth, R. W. (1992). A meta-analytical structural equations analysis of a model of employee turnover. *Journal of Applied Psychology*, 77, 890–909.

Hom, P. W., & Griffeth, R. W. (1991). Structural equations modeling test of a turnover theory: Cross–sectional and longitudinal analyses. *Journal of Applied Psychology*, 76, 350–366.

Hom, P. W., & Griffeth, R. W. (1995). *Employee Turnover*. Cincinnati, OH: South/Western.

Hom, P. W., Griffeth, R. W., Palich, L. E., & Bracker, J. S. (1993). *Realistic Job Previews: Two-Occupation Test of Mediating Processes*. Tempe, AZ: College of Business, Arizona State University.

Hom, P. W., Griffeth, R. W., & Sellaro, C. L. (1984). The validity of Mobley's 1977 model of employee turnover. *Organizational Behavior and Human Performance*, 34, 141–174.

Hom, P. W., & Hulin, C. L. (1981). A competitive test of the prediction of reenlistment by several models. *Journal of Applied Psychology*, 66(1), 23–39.

Hom, P. W., & Kinicki, A. J. (2001). Toward a greater understanding of how dissatisfaction drives employee turnover. *Academy of Management Journal*, 44, 975–987.

Hom, P. W., Lee, T. W., Shaw, J. D., & Hausknecht, J. P. (2017). One hundred years of employee turnover theory and research. *Journal of Applied Psychology*, 102, 530–545.

Hom, P. W., Mitchell, T. R., Lee, T. W., & Griffeth, R. W. (2012). Reviewing employee turnover: Focusing on proximal withdrawal states and an expanded criterion. *Psychological Bulletin*, 138, 831–858.

Homans, G. C. (1961). *Social Behavior: Its Elementary Forms*. New York: Harcourt, Brace & World.

Hulin, C. L. (1991). Adaptation, persistence, and commitment in organizations. In M. D. Dunnette & L. M. Hough (Eds.), *Handbook of Industrial and Organizational Psychology* (2nd ed., pp. 445–505). Palo Alto, CA: Consulting Psychologists Press.

Hulin, C. L., & Blood, M. R. (1968). Job enlargement, individual differences, and worker responses. *Psychological Bulletin*, 69, 41–55.

Hulin, C. L., Roznowski, M., & Hachiya, D. (1985). Alternative opportunities and withdrawal decisions: Empirical and theoretical discrepancies and an integration. *Psychological Bulletin*, 97, 233–250.

Ilgen, D. R., & Dugoni, B. L. (1977). *Initial Orientation to the Organization*. Paper presented at the Annual Meeting of the Academy of Management, Kissimmee, Florida (August).

Jackofsky, E. F. (1984). Turnover and job performance: An integrated process model. *Academy of Management Review*, 9, 74–83.

Jackofsky, E. F., & Slocum, J. W. (1987). A causal analysis of the impact of job performance on the voluntary turnover process. *Journal of Occupational Behavior*, 8(3), 263–270.

James, L. R., Mulaik, S. A., & Brett, J. M. (1982). *Causal Analysis: Assumptions, Models, and Data*. Beverly Hills, CA: Sage.

Jaros, S. J., Jermier, J. M., Koehler, J. W., & Sincich, T. (1993). Effects of continuance, affective, and moral commitment on the withdrawal process: An evaluation of eight structural models. *Academy of Management Journal*, 36, 951–995.

Jiang, K., Liu, D., McKay, P. F., Lee, T. W., & Mitchell, T. R. (2012). When and how is job embeddedness predictive of turnover? A meta-analytic investigation. *Journal of Applied Psychology*, 97(5), 1077–1096.

Kammeyer-Mueller, J. D., Wanberg, C. R., Glomb, T. M., & Ahlburg, D. (2005). The role of temporal shifts in turnover processes: It's about time. *Journal of Applied Psychology*, 90(4), 644–658.

Kelley, H. H., & Thibaut, J. W. (1978). *Interpersonal Relations: A Theory of Interdependence*. New York: Wiley.

Kiesler, C. A., & Sakumura, J. (1966). A test of a model for commitment. *Journal of Personality and Social Psychology*, 3, 349–353.

Laker, D. R. (1991). Job search, perceptions of alternative employment and the turnover decision. *Journal of Applied Business Research*, 7, 6–16.

Lawler, E. E. (1981). *Pay and Organizational Development*. Reading, MA: Addison-Wesley.

Lee, T. W. (1988). How job satisfaction leads to employee turnover. *Journal of Business and Psychology*, 2, 263–271.

Lee, T. W., Hom, P. W., Eberly, M. B., Li, J., & Mitchell, T. R. (2017). On the next decade of research in voluntary employee turnover. *Academy of Management Perspectives*, 31(3), 201–221.

Lee, T. W., & Mitchell, T. R. (1994). An alternative approach: The unfolding model of voluntary employee turnover. *Academy of Management Review*, 19, 51–89.

Lee, T. W., Mitchell, T. R., Holtom, B. C., McDaniel, L. S., & Hill, J. W. (1999). The unfolding model of voluntary turnover: A replication and extension. *Academy of Management Journal*, 42, 450–462.

Lee, T. W., Mitchell, T. R., Wise, L., & Fireman, S. (1996). An unfolding model of voluntary employee turnover. *Academy of Management Journal*, 39, 5–36.

Lee, T. W., & Mowday, R. T. (1987). Voluntarily leaving an organization: An empirical investigation of Steers and Mowday's model of turnover. *Academy of Management Journal*, 30, 721–743.

Locke, E. A. (1976). The nature and causes of job satisfaction. In M. D. Dunnette (Ed.), *Handbook of Industrial and Organizational Psychology* (pp. 1297–1350). Chicago, IL: Rand McNally.

Louis, M. R. (1980). Surprise and sense making: What newcomers experience in entering unfamiliar organizational settings. *Administrative Science Quarterly*, 25, 226–251.

Maertz, C. P., & Campion, M. A. (2004). Profiles in quitting: Integrating process and content turnover theory. *Academy of Management Journal*, 47, 566–582.

March, J. G., & Simon, H. A. (1958). *Organizations*. New York: Wiley.

Martin, Jr., T. N. (1979). A contextual model of employee turnover intentions. *Academy of Management Journal*, 22, 313–324.

Meglino, B. M., DeNisi, A. S., Youngblood, S. A., & Williams, K. J. (1988). Effects of realistic job previews: A comparison using an enhancement and a reduction preview. *Journal of Applied Psychology*, 73, 259–266.

Michaels, C. E., & Spector, P. E. (1982). Causes of employee turnover: A test of the Mobley, Griffeth, Hand, and Meglino model. *Journal of Applied Psychology*, 67, 53–59.

Miller, H. E., Katerberg, R., & Hulin, C. L. (1979). Evaluation of the Mobley, Horner, and Hollingsworth model of employee turnover. *Journal of Applied Psychology*, 64, 509–517.

Mitchell, T. R., Holtom, B. C., Lee, T. W., Sablynski, C. J., & Erez, M. (2001). Why people stay: Using job embeddedness to predict voluntary turnover. *Academy of Management Journal*, 44, 1102–1121.

Mobley, W. H. (1977). Intermediate linkages in the relationship between job satisfaction and employee turnover. *Journal of Applied Psychology*, 62, 237–240.

Mobley, W. H. (1982). *Employee Turnover: Causes, Consequences, and Control*. Reading, MA: Addison-Wesley.

Mobley, W. H., Griffeth, R. W., Hand, H. H., & Meglino, B. M. (1979). Review and conceptual analysis of the employee turnover process. *Psychological Bulletin*, 86, 493–522.

Mobley, W. H., Horner, S. O., & Hollingsworth, A. T. (1978). An evaluation of precursors of hospital employee turnover. *Journal of Applied Psychology*, 63, 408–414.

Morgeson, F. P., Mitchell, T. R., & Liu, D. (2015). Event system theory: An event-oriented approach to the organizational sciences. *Academy of Management Review*, 40(4), 515–537.

Morrell, K., Loan-Clarke, J., Arnold, J., & Wilkinson, A. (2008). Mapping the decision to quit: A refinement and test of the unfolding model of voluntary turnover. *Applied Psychology: An International Review*, 57(1), 128–150.

Morrell, K. M., Loan-Clarke, J., & Wilkinson, A. J. (2004). Organisational change and employee turnover. *Personnel Review*, 33(2), 161–173.

Motowidlo, S. J., & Lawton, G. W. (1984). Affective and cognitive factors in soldiers' reenlistment decisions. *Journal of Applied Psychology*, 69, 157–166.

Mowday, R. T., Koberg, C. S., & McArthur, A. W. (1984). The psychology of the withdrawal process: A cross–Validation test of Mobley's intermediate linkages model of turnover in two samples. *Academy of Management Journal*, 27, 79–94.

Mowday, R. T., Porter, L. W., & Steers, R. M. (1982). *Employee–Organization Linkages*. New York: Academic Press.

Muchinsky, P. M., & Morrow, P. C. (1980). A multidisciplinary model of voluntary employee turnover. *Journal of Vocational Behavior*, 17(3), 263–290.

O'Reilly, C. A., & Chatman, J. (1986). Organizational commitment and psychological attachment: The effects of compliance, identification, and internalization. *Journal of Applied Psychology*, 71, 492–499.

Park, T. Y., & Shaw, J. D. (2013). Turnover rates and organizational performance: A meta-analysis. *Journal of Applied Psychology*, 98, 268–309.

Peters, L. H., Jackofsky, E. E., & Salter, J. R. (1981). Predicting turnover: A comparison of part-time and full-time employees. *Journal of Occupational Behavior*, 2, 89–98.

Pettman, B. O. (1973). Some factors influencing labour turnover: A review of research literature. *Industrial Relations Journal*, 4(3), 43–61.

Porter, L. W., & Steers, R. M. (1973). Organizational, work, and personal factors in employee turnover and absenteeism. *Psychological Bulletin*, 80, 151–176.
Premack, S. L., & Wanous, J. P. (1985). A meta-analysis of realistic job preview experiments. *Journal of Applied Psychology*, 70, 706–719.
Price, J. L. (1977). *The Study of Turnover*. Ames, IA: Iowa State University Press.
Price, J. L., & Bluedorn, A. C. (1979). Test of a causal model of turnover from organizations. In D. Dunkerley & G. Salaman (Eds.), *The International Yearbook of Organizational Studies (pp. 217–236)*. London: Routledge & Kegan Paul.
Price, J. L., & Mueller, C. W. (1981). A causal model of turnover for nurses. *Academy of Management Journal*, 24, 543–565.
Price, J. L., & Mueller, C. W. (1986). *Absenteeism and Turnover of Hospital Employees*. Greenwich, CT: JAI Press.
Purl, J., Hall, K. E., & Griffeth, R. W. (2016). A diagnostic methodology for discovering the reasons for employee turnover using shocks and events. In G. Saridakis & C. Cooper (Eds.), *Research Handbook on Employee Turnover* (pp. 213–246). Northhampton, MA: Edward Elgar.
Rokeach, M. (1973). *The Nature of Human Values*. New York: Free Press.
Rosse, J. G., & Hulin, C. L. (1985). Adaptation to work: An analysis of employee health, withdrawal, and change. *Organizational Behavior and Human Decision Processes*, 36(3), 324–347.
Rosse, J. G., & Miller, H. E. (1984). Relationship between absenteeism and other employee behaviors. In P. S. Goodman & R. S. Atkin (Eds.), *Absenteeism: New Approaches to Understanding, Measuring, and Managing Employee Absence (pp. 194–228)*. San Francisco, CA: Jossey-Bass.
Rousseau, D. (1985). Issues in level in organizational research: Multi-level and cross-level perspectives. In L. L. Cummings & B. M. Staw (Eds.), *Research in Organizational Behavior (vol. 7, pp. 1–37)*. Greenwich, CT: JAI Press.
Rusbult, C. E., & Farrell, D. (1983). A longitudinal test of the investment model: The impact of job satisfaction, job commitment, and turnover of variations in rewards, costs, alternatives, and investments. *Journal of Applied Psychology*, 68, 429–438.
Sager, J., Griffeth, R. W., & Hom, P. W. (1992). *A Structural Model Assessing the Validity of Turnover Cognitions*. Denton, TX: Department of Marketing, University of North Texas.
Salancik, G. R., & Pfeffer, J. (1978). Social information processing approach to job attitudes and task design. *Administrative Science Quarterly*, 23, 224–253.
Schneider, J. (1976). The "greener grass" phenomenon: Differential effects of a work context alternative on organizational participation and withdrawal intentions. *Organizational Behavior and Human Performance*, 16, 308–333.
Shadish, W. R., Cook, T. D., & Campbell, D. T. (2002). *Experimental and Quasi-Experimental Design for Generalized Causal Inference*. Boston, MA: Houghton Mifflin.
Sheridan, J. E. (1985). A catastrophe model of employee withdrawal leading to low job performance, high absenteeism, and job turnover during the first year of employment. *Academy of Management Journal*, 28, 88–109.
Sheridan, J. E., & Abelson, M. A. (1983). Cusp catastrophe model of employee turnover. *Academy of Management Journal*, 26, 418–436.
Simon, H. A. (1947). *Administrative Behavior*. New York: Free Press.
Smith, P. C., Kendall, L. M., & Hulin, C. L. (1969). *The Measurement of Satisfaction in Work and Retirement*. Chicago, IL: Rand McNally.

Spencer, D. G., Steers, R. M., & Mowday, R. T. (1983). An empirical test of the inclusion of job search linkages into Mobley's model of the turnover decision process. *Journal of Occupational Psychology*, 56(2), 137–144.

Steel, R. P., & Griffeth, R. W. (1989). The elusive relationship between perceived employment opportunity and turnover behavior: A methodological or conceptual artifact? *Journal of Applied Psychology*, 74, 846–854.

Steel, R. P., Lounsbury, J., & Horst, W. (1981). A test of the internal and external validity of Mobley's model of employee turnover. In T. Martin & R. Osborn (Eds.), *Proceedings of the 24th Annual Conference of the Midwest Academy of Management* (pp. 333–345). Carbondale, IL: College of Business Administration, Southern Illinois University.

Steers, R. M., & Mowday, R. T. (1981). Employee turnover and postdecision accommodation processes. In L. L. Cummings & B. M. Staw (Eds.), *Research in Organizational Behavior (vol. 3, pp. 235–281)*. Greenwich, CT: JAI Press.

Tein, J.-Y., Sandler, I. N., & Zautra, A. J. (2000). Stressful life events, psychological distress, coping, and parenting of divorced mothers: A longitudinal study. *Journal of Family Psychology*, 14(1), 27–41.

Thibaut, J. W., & Kelley, H. H. (1959). *The Social Psychology of Groups*. New York: Wiley.

Wagner, B. M., Compas, B. E., & Howell, D. C. (1988). Daily and major life events: A test of an integrative model of psychosocial stress. *American Journal of Community Psychology*, 16, 189–205.

Wanous, J. P. (1973). Effects of realistic job preview on job acceptance, job attitudes, and job survival. *Journal of Applied Psychology*, 58, 327–332.

Wanous, J. P. (1980). *Organizational Entry: Recruitment, Selection and Socialization of Newcomers*. Reading, MA: Addison-Wesley.

Wanous, J. P. (1992). *Organizational Entry* (2nd ed.). New York: Addison-Wesley.

Wanous, J. P., Poland, T. D., Premack, S. L., & Davis, K. S. (1992). The effects of met expectations on newcomer attitudes and behaviors: A review and meta-analysis. *Journal of Applied Psychology*, 77, 288–297.

Withey, M. J., & Cooper, W. H. (1989). Predicting exit, voice, loyalty, and neglect. *Administrative Science Quarterly*, 34, 521–539.

Wiggins, J. S. (1973). *Personality and Prediction: Principles of Personality Assessment*. Menlo Park, CA: Addison-Wesley.

Winship, C., & Mare, R. D. (1992). Models for sample selection bias. *Annual Review of Sociology*, 18, 327–350.

Youngberg, C. F. (1963). *An Experimental Study of Job Satisfaction and Turnover in Relation to Job Expectations and Self-Expectations*. Ph.D. dissertation, New York University, New York.

Youngblood, S. A., Mobley, W. H., & Meglino, B. M. (1983). A longitudinal analysis of the turnover process. *Journal of Applied Psychology*, 68, 507–516.

5
THE PSYCHOLOGY OF STAYING
Job Embeddedness

Given a century-long preoccupation with why employees quit (Hom, Lee, Shaw, & Hausknecht, 2017), turnover scholars have neglected why they stay, presuming that the reasons for leaving are simply *mirror opposites* of reasons for staying (Lee, Burch, & Mitchell, 2014). After all, one either stays or leaves as they are opposite actions. Yet Mitchell, Holtom, Lee, Sablynski, and Erez (2001) challenged this prevailing wisdom, arguing that the psychology of staying differs from that of leaving and that their reasons can differ. According to this logic, one may leave because of low pay but not necessarily stay for the sake of good pay (instead staying for the camaraderie of one's coworkers). Specifically, Mitchell et al. (2001) pioneered "job embeddedness" to represent a broad constellation of forces constraining people from leaving, and liken it to "a net or web in which an individual can become stuck" (p. 1104). Although recognizing that people can be "enmeshed or embedded in many different ways" (p. 1104), they identified three prime embedding forces: (1) *fit* to a job or community; (2) *links* (social ties) to workplace or community constituents; and (3) *sacrifice*—job or community amenities or benefits relinquished by leaving. While job fit, links, and sacrifice overlap with existing explanatory constructs (imperfectly; Yao, Lee, Mitchell, Burton, & Sablynski, 2004), this breakthrough conceptualization uniquely highlights the role of community fit, links, and sacrifices (collectively called "community embeddedness") for sustaining retention. Other than labor market conditions, classic theories have generally neglected how external influences affect leaving (Hom & Griffeth, 1995; Mobley, 1982; Price & Mueller, 1981; Rusbult & Farrell, 1983).

Several other features are worth noting about this theory. For one, Mitchell and Lee (2001) presume that embedding forces exert additive and compensatory effects. Thus, an employee may remain in a low-paid, boring job if they have many close friends at work or would have to give up valued perks (e.g., tuition reimbursement).

Moreover, Mitchell and Lee (2001) construe job embeddedness as a state of inertia: "most of the time, [staying] is not even seen or considered as a choice process" (p. 213).

Since its inception, Mitchell et al.'s (2001) theory has caused a paradigmatic shift, redirecting turnover theory and research toward identifying forces inducing incumbents to stay in varied work roles and settings. Sustaining their contention that exclusive focus on leaving forces limits predictability, a plethora of studies attest to job embeddedness's incremental validity for predicting turnover, after controlling standard turnover predictors (e.g., job attitudes, perceived alternatives; Jiang, Liu, McKay, Lee, & Mitchell, 2012; Lee, Mitchell, Sablynski, Burton, & Holtom, 2004; Mitchell et al., 2001). Moreover, meta-analytic regression (Jiang et al., 2012) further demonstrated that both organizational and community embeddedness made separate but unique contributions toward turnover prediction (after controlling common turnover antecedents). Further, Mitchell et al.'s (2001) theory has inspired wide-ranging research on different embedding forces, embeddedness forms, and other behavioral effects (Holtom, Mitchell, Lee, & Eberly, 2008; Hom, 2011; Lee et al., 2004). We next review these separate research streams.

Additional Embedding Forces

Early embeddedness research studied the impact of the three original embedding dimensions (fit, links, and sacrifice; Holtom et al., 2008; Lee et al., 2004; Mitchell et al., 2001), though customizing measures to capture idiosyncratic forces representing those dimensions. To illustrate, Mitchell et al.'s (2001) job-fit measure assessed professional growth opportunities among hospital staff but not grocery store clerks (who lacked such prospects), while Hom et al. (2009) adapted Mitchell et al.'s (2001) job-sacrifice questions to capture perks available to Chinese managers (e.g., housing subsidy). Early on, Mitchell and his colleagues (Mitchell et al., 2001; Mitchell & Lee, 2001) implied that their original taxonomy of embedding dimensions was incomplete. To illustrate, Mitchell et al. (2001) noted that "having a great boss may be hard to give up" (p. 1116), suggesting that the *quality* of links (e.g., at-work friends, mentors, extended family in the community) reflects forces for staying neglected by the number of links (cf. Holtom et al., 2008).

Given that turnover and embeddedness research historically sampled employees from the United States, Canada, England, and Australia (UCEA; Maertz, Stevens, & Campion, 2003), Ramesh and Gelfand (2010) sought to generalize job embeddedness to a collectivist country (India). Apart from testing the original embeddedness construct, they expanded the construct space by introducing "family embeddedness" to capture family forces for staying or leaving (e.g., family pressures to leave, family opinions about family member's employer) more salient in collectivist cultures. They defined family embeddedness as embodying: (1) *family links* (family connections to workplace constituents); (2) *family fit* (family views of how well the company fits the employed family member); and (3) *family sacrifice* (the job benefits family would lose if the family member quits). They found that family embeddedness explains additional variance in call center turnover beyond job embeddedness in both India and the United States.

Extending Ramesh and Gelfand's (2010) notion of family embeddedness in workplaces, Feldman, Ng, and Vogel (2012) promulgated family embeddedness in the *community at large*, which can embed an employee *by proxy*. "Embedding by proxy" (later called "family embeddedness in a community" by Kiazad, Holtom, Hom, & Newman, 2015) occurs when "an individual is embedded indirectly by the costs of leaving one's own job for the family unit as a whole" (p. 211). They note that family members (spouse, offspring, aging parents, shared custody arrangements) can embed the employee indirectly. To illustrate, an employee may stay because his or her leaving would disrupt spousal careers (e.g., spouses own a business serving their own clientele [e.g., CPA, physician]) or children's education. Feldman et al. (2012) differentiate between embeddedness by proxy and community embeddedness, noting that the former reflects a family's community attachment rather than an employee's own community attachment. Thus, an employee may stay—even in a community he or she personally finds disagreeable (due to poor weather or recreational opportunities)—because his or her family prefers local schools or employment opportunities.

Further increasing the comprehensiveness of the embeddedness construct, Felps et al. (2009) advanced "coworker embeddedness" as an additional embedding force, whose absence can trigger "turnover contagion"—where turnover spreads throughout a workgroup. They theorized that when many colleagues actively seek other employment or actually leave (because they are poorly embedded), they emit observable cues (e.g., public expressions of job discontent or resignations, noticeable absences to interview elsewhere) that signal the "salience and perceived viability of leaving" to other remaining employees (p. 547). These employees in turn may look or leave, prompted by social comparison processes whereby "the act of perceiving another person's behavior creates a tendency to behave similarly oneself" (p. 547). In line with their thesis, they found that the average level of job embeddedness within a unit (department, bank branch) reduces individual unit members' turnover (controlling for a member's own job embeddedness). More embedded coworkers thus decreased individual turnover. Moreover, Felps et al. (2009) showed that job search mediated this effect: lower coworker embeddedness increased a focal employee's leaving by increasing coworkers' job search.

Similarly, Ng and Feldman (2013) identified employees' perceptions of their supervisors' job embeddedness as another embedding force, examining how the trajectory of change over time of those perceptions affect employees' own job embeddedness. According to social information processing theory (Salancik & Pfeffer, 1978), increasing supervisory embeddedness furnishes positive social cues about the organization—"that the organization has admirable qualities, which attract veteran managers to stay" (p. 653). When perceiving escalating embeddedness by superiors, subordinates may infer (or even witness) their supervisors experiencing positive events (e.g., promotion, pay raise) reinforcing staying. By implication, "these signals positively color employees' perceptions of the advantages of being embedded" (p. 652). What is more, increasingly embeddedness by firm representatives (aka supervisors) "sends positive signals to employees that the firm will continue to be a competent, viable, and ongoing business enterprise" (p. 655), boosting employees' job security. Finally, that supervisors are not "abandoning ship" removes a shock that can trigger subordinate turnover (Lee & Mitchell, 1994). After all, supervisory departures may arouse anxiety among subordinates who fret over how their career future might be negatively impacted and may thus feel quit-prone (Ballinger, Lehman, & Schoorman, 2010; Shapiro, Hom, Shen & Agarwaal, 2016). In support, Ng and Feldman (2013) found that increasing perceived supervisor embeddedness over time was positively related to a trajectory of rising employee embeddedness.

Embeddedness Forms

Embeddedness investigators have also generalized Mitchell et al.'s theory to explain persistence in work roles besides a particular job in organizations (Kiazad et al., 2015; Ng & Feldman, 2007; Tharenou & Caulfield, 2010). Specifically, Ng and Feldman (2007) proposed differentiating between on-the-job (OTJ) and organizational embeddedness, claiming that Mitchell et al. (2001) conflate two distinct forms of embeddedness. That is, an employee may be embedded in one form but not necessarily the other. To illustrate, an employee may be embedded in an organization because he or she fits the organization's values, has many links spanning different departments and hierarchical levels, and would lose key corporate benefits by leaving (e.g., pension, vacation days). However, this employee may not be embedded in their particular job because they find work tasks meaningless, has few links to coworkers in the work group, and would give up few job perks (e.g., access to private restroom) if they leave. Because jobs are nested within organizations, OTJ embeddedness often engenders higher retention in organizations. Ng and Feldman (2007) note that employees highly embedded in a job may quit if employers transfer (or promote) them to less satisfying jobs or jobs that they perform less effectively (e.g., effective salesman becomes a less competent supervisor).

Feldman and Ng (2007) also introduced "occupational embeddedness"—or the totality of forces embedding incumbents in their occupational field. This form of embeddedness differs from OTJ and organizational embeddedness as incumbents embedded in their profession may leave a job or workplace to advance their professional competency. Adopting Mitchell et al.'s (2001) original dimensions, Feldman and Ng noted that people are embedded in occupations by way of fit (satisfying occupational demands), links (involvement in professional societies), and sacrifice (forsaking human capital investments by leaving the occupational field). Ng and Feldman (2009) demonstrated that occupational embeddedness explains unique variance in performance, counterproductive work behaviors (CWBs), and creativity above and beyond organizational embeddedness.

International scholars have also generalized job embeddedness to explain why expatriates stay or leave international assignments. Specifically, Tharenou and Caulfield (2010) define host-country embeddedness to comprise community embeddedness (where expatriates feel embedded in their host country because they fit the local culture, form many links to local citizens [as do their family members], and would sacrifice a satisfying social life if they return home) and career embeddedness (they would experience considerable career sacrifices repatriating, they find fit between their career goals and host country opportunities, and they form valuable career host-country links). Sampling Australian (self-initiated) expatriates, they documented that both forms of host-country embeddedness reduce their intentions to return home.

Exploring a novel effect of expatriate embeddedness, Kraimer, Shaffer, Harrison, and Ren (2012) demonstrated that such embeddedness increases repatriates' departures from their parent corporation. Applying identity strain theory, they argued that expatriates strongly embedded in their host country form a stronger expatriate identity (i.e., construing themselves as international employees). Upon returning home, these repatriates may feel identity strain (conflict between their international and repatriate identities) when they perceive job deprivation relative to their non-international peers (i.e., perceiving that their organization furnishes few—if any—appreciable benefits relative to peers who stayed home). Their predictions were corroborated with a sample of 112 repatriated employees representing various nationalities.

Other Direct and Moderating Effects by Job Embeddedness

Apart from its retention effects, Lee et al. (2004) demonstrated that job embeddedness (especially on-the-job rather than off-the-job embeddedness) can increase job performance and organizational citizenship. Since March and Simon (1958), organizational scholars have long formulated separate models to explain employees' decisions to participate and perform. Wheeler and his colleagues (Halbesleben & Wheeler, 2008; Wheeler, Harris, & Sablynski, 2012), however, argue that job embeddedness can also underlie job performance according to conservation of resources (COR) theory (Hobfoll, 1989, 2001). This theory holds that people strive to acquire, protect, and retain resources, which help them meet external demands, achieve desired goals, or protect against future resource losses. COR theory further submits that resource losses arouse greater affect or behavior more than does equivalent resource gain ("primacy of loss" motive) and that people invest resources to protect or accumulate resources ("resource investment" motive). Further, people amassing more resources better cope with resource losses, while enabling them to bundle resources together to create more resources ("resource caravan").

Applying COR theory, Wheeler and colleagues liken job embeddedness (JE) to a resource caravan—or a state of ample resources—whereby links represent social resources from others, fit reflects felt belongingness in a firm and community, and sacrifice depicts job or community benefits lost when leaving these contexts. They further envisioned that "employees invest [organizational] JE resources into job performance as a means to attain future resources, which replenish and build future organizational JE" (Wheeler et al., 2012, p. 249). Similarly, Wheeler and colleagues reasoned that a resource caravan based on high community JE also boosts performance by furnishing external resources into investment in performance and fueling work motivation to protect community JE resources that are lost if employees are fired for poor performance and forced to relocate. When JE is low, however, employees' resources are depleted and thus cannot be devoted toward higher performance. In support, Wheeler et al. (2012) found that both organizational and community JE explained unique variance in self-rated performance among hospital personnel. These performance effects concur with longstanding research that organizational commitment (especially affective commitment—committing to organizations one wants to rather than because one has to or needs to; Meyer & Allen, 1997) can improve not only organizational participation, but also job performance (and organizational citizenship; Meyer, Stanley, Herscovitch, & Topolnytsky, 2002).

Besides direct effects on outcomes, job embeddedness can moderate the effects of outcome's antecedents (Lee et al., 2014). A preliminary analysis by Mitchell and Lee (2001) first established that job embeddedness buffers against the effects of turnover drivers (namely, various types of shocks; Lee & Mitchell, 1994), finding that "highly job embedded people who experience shocks have fewer plans about leaving than people who are low on embeddedness and who experience a shock" (p. 227). Further corroborating a buffering effect, Burton, Holtom, Sablynski, Mitchell, and Lee (2010) documented that on-the-job (OTJ) embeddedness can attenuate the detrimental effects of workplace shocks (i.e., negative job events inducing thoughts of leaving, such as unexpected negative performance review, lower-than-expected raises, being passed over for promotion). While such shocks may motivate leaving, they may also drive poorer performance or worse organizational citizenship behavior (OCB) prior to—or instead of—leaving (Hulin, Roznowski, & Hachiya, 1985). As predicted, Burton et al. (2010) found that negative job shocks decreased job performance and OCBs for employees in a large financial institution who have low OTJ embeddedness. Yet the reverse effects were true for employees having high OTJ embeddedness—negative shocks did not lower performance or OBCs.

Multifocal Model of Job Embeddedness

Integrating varied forms of work-focused embeddedness (i.e., OTJ, organizational, and occupational), Kiazad et al. (2015) extended COR theory to explicate how their antecedents and consequences differ (see Figure 5.1). Following Wheeler et al. (2012), their multifocal embeddedness framework (MEF) infers from the primary of loss COR tenet that "people stay to retain resources that hold intrinsic (sacrifices) or instrumental (fit and links) value as resource loss is distressing" (p. 642). Similarly, MEF theory also adopts the COR resource investment principle that "JE promotes

Off-The-Job Characteristics that Supply Embedding Resources

Level 3 — • Community characteristics

Level 2 —
Off-The-Job Characteristics that Supply Embedding Resources
• Near by extended family
• Professional communities

Organizational Practices that Supply Embedding Resources
• Skill-enhancing HPWPs
• Opportunity-enhancing HPWPs
• Motivation-enhancing HPWPs

P5 P4 P6 P1-3

Level 1 —
Work-Based Embeddedness Foci
• Occupational embeddedness
• Organizational embeddedn ess
• On-the-job embeddedness

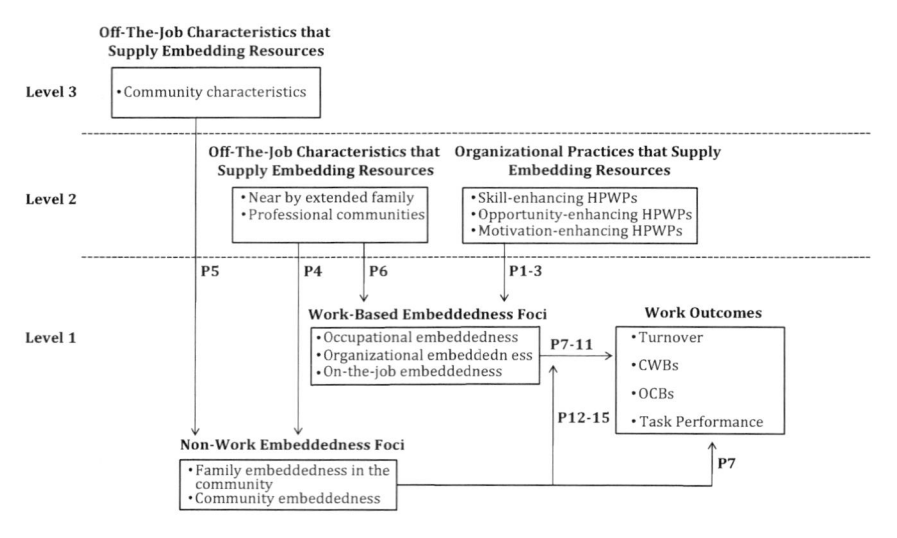

P7-11

Work Outcomes
• Turnover
• CWBs
• OCBs
• Task Performance

P12-15

Non-Work Embeddedness Foci
• Family embeddedness in the community
• Community embeddedness

P7

FIGURE 5.1 Conservation of Resources Multi-Foci Theory of Job Embeddedness

performance because instrumental resources (fit and links) enable employees to fulfill job responsibilities more effectively, enabling them to acquire more resources" (p. 642).

Building upon prior theorizing about work-based embeddedness forms, Kiazad et al. (2015) thus conceptualized how high-performance work practices (HPWPs) differentially affect them. To illustrate, they maintain that opportunity-enhancing HPWPs (e.g., employee empowerment, self-managing teams; Gardner, Wright, & Moynihan, 2011) bolster all three forms of work-based embeddedness, though most increasing organizational embeddedness. Such HPWPs sustain fit (e.g., quality improvement groups and suggestion systems promote demands–abilities PO fit), links (e.g., working parties and joint management–worker committees broaden links to other departments and higher management levels), and sacrifice (e.g., empowering practices create felt control and status [COR resources] that are surrendered by leaving). Kiazad et al. further claim that opportunity-enhancing HPWPs boost *organizational* embeddedness more than OTJ or occupational embeddedness, because employee involvement and job rotation integrate employees into the larger firm-wide social system and thus furnish them wider-ranging social capital. Because firm-specific social capital has limited transferability, opportunity-enhancing HPWPs may thus embed incumbents in an organization more than a particular job or occupation.

Moreover, MEF theory clarifies how the three work-based embedding forms differentially affect varied work outcomes (e.g., turnover, performance). To illustrate, this formulation envisions organizational embeddedness most deterring quits because organization-embedded incumbents derive more resources from their organization than from their job or occupational field per se. After all, leaving a particular firm would not drastically reduce their occupational resources (e.g., surrendering professional connections or occupational skills) or job-based resources (as leavers can assume similar jobs requiring similar KSAs and offering similar intrinsic rewards at other companies).

From COR theory, MEF theory also proposes that individuals embedded in all three work-based embedding forms are "motivated to invest time and effort toward superior task performance to acquire (or protect) resources that enable them to meet professional goals" (Kiazad et al., 2015, p. 650). Because resources are profitably invested (for maximizing "returns") when useful for a given purpose (e.g., meet performance goals or OCB expectations), this perspective further maintains that job embeddedness boosts job performance *most* because job-embedded incumbents have the skills and abilities to meet job demands (job fit) and local relationships (job links) to fulfill performance goals (e.g., tips or help completing tasks), while feeling induced to build upon an already sizeable stock of job-based resources (e.g., attaining larger bonuses). By contrast, employees embedded in occupations or firms strive for greater accomplishments in professions (e.g., achieve office in professional associations) or organizations (e.g., attain executive posts). Indeed, investing resources in occupational or organizational domains (e.g., by participating in professional societies or cross-functional teams) can deplete resources, such as time and effort, available for task performance. To maximize return on investments in these other embedding foci, organization- or occupation-embedded incumbents are thus reluctant to make inordinate investments into performance. After all, intense focus on performing a job superbly can lessen organizational mobility (as supervisors are loathe to promote their best performers) or professional mobility (as employee may develop greater competencies to perform a job at the end of expense of growing professionally, such as professors neglecting scholarly pursuits and trailing scholarly advances in their field when entering university administration).

Extending the embeddedness literature (Lee et al., 2014), Kiazad et al.'s (2015) perspective further specifies how non-work embedding foci can moderate how work-based embedding foci differentially affect different work outcomes. According to MEF theory, community and family community embeddedness can reinforce the positive impact of work-based embeddedness on retention. When employees or their families are embedded in a community, they "stay to protect resources available to their family and to them indirectly (i.e., harmonious family relations, spousal income supplement)" (Kiazad et al., 2015, p. 651). According to the primacy of loss COR tenet, employees are doubly motivated to stay when they are also embedded by work-based fit, links, and sacrifice (to retain resources from work domains). In contrast, community and FEC embeddedness weakens the positive effects of work-based embeddedness on OCBs. That is, employees (or their families) highly embedded in communities have less time or energy available for OCBs as they are overly involved in community roles or activities (e.g., civil or church duties). They are also less capable of acquiring resources through OCBs (e.g., enhanced reputation as good citizens) as community (or family) fit to local clubs or institutions has little instrumental value enabling them to help coworkers or implement new ideas for workplace improvements.

In summary, MEF theory furnishes parsimonious theoretical COR mechanisms to explain job embeddedness' etiology and effects, addressing the absence of a compelling or integrative theory underlying this construct (Lee et al., 2014). Moreover, MEF theory reconceives the original view of job embeddedness as a passive state of being stuck (Mitchell et al., 2001), contending that embedded incumbents proactively "protect against resource loss, recover from losses, and gain resources" (Hobfoll, 2001, p. 349). Further, this model elucidates why people become embedded in certain foci—namely, to "avoid losing resources that hold intrinsic (sacrifices) or instrumental (fit and links) value in those contexts" (Kiazad et al., 2015, p. 652). Finally, this model offers new insight into heretofore overlooked interactions between off-the-job embeddedness and work-based embeddedness, envisioning synergistic effects on retention but counteractive effects on performance.

Because Kiazad et al. (2015) derived their MEF framework from a conceptual synthesis of the empirical literature, certain structural MEF linkages were corroborated in past studies (e.g., observed relationships between OTJ embeddedness and turnover). All the same, no study has yet to test the model in its entirety. Moreover, this model focused on community and family embeddedness in the community, yet overlooked family job embeddedness that may represent off-the-job forces distinct from the former embedding forms. A family may be embedded in a community but not necessarily in a family member's workplace (Ramesh & Gelfand, 2010). Indeed, family job embeddedness may demonstrate stronger interactive effects with work-based embeddedness. When a family is also embedded in workplaces (e.g., family receives job benefits and befriends company personnel), job-embedded employees more likely stay to avoid the loss of job benefits valued by themselves and their families. Further research should also directly verify MEF's underlying theoretical mechanisms—namely, incumbents' motivation to accumulate, protect, or recoup (lost) resources (Hobfoll, 2001).

Proximal Withdrawal State Theory (PWST)

Complementing Mitchell et al.'s (2001) original notion of contextual forces embedding incumbents in jobs, Hom, Mitchell, Lee, and Griffeth (2012) promulgated motivational states for staying (and leaving) to capture the phenomenology of being embedded or "stuck" in a job. Adopting Meyer, Becker, and Vandenberghe's (2004) view that a mindset to pursue a course of action depends on its purposes (staying vs. leaving) and locus of causality, Hom et al. (2012) propose psychological states to participate in—or withdraw from— organizations based on employee preference to stay or leave and perceived volitional control over those preferences. Crossing high and low scores on both dimensions, they derived four proximal states in Figure 5.2: enthusiastic stayers (people who want to and can stay); enthusiastic leavers (people who want to leave

The Psychology of Staying 131

PERCEIVED EMPLOYEE CONTROL

	High Control	Low Control
Prefer to Stay	**Enthusiastic Stayer** "I want to stay and I can stay"	**Reluctant Leaver** "I want to stay but I must leave"
Prefer to Leave	**Enthusiastic Leaver** "I want to leave and I can leave"	**Reluctant stayer** "I want to leave but I must stay"

EMPLOYEE PREFERENCE TO STAY OR LEAVE

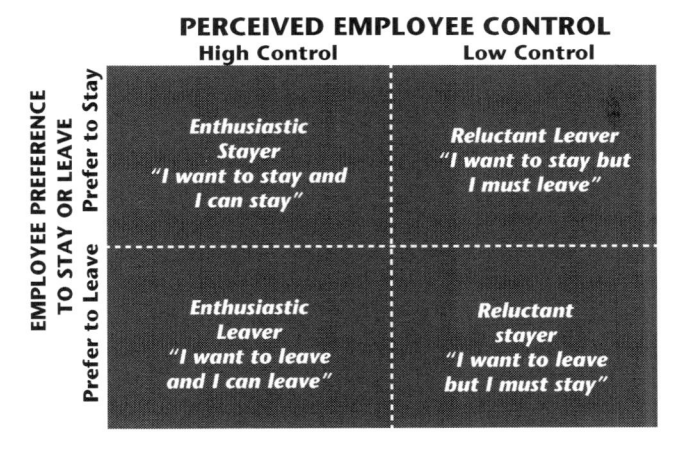

FIGURE 5.2 Prime Proximal Withdrawal States

Proximal Withdrawal States Theory (PWST)

Distal Influence (e.g., Job Characteristics) → Intermediate Antecedents (e.g., Job Satisfaction, Perceived Alternatives, Commitment, Job Embeddedness) → Direct Antecedent (Job Search and Intent to Quit) → Actual Turnover (Voluntarily Leave or Not)

Proximal Withdrawal States
- Preference of Leaving/Staying
- Volitional Control

Types of Leaving
Turnover Speed Exit
Destination

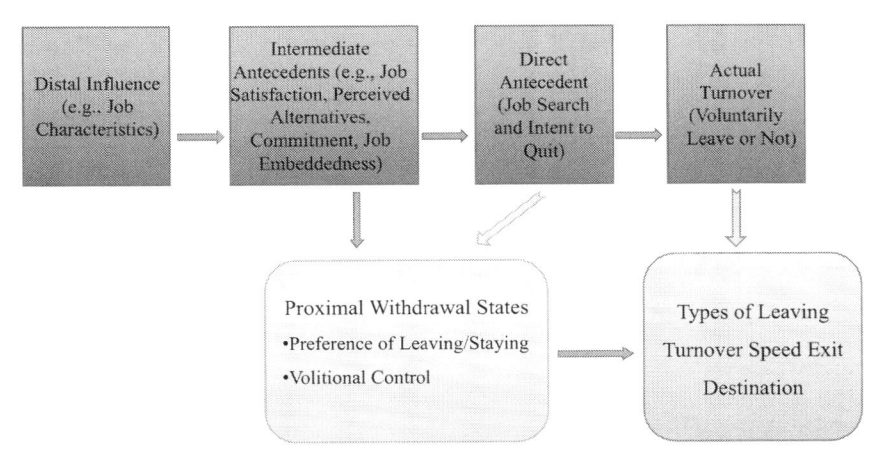

FIGURE 5.3 Proximal Withdrawal States Theory

and can leave); reluctant stayers (people who want to leave but feel that they must stay); and reluctant leavers (people who want to stay but feel that they must leave).

To improve turnover predictability (which rarely exceeds 25% of explained variance; Lee & Mitchell, 1994; Maertz & Campion, 1998), Hom et al. (2012) expanded both turnover's direct antecedents and its criterion space. As shown in Figure 5.3, most theories identify new predictors at various stages or steps during the withdrawal process, whereby environmental and organizational influences (e.g., unemployment rate, job characteristics, external shocks) represent distal causes that influence turnover via intermediate causes (e.g., job attitudes, perceived alternatives; Lee & Mitchell, 1994; Mobley, Griffeth, Hand, & Meglino, 1979; Price & Mueller, 1986; Steers & Mowday, 1981). Hom et al. (2012) propose "proximal withdrawal states" (PWS), interposing them as immediate antecedents of leaving. Corresponding to these proximal predictors, Hom et al. expanded the criterion domain to include types of leaving (voluntary vs. involuntary quits) and staying (enthusiastic vs. reluctant staying), turnover destinations (where leavers end up when they leave), and turnover speed (how quickly people leave once they decide to leave; Lee, Mitchell, Holtom, McDaniel, & Hill, 1999). Apart from improving turnover predictions, PWS mindsets may also underlie other workplace behaviors (e.g., performance, OCBs), consistent with past demonstrations that job embeddedness and organizational commitment (representing staying mindsets; Herscovitch & Meyer, 2002) can affect employees' decision to perform (Lee et al., 2004; Meyer et al., 2004). We next describe more fully these prime PWS states.

Reluctant Staying

Although conventional embeddedness thought conflates them (Holtom et al., 2008; Lee et al., 2014), PWST suggests that reluctant stayers arise from different embedding forces than do enthusiastic stayers and behave differently at work. To illustrate, reluctant stayers may stay in a job they misfit or dislike because they would face considerable job or community sacrifices if they leave (e.g., surrender valued fringe benefits or give up good weather). While staying (like enthusiastic stayers, until they can get another job or their children leave for college), reluctant stayers may perform worse, exhibit more work avoidance behaviors (WABs), and engage in fewer OCBs but more counterproductive work behaviors (CWBs). Commitment scholars are documenting such dysfunctional reactions by people afflicted by continuance commitment (CC) mindsets (Gellatly, Meyer, & Luchak, 2006; Meyer, Morin, & Vandenberghe, 2015, Meyer, Stanley, & Parfyonova, 2012). All the same, this mindset reflects only incumbents who feel that they cannot leave because they would lose too many job benefits or become unemployed. PWST proposes other costs that commitment theorists overlook, such as loss of community benefits for employees or their families (Feldman et al., 2012). Further, CC mindsets fail to reflect strong desires for leaving, capturing instead weak preferences for staying (aka low affective commitment). After all, preferences for staying and leaving are not perfectly (inversely) related as some people can feel ambivalence (having strong feelings for both staying and leaving).

Reluctant Leaving

Traditionally, turnover researchers omitted "involuntary turnover"—or employer-mandated departures, such as dismissals, layoffs, and retirement—from their theory and research as they sought to understand the etiology of voluntary quits. By comparison, PWST proposes that taking into account reluctant leaving mindsets prompted by such personnel actions can improve predictions of an expanded turnover criterion that includes both voluntary and involuntary quits (Batt & Colvin, 2011; Campion, 1991). What is more, PWST suggests reluctant leaving mindsets (reflecting job insecurity) can be induced by *future expectations* of impending involuntary terminations. Such prospective leavers may engage in WABs, CWBs, quit, or even contest or postpone their impending terminations. Further, Hom et al. (2012) recognize that normative pressures (e.g., arising from spousal relocations) or social obligations (e.g., leaving labor market to care for elderly parents) also prompt reluctant leaving states. While employers did not mandate their departures, such leavers nonetheless feel *less* control over their quit decisions when paternal or external authorities (e.g., parents, coaches) urge them to quit. According to Ryan and Deci (2000), external regulation (complying with others' demands to stay or leave to receive rewards or avoid punishments) and introjected regulation (enacting participation actions to avoid felt guilt or anxiety) represent extrinsic motivation rather than self-determination.

Enthusiastic Staying

Although not explicitly named, turnover theorists assume that this mindset reflects positive job attitudes, such as high job satisfaction (Mowday, Porter, & Steers, 1982) or high affective organizational commitment (Meyer & Herscovitch, 2001), given their implicit assumption that the preference for staying is merely the polar opposite of the preference for leaving. Presumably, enthusiastic stayers want to stay because they feel positive affect toward their job or firm, while employees wanting to leave feel negative affect. While job attitudes may represent a single bipolar dimension, Hom et al. (2012) envision enthusiastic staying and leaving as distinct mindsets for their underlying motives are not necessarily mirror opposites. They may even coexist for ambivalent incumbents who feel highly satisfied with their job (sustaining enthusiastic staying), while feeling enticed to leave (assuming enthusiastic leaving) by highly attractive alternative jobs or geographic locations. In line with research on the behavioral effects of incumbents feeling strong affective commitment (a type of enthusiastic staying; Gellatly et al., 2006; Sinclair, Tucker, Cullen, & Wright, 2005; Wasti, 2005), PWST predicts that enthusiastic stayers would exhibit higher performance and more OCBs, while refraining from WABs and CWBs.

Enthusiastic Leaving

PWST posits an enthusiastic leaving state—which reflects both desire and ability to leave—and is broader and more fundamental than traditional notions of quit intentions, such as withdrawal cognitions (representing general thoughts about leaving) or choice intentions (decisions to accept an alternative over the current job; Mobley et al., 1979; Steel, 2002). This mindset initiates a withdrawal sequence involving the formation of various intentions (or goals) to enact a series of intermediate behaviors and successfully executing them before actually departing. For those pursuing alternatives (e.g., another job, law school, full-time parenting), enthusiastic leavers must first identify prospective alternatives (and solicit information about them), apply for acceptable alternatives, and acquire them (Steel, 2002). Even those leaving without job offers or alternatives in hand must perform various tasks, such as notifying managers of their plan to quit, training replacements, participating in exit interviews, and cleaning out one's desk (Klotz & Bolino, 2016). In short, this mindset predates quit intentions and initiates a host of WABs, including lower performance (Sturman & Trevor, 2001) and less OCBs (Chen, Hui, & Sego, 1998).

Antecedents of Staying/Leaving Preferences

Following motivational forces (Maertz & Campion, 2004) and embeddedness (Feldman et al., 2012; Mitchell et al., 2001) theories, Hom et al. (2012) speculated about the etiology of the PWS mindsets by theorizing how these forces affect staying/leaving preferences and perceived volition, the key dimensions underlying mindsets. As Figure 5.4, they proposed that *affective forces* underpin preferences to stay or leave. Thus, employees prefer to stay if they experience positive affective forces when they fit the job or organization (Mitchell & Lee, 2001) or prefer to leave if they experience negative affective forces due to negative workplace shocks (Lee et al., 1999; Maertz & Campion, 2004). What is more, they may want to stay due to *calculative* forces—forming positive expectations about desirable future work roles (e.g., promotions or transfers; Mobley et al., 1979). Moreover, constituent forces (Maertz & Griffeth, 2004) can shape preferences to stay or leave. That is, close relationships on and off the job (link number or quality; Holtom et al., 2008; Mitchell et al., 2001) can boost preferences to stay, while bullying colleagues or abusive (or bigoted) supervisors can increase preferences to leave (McKay et al., 2007; Roberson, 2004; Tepper, 2000).

Moral forces—moral obligations to stay (Maertz & Campion, 2004)—may also boost employee preferences for staying or leaving if such decisions accord with their personal values. To illustrate, employees in nonprofit organizations (charities, firefighting, drug rehabilitation) may stay if they believe their work can make a positive difference in other people's lives (Grant, 2007), while they may want to leave if they cannot have such impact (e.g., nurses leaving understaffed hospitals to provide superior patient care elsewhere). Moreover, alternative forces—highly attractive work or unpaid alternatives elsewhere (Maertz & Griffeth, 2004)—may prompt desires to leave even among even satisfied employees (Lee et al., 1996, 1999). Finally, embedding human resource management (HRM) practices (e.g.,

STATE ANTECEDENTS

PREFERENCE ANTECEDENTS
- AFFECTIVE FORCES
  - Job Fit
  - Inital Job Attitudes
  - Negative Workplace Shocks
- CALCULATIVE FORCES
- CONSTITUENT FORCES
  - On- and Off-The-Job Links
  - Tumover Contagion
  - Bullying Co-Workers
  - Abusive Supervisors
  - Racial or Gender Harassment
- MORAL/ETHICAL FORCES
- EMBEDDING HRM PRACTICES
  - High Involvement Work Structures
  - Workforce Inducements
  - Workforce Investments
- ALTERNATIVE FORCES
  - Desirable Work or Extrawork Altematives
    - Personal Shocks
    - Spontaneous Job Offers

CONSTRAINT ANTECEDENTS
- LEGAL FORCES
  - Employer Pressure to Leave
  - Employment Contracts
- NORMATIVE FORCES
  - External Pressure
  - Workplace Pressure
- BEHAVORIAL FORCES
  - Job Sacrifices
  - Community & Family Sacrifices
- ALTERNATIVE FORCES
  - Few or Undesirable Job Altemafives
- JOB PROTECTION FORCES
  - Unionizafion
  - Tenure/Seniority Protections
- PERFORMANCE-ENHANCING HRM
  - Contingent Rewards
  - Perfomance Montoring
- JUST TERMINATION PRACTICES

PROXIMAL WITHDRAWAL STATES
- STAY/LEAVE PREFERENCE
- DECISION CONTROL

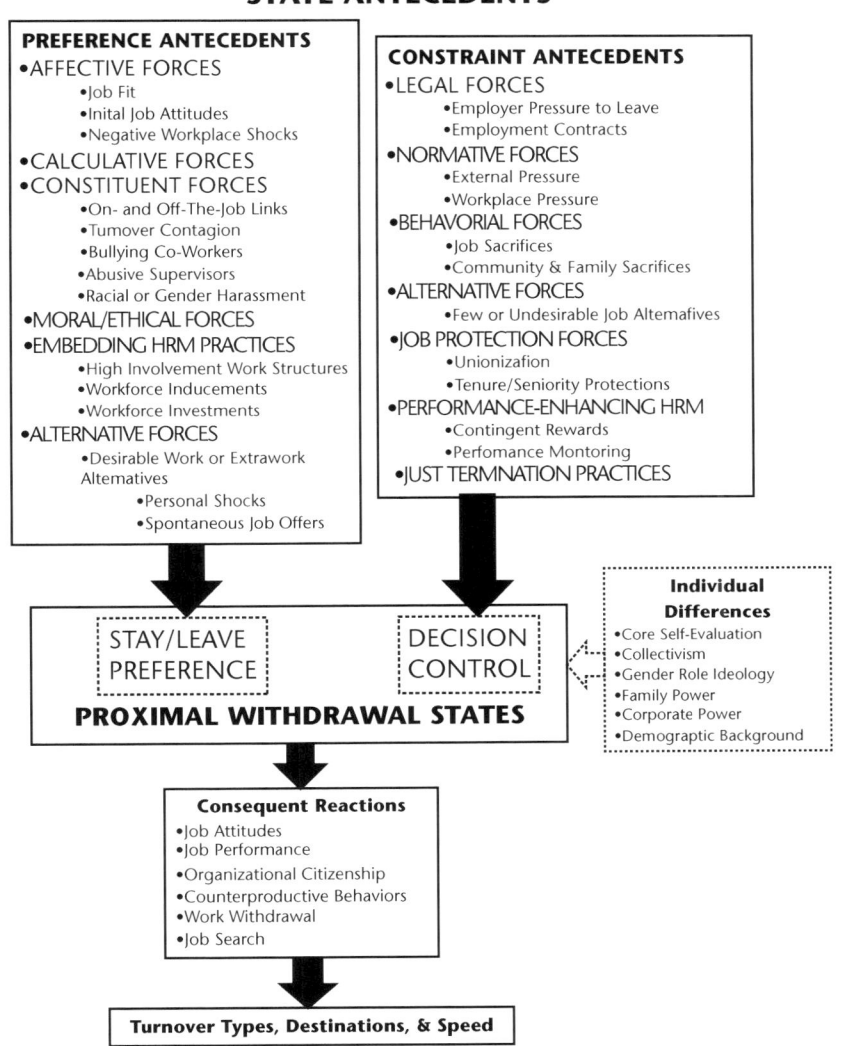

Individual Differences
- Core Self-Evaluation
- Collectivism
- Gender Role Ideology
- Family Power
- Corporate Power
- Demograptic Background

Consequent Reactions
- Job Attitudes
- Job Performance
- Organizational Citizenship
- Counterproductive Behaviors
- Work Withdrawal
- Job Search

Turnover Types, Destinations, & Speed

FIGURE 5.4 Antecedents of Proximal Withdrawal States

empowerment, self-managing teams, developmental opportunities) may increase staying preferences (Trevor & Nyberg, 2008).

Hom et al. (2012) contend that consideration of reluctant staying and leaving mindsets can improve turnover prediction and understanding as prevailing views presume that employees are either enthusiastic stayers or leavers. Attesting to their view, Li, Lee, Mitchell, Hom, and Griffeth (2016) demonstrated that common turnover predictors (e.g., job satisfaction, job embeddedness) more accurately predict turnover among enthusiastic stayers and leavers than among reluctant stayers and leavers.

Antecedents of Perceived Volitional Control

In line with traditional thinking, Hom et al. (2012) recognize that *legal* forces can lessen employees' decisions to stay or leave. That is, employers (especially in the United States) have the legal authority to terminate employees' employment (via firings or layoffs, just as employees have the freedom to quit according to the employment-at-will doctrine), although such authority may be constrained by job protections (e.g., civil service protections, unionization, tenure). By the same token, employers also invoke legal forces by using employment contracts to forestall or postpone employees' departures (e.g., teachers, soldiers; Maertz & Campion, 2004). What is more, PWST posits *normative* forces—namely, social pressures from colleagues, friends, or family to stay or leave (Maertz & Griffeth, 2004). Turnover researchers have long established that employees quit or relocate due to their job's interference with their ability to participate in family functions (Hom & Kinicki, 2001), spousal relocations (Lee et al., 1996), or family hardships incurred by living in disagreeable communities (e.g., living abroad, unsafe neighborhoods; Shaffer & Harrison, 2001). These turnover drivers imply that normative forces underlie their effects as family members may exhort employees to quit jobs, allowing them to more fully participate in family activities, allowing spouses to assume better jobs elsewhere, or enabling families to escape inhospitable living conditions (e.g., polluted and dirty cities abroad).

Following traditional viewpoints (Mobley, 1977; Rusbult & Farrell, 1983), Hom et al. (2012) submit *behavioral* forces—what employees would surrender if they quit their job, such as job benefits or a corner office—which reduce quit propensity. As a form of external regulation based on sanctions (Ryan & Deci, 2000), behavioral forces may impose extreme costs on leaving, diminishing volitional control by making incumbents feel that they *must* stay (cf. Herscovitch & Meyer, 2002). Following embeddedness theory (Mitchell & Lee, 2001), Hom et al. (2012) expanded those forces to include community sacrifices—or personal costs of leaving a community—such as giving up valued water sports when moving to Kansas City. Further, PWST recognizes that employees' families may also suffer when employees relocate (i.e., family sacrifices) as they may lose job benefits available to families (e.g., tuition assistance for employees' offspring; Ramesh & Gelfand, 2010) or community amenities, such as spousal employment opportunities and excellent neighborhood schools for children (Feldman et al., 2012). Besides such turnover costs, PWS theorists note that low *alternative* forces—or the absence of job alternative or desirable ones—can reduce incumbents' beliefs that they can quit. High unemployment or low movement capital (i.e., lack of marketable skills or experience) may lessen their perceptions that they can quit (Steel, 2002; Trevor, 2001).

Further, job protection systems (e.g., unionization, faculty tenure) can curb arbitrary managerial decisions to dismiss or lay off staff, increasing employees' felt freedom to stay (Batt & Colvin, 2011). Moreover, firms implementing fair termination procedures (e.g., appeal opportunities, ample severance pay, outplacement services) may increase employees' perception that they have some "choice" over leaving by having the chance to challenge termination decisions or by attaining desirable employment alternatives given firm investments in their employability ("positive involuntary turnover"; Manz, Fugate, Hom, & Millikin, 2015). Lastly, performance-enhancing HRM practices (e.g., performance monitoring, rank-and-yank appraisals, contingent pay; Batt & Colvin, 2011) can lessen felt control over staying, especially among marginal performers (Shaw, Dineen, Fang, & Vellella, 2009).

PWS Subtypes

Hom et al. (2012) also identified subgroups for the prime PWS states, as shown in Figure 5.5, based on salient PWS antecedents, while theorizing how they might differ in work outcomes.

Enthusiastic Staying Subtypes

They identified three subtypes: (1) engaged stayers; (2) embedded engaged stayers; and (3) slackers. Engaged stayers are intrinsically embedded in a job by affective forces (e.g., person–job fit, strong workplace links), calculative forces, and/or moral forces. As Table 5.1 shows, they perform effectively, exhibit more OCBs,

Proximal Withdrawal States (PWS) Model

Perceived Employee Control

		High Control	Low Control
Preference to Stay or Leave	Prefer to stay	**Enthusiastic Stayer** - Engaged Stayers - Embedded Stayers - Slackers	**Reluctant Leaver** - Involuntary Leavers - Retirement - Coerced Leavers
	Prefer to leave	**Enthusiastic Leaver** - Planned Leavers - Negative Job Shock Leavers - Job Offer Leavers - Dissatisfied Leavers	**Reluctant Stayer** - Contractual Stayers - Trapped Stayers

FIGURE 5.5 Proximal Withdrawal Subtypes

TABLE 5.1 Theoretical Summary and Integration

Withdrawal States and Subtypes	Immediate Antecedents	Consequent Attitudes and Behaviors	Time to Leave	Turnover Destinations
1. Enthusiastic Stayers				
Engaged Stayers	High affective, calculative, or constituent force	Good performance, OCBs, less CWBs and WABs; positive JS and OC	Slow	Retirement destinations, disability (disease, injury, infirmity), death, or unsolicited job offer
Embedded Engaged Stayers	High affective, calculative, or constituent force *and* high sacrifices or normative forces to stay	Same as engaged stayers	Slower than engaged stayers	Retirement destinations, disability, death, or unsolicited job offer
Slackers	NS job overfit or DA job fit (but low D&A) *and* high job/community sacrifice or low alternative force (no better jobs)	Poor performance, less OCBs and WABs; average JS and OC	Slow	Retirement destinations, disability, death, or no options (due to dismissal or layoff)
2. Reluctant Stayers				
Trapped Stayers	Low affective, calculative, or constituent force *and* high normative force to stay, high sacrifices, or low alternative force (no jobs)	Marginal performance, WABs, CWBs, less OCBs, job search; negative JS and OC	Moderate (removal of exit barriers)	Another job, unpaid work (e.g., full-time caretaker), or non-work option (e.g., MBA enrollment)
Contractual Stayers	Low affective or calculative force *and* high legal force (employment contract)	Minimally acceptable performance, less OCBs, little CWBs or WABs; somewhat negative JS and OC	Moderate (contract duration)	Another job, unpaid work, non-work, or no option

(*Continued*)

TABLE 5.1 (Cont.)

Withdrawal States and Subtypes	Immediate Antecedents	Consequent Attitudes and Behaviors	Time to Leave	Turnover Destinations
3. Enthusiastic Leavers				
Voluntary Leaving Subtypes:				
Path 1 (Plan)	High alternative force	Adequate to good performance, OCBs, less CWBs or WABs; continued positive JS and OC	Implement plan soon after shock	Retirement destinations, unpaid work, non-work, or no option
Path 2 (Negative Job Shock)	Low affective (image violation) or constituent (bullies, bad bosses) force	Poor performance, CWBs; negative JS and OC	Very quickly (just quits)	No option
Path 3 (Job Offer)	High alternative force (unsolicited job inquiry or offer)	Adequate to good performance, OCBs, less CWBs or WABs; continued positive JS and OC	Moderate	Another (better) job
Path 4 (Dissatisfaction)	Low affective (initial negative JS and OC), calculative, or constituent force	Poor performance, WABs, job search, less OCBs, CWBs; more negative JS and OC	Slower	Another job
4. Reluctant Leavers	All subtypes below should have high affective, calculative, or constituent force to stay *and* a force(s) to leave			

(*Continued*)

TABLE 5.1 (Cont.)

Withdrawal States and Subtypes	Immediate Antecedents	Consequent Attitudes and Behaviors	Time to Leave	Turnover Destinations
Involuntary Leavers	High legal force to leave (suspected or anticipated terminations)	Poor performance (or attempts to upgrade performance), WABs, job search; increasingly negative JS and OC	Faster to quick	No option (or another job if lined up before leaving) or poor options
Traditional Retiring Leavers	High legal force to leave *and* moderate to high alternative forces (pension eligibility, early retirement incentives)	Moderate to good performance, OCBs, little CWBs or WABs; above-average JS and OC	Slower	Bridge employment, unpaid work (e.g., volunteer), non-work, or no option
Coerced Leavers	High normative force to leave (e.g. pressing family care duties, spousal relocations, family dislocations)	Moderate to good performance, OCBs, little CWBs or WABs; likely positive JS and OC	Moderate to slow	Another job, unpaid work, or non-work option (less desirable options)
Resistant Leavers	High legal forces to leave *and* high normative pressure to stay, high sacrifice, or lack of desirable jobs	Resistance, poor performance (or attempts to upgrade performance), WABs, job search; increasingly negative JS and OC	Moderate to slow	No option (or another job lined up before leaving), possible reinstatement

Note: NS = needs–supplies; DA = demands–abilities; JS = job satisfaction; OC = affective organizational commitment; OCBs = organizational citizenship behaviors; WABs = work avoidance behaviors (e.g., absences, tardiness); CWBs = counterproductive work behaviors; D = demands; A = abilities.

and avoid CWBs. When they are also embedded by behavioral forces (becoming embedded engaged stayers), they behave similarly but may stay longer given that both intrinsic and extrinsic forces embed them. Both may stay indefinitely until some shock (e.g., retirement, spousal relocation, disability) dislodges them.

By contrast, slackers primarily stay for extrinsic reasons, such as stress-free, well-paid, and secure jobs. They predominate the workforces of companies practicing overinvestment employee–organizational relationships (EOR; high corporate inducements for minimal worker contributions; Tsui, Pearce, Porter & Tripoli, 1997) (e.g., Chinese state-owned enterprises, unionized firms; Hom et al., 2009; Shaw et al., 2009). Because they do not find their job intrinsically rewarding, they may only perform tasks specified in their job descriptions (avoiding OCBs) and perform well enough to escape being fired. As Hom et al. (2012) envision, "slackers are loyal to their paycheck, are disengaged, and are low performers with few chances of leaving voluntarily" (p. 842). They plan to retire (sooner rather than later), assuming their employer can afford their labor or marginal performance.

Reluctant Staying Subtypes

Hom et al. (2012) identified two subtypes of reluctant stayers who want to leave a job lacking in affective, constituent, or calculative forces but must stay due to extrinsic constraints (e.g., employment contracts, high unemployment, community sacrifices): (1) *trapped stayers*; and (2) *contractual stayers*. The former stayers experience few intrinsic rewards for staying (low job or PO fit) and thus exhibit more WABs and CWBs (see Table 5.1). They are marginal performers who are stuck until exit barriers are lifted. Once barriers are lifted (e.g., improving job market, spouse graduates from law school), trapped stayers readily leave. Contractual stayers, however, stay to fulfill employment contracts and may feel less dissatisfaction or job misfit because they had freely entered into those contracts. Bound by legal forces to stay (for a fixed duration) and satisfactorily meet job requirements, they differ from trapped stayers by avoiding CWBs and WABs, while performing their jobs better than the latter.

Enthusiastic Leaving Subtypes

Following Lee and Mitchell's (1994) unfolding model, Hom et al. (2012) identified four subtypes based on their four turnover paths—namely, dissatisfied leavers (Path 4) and three kinds of shock-driven leavers (Paths 1–3). Low affective forces induce Path-4 leavers to follow a conventional path by which they locate and obtain more satisfying work or nonwork alternatives before leaving (Hom & Kinicki, 2001; Lee et al., 1999; Mobley, 1977). Turnover researchers have long documented their dysfunctional behavioral syndrome: high WABs and CWBs but low job performance and OCBs (Chen et al., 1998; Dalal, Lam, Weiss, Welch, & Hulin, 2009; Harrison, Newman, & Roth, 2006; Hom & Kinicki, 2001). Resembling the prototypical leaver (March & Simon, 1958; Mobley et al., 1979), they often end up with another alternative before or after leaving (Lee et al., 1999, 2008).

According to Lee and Mitchell (1994), different types of shocks induce different turnover paths and thus different enthusiastic leaving subtypes. Path 1 leavers experience a shock (precipitating event) that activates a preexisting plan to quit, such as exiting a part-time job when graduating college or leaving the workforce when bearing a child, while Path 3 leavers receive an unsolicited job interview or offer. Unlike Path 4 leavers, they are not dissatisfied with their job as external shocks (often more desirable alternatives, such as better job offers) caused them to think about leaving. Hom et al. (2012) argued that they are "pulled away by attractive roles ... rather than pushed away from dissatisfying work" (p. 843). Consequently, these leavers would not exhibit CWBs, WABs, poor performance, or low OCBs. Quite likely, Path 1 leavers will end up in nonemployment destinations, while Path 3 leavers will leave for another job. Finally, Path 2 leavers exit due to some negative job shock (e.g., poor performance review, being passed over for promotion; Burton et al., 2010), occasioning negative affect (e.g., anger, fear; Maertz & Campion, 2004). Because they often leave quickly without job offers in hand (headed toward no immediate work destinations), they have less time to engage in dysfunctional behaviors (e.g., sabotage, theft), though they may insult their supervisors or exit without prior notification of their leaving (Klotz & Bolino, 2016).

Reluctant Leaving Subtypes

Depending on antecedent forces, Hom et al. (2012) identified four subtypes: (1) involuntary leavers; (2) traditional retiring leavers; (3) coerced leavers; and (4) resistant leavers. Fitting the classic definition of employer-initiated departures (Maertz & Campion, 1998), involuntary leavers embody those whom employers are firing or laying off. PWST expands this category to include employees who *anticipate* that they might lose employment (engrossing them in feelings of job insecurity), perhaps because employers have previously laid off staff (Trevor & Nyberg, 2008) or employers implement performance-enhancing HRM practices that repeatedly evaluate their performance harshly (Batt & Colvin, 2011). While they may misbehave upon learning or suspecting impending job loss, involuntary leavers may have little time to retaliate against employers (who often promptly remove them from the premises) by committing CWBs or WABs.

Given that their longevity implies that they have consistently satisfied job demands (demands–ability job fit) and have enough time to internalize organizational values (PO fit), *prospective retirees* may perform effectively and engage in more OCBs—notably, lasting institutional contributions and mentoring younger generations (reinforced by growing death awareness; Grant & Wade-Benzoni, 2009). Although not mandated by firms to leave, *coerced leavers* may feel compelled to leave by external referents, such as spouses, parents, or authorities in other social systems (e.g., varsity team coaches, professors, religious communities). They can offer rewards or sanctions to incumbents to prompt compliance with demands to quit (e.g., parents can demand teenagers quit work to focus on their schooling, relocating spouses may threaten divorce if employees do not quit and follow them). Relying on introjected regulation (Ryan & Deci, 2000), external referents can exhort employees to leave workplaces to fulfill some social or family obligations. To illustrate, Mexican women may exit the labor market to assuage their guilt for failing to abide by the feminine ideal symbolized by the virgin mother ("marianismo") in their culture that prescribes that they should center their lives around marriage and motherhood (Tiano, 1994). Because significant others outside the organization are compelling them to leave desired jobs, coerced leavers may possess positive job attitudes like enthusiastic leavers. While eventually leaving, they may nonetheless not manifest dysfunctional behaviors shown by dissatisfied leavers, such as high CWBs and WABs (or low performance and OCBs). Finally, resistant leavers feel pressured by employers to leave but face opposing normative or behavioral forces to stay. Their families may, however, exhort them to stay so that spouses can maintain access to valued job benefits (e.g., healthcare coverage) and teenage children can continue their friendships and attending excellent schools. To keep their job, these employees might improve their performance, appeal their superior's decision, file lawsuits, or solicit support from powerful allies (e.g., union officials).

Several studies recently evaluated Hom et al.'s (2012) formulation. Woo and Allen (2014) first tested the PWS taxonomy with latent profile analysis (LPA), using queries about quit intentions, job search, and reasons for staying or leaving (e.g., work life quality, career benefits, alternatives) as latent class indicators. They identified embedded and detached stayers and dissatisfied and script-driven seekers, corresponding to Hom et al.'s (2012) enthusiastic and reluctant stayers and (affect- and shock-driven) enthusiastic leavers, respectively. Directly assessing PWS states, Li et al. (2016) observed that reluctant stayers and enthusiastic leavers are similar in job attitudes and job embeddedness as are reluctant leavers and enthusiastic stayers. These results upheld the PWS tenet that reluctant leavers differ from enthusiastic leavers and that reluctant stayers differ from enthusiastic stayers. Moreover, they found that job satisfaction, job embeddedness, and quit intentions more accurately predict turnover among enthusiastic stayers and leavers. Yet they poorly predict turnover among reluctant stayers and leavers, suggesting that perceived volitional control represents a neglected boundary condition limiting the predictive efficacy of turnover and job embeddedness models.

The Dark Side of Job Embeddedness

Using latent growth modeling (LGM), Ng and Feldman (2010) first observed declines in social capital development behaviors over time among highly embedded managers. Presumably, embedded managers lose interest in developing additional social capital as they move up the corporate ladder. Amassing social capital helped speed their promotions through lower managerial ranks. Yet once they near the top of the management hierarchy, they foresee fewer available promotions, reducing their motivation to build more social capital. Moreover, embedded managers have established a wide network of social contacts and maintaining this vast network requires substantial time and energy, decreasing their ability to cultivate new relationships.

Surveying U.S. and Chinese managers and professionals on three occasions, Ng and Feldman (2012) observed that increasing organizational embeddedness over time was related to a rising trajectory of work–family conflict, using LGM tests. They theorized a depletion mechanism whereby escalating organizational embeddedness increases employees' work responsibilities (e.g., engaging in more OCBs due to greater PO fit and links) and work motivation (to safeguard accumulated benefits), depleting the time and energy available for family functions. They also found that increasing community embeddedness is also positively related to rising work–family conflict. Applying a similar depletion mechanism, they argued that community embeddedness (e.g., volunteer work, community leadership) reduces one's ability to satisfy family demands. Yet such individuals are likely to *blame* their job for causing the work–family conflict, perceiving work demands as intrusive on non-work domains. Based on this logic, increasing community embeddedness thus increases perceptions that work interferes with family life.

Finally, Allen, Peltokorpi, and Rubenstein (2016) documented the personal negative outcomes that befall employees "stuck" in adverse work environments. They first documented that embedded employees are less quit-prone despite adverse conditions (e.g., abusive supervision). While staying to safeguard ample resources (job sacrifices), embedded employees, however, suffer ill effects when continually exposed to stressors, according to Allen et al. (2016). Specifically, they found that embedded employees experiencing abusive supervision or high job insecurity reported worse physical health symptoms and sleeping, as well as more emotional exhaustion.

References

Allen, D. G., Peltokorpi, V., & Rubenstein, A. L. (2016). When "embedded" means "stuck": Moderating effects of job embeddedness in adverse work environments. *Journal of Applied Psychology*, 101(12), 1670–1686.
Ballinger, G. A., Lehman, D., & Schoorman, F. D. (2010). Leader–member exchange and turnover before and after succession events. *Organizational Behavior and Human Decision Processes*, 113, 25–36.
Batt, R., & Colvin, A. (2011). An employment systems approach to turnover: Human resources practices, quits, dismissals, and performance. *The Academy of Management Journal*, 54(4), 695–717.

Burton, J., Holtom, B. C., Sablynski, C., Mitchell, T. R., & Lee, T. W. (2010). The buffering effects of job embeddedness on negative shocks. *Journal of Vocational Behavior*, 76, 42–51.

Campion, M. A. (1991). Meaning and measurement of turnover: Comparison of alternative measures and recommendations for research. *Journal of Applied Psychology*, 76, 199–212.

Chen, X.-P., Hui, C., & Sego, D. J. (1998). The role of organizational citizenship behavior in turnover: Conceptualization and preliminary tests of key hypotheses. *Journal of Applied Psychology*, 83(6), 922–931.

Dalal, R., Lam, H., Weiss, H., Welch, E., & Hulin, C. (2009). A within-person approach to work behavior and performance: Concurrent and lagged citizenship-counterproductivity associations, and dynamic relationships with affect and overall job performance. *Academy of Management Journal*, 52, 1051–1066.

Feldman, D. C., & Ng, T. W. H. (2007). Careers: Mobility, embeddedness, and success. *Journal of Management*, 33(3), 350–377.

Feldman, D. C., Ng, T. W. H., & Vogel, R. (2012). Off-the-job embeddedness: A reconceptualization and agenda for future research. *Research in Personnel and Human Resource Management*, 31, 209–251.

Felps, W., Mitchell, T. R., Hekman, D. R., Lee, T. W., Holtom, B. C., & Harman, W. S. (2009). Turnover contagion: How coworkers' job embeddedness and job search behaviors influence quitting. *Academy of Management Journal*, 52(3), 545–561.

Gardner, T. M., Wright, P. M., & Moynihan, L. M. (2011). The impact of motivation, empowerment, and skill enhancing practices on aggregate voluntary turnover: The mediating effect of collective affective commitment. *Personnel Psychology*, 64, 315–350.

Gellatly, I. R., Meyer, J. P., & Luchak, A. A. (2006). Combined effects of the three commitment components on focal and discretionary behaviors: A test of Meyer and Herscovitch's propositions. *Journal of Vocational Behavior*, 69, 331–345.

Grant, A. M. (2007). Relational job design and the motivation to make a prosocial difference. *Academy of Management Review*, 32, 393–417.

Grant, A. M., & Wade-Benzoni, K. A. (2009). The hot and cool of death awareness at work: Mortality cues, aging, and self-protective and prosocial motivations. *The Academy of Management Review*, 34(4), 600–622.

Halbesleben, J. R. B., & Wheeler, A. R. (2008). The relative roles of engagement and embeddedness in predicting job performance and intention to leave. *Work & Stress*, 22(3), 242–256.

Harrison, D. A., Newman, D. A., & Roth, P. L. (2006). How important are job attitudes? Meta-analytic comparisons of integrative behavioral outcomes and time sequences. *Academy of Management Journal*, 49, 305–325.

Herscovitch, L., & Meyer, J. P. (2002). Commitment to organizational change: Extension of a three-component model. *Journal of Applied Psychology*, 87(3), 474–487.

Hobfoll, S. E. (1989). Conservation of resources: A new attempt at conceptualizing stress. *American Psychologist*, 44(3), 513–524.

Hobfoll, S. E. (2001). The influence of culture, community, and the nested-self in the stress process: Advancing conservation of resources theory. *Applied Psychology: An International Review*, 50(3), 337–370.

Holtom, B. C., Mitchell, T. R., Lee, T. W., & Eberly, M. B. (2008). Turnover and retention research: A glance at the past, a closer review of the present, and a venture into the future. *Academy of Management Annals*, 2, 231–274.

Hom, P. W. (2011). Organizational exit. In S. Zedeck (Ed.), *Handbook of Industrial and Organizational Psychology* (vol. 2, pp. 67–117). Washington, DC: American Psychological Association.

Hom, P. W., & Griffeth, R. W. (1995). *Employee Turnover.* Cincinnati, OH: South/Western.

Hom, P. W., & Kinicki, A. J. (2001). Toward a greater understanding of how dissatisfaction drives employee turnover. *Academy of Management Journal*, 44, 975–987.

Hom, P. W., Lee, T. W., Shaw, J. D., & Hausknecht, J. P. (2017). One hundred years of employee turnover theory and research. *Journal of Applied Psychology*, 102, 530–545.

Hom, P. W., Mitchell, T. R., Lee, T. W., & Griffeth, R. W. (2012). Reviewing employee turnover: Focusing on proximal withdrawal states and an expanded criterion. *Psychological Bulletin*, 138, 831–858.

Hom, P. W., Tsui, A. S., Wu, J. B., Lee, T. W., Zhang, A. Y., Fu, P. P., & Li, L. (2009). Explaining employment relationships with social exchange and job embeddedness. *Journal of Applied Psychology*, 94, 277–297.

Hulin, C. L., Roznowski, M., & Hachiya, D. (1985). Alternative opportunities and withdrawal decisions: Empirical and theoretical discrepancies and an integration. *Psychological Bulletin*, 97, 233–250.

Jiang, K., Liu, D., McKay, P. F., Lee, T. W., & Mitchell, T. R. (2012). When and how is job embeddedness predictive of turnover? A meta-analytic investigation. *Journal of Applied Psychology*, 97(5), 1077–1096.

Kiazad, K., Holtom, B. C., Hom, P. W., & Newman, A. (2015). Job embeddedness: A multifoci theoretical extension. *Journal of Applied Psychology*, 100, 641–659.

Klotz, A. C., & Bolino, M. C. (2016). Saying goodbye: The nature, causes, and consequences of employee resignation styles. *Journal of Applied Psychology*, 101(10), 1386–1404.

Kraimer, M. L., Shaffer, M. A., Harrison, D. A., & Ren, H. (2012). No place like home? An identity strain perspective on repatriate turnover. *Academy of Management Journal*, 55(2), 399–420.

Lee, T. H., Gerhart, B., Weller, I., & Trevor, C. O. (2008). Understanding voluntary turnover: Path-specific job satisfaction effects and the importance of unsolicited job offers. *Academy of Management Journal*, 51(4), 651–671.

Lee, T. W., Burch, T. C., & Mitchell, T. R. (2014). The story of why we stay: A review of job embeddedness. *Annual Review of Organizational Psychology and Organizational Behavior*, 1, 199–216.

Lee, T. W., & Mitchell, T. R. (1994). An alternative approach: The unfolding model of voluntary employee turnover. *Academy of Management Review*, 19, 51–89.

Lee, T. W., Mitchell, T. R., Holtom, B. C., McDaniel, L. S., & Hill, J. W. (1999). The unfolding model of voluntary turnover: A replication and extension. *Academy of Management Journal*, 42, 450–462.

Lee, T. W., Mitchell, T. R., Sablynski, C. J., Burton, J. P., & Holtom, B. C. (2004). The effects of job embeddedness on organizational citizenship, job performance, volitional absences, and voluntary turnover. *Academy of Management Journal*, 47(5), 711–722.

Lee, T. W., Mitchell, T. R., Wise, L., & Fireman, S. (1996). An unfolding model of voluntary employee turnover. *Academy of Management Journal*, 39, 5–36.

Li, J., Lee, T. W., Mitchell, T. R., Hom, P. W., & Griffeth, R. W. (2016). The effects of proximal withdrawal states on job attitudes, job searching, intent to leave, and employee turnover. *Journal of Applied Psychology*, 101(10), 1436–1456.

Maertz, C. P., & Campion, M. A. (1998). 25 years of voluntary turnover research: A review and critique. In C. L. Cooper & I. T. Robertson (Eds.), *International Review of Industrial and Organizational Psychology* (vol. 13, pp. 49–81). New York: Wiley.

Maertz, C. P., & Campion, M. A. (2004). Profiles in quitting: Integrating process and content turnover theory. *Academy of Management Journal*, 47, 566–582.

Maertz, C. P., & Griffeth, R. W. (2004). Eight motivational forces and voluntary turnover: A theoretical synthesis with implications. *Journal of Management*, 30, 667–683.

Maertz, C. P., Stevens, M. J., & Campion, M. A. (2003). A turnover model for the Mexican maquiladoras. *Journal of Vocational Behavior*, 63, 111–135.

Manz, C. C., Fugate, M., Hom, P. W., & Millikin, J. P. (2015). When having to leave is a "good thing": A case for positive involulntary turnover. *Organizational Dynamic*, 44(1), 57–64.

March, J. G., & Simon, H. A. (1958). *Organizations*. New York: Wiley.

McKay, P. F., Avery, D. R., Tonidandel, S., Morris, M. A., Hernandez, M., & Hebl, M. R. (2007). Racial differences in employee retention: Are diversity climate perceptions the key? *Personnel Psychology*, 60, 35–62.

Meyer, J. P., & Allen, N. J. (1997). *Commitment in the Workplace: Theory, Research, and Application*. Thousand Oaks, CA: Sage.

Meyer, J. P., Becker, T. E., & Vandenberghe, C. (2004). Employee commitment and motivation: A conceptual analysis and integrative model. *Journal of Applied Psychology*, 89(6), 991–1007.

Meyer, J. P., & Herscovitch, L. (2001). Commitment in the workplace: Toward a general model. *Human Resource Management Review*, 11(3), 299–326.

Meyer, J. P., Morin, A. J., & Vandenberghe, C. (2015). Dual commitment to organization and supervisor: A person-centered approach. *Journal of Vocational Behavior*, 88, 56–72.

Meyer, J. P., Stanley, D. J., Herscovitch, L., & Topolnytsky, L. (2002). Affective, continuance and normative commitment to the organization: A meta-analysis of antecedents, correlates, and consequences. *Journal of Vocational Behavior*, 61, 20–52.

Meyer, J. P., Stanley, L. J., & Parfyonova, N. M. (2012). Employee commitment in context: The nature and implication of commitment profiles. *Journal of Vocational Behavior*, 80(1), 1–16.

Mitchell, T. R., Holtom, B. C., Lee, T. W., Sablynski, C. J., & Erez, M. (2001). Why people stay: Using job embeddedness to predict voluntary turnover. *Academy of Management Journal*, 44, 1102–1121.

Mitchell, T. R., & Lee, T. W. (2001). The unfolding model of voluntary turnover and job embeddedness: Foundations for a comprehensive theory of attachment. *Research in Organizational Behavior*, 23, 189–246.

Mobley, W. H. (1977). Intermediate linkages in the relationship between job satisfaction and employee turnover. *Journal of Applied Psychology*, 62(2), 237–240.

Mobley, W. H. (1982). *Employee Turnover: Causes, Consequences, and Control*. Reading, MA: Addison-Wesley.

Mobley, W. H., Griffeth, R. W., Hand, H. H., & Meglino, B. M. (1979). Review and conceptual analysis of the employee turnover process. *Psychological Bulletin*, 86, 493–522.

Mowday, R. T., Porter, L. W., & Steers, R. M. (1982). *Employee–Organization Linkages*. New York: Academic Press.

Ng, T. W. H., & Feldman, D. C. (2007). Organizational embeddedness and occupational embeddedness across career stages. *Journal of Vocational Behavior*, 70, 336–351.

Ng, T. W. H., & Feldman, D. C. (2009). Age, work experience, and the psychological contract. *Journal of Organizational Behavior*, 30, 1053–1075.

Ng, T. W. H., & Feldman, D. C. (2010). The effects of organizational embeddedness on development of social capital and human capital. *Journal of Applied Psychology*, 95(4), 696–712.

Ng, T. W. H., & Feldman, D. C. (2012). The effects of organizational and community embeddedness on work-to-family and family-to-work conflict. *Journal of Applied Psychology*, 97(6), 1233–1251.

Ng, T. W. H., & Feldman, D. C. (2013). Changes in perceived supervisor embeddedness: Effects on employees' embeddedness, organizational trust, and voice behavior. *Personnel Psychology*, 663, 645–685.

Price, J. L., & Mueller, C. W. (1981). A causal model of turnover for nurses. *Academy of Management Journal*, 24, 543–565.

Price, J. L., & Mueller, C. W. (1986). *Absenteeism and Turnover of Hospital Employees*. Greenwich, CT: JAI Press.

Ramesh, A., & Gelfand, M. J. (2010). Will they stay or will they go? The role of job embeddedness in predicting turnover in individualistic and collectivistic cultures. *Journal of Applied Psychology*, 95(5), 807–823.

Roberson, L. (2004). On the relationship between race and turnover. In R. W. Griffeth & P. W. Hom (Eds.), *Innovative Theory and Empirical Research on Employee Turnover* (pp. 211–229). Greenwich, CT: Information Age.

Rusbult, C. E., & Farrell, D. (1983). A longitudinal test of the investment model: The impact of job satisfaction, job commitment, and turnover of variations in rewards, costs, alternatives, and investments. *Journal of Applied Psychology*, 68, 429–438.

Ryan, R. M., & Deci, E. L. (2000). Intrinsic and extrinsic motivations: Classic definitions and new directions. *Contemporary Educational Psychology*, 25(1), 54–67.

Salancik, G. R., & Pfeffer, J. (1978). Social information processing approach to job attitudes and task design. *Administrative Science Quarterly*, 23, 224–253.

Shaffer, M. A., & Harrison, D. A. (2001). Forgotten partners of international assignments: Development and test of a model of spouse adjustment. *Journal of Applied Psychology*, 86(2), 238–254.

Shapiro, D. L., Hom, P. W., Shen, W., & Agarwal, R. (2016). How do leader departures affect subordinates' organizational attachment? A 360-degree relational perspective. *The Academy of Management Review*, 41(3), 479–502.

Shaw, J. D., Dineen, B. R., Fang, R., & Vellella, R. F. (2009). Employee–organization exchange relationships, HRM practices, and quit rates of good and poor performers. *Academy of Management Journal*, 52(5), 1016–1033.

Sinclair, R. R., Tucker, J. S., Cullen, J. C., & Wright, C. (2005). Performance differences among four organizational commitment profiles. *Journal of Applied Psychology*, 90(6), 1280–1287.

Steel, R. P. (2002). Turnover theory at the empirical interface: Problems of fit and function. *Academy of Management Review*, 27, 346–360.

Steers, R. M., & Mowday, R. T. (1981). Employee turnover and postdecision accommodation processes. In L. L. Cummings & B. M. Staw (Eds.), *Research in Organizational Behavior* (vol. 3, pp. 235–282). Greenwich, CT: JAI Press.

Sturman, M. C., & Trevor, C. O. (2001). The implications of linking the dynamic performance and turnover literatures. *Journal of Applied Psychology*, 86(4), 684–696.

Tepper, B. J. (2000). Consequences of abusive supervision. *Academy of Management Journal*, 43, 178–190.

Tharenou, P., & Caulfield, N. (2010). Will I stay or will I go? Explaining repatriation by self-initiated expatriates. *Academy of Management Journal*, 53(5), 1009–1028.

Tiano, S. (1994). *Patriarchy on the Line: Labor, Gender, and Ideology in the Mexican Maquila Industry*. Philadelphia, PA: Temple University Press.

Trevor, C. O. (2001). Interactions among actual ease-of-movement determinants and job satisfaction in the prediction of voluntary turnover. *Academy of Management Journal*, 44(4), 621–638.

Trevor, C. O., & Nyberg, A. J. (2008). Keeping your headcount when all about you are losing theirs: Downsizing, voluntary turnover rates, and the moderating role of HR practices. *Academy of Management Journal*, 51(2), 259–276.

Tsui, A. S., Pearce, J. L., Porter, L. W., & Tripoli, A. M. (1997). Alternative approaches to the employee–organization relationship: Does investment in employees pay off? *Academy of Management Journal*, 40(5), 1089–1997.

Wasti, S. (2005). Commitment profiles: Combinations of organizational commitment forms and job outcomes. *Journal of Vocational Behavior*, 67, 290–308.

Wheeler, A. R., Harris, K. J., & Sablynski, C. J. (2012). How do employees invest abundant resources? The mediating role of work effort in the job-embeddedness/job-performance relationship. *Journal of Applied Social Psychology*, 42(Suppl. 1), E244–E266.

Woo, S. E., & Allen, D. G. (2014). Toward an inductive theory of stayers and seekers in the organization. *Journal of Business and Psychology*, 29(4), 683–703.

Yao, X., Lee, T. W., Mitchell, T. R., Burton, J. P., & Sablynski, C. S. (2004). Job embeddedness: Current research and future directions. In R. W. Griffeth & P. W. Hom (Eds.), *Understanding Employee Retention and Turnover* (pp. 153–187). Greenwich, CT: Information Age.

6

NEW PERSPECTIVES ON CLASSIC TURNOVER ANTECEDENTS

In this chapter, we review promising approaches that advance the understanding of organizational withdrawal by elaborating new perspectives on classic turnover theories, models, constructs, or processes. Drawing from foundational work on how job attitudes, particularly job satisfaction and organizational commitment, drive the desire to leave, how perceptions of the ability to attain desirable alternatives drives the ease of leaving, and how the complex nature of job performance influences these processes, we focus on research about commitment profiles, job satisfaction trajectories, job performance, and ease of movement. These perspectives are important in their own right and also may provoke the revision of more complete theoretical formulations of withdrawal.

Organizational Commitment: Commitment Profiles

Central to all conceptualizations of turnover is that poor attitudes stimulate the termination process. Positing that commitment to company values and goals undermines thoughts of withdrawal (Mowday, Porter, & Steers, 1982), theorists of turnover (Price & Mueller, 1986; Steers & Mowday, 1981) have incorporated organizational commitment. Early meta-analyses found that commitment predicts withdrawal cognitions (Hom, Caranikas-Walker, Prussia, & Griffeth, 1992; Mathieu & Zajac, 1990), while confirmatory factor analyses affirmed its conceptual independence from other work-related attitudes such as job satisfaction (Brooke, Russell, & Price, 1988; Mathieu & Farr, 1991). Scholars of commitment universally contend that commitment predicts quits more accurately than does job satisfaction (Porter, Steers, Mowday, & Boulian, 1974) because resignation implies a rejection of the company, not necessarily of the job, which can be assumed elsewhere (Hom & Hulin, 1981).

The popularity of the notion of organizational commitment extends over decades. Becker (1960) first formally analyzed this construct and proposed the side bet notion, wherein several conditions under which "side bets" are made by the employee, organization, and culture encourage an employee to stay on the job. For example, generalized cultural expectations, impersonal bureaucratic arrangements, individual adjustments to social positions, and face-to-face interactions all bind an employee to the company "by default." In the 1970s, Porter and his colleagues (Mowday et al., 1982; Porter et al., 1974) advanced a new conceptualization, specifying commitment as comprising: (1) a strong belief in and acceptance of the organization's goals and values; (2) a willingness to exert considerable effort on behalf of the organization; and (3) a strong desire to maintain membership in the organization. They developed the organizational commitment questionnaire (OCQ) to assess this concept, and the OCQ eventually became the leading index for testing hypotheses about attachments to companies (see Mathieu & Zajac, 1990). Undertaking a longitudinal test, Porter et al. (1974) first demonstrated that commitment more effectively differentiated stayers and leavers than did job satisfaction. Later, Porter, Crampon, and Smith (1976) showed that differences in commitment between stayers and leavers grow as the time-lag between turnover and assessments of commitment shrinks.

Subsequently, Steers (1977) proposed and conducted a two-sample test of a model in which organizational commitment mediated three classes of antecedents (personal traits, such as need for achievement and age; job characteristics, such as task identity and feedback; and work experiences, such as group cohesion) and multiple consequences (quit intentions, attendance, turnover, and job performance). The relationship of commitment to turnover ($r = -.17$, $p \leq .05$) was relatively modest; still, Steers's framework initiated numerous scholarly explorations of the causes and outcomes of commitment. In a comprehensive meta-analysis, Mathieu and Zajac (1990) summarized studies on commitment's antecedents and consequences, organizing the results according to an expanded framework based on Steers (1977), and finding that committed employees quit less often ($r = -.28$) than do uncommitted employees. Similarly, turnover meta-analyses have reported commitment–turnover correlations corrected for predictor unreliability and sampling error of $-.27$ (Griffeth, Hom, & Gaertner, 2000) and $-.29$ (Rubenstein, Eberly, Lee, & Mitchell, 2018).

Despite its impressive pattern of relationships, organizational commitment research garnered criticisms on grounds of measurement and conceptualization. Though commitment predicts quits better than does job satisfaction, Mobley, Griffeth, Hand, and Meglino (1979) expressed reservations that the inclusion of intentions to quit on the OCQ scale possibly inflated its predictive validity. Hom and his colleagues (Hom & Hulin, 1981; Hom, Katerberg, & Hulin, 1979) statistically removed an independent measure of intentions to quit from correlations between turnover and attitudes. After those decisions were partialled out, correlations between commitment and quitting did *not* surpass correlations between satisfaction and quitting. Hom and Hulin (1981) thus concluded "that the predictive power of OC resides not in its assessing a more relevant employee attitude but in its assessing intention to withdraw from the organization" (p. 34). Subsequently, Bozeman and Perrewé (2001) used confirmatory factor analysis to identify six OCQ items overlapping with turnover cognitions items and recommended removing these items from the scale when studying turnover.

Over the years, other conceptualizations of commitment have surfaced. Reichers (1985) reconceptualized commitment in terms of different constituents, recognizing the influences (values and goals) of multiple reference groups (constituency) and roles in organizations. She posited three definitions: (1) side bets, or the rewards and costs of membership in an organization; (2) attributions, or the binding of the individual to behavior; and (3) congruence between the goals of the individual and the organization. This concept of "multiple commitments" is a significant theoretical milestone, refining as it does the original global conception of commitment (see Porter et al., 1974) by delineating its multiple facets. O'Reilly and Chatman (1986) also specified three dimensions of commitment to an organization: (1) compliance (instrumental involvement for extrinsic rewards); (2) identification (involvement based on desire for affiliation); and (3) internalization (involvement predicated on congruence between the values of the individual and the company). They developed an instrument to measure these bases and administered a survey to university personnel. Predictably, factor analysis substantiated three separate factors, and the survey showed that commitment based on internalization or identification increased organizational citizenship and decreased turnover. Compliance, however, weakened decisions to remain with the organization.

Similarly, Allen and Meyer (1993) identified three kinds of commitment: affective, continuance, and normative. Affective attachment corresponds to Porter's conception; continuance refers to the economic side bet approach espoused by Becker (1960); normative commitment, which is defined as moral responsibility to the organization, extends past perspectives. In two studies, Allen and Meyer developed measures of this multidimensional construct and then estimated relationships between these forms and antecedents of commitment. Results differentiated these forms, showing them to be rooted in disparate causes. Despite varying terminology, three dominant dimensions of commitment emerged: (1) attitudinal (internalization, identification [O'Reilly & Chatman, 1986] and affective [Allen & Meyer, 1993]); (2) calculative (compliance [O'Reilly & Chatman, 1986] and continuance [Allen & Meyer, 1993]); and (3) normative (Allen & Meyer, 1993). Differentiating attitudinal from calculative commitments, Mathieu and Zajac's (1990) meta-analysis revealed that attitudinal commitment correlated with job satisfaction and quit decisions more than did calculative commitment.

Recently, Klein, Molloy, and Brinsfield (2012) reconceptualized commitment by focusing on the types and targets of psychological bonds. They more narrowly defined commitment as a volitional bond grounded in dedication to and responsibility for a particular target. Similar to empirical efforts to separate items in commitment measures that overlap extensively with items measuring withdrawal cognitions, this definition conceptually distinguishes commitment bonds from retention and also facilitates simultaneous examination of multiple commitments. Klein et al. (2012)

also proposed a continuum of attachment bonds ranging from lower to higher in psychological involvement with the target: acquiescence, instrumental, commitment, and identification. Commitment bonds are volitional (as opposed to acquiescence or instrumental bonds, which may be coerced or grounded in avoiding significant loss), entail dedication to and responsibility for the target, and are most closely aligned with, yet distinct from, prior affective and normative conceptualizations of commitment. Importantly for our purposes, this conceptualization of commitment is conceptually distinct from retention, especially when focused on targets other than the organization. Nevertheless, an expected outcome of commitment bonds targeted at the organization is continuance: the motivation to continue the attachment bond that includes intentions and behaviors associated with continuing the attachment (Klein et al., 2012). Thus, we would still expect commitment bonds to the organization to be inversely associated with turnover.

This discussion of types and targets of commitment leads into one of the most interesting trends in commitment research with implications for understanding turnover: commitment profiles. Different types of organizational commitment (e.g., affective, normative, or continuance commitment) have most often been considered as individual predictor or outcome variables, or, less frequently, in terms of their interactions with each other in predicting outcomes (Gellatly, Meyer, & Luchak, 2006; Kabins, Xu, Bergman, Berry, & Willson, 2016). More recently, researchers are taking advantage of methodological approaches to developing person-centered profiles in which individuals are classified based on multiple types of commitment simultaneously (Kabins et al., 2016; Meyer & Parfyonova, 2010). Meyer, Stanley, and Parfyonova (2012) identified seven commonly identified profiles considering affective, normative, and continuance commitment: (1) high, (2) medium, and (3) low profiles with generally similar levels across the three types of commitment; (4) an affective dominant profile; (5) a continuance dominant profile; (6) an affective and normative dominant profile; and (7) a normative and continuance dominant profile. Kabins et al. (2016) further classified these as values-based profiles associated with a desire to stay connected and lower turnover (high, affective dominant, affective and normative dominant), exchange-based profiles associated with obligations to stay connected and modestly lower turnover (continuance dominant, normative and continuance dominant), and weak profiles with little motivation to stay connected (low, moderate), although the exchange-based profiles did not emerge in their multilevel latent profile analysis of meta-analytical data.

As an example of a profile-driven approach, Stanley, Vandenberghe, Vandenberg, and Bentein (2013) posited three profile-driven explanatory mechanisms for the link between commitment profiles and turnover: a self-determination theory perspective (Ryan & Deci, 2000) that profiles associated with internal motivations for staying are more strongly (inversely) related to turnover; an ease and desirability of movement perspective (March & Simon, 1958) that these motives act as independent forces influencing commitment profiles; and a contextual perspective that profiles driven by high levels of affective commitment shape the meaning of other components of profiles (Gellatly et al., 2006). This latter perspective is consistent with Kabins et al.'s (2016) contention that the overall experience of commitment is driven by affective commitment. In a sample of 712 alumni of a Belgian university, Stanley et al. (2013) used latent profile analysis to identify profiles and negative binomial regression with logistic regression to test their relationships with turnover. Their analysis identified six clusters: committed; moderately committed; not committed; affective and normative dominant; continuance dominant; and affective dominant. The not committed profile had significantly higher turnover than the committed, affective dominant, and affective and normative dominant profiles.

Stanley et al. (2013) suggested future research consider the effects of commitment profile change over time. Taking up that challenge, Xu and Payne (2018) adopted a three-step approach to latent profile analysis (Asparouhov & Muthen, 2014) and, in a sample of U.S. Army officers completing four surveys over a four-year period, examined the stability of commitment profiles over four years and the effects of commitment profiles on turnover up to three years later, also modeling turnover behavior in terms of the risk of leaving based on duration of staying within the organization. In their cross-sectional samples, they retained four profiles; two they characterized as weak commitment profiles (e.g., medium affective commitment) and two as values-based profiles (e.g., high affective commitment; Kabins et al., 2016). An exchange-based profile did not emerge in any of the samples. This latter finding, although at odds with commitment theory, is consistent with Kabins et al.'s (2016) meta-analytic results. It may be consistent with Klein et al.'s (2012) model of attachment bonds contending that instrumental and commitment bonds are different forms of attachment. Across the four waves, similar profiles emerged suggesting that the structure of the profiles was quite stable over four years (Xu & Payne, 2018). Similarly, relatively few individuals changed commitment profiles over the four-year period, suggesting substantial temporal stability.

Regarding relationships with turnover, Xu and Payne (2018) found that turnover and tenure varied systematically with commitment profiles and profile change. Specifically, values-based commitment profiles had significantly higher tenure, lower turnover rates, and lower turnover hazard compared with weak commitment profiles. The Kabins et al. (2016) multilevel meta-analysis similarly found that values-based commitment profiles had lower turnover rates than weak commitment profiles. Over time, Xu and Payne (2018) found that the survival probabilities for the four profiles decreased; however, the speed of the decrease varied among the four profiles. Survival probabilities for the value-based profiles decreased slowly over time, whereas survival probabilities for the weak commitment profiles dropped more sharply over time. For example, half of the individuals in a medium affective and low continuance commitment profile turned over by the fourth year. Similarly, individuals who maintained value-based profile membership over time were less likely to leave, and survival probabilities for those who maintained weak commitment profiles decreased sharply relative to those maintaining values-based profiles. Xu and Payne's (2018) results also showed that transition patterns from lower to higher commitment profiles (e.g., greater affective commitment) were associated with higher survival probabilities than transition patterns from higher to lower commitment profiles. For example, the survival probabilities of these latter individuals quickly dropped to zero.

Expanding beyond commitment profiles, there is promise in person-centered approaches for uncovering other constellations of profiles as they pertain to turnover. For example, Woo and Allen (2014) took an inductive approach to describe profiles of stayers and (job) seekers taking into account quit intentions, job search behaviors, and reasons for seeking. In a sample of 583 individuals residing and working full-time in the United States, they used latent class cluster analysis that identified four clusters: (1) *embedded stayers* who expressed the lowest thoughts of leaving, plans to leave, and job search behavior, and the highest endorsement for socio-emotional attachment; (2) *detached stayers* who had higher turnover intentions and job search behavior than embedded stayers (although lower than subsequent clusters), but relatively low socio-emotional attachment; (3) *dissatisfied stayers* who most often thought about leaving and planned to leave, and engaged in job search more than the prior two clusters, as well as the lowest endorsement for socio-emotional attachment; and (4) *script-driven seekers* who most often sought and secured other job offers, while most citing external reasons for leaving. Woo and Allen (2014) concluded that these clusters could be distinguished in terms of direction of action (i.e., intentions to stay or leave) and concreteness of action (tangible vs. abstract plans). Thus, future person-centered research may involve identifying participation or withdrawal clusters or profiles of individuals with similar motives and circumstances.

Job Satisfaction: Satisfaction Trajectories

As noted above, central to all conceptualizations of turnover is that poor attitudes stimulate the termination process. Traditional thinking (e.g., March & Simon, 1958; Mobley, 1977; Porter & Steers, 1973; Price, 1977) asserts that job dissatisfaction prompts turnover cognitions, presuming that a dissatisfying work environment motivates the desire to escape (Hulin, 1991). The focus on job satisfaction is deeply engrained in turnover scholarship and derives directly from the original formulation of March and Simon's (1958) theory of organizational equilibrium. In that model, in which the perceived desirability and the perceived ease of movement are the two most important considerations in an individual's decision to continue participating in the organization, the primary factor influencing perceived movement desirability is the individual's satisfaction with the job. That is, job satisfaction reduces desirability of movement. March and Simon (1958) identified three sources of job satisfaction. First, conformity of job characteristics to self-image enhances job satisfaction: "Dissatisfaction arises from a disparity between reality and the ego-ideal held by the individual. The greater the disparity, the more pronounced the desire to escape from the situation" (p. 94). Relevant self-image dimensions—namely, self-evaluations of independence, worth, and competencies or interests—are then satisfied (or frustrated) by supervisory practices, wages, participation in job assignment, and educational level. Besides person–job fit, predictability in instrumental relationships on the job and compatibility of work requirements with other role requirements (which hinges on congruency of work time patterns with those of other roles) promote job satisfaction.

Job satisfaction is the most widely studied predictor of turnover (Holtom, Mitchell, Lee, & Eberly, 2008). The focus on job (dis)satisfaction as the most important attitudinal predictor of turnover has been so influential and pervasive that it ultimately led to concerns that satisfaction-driven turnover became a dominant paradigm that overestimated satisfaction's role and importance. For example, commitment scholars, as noted above, contended that organizational commitment was conceptually and empirically more strongly linked with turnover, while turnover scholars developed models to explicitly explore non-satisfaction paths to turnover (e.g., the unfolding model; Lee & Mitchell, 1994). Indeed, Allen, Bryant, and Vardaman (2010) called the idea that "people quit because they are dissatisfied with their jobs" one of the prime managerial myths and misconceptions about turnover. Indeed, recent studies based on interviews with former employees reveal that job dissatisfaction is the driving force in fewer than half of individual turnover decisions (Lee, Mitchell, Holtom, McDaniel, & Hill, 1999).

Still, job dissatisfaction remains one of the most *consistent* attitudinal predictors of turnover. In Griffeth et al.'s (2000) meta-analysis, the correlation between job satisfaction and turnover corrected for sampling and measurement errors is −.22. This correlation in Rubenstein et al.'s (2018) meta-analysis is −.28. Although our focus is on overall job satisfaction, there is also considerable evidence that various facets of satisfaction are also consistently, if more modestly, related to turnover—for example, supervisor satisfaction −.13; coworker satisfaction −.13; pay satisfaction −.08 (Griffeth et al., 2000). Based on this "discouraging" state of affairs, a new trend in research on attitudinal effects on turnover is to consider the dynamic nature of how job satisfaction changes over time and how its trajectory may also affect turnover decisions.

Indeed, Rubenstein et al. (2018) concluded their meta-analysis by explicitly calling for turnover researchers to focus future efforts on examining how turnover antecedents grow, decline, or stagnate over time. They note that most research underlying their meta-analysis is based on a static cohort approach assessing turnover antecedents on only one occasion (Steel, 2002). This methodology for studying turnover is so pervasive that Allen, Hancock, Vardaman, and McKee (2014) referred to it as a "dominant analytical mindset," despite longitudinal findings that the assumption that attitudinal antecedents are largely stable is not realistic, as they often fluctuate and their changes are systematically meaningful (Kammeyer-Mueller, Wanberg, Glomb, & Ahlburg, 2005). Thus, Rubenstein et al. (2018)

emphasize that a dynamic perspective assessing temporal shifts in causal influences may increase understanding of turnover decisions.

As Kammeyer-Mueller et al. (2005) note, turnover scholars have long acknowledged temporal dynamics in turnover theory—for example, models envisioning a progression of withdrawal behaviors (Hulin, 1991) or predicting turnover speed (Lee et al., 1999). In an early test, Kammeyer-Mueller et al. (2005) examined a turnover model with five waves of predictor data. In a sample of 932 newcomers, 606 of whom responded to all surveys, dynamic work satisfaction predicted employment duration and there was a marginally significant trend for work satisfaction to decline among leavers compared to stayers.

Although some turnover theory acknowledges the likelihood that satisfaction can change—for example, in response to job changes or shocks (Lee & Mitchell, 1994; Mobley, 1982b)—there is little consideration of how and why these changes might influence turnover differently or uniquely relative to absolute levels of satisfaction. Consider this example, paraphrased from Chen, Ployhart, Cooper-Thomas, Anderson, and Bliese (2011): two employees report a 4 on a five-point satisfaction scale. Extant turnover theory suggests these employees should report similar intentions to turnover and have a similar likelihood of actually turning over. However, what if one employee has recently changed from a 3 to a 4, while the other has recently changed from a 5 to a 4? We might expect that the employee experiencing declining job satisfaction would differ in meaningful ways in terms of turnover intentions and likelihood of turnover relative to the employee experiencing increasing job satisfaction, even though their levels of satisfaction are the same.

Chen et al. (2011) attempted to provide a theoretical account of job satisfaction change and turnover. They focus their model on explaining the dynamic nature of job satisfaction and turnover intentions. For example, Chen et al. (2011) explain how prospect theory (Kahneman & Tversky, 1979, 1984) suggests that change in subjective experiences is likely to be at least as salient as absolute levels, and that decreases in job satisfaction will be more salient and carry more meaning than increases. At the same time, trajectories may provide a sense of the velocity or direction of the likely future direction of circumstances (Chen et al., 2011; Hsee & Abelson, 1991). Thus, individuals experiencing declining job satisfaction may grow to expect that circumstances will continue to worsen, with the opposite true in the case of increasing job satisfaction, akin to spirals (Lindsley, Brass, & Thomas, 1995). This is consistent with arguments that the likelihood of amelioration moderates the effects of justice perceptions on withdrawal (Aquino, Griffeth, Allen, & Horn, 1997), while also suggesting that consistent or sharp trends or trajectories may influence perceptions of the likelihood of amelioration. Applying the conservation of resources perspective, Chen et al. (2011) further suggest that declining job satisfaction is particularly likely to create emotional distress, and presumably higher turnover intentions (Hobfoll, Johnson, Ennis, & Jackson, 2003).

Chen et al. (2011) tested these ideas using mixed effects growth models in three longitudinal samples: 725 British Army soldiers during military training; 198 employees who joined a multinational consulting firm; and 800 U.S. Army soldiers stationed in Europe. In each sample, they found that job satisfaction and turnover intentions both changed over time for many participants, and that average job satisfaction level (across waves) had a negative relationship with changes in turnover intentions. They also found that job satisfaction *change* was negatively related to turnover intentions change, explaining up to 16% of the variance in turnover intentions change beyond control variables. Although turnover intentions are psychologically proximal antecedents of turnover that typically explain the most variance in turnover decisions, they are far from perfect predictors of turnover behavior (Allen, Weeks, & Moffitt, 2005; Vardaman, Taylor, Allen, Gondo, & Amis, 2015). Thus, the most relevant analysis by Chen et al. (2011) for our purposes used actual voluntary turnover data from the first sample. They found that the temporal change in turnover intentions over time, rather than their average level during this period, predicted actual turnover. Job satisfaction change only predicted turnover through an indirect effect on turnover intentions change. Thus, job satisfaction change influences turnover above and beyond job satisfaction level indirectly via turnover intentions change. Interestingly, job satisfaction decline and improvement showed no significant differences. A fourth sample of 85 MBA students replicated the finding that job satisfaction change is related to turnover intentions change with turnover intentions measured subsequently to job satisfaction.

Focusing on turnover behavior as the outcome, Liu, Mitchell, Lee, Holtom, & Hinkin (2012) considered employees' and business units' job satisfaction trajectories over time, as well as variability of employees' job satisfaction trajectories. Liu et al. (2012) contend that business unit satisfaction trajectories, as well as within-unit variance in employee job satisfaction trajectories (i.e., dispersion), furnish additional informational and social cues individuals use for interpreting their own work experiences. They collected job satisfaction data from 5,270 employees from 175 business units of a U.S. recreation and hospitality organization three times over six-month intervals, with turnover data collected one year later. Using hierarchical generalized linear modeling, they found that individual and unit-level job satisfaction trajectories were negatively related to individual turnover, and that unit-level job satisfaction trajectory was negatively related to unit-level turnover rate. Thus, Liu et al. (2012) demonstrate that satisfaction trajectories do indeed influence turnover over and above satisfaction levels, and extend this line of thinking to unit-level turnover rates as well as individual turnover decisions. They also note that the traditional static individual-level predictor approach explained only 5% of the variance in individual turnover, while the dynamic multilevel approach incorporating individual and unit-level trajectories explained 43% of the variance in individual turnover. Liu et al.'s (2012) study also shows the importance of social context: when an employee is "out of step" with their work context (i.e., this individual's own satisfaction trajectory is moving in the opposite direction of the unit-level satisfaction trajectory), the unit-level trend dampens the impact of his or her personal attitudinal trajectory on turnover decisions.

Much of the existing research on job satisfaction trajectories focuses on organizational newcomers, perhaps because of the tendency for them to enter with high expectations and to experience attitude declines soon thereafter (a "honeymoon-hangover" effect; Boswell, Boudreau, & Tichy, 2005). Following this trend, Wang, Hom, and Allen (2017) examined how organizational socialization activities affect job satisfaction trajectories, turnover intentions trajectories, and turnover behavior. They studied new hires in a large entertainment and gaming organization, surveying employees four times and collecting data on their turnover. Their results affirmed the hangover effect in that the average job satisfaction trajectory is negative. Most relevant for our purposes, job satisfaction trajectories were inversely related to turnover intentions trajectories, which were positively related to turnover behavior. The authors also concluded that job satisfaction and quit intention trajectories translated how socialization tactics, specifically those focused on the social context, aggravated hangover effects on turnover. Given the mediating role of turnover intentions trajectories found in multiple studies, an important avenue for future research is to assess the extent to which this withdrawal process operates in a similar or different manner from more static processes. Wang et al. (2017) also demonstrated interesting curvilinear relationships, showing that socialization tactics are inversely related to job satisfaction trajectories at low to moderate levels; however, at higher levels, socialization tactics begin to slow satisfaction declines. Indeed, extensive socialization tactics focused on the social context can dampen the hangover effect and reduce newcomer turnover.

Given the promise of considering the role of job satisfaction trajectories for understanding turnover, there is likely promise in considering the dynamic effects of other turnover antecedents as well. For example, there is emerging research demonstrating that employees experiencing steeper declines over time in organizational commitment more likely quit (Bentein, Vandenberghe, Vandenberg, & Stinglhamber, 2005); that leavers become progressively less committed over time in comparison to stayers who have more stable commitment trajectories (Kammeyer-Mueller et al., 2005); and that changing commitment profiles are also related to turnover (Xu & Payne, 2018).

Rubenstein et al. (2018) encourage building on these results by considering how other turnover antecedents such as absenteeism, job search, job embeddedness, or work–life conflict show dynamic trajectories that may predict quitting. Justice, in particular, is a construct with a burgeoning body of research investigating its dynamic qualities that is likely related to turnover processes. For example, Hausknecht, Sturman, and Roberson (2011) found employee justice perceptions varied over a year, while Matta, Scott, Colquitt, Koopman, and Passantino (2017) found justice perceptions to vary within just a three-week period, and Rubenstein, Allen, and Bosco (2019) found in a study of 4,348 banking employees that justice trajectories over a four-year period interacted with justice levels in predicting voluntary turnover. These studies suggest further inquiries into temporal changes in other turnover antecedents as well as their interactive and curvilinear effects. Given encouraging findings noted here, as well as Kammeyer-Mueller et al.'s (2005) demonstration that a model including trajectories of several turnover antecedents improved turnover variance explained by the static model by over 100%, future research into change trajectories in the turnover process is clearly warranted.

Job Performance: Complex Relationships

Although turnover research has largely been concerned with how many people leave and identifying the antecedents and processes that influence that decision, it also matters, of course, *who* is leaving (Allen, 2008). For that reason, there is an important stream of research addressing the relationship between job performance and turnover—if high performers are more likely to quit, then turnover is far more problematic than if low performers are leaving. This literature has evolved in several ways to clarify the role of job performance in the turnover process. Initially, the focus was on considering job performance in conjunction with turnover to conceptualize and define functional or dysfunctional turnover (as discussed earlier in Chapter 1).

Researchers then sought to determine if performance and voluntary turnover were reliably related and to identify the sign of this relationship. Early studies characterized this relationship as *negative*: poor performers quit more often (e.g., see Keller, 1984; McEvoy & Cascio, 1987; Sheridan & Vredenburgh, 1978; Stumpf & Dawley, 1981); *positive*: good performers quit more often (e.g., see Allison, 1974; Bassett, 1967; Blau & Schoenherr, 1971; Lazarsfeld & Thielens, 1958; Pavalko, 1970; Pederson, 1973); or even *indeterminate* (e.g., see Bluedorn & Abelson, 1981; Mobley, 1982a; Price, 1977). Adding to this confusion, some researchers characterized this relationship as *zero* (Martin, Price, & Mueller, 1981). Ultimately, meta-analyses (Bycio, Hackett, & Alvares, 1990; Griffeth et al., 2000; McEvoy & Cascio, 1987; Rubenstein et al., 2018; Williams & Livingstone, 1994) have largely demonstrated an *inverse* correlation between performance and turnover—for example, corrected correlations of −.17 (Griffeth et al., 2000) and −.21 (large outlier included; Hom, Roberson, & Ellis, 2008) or −.08 (outlier excluded; Rubenstein et al., 2018).

However, meta-analyses have also identified moderators of the correlation between performance and turnover, and acknowledge that null or positive correlations are possible under certain conditions. For one, short time lapses between measurements of performance and turnover attenuated their association (McEvoy & Cascio, 1987). Explaining this moderation, McEvoy and Cascio argued that the relationship appears only after employees decide to leave. After that decision is formed, job performance declines precipitously before the employee quits. Contrary to this finding, Griffeth et al. (2000) found the relationship significantly more negative with turnover lags shorter than one year compared with lags greater than one year. McEvoy and Cascio also found that national unemployment rates affect the correlation, with job scarcity increasing it so that it becomes more *negative*. Williams and Livingstone (1994) found that contingent pay systems strengthen correlations between performance and quitting, with incentive pay accelerating exits by marginal performers. Griffeth et al. (2000) uncovered an even starker contrast with a negative performance–turnover relationship with reward contingencies and a positive relationship in conditions of no reward contingency. Rubenstein et al. (2018) found that the performance–turnover relationship was strengthened in contexts where the mean withdrawal cognitions surrounding the individual were higher, suggesting a social or contagion-based mechanism.

Whereas the bulk of this research focuses on voluntary turnover, Jackofsky (1984) initiated investigations combining voluntary and involuntary quits to posit a curvilinear U-shaped relationship between performance and overall turnover. Extrapolating March and Simon's (1958) theory, Jackofsky reasoned that at low performance levels, involuntary turnover (dismissal) is high. As performance increases to some middle level, both involuntary and voluntary exits decline, presumably because average performers cannot easily find alternatives, but neither do they face dismissal. As performance increases beyond the middle range, however, voluntary turnover increases because good performers can change jobs easily. Testing this curvilinear hypothesis, Jackofsky, Ferris, and Breckenridge (1986) found significant U-shaped curves that accounted for 3% and 17.6% of the turnover variance among accountants and truck drivers, respectively. This study is noteworthy because truckers' performance was measured objectively, by the revenue earned. Later, Mossholder, Bedeian, Norris, Giles, and Field (1988) replicated those curvilinear relationships in a study of operative electronic employees and textile supervisors. Williams and Livingstone's (1994) meta-analysis summarized results from eight studies and found that curvilinear relationships between performance and turnover hold reliably.

Subsequent research also considered the likelihood that the desirability of job movement, defined as job satisfaction, interacts with performance to affect turnover. Given their potentially greater mobility, effective performers may more easily translate their dissatisfaction with the job into departure than can poor performers: "Thus, the negative relationship between satisfaction and turnover should be stronger for higher, as compared to lower, performers" (Jackofsky, 1984, p. 79). Mossholder et al. (1988) tested this prediction with two samples and found that the interaction held for operators, accounting for 1% of the turnover variance, but not for textile supervisors. Opposing Jackofsky's increased alternatives perspective, Lance (1988) advanced a contingent rewards rationale (Dreher, 1982; Spencer & Steers, 1981), theorizing that there is a stronger negative relationship between job satisfaction and turnover for *poor* performers than there is for good performers. Supposedly, most firms retain the good performers by rewarding them more generously than they reward poor performers, which decreases the latter's morale (Zenger, 1992). Poor performers are more likely to be "pushed" from the job by dissatisfaction; good performers are readily "pulled" from their present jobs by factors unrelated to their own satisfaction, by, for instance, unsolicited job offers, movement to a higher-level job with another company, or incidental job search resulting in an alternative employment opportunity. Using turnover intentions as a dependent variable, Lance sustained the contingent rewards hypothesis for first-line supervisory and hourly technical groups, but not for other occupational groups.

Subsequent investigations have extended these lines of inquiry as well as moving in newer directions. Trevor, Gerhart, and Boudreau (1997) explicitly set out to extend the work on curvilinearity and moderators in the job performance–turnover relationship. These authors integrated several important points from prior work: that the relationship between desirability of movement and turnover likely depends on the nature of reward systems; that ease and desirability of movement should be considered simultaneously; and that the performance–turnover relationship may be nonlinear. Consistent with Jackofsky's (1984) perspective, Trevor et al. (1997) proposed a curvilinear relationship in which *voluntary turnover* would be highest among low performers, who presumably find their low performance dissatisfying and also likely receive less recognition and fewer rewards, and among high performers, whose performance provides them numerous employment alternatives. However, they also proposed that this link would depend on the extent to which higher performers actually receive greater rewards, using salary growth as in indicator of underlying pay-for-performance linkages. Similarly, they proposed that promotions would indicate underlying reward-for-performance linkages as well as serving as an externally verifiable signal regarding performance; thus, promotions could attenuate desire to leave while also promoting the ease of leaving.

Sampling 5,143 exempt employees from a single organization, Trevor et al. (1997) observed an inverse correlation between job performance and voluntary turnover ($r = -.20$). More importantly, they confirmed significant curvilinearity with turnover probability greater for the lowest and highest performers relative to average performers, thus confirming nonlinear performance–turnover relationships. They also found a significant moderating effect of salary growth such that when salary growth was lower, turnover probability for the highest performers was greater; however, when salary growth was higher, top performer turnover probability was lower. The results regarding the moderation of promotions were more difficult to interpret, but appeared to facilitate low performer ease of movement, perhaps by providing an external signal of employability.

Around the same time period, Allen and Griffeth (199 similar model. Their approach emphasizes that job pe· simultaneous and sometimes conflicting effects on perceiv. of leaving, while also identifying two key moderators. Impe explicitly incorporated key theoretical mediators into the process; . instead of assuming that higher performers perceive more alternatives, pe. alternatives are explicitly assessed. Similarly, they positioned turnover intentio. as the proximal antecedent to turnover behavior, consistent with other turnover theorizing.

In Allen and Griffeth's (1999) multi-route model, they described three pathways by which job performance influences turnover. One is through cognitive and affective evaluations of the desire to leave the organization. In general, high job performance is likely to reduce the desire to leave by increasing intrinsic satisfaction, improving job-related attitudes such as satisfaction and commitment associated with presumably greater rewards and recognition, and increased opportunities for internal opportunities, especially in larger organizations. This negative relationship with desirability of movement would then make the withdrawal process and subsequent turnover less likely, consistent with the general negative performance–turnover relationship often found. Importantly, though, this path is moderated by the extent to which rewards, recognition, and internal opportunities are truly contingent on performance, consistent with Trevor et al.'s (1997) positioning of pay-for-performance indicators.

The second pathway is through actual and perceived job market mobility. Higher job performance likely increases the number and quality of alternative jobs an individual could acquire. This positive relationship with ease of movement would make the withdrawal process, especially job market scanning and job search behaviors, and subsequent turnover more likely. Conflicting directions of the desirability of movement and ease of movement pathways may account for the mixed findings observed regarding the direct performance–turnover relationship. At the same time, this pathway likely depends on the extent to which alternative employers are able to identify and verify high performance, what Allen and Griffeth (1999) refer to as "visibility of performance." Trevor et al. (1997) suggest that promotions could serve as a visible indicator of high performance. Incumbents in many occupations cannot provide any objective documentation of their work achievements to other prospective employers, who must rely on less trustworthy résumés or references to discern an applicant's credentials. University professors, for example, can list scholarly publications to document (and publicize) their accomplishments, and Schwab (1991) found that accomplished scholars more readily quit for other academic posts. The achievements of many professionals such as professional athletes, top executives, and scientists and engineers may be visible or objectively verifiable; those of incumbents in other jobs may not.

Allen and Griffeth's (1999) multi-route model also suggests a more direct path from job performance to turnover in response to performance-related shocks. The unfolding model of turnover (Lee & Mitchell, 1994) suggests that many turnover decisions are not a result of job dissatisfaction or an intensive search for alternatives; instead, particularly jarring events may lead individuals to reconsider their employment relationship. There are likely numerous performance-related shocks that could trigger consideration of leaving. For example, low performance resulting in negative or particularly harsh performance feedback could trigger the withdrawal process; conversely, a high performer who was previously quite satisfied could receive an unsolicited job offer that leads directly to quitting, or a high performer whose performance feedback does not seem commensurate with contributions could develop turnover intentions.

Taken together, this model suggests considering the simultaneous effects of reward contingencies and performance visibility. When reward contingencies are high and performance visibility is low, we expect the traditional negative performance–turnover relationship: high performers are being rewarded appropriately yet their high performance does not necessarily provide additional labor market opportunities. When reward contingencies are low and performance visibility is high, we might expect a problematic positive relationship: high performers are not being rewarded for their extra contributions and they are able to document their value to prospective employers. When both are high or low, effects are complex, may result in weak observed relationships because of contrasting influences, and the turnover of high performers likely depends on other contextual factors, such as labor market conditions.

Allen and Griffeth (2001) tested elements of this model in a sample of 130 employees of a medical services organization. Job performance was not significantly correlated with turnover in their sample. A structural equation modeling test demonstrated that job performance was positively associated with perceived alternatives, which increased turnover intentions and subsequent turnover behavior, consistent with the ease-of-movement pathway. However, although job satisfaction was negatively related to turnover, job performance was not significantly related to job satisfaction in this sample. Adding moderators provided a more nuanced picture as both moderating effects were significant. The relationship between job performance and satisfaction was significantly positive under high contingent rewards, and negative but not significant under low contingent rewards; the relationship between performance and perceived alternatives was significantly positive under high visibility, and negative but not significant under low visibility. These complex contrasting effects explain the lack of bivariate correlation between performance and turnover, and subsequent exploration of the data showed a remarkable contrast in the performance–turnover relationship for individuals reporting high contingent rewards and low performance visibility ($r = -.33$) compared with those reporting low contingent rewards and high performance visibility ($r = .32$). Consistent with Allen and Griffeth's (1999) predictions, high performers less often quit (than lower performers) under the former circumstances but more likely quit under the latter circumstances.

Salamin and Hom (2005) extended these perspectives in a large ($N = 11,098$) sample of Swiss bankers. Although, like Trevor et al. (1997), they considered pay growth as an indicator of contingent rewards, they also considered merit bonuses as a potentially more relevant moderator, because merit bonuses are more contingent on performance than are base pay increases, consistent with the idea of maximally contingent incentives (Harrison, Virick, & William, 1996). Similarly, while Salamin and Hom (2005) included promotions as an indicator of movement capital (again, like Trevor et al., 1997), they also incorporated multilevel promotions as a potentially more powerful signal to the labor market about worker productivity. Performance and turnover exhibited the typical negative bivariate correlation ($r = -.20$) in their sample. Using Cox regression, Salamin and Hom (2005) replicated a significant curvilinear performance–turnover relationship in which there was a generally increasingly positive relationship between job performance and job survival rates, except for top performers who exhibited a decreasing survival rate and remained employed for a shorter duration than those just below them on the performance metric.

With respect to moderation, salary growth did not moderate the relationship between performance and turnover hazard; however, bonus pay did moderate such that top performers are more likely to quit when they receive no bonus pay but are less likely to quit with significant bonuses. Neither promotions nor multilevel promotions were significant moderators; however, promotion rate decreased turnover risk, while multilevel promotions *increased* turnover risk substantially. Thus, even though multilevel promotions did not moderate the performance–turnover relationship, they may serve as strong external signals of competence and movement capital.

Given that performance is dynamic rather than static, it is crucial to attend to the dynamic nature of performance in considering how performance relates to turnover (Harrison et al., 1996). For example, Harrison et al. (1996) demonstrated in a sample of field sales representatives that current performance better predicts voluntary turnover than average performance, and also that the slope of change in performance from month to month (performance velocity) improved the prediction of turnover risk, similar to the research on satisfaction trajectories reviewed earlier. Sturman and Trevor (2001) extended the examination of performance trends over longer time periods of up to eight months. They also considered the possibility that dynamic and current performance could interact to influence turnover, suggesting that performance trends would be more important for lower current performers than higher. Sturman and Trevor (2001) used hierarchical linear modeling and proportional hazards analysis to test hypotheses in a multistate sample of 1,413 loan originators from a financial services organization. Consistent with prevailing theory, current performance was negatively related to the likelihood of voluntary turnover. The two-month trend in performance was also negatively related to the likelihood of voluntary turnover, as was the consideration of longer performance trends of up to eight months. These findings suggest considerable robustness to the idea that performance trends are important for understanding the role of job performance in individual turnover decisions. Further, current performance and performance trend interacted significantly such that the negative relationship between performance trend and turnover likelihood was *strong* when current job performance was lower but weak when current performance was higher.

Attempting to integrate prior work with the shock-driven perspective of the unfolding model, Becker, Cropanzano, and Sanfey (2011) suggested that lower performers are especially susceptible to shocks associated with downward performance change. Allen and Griffeth (1999) suggested performance-related shocks as one pathway connecting job performance to turnover, and Becker et al. (2011) specify performance ratings changes, especially downward changes, as likely to represent performance-related shocks. They estimated proportional hazards rate models in a sample of 1,755 individuals entering a division of a Fortune 500 engineering technology company. The overall relationship between performance level and turnover was negative and there was a significant curvilinear relationship, although it more closely resembled the Salamin and Hom (2005) curve where the inflection occurs at the highest levels of performance, as opposed to the more pronounced U-shape observed by Trevor et al. (1997). However, performance change did not significantly add to the prediction of turnover. There was, though, a significant interaction effect between performance level and performance change, suggesting that low performers' turnover was more affected by performance change, consistent with Sturman and Trevor (2001). In sum, Becker et al. (2011) showed that individuals more likely quit subsequent to declining performance ratings, especially for already low performers.

Finally, evidence suggests the performance–turnover relationship may vary across cultures (Sturman, Shao, & Katz, 2012). This is an important avenue for exploration given the U.S.-centric perspective of turnover research in major management and psychology journals (Allen & Vardaman, 2017). Allen and Vardaman (2017) suggested culture should influence turnover process through impacts on employee expectations regarding working conditions, employment terms, managerial roles, and psychological contracts; the relative salience of attitudes; the interpretation of organizational communication; and the relative value of work and familial roles and responsibilities. All of these are likely intertwined with processes linking job performance and turnover. The Salamin and Hom (2005) study investigated the performance–turnover relationship in Switzerland and replicated the curvilinear relationship found in prior work. This is an important replication that assesses generalizability to another cultural context, especially given relatively high labor mobility, cultural norms for performance excellence, strong employment protections, preferences for internal hiring, and higher collectivism relative to the United States (Salamin & Hom, 2005). Still, Switzerland is not maximally culturally divergent from the United States, and additional international research is valuable.

Sturman et al. (2012) investigated the performance–turnover relationship in a sample of 3,211 white-collar employees of a multinational organization across 24 countries. Although they generally expected a curvilinear relationship to generalize across country contexts, they also expected variation in the nature of this relationship. They examined the cultural dimensions of in-group collectivism, power distance, uncertainty avoidance, and performance orientation (Hofstede, 1980; House, Hanges, Javidan, Dorfman, & Gupta, 2004). More specifically, Sturman et al. (2012) posited that the performance–turnover relationship and observed curvilinearity would be weaker in more collectivist, higher power distance, and higher uncertainty avoidance cultures, but stronger in higher performance orientation cultures. They observed the familiar negative correlation between performance and voluntary turnover ($r = -.11$) across the sample. Using hierarchical linear modeling with a Bernoulli model, analogous to logistic regression, they demonstrated a significant negative linear relationship as well as a significant curvilinear relationship across countries.

Sturman et al. (2012) also found significant across-country differences, and significant results consistent with hypotheses for all four cultural dimensions. In particular, the familiar U-shaped or J-shaped turnover–performance curves appeared in cultures characterized by low collectivism, low power distance, low uncertainty avoidance, or high performance orientation (all generally consistent with U.S. culture). Alternatively, high collectivist, high power distance, high uncertainty avoidance, and low performance orientation cultures showed less pronounced performance–turnover curvatures. Sturman et al. (2012) thus concluded "that there is a generalizable nonlinear relationship between performance and turnover, characterized by a quadratic functional form that is moderated by cultural dimensions" (p. 56). The next step for research in this domain may be to assess the cross-cultural generalizability of complex models incorporating moderators such as reward contingency and performance visibility as well as dynamic performance trajectories.

Movement Ease: Does It Explain Quits?

Drawing from a well-established tenet that "under nearly all conditions the most accurate single predictor of labor turnover is the state of the economy," March and Simon (1958, p. 100) positioned perceived ease of movement as one of the primary mechanisms underpinning individual decisions to continue organizational participation. They proposed that ample extra-organizational alternatives promote perceived ease of movement. In turn, business activity, personal attributes (e.g., age, sex, education, and tenure), and number of firms visible determine the number of perceived alternatives. March and Simon (1958) further conceptualized that company prestige, company size, production of a well-known product, number of high-status occupations and employees, and rapid growth influence a firm's visibility. In addition, the individual's residence and number of outside organizations to which she belongs increase her personal contacts, which expands the number of visible firms.

Because companies also scan people, an individual's own visibility increases the number of organizations seeking to employ her. Such visibility among individuals may depend on the heterogeneity of personal contacts, high social status, and individual uniqueness. March and Simon (1958) theorized that an individual's propensity to seek employment boosts the number of visible companies. Job satisfaction and habituation in turn shape the propensity to search: "Dissatisfaction makes movement more desirable and also (by stimulating search) makes it appear more feasible" (p. 105). By contrast, habituation to a particular job, which mounts with age and job tenure, diminishes the propensity to search.

Although few studies have directly tested March and Simon's model in its entirety, their conceptualization nonetheless influenced successive generations of theorists. Although a cornerstone for most theories, various indicators of movement ease—whether objective (e.g., unemployment rates) or subjective (e.g., employee perceptions of alternatives)—modestly predict *individual* turnover decisions. For example, Griffeth et al.'s (2000) meta-analysis found a corrected correlation between perceived alternatives and turnover of .15, while Rubenstein et al. (2018) found a corrected correlation of .23. Such findings are statistically significant and meaningful, but considerably weaker than other predictors. This state of affairs is surprising given the prominent place of job mobility in turnover theories and the common-sense notion that individuals with more alternatives are more likely to take advantage of them. Below, we summarize the impact of this thinking on several classic turnover theories and review more recent work that demonstrates the persistent influence of March and Simon's explanatory scheme and attempts to refine perceived ease of movement in turnover models.

Reviewing empirical tests on job alternatives, Hulin, Roznowski, and Hachiya (1985) concluded that perceptual estimates of labor market prospects have predicted turnover poorly, whereas aggregate labor market statistics, such as unemployment rates, predicted turnover rates consistently and strongly (although not necessarily individual turnover decisions). To account for such discrepant findings, they proposed that work alternatives can directly affect job satisfaction, a reversal of the longstanding premise that satisfaction influences alternatives by initiating search. This important interplay among job search, perceptions of alternatives, and attitudes was described in a cybernetic model by Steel (2002), a model addressed in depth in Chapter 7. Hulin et al. (1985) suggested that job opportunities directly induce turnover because employees quit when they are *certain* about securing other employment, not because they surmise from local unemployment data that there is a *probability* of a job. This reconceptualization envisioned a different role in the turnover process for job opportunities, and they hypothesized three mechanisms to explain why perceived alternatives might minimally affect individual turnover.

One is that different economies produce different workforces. Hulin et al. (1985) argued that economic expansion attracts casual or marginal workers into the labor force. They do not normally work regularly, but prosperous times lure them into full-time employment because the job surplus drives up wages (and relaxes hiring standards). Nevertheless, marginal employees do not plan to stay employed for very long. After accumulating enough funds, they will quit to pursue more pleasurable or less stressful avocations. Given their weak orientation toward work, these workers are unlikely, when quitting, to engage in the complex cognitive processes theorized by turnover scholars. A second is that economic activities, such as employment levels, directly influence job satisfaction. High unemployment reduces individuals' comparison levels for alternatives (Thibaut & Kelly, 1959), thus bolstering job satisfaction. By comparison, low unemployment and plentiful alternatives promote dissatisfaction and intentions to quit. During prosperous economies, foregone alternatives become "opportunity costs" that employees incur to maintain membership in their present organization. The third mechanism is that job opportunities affect turnover directly and not necessarily through intentions to quit. Presumably, most employees do not quit merely on the chance of finding an alternative, but when they have actual job offers. The more jobs there are available, the more likely dissatisfied employees can find and obtain other jobs, allowing them to leave unsatisfactory positions. Hulin et al. (1985) further noted that many leavers may leave the labor force to engage in other activities rather than quit for another job, which may also explain why perceptions of job alternatives poorly translate into departures. Hulin et al. (1985) thus advanced multiple mechanisms to clarify why ease of movement, as originally conceived by March and Simon (1958), may not underpin quit decisions—especially by marginal drifters and leavers seeking alternatives other than work.

Another research stream focused on the conceptualization and operationalization of perceived alternatives to work, raising construct and measurement issues to the fore. Perceived alternatives and economic opportunities constitute different conceptualizations at different levels of analysis about the availability of jobs. Economic opportunities refer to an objective condition about job availability and may affect turnover or moderate its influences. By contrast, perceived alternatives represent an employee's perceptions of the labor market. In much organizational research, the effects of perceived alternatives on individual turnover are weaker or less consistent relative to labor-economic findings of strong effects of unemployment rates on quit rates.

Griffeth and Hom (1988) proposed that imprecision, ambiguity, and diversity in operationalizations of perceived alternatives possibly understated its effects on turnover. Different conceptualizations of movement ease in various theories spawned alternative representations. March and Simon (1958), Price and Mueller (1981, 1986), and Steers and Mowday (1981) considered the number and availability of job opportunities, whereas Farrell and Rusbult (1981) emphasized their quality. Mobley (1977), Mobley, Horner, and Hollingsworth (1978), and Mobley et al. (1979) stressed both attainability and desirability of alternatives, whereas Billings and Wemmerus (1983) construed perceived alternatives as a personal attribute, hope, arguing that an employee may be optimistic that viable alternatives exist without necessarily knowing the actual number or quality of those alternatives.

Inviting more confusion, empirical operationalizations often misrepresent corresponding conceptual definitions. Price and Mueller (1981, 1986) embraced both number and availability of alternatives, but their measure combined a subjective estimation of job vacancies in the labor market and a personal estimation of the chances of finding alternatives (i.e., they were measuring hope). Most models imply that specific positions lure employees away from their present job (Hulin et al., 1985), but existing measures often reference vague, general impressions of alternatives (see Youngblood, Mobley, & Meglino, 1983). Indeed, the typical measurement is determined by simply asking employees to estimate the probability of finding an acceptable alternative (see Mobley et al., 1978).

Griffeth and Hom (1988) compared the relative validity of several operationalizations of perceived alternatives within the context of Mobley et al.'s (1979) turnover model. They found that no measure of perceived alternatives made a significant independent contribution to the prediction of turnover beyond job satisfaction and expected utility of the present job. Surprisingly, perceptions of specific jobs predicted intentions to quit *less accurately* than did more general perceptions of the labor market. Though a pioneering effort, perceived alternatives may have limited influence on decisions to quit for their sample of nurses (who may quit for alternatives apart from work or look for other employment *after* quitting), and deficient representation of alternatives (considering only major hospitals within the metropolitan area, thereby excluding smaller hospitals and jobs outside the city or in different states) likely weakened their measures of perceived alternatives.

Steel and Griffeth (1989) proposed that methodological artifacts may attenuate observed relationships between perceived alternatives and turnover. One methodological problem is the predominance of occupationally homogeneous samples in research on turnover, which may restrict variance in perceptions of employment opportunities. Indeed, Allen et al. (2014), in their review of turnover analytical mindsets in 406 articles with 447 turnover studies, concluded that the average sample was 95% from one occupational group; the median was 100%. Testing the impact of occupational homogeneity, Steel and Griffeth

(1989) correlated unemployment rates and correlations (derived from various studies) between perceived alternatives and quits. They hypothesized an inverse relationship between joblessness and perceived alternatives–turnover correlations because as jobs become more plentiful, perceived alternatives should more strongly induce turnover. They were right: correlations between alternatives and turnover themselves inversely correlated with national, regional, and industrial unemployment statistics.

Contrary to the hypothesis, the correlations between alternatives and turnover *positively* covaried with occupational unemployment. Suspecting bias, because 8 of 14 occupational studies had sampled nurses, they sorted the studies into two subgroups, nurses and other workers, and recomputed statistics. They found that occupational joblessness correlated *negatively* with correlations between perceived alternatives and quits for the non-nursing sample ($r = .76, p < .05$), as originally predicted, and positively for the nurses ($r = .83, p < .05$). They reasoned that because the nursing labor market is persistently strong, nurses can readily enter and exit the workforce with minimal job search and need for job comparison. Because nurses "take the job market for granted," perceptions of alternatives do not dominate their decisions to quit (Griffeth & Hom, 1988; Mowday, Koberg, & McArthur, 1984).

Poor instrumentation also perhaps weakened the observable influence of perceived alternatives on turnover. According to Steel and Griffeth (1989), most studies (59%) used single-item ratings by deficient and unreliable measures to operationalize perceived alternatives. Although focused more broadly, Allen et al.'s (2014) dominant analytical mindset (DAM) review found that 51% of studies continue to rely on single-item measures of turnover predictors and 35% reported no assessment of reliability. Thus, Steel and Griffeth's (1989) admonitions for future research on perceived alternatives to sample a wider range of jobs and occupations and improve operationalization likely remain important.

To improve measurement of perceived alternatives, Griffeth, Steel, Allen, and Bryan (2005) developed a multidimensional measure of job market perceptions, the Employment Opportunity Index (EOI; for the full EOI scale, see Table 6.1). In contrast to the trend identified by Steel and Griffeth (1989) and Allen et al. (2014) toward relatively simplistic one-item or short unidimensional multi-item scales, Griffeth et al. (2005) developed a rich multidimensional measure. Grounded in several prior research streams and theoretical perspectives (e.g., Jackofsky & Peters, 1983; March & Simon, 1958; Steel & Griffeth, 1989), the EOI incorporates five dimensions of labor market cognitions: ease of movement; desirability of movement; crystallization of alternatives; networking; and mobility. Ease and desirability of movement are derived from March and Simon's (1958) theory of organizational equilibrium, and tap both the quantity and relative quality of available alternatives. Crystallization of alternatives captures the notion that concrete alternatives such as a job offer in hand are more likely to lead to action than vague perceptions of a favorable job market (Griffeth & Hom, 1988).

The networking dimension recognizes the role that contacts, job availability information, and social processes play in the job search process (Fernandez, Castilla, & Moore, 2000). Finally, mobility captures the notion that there may be circumstances that prevent individuals from leaving a job even if there are plentiful desirable alternatives available, analogous to the idea of being embedded, in this case focused on personal or off-the-job factors (Lee, Mitchell, Sablynski, Burton, & Holtom, 2004).

Across three studies, including university faculty and staff, department store employees, and employees of an insurance company, Griffeth et al. (2005) developed and provided validation evidence regarding the multidimensional EOI. After arriving at a five-factor 14-item model with acceptable reliability, several tests showed patterns of correlations with traditional alternative scales, theoretically similar and dissimilar constructs, the withdrawal process, and actual turnover that were largely consistent with predictions regarding convergent and discriminant

TABLE 6.1 Employment Opportunity Index (EOI)

Ease of Movement
There simply aren't very many jobs for people like me in today's job market. (R)
Given my qualifications and experience, getting a new job would not be very hard at all.
I can think of a number of organizations that would probably offer me a job if I was looking.

Desirability of Movement
If I looked for a job, I would probably wind up with a *better* job than the one I have now.
By and large, the jobs I could get if I left here are *superior* to the job I have now.
Most of the jobs I could get would be an *improvement* over my present circumstances.

Networking
I have a far-reaching "network" of contacts that could help me find out about other job opportunities.
I have contacts in other companies who might help me line up a new job.
My work and/or social activities tend to bring me in contact with a number of people who might help me line up a new job.

Crystallization of Alternatives
Right now, I have a job offer "on the table" from another employer, if I choose to take it.
I have found a better alternative than my present job.

Mobility
I am unable to move to another place of residence now even if a better job came along. (R)
My spouse's career makes it very difficult for me to leave. (R)
There are factors in my personal life (e.g., school-age children, relatives, etc.) that make it very difficult for me to leave in the near future. (R)

(R) = item is reverse-scored

validity. Logistic regression models including the EOI explained significantly more variance in turnover behavior, and the EOI showed a 25% improvement in the prediction of turnover beyond job attitudes and traditional perceived alternative measures. The results also suggested the presence of job search micro-processes that demonstrate the potential in considering EOI dimensions at different points in the turnover process.

Economic opportunity is the objective counterpart to perceived alternatives. Unlike labor-economic studies on this macro-construct, organizational scholars were slower to examine how economic opportunity affects turnover among individuals, although there are examples. Gerhart (1987) found that regional unemployment rates moderate correlations between satisfaction and turnover. In a meta-analysis, Carsten and Spector (1987) correlated unemployment rates with correlations between satisfaction and turnover, and also found that economic expansions facilitate translation of dissatisfaction about the job into departure. Dreher and Dougherty (1980) found job competition, statistics on which they obtained from the U.S. Department of Labor's (1976) *Occupational Outlook Quarterly*, did *not* affect turnover through any interaction with attitudes about the job. Their classification of employment opportunity is noteworthy because the *Occupational Outlook* provided independent evaluations of the supply and demand for most professional and technical jobs. A major drawback is that these projections are made on a national basis, whereas local or regional job markets may better disclose any moderation of relationships between satisfaction and quitting. Using local unemployment statistics, Youngblood, Baysinger, and Mobley (1985) did find that *both* job satisfaction and joblessness affect turnover and that the relationship between job satisfaction and turnover strengthens during prosperous economic times.

Hom et al. (1992) used meta-analysis to cumulate studies testing Mobley et al.'s (1978) model. They grouped studies by various indices of unemployment to test the way in which unemployment moderates various pathways through the model. Occupational unemployment moderated the pathway between decisions to quit and turnover more than did other joblessness statistics. All forms of unemployment nevertheless conditioned the pathway between satisfaction and withdrawal cognitions (search intentions, quit intentions), although they also exerted an opposite, moderating impact. That is, depressed occupational labor markets decreased the pathway between satisfaction and thoughts of quitting but heightened the impact of satisfaction on search and quit intentions. In contrast, national and regional unemployment reinforced the pathway between satisfaction and thoughts of quitting while reducing the pathway between satisfaction and decisions to quit. What is more, national unemployment weakened the probability of a relationship between alternatives and withdrawal cognitions, whereas occupational joblessness increased them. All forms of unemployment moderated the pathway between search intentions and decisions to quit, though in contrary directions. Expansive occupational markets reinforced this linkage, but prosperous regional and national markets diminished it.

More recently, Rubenstein et al. (2018) meta-analytically assessed national unemployment rates as a moderator of relationships between 15 turnover antecedents and turnover. Although most moderating effects were not significant, results suggested that the relationship between education and turnover is more positive when unemployment rates are higher, whereas the relationship between stress/exhaustion and turnover becomes less positive when unemployment rates are higher. These contrasting moderating results suggest unemployment rates might have different effects on turnover driven by opportunity (e.g., for educated individuals) than that driven by job dissatisfaction (e.g., under conditions of stress or exhaustion).

Trevor (2001) expanded the focus on actual (as opposed to perceived) ease of movement. As opposed to considering actual ease of movement either from the perspective of general job availability, as in studies assessing unemployment rates, or of individual mobility-enhancing attributes, such as education, he considered both simultaneously. Trevor (2001) also provided a direct test of one of March and Simon's (1958) foundational ideas: that turnover decisions are a joint function of the ease and desirability of movement. Thus, he assessed interaction effects among job satisfaction (as an indicator of desirability of movement) and indicators of actual ease of movement that capture general job availability and individual movement capital. Drawing on human capital (Bretz, Boudreau, & Judge, 1994) and signaling (Spence, 1973) theories, Trevor (2001) identified education, cognitive ability, and occupation-specific training as proxies for movement capital.

Using data on 5,506 individuals from the National Longitudinal Survey of Youth (NLSY; Center for Human Resource Research, 1995), Trevor (2001) tested proposed interaction effects using survival analysis with a proportional hazards rate model (Cox, 1972). Reasoning that local unemployment rates may be more appropriate for some occupation, such as blue-collar jobs, whereas occupational unemployment rates may be more appropriate for higher-level jobs with broader regional labor markets, he constructed a composite measure incorporating both local and occupational unemployment rates. Results demonstrated that the negative effects of job satisfaction on voluntary turnover and the positive effects of unemployment rates on turnover are stronger when all three movement capital indicators (education, cognitive ability, and occupation-specific training) are higher. The results also suggest that the negative effects of job satisfaction on voluntary turnover were greater when unemployment rates are lower. These results emphasize the importance of considering the interactive effects of movement ease and desirability for predicting turnover, as well as the potential for capturing actual movement ease with movement capital proxies. Trevor (2001) suggests additional research on other indicators of movement capital, such as promotions, certifications, or certain types of highly visible performance.

References

Allen, D. G. (2008). *Retaining Talent: A Guide to Analyzing and Managing Employee Turnover*. SHRM Foundation Effective Practice Guidelines Series, 1–43.

Allen, D. G., Bryant, P. C., & Vardaman, J. M. (2010). Retaining talent: Replacing misconceptions with evidence-based strategies. *Academy of Management Perspectives*, 24, 48–65.

Allen, D. G., & Griffeth, R. W. (2001). Test of a mediated performance–turnover relationship highlighting the moderating roles of visibility and reward contingency. *Journal of Applied Psychology*, 86, 1014–1021.

Allen, D. G., & Griffeth, R. W. (1999). Job performance and turnover: A review and integrative multi-route model. *Human Resource Management Review*, 9(4), 525–548.

Allen, D. G., Hancock, J. I., Vardaman, J. M., & McKee, D. N. (2014). Analytical mindsets in turnover research. *Journal of Organizational Behavior*, 35, 61–68.

Allen, D. G., & Vardaman, J. M. (2017). Recruitment and retention across cultures. *Annual Review of Organizational Psychology and Organizational Behavior*, 4, 153–181.

Allen, D. G., Weeks, K. P., & Moffitt, K. R. (2005). Turnover Intentions and voluntary turnover: The moderating roles of self-monitoring, locus of control, proactive personality, and risk aversion. *Journal of Applied Psychology*, 90(5), 980–990.

Allen, N., & Meyer, J. P. (1993). Organizational commitment: Evidence of career stage effects? *Journal of Business Research*, 26(1), 49–61.

Allison, P. D. (1974). *Inter-Organizational Mobility of Academic Scientists*. Paper presented at annual meeting of the American Sociological Association, Montreal, Canada.

Aquino, K., Griffeth, R. W., Allen, D. G., & Horn, P. W. (1997). Integrating justice constructs into the turnover process: A test of a referent cognitions model. *Academy of Management Journal*, 40, 1208–1227.

Asparouhov, T., & Muthén, B. (2014). Auxiliary variables in mixture modeling: Three-step approaches using Mplus. *Structural Equation Modeling: A Multidisciplinary Journal*, 21, 329–341.

Bassett, G. A. (1967). *A Study of Factors Associated with Turnover of Exempt Personnel*. Crotonville, NY: General Electric.

Becker, H. S. (1960). Notes on the concept of commitment. *American Journal of Sociology*, 66, 32–42.

Becker, W. J., Cropanzano, R., & Sanfey, A. G. (2011). Organizational neuroscience: Taking organizational theory inside the neural black box. *Journal of Management*, 37(4), 933–961.

Bentein, K., Vandenberghe, C., Vandenberg, R., & Stinglhamber, F. (2005). The role of change in the relationship between commitment and turnover: A latent growth modeling approach. *Journal of Applied Psychology*, 90(3), 468–482.

Billings, R., & Wemmerus, V. (1983). The role of alternatives in process models of employee withdrawal. *Proceedings of the 26th Annual Conference of the Midwest Academy of Management*, 18–29.

Blau, P. M., & Schoenherr, R. (1971). *The Structure of Organizations*. New York: Basic Books.

Bluedorn, A., & Abelson, M. (1981). *Employee Performance and Withdrawal from Work*. Unpublished manuscript, College of Business Administration, Pennsylvania State University.

Boswell, W. R., Boudreau, J. W., & Tichy, J. (2005). The relationship between employee job change and job satisfaction: The honeymoon-hangover effect. *Journal of Applied Psychology*, 90, 882–892.

Bozeman, D. P., & Perrewé, P. L. (2001). The effect of item content overlap on organizational commitment questionnaire–turnover cognitions relationships. *Journal of Applied Psychology*, 86(1), 161–173.

Bretz, Jr., R. D., Boudreau, J. W., & Judge, T. A. (1994). Job search behavior of employed managers. *Personnel Psychology*, 47(2), 275–301.

Brooke, P., Russell, D. W., & Price, J. L. (1988). Discriminant validation of measures of job satisfaction, job involvement, and organizational commitment. *Journal of Applied Psychology*, 73, 139–145.

Bycio, P., Hackett, R. D., & Alvares, K. M. (1990). Job performance and turnover: A review and meta-analysis. *Applied Psychology, An International Review*, 39(1), 47–76.

Carsten, J. M., & Spector, P. E. (1987). Unemployment, job satisfaction, and employee turnover: A meta-analytic test of the Muchinsky model. *Journal of Applied Psychology*, 72, 374–381.

Center for Human Resource Research. (1995). *National Longitudinal Survey of Youth*. Columbus, OH: Ohio State University.

Chen, G., Ployhart, R. E., Cooper Thomas, H., Anderson, N., & Bliese, P. D. (2011). The power of momentum: A new model of dynamic relationships between job satisfaction change and turnover intentions. *Academy of Management Journal*, 54(1), 159–181.

Cox, D. R. (1972). Regression models and life tables. *Journal of Royal Statistical Society B*, 34, 187–220.

Dreher, G. F. (1982). The role of performance in the turnover process. *Academy of Management Journal*, 25, 137–147.

Dreher, G. F., & Dougherty, T. W. (1980). Turnover and competition for expected job openings: An exploratory analysis. *Academy of Management Journal*, 23, 766–772.

Farrell, D., & Rusbult, C. E. (1981). Exchange variables as predictors of job satisfaction, job commitment, and turnover: The impact of rewards, costs, alternatives, and investments. *Organizational Behavior and Human Performance*, 28, 78–95.

Fernandez, R., Castilla, E., & Moore, P. (2000). Social capital at work: Networks and employment at a phone center. *American Journal of Sociology*, 105(5), 1288–1356.

Gellatly, I. R., Meyer, J. P., & Luchak, A. A. (2006). Combined effects of the three commitment components on focal and discretionary behaviors: A test of Meyer and Herscovitch's propositions. *Journal of Vocational Behavior*, 69, 331–345.

Gerhart, B. (1987). How important are dispositional factors as determinants of job satisfaction? Implications for job design and other personnel programs. *Journal of Applied Psychology*, 72(3), 366–373.

Griffeth, R. W., & Hom, P. W. (1988). A comparison of different conceptualizations of perceived alternatives in turnover research. *Journal of Organizational Behavior*, 9, 103–111.

Griffeth, R. W., Hom, P. W., & Gaertner, S. (2000). A meta-analysis of antecedents and correlates of employee turnover: Update, moderator tests, and research implications for the next millennium. *Journal of Management*, 26, 463–488.

Griffeth, R. W., Steel, R. P., Allen, D. G., & Bryan, N. (2005). The development of a multidimensional measure of job market cognitions: The employment opportunity index (EOI). *Journal of Applied Psychology*, 90, 335–349.

Harrison, D. A., Virick, M., & William, S. (1996). Working without a net: Time, performance, and turnover under maximally contingent rewards. *Journal of Applied Psychology*, 81(4), 331–345.

Hausknecht, J. P., Sturman, M. C., & Roberson, Q. M. (2011). Justice as a dynamic construct: Effects of individual trajectories on distal work outcomes. *Journal of Applied Psychology*, 96(4), 872–880.

Hobfoll, S. E., Johnson, R. J., Ennis, N., & Jackson, A. P. (2003). Resource loss, resource gain, and emotional outcomes among inner city women. *Journal of Personality and Social Psychology*, 84(3), 632–643.

Hofstede, G. (1980). Motivation, leadership and organizations. *Organizational Dynamics*, 9, 42–63.

Holtom, B. C., Mitchell, T. R., Lee, T. W., & Eberly, M. B. (2008). Turnover and retention research: A glance at the past, a closer review of the present, and a venture into the future. *Academy of Management Annals*, 2, 231–274.

Hom, P. W., Caranikas-Walker, F., Prussia, G. E., & Griffeth, R. W. (1992). A meta-analytical structural equations analysis of a model of employee turnover. *Journal of Applied Psychology*, 77, 890–909.

Hom, P. W., & Hulin, C. L. (1981). A competitive test of the prediction of reenlistment by several models. *Journal of Applied Psychology*, 66(1), 23–39.

Hom, P. W., Katerberg, Jr., R., & Hulin, C. L. (1979). Comparative examination of three approaches to the prediction of turnover. *Journal of Applied Psychology*, 64, 280–290.

Hom, P. W., Roberson, L., & Ellis, A. D. (2008). Challenging conventional wisdom about who quits: Revelations from corporate America. *Journal of Applied Psychology*, 93, 1–34.

House, R. J., Hanges, P. J., Javidan, M., Dorfman, P. W., & Gupta, V. (Eds.). (2004). *Culture, Leadership, and Organizations: The GLOBE Study of 62 Societies*. Thousand Oaks, CA: Sage.

Hsee, C. K., & Abelson, R. P. (1991). Velocity relation: Satisfaction as a function of the first derivative of outcome over time. *Journal of Personality and Social Psychology*, 60(3), 341–347.

Hulin, C. L. (1991). Adaptation, persistence, and commitment in organizations. In M. D. Dunnette & L. M. Hough (Eds.), *Handbook of Industrial and Organizational Psychology* (2nd ed., pp. 445–505). Palo Alto, CA: Consulting Psychologists Press.

Hulin, C. L., Roznowski, M., & Hachiya, D. (1985). Alternative opportunities and withdrawal decisions: Empirical and theoretical discrepancies and an integration. *Psychological Bulletin*, 97, 233–250.

Jackofsky, E. F. (1984). Turnover and job performance: An integrated process model. *Academy of Management Review*, 9, 74–83.

Jackofsky, E. F., Ferris, K. R., & Breckenridge, B. G. (1986). Evidence for a curvilinear relationship between job performance and turnover. *Journal of Management*, 12(1), 105–111.

Jackofsky, E. F., & Peters, L. H. (1983). The hypothesized effects of ability in the turnover process. *Academy of Management Review*, 8, 46–49.

Kabins, A. H., Xu, X., Bergman, M. E., Berry, C. M., & Willson, V. L. (2016). A profile of profiles: A meta-analysis of the nomological net of commitment profiles. *Journal of Applied Psychology*, 101(6), 881–904.

Kahneman, D., & Tversky, A. (1979). Prospect theory: An analysis of decisions under risk. *Econometrica*, 2, 313–327.

Kahneman, D., & Tversky, A. (1984). Choices, values, and frames. *American Psychologist*, 39, 341–350.

Kammeyer-Mueller, J. D., Wanberg, C. R., Glomb, T. M., & Ahlburg, D. (2005). The role of temporal shifts in turnover processes: It's about time. *Journal of Applied Psychology*, 90(4), 644–658.

Keller, R. T. (1984). The role of performance and absenteeism in the prediction of turnover. *Academy of Management Journal*, 27, 176–183.

Klein, H., Molloy, J., & Brinsfield, C. (2012). Reconceptualizing workplace commitment to redress a stretched construct: Revisiting assumptions and removing confounds. *Academy of Management Review*, 37, 130–151.

Lance, C. E. (1988). Job performance as a moderator of the satisfaction-turnover intention relation: An empirical contrast of two perspectives. *Journal of Organizational Behavior*, 9(3), 271–280.

Lazarsfeld, P. F., & Thielens, W. (1958). *The Academic Mind: Social Scientists in a Time of Crisis*. Glencoe, IL: The Free Press.

Lee, T. W., & Mitchell, T. R. (1994). An alternative approach: The unfolding model of voluntary employee turnover. *Academy of Management Review*, 19, 51–89.

Lee, T. W., Mitchell, T. R., Holtom, B. C., McDaniel, L. S., & Hill, J. W. (1999). The unfolding model of voluntary turnover: A replication and extension. *Academy of Management Journal*, 42, 450–462.

Lee, T. W., Mitchell, T. R., Sablynski, C. J., Burton, J. P., & Holtom, B. C. (2004). The effects of job embeddedness on organizational citizenship, job performance, volitional absences, and voluntary turnover. *Academy of Management Journal*, 47(5), 711–722.

Lindsley, D. H., Brass, D. J., & Thomas, J. B. (1995). Efficacy-performance spirals: A multilevel perspective. *Academy of Management Review*, 20, 645–678.

Liu, D., Mitchell, T. R., Lee, T. W., Holtom, B. C., & Hinkin, T. R. (2012). When employees are out of step with coworkers: How job satisfaction trajectory and dispersion influence individual- and unit-level voluntary turnover. *Academy of Management Journal*, 55, 1360–1380.

March, J. G., & Simon, H. A. (1958). *Organizations*. New York: Wiley.

Martin, T. N., Price, J. L., & Mueller, C. W. (1981). Job performance and turnover. *Journal of Applied Psychology*, 66, 116–119.

Mathieu, J. E., & Farr, J. L. (1991). Further evidence for the discriminant validity of measures of organizational commitment, job involvement, and job satisfaction. *Journal of Applied Psychology*, 76, 127–133.

Mathieu, J. E., & Zajac, D. (1990). A review and meta-analysis of the antecedents, correlates, and consequences of organizational commitment. *Psychological Bulletin*, 108, 171–194.

Matta, F. K., Scott, B. A., Colquitt, J. A., Koopman, J., & Passantino, L. G. (2017). Is consistently unfair better than sporadically fair? An investigation of justice variability and stress. *Academy of Management Journal*, 60(2), 743–770.

McEvoy, G. M., & Cascio, W. F. (1987). Do good or poor performers leave? A meta-analysis of the relationship between performance and turnover. *Academy of Management Journal*, 30, 744–762.

Meyer, J. P., & Parfyonova, N. M. (2010). Normative commitment in the workplace: A theoretical analysis and re-conceptualization. *Human Resource Management Review*, 20, 283–294.

Meyer, J. P., Stanley, L. J., & Parfyonova, N. M. (2012). Employee commitment in context: The nature and implication of commitment profiles. *Journal of Vocational Behavior*, 80, 1–16.

Mobley, W. H. (1977). Intermediate linkages in the relationship between job satisfaction and employee turnover. *Journal of Applied Psychology*, 62, 237–240.

Mobley, W. H. (1982a). *Employee Turnover: Causes, Consequences, and Control*. Reading, MA: Addison-Wesley.

Mobley, W. H. (1982b). Some unanswered questions in turnover and withdrawal research. *Academy of Management Review*, 7, 111–116.

Mobley, W. H., Griffeth, R. W., Hand, H. H., & Meglino, B. M. (1979). Review and conceptual analysis of the employee turnover process. *Psychological Bulletin*, 86(3), 493–522.

Mobley, W. H., Horner, S. O., & Hollingsworth, A. T. (1978). An evaluation of precursors of hospital employee turnover. *Journal of Applied Psychology*, 63, 408–414.

Mossholder, K. W., Bedeian, A. G., Norris, D. R., Giles, W. F., & Field, H. S. (1988). Job performance and turnover decisions: Two field studies. *Journal of Management*, 14(3), 403–414.

Mowday, R. T., Koberg, C. S., & McArthur, A. W. (1984). The psychology of the withdrawal process: A cross–Validation test of Mobley's intermediate linkages model of turnover in two samples. *Academy of Management Journal*, 27, 79–94.

Mowday, R. T., Porter, L. W., & Steers, R. M. (1982). *Employee–Organization Linkages*. New York: Academic Press.

O'Reilly, C. A., & Chatman, J. (1986). Organizational commitment and psychological attachment: The effects of compliance, identification, and internalization. *Journal of Applied Psychology*, 71, 492–499.

Pavalko, R. M. (1970). Recruitment to teaching: Patterns of selection and retention. *Sociology of Education*, 43, 340–353.

Pederson, D. G. (1973). Approximate method of sampling on multinomial population. *Population Biometrics*, 29, 814–821.

Porter, L. W., Crampon, W. J., & Smith, F. J. (1976). Organizational commitment and managerial turnover: A longitudinal study. *Organizational Behavior and Human Performance*, 15, 87–98.

Porter, L. W., & Steers, R. M. (1973). Organizational, work, and personal factors in employee turnover and absenteeism. *Psychological Bulletin*, 80, 151–176.

Porter, L. W., Steers, R. M., Mowday, R. T., & Boulian, P. V. (1974). Organizational commitment, job satisfaction, and turnover among psychiatric technicians. *Journal of Applied Psychology*, 59, 603–609.

Price, J. L. (1977). *The Study of Turnover*. Ames, IA: Iowa State University Press.

Price, J. L., & Mueller, C. W. (1981). A causal model of turnover for nurses. *Academy of Management Journal*, 24, 543–565.

Price, J. L., & Mueller, C. W. (1986). *Absenteeism and Turnover of Hospital Employees*. Greenwich, CT: JAI Press.

Reichers, A. E. (1985). A review and reconceptualization of organizational commitment. *Academy of Management Review*, 10, 465–476.

Rubenstein, A. L., Allen, D. G., & Bosco, F. A. (2019). What's past (and present) is prologue: Interactions between justice levels and trajectories predicting behavioral reciprocity. *Journal of Management*, 45(4), 1569–1594.

Rubenstein, A. L., Eberly, M. B., Lee, T. W., & Mitchell, T. R. (2018). Surveying the forest: A meta-analysis, moderator investigation, and future-oriented discussion of the antecedents of voluntary employee turnover. *Personnel Psychology*, 71(1), 23–65.

Ryan, R. M., & Deci, E. L. (2000). Intrinsic and extrinsic motivations: Classic definitions and new directions. *Contemporary Educational Psychology*, 25(1), 54–67.

Salamin, A., & Hom, P. W. (2005). In search of the elusive U-shaped performance–turnover relationship: Are high performing Swiss bankers more liable to quit? *Journal of Applied Psychology*, 90, 1204–1216.

Schwab, D. P. (1991). Contextual variables in employee performance–turnover relationships. *Academy of Management Journal*, 34, 966–975.

Sheridan, J. E., & Vredenburgh, D. J. (1978). Usefulness of leadership behavior and social power variables in predicting job tension, performance, and turnover of nursing employees. *Journal of Applied Psychology*, 63, 89–95.

Spence, M. (1973). Job market signaling. *Quarterly Journal of Economics*, 87, 355–374.
Spencer, D. G., & Steers, R. M. (1981). Performance as a moderator of the job satisfaction–turnover relationship. *Journal of Applied Psychology*, 66, 511–514.
Stanley, L., Vandenberghe, C., Vandenberg, R., & Bentein, K. (2013). Commitment profiles and employee turnover. *Journal of Vocational Behavior*, 82, 176–187.
Steel, R. P. (2002). Turnover theory at the empirical interface: Problems of fit and function. *Academy of Management Review*, 27, 346–360.
Steel, R. P., & Griffeth, R. W. (1989). The elusive relationship between perceived employment opportunity and turnover behavior: A methodological or conceptual artifact? *Journal of Applied Psychology*, 74, 846–854.
Steers, R. M. (1977). Antecedents and outcomes of organizational commitment. *Administrative Science Quarterly*, 22(1), 46–56.
Steers, R. M., & Mowday, R. T. (1981). Employee turnover and postdecision accommodation processes. In L. L. Cummings & B. M. Staw (Eds.), *Research in Organizational Behavior* (vol. 3, pp. 235–281). Greenwich, CT: JAI Press.
Stumpf, S. A., & Dawley, P. K. (1981). Predicting voluntary and involuntary turnover using absenteeism and performance indices. *Academy of Management Journal*, 24, 148–163.
Sturman, M. C., Shao, L., & Katz, J. (2012). The effect of culture on the curvilinear relationship between performance and turnover. *Journal of Applied Psychology*, 97, 46–62.
Sturman, M. C., & Trevor, C. O. (2001). The implications of linking the dynamic performance and turnover literatures. *Journal of Applied Psychology*, 86(4), 684–696.
Thibaut, J. W., & Kelly, H. H. (1959). *The Social Psychology of Groups*. New York: Wiley.
Trevor, C. O. (2001). Interactions among actual ease-of-movement determinants and job satisfaction in the prediction of voluntary turnover. *Academy of Management Journal*, 44(4), 621–638.
Trevor, C. O., Gerhart, B., & Boudreau, J. W. (1997). Voluntary turnover and job performance: Curvilinearity and the moderating influences of salary growth and promotions. *Journal of Applied Psychology*, 82(1), 44–61.
U.S. Department of Labor. (1976). *Occupational Outlook Quarterly*, 20, 2–28.
Vardaman, J. M., Taylor, S. G., Allen, D. G., Gondo, M. B., & Amis, J. M. (2015). Translating intentions to behavior: The interaction of network structure and behavioral intentions in understanding employee turnover. *Organization Science*, 26, 1177–1191.
Wang, D., Hom, P. W., & Allen, D. G. (2017). Coping with newcomer hangover: How socialization tactics affect declining job satisfaction during early employment. *Journal of Vocational Behavior*, 100, 196–210.
Williams, C. R., & Livingstone, L. P. (1994). A second look at the relationship between performance and voluntary turnover. *Academy of Management Journal*, 37, 269–298.
Woo, S., & Allen, D. G. (2014). Toward an inductive theory of stayers and seekers in the organization. *Journal of Business & Psychology*, 29(4), 683–703.
Xu, X., & Payne, S. C. (2018). Predicting retention duration from organizational commitment profile transitions. *Journal of Management*, 44(5), 2142–2168.
Youngblood, S., Baysinger, B., & Mobley, W. (1985). *The Role of Unemployment and Job Satisfaction on Turnover: A Longitudinal Study*. Paper presented at the National Meeting of the Academy of Management, San Diego, California (August).
Youngblood, S. A., Mobley, W. H., & Meglino, B. M. (1983). A longitudinal analysis of the turnover process. *Journal of Applied Psychology*, 68, 507–516.
Zenger, T. R. (1992). Why do employers only reward extreme performance? Examining the relationships among performance, pay, and turnover. *Administrative Science Quarterly*, 37, 198–219.

7
RESEARCH STREAMS ON UNDERSTUDIED TURNOVER ANTECEDENTS

This chapter focuses on promising explanatory constructs that turnover theorists have given short shrift—either theoretically or empirically. In particular, we consider job search, which is a long-theorized antecedent in classic and contemporary turnover theories (Hom & Kinicki, 2001; Lee & Mitchell, 1994; March & Simon, 1958; Mobley, 1977; Mobley, Griffeth, Hand, & Meglino, 1979; Steers & Mowday, 1981) but whose conceptualization (including its antecedents and consequences) has been limited (Blau, 1993; Steel, 2002; Swider, Boswell, & Zimmerman, 2011). Moreover, we consider leadership characteristics that have been narrowly examined historically by turnover theorists (focusing mostly on subordinate attitudes toward leaders or their leader–member exchange; Griffeth, Hom, & Gaertner, 2000) or overlooked by embeddedness theorists (Mitchell, Holtom, Lee, Sablynski, & Erez, 2001). In particular, we consider how attraction to or identification with leaders can help retain employees by buffering them against shocks (Waldman, Carter, & Hom, 2015) but also how such embedding forces can uproot subordinates when leaders exit (Ballinger, Lehman & Schoorman, 2010; Li, Hausknecht, & Dugoni, 2018; Shapiro, Hom, Shen, & Agarwal, 2016). Drawing from the nascent literature on mate guarding and turnover cues, we further consider how leaders may enact "employee guarding" to retain potential defectors (Gardner, Munyon, Hom & Griffeth, 2018a) as well as identify potential defections (Gardner, Van Iddekinge, & Hom, 2018b).

Further, early research by Krackhardt and Porter (1986) first noted how members of employees' networks of workplace ties can influence turnover, departing from traditional preoccupation with coworker satisfaction or commitment (Griffeth et al., 2000; Meyer, Stanley, Herscovitch, & Topolnytsky, 2002; Mobley et al., 1979). This research stream has evolved independently of turnover theory and research, demonstrating that network centrality is a prime turnover antecedent

(Feeley & Barnett, 1997; Feeley, Hwang & Barnett, 2008). Recently, turnover scholars began incorporating network measures to demonstrate their incremental validity beyond traditional turnover antecedents (Hom & Xiao, 2011; Mossholder, Settoon, & Henagan, 2005; Vardaman, Taylor, Allen, Gondo, & Amis, 2015) as well as clarifying their role in the turnover process (Porter, Woo, & Campion, 2016). Departing from traditional overemphasis on environmental causes of turnover (mediated via job attitudes; Price & Mueller, 1981), turnover researchers have also generally ignored personality or dispositional causes (Hom, Lee, Shaw, & Hausknecht, 2017) (given their historic poor predictions; Griffeth & Hom, 1988), though acknowledging predictive efficacy of weighted application blanks (or biodata; Griffeth & Hom, 2001) or other individual differences (without specifying personality traits; Mobley et al., 1979; Steers & Mowday, 1981). Yet demonstrations of the predictive validity of the Big Five personality traits (Barrick & Mount, 1991) has reinvigorated interest in how personality traits (Zimmerman, 2008), and other related traits (e.g., locus of control; Allen, Weeks, & Moffitt, 2005; Woo, 2011), can underlie quit propensity.

Job Search Mechanism

March and Simon (1958) first recognized that job search increases ease of movement by expanding the number of perceived extra-organizational alternatives. Building on this rudimentary view, Mobley (1977) intuitively conceived a *prevailing* process by which job search culminates in higher turnover. He envisioned that employees who become dissatisfied with their job first contemplate job search's "subjective expected utility" (SEU, projecting its benefits, such as finding comparable jobs, as well as its costs) and turnover costs (e.g., losing valued job benefits). Should employees form positive search SEUs and foresee few prohibitive costs for quitting, they may then develop search intentions that prompt an active job search. Job searches may then generate alternative jobs that are then compared with the existing job. If this comparison favors one or more job offers, they then quit upon choosing a particular offer. Inspired by this formulation, most studies find that search intensity and different methods of job search predict turnover moderately well (Blau, 1993; Griffeth et al., 2000). A few tests fully assessing Mobley's (1977) job search sequence partially upheld this mechanism, such as demonstrating that search SEU underlies search or intensive searches boost comparison between alternative jobs with the current job (Hom & Griffeth, 1991; Hom & Kinicki, 2001; Lee, 1988).

All the same, a broad body of evidence increasingly disputes the prominent theoretical role accorded to job search by Mobley (1977). Specifically, comprehensive literature reviews later conclude that employee perceptions of job alternatives, which are direct byproducts of search, *poorly* predict turnover (Hulin, Roznowski, & Hachiya, 1985; Steel & Griffeth, 1989). While such findings suggest that many leavers' decisions to exit do not hinge on employment prospects (e.g., marginal drifters; Hulin et al., 1985), common static cohort research designs also imprecisely capture labor market perceptions for they often sample many respondents who are not interfacing with sources of labor market information, such as stayers (Steel, 2002). What is more, some employees—especially in high-demand occupational fields (e.g., nursing)—may quit without *first* pursuing alternative jobs (Hom & Griffeth, 1991; Steers & Mowday, 1981). Further, some employees receive unsolicited job opportunities without undergoing a search, according to unfolding model research (Lee, Mitchell, Holtom, McDaniel, & Hill, 1999; Lee, Mitchell, Wise, & Fireman, 1996). The unfolding model identifies a turnover path (No. 3) in which unsolicited job interviews or offers ("external shocks") can induce leaving even among satisfied incumbents. Finally, Boswell, Boudreau, and Dunford (2004) established that some employees pursue alternatives to achieve greater leverage with their employers. Rather than trying to leave, they seek job offers to improve their lot (e.g., securing counter-offers), thus contesting classic views that job search represents a withdrawal stage initiated by dissatisfaction and that culminates in quits (Mobley, 1977; Mobley et al., 1979; Steers & Mowday, 1981). Boswell et al. (2004) observed that only employees soliciting jobs to leave later quit, while those seeking leverage tend not to quit. Indeed, an online survey revealed that 74% of workers claimed they were "always hunting" even though 51% feel satisfied with their job (Trusty, Allen, & Fabian, 2019).

Evolutionary Job Search

In light of growing discordant evidence against traditional thinking (Mobley, 1977; Steers & Mowday, 1981), Steel (2002) revised these models by introducing a cybernetic search process incorporating explanations for why people search when they are not necessarily dissatisfied or why they leave without job offers in hand (what he terms the "no-search exception"; see Figure 7.1). Extending prevailing formulations (Mobley, 1977; Steers & Mowday, 1981), he delineated three stages of the search process. An initial stage involves "passive scanning" of the labor market whereby employees (including those not planning to leave) casually browse news about the job market (e.g., read media accounts about the unemployment rate). Some employees next progress to a second stage ("focused search"), where they seek *specific* information about prospective job options (e.g., read job ads in trade journals). After identifying a viable set of alternatives, employees may progress to a third stage and directly "contact prospective employers" where they can learn about specific jobs as well as their own employability.

Steel (2002) further conceptualizes labor market information as hierarchically multilayered such that job-seekers expend more effort as they pass through search stages to penetrate less accessible but more particularistic (and more useful) information. Given "dynamic learning," job-seekers' labor market and employability perceptions change over time and become more realistic as they progress through search stages. Steel's cybernetic submodel also allows for

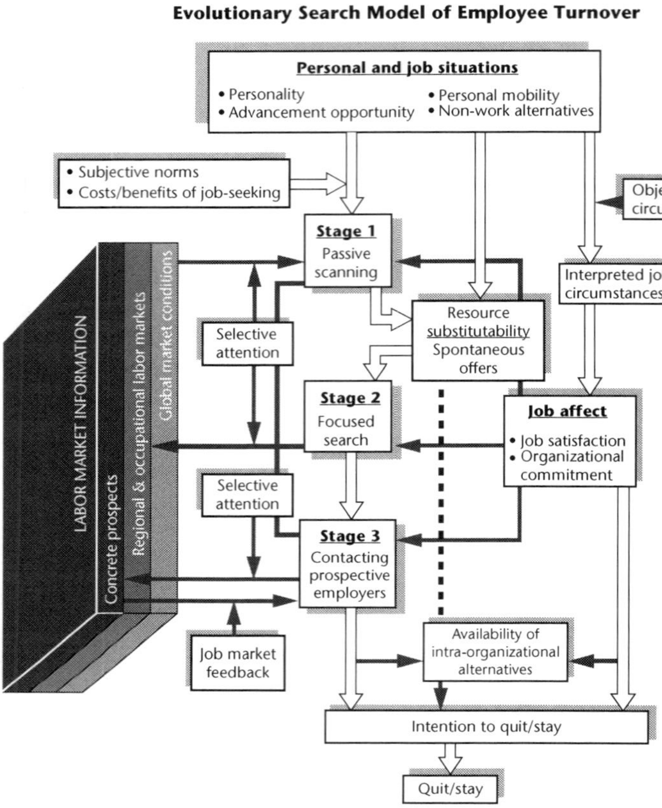

184 Understudied Turnover Antecedents

Evolutionary Search Model of Employee Turnover

FIGURE 7.1 Steel's (2002) Evolutionary Search Model of Employee Turnover

negative feedback loops such that job-seekers receiving negative feedback about job availability or their employability may cause them to reassess their current job, including reversing their initial decision to leave. Because labor market perceptions change so dramatically when job-seekers accumulate more realistic knowledge about jobs and employability, it is not surprising that one-time assessments of employee perceptions of alternatives by static cohort research designs poorly predict turnover. After all, such views are often inaccurate when coming from survey participants who are not soliciting labor market information or merely scanning such data (Steel, 2002).

Finally, Steel (2002) envisions how resource substitutability and spontaneous offers can explain why some leavers do not seek alternatives before exiting, which he calls the "no-search exceptions." If a person has substitute resources (e.g., alternative income sources), he or she can bypass job search and directly quit. Examples include employees quitting to enroll in law schools as they have sufficient savings or loans to cover educational expenses or those leaving the labor force to start a family (depending on partner wages for support). Further, Steel (2002) identifies non-attitudinal causes of job search, such as personal mobility, subjective norm, and job search SEU. To illustrate, employees may quit to follow a relocating spouse (complying with spousal pressure to quit) and find work afterwards, while others may secure other job offers to improve their negotiating leverage with employers (Bretz, Boudreau, & Judge, 1994).

To our knowledge, turnover researchers have yet to test Steel's model in its entirety, although some researchers are tracking how job search changes over time for prospective leavers (Kammeyer-Mueller, Wanberg, Glomb, & Ahlburg, 2005). Nonetheless, unemployment scholars have most pioneered repeated-measures surveys about how job-seekers attain re-employment and corroborated certain dynamic propositions in Steel's (2002) theory. To illustrate, Wanberg, Zhu, and van Hooft (2010) surveyed unemployed people's job search daily for three weeks and found that daily fluctuations in perceived progress in job search bolsters positive affect and re-employment self-efficacy during the same day, while reducing time spent on job search the next day. Later, Wanberg, Zhu, Kanfer, and Zhang (2012) monitored job search among the unemployed weekly for 20 weeks. Their study reported a curvilinear relationship between search intensity and time such that this effort declines during the first 10 weeks and intensifies later. Going beyond Steel's (2002) theory (and other turnover models), these authors scrutinized motivational traits (i.e., *approach* orientation representing individuals "who engage in goal striving for personal growth and developing competencies" vs. *avoidance* orientation for those "who strive to avoid failure, preserve resources, and protect self-concept"; Wanberg et al., 2012, p. 264) and self-regulatory states (motivational control, which is the "intentional cognitive redirection of attention, use of goal setting, and/or use of environmental management strategies to stay on course," and self-defeating cognitions, which represent felt hopelessness and negative expectations about successful job search; Wanberg et al., 2012, p. 266). They investigated how these traits and states affect job search intention and mental health, which in turn can underpin successful searches.

Specifically, Wanberg et al. (2012) learned that seekers adopting approach motivation more often enacted motivational control during these weeks, while those that have an avoidance motivation engaged in less motivational control but experienced more self-defeating cognitions. What is more, more motivational control in a given week boosts hours job-hunting and mental health (less anxiety and depression) in the same week, while self-defeating cognitions in a week diminish mental health in the same week. By and large, these self-regulatory states mediate how motivational traits influence search effort and mental health. Finally, average search hours during unemployment increase re-employment speed and average number of weekly interviews, whereas initial positive mental health also increases job interviews.

While repeated-measures search studies among the unemployed can deepen insight into the role that job search plays in the turnover process (Wanberg et al., 2012), employed job-seekers do not face the same deadline pressures to find jobs as do the unemployed whose unemployment insurance can run out. Rather, their job search may "leisurely" transpire over a longer time frame that enables them to find superior alternatives rather than the first job offer they can secure. Indeed, repeatedly surveying employees about job search may prove difficult for this longitudinal design may require a sufficient number of active job-seekers interfacing with the labor market (Steel, 2002). Otherwise, repeated-measures search research may be limited to incumbents at certain career stages in some occupational fields, such as junior auditors in public accounting firms who earned their CPA or six-year assistant professors going up for tenure. Nonetheless, Wanberg et al.'s (2012) investigation highlights how motivational traits and self-regulatory states can help job-seekers more successfully attain job offers (allowing them to quit), which can supplement the prevailing focus on search methods and network sources of job leads by turnover scholars (Griffeth, Steel, Allen, & Bryan, 2005).

Leadership Influences

Leader Affect and Relationship Quality

Historically, turnover and embeddedness theorists have de-emphasized leadership influences (Hulin et al., 1985; Mobley, 1977; Rusbult & Farrell, 1981; Steers & Mowday, 1981), relegated them to distal antecedents of more central—more potential—antecedents (e.g., job attitudes; Mobley et al., 1979; Steers & Mowday, 1981), or deemed them a mere subset of a larger class of antecedents (e.g., one of many job dissatisfaction facets, one of many embedding links, or a particular shock activating turnover path 2; Lee & Mitchell, 1994; Mitchell & Lee, 2001). Such insignificance in classic and modern-day perspectives on leaving and staying contributed to longstanding neglect in empirical research on leadership drivers of turnover (Waldman et al., 2015). What is more, existing turnover studies on leadership narrowly scrutinized employees' attitudes toward leaders or quality of their relationship with leaders (notably, leader–member exchange [LMX]; Graen & Ginsburgh, 1977), uncovering modest correlations (Griffeth et al., 2000; Rubenstein, Eberly, Lee, & Mitchell, 2018). Such findings challenge the prevailing managerial wisdom that "people quit bosses, not jobs" (Reina, Rogers, Peterson, Byron, & Hom, 2018; Waldman et al., 2015), given widespread beliefs that supervisors exert *dominant* control over employees' immediate work environs and thus influence other well-established turnover drivers (e.g., pay, promotions; Rubenstein et al., 2018).

All the same, turnover and embeddedness scholars are beginning to revisit leadership influences, capitalizing on the creative renaissance in modern leadership theory and research. Moving beyond conventional findings that leader–member exchange (LMX) decreases turnover (Dulebohn, Bommer, Liden, Brouer, &

Ferris, 2012), Seo, Nahrgang, Carter, and Hom (2018) thus investigated how LMX configurations—or the mix of high and low LMX relationships within a leader's work group—can affect the overall rate of group attrition (i.e., collective turnover). Examining LMX relationships within work groups in a Chinese hospitality organization, they identified four LMX configurations: (1) *bimodal configuration* (where a leader forms high LMX with 50% of her subordinates and low LMX with the other 50%); (2) *fragmented configuration* (where a leader forms a unique LMX relationship with each member); (3) *solo-status low LMX configuration* (where a few members have low LMX, while most have high LMX); and (4) *solo-status high LMX configuration* (where a few members have high LMX, whereas most have low LMX). They observed higher collective turnover and lower average organizational commitment in bimodal LMX configurations (comprising equal-sized high and LMX subgroups, which can evolve into fault lines weakening group solidarity). By contrast, collective turnover is lowest and mean commitment level is highest for solo-status low LMX (where most members have high LMX) and fragmented configurations (where leaders form unique relationships with each member, preventing emergence of LMX subgroups [comprising members with identical LMXs] that impede teamwork and commitment to the team as a whole).

Leader Motivational Behaviors

Focusing on how leadership behaviors affect subordinate loyalty, Waldman et al. (2015) examined the direct and cross-level effects of transformational leadership, whereby leaders transform followers to seek organizational goals over self-interests. According to embeddedness theory (Mitchell et al., 2001), transformational leaders might embed followers by promoting job fit and links. That is, such leaders use idealized influence to induce followers to identify with organizational values and goals, boosting person–firm fit. Such leaders also forge stronger links when exhibiting individualized consideration toward followers. Beyond this, Sluss and Ashforth's (2007) relational identification theory (extent to which an individual defines oneself in terms of role relationships) implies that such leaders' attributed charisma may induce followers to admire and trust them, thereby motivating followers to self-identify themselves as the *leader's followers*. Because leaders are organizational representatives, this role identification may reinforce organizational identification and thus loyalty (Mael & Ashforth, 1992). All told, transformational leadership may directly lower subordinates' quit propensity by invoking stronger fit, links, and company identification.

Besides decreasing quit propensity, Waldman et al. (2015) envisioned that transformational leaders can dissuade followers deciding to quit (for whatever reason) from enacting their decisions. Specifically, leaders can inspire hope about distressing working conditions (e.g., layoff shocks; Trevor & Nyberg, 2008) by assuaging followers' fears and inspiring optimism about a brighter future. While unable to address all turnover causes (e.g., spousal relocations or leaving to care for family members; Lee & Mitchell, 1994), transformational leaders might lessen the chances that followers will follow through on their initial decisions to leave due to negative job shocks (a major turnover path).

Surveying Chinese work groups, Waldman et al.'s (2015) multilevel statistical tests established that transformational leadership reduces collective turnover (after controlling other turnover and leadership antecedents) by diminishing group-level quit intentions. Moreover, they documented a cross-level moderating effect, whereby transformational leadership disrupts the translation of followers' quit intentions into actual turnover. That is, they found that transformational leadership *attenuates* positive relationships between quit intentions and voluntary quits. Their finding not only revealed broader—if not more potent—effects than past leadership attrition studies, but also identified a circumstance for why quit intentions do not inevitably culminate in quits (aka boundary condition; Allen et al., 2005).

Along these lines, Reina et al. (2018) further documented that how leaders deploy influence tactics to motivate subordinates to comply with their requests may also affect the latter's quit propensity. They showed that managers who regularly use inspirational appeals (that arouse strong emotions by appealing to subordinates' values or ideals) to motivate subordinates also enhance their job loyalty (by promoting job engagement and job satisfaction). By comparison, managers who often pressure subordinates to obey orders or achieve performance standards (e.g., using persistent reminders, threats, or warnings) actually impel subordinates to quit (by decreasing their job engagement and job satisfaction).

Leader Humility

Still, another new research avenue on leader turnover effects is the emerging scholarship on leaders' expressed humility, reflecting their: "(a) manifested willingness to view oneself accurately, (b) displayed appreciation of others' strengths and contributions, and (c) teachability" (Owens, Johnson, & Mitchell, 2013, p. 1518). Owens and colleagues argued that leaders who hold a realistic view of themselves (including recognizing their shortcomings), are receptive to subordinates' ideas, and giving subordinates due credit for their contributions will improve subordinates' feelings toward the leader and the job. Such enhanced job satisfaction should strengthen retention, according to turnover research (Griffeth et al., 2000). Testing this inference in a U.S. health services organization, Owens et al. (2013) demonstrated that subordinates who perceive their supervisors to be humble feel higher job satisfaction and thus less likely quit.

Generalizing Owens et al.'s (2013) finding to China, Ou, Seo, Choi, and Hom (2017) later found that Chinese executives' humility also diminishes quits among their direct reports (i.e., middle managers [MMs]) by raising MMs' job satisfaction (i.e., top executive humility → MM satisfaction → MM quits). They argued that such findings suggest that humble executives better satisfy MM needs for competency (by valuing MM abilities and recognizing MM accomplishments), autonomy (by involving MMs in decision-making), and relatedness (by respecting MMs as equals). Ou et al. (2017) further investigated how divisiveness among executives within top management teams (TMTs) can moderate the effects of executive humility on MM retention. To capture team disharmony, they assessed TMT demographic fault lines, which represent the extent to which teams comprise homogeneous subgroups whose members are alike on multiple demographic attributes. For example, TMT conflicts may arise when one subgroup comprise exclusively older Cantonese-speaking male executives and another comprises younger female executives fluent in Mandarin.

In particular, Ou et al. (2017) theorized that TMT fault lines weaken the beneficial impact of executive humility on MM job satisfaction by creating coordination difficulties for MM subunits reporting to different executives (aka TMT members). To illustrate, MM subordinates of antagonistic TMT members (or subgroups) may withhold useful information from one another, compete for resources due to conflicting subunit goals, or distrust MMs in other units. Consequently, TMT demographic fault lines impair collaboration among MM subunits, essential for implementing TMT strategic goals. Moreover, poor interdepartmental cooperation imposes more stress on MMs, who must spend more time monitoring MMs in other subunits to ensure they meet their commitments or expend extra resources as buffers should other subunits fail to do so. This added stress hampers MMs' ability to fulfill other job duties, threatening them with loss of rewards and recognition. Further, MMs may regard TMTs plagued by fault lines (or their effects) as collectively incompetent and deduce that their own superiors (TMT members) are also inept. When seeing leaders as inept, followers may interpret a leader's humility as signaling indecisiveness and timidity rather than a positive leadership attribute.

Beyond this, Ou et al. (2017) envisioned TMT fault lines dampening the (negative) impact of MM satisfaction on MM leaving. Conceivably, MMs may witness more disengagement and withdrawal by leaders (e.g., job-seeking; Ng & Feldman, 2013) given the latter's membership in dysfunctional TMTs. Social cues signaling impending leader departures may in turn induce MMs to feel anxious about future workplace changes as they anticipate potential loss of a valued leader and her social capital (Li et al., 2018; Shapiro et al., 2016). In addition, MMs may foresee a less favorable career path as they—prospective candidates themselves for executive posts—may dread promotion to strife-ridden TMTs. In support, Ou et al. (2017) concluded that TMT fault lines do diminish the positive impact of executive humility on MM satisfaction, while attenuating how MM satisfaction lessens MM quits.

Leader Attempts to Predict and Prevent Turnover

Focusing more directly on leader effects on subordinate turnover, Gardner et al. (2018a) argued that managers often feel "psychological ownership" toward subordinates (i.e., feeling that they own and control use of "their" human resources) and behave "territorially" (i.e., establishing and defending exclusive usage of their proprietary resources) when other employers attempt to poach subordinates. To identify how managers "guard" subordinates against losing them to other firms, Gardner et al. (2018a) drew from the mate guarding literature identifying how individuals preserve romantic relationships by preventing encroachment by romantic rivals or mates' defection to them. From that research, Gardner et al. (2018a) developed a measure of "employee guarding" to capture managers' attempt to defend and safeguard their agentic human resources from expropriation by other firms. While subordinates may leave for other reasons (e.g., return to school, assume domestic duties full-time; Lee & Mitchell, 1994), Gardner et al. (2018a) hypothesized that managers most resort to guarding tactics when subordinates join competing firms for such defections enrich competitors' human capital or supply them proprietary secrets.

Gardner et al. (2018a) adapted mate guarding items to assess how managers prevent employees from quitting for other workplaces. Surveying managers, they identified 40 common tactics (from an initial list of 74 guarding items) reflecting two factors according to factor analysis—namely, "persuasion" (tactics to deter leaving by using reason, fear induction, coercion or reward, such as "I told him/her that another employer was not well managed" and "I asked him/her to explain their time away from the workplace") and "nurturing" (tactics based on expressions of cultivating, caring for, and cherishing subordinates and their contributions, such as "I went out of my way to be kind and caring" and "I publicly praised him/her for their work").

To clarify etiology of employee guarding, Gardner et al. (2018a) had managers from a multinational firm describe their use of guarding tactics toward a particular subordinate (using an abbreviated 17-item scale), who in turn completed a cognitive ability test. When managers expected this subordinate to possibly defect in the near future, they more often engaged in nurturing and persuasion guarding tactics. Managers also most often engaged in nurturing when the potential defector had high cognitive ability. What warrants future research is whether such guarding tactics actually do discourage employee defections, though evolutionary psychologists suggest that mate guarding may prove ineffective, often enacted "too late" (Buss & Schmitt, 2018).

To deploy guarding tactics expeditiously, Gardner et al. (2018b) believed that managers must first detect whether subordinates are actually attempting to quit. They thus sought to pinpoint "pre-quitting behaviors" (PQBs) exiting employees unwittingly "leak" as they progress through the withdrawal process and can be *observed* by others (including managers). They reasoned that prospective leavers may emit behavioral cues (or PQBs) as they transition across the major stages in the turnover process, such as: (a) deteriorating job attitudes (expressed as job complaints and less OCBs); (b) search for alternatives (e.g., missing work to visit other employers, internet job searches at work); and (c) crystallization of quit decisions (e.g., make fewer calls to generate new sales, confide impending exit to colleagues).

To identify PQBs, they asked business students to recall a time they had quit and report what visible behaviors they emitted when leaving, while asking managers to recall behaviors they noticed about employees before they departed. These participants generated 931 behaviors. After eliminating redundant, unclear, or non-behavioral items, Gardner and another judge independently sorted the remaining 623 PQBs into 116 clusters of similar behaviors and wrote a single PQB item to best capture that cluster. To prune the item pool, Gardner et al. (2018b) recruited additional samples of managers to rate how frequently PQBs occur among departing subordinates. Specifically, they identified 13 PQBs strongly representing a single factor (e.g., "their work productivity has decreased more than usual," "they have been less willing to commit to long-term timelines than usual") according to exploratory factor analysis of survey responses, while also deleting rare PQBs. Testing predictive validity, they next had funeral directors describe PQBs by one of their subordinates and later reported that subordinate's employment status 13 months afterwards. Encouragingly, Gardner et al. (2018b) observed that PQBs predicted future subordinate turnover, explaining additional variance in turnover beyond subordinates' demographic traits, job performance, and managerial expectations of subordinate leaving.

Leader Departures

While scholars increasingly affirm the maxim that "people quit bosses, not jobs," others conversely realize that people also quit if bosses quit (Kacmar, Andrews, Van Rooy, Steilberg, & Cerrone, 2006; Ng & Feldman, 2013). Presumably, a leader's departure prompts subordinates to feel more uncertainty and worry about their fate in the workplace without the leader (Shapiro et al., 2016). When feeling strong negative affect (e.g., anxiety, fear) and anticipating a more dismal future in the workplace (i.e., pessimism about attaining career goals or values without the departed leader's resources and help), subordinates may contemplate leaving (Shapiro et al., 2016). In support, Kacmar et al. (2006) observed greater crew turnover in fast-food restaurants when supervisors depart, while Ng and Feldman (2013) found that subordinates who notice deteriorating job embeddedness among supervisors over time become increasingly less embedded in their job. Sampling 287 units of a hospitality corporation, Li et al. (2018) recently demonstrated that departures of *high-performing* general managers bolster unit-level turnover among core employees (who perform central operational duties) and that unit-level turnover rate *increases* for months afterwards. This rising trajectory of collective

192 Understudied Turnover Antecedents

turnover was, however, reversed if a general manager from another unit replaced the departing leader.

Refining this "leader departure" effect, other scholars envision how this effect may hinge on followers' LMX with departing leaders (Ballinger et al., 2010; Shapiro et al., 2016). Ballinger et al. (2010) thus noted that high LMX with a leader ordinarily embeds employees in organizations but can become "a force that drives employee turnover" if the leader exits (p. 25). They reasoned that subordinates that have high LMX with a leader feel most "shock" when that leader exits and more readily quit as they anticipate a more dismal fate without that leader (losing access to the leader's social capital). By contrast, subordinates that have *low* LMX with the departing leader feel more optimistic and remain as they may envision a better relationship with the incoming leader. In support, Ballinger et al. (2010) demonstrated that veterinary hospital employees that have high LMX with the medical director quit more often if the director leaves, whereas those that have low LMX with the exiting director are less quit-prone.

Extending Ballinger et al.'s (2010) theoretical analysis, Shapiro et al. (2016) conceive additional moderators of leader departure effects—namely: (a) subordinate's organizational identification; (b) corporate-wide developmental network; and (c) turnover contagion (see Figure 7.2). Subordinates that have high-LMX leaders tend to identify with them (i.e., perceived oneness with leaders) but may also develop greater organizational identification (Shapiro et al., 2016). Because they see leaders as organizational agents, they may interpret favorable treatment from high-LMX leaders as indirectly stemming from the organization itself. They may thus attribute greater benevolence to the organization and thus identify with the organization via anthropomorphization (Sluss & Ashforth, 2008). More than

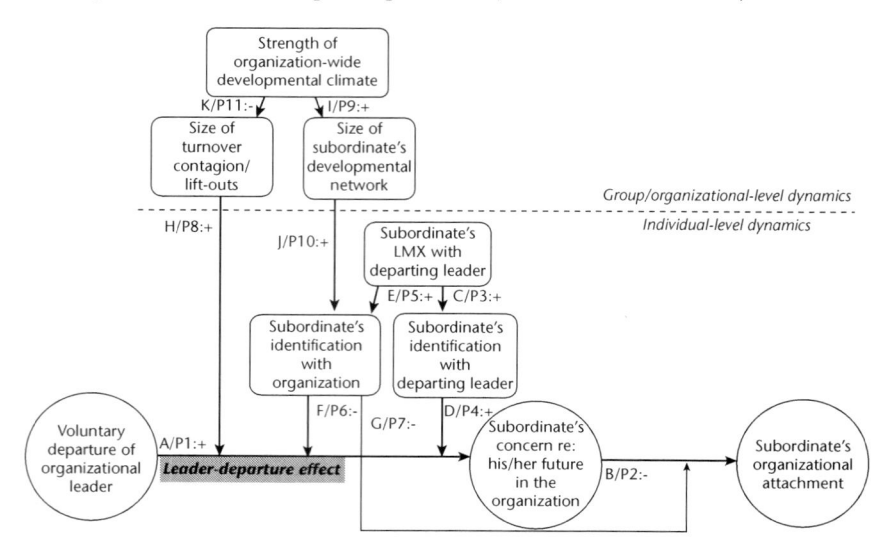

FIGURE 7.2 A 360-Degree Relational Perspective on Leader Departure Effects

this, subordinates in high-LMX relationships may especially help leaders achieve unit goals through higher productivity and organizational citizenship. Such exceptional unit contributions facilitate attainment of organizational goals as unit and organizational goals are generally congruent. To maintain self-consistency between "who they are ... and what they do," high-performing subordinates may thus infer that they "also must identify with the organization" when performing tasks on behalf of the organization (Sluss, Ployhart, Cobb, & Ashforth, 2012, p. 955). Shapiro et al. (2016) further maintain that organizational identification furnishes employees with a strong "psychological anchor" that discourages quit intentions because they feel more "empowered as a result of having little dependence on, or need for, any one individual, including any specific leader" (p. 488).

In addition, Shapiro et al. (2016) promulgate "organization-wide developmental climate"—or "shared perceptions regarding the extent to which career development and psycho-social support-related developing behaviors occur in an organization in directions that are lateral, bottom-up, and/or top-down, and the extent to which such behaviors are expected, desired, systematically procedurally supported, and rewarded" (p. 491)—as another condition suppressing leader departure effects. Organizations promoting developmental climates value and reward mentoring, encouraging employees (not just managers) to mentor others and role model such behaviors for others. When developmental climates flourish, subordinates' developmental networks expand to include a wider array of high-quality developers (e.g., higher-ranked authorities, peers, subordinates) besides immediate superiors, rendering them less dependent on superiors and less distressed when superiors—who are merely one constituent of their developmental network—leave the organization.

The size of a subordinate's constellation of developmental relationships in turn strengthens his or her organizational identification. After all, their mentors may "talk up" the company in which their networks are nested (Sluss & Ashforth, 2008) and thus increase the company's image and attractiveness, boosting identification (Kreiner & Ashforth, 2004). Moreover, subordinates may project their mentors' caring qualities onto the organization and thus more closely identify with the organization via anthropomorphization (Sluss & Ashforth, 2008). Finally, positive affect from relational identification with mentors (members "nested" within organizations) can transfer to the organization and thus sustain organizational identification (Sluss & Ashforth, 2008). Following Trevor and Nyberg's (2008) finding that "embedding human resources" buffers against shocks, Shapiro et al. (2016) thus deduce that subordinates' enlarged mentoring networks blunt the impact of leader departures as ample high-quality connections confer many resources (e.g., valuable career and psychosocial support that substitute for the loss of the leader's resources) that embed them in firms.

Finally, Shapiro et al. (2016) identify turnover contagion, where a subordinate feels quit-prone when many colleagues are deserting the workplace, as a moderator exacerbating the leader departure effect. When members of the same work group exit for the *same* workplace destination, this type of collective turnover is known as "lift outs" (Groysberg & Abrahams, 2006). Shapiro et al. (2016) theorized that mass exits emit social cues legitimizing and boosting the attractiveness of leaving. Subordinates left behind may infer that leavers are dissatisfied with the job, which may alert them to disagreeable features in their own job. Indeed, departing coworkers may openly disparage the current workplace to self-justify their leaving (Bartunek, Huang, & Walsh, 2008), which can diminish how remaining employees feel about their own job. Moreover, awareness of leavers' superior job offers may make the current job seem worse by comparison because attractive alternatives "increase adaptation levels and decrease job satisfaction" (Hulin et al., 1985, p. 243). All told, social cues emitted by exiting coworkers may reinforce subordinates' initial concern over their fate in the workplace, first prompted by the leader's departure and contribute to the impression that all are "abandoning [a sinking] ship" (Ng & Feldman, 2013, p. 655).

Social Networks

Disputing predominant views that turnover occurs atomistically within work groups, Krackhardt and Porter (1986) first deployed social network analysis to demonstrate that an individual's turnover may be influenced by turnover among members in his or her communication network (aka turnover contagion). In particular, Krackhardt and Porter (1986) argued that one's quit decision is most influenced by another coworker's leaving if one sees the other as "structurally equivalent," both of them occupying work roles where they have similar informal communication patterns. For example, two first-line supervisors are structurally equivalent as they issue advice or orders to rank-and-file hourly workers while reporting to middle managers (not necessarily the same persons).

Surveying fast-food employees in three restaurants, Krackhardt and Porter (1986) assessed *perceived* social networks by asking them to list whom people go to for help and advice at their restaurants. They next derived measures of (perceived) structural equivalence between each pair of employees and found that turnover tends to co-occur among structurally equivalent pairs. Provocatively, they concluded that turnover is "concentrated in patterns that can be delineated by role similarities in a communication network" (p. 54). Although long delayed, this landmark study ultimately inspired subsequent research on social networks (Ballinger, Cross, & Holtom, 2016; Feeley & Barnett, 1997; Mossholder et al., 2005) and turnover contagion (Felps et al., 2009).

In particular, later turnover researchers identified network centrality (an occupant's centrality in social networks in workplaces), generally assessing the volume of contacts from which an employee receives expressive or instrumental resources (aka "degree centrality"). To illustrate, Feeley and Barnett (1997) demonstrated that an erosion model best predicts turnover (assessing network centrality as the fewest number of links to reach all network members), concluding that employees "located on the … periphery of the network would be more likely to leave their organization" (p. 383). Replicating this erosion model, Feeley (2000) found that network centrality in a communication network (where respondents reported the number of different organizational contacts they regularly speak to about work or non-work topics) also predicts turnover. Surveying fast-food restaurant staff, Feeley et al. (2008) further established that more friendship ties (based on peer nomination or "out-degree" centrality in friendship networks), but not centrality in the advice network with peers, deter quits. Consistent with Feeley et al.'s erosion model, Mossholder et al. (2005) further established that an employee's centrality in the workplace communication network (reflecting the volume of coworkers soliciting that employee for advice or gossip about the firm; aka "in-degree centrality") also portends that employee's job longevity.

Following recommendations by embeddedness scholars to investigate the quality of links and their interconnectivity (Holtom, Mitchell, Lee, & Eberly, 2008), Hom and Xiao (2011) sought to more fully assess Chinese nationals' professional *guanxi* networks using Burt's (1997a, 1997b) methodology to capture *network closure*, which includes contact interconnectivity (or network constraint), tie strength, and diversity of network resources (using multiple name generators to identify contacts supplying various resources, such as sponsorship and political aid). They noted that Burt's approach more thoroughly assesses the quintessential family-like "network of personally defined reciprocal bonds" prevalent in China (Redding, Norman, & Schlander, 1993, p. 656) that are:

> (a) strong, (b) *multiplex* conduits for *both* socio-emotional and material resources ... (c) embedded in third-party ties or affiliations (sharing alma maters or hometowns, for example), (d) span different social systems (e.g., job, family), and (e) bound by normative obligations for reciprocity and long-term continuity.
>
> *(Hom & Xiao, 2011, p. 188, emphasis in original)*

Hom and Xiao (2011) further noted that *guanxi* networks include *cross-system* ties between contacts from different social systems (i.e., family members have workplace ties, entrepreneurs enlist local government officials to their boards or hire their relatives).

Hom and Xiao (2011) theorized that *guanxi* networks promote job loyalty for several reasons. That is, Chinese citizens' workplace ties are often strong and interconnected (which strengthen direct ties due to third-party affiliations; Krackhardt, 1998) and strong ties should reinforce staying according to job embeddedness theory. Moreover, strong and dense ties among *guanxi* contacts should enhance Chinese identification with ingroup networks as collectivists define themselves "in terms of connections and role relationships with significant others" (Brewer & Chen, 2007, p. 136). Their identification with workplace networks may in turn foster staying as these networks are embedded within workplaces (Burt, 2001). Moreover, Chinese nationals remain in closed workplace networks to partake in greater communal resources available from dense networks, while feeling more normative pressure to stay as interlocked members can more readily monitor and sanction potential defection. Finally, ties between network contacts from different social systems further discourage turnover. After all, Chinese culture or institutions promote cross-system ties. To illustrate, employees in state-owned firms may live in company housing (facilitating family interactions with other workers and families), work for family businesses (where one's associates are family members), join businesses sponsoring family or social events (building family-work ties), or treat business associates as family members (inviting them to family dinners or events to strengthen intimate ties). Extending Ramesh and Gelfand's (2010) notion of family embeddedness, a Chinese national may thus feel inhibited from leaving as such turnover severs ties between family and work contacts. Sampling employees from two high-tech firms in China, Hom and Xiao (2011) thus documented that network closure reduces voluntary quits among Chinese citizens.

Extending this line of inquiry, Vardaman et al. (2015) creatively envisioned how network centrality moderates the impact of quit decisions on actual turnover. Based on temporal construal theory (that people undervalue the costs of future events), they hypothesize that centrality in advice and friendship networks (reflecting accumulated social capital) most discourages prospective leavers from enacting their initial quit decisions when they approach the date when they must make a final, irrevocable, and public decision to actually leave. Presumably, central network occupants more carefully deliberate on the full costs of surrendering amassed social capital (i.e., more access to knowledge, rewards or influence for greater expertise, more friendships or obligations) when nearing the time of actual leaving, discouraging them from following through on their original intentions to quit. By contrast, network centrality exerts weaker moderating effects when actual departures are delayed into the distant future because central network participants discount social capital losses for remote events. In support, Vardaman et al. (2015) found that teachers' (in-degree) advice-giving centrality (based on peer nominations) lessens the positive effect of turnover intentions on actual turnover, whereas both in-degree and out-degree (based on respondents' perceptions) friendship centrality weakens the influence of turnover intentions on turnover.

Finally, Ballinger et al. (2016) identified other social capital forms that incumbents accumulate, such as reputation and brokerage, that embed them in jobs but are neglected by existing network and embeddedness inquiries into the volume of an employee's workplace contacts (i.e., degree centrality or links; Mitchell et al., 2001). Specifically, they examined (incoming) eigenvector centrality, which captures how well an employee is connected to contacts with many network ties. According to social network research, a person connected to highly sought-out others may become reputed as an "expert to whom experts turn" (Burt & Merluzzi, 2014, p. 164). Social network studies determine that employees with high eigenvector centrality are effective leaders, enjoy greater reputations, and receive more help from others (Ballinger et al., 2016). Because network reputation confers many resources, those high in eigenvector centrality should be more loathe to quit and thus surrender such resources.

Ballinger et al. (2016) further argue that "structural holes"—where employees link disconnected social networks—allow employees to become "brokers" (Burt, 1992). That is, they can act as gatekeepers controlling the flow of information between disparate parties as well as derive more innovative ideas when integrating non-redundant information from these groups. When people bridge disparate groups, they are better performers, promoted more often, and earn higher pay (Ballinger et al., 2016; Burt, 1992, 2005). Because brokering positions in networks is not readily transferrable to new companies, brokers tend to stay to avoid losing such social capital. As theorized, Ballinger et al. (2016) documented that employees with high eigenvector centrality in networks more likely stay. Yet they found that structural holes most deter leaving among executives than contributors (e.g., engineers, consultants) because the former depend more on brokerage to perform their jobs than do the latter.

Personality Influences

Although recognized by March and Simon (1958) and Mobley et al. (1979), comprehensive turnover (and embeddedness) theories since then have largely neglected personality influences (Hom & Griffeth, 1995; Hulin et al., 1985; Lee & Mitchell, 1994; Mitchell et al., 2001; Price & Mueller, 1981, 1986; Steers & Mowday, 1981) or inadequately explained their impact (Zimmerman, Swider, Woo, & Allen, 2016). Despite their conspicuous absence from prevailing theories, turnover researchers are increasingly investigating personality variables, heartened by Barrick and Mount's (1991) seminal meta-analytical demonstration of the validity of the "Big Five" personality traits (i.e., openness to experience, conscientiousness, extraversion, agreeableness, and neuroticism). They concluded that conscientiousness is a "consistently valid predictor of all occupational groups ... and for all criterion types" (personnel data, including turnover or tenure; pp. 17–18). Using a path analytical meta-analysis, Zimmerman (2008) later established that emotional stability most predicts (negatively) employees' quit intentions, while conscientiousness and agreeableness most predict (negatively) actual turnover (after controlling quit intentions, job satisfaction, and job performance).

Apart from the Big Five personality traits, turnover researchers sporadically explored other personality qualities (e.g., locus of control, achievement drive), often investigating how they moderate the impact of turnover antecedents (Griffeth & Hom, 1988; Mowday, Porter, & Stone, 1978; Mowday & Spencer, 1981). Much later, Allen et al. (2005) theorized that personality factors can clarify why quit intentions modestly predict turnover despite its theoretical prominence as the most proximal turnover antecedent (Griffeth et al., 2000). They showed that the intention–turnover relationship is stronger for low self-monitors (who express what they think and feel and act accordingly rather than comply with social norms) and those lower in risk aversion (who risk exiting a familiar job for alternatives where success or satisfaction is not fully known). Further, they noticed that employees with high locus of control (who believe they are masters of their fate) will act on their quit intentions as they believe that they can readily obtain alternatives.

Cognitive-Affective Processing System Theory

To furnish a more complete and integrative explanatory account for how personality variables (and other individual differences) affect withdrawal behaviors, Zimmerman et al. (2016) applied Mischel and Shoda's (1995, 1998) cognitive-affective processing system (CAPS). Focusing on the "situated person," CAPS envisions that individuals interpret the same situational condition differently but nevertheless consistently. That is, they exhibit stable "situational profiles" such that if certain situations occur, they will respond in the same manner. When encountering certain situations, individuals will interpret their experience by accessing relevant cognitions and affective states known as "cognitive-affective units" (CAUs) to generate a behavioral response. CAPS identifies five types of CAUs: (1) encodings; (2) expectancies and beliefs; (3) affects; (4) goals and values; and (5) competencies and self-regulatory plans. CAUs affect one another as mediators as well as moderators between a prior CAU and eventual behavior.

Applying this theory, Zimmerman et al. (2016) posit CAUs that correspond to prime explanatory constructs in turnover and embeddedness theories and explain how personality traits affect those causal antecedents (see Figure 7.3). According to CAPS, encodings represent how individuals construe or interpret themselves, other people (and interpersonal interactions), momentary events, or situations (external or internal) by cognitively applying mental constructs to derive meaning (Mischel & Shoda, 1995). From CAPS and personality theory, Zimmerman et al. (2016) thus deduce that proactive personalities may encode unsolicited job offers as an opportunity for career growth and more likely quit following turnover path 3 (Lee & Mitchell, 1994). By comparison, neurotics may overly attend to negative features of their job and more likely develop job dissatisfaction, which increases their quit propensity (Mobley, 1977). Based on CAPS, Zimmerman et al. (2016) further theorize how personality attributes affect "expectancies and beliefs" CAUs—notably, expectancy that withdrawal can lead to certain outcomes and perceived control over withdrawal decisions. To illustrate, they envision that incumbents open to experience may regard staying long-term in a job as costly, while regarding job-hopping as offering opportunities to grow (aka hobos; Woo, 2011). Additionally, Zimmerman et al. (2016) argue that individuals high in core

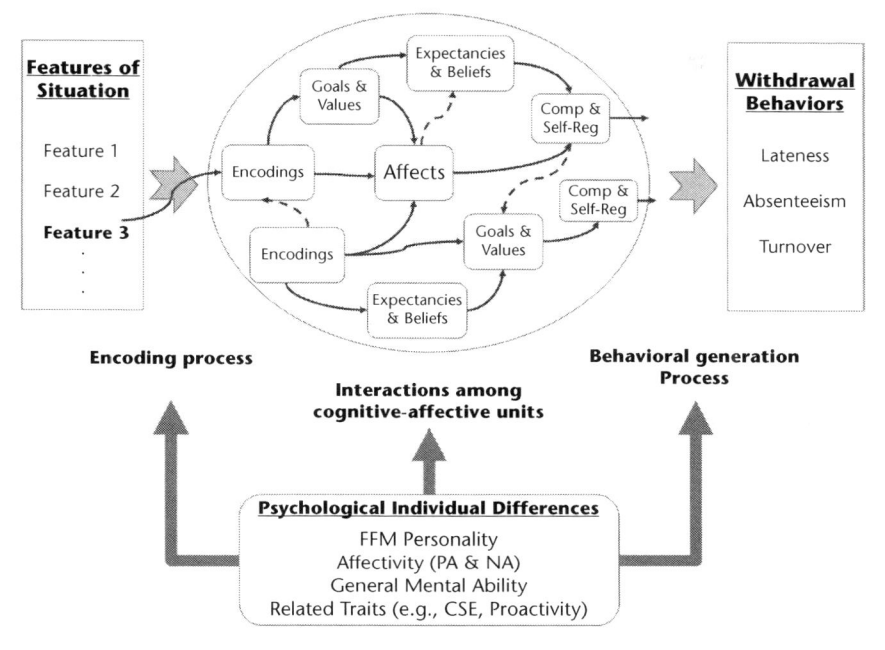

FIGURE 7.3 Zimmerman, Swider, Woo, and Allen's (2016) Theory of How Psychological Individual Differences Affect Withdrawal via Cognitive-Affective Units (FFM = Five-Factor Model; PA = positive affectivity; NA = negative affectivity; CSE = core self-evaluation; Comp = competencies; Self-Reg = self-regulatory plans)

self-evaluation may feel more control over the decision to stay or leave (Hom, Mitchell, Lee, & Griffeth, 2012).

Zimmerman et al. (2016) also conceptualize how personality dispositions affect "affective responses to psychological situations"—aka "affects CAU" (Mischel & Shoda, 1995, 1998). Because internals feel in control of what happens in their work lives, they should feel job satisfaction and engaged in work roles they help create (discouraging them from leaving; Hom & Griffeth, 1991). By contrast, agreeable employees feel more job satisfaction as they more easily form positive relationships at work, increasing their propensity to stay due to constituent forces (Maertz & Campion, 2004). As for "goals and values CAU," Zimmerman et al. (2016) speculate that employees open to experience may find higher person–organization fit in innovative cultures (becoming more embedded; Mitchell & Lee, 2001), while extraverts better match to team-oriented cultures. Their theory also notes that *others*' values and goals can represent CAUs influencing employees' quit decisions. For example, agreeable incumbents may acquiesce to the will or values of family members who exhort them to quit to assume more domestic duties or relocate elsewhere (Hom et al., 2012). Finally, Zimmerman et al.'s (2016) CAPS perspective maintains that personality traits can prompt withdrawal via self-regulatory plans (i.e., self-regulation of one's behavior via self-imposed standards, consequences, and self-reinforcement; Neck, Manz, & Houghton, 2019) and competencies. Engaging in strategic planning (e.g., deliberating on long-term action consequences), conscientious employees are more prone to follow turnover path 1 when leaving (i.e., enact preexisting plans to quit once certain circumstances occur; Lee & Mitchell, 1994; Maertz & Campion, 2004). Lacking impulse control, neurotics more likely impulsively quit due to negative job shocks (Lee et al., 1996, 1999).

Zimmerman et al.'s (2016) CAPS framework represents a major theoretical development addressing a conspicuous gap in theories of leaving and staying that neglect personality effects or deficiently explain their effects. While practitioners have long relied on personnel selection (including personality assessments; Russell, 2013), they have primarily focused on predicting turnover rather than explaining its occurrences. Thus, personality testing has often lacked grounding in theory or overestimated predictive power by selectively choosing the best personality item predictors from a large battery of item predictors (much like weighted application blanks; Griffeth & Hom, 2001). Or else, consultants failed to properly validate their personality tests or allowed independent inquiries of their predictive validity (that can yield peer-reviewed publications in academic journals). Not surprisingly, most withdrawal scholars thus shunned personality testing in their theory or research given such empiricism (and hucksterism) about their predictive effectiveness. Just as Staw (2016) has redirected the organizational behavior field away from its historical preoccupation with situational influences toward recognition of individual differences, Zimmerman et al.'s (2016) theory may likewise nudge turnover theory and research toward greater consideration of personality traits (and other individual differences) and their indispensable role in the withdrawal process.

References

Allen, D. G., Weeks, K. P., & Moffitt, K. R. (2005). Turnover intentions and voluntary turnover: The moderating roles of self-monitoring, locus of control, proactive personality, and risk aversion. *Journal of Applied Psychology*, 90(5), 980–990.

Ballinger, G. A., Cross, R., & Holtom, B. C. (2016). The right friends in the right places: Understanding network structure as a predictor of voluntary turnover. *Journal of Applied Psychology*, 101(4), 535–548.

Ballinger, G. A., Lehman, D, & Schoorman, F. D. (2010). Leader–member exchange and turnover before and after succession events. *Organizational Behavior and Human Decision Processes*, 113, 25–36.

Barrick, M. R., & Mount, M. K. (1991). The Big Five personality dimensions and job performance: A meta-analysis. *Personnel Psychology*, 44, 1–26.

Bartunek, J. M., Huang, Z., & Walsh, I. J. (2008). The development of a process model of collective turnover. *Human Relations*, 61(1), 5–38.

Blau, G. (1993). Further exploring the relationship between job search and voluntary individual turnover. *Personnel Psychology*, 46, 313–330.

Boswell, W. R., Boudreau, J. W., & Dunford, B. B. (2004). The outcomes and correlates of job search objectives: Searching to leave or searching for leverage? *Journal of Applied Psychology*, 89(6), 1083–1091.

Bretz, Jr, R. D., Boudreau, J. W., & Judge, T. A. (1994). Job search behavior of employed managers. *Personnel Psychology*, 47(2), 275–301.

Brewer, M. B., & Chen, Y.-R. (2007). Where (who) are collectives in collectivism? Toward conceptual clarification of individualism and collectivism. *Psychological Review*, 114(1), 133–151.

Burt, R. S. (1992). *Structural Holes*. Cambridge, MA: Harvard University Press.

Burt, R. S. (1997a). The contingent value of social capital. *Administrative Science Quarterly*, 42, 339–365.

Burt, R. S. (1997b). A note on social capital and network content. *Social Networks*, 19, 355–373.

Burt, R. S. (2001). Attachment, decay, and social network. *Journal of Organizational Behavior*, 22(6), 619–643.

Burt, R. S. (2005). *Brokerage and Closure*. Oxford: Oxford University Press.

Burt, R. S., & Merluzzi, J. (2014). Embedded brokerage. *Research in the Sociology of Organizations*, 37, 159–175.

Buss, D. M., & Schmitt, D. P. (2018). Mate preferences and their behavioral manifestations. *Annual Review of Psychology*, 70, 23.1–23.34.

Dulebohn, J. H., Bommer, W. H., Liden, R. C., Brouer, R. L., & Ferris, G. R. (2012). A meta-analysis of antecedents and consequences of leader–member exchange: Integrating the past with an eye toward the future. *Journal of Management*, 38(6), 1715–1759.

Feeley, T. H. (2000). Testing a communication network model of employee turnover based on centrality. *Journal of Applied Communication Research*, 28(3), 262–277.

Feeley, T. H., & Barnett, G. A. (1997). Predicting employee turnover from communication networks. *Human Communication Research*, 23, 370–387.

Feeley, T. H., Hwang, J., & Barnett, G. A. (2008). Predicting employee turnover from friendship networks. *Journal of Applied Communication Research*, 36(1), 56–73.

Felps, W., Mitchell, T. R., Hekman, D., Lee, T. W., Holtom, B. C., & Harman, W. S. (2009). Turnover contagion: How coworkers' job embeddedness and coworkers' job search behaviors influence quitting. *Academy of Management Journal*, 52, 545–561.

Gardner, T. M., Munyon, T. P., Hom, P. W., & Griffeth, R. W. (2018a). When territoriality meets agency: An examination of employee guarding as a territorial strategy. *Journal of Management*, 447, 2580–2610.

Gardner, T. M., Van Iddekinge, C. H., & Hom, P. W. (2018b). If you've got leavin' on your mind: The identification and validation of pre-quitting behaviors. *Journal of Management*, 44(8), 3231–3257.

Graen, G. B., & Ginsburgh, S. (1977). Job resignation as a function of role orientation and leader acceptance: A longitudinal investigation of organizational assimilation. *Organizational Behavior and Human Performance*, 19, 1–17.

Griffeth, R. W., & Hom, P. W. (1988). Locus of control and delay of gratification as moderators of employee turnover. *Journal of Applied Social Psychology*, 18, 1318–1333.

Griffeth, R. W., & Hom, P. W. (2001). *Retaining Valued Employees*. Thousand Oaks, CA: Sage.

Griffeth, R. W., Hom, P. W., & Gaertner, S. (2000). A meta-analysis of antecedents and correlates of employee turnover: Update, moderator tests, and research implications for the next millennium. *Journal of Management*, 26, 463–488.

Griffeth, R. W., Steel, R. P., Allen, D. G., & Bryan, N. (2005). The development of a multidimensional measure of job market cognitions: The Employment Opportunity Index (EOI). *Journal of Applied Psychology*, 90, 335–349.

Groysberg, B., & Abrahams, R. (2006). Lift outs: How to acquire a high-functioning team. *Harvard Business Review*, 84(12), 133–140.

Holtom, B. C., Mitchell, T. R., Lee, T. W., & Eberly, M. B. (2008). Turnover and retention research: A glance at the past, a closer review of the present, and a venture into the future. *The Academy of Management Annals*, 2(1), 231–274.

Hom, P. W., & Griffeth, R. W. (1991). Structural equations modeling test of a turnover theory: Cross-sectional and longitudinal analyses. *Journal of Applied Psychology*, 76, 350–366.

Hom, P. W., & Griffeth, R. W. (1995). *Employee Turnover*. Cincinnati, OH: South/Western.

Hom, P. W., & Kinicki, A. J. (2001). Toward a greater understanding of how dissatisfaction drives employee turnover. *Academy of Management Journal*, 44, 975–987.

Hom, P. W., Lee, T. W., Shaw, J. D., & Hausknecht, J. P. (2017). One hundred years of employee turnover theory and research. *Journal of Applied Psychology*, 102(3), 530–545.

Hom, P. W., Mitchell, T. R., Lee, T. W., & Griffeth, R. W. (2012). Reviewing employee turnover: Focusing on proximal withdrawal states and an expanded criterion. *Psychological Bulletin*, 138, 831–858.

Hom, P. W., & Xiao, Z. (2011). Embedding social capital: How *guanxi* ties reinforce Chinese employees' retention. *Organizational Behavior and Human Decision Processes*, 116, 188–202.

Hulin, C. L., Roznowski, M., & Hachiya, D. (1985). Alternative opportunities and withdrawal decisions: Empirical and theoretical discrepancies and an integration. *Psychological Bulletin*, 97(2), 233–250.

Kacmar, K. M., Andrews, M. C., Van Rooy, D. L., Steilberg, R. C., & Cerrone, S. (2006). Sure everyone can be replaced … but at what cost? Turnover as a predictor of unit-level performance. *Academy of Management Journal*, 49, 133–144.

Kammeyer-Mueller, J. D., Wanberg, C. R., Glomb, T. M., & Ahlburg, D. (2005). The role of temporal shifts in turnover processes: It's about time. *Journal of Applied Psychology*, 90(4), 644–658.

Krackhardt, D. (1998). Simmelian ties: Super strong and sticky. In R. M. Kramer & M. A. Neale (Eds.), *Power and Influence in Organizations* (pp. 21–38). Thousand Oaks, CA: Sage.

Krackhardt, D., & Porter, L. W. (1986). The snowball effect: Turnover embedded in communication networks. *Applied Psychology*, 71, 50–55.

Kreiner, G. E., & Ashforth, B. E. (2004). Evidence toward an expanded model of organizational identification. *Journal of Organizational Behavior*, 25(1), 1–27.

Lee, T. W. (1988). How job satisfaction leads to employee turnover. *Journal of Business and Psychology*, 2, 263–271.

Lee, T. W., Mitchell, T. R., Holtom, B. C., McDaniel, L., & Hill, J. (1999). The unfolding model of voluntary turnover: A replication and extension. *Academy of Management Journal*, 42, 450–462.

Lee, T. W., & Mitchell, T. R. (1994). An alternative approach: The unfolding model of voluntary employee turnover. *The Academy of Management Review*, 19(1), 51–89.

Lee, T. W., Mitchell, T. R., Wise, L., & Fireman, S. (1996). An unfolding model of voluntary employee turnover. *Academy of Management Journal*, 39, 5–36.

Li, H. J., Hausknecht, J. P., & Dugoni, L. (2018). Initial and long-term change in unit-level turnover following leader succession: Contingent effects of outgoing and incoming leader characteristics. *Organizational Science*, in press.

Mael, F., & Ashforth, B. E. (1992). Alumni and their alma mater: A partial test of the reformulated model of organizational identification. *Journal of Organizational Behavior*, 13(2), 103–123.

Maertz, C. P., & Campion, M. A. (2004). Profiles in quitting: Integrating process and content turnover theory. *Academy of Management Journal*, 47, 566–582.

March, J. G., & Simon, H. A. 1958. *Organizations*. New York: Wiley.

Meyer, J. P., Stanley, D. J., Herscovitch, L., & Topolnytsky, L. (2002). Affective, continuance and normative commitment to the organization: A meta-analysis of antecedents, correlates, and consequences. *Journal of Vocational Behavior*, 61, 20–52.

Mischel, W., & Shoda, Y. (1995). A cognitive-affective system theory of personality: Reconceptualizing situations, dispositions, dynamics, and invariance in personality structure. *Psychological Review*, 102(2), 246–268.

Mischel, W., & Shoda, Y. (1998). Reconciling processing dynamics and personality dispositions. *Annual Review of Psychology*, 49, 229–258.

Mitchell, T. R., Holtom, B. C., Lee, T. W., Sablynski, C. J., & Erez, M. (2001). Why people stay: Using job embeddedness to predict voluntary turnover. *Academy of Management Journal*, 44, 1102–1121.

Mitchell, T. R., & Lee, T. W. (2001). The unfolding model of voluntary turnover and job embeddedness: Foundations for a comprehensive theory of attachment. *Research in Organizational Behavior*, 23, 189–246.

Mobley, W. H. (1977). Intermediate linkages in the relationship between job satisfaction and employee turnover. *Journal of Applied Psychology*, 62(2), 237–240.

Mobley, W. H., Griffeth, R. W., Hand, H. H., & Meglino, B. M. (1979). Review and conceptual analysis of the employee turnover process. *Psychological Bulletin*, 86, 493–522.

Mossholder, K. W., Settoon, R. P., & Henagan, S. C. (2005). A relational perspective on turnover: Examining structural, attitudinal, and behavioral predictors. *Academy of Management Journal*, 48(4), 607–618.

Mowday, R. T., Porter, L. W., & Stone, E. F. (1978). Employees characteristics as predictors of turnover among female clerical employees in two organizations. *Journal of Vocational Behavior*, 12, 321–332.

Mowday, R. T., & Spencer, D. G. (1981). The influence of task and personality characteristics on employee turnover and absenteeism incidents. *Academy of Management Journal*, 24, 634–642.

Neck, C., Manz, C., & Houghton, J. (2019). *Self-Leadership: The Definitive Guide to Personal Excellence*. Thousand Oaks, CA: Sage.

Ng, T. W. H., & Feldman, D. C. (2013). Changes in perceived supervisor embeddedness: Effects on employees' embeddedness, organizational trust, and voice behavior. *Personnel Psychology*, 663, 645–685.

Ou, A. Y., Seo, J., Choi, D., & Hom, P. W. (2017). When can humble top executives retain middle managers? The moderating role of top management team faultlines. *Academy of Management Journal*, 60(5), 1915–1931.

Owens, B. P., Johnson, M. D., & Mitchell, T. R. (2013). Expressed humility in organizations: Implications for performance, teams, and leadership. *Organization Science*, 24(5), 1517–1538.

Porter, C. M., Woo, S. E., & Campion, M. A. (2016). Internal and external networking differentially predict turnover through job embeddedness and job offers. *Personnel Psychology*, 69(3), 635–672.

Price, J. L., & Mueller, C. W. (1981). A causal model of turnover for nurses. *Academy of Management Journal* 24, 543–565.

Price, J. L., & Mueller, C. W. (1986). *Absenteeism and Turnover of Hospital Employees.* Greenwich, CT: JAI Press.

Ramesh, A., & Gelfand, M. J. (2010). Will they stay or will they go? The role of job embeddedness in predicting turnover in individualistic and collectivistic cultures. *Journal of Applied Psychology*, 95(5), 807–823.

Redding, S., Norman, A., & Schlander, A. (1993). The nature of individual attachment to the organization: A review of East Asian variations. In M. Dunnette & L. Hough (Eds.), *Handbook of Industrial and Organizational Psychology* (vol. 4, pp. 647–688). Palo Alto, CA: CA Consulting Psychology Press.

Reina, C., Rogers, K., Peterson, S., Byron, K., & Hom, P. W. (2018). Quitting the boss? The role of manager influence tactics and employee emotional engagement in voluntary turnover. *Journal of Leadership and Organizational Studies*, 25(1), 5–18.

Rubenstein, A. L., Eberly, M. B., Lee, T. W., & Mitchell, T. R. (2018). Surveying the forest: A meta-analysis, moderator investigation, and future-oriented discussion of the antecedents of voluntary employee turnover. *Personnel Psychology*, 71(1), 23–65.

Rusbult, C. E., & Farrell, D. (1981). Exchange variables as predictors of job satisfaction, job commitment, and turnover: The impact of rewards, costs, alternatives, and investments. *Organizational Behavior and Human Performance*, 28(1), 78–95.

Russell, C. J. (2013). Is it time to voluntarily turn over theories of voluntary turnover? *Industrial and Organizational Psychology*, 6, 156–173.

Seo, J. J., Nahrgang, J. D., Carter, M. Z., & Hom, P. W. (2018). Not all differentiation is the same: Examining the moderating effects of leader–member exchange (LMX) configurations. *Journal of Applied Psychology*, 103(5), 478–495.

Shapiro, D. L., Hom, P. W., Shen, W., & Agarwal, R. (2016). How do leader departures affect subordinates' organizational attachment? A 360-degree relational perspective. *The Academy of Management Review*, 41(3), 479–502.

Sluss, D. M., & Ashforth, B. E. (2007). Relational identity and identification: Defining ourselves through work relationships. *Academy of Management Review*, 32(1), 9–32.

Sluss, D. M., & Ashforth, B. E. (2008). How relational and organizational identification converge: Processes and conditions. *Organization Science*, 19(6), 807–823.

Sluss, D. M., Ployhart, R. E., Cobb, M. G., & Ashforth, B. E. (2012). Generalizing newcomers' relational and organizational identifications: processes and prototypicality. *Academy of Management Journal*, 55(4), 949–975.

Staw, B. M. (2016). Stumbling toward a social psychology of organizations: An autobiographical look at the direction of organizational research. *Annual Review of Organizational Psychology and Organizational Behavior*, 3, 1–19.

Steel, R. P. (2002). Turnover theory at the empirical interface: Problems of fit and function. *Academy of Management Review*, 27, 346–360.

Steel, R. P., & Griffeth, R. W. (1989). The elusive relationship between perceived employment opportunity and turnover behavior: A methodological or conceptual artifact? *Journal of Applied Psychology*, 74, 846–854.

Steers, R. M., & Mowday, R. T. (1981). Employee turnover and postdecision accommodation processes. In L. L. Cummings & B. M. Staw (Eds.), *Research in Organizational Behavior* (vol. 3, pp. 235–282). Greenwich, CT: JAI Press.

Swider, B. W., Boswell, W. R., & Zimmerman, R. D. (2011). Examining the job search–turnover relationship: The role of embeddedness, job satisfaction, and available alternatives. *Journal of Applied Psychology*, 96(2), 432–441.

Trevor, C. O., & Nyberg, A. J. (2008). Keeping your headcount when all about you are losing theirs: Downsizing, voluntary turnover rates, and the moderating role of HR practices. *Academy of Management Journal*, 51(2), 259–276.

Trusty, J., Allen, D. G., & Fabian, F. (2019). Hunting while working: An expanded model of employed job search. *Human Resource Management Review*, 29(1), 28–42.

Vardaman, J. M., Taylor, S., Allen, D. G., Gondo, M. B., & Amis, J. (2015). Translating intentions to behavior: The interaction of network structure and behavioral intentions in understanding employee turnover. *Organization Science*, 26(4), 1177–1191.

Waldman, D. A., Carter, M. Z., & Hom, P. W. (2015). A multilevel investigation of leadership and turnover behavior. *Journal of Management*, 41(6), 1724–1744.

Wanberg, C. R., Zhu, J., Kanfer, R., & Zhang, Z. (2012). After the pink slip: Applying dynamic motivation frameworks to the job search experience. *Academy of Management Journal*, 55(2), 261–284.

Wanberg, C. R., Zhu, J., & van Hooft, E. A. J. (2010). The job search grind: Perceived progress, self-reactions, and self-regulation of search effort. *Academy of Management Journal*, 53(4), 788–807.

Woo, S. E. (2011). A study of Ghiselli's hobo syndrome. *Journal of Vocational Behavior*, 79(2), 461–469.

Zimmerman, R. D. (2008). Understanding the impact of personality traits on individuals' turnover decisions: A meta-analytic path model. *Personnel Psychology*, 61(2), 309–348.

Zimmerman, R. D., Swider, B. W., Woo, S. E., & Allen, D. G. (2016). Who withdraws? Psychological individual differences and employee withdrawal behaviors. *Journal of Applied Psychology*, 101(4), 498–519.

8
METHODOLOGICAL APPROACHES IN TURNOVER RESEARCH

In this chapter, we review prevailing methodologies for turnover research. Specifically, we describe various methods for estimating predictive accuracy of turnover predictors and for testing turnover models.

Standard Research Practice (SRP)

Steel (2002) coined the term "standard research practice" to describe the predominant methodology by turnover researchers. Pioneered by Hulin (1966) and Mobley, Horner, and Hollingsworth (1978), researchers often use a "static cohort method" whereby they would sample a cohort of current or new employees and assess prospective turnover antecedents (e.g., job attitudes, personality attributes) on *one occasion* (or time period) using surveys, application blanks, or tests. Researchers would later retrieve information about this cohort's current employment status by soliciting personnel records. They then create a criterion score, which denotes whether study participants voluntarily quit since predictor assessments or have remained employed since. Figure 8.1 illustrates this longitudinal design, representing predictor assessments at Time-1 and criterion assessment at Time-2. Finally, researchers statistically relate this *static* criterion (denoting "an individual's standing at a *single instance in time*"; Steel, 2002, p. 347, emphasis in original) to earlier predictor scores using ordinary least squares (OLS) regression analysis. Statistical tests thus estimate whether predictors significantly and appreciably foreshadow employees' subsequent turnover behavior.

Although increasingly criticized (Allen, Hancock, Vardaman, & Mckee, 2014; Mobley, 1982; Steel, 2002), SRP nonetheless represents a major methodological improvement over past turnover studies (Hom, Lee, Shaw, & Hausknecht, 2017). In particular, SRP insured a temporal lag between

Standard Research Practice
Measurement Window

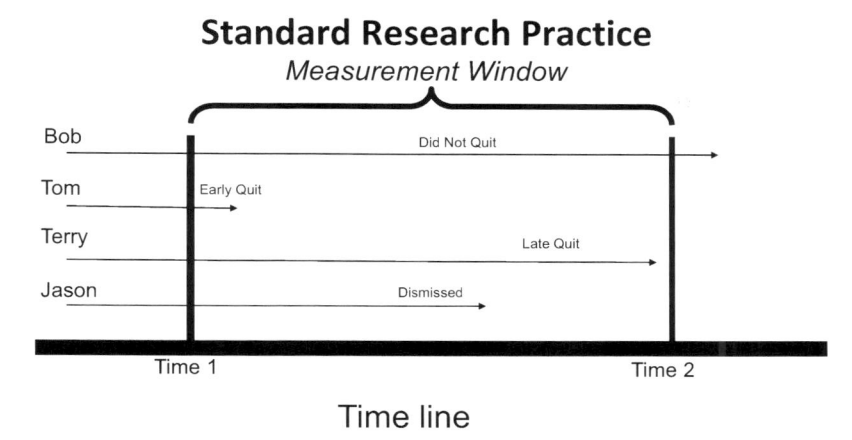

```
Bob    |—————————Did Not Quit—————————→|
Tom    | Early Quit
       |→
Terry  |                    Late Quit
       |————————————————————→
Jason  |           Dismissed
       |————————→
       Time 1                    Time 2
```

Time line

FIGURE 8.1 Standard Research Practice

predictor and turnover assessments, increasing confidence that predictors truly foreshadow—if not causally influence—turnover (i.e., internal validity). Modern turnover researchers also more carefully established that their criterion reflects "voluntary leaving" rather than all forms of leaving (e.g., layoffs, terminations; Hom & Griffeth, 1995). Further, contemporary researchers more assiduously avoided confounding individual-level with aggregate-level relationships (Hulin, Roznowski, & Hachiya, 1985).

Dominant Analytical Mindset (DAM)

Extending Steel's (2002) critique, Allen et al. (2014) sought to identify a dominant "analytical mindset" representing popular methodological choices by turnover researchers for research designs, data collection and measurement strategies, and analytical techniques. Reviewing 447 empirical studies over the past 52 years, they identified characteristics of a turnover DAM. Specifically, they concluded that turnover studies are primarily done in field settings (99%) with quantitative designs. Sustaining Steel's (2002) view, the most popular research design is the static cohort design (49%). Turnover researchers thus largely used correlational designs (86%), with few deploying experimental or quasi-experimental designs. Moreover, 84% of studies investigated the individual level of analysis, with 5% being multilevel. For data collection and measurement, 79% of studies relied on survey measures to assess turnover predictors, using idiosyncratic scales (73%) that lack construct validity (75%). Most investigations collected information about voluntary turnover 12 months since survey administration. Finally, the most common data analytical techniques are OLS or logistic regression (58%), while investigators generally tested moderation with multiple regression and mediation with the Baron–Kenny step approach or structural equation modeling (SEM).

In summary, Allen et al. (2014) concluded that a DAM predominates in turnover research: "the bulk of turnover research is quantitative, conducted in field settings, at the individual level of analysis, utilizing correlational designs, with a heavy reliance on survey measures and regression-based methods" (pp. 876, 878). These methodological choices are narrower than those made in organizational behavior and human resource research. Echoing Steel (2002), they concluded that a turnover DAM may prevent researchers from adequately assessing the process by which turnover unfolds (failing to verify a key tenet in many turnover theories) but also constraining the type of research questions explored and thus stifling theoretical creativity.

Statistical Methods of Turnover Prediction

Over the years, methodologists have often pioneered new statistical methods for management scholarship (notably, organizational behavior) by first demonstrating their methodological advantages for predicting turnover or evaluating turnover (or commitment) models (Hom, Caranakis-Walker, Prussia, & Griffeth, 1992; Huselid & Day, 1991; Lance, Vandenberg, & Self, 2000; Lee & Mitchell, 1994; Morita, Lee, & Mowday, 1989, 1993; Sturman & Trevor, 2001; Williams & Podsakoff, 1989). We first review their applicability for predicting turnover, while later reviewing their utility for theory verification.

Logistic Regression

Although the statistical method of choice among early scholars (Hom & Griffeth, 1995), authors 30 years ago began condemning OLS regression for predicting a binary dependent variable such as turnover (Harrison & Hulin, 1989; Huselid & Day, 1991) because it produces severe statistical problems. First, predicted turnover values may fall outside 0–1 boundaries, generating meaningless results. Second, heteroscedastic and non-normal errors derived from analysis of a dichotomous dependent variable may invalidate coefficient t-tests. Third, estimates of the marginal effects of an independent variable may be biased because they depend on the mean value of the dependent variable. Illustrating this pitfall, Huselid and Day (1991) showed divergent conclusions yielded by OLS and logistic regression analyses.

Survival Analysis

While logistic regression more appropriately analyzes categorical criterion, this method (like OLS regression) ignores relevant information about *when*—not just if—employees quit (Morita et al., 1989, 1993; Peters & Sheridan, 1988; Singer & Willett, 1991). Unless one is investigating entering employees, the dates for beginning and ending a standard cross-sectional study (i.e., occasions for assessing predictors and criterion) are typically arbitrary. Yet the particular temporal lag chosen (aka "measurement window" in Figure 8.1) can dramatically alter a study's findings on statistical relationships between predictors and quitting (Murnane, Singer, & Willett, 1989). Short measurement periods weaken estimated predictor–turnover relationships because fewer employees leave in any brief period and proportionally fewer quitters shrink turnover variance. By contrast, more employees may quit over a longer time period; the resulting higher turnover variance can bolster correlations, assuming predictors' causal impact has not eroded over time (Harrison & Hulin, 1989). Consequently, the predictive efficacy of turnover determinants may hinge more on arbitrarily chosen measurement intervals than on their true predictive validity. Indeed, Carsten and Spector (1987) estimated a −.51 correlation between the measurement window and satisfaction–turnover relationships, indicating that job satisfaction best predicts quits when the time span is short. Similarly, Griffeth, Hom, and Gaertner (2000) reported stronger performance–turnover correlations when the measurement window was less than 12 months ($r = -.26$) than when it was 12 months or longer ($r = -.14$).

The SRP design also distorts results by arbitrarily dictating which study participants are stayers and which are leavers (Murnane et al., 1989; Peters & Sheridan, 1988). Stayers are merely those employees who had not yet quit by the time the study ended (e.g., "Bob" in Figure 8.1); leavers are those leaving during the study period (e.g., "Tom" and "Terry" in Figure 8.1). If a study had ended earlier, some leavers—who had not quit by that time—would have been classified as stayers (e.g., "Terry" in Figure 8.1); a study ending later would result in more stayers becoming leavers (Steel, 2002). Such shifting employment status (and hence changing base rate and criterion variance) spuriously alters estimated predictive validity of turnover causes (Morita et al., 1993; Peters & Sheridan, 1988).

Most of all, this static cohort design neglects the *timing* of resignations (Morita et al., 1989), treating an employee who quits after 10 years of tenure the same as one who quits after a few days of employment (e.g., "Tom" and "Terry" in Figure 8.1; Murnane et al., 1989). This methodological tradition thus precluded consideration of the temporal process of change implicit in contemporary theories, overlooking how turnover causes shift over time and their dynamic relationships (Mobley, 1982; Morita et al., 1993; Rubenstein, Eberly, Lee, & Mitchell, 2018). Prevailing turnover research thus mostly attempts to predict *whether* turnover occurs (Williams, 1990), not *when* turnover occurs. Consequently, the standard design and OLS regression analysis may poorly address settings or occupations where quit rates exceed 100%, such as found among part-time fast-food restaurant staff (Krackhardt & Porter, 1985) or Mexican workers in export-oriented manufacturing (Miller, Hom, & Gomez-Mejia, 2001). For such jobs, predictions of *when* employees will quit rather than *if* they will quit would prove invaluable (Murnane et al., 1989).

To offset such methodological inadequacies, methodologists introduced "survival analysis" to examine turnover timing (Morita et al., 1989, 1993; Murnane et al., 1989; Peters & Sheridan, 1988). This technique comprises a family of actuarial methods from the biomedical life sciences to track the life expectancies of patients with life-threatening diseases. By treating employment duration as analogous to a lifetime, survival analysis can trace retention rates during employment, estimate quit rates at various stages of tenure, and identify peak termination periods (Singer & Willett, 1991). The prime dependent variable is the time elapsed between a starting point (e.g., organizational entry, predictor assessment) and occurrence of an event (namely, voluntary exits), thus reflecting when employees quit (unlike standard regression methods). Survival analysis focuses on two prime statistics: the *survival rate* (probability that employees remain employed at a particular occasion) and *hazard rate* (probability that employees will quit at a given time given they had stayed until that time; Singer & Willett, 1991).

We describe two types of survival analyses, which differ in whether they assess time as a discrete (e.g., employment duration defined monthly) or continuous variable. For discrete time assessment, the *discrete-time hazard* ($h[t_j]$) is the *conditional probability* that an employee i will experience the event (i.e., voluntarily quit) in time period j given that he or she did not experience it earlier (i.e., stayed up to that time; Singer & Willett, 2003). Put differently:

$h(t_j)$ = (number of employees voluntarily leaving during time j) ÷ (number of employees who still remain during time j [aka "risk set" who are at *risk* of experiencing the event])

For the sake of illustration, we report a "life table" tracing the "event histories" of newly hired nurses from their entry date (when none had yet to experience the event—i.e., voluntary quit) through the end of their first year of employment. This table divides nurses' first year of employment into discrete monthly periods and reports: (1) the number of nurses employed at the beginning of the month (i.e., the "risk set" at risk of voluntarily leaving during the month); and (2) the number of nurses who voluntarily quit during the month, and those who are "censored" during this time. *Censored observations* represent employees whose event time (or date of voluntary leaving) is unknown. Survival analyses retain employees who involuntarily left (e.g., dismissals, retirement, layoffs) before they can voluntarily quit, as well as those remaining employed after the measurement window closes (145 nurses). *When* involuntary leavers and stayers voluntarily leave is thus unknown as they never experience this event during the study (Morita et al., 1993). Unlike traditional procedures, survival analysis can partially use data from involuntary quitters. It includes their data in time periods that they had completed (their retention time is at least their dismissal date) but discards their data from time periods they had missed.

Each successive risk set is the prior month's risk set, excluding those who voluntarily and involuntary quit (those experiencing the event and those who became censored). From the life table in Figure 8.2, we compute the hazard probability for each time period shown in the bottom panel. For example, the hazard probability for the fourth month is 2.56% (or 4 leavers divided by 156 nurses constituting the risk set for that period)—or percent of that period's risk set leaving that period. The hazard function plotted in Figure 8.3 represents a set of $h(t_j)$'s that describes the risk of turnover occurrence at each time period, revealing when turnover most occurs.

Life Table: Employment History of New Nurses

Time Period (Job Tenure)	Incumbents at Risk at Beginning of Time Period	Voluntary Quits (Event)	Censored at End of Time Period
0-1 Month	158	1	0
1-2 Months	157	0	0
2-3 Months	157	1	0
3-4 Months	156	4	0
4-5 Months	152	2	0
5-6 Months	150	1	2 (2 Dismissed; Voluntary Quit Date is Unknown)
6-7 Months	147	2	0
7-8 Months	145	2	0
8-9 Months	143 (Risk Set at 8-9 Months)	2 (2 Experienced Event)	0
9-10 Months	141	1	1
10-11 Months	139	2	0
11-12 Months	137	0	0
12-13 Months	137	2	135 (135 Remain Employed When Study Ended — Quit Date is Unknown)

Conditional Risk of Turnover Occurrence

Time Period (Tenure)	Incumbents at Risk at Beginning of Time Period	Voluntary Quits (Event)	Censored at End of Time Period	Hazard Probability
0-1 Month	158	1	0	0.0063
1-2 Months	157	0	0	0.0000
2-3 Months	157	1	0	0.0064
3-4 Months	156	4	0	0.0256 — $h(t_3) = \frac{4}{156}$
4-5 Months	152	2	0	0.0132
5-6 Months	150	1	2	0.0067
6-7 Months	147	2	0	0.0136
7-8 Months	145	2	0	0.0138
8-9 Months	143	2	0	0.0140
9-10 Months	141	1	1	0.0071
10-11 Months	139	2	0	0.0144 (1.4% Probability of Quitting Given that Nurse Stayed 10 Months)
11-12 Months	137	0	0	0.0000
12-13 Months	137	2	135	0.0146

FIGURE 8.2 Computing Hazard Rates for New Nurses

For new nurses, their highest probability of leaving during the first year occurs during their third month of employment after they had completed "probation."

Equally informative, the survival rate ($S[t_j]$) is the probability that an employee i will stay (or "survive") past time period j (Singer & Willett, 2003). That is:

Discrete-Time Hazard Function

Hazard Function

[Graph showing h(t) vs Month of Employment, ranging from 0 to 12 months, with h(t) values between 0.0000 and 0.0300]

Probability of Staying for New Nurses

Survival Function

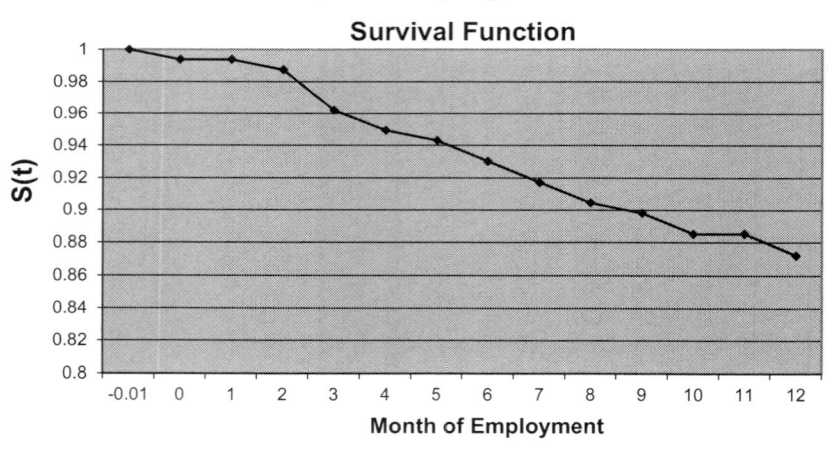

[Graph showing S(t) vs Month of Employment, ranging from -0.01 to 12 months, with S(t) values declining from 1 to approximately 0.87]

FIGURE 8.3 Survival Analysis: Hazard and Survival Functions

$S(t_j)$ = (number of employees remaining by end of time period j) ÷ (all employees)

Singer and Willett (2003) proposed computing $S(t_j)$ as $S(t_{j-1}) \times [1-h(t_j)]$ when there are censored observations. Figure 8.3 shows the survival function, which represents a set of $S(t_j)$'s, while Figure 8.4 reports data for computing $S(t_j)$'s. To illustrate, survival probability for the fourth time interval is 96.2%, which is the survival probability for the previous third interval (.9873) multiplied by 1 minus the hazard probability for the fourth time interval (.0256). According to this function, 88.5% of new nurses survived during their first year of work.

Discrete-Time Survival Probability = Probability that nurse i will stay beyond time j (Did Not Quit)

$$S(t_j) = S(t_{j-1}) [1-h(t_j)]$$

Month of Employment	Nurses at Risk at Beginning of Month	Voluntary Quits (Event)	Censored at End of Month	Hazard Probability	Survival Probability
0-1 Month	158	1	0	0.0063	0.9937
1-2 Months	157	0	0	0.0000	0.9937
2-3 Months	157	1	0	0.0064	0.9873
3-4 Months	156	4	0	0.0256	0.9620
4-5 Months	152	2	0	0.0132	0.9494
5-6 Months	150	1	2	0.0067	0.9430
6-7 Months	147	2	0	0.0136	0.9302
7-8 Months	145	2	0	0.0138	0.9174
8-9 Months	143	2	0	0.0140	0.9045
9-10 Months	141	1	1	0.0071	0.8981
10-11 Months	139	2	0	0.0144	0.8852
11-12 Months	137	0	0	0.0000	0.8852
12-13 Months	137	2	135	0.0146	0.8723

Annotations: $S(t_1) = 1.0(1-.0063)$; $S(t_3) = .9873(1-.0256)$; 88.5% Survived by end of 11th month

FIGURE 8.4 Life Table for Computing Survival Probabilities

For discrete time, we use discrete-time hazard models to estimate how the entire hazard profile (the "dependent variable") is a function of predictor variables. From Hom, Griffeth, Palich, and Bracker (1998), Figure 8.5 plots hazard and survival profiles (reflecting job survival) for two groups of new nurses—one comprising nurses who received a realistic job preview (RJP) during orientation and another group who did not receive the RJP (control group). Visual inspection suggests that RJP nurses had lower hazards of leaving than did control nurses, as well as higher job survival than the latter. To statistically estimate the relationship between the RJP predictor variable and the hazard function, statisticians prefer transforming the discrete-time hazard, which otherwise yields inadmissible values (as it is a conditional probability that must lie between 0 and 1), and thus facilitate comparisons between groups having different predictor scores. In particular, discrete-hazard survival analysis assesses the natural logarithm of the odds, where odds represent the ratio of the probability of leaving divided by the probability of staying. Known as the *logit transformation*, this analysis uses logistic regression to estimate the following equation:

$$\text{Logit } h(t_j) = [\alpha_1 D_1 + \alpha_2 D_2 + \ldots + \alpha_j D_j] + \beta_1 X_1 + \beta_2 X_2 + \ldots + \beta_P X_P.$$

with time period j and where Ds represent dummy variables representing different time periods (1 to J), Xs represent predictors (from 1 to P), αs represent intercepts reflecting the logit hazard (or "log odds of turnover occurrence") at a particular time, and βs assess the effect of a unit difference in a predictor on turnover occurrence (Singer & Willett, 2003). This statistical model specifies that the logit hazard function has an identical *shape* across groups varying in predictor scores,

214 Methodological Approaches

Hazard Function

Survival Function

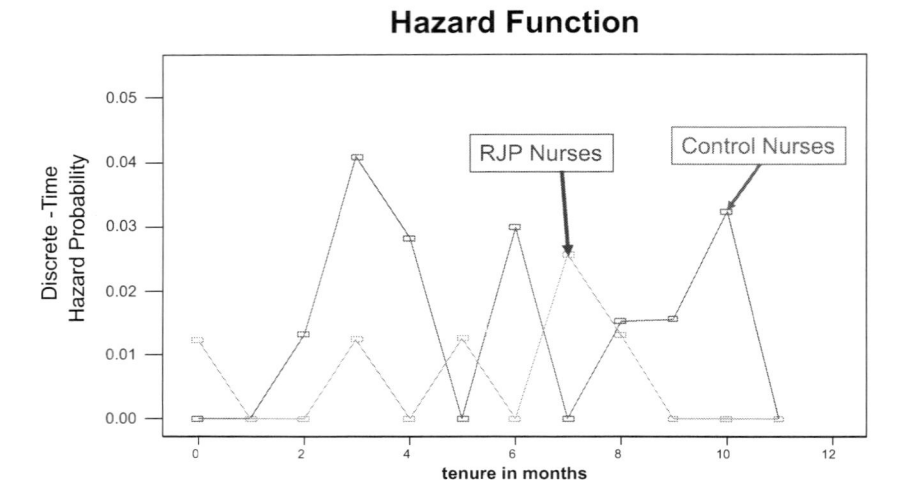

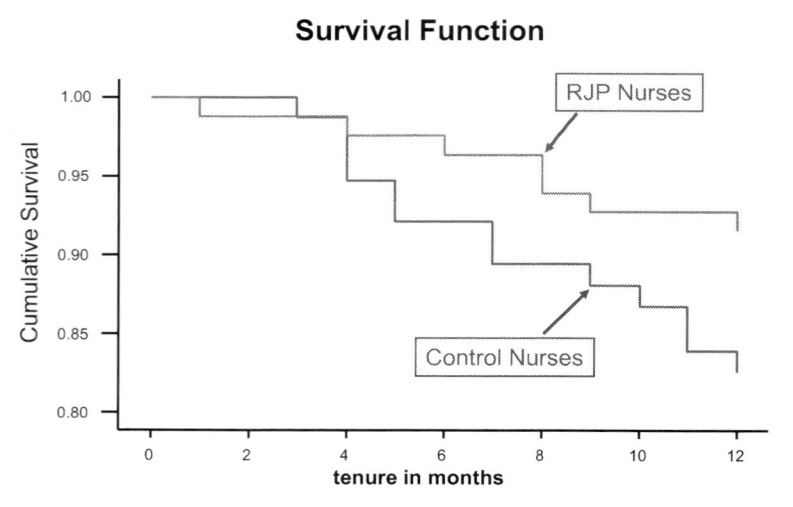

FIGURE 8.5 Hazard and Survival Functions between Treatment and Control Groups (New Nurses Receiving Job Previews or No Previews)

that *distance* between groups' functions is identical in every time, and that vertical displacement between group functions reflects a predictor's effect (Singer & Willett, 2003). Figure 8.6 displays the logit hazard functions for RJP and control nurses. That RJP nurses' hazard function is lower (displayed downward) compared to that for control nurses (whose function represents a baseline) suggests that the RJP reduced nurses' quit rate. Discrete-time hazard regression analysis determined that the RJP predictor variable (where RJP is coded as 1 and control is coded as 0) marginally reduced turnover ($p \leq .10$). Its regression coefficient (B) was −.767,

Methodological Approaches **215**

Logit Hazard by Experimental Group

Logit Hazard = Logarithm of Odds

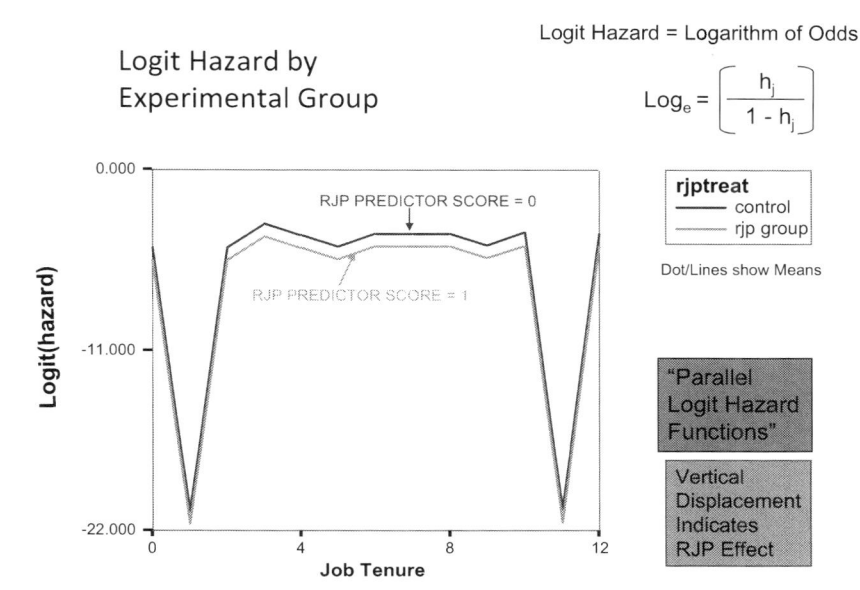

$$\text{Log}_e = \left[\frac{h_j}{1-h_j}\right]$$

FIGURE 8.6 Discrete-Hazard Survival Analysis Demonstrating RJP Effect on Nursing Turnover

which translates into an odds ratio (e^B) of .464. Put differently, the odds of voluntary quits for RJP nurses is 46% of the odds of quits for control nurses. Alternatively, the reciprocal of the odds ratios indicates that the odds of quitting are 2.16 higher for control than RJP nurses.

Cox Regression Model

For events occurring in continuous time, turnover researchers resort to the Cox regression model (often known as the "proportional hazard" model; Singer & Willett, 2003) to model the relationship between the entire hazard profile and predictors. This model assumes that an event occurs during a precise instance in time, such as quitting a job at 6:30 p.m. on March 27, 2019. Yet an infinite number of such instances exist for continuous time measurement that can always be divided into finer and finer intervals (e.g., nanosecond). Importantly, the probability of observing any particular event time is infinitesimally small, approaching 0 as time intervals shrink. For continuous time, Cox regression thus estimates a different hazard function as the hazard (or risk of event occurrence) is no longer a conditional probability, but a *rate per unit time*—or number of turnover events occurring during a time period—which can exceed 1.0. Rather than logit transformation, Cox regression predicts the logarithmic transformation of the hazard:

$$\text{Log } h(t_{ij}) = \log h_0(t_j) + [\beta_1 X_{1ij} + \beta_2 X_{2ij} + \ldots + \beta_p X_{pij}]$$

where log $h_0(t)$ represents the baseline hazard function (or log hazard profile when all predictor values equal 0) and the second part represents a weighted combination of predictors. Like discrete-time regression, this model assumes *parallel* log hazard functions for different individuals. Regression coefficients also index vertical displacement of (log) hazard profiles, estimating amount of elevation of the log hazard profile for a one-unit difference in predictor scores.

For greater interpretability, we can transform Cox predictor coefficients by antilogging (e^β), yielding "hazard ratios" that gauge the effect of a one-unit difference in a predictor on raw hazard. For illustration, we used Cox regression to estimate RJP impact on beginning nurses' job survival, deriving a regression coefficient of −.758 for the RJP predictor (which coded control nurses as 0s and RJP nurses as 1s) and thus an .469 hazard ratio. Figure 8.7 displays the estimated continuous-time hazard functions for RJP and control nurses. According to the hazard ratio, the estimated hazard of leaving for RJP nurses is .469 times that for control nurses. Put differently, the estimated hazard for control nurses is 2.13 times (1/hazard ratio) greater than that for RJP nurses. For hazard ratios close to 1.0, the following formula for computing the percentage change in hazard rates for unit change in a predictor may improve interpretability: $\%h(t) = 100 \times (e^\beta - 1)$. In our running example, the RJP (a unit predictor increase from 0) diminishes the hazard of leaving by 59.8% (Allison, 1984).

Apart from static predictor values, Cox regression can handle predictors whose values change over time (Hom & Kinicki, 2001). Because proportional hazard models assume that predictor effects are constant over time (hence parallel hazard profiles), this assumption can be tested by adding predictor × time interaction terms in Cox regression models. Fully parameterized hazard models, however, do not assume constant hazards. These models, however, are less accessible and

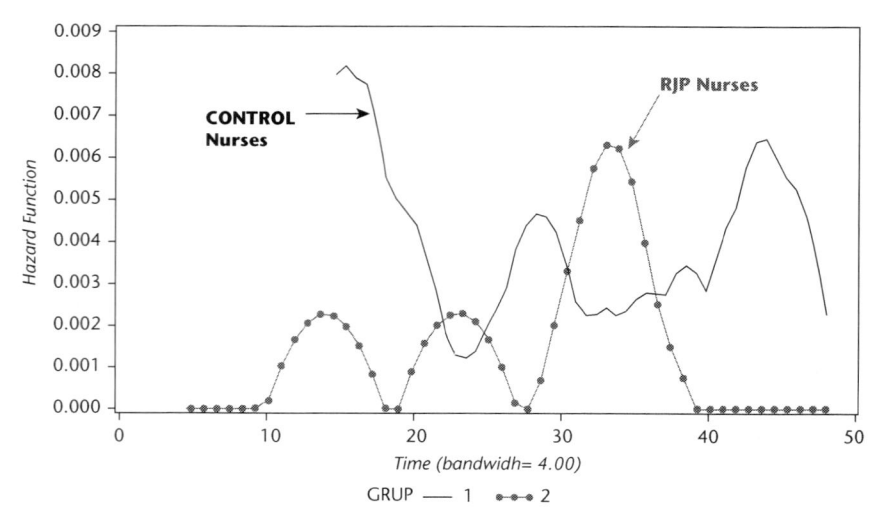

FIGURE 8.7 Estimated Continuous Hazard Functions for RJP and Control Nurses

require fitting a functional form for the hazard function (see O'Reilly, Caldwell, & Barnett, 1989). Finally, investigators can perform stratified analyses, allowing different subgroups to have different rather than identical baseline hazard functions.

In conclusion, survival analysis offers a powerful technique for examining the temporal dimension of the withdrawal process. This method is superior to regression methods that predict a static binary turnover criterion by revealing that a predictor may affect not just turnover occurrence, but also its timing. Moreover, traditional analytical procedures neglect how a causal antecedent may have varying effects on turnover over time (which can be estimated by adding predictor × time interactions to Cox regression; Salamin & Hom, 2005). Moreover, inclusion of a dichotomous dependent variable (turnover) into OLS regression violates statistical assumptions of continuous dependent variable and normally distributed errors, producing biased estimates (Huselid & Day, 1991). Morita et al. (1993) showed how such violations invalidated conclusions by OLS regression analysis compared with survival analysis. Survival analysis also treats missing or censored data more efficiently, while including cases of involuntary leaving (Morita et al., 1989).

Random Coefficient Modeling for Assessing Predictor Change

Temporal shifts in turnover causes have long captivated scholarly attention when pioneers such as Charles Hulin (1966) and Lyman Porter (Porter, Crampon, & Smith, 1976) showed that the algebraic difference between measures of job attitudes on two separate occasions can predict turnover. Indeed, Rusbult and Farrell (1983) uncovered such sizeable correlations between antecedent difference scores and turnover (e.g., computing an adjusted R^2 of .65 when regressing turnover onto difference scores for model variables) that they concluded that "it is the *process of change*—declining rewards, increasing costs, divestiture (i.e., declining investment size), and improving alternative quality—that distinguishes between those who stay and those who leave" (p. 437, emphasis in original). Despite such remarkable findings, contemporary methodologists condemned difference (and residual gain) scores, noting that they are unreliable, inversely related to pretest scores, cannot explain unique variance beyond their components, and are subject to regression-toward-the-mean artifacts (Edwards, 1994a, 2002; Irving & Meyer, 1999).

Rather, a form of multilevel modeling known as "random coefficient modeling" (RCM) has become the method of choice for analyzing panel (repeated-measures) data to estimate trajectories of change for turnover predictors and their ability to predict turnover (Hom & Haynes, 2007; Sturman & Trevor, 2001). Relying on panel data (where respondents are assessed three or more times), RCM treats repeated assessments of a turnover predictor as an outcome of the timing of their measurement. To illustrate, we surveyed employees on three occasions, assessing their job satisfaction (see Figure 8.8). To estimate an employee's change in job satisfaction over time, we regress job satisfaction onto time, generating an intercept term (representing Time-1 level of job satisfaction—or its initial status) and a slope term (reflecting "rate of

Interindividual Differences in Change

- Differences in Growth Trajectories Across Individuals

- Subjects 4 and 46 Have Different Intercepts and Different Slopes

SUBJECT 4

Job Satisfaction = 3.25 -0.25 (Time)

SUBJECT 46

Job Satisfaction = 2.17 + 0.38 (Time)

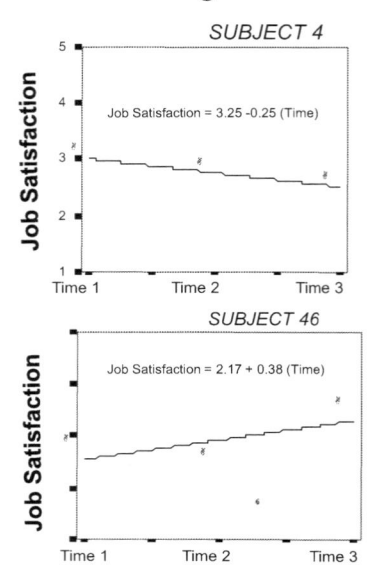

FIGURE 8.8 Individual Variability in Regression Equations

change per unit time"—or amount of change in satisfaction per unit time). The slope parameter—otherwise known as a "growth" trajectory (borrowing a term from developmental psychology)—thus captures temporal change rather than classic difference score (Edwards, 1994b). Note that RCM allows for different trajectories for different people whose intercepts and slopes may differ (see Figure 8.8).

While focusing on individual trajectories (i.e., *within-person* change), RCM also estimates interindividual differences in those trajectories (i.e., *between-person* differences in change). To illustrate, Figure 8.9 reports separate regressions (regressing job satisfaction onto time) for different respondents. These individual regression analyses reveal individual differences in intercept and slope terms. RCM can identify factors that underlie individual variability in growth parameters. To do so, RCM estimates two submodels simultaneously: a level 1 model describing how each person changes over time and a level 2 model that describes how those changes vary across persons (and hinge on other variables differentiating them). A level 1 submodel for an individual's change in job satisfaction (Y) is:

$$Y_{ij} = \pi_{0i} + \pi_{1i}(Time_j) + \varepsilon_{ij}$$

where i indexes persons and j indexes occasions of measurement. Growth parameters are $\pi_{0i} + \pi_{1i}$ where:

π_{0i} = the intercept of the change trajectory for individual i
and

π_{1i} = the slope of the change trajectory for individual i

Methodological Approaches 219

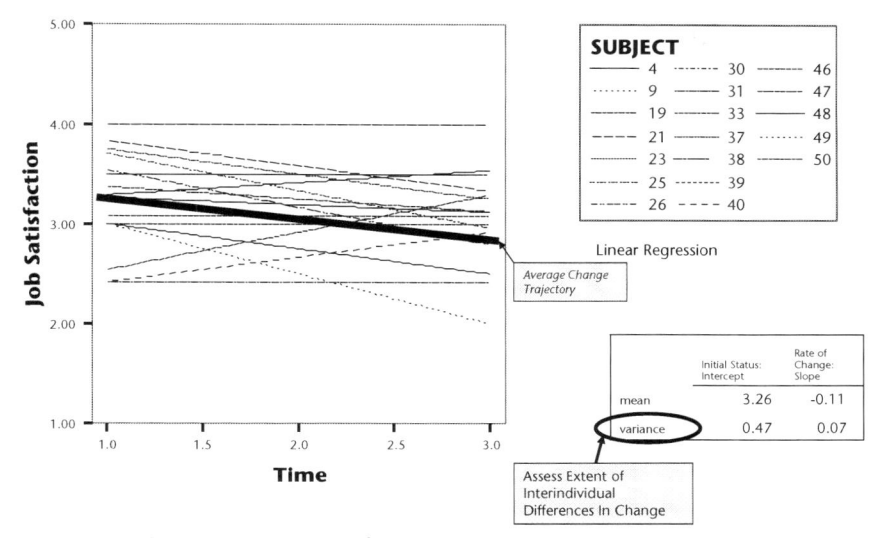

FIGURE 8.9 Average Trajectory and Between-Person Variance in Trajectory

or the rate at which individual i's job satisfaction changes over time. For interpretability of the intercept, the time scale is usually "centered" (i.e., the first measurement is scaled at zero) so that the intercept equals the job satisfaction score at the first assessment. ε_{ij} represents the deviation of the individual's actual job satisfaction score from the trajectory and reflects measurement error and score variations not explained by time. Moreover, RCM estimates the level 1 residual variance (σ^2_ε), which reflects scatter of residual scores around individual i's change trajectory.

To determine why individuals vary in change trajectory, RCM estimates a level 2 submodel that seeks to explain interindividual differences in growth parameters with between-person (aka level 2) predictors. Assuming the same functional relationship between a turnover antecedent (e.g., job satisfaction) and time, individuals are presumed to have different level 1 intercept and slope parameters. The level 2 model in turn regresses individual growth parameters onto level 2 predictors to explain between-person variation in the job satisfaction trajectory.

To illustrate how RCM can assess the relationship between the change trajectory of a turnover antecedent and turnover, we report a multilevel analysis of a longitudinal survey of organizational commitment among new 924 casino workers (Wang, Hom, & Allen, 2017). For RCM, we used Raudenbush and Bryk's (2002) hierarchical linear modeling (HLM) program. We thus estimated a level 1 equation regressing commitment (COMMIT) onto time of measurement:

$$COMMIT_{ij} = \pi_{0i} + \pi_{1j}(Time_j) + \varepsilon_{ij}$$

and level 2 equations specifying $QUIT_i$ (employment status coding leavers as 1 and stayers as 0) as a "predictor" of growth parameters. Specifically, we estimate how turnover is related to commitment intercepts by estimating:

$$\pi_{0i} = \gamma_{00} + \gamma_{01}(QUIT_i) + \zeta_{0i}$$

where γ_{00} represents the population average of level 1 intercepts for individuals when level 2 predictor (QUIT) scores equal zero (aka stayers) and γ_{01} represents the "effect" of turnover on commitment intercepts. We further compute another equation assessing how turnover is related to the slope of the commitment trajectory with the following:

$$\pi_{1j} = \gamma_{10} + \gamma_{11}(QUIT_i) + \zeta_{1i}$$

where γ_{10} represents the population average of individuals' slopes when their level 2 predictor scores (QUIT) equal zero and γ_{11} represents the "effect" of turnover on individuals' commitment slope. ζ_{0i} represents the level 2 residual or between-person variation in intercept not explained by level 2 predictors, while ζ_{1i} represents the level 2 residual or between-person variation in slope not explained by level 2 predictors.

The HLM test for the second-level model predicting intercepts yielded the following: $\gamma_{00} = 4.61$ ($p < .05$) and $\gamma_{01} = -.09$ ($p > .05$). That is, turnover did not "affect" initial commitment as stayers and leavers did not differ in Time-1 measurement of commitment levels ($\gamma_{01} = -.09$). At Time-1, these two groups reported similar commitment levels. However, the second-level model predicting slopes yielded $\gamma_{10} = -.01$ ($p < .05$), indicating that commitment declined for the entire sample, and $\gamma_{11} = -.01$ ($p < .05$), indicating that leavers (whose QUIT score is "higher") exhibit greater commitment decline than do stayers. Figure 8.10 reveals how slopes vary between stayers and leavers. In other words, casino workers whose commitment to the organization fall more precipitously during the initial period of employment more readily quit their job.

For a more familiar analysis treating turnover as a dependent variable, HLM users can generate Bayes estimates of growth parameters to predict turnover (Wang et al., 2017). To illustrate, we regressed casino workers' turnover onto Bayes estimates of their commitment slope (Raudenbush & Bryk, 2002) with logistic regression, which yielded a $B = -24.71$ ($p < .05$). According to the formula $(e^B - 1) \times 100$ (Allison, 1995), a one-unit *increase* in the commitment slope (or less negative slope) translates into a 100% decrease in turnover *odds* (ratio of the probability of leaving divided by probability of staying).

Using RCM tests, turnover researchers increasingly document that the trajectory of change of turnover antecedents can explain additional variance in turnover beyond that by their static scores (e.g., job satisfaction, job performance; Chen, Ployhart, Thomas, Anderson, & Bliese, 2011; Kammeyer-Mueller, Wanberg, Glomb, & Ahlburg, 2005; Liu, Mitchell, Lee, Holtom, & Hinkin, 2012; Sturman & Trevor, 2001). While not necessarily demonstrating that change trajectories are

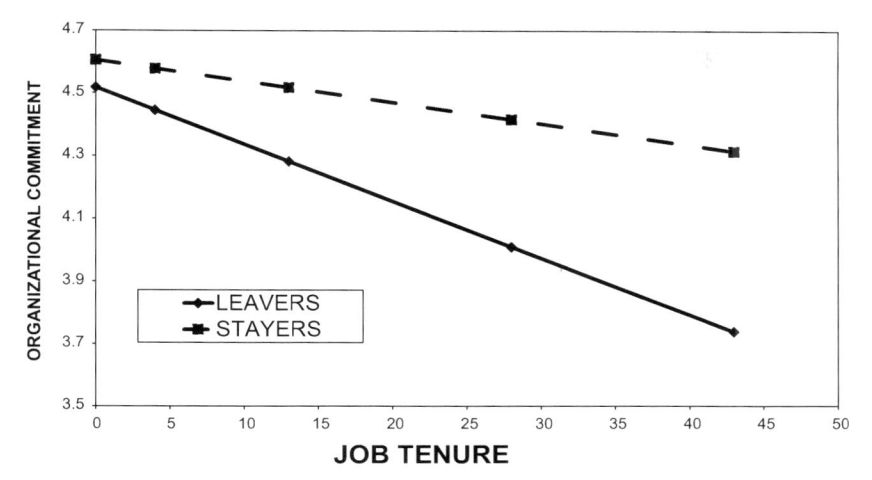

FIGURE 8.10 Trajectory of Change for Organizational Commitment between Stayers and Leavers

more powerful predictors than are static predictors (cf. Rusbult & Farrell, 1983), RCM tests are attesting to the long-held wisdom that they offer insight into the turnover process and can improve predictive validity (Mobley, 1982; Steel, 2002).

Testing Causal Models of the Turnover Process

Since the modern era of turnover theory and research began in the 1970s (Mobley, 1977; Price, 1977; Price & Mueller, 1981), researchers began testing theorized structural networks among turnover determinants in addition to estimating their ability to forecast turnover (Hom et al., 2017). Apart from breadth and scope, turnover theorists since March and Simon (1958) formulate elaborate networks of structural associations among model variables (Hom & Griffeth, 1995; Hulin et al., 1985; Mobley, Griffeth, Hand, & Meglino, 1979; Price & Mueller, 1981; Steers & Mowday, 1981). Early tests relied on exploratory path analysis to assess structural relationships by regressing each turnover determinant onto *all* determinants occurring earlier in a temporal sequence for withdrawal (Lee, 1988; Mobley et al., 1978; Price & Mueller, 1981). Such path analyses did not, however, represent confirmatory analysis, which prescribes testing theoretically dictated pathways, not every possible one (James, Mulaik, & Brett, 1982). Apart from such misuse, early researchers generally neglected to validate pathways omitted by their formulations ("the omitted parameters test"; James et al., 1982). Most theories, especially parsimonious ones, imply the *absence* of causal connections, in addition to explicitly specifying connections. Yet the validity of so-called null pathways usually went untested. Further, early path analyses rarely controlled random measurement error, which biases parameter estimates (Williams & Hazer, 1986).

Structural Equation Modeling (SEM)

Increasingly, turnover researchers began applying structural equation modeling (SEM) to overcome the aforementioned shortcomings of *exploratory* path analysis. Testing both non-zero and null structural pathways *theorized a priori* (James et al., 1982), SEM tests simultaneously estimate the validity of the former by computing path coefficients and the validity of the latter by generating overall model fit statistics (Hom et al., 1992). Using SEM to set measurement parameters based on scale reliabilities (Williams & Hazer, 1986), SEM can also more accurately estimate causal effects among constructs by controlling random measurement error (testing a "manifest variables" structural model).

More ambitiously, some turnover researchers more fully exploited the power of SEM by testing "latent variables" (LV) structural models. Going beyond a priori specification of structural relationships among turnover antecedents, LV structural models further specify how a set of indicators represent each construct. To illustrate, Figure 8.11 reports an LV structural model by Hom and Kinicki (2001), in which latent variables (factors) are depicted with ellipses and manifest variables (indicators) with boxes. Straight arrows from ellipses to boxes represent indicator loadings on latent variables; straight arrows among ellipses represent causal effects among latent variables. The measurement submodel prescribes a certain pattern of factor loadings between indicators and latent factors. The structural submodel of the LV model depicts theorized structural relations among factors and thus essentially embodies the substantive theory.

Using multiple indicators, SEM analysis of LV structural models more accurately estimates structural relationships by disattenuating causal parameters from random errors of measurement (Dwyer, 1983). Excepting programmatic research by Price and Mueller (1981, 1986), turnover researchers have rarely carefully validated their operationalizations of explanatory constructs (Allen et al., 2014). SEM tests, however, prompt researchers to pay greater attention to their measures and toward validating them as flawed measures can undermine theory verification.

SEM analysis then simultaneously estimates both measurement and structural models, which together constitute the LV structural model. Using one of several estimation methods (e.g., maximum likelihood), SEM simultaneously derives estimates for measurement and causal parameters that maximally recompute observed covariances. We interpret omnibus fit indices and parameter estimates to judge model fit. Significant (sizeable) factor loadings uphold the measurement submodel, while significant causal parameters (carrying the correct signs) uphold the structural submodel. While SEM users often interpret omnibus fit statistics (e.g., chi-square test) to judge overall fit of the model, they rarely regard them as direct tests of the validity of null parameters (James et al., 1982). Rather, they further test alternative versions of the structural model that adds superfluous structural pathways (Aquino, Griffeth, Allen, & Hom, 1997), such as direct effect of job dissatisfaction onto turnover in Figure 8.11. SEM assessment of alternative

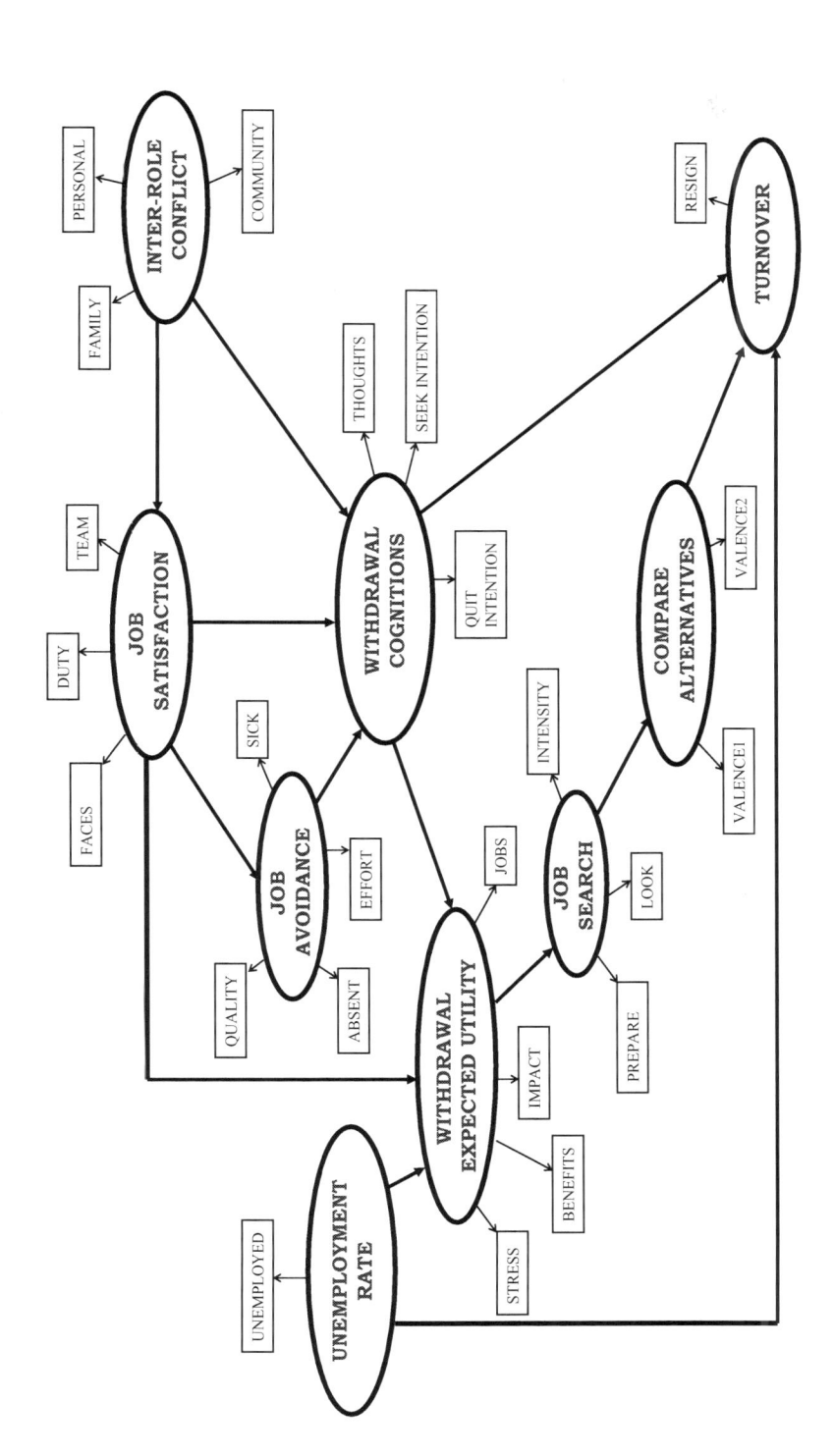

FIGURE 8.11 Hom and Kinicki's (2001) Latent Variables Structural Model

models revealing extra paths to be non-significant (or little improvement in model fit) would further corroborate the original structural model. Further, Anderson and Gerbing (1988) suggested testing various alternative measurement models to find the best-fitting one, adopting a two-stage procedure testing and refining the measurement model before evaluating the structural model (Hom & Griffeth, 1991). Though exploratory, separate estimation (including respecification) of the measurement model before assessing the structural model may reduce "interpretational confounding."

SEM Panel Analysis

Turnover theories also presume causal order or direction among their explanatory constructs (Mobley, 1977; Price & Mueller, 1981), yet those causal priorities are rarely validated. Generally speaking, turnover researchers often used correlational research designs to verify turnover models (Allen et al., 2014). Yet assessing antecedent and consequent constructs concurrently yields weak evidence for their causal direction (Mobley, 1982). While unable to rival true experimentation for causal inference, panel designs—repeated measurement of turnover determinants—might estimate the magnitude and direction of their causal effect more accurately than ubiquitous cross-sectional designs (Aronson, Ellsworth, Carlsmith, & Gonzales, 1990; Dwyer, 1983). To establish causal direction, some scholars assessed cross-lagged relationships between turnover antecedents, assessing them on several occasions. Early tests applied cross-lagged regression (Bateman & Strasser, 1983, 1984) or path analysis (Curry, Wakefield, Price, & Mueller, 1986; Farkas & Tetrick, 1989) to evaluate the lagged causal impact of Time-1 variables on Time-2 variables. For example, Curry et al. (1986) assessed job satisfaction and organizational commitment on two occasions, although disputing their causal relationship as they detected no lagged effects between them. Because turnover theories generally neglect causal lag times (Sheridan & Abelson, 1983), some scholars have used cross-lagged designs (with multiple waves of variable assessment) to empirically identify the timing or duration of causal effects (Hom & Griffeth, 1991).

In a methodological advance, Williams and Podsakoff (1989) introduced latent variables SEM as a superior procedure for analyzing longitudinal repeated-measures data that controls random errors of measurement and autocorrelated measurement errors to more precisely estimate structural parameters (Anderson & Williams, 1992; Dwyer, 1983). To illustrate, we might try to establish causal priority between two latent constructs: job satisfaction and organizational commitment. We would undertake a panel survey and measure these constructs, using multiple indices, on at least two occasions. Then we test an LV structural model, such as shown in Figure 8.12. To control autocorrelated measurement errors, this model estimates correlations between measurement errors across occasions (portrayed by connecting arrows impinging on boxes; Hom & Griffeth, 1991). This model

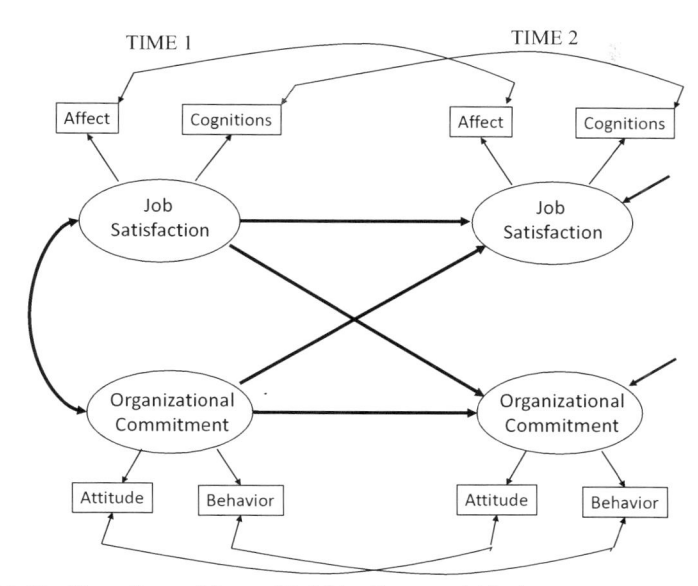

FIGURE 8.12 Cross-Lagged Latent Variables Structural Mode

also specifies the time-lagged effect of each variable onto itself, the source of its temporal stability. For instance, Time-1 satisfaction is depicted as impacting Time-2 satisfaction. The specification of the effects of Time-1 satisfaction on Time-2 commitment and of the impact of Time-1 commitment on Time-2 satisfaction, in this model, estimates lagged causal effects. We can estimate this model and use it as a baseline for nested comparisons to verify causal direction.

Figure 8.13 shows such nested comparison models omitting their measurement submodels. As a baseline model, the first model (*reciprocal causation*) posits a lagged reciprocal causation between attitudes. Assuming that the baseline model fits data, we compare it to the *satisfaction causation* model, specifying only a lagged satisfaction effect. If this model matches the baseline model's fit and its causal parameter is significant, we might conclude that satisfaction "causes" commitment. If the *commitment causation* model approximates the baseline model's fit better than does the satisfaction causation model and yields a significant commitment lagged influence, we might claim that commitment "affects" satisfaction. Reciprocal causation is, however, indicated by superior fit in the baseline model relative to the other two nested models and significant estimates for both of its two lagged causal parameters. All causal lagged effects are refuted if the baseline model badly fits data and yields no significant cross-lagged causal effects between the two attitudes.

Simple longitudinal models of causation between a few antecedents are likely misspecified because they may exclude many causes, including shared causes of measured antecedents (Anderson & Williams, 1992). If stable, these unmeasured

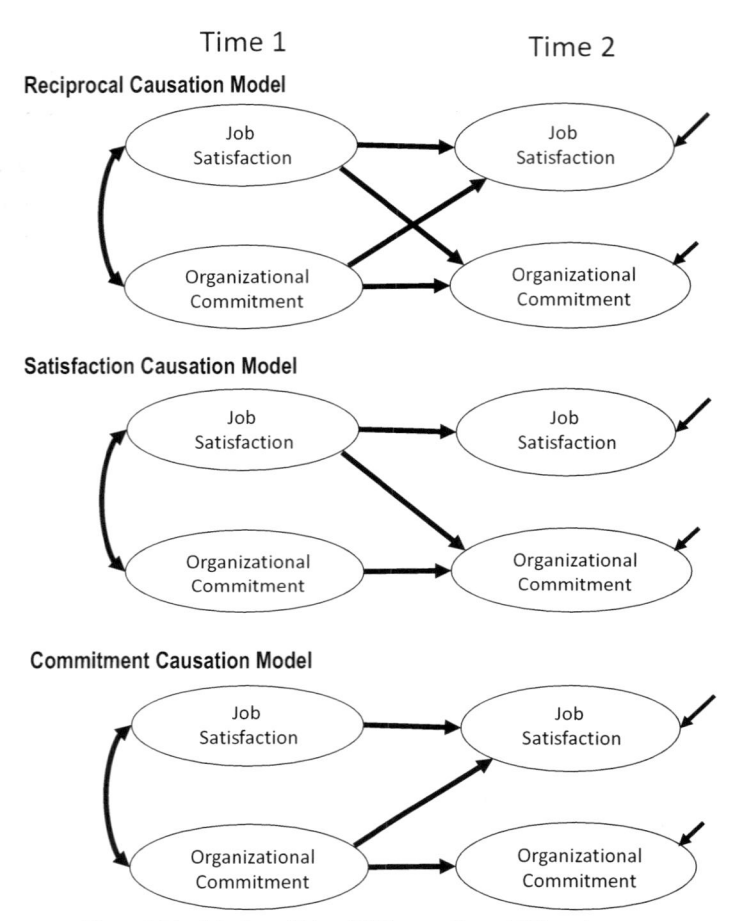

FIGURE 8.13 Nested Models Specifying Different Causal Directions

causes can induce correlations between disturbances across time periods and thus distort estimated lagged causal effects. To illustrate, Anderson and Williams compared two panel models of reciprocal effects between satisfaction and commitment, one with and one without correlated disturbances. The model specifying no correlated disturbances—an invalid assumption given the exclusion of many attitudinal causes—estimated lagged causal effects; the (correct) model, which did have correlated disturbances (to represent omitted causes), revealed few lagged effects. Consequently, Anderson and Williams recommended that SEM users estimate between-time (and within-time) correlations among disturbances if their panel models exclude relevant (and stable) causes. By taking into account disturbance correlations, SEM tests of even misspecified models that omit relevant causes may more accurately assess lagged causal influences.

Because temporal parameters are missing from turnover models (Miller, Katerberg, & Hulin, 1979), cross-lagged panel SEM analysis might empirically estimate causal lags (cf. Sims & Szilagyi, 1979). To illustrate, Williams and Podsakoff (1989) applied SEM analysis to estimate causal lag times from several waves of observations taken at equal time intervals. A three-wave LV panel model specifying causal influence from satisfaction to commitment is shown in Figure 8.14. Like a two-wave model, this model specifies covariances between measurement errors and autoregressive effects between adjacent time periods. Assuming that satisfaction causes commitment (and not the reverse), this model estimates brief (*first-order* effects between adjacent periods: Time-1 satisfaction → Time-2 commitment) and extended (*second-order* effects: Time-1 satisfaction → Time-3 commitment) lagged effects by satisfaction. This empirical approach is not without its limitations. We can rely on background knowledge and intuition, but specification of survey timing is still arbitrary. If measurement lags are too long, we miss the causal duration (Curry et al., 1986; Farkas & Tetrick, 1989) and falsely conclude that there is no lagged causation (Anderson & Williams, 1992).

Latent Growth Modeling (LGM)

Although RCM can estimate the predictive validity of turnover antecedents' change trajectories (Chen et al., 2011; Liu et al., 2012), latent growth modeling (LGM; Chan, 1998; Duncan, Duncan, Strycker, Li, & Alpert, 1999) can more directly test the structural networks among causal antecedents (often delineated in process models of turnover) by capturing how antecedents' trajectories are themselves interrelated (i.e., dynamic relationships; Chan & Schmitt, 2000) and can underpin leaving (Bentein, Vandenberg, Vandenberghe, & Stinglhamber, 2005; Lance et al., 2000). Given

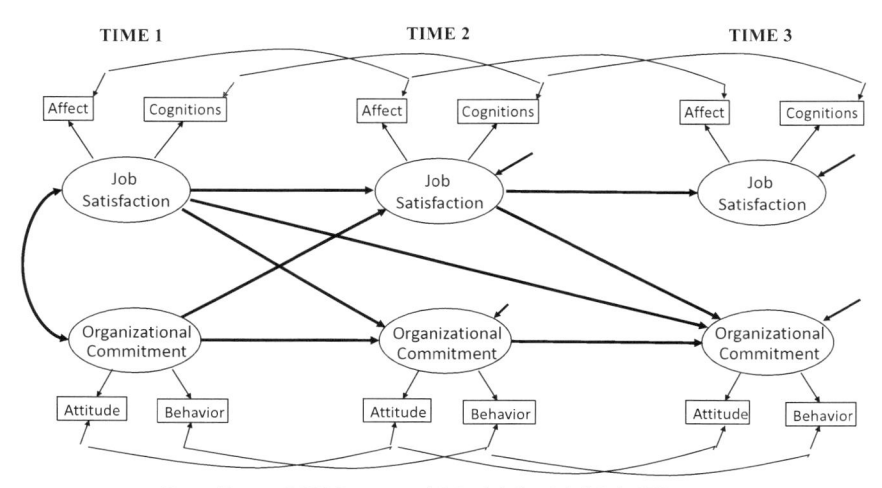

FIGURE 8.14 Cross-Lagged LV Structural Model for Multiple Waves

228 Methodological Approaches

multiwave (time-structured) assessments of a turnover cause (Singer & Willett, 2003), LGM can estimate interindividual variability in its change trajectory (both its intercept and slope) and assess how its growth parameters are related to other variables (static or dynamic antecedents or consequents). We discuss two variants of LGM modeling: first-order factor (FOF) and second-order factor (SOF) LGM (Lance et al., 2000).

FOF LGM resembles confirmatory factor analysis (CFA) by representing the intercept and slope of a change trajectory as latent growth factors underpinning repeated measurements of a given turnover antecedent. Figure 8.15 depicts a FOF growth model predicting an outcome. The antecedent variable is assessed on three (equally spaced) occasions (i.e., Y1–Y3), while the outcome is measured on a fourth occasion (Y4). Like CFA, Y indicators of a turnover antecedent reflect two latent growth factors—namely, the intercept and slope of its change trajectory. Unlike CFA, Y indicators on different occasions have fixed (not estimated) factor loadings on intercept and slope factors. To identify the intercept factor, all indicators have a fixed loading of 1.0 for this factor. To identify a linear slope, we fix Time-1 indicator's factor loading on the slope factor at 0, fix the second indicator's loading at 1, and fix the third indicator's loading at 2. These slope loadings represent a linear relationship between the variable and (equal-spaced) measurement occasions because these loadings fall along a straight line when plotted against time. Each variable's indicator on a particular occasion thus reflects both intercept and slope factors, as well as measurement error. Although individual growth scores are not directly computed, FOF LGM can estimate their variance (σ^2) and mean (μ) as well as their structural effects (β).

For illustration, we report a test of Ajzen's (1991) theory of planned behavior (TPB), which posits that perceived behavioral control and behavioral intentions primarily determine behavior. Intentions in turn are a function of attitude toward the act, the subjective norm, and perceived behavioral control. Ajzen and Madden (1986) established that the TPB model can accurately predict and explain students'

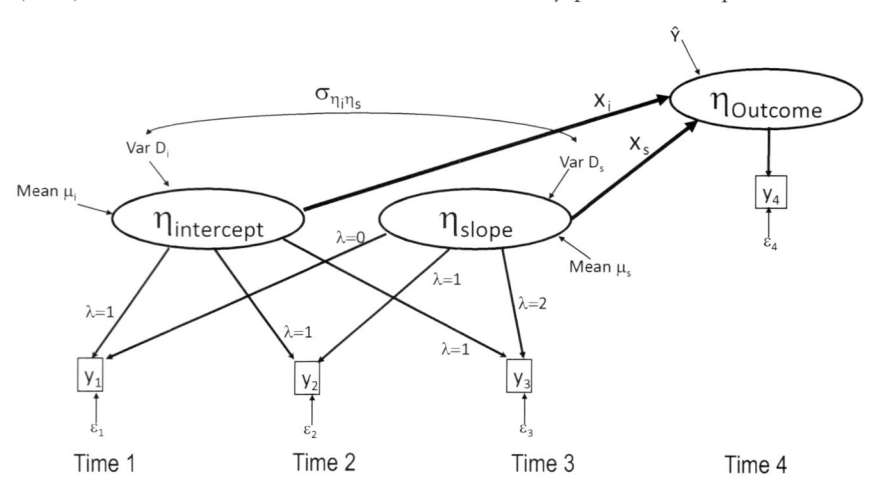

FIGURE 8.15 First-Order Factor Latent Growth Model

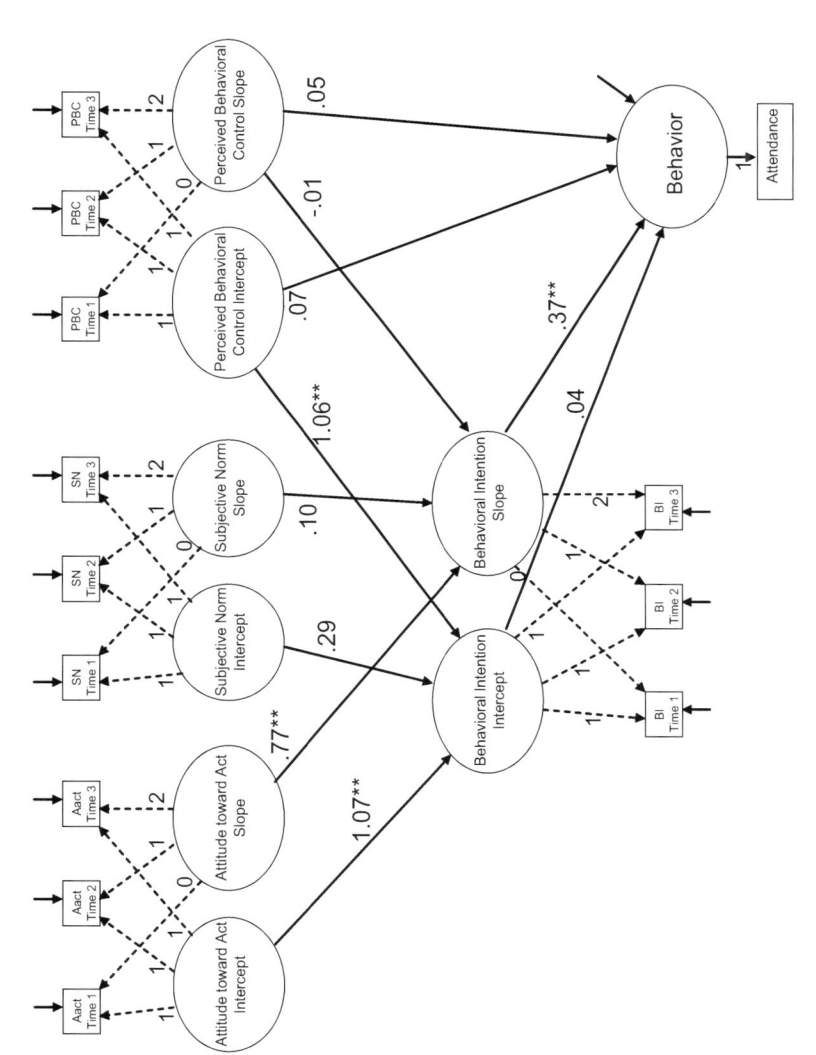

FIGURE 8.16 Using FOF LGM to Test Dynamic Relationships in Ajzen's (1991) Theory of Planned Behavior

class attendance. Extending that cross-sectional test, we try to validate the TPB model with FOF LGM by surveying 245 undergraduates monthly (three times) about TPB components for an entire seminar. In particular, we sought evidence about whether or not the dynamic relationships between TPB components (i.e., correlations between change trajectories; Lance et al., 2000) correspond to the theorized TPB structural network traditionally verified by cross-sectional designs. We thus tested a dynamic TPB model in Figure 8.16, specifying that each TPB component's intercept and slope scores would *similarly* influence downstream TPB components.

LGM tests found adequate overall fit for this dynamic TPB model (according to standard SEM fit statistics). This analysis revealed significant declines in attitude toward class attendance, subjective pressure for attendance, perceived control over attendance, and attendance intentions during the semester. Sustaining dynamic effects, this LGM also showed that increasing favorable attitudes toward class attendance is positively related to rising attendance intentions over time, which in turn is positively related to actual class attendance (self-reported at Time-4). We, however, detected no effects by change trajectories for the subjective norm or perceived behavioral control.

Second-Order Factor (SOF) Latent Growth Modeling

While FOF LGM can directly test long-held assumptions that changes in distal turnover causes "induce" turnover or changes in proximal causes (Hom & Griffeth, 1991; Mobley, 1982), SOF LGM additionally controls for potential shifts in indicators' psychometric properties, which may masquerade as genuine variable change (Chan, 1998, 2002; Vandenberg & Lance, 2000). That is, "beta" and "gamma" changes in instrumentation can threaten valid inferences about true ("alpha") change (Chan, 2002). Beta change represents scale recalibration over time (e.g., respondents interpret a rating scale differently over time), whereas gamma change represents changes in the meaning of a measure over time (e.g., respondents define a construct they are evaluating differently over time; Vandenberg & Self, 1993).

To probe such artifactual changes, Vandenberg and Lance (2000) suggest testing the indicators' longitudinal measurement invariance before assessing temporal change in constructs, using CFA. To illustrate, Figure 8.17 shows a measurement model whereby a single latent construct is assessed by three indicators on three separate occasions. This model specifies each occasion as a latent factor assessed by three indicators. Each indicator is a function of its loading on the occasion factor (λ), an intercept (τ, useful for comparing mean-level variable changes over time), and measurement error (δ). Further, the model allows for covariance (θ) between the same indicator over time to assess autocorrelated measurement errors.

Vandenberg and Lance (2000) prescribed a series of tests of nested versions of this measurement model to assess artifactual psychometric shifts. They suggest first testing "configural invariance" to check for gamma change by assessing the fit of the measurement model in Figure 8.17 without imposing any equality constraints on

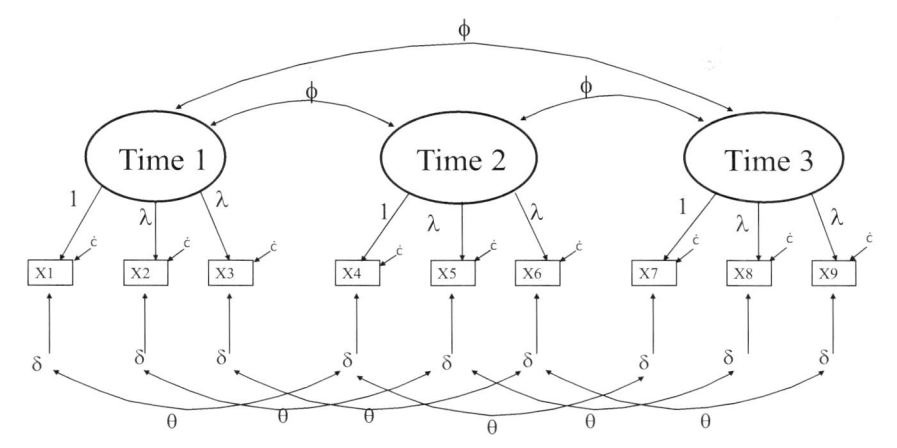

FIGURE 8.17 Longitudinal Measurement Model for Indicators Assessing the Same Construct

its parameters (e.g., all factor loadings—excepting those for reference indicators—are free to vary across occasions). Should this model fit data (according to omnibus fit indices and significant factor loadings), we would conclude that the pattern of factor loadings (and number of substantive factors, which is one in this example) is stable over time. Should this baseline model fail to fit data, we would not proceed to investigate change in this construct as it would be meaningless to examine its change when its indicators lack configural invariance (Lance et al., 2000).

After verifying configural invariance, Vandenberg and Lance (2000) prescribed testing a nested model constraining factor loadings for each indicator to be the same over time. Comparison between this model with the baseline model assesses beta change by determining whether indicators have stable validity and reflect the latent construct with the same precision over time. Should this second model fit as well as the (well-fitting) baseline model, we accept this more constrained model (due to parsimony) and conclude "metric invariance"—that factor loadings are identical over time (disputing beta change). After demonstrating both configural and metric invariance, we next evaluate whether indicant intercepts are stable over time to ascertain whether measures are calibrated equivalently to their underlying constructs with respect to location parameters across measurement occasions (Lance et al., 2000, p. 109). Specifically, we evaluate a third measurement model constraining each indicator's intercept to be constant over time (assessing "scalar invariance"). This model is nested within the second model as it retains the latter's time-invariant factor loadings. Scalar invariance exists if the third model fits data as closely as does the second model. In short, turnover researchers might first establish longitudinal measurement invariance (ruling out beta and gamma changes) before investigating change trajectories or mean changes over time in their explanatory constructs (Lance et al., 2000).

232 Methodological Approaches

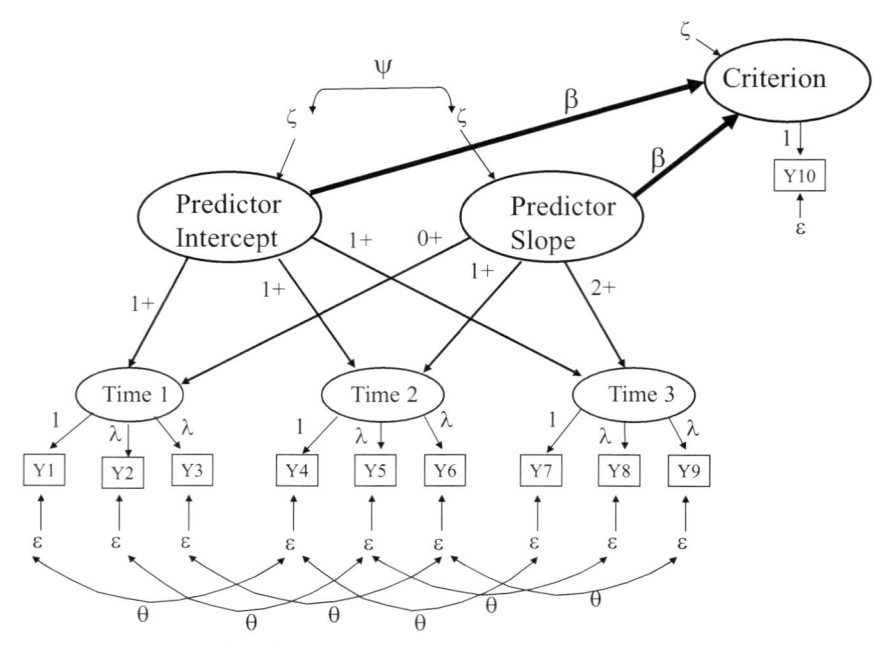

FIGURE 8.18 Second-Order Factor Latent Growth Model

After performing measurement invariance tests (identifying a well-fitting measurement submodel), researchers next estimate the slope and intercept for the underlying substantive construct with a SOF LGM model that incorporates the final (most constrained) measurement model. Figure 8.18 depicts a SOF LGM model, specifying growth parameters as "second-order" factors, which in turn affect "first-order" occasion factors (defined by a set of indicators gauging the same substantive construct collected on the same occasion). This model relates occasion to growth factors with a fixed set of second-order factor loadings, like those relating growth factors to indicants on different occasions in FOF LGM. For SOF LGM, we adopt the same factor structure relating occasion factors to indicators from the final model from measurement invariance tests, while imposing its equality constraints. By incorporating such measurement parameters, SOF LGM can control for the biasing effects of random measurement error and autocorrelated errors when estimating a construct's growth parameters (and their relationships with other constructs). Importantly, SOF LGM tests can also control for partial measurement invariance when measurement invariance tests identify a few factor loadings or intercepts varying over time.

To illustrate, we report SOF LGM findings from a panel survey of 290 working students whose withdrawal cognitions (i.e., thoughts of leaving, search intentions, and quit intentions; Hom & Griffeth, 1991) are assessed monthly for three months. Measurement invariance tests had established configural and

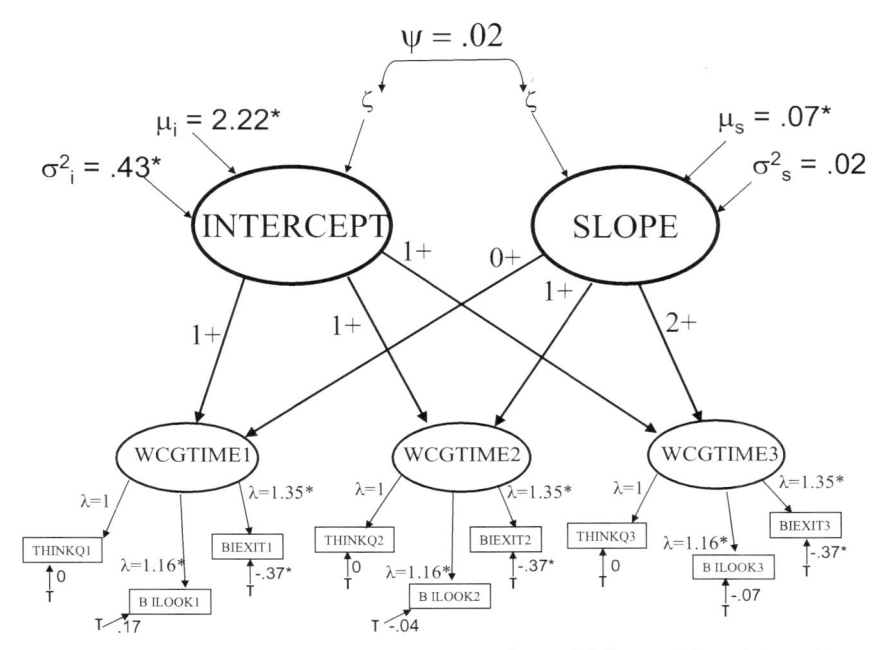

FIGURE 8.19 Second-Order Factor Latent Growth Model for Withdrawal Cognitions

metric invariance for these indicants as well as partial scalar invariance. The SOF LGM test incorporated these specifications for factor loadings and intercepts when assessing growth parameters. Omnibus fit statistics sustained this model (e.g., comparative fit index = .916; Bollen IFI = .928; NFI = .916; RMR = .054), while Figure 8.19 reports the parameter estimates. As noted, all factor loadings are significant and invariant over time, although intercepts for one indicator (i.e., search intentions) varied over time. Importantly, this test revealed that the average Time-1 withdrawal cognitions to be 2.22 as well as significant intercept variance (.43). The average slope was .07 (indicating rising withdrawal cognitions over time), though there were no significant individual differences in slope (.02).

We next added an outcome variable to this SOF LGM model—namely, working students' Time-4 withdrawal cognitions (assessed in a fourth survey). This expanded SOF LGM determined whether withdrawal cognitions' intercept and slope during the prior three months can predict later withdrawal cognitions. Omnibus fit statistics affirmed this model (e.g., NFI = .914; CFI = .929), while Figure 8.20 reveals that Time-1 withdrawal cognitions and its ascending trajectory from Time-1 to Time-3 boosted Time-4 withdrawal cognitions. That is, working students formed stronger Time-4 withdrawal cognitions when they had stronger Time-1 withdrawal cognitions and when their withdrawal cognitions intensified over time.

234 Methodological Approaches

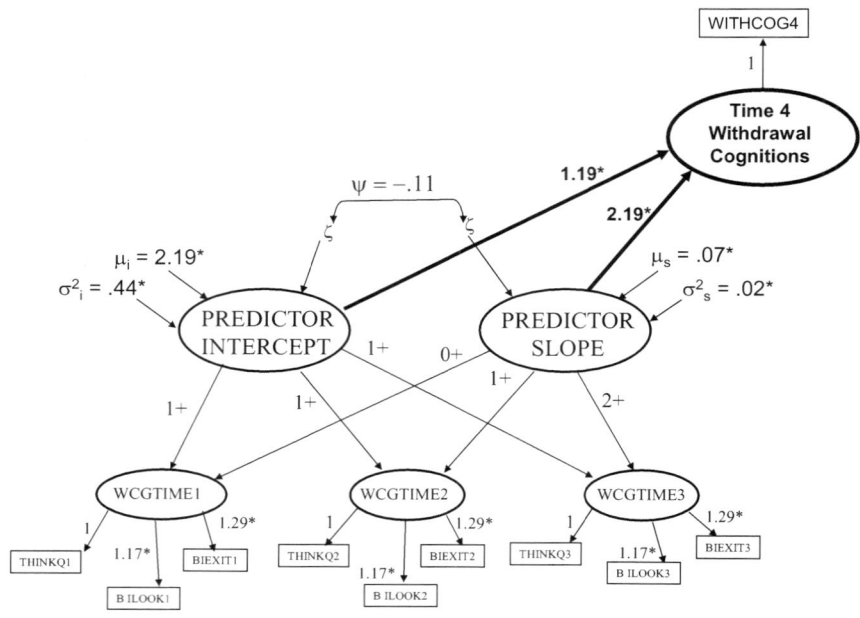

FIGURE 8.20 Second-Order Factor LGM Model Predicting Time-4 Withdrawal Cognitions

While still remarkably rare (e.g., .5%; Allen et al., 2014), LGM tests can generate stronger causal evidence for theories (Pitariu & Ployhart, 2010) by directly demonstrating that temporal shifts in mediating variables translate the impact of distal antecedents onto quit intentions or turnover (Bentein et al., 2005; Lance et al., 2000). Nevertheless, such tests require extensive data collection as they demand three or more waves of measures on model variables that are time-structured (although not necessarily equal-spaced observations; Singer & Willett, 2003). Importantly, researchers must judiciously select time periods (and measurement lags) where they can observe temporal change among turnover antecedents. Not surprisingly, many panel studies (including recent ones) sampled beginning employees whose job perceptions or attitudes may most change during early employment (Chen et al., 2011; Hom & Griffeth, 1991; Lance et al., 2000; Porter, Steers, Mowday, & Boulian, 1974; Youngblood, Mobley, & Meglino, 1983). Alternatively, researchers can sample existing employees and insure that they can observe change by surveying them over long time periods or moments when change may likely occur (e.g., after some momentous workplace event, such as layoffs; Trevor & Nyberg, 2008). Despite their methodological strengths for capturing dynamic processes implicit in many turnover models (Allen et al., 2014; Steel, 2002), LGM methodology may not realize its potential for theory-testing when temporal change is not discernible on key or many model variables.

Applying Other Research Methods

Besides advocating more latent growth modeling and survival analysis, Allen et al. (2014) proposed other uncommon methods to break away from orthodox turnover DAM. In particular, they recommended more qualitative research as only 1% of turnover studies they reviewed were exclusively qualitative. As Lee and his colleagues (Lee, Mitchell, Holtom, McDaniel, 1999; Lee, Mitchell, Wise, & Fireman, 1996) illustrated, qualitative research can "provide richer, deeper accounts of turnover and its associated processes … uncover[ing] nuances in the turnover process that cannot be discovered through using the DAM" (Allen et al., 2014, p. 878). They also suggested more multilevel modeling to "more fully consider group, business unit, organization, and even cultural constructs that could influence individual turnover decisions" (p. 879). Further, Allen and colleagues prescribed more experimental and quasi-experimental research to verify causality and mediation envisioned in turnover formulations. Field experiments can also help validate the efficacy of interventions to reduce turnover, which can lend greater credence to practical advice. Finally, they advise diversifying measurement methods beyond surveys, such as using more diaries, interviews, observations, or objective indicators to assess model variables.

References

Ajzen, I. (1991). The theory of planned behavior. *Organizational Behavior and Human Decision Processes*, 50, 179–211.

Ajzen, I., & Madden, T. J. (1986). Prediction of goal-directed behavior: Attitudes, intentions, and perceived behavioral control. *Journal of Experimental Social Psychology*, 22(5), 453–474.

Allen, D. G., Hancock, J. I., Vardaman, J. M., & Mckee, D. N. (2014). Analytical mindsets in turnover research. *Journal of Organizational Behavior*, 35, S61–S86. doi:10.1002/job.1912.

Allison, P. D. (1984). *Event History Analysis: Regression for Longitudinal Event Data*. Beverly Hills, CA: Sage.

Allison, P. D. (1995). *Survival Analysis Using SAS: A Practical Guide*. Cary, NC: SAS Institute.

Anderson, J. C., & Gerbing, D. W. (1988). Structural equation modeling in practice: A review and recommended two-step approach. *Psychological Bulletin*, 103(3), 411–423.

Anderson, S. E., & Williams, L. J. (1992). Assumptions about unmeasured variables with studies of reciprocal relationships: The case of employee attitudes. *Journal of Applied Psychology*, 77(5), 638–650.

Aquino, K., Griffeth, R. W., Allen, D. G., & Hom, P. W. (1997). Integrating justice constructs into the turnover process: A test of a referent cognitions model. *Academy of Management Journal*, 40(5), 1208–1227.

Aronson, E., Ellsworth, P. C., Carlsmith, J. M., & Gonzales, M. H. (1990). *Methods of Research in Social Psychology*. New York: McGraw-Hill.

Bateman, T. S., & Strasser, S. (1983). A cross-lagged regression test of the relationships between job tension and employee satisfaction. *Journal of Applied Psychology*, 68(3), 439–445.

Bateman, T. S., & Strasser, S. (1984). A longitudinal analysis of the antecedents of organizational commitment. *Academy of Management Journal*, 27(1), 95–112.

Bentein, K., Vandenberg, R., Vandenberghe, C., & Stinglhamber, F. (2005). The role of change in the relationship between commitment and turnover: A latent growth modeling approach. *Journal of Applied Psychology*, 90, 468–482.

Carsten, J. M., & Spector, P. E. (1987). Unemployment, job satisfaction, and employee turnover: A meta-analytic test of the Muchinsky model. *Journal of Applied Psychology*, 72, 374–381.

Chan, D. (1998). The conceptualization and analysis of change over time: An integrative approach incorporating longitudinal mean and covariance structures analysis (LMACS) and multiple indicator latent growth modeling (MLGM). *Organizational Research Methods*, 1, 421–483.

Chan, D. (2002). Latent growth modeling. In F. Drasgow & N. Schmitt (Eds.), *Measuring and Analyzing Behavior in Organizations* (pp. 302–349). San Francisco, CA: Jossey-Bass.

Chan, D., & Schmitt, N. (2000). Interindividual differences in intraindividual changes in proactivity during organizational entry: A latent growth modeling approach to understanding newcomer adaptation. *Journal of Applied Psychology*, 85, 190–210.

Chen, G., Ployhart, R., Thomas, H., Anderson, N., & Bliese, P. (2011). The power of momentum: A new model of dynamic relationships between job satisfaction and turnover intentions. *Academy of Management Journal*, 54, 159–181.

Curry, J. P., Wakefield, D. S., Price, J. L., & Mueller, C. W. (1986). On the causal ordering of job satisfaction and organizational commitment. *Academy of Management Journal*, 29, 847–858.

Duncan, T., Duncan, S., Strycker, L., Li, F., & Alpert, A. (1999). *An Introduction to Latent Variable Growth Curve Modeling*. Mahwah, NJ: Lawrence Erlbaum.

Dwyer, J. (1983). *Statistical Models for the Social and Behavioral Sciences*. New York: Oxford University Press.

Edwards, J. R. (1994a). The study of congruence in organizational behavior research: Critique and a proposed alternative. *Organizational Behavior and Human Decision Processes*, 58, 51–100.

Edwards, J. R. (1994b). Regression analysis as an alternative to difference scores. *Journal of Management*, 20, 683–689.

Edwards, J. R. (2002). Alternatives to difference scores. In F. Drasgow & N. Schmitt (Eds.), *Measuring and Analyzing Behavior in Organizations* (pp. 350–400). San Francisco, CA: Jossey-Bass.

Farkas, A., & Tetrick, L. (1989). A three-wave longitudinal analysis of the causal ordering of satisfaction and commitment on turnover decisions. *Journal of Applied Psychology*, 74, 855–868.

Griffeth, R. W., Hom, P. W., & Gaertner, S. (2000). A meta-analysis of antecedents and correlates of employee turnover: Update, moderator tests, and research implications for the next millennium. *Journal of Management*, 26, 463–488.

Harrison, D. A., & Hulin, C. L. (1989). Investigations of absenteeism: Using event history models to study the absence-taking process. *Journal of Applied Psychology*, 74(2), 300–316.

Hom, P. W., Caranikas-Walker, F., Prussia, G. E., & Griffeth, R. W. (1992). A meta-analytical structural equations analysis of a model of employee turnover. *Journal of Applied Psychology*, 77, 890–909.

Hom, P. W., & Griffeth, R. W. (1991). Structural equations modeling test of a turnover theory: Cross-sectional and longitudinal analyses. *Journal of Applied Psychology*, 76, 350–366.

Hom, P. W., & Griffeth, R. W. (1995). *Employee Turnover*. Cincinnati, OH: South/Western.

Hom, P. W., Griffeth, R. W., Palich, L. E., & Bracker, J. S. (1998). An exploratory investigation into theoretical mechanisms underlying realistic job previews. *Personnel Psychology*, 51, 421–451.

Hom, P. W., & Haynes, K. (2007). Applying advanced panel methods to strategic management research: A tutorial. In D. Ketchen & D. Bergh (Eds.), *Research Methodology in Strategy and Management* (vol. 4, pp. 193–272). Amsterdam: Elsevier.

Hom, P. W., & Kinicki, A. (2001). Toward a greater understanding of how dissatisfaction drives employee turnover. *Academy of Management Journal*, 44, 975–987.

Hom, P. W., Lee, T. W., Shaw, J. D., & Hausknecht, J. P. (2017). One hundred years of employee turnover theory and research. *Journal of Applied Psychology*, 102(3), 530–545.

Hulin, C. L. (1966). Job satisfaction and turnover in a female clerical population. *Journal of Applied Psychology*, 50(4), 280–285.

Hulin, C. L., Roznowski, M., & Hachiya, D. (1985). Alternative opportunities and withdrawal decisions: Empirical and theoretical discrepancies and an integration. *Psychological Bulletin*, 97(2), 233–250.

Huselid, M. A., & Day, N. E. (1991). Organizational commitment, job involvement, and turnover: A substantive and methodological analysis. *Journal of Applied Psychology*, 76, 380–391.

Irving, P., & Meyer, J. (1999). On using residual and difference scores in the measurement of congruence: The case of met expectation research. *Personnel Psychology*, 52, 85–95.

James, L. R., Mulaik, S. A., & Brett, J. M. (1982). *Causal Analysis: Assumptions, Models, and Data*. Beverly Hills, CA: Sage.

Kammeyer-Mueller, J., Wanberg, C., Glomb, T., & Ahlburg, D. (2005). Turnover processes in a temporal context: It's about time. *Journal of Applied Psychology*, 90, 644–658.

Krackhardt, D., & Porter, L. W. (1985). When friends leave: A structural analysis of the relationship between turnover and stayers' attitudes. *Administrative Science Quarterly*, 30, 242–261.

Lance, C. E., Vandenberg, R. J., & Self, R. M. (2000). Latent growth models of individual change: The case of new-comer adjustment. *Organizational Behavior and Human Decision Processes*, 83, 107–140.

Lee, T. W. (1988). How job satisfaction leads to employee turnover. *Journal of Business and Psychology*, 2, 263–271.

Lee, T. W., & Mitchell, T. R. (1994). An alternative approach: The unfolding model of voluntary employee turnover. *The Academy of Management Review*, 19(1), 51–89.

Lee, T. W., Mitchell, T. R., Holtom, B. C., McDaniel, L., & Hill, J. (1999). The unfolding model of voluntary turnover: A replication and extension. *Academy of Management Journal*, 42, 450–462.

Lee, T. W., Mitchell, T. R., Wise, L., & Fireman, S. (1996). An unfolding model of voluntary employee turnover. *Academy of Management Journal*, 39, 5–36.

Liu, D., Mitchell, T. R., Lee, T. W., Holtom, B. C., & Hinkin, T. (2012). When employees are out of step with coworkers: How job satisfaction trajectory and dispersion influence individual- and unit-level voluntary turnover. *Academy of Management Journal*, 55, 1360–1380.

March, J. G., & Simon, H. A. (1958). *Organizations*. New York: Wiley.

Miller, H. E., Katerberg, R., & Hulin, C. L. (1979). Evaluation of the Mobley, Horner, and Hollingsworth model of employee turnover. *Journal of Applied Psychology*, 64, 509–517.

Miller, J., Hom, P. W., & Gomez-Mejia, L. (2001). The high cost of low wages: Does maquiladora compensation reduce turnover? *Journal of International Business Studies*, 32(3), 585–595.

Mobley, W. H. (1977). Intermediate linkages in the relationship between job satisfaction and employee turnover. *Journal of Applied Psychology*, 62, 237–240.

Mobley, W. H. (1982). *Employee Turnover: Causes, Consequences, and Control*. Reading, MA: Addison-Wesley.

Mobley, W. H., Griffeth, R. W., Hand, H. H., & Meglino, B. M. (1979). Review and conceptual analysis of the employee turnover process. *Psychological Bulletin*, 86, 493–522.

Mobley, W. H., Horner, S. O., & Hollingsworth, A. T. (1978). An evaluation of precursors of hospital employee turnover. *Journal of Applied Psychology*, 63, 408–414.

Morita, J. G., Lee, T. W., & Mowday, R. T. (1989). Introducing survival analysis to organizational researchers: A selected application to turnover research. *Journal of Applied Psychology*, 74, 280–292.

Morita, J. G., Lee, T. W., & Mowday, R. T. (1993). The regression-analog to survival analysis: A selected application to turnover research. *Academy of Management Review*, 36, 1430–1464.

Murnane, R. J., Singer, J. D., & Willett, J. B. (1989). The influences of salaries and "opportunity costs" on teachers' career choices: Evidence from North Carolina. *Harvard Educational Review*, 59, 325–346.

O'Reilly, C. A., Caldwell, D. F., & Barnett, W. P. (1989). Work group demography, social integration, and turnover. *Administrative Science Quarterly*, 34, 21–37.

Peters, L. H., & Sheridan, J. E. (1988). Turnover research methodology: A critique of traditional designs and a suggested survival model alternative. In K. M. Rowland & G. R. Ferris (Eds.), *Research in Personnel and Human Resource Management* (vol. 6, pp. 231–262). Greenwich, CT: JAI Press.

Pitariu, A. H., & Ployhart, R. E. (2010). Explaining change: Theorizing and testing dynamic mediated longitudinal relationships. *Journal of Management*, 36(2), 405–429.

Porter, L. W., Crampon, W. J., & Smith, F. J. (1976). Organizational commitment and managerial turnover: A longitudinal study. *Organizational Behavior and Human Performance*, 15, 87–98.

Porter, L. W., Steers, R. M., Mowday, R. T., & Boulian, P. V. (1974). Organizational commitment, job satisfaction, and turnover among psychiatric technicians. *Journal of Applied Psychology*, 59, 603–609.

Price, J. L. (1977). *The Study of Turnover*. Ames, IA: Iowa State University Press.

Price, J. L., & Mueller, C. W. (1981). A causal model of turnover for nurses. *Academy of Management Journal*, 24, 543–565.

Price, J. L., & Mueller, C. W. (1986). *Absenteeism and Turnover of Hospital Employees*. Greenwich, CT: JAI Press.

Raudenbush, S., & Bryk, A. (2002). *Hierarchical Linear Models*. Thousand Oaks, CA: Sage.

Rubenstein, A. L., Eberly, M. B., Lee, T. W., & Mitchell, T. R. (2018). Surveying the forest: A meta-analysis, moderator investigation, and future-oriented discussion of the antecedents of voluntary employee turnover. *Personnel Psychology*, 71(1), 23–65.

Rusbult, C., & Farrell, D. (1983). A longitudinal test of the investment model. *Journal of Applied Psychology*, 68, 429–438.

Salamin, A., & Hom, P. W. (2005). In search of the elusive U-shaped performance–turnover relationship: Are high performing swiss bankers more liable to quit? *Journal of Applied Psychology*, 90(6), 1204–1216.

Sheridan, J. E., & Abelson, M. A. (1983). Cusp catastrophe model of employee turnover. *Academy of Management Journal*, 26, 418–436.

Sims, H. P., & Szilagyi, A. D. (1979). Time lags in leader reward research. *Journal of Applied Psychology*, 64(1), 71–76.

Singer, J., & Willett, J. (2003). *Applied Longitudinal Data Analysis*. New York: Oxford University Press.

Singer, J. D., & Willett, J. B. (1991). Modeling the days of our lives: Using survival analysis when designing and analyzing longitudinal studies of duration and the timing of events. *Psychological Bulletin*, 110(2), 268–290.

Steel, R. P. (2002). Turnover theory at the empirical interface: Problems of fit and function. *Academy of Management Review*, 27, 346–360.

Steers, R. M., & Mowday, R. T. (1981). Employee turnover and postdecision accommodation processes. In L. L. Cummings & B. M Staw (Eds.), *Research in Organizational Behavior* (vol. 3, pp. 235–282). Greenwich, CT: JAI Press.

Sturman, M., & Trevor, C. (2001). The implications of linking the dynamic performance and turnover literatures. *Journal of Applied Psychology*, 86, 684–696.

Trevor, C. O., & Nyberg, A. J. (2008). Keeping your headcount when all about you are losing theirs: Downsizing, voluntary turnover rates, and the moderating role of HR practices. *Academy of Management Journal*, 51(2), 259–276.

Vandenberg, R., & Lance, C. (2000). A review and synthesis of the measurement invariance literature: Suggestions, practices, and recommendations for organizational research. *Organizational Research Methods*, 3, 4–69.

Vandenberg, R., & Self, R. (1993). Assessing newcomers' changing commitments to the organization during the first 6 months of work. *Journal of Applied Psychology*, 78, 557–568.

Wang, D., Hom, P. W., & Allen, D. G. (2017). Coping with newcomer "hangover": How socialization tactics affect declining job satisfaction during early employment. *Journal of Vocational Behavior*, 100, 196–210.

Williams, C. R. (1990). Deciding when, how, and if to correct turnover correlations. *Journal of Applied Psychology*, 75, 732–737.

Williams, L., & Podsakoff, P. (1989). Longitudinal field methods for studying reciprocal relationships in organizational behavior research: Toward improved causal analysis. In L. L. Cummings & B. M. Staw (Eds.), *Research in Organizational Behavior* (pp. 247–292). Greenwich, CT: JAI Press.

Williams, L. J., & Hazer, J. T. (1986). Antecedents and consequences of satisfaction and commitment in turnover models: A reanalysis using latent variable structural equation methods. *Journal of Applied Psychology*, 71, 219–231.

Youngblood, S., Mobley, W., & Meglino, B. (1983). A longitudinal analysis of the turnover process. *Journal of Applied Psychology*, 68, 507–516.

9
CONTROLLING TURNOVER

Given the direct and indirect costs associated with employee turnover, it is important for organizational leaders to be able to draw on the extensive body of turnover research to enact evidence-based retention strategies. However, popular turnover management advice too often rests on case studies, anecdotal evidence, dubious empirical underpinnings, or managerial myths and misconceptions (Allen, Bryant, & Vardaman, 2010). We do not focus here on the general management of turnover antecedents such as employee attitudes that have been extensively covered elsewhere in this book and represent generic best practices. Many organizations already regularly survey employees to track well-documented antecedents such as job satisfaction or employee engagement, or use personnel record data on variables such as promotion history to identify likely turnover problem areas (Lee, Hom, Eberly, & Li, 2017). Instead, we focus on a few specific areas of practice with strong bodies of supporting research and clear managerial implications. Allen et al. (2010) provide a useful summary of evidence-based human resource management strategies for managing turnover (Table 9.1). We begin with robust methods of controlling turnover even before employees are hired during the recruitment and selection process. We then discuss several approaches to managing incumbent employee turnover, ranging from early onboarding practices to newer models capitalizing on advances in data analytics. Finally, we discuss promising approaches to identifying leavers before they leave.

Realistic Job Previews (RJPs)

Existing academic inquiry has consistently demonstrated that providing job applicants with realistic and balanced information about a job and about the organization (realistic job preview, RJP) consistently reduces their likelihood

TABLE 9.1 Evidence-Based HR Management Strategies for Reducing Turnover

Recruitment (Breaugh & Starke, 2000)	• Providing a realistic job preview (RJP) during recruitment or orientation improves retention. • Employees hired through employee referrals tend to have better retention than those hired through other recruitment sources.
Selection (Griffeth & Hom, 2001; Hunter & Hunter, 1984; Kristof-Brown, Zimmerman, & Johnson, 2005)	• Biodata (biographical data) and weighted application blanks (WABs) can be used during the selection process to predict who is most likely to quit. • Assessing fit with the organization and job during selection improves subsequent retention.
Socialization (Allen, 2006; Kammeyer-Mueller & Wanberg, 2003)	• Involve experienced organization insiders as role models, mentors, or trainers. • Provide new hires with positive feedback as they adapt. • Structure orientation activities so that groups of new hires experience them together. • Provide clear information about the stages of the socialization process.
Training and development (Hom & Griffeth, 1995)	• Offering training and development opportunities generally decreases the desire to leave; this may be particularly critical in certain jobs that require constant skills updating. • Organizations concerned about losing employees by making them more marketable should consider job-specific training and linking developmental opportunities to tenure.
Compensation and rewards (Griffeth & Hom, 2001; Heneman & Judge, 2006)	• Lead the market for some types of rewards and some positions in ways that fit with business and HR strategy. • Tailor rewards to individual needs and preferences. • Promote justice and fairness in pay and reward decisions. • Explicitly link rewards to retention.
Supervision (Aquino, Griffeth, Allen, & Hom, 1997; Griffeth, Hom, & Gaertner, 2000; Tepper, 2000)	• Train supervisors and managers on how to lead and how to develop effective relationships with subordinates and other retention management skills. • Evaluate supervisors and managers on retention. • Identify and remove abusive supervisors.
Engagement (Ramsay, 2006; Vance, 2006)	• Design jobs to increase meaningfulness, autonomy, variety, and coworker support. • Hire internally where strategically and practically feasible. • Provide orientation that communicates how jobs contribute to the organizational mission and helps new hires establish relationships. • Offer ongoing skills development. • Consider competency-based and pay-for-performance systems. • Provide challenging goals. • Provide positive feedback and recognition of all types of contributions.

Source: Allen et al. (2010, p. 57, Table 3)

of subsequently turning over (Barber, 1998; Breaugh & Starke, 2000; Wanous, 1980). Although consistent, the effect sizes are modest (McEvoy & Cascio, 1985, $r = -.09$; Premack & Wanous, 1985, $r = -.06$; Phillips, 1998, $r = -.06$), there are questions about the primary mechanisms by which RJPs influence turnover, and there may be important moderators at play (Earnest, Allen, & Landis, 2011).

Theoretical Explanations

Met Expectations

The prevailing explanation for the efficacy of RJPs is derived from the theory of met expectations (Porter & Steers, 1973). Presumably, new employees hold naive and inflated expectations about their new jobs (Wanous, 1980) and later are shocked to learn that their new work roles do not conform to their initial expectations (Breaugh & Starke, 2000; Dean, Ferris, & Konstans, 1988). Unmet expectations, in turn, induce dissatisfaction and resignations (Fedor, Buckley, & Davis, 1997; Premack & Wanous, 1987). RJPs can forestall the reality shock by forewarning newcomers about the unpleasant realities of the work. With initial expectations deflated, the job can more easily meet newcomers' expectations and disillusionment and organizational withdrawal be prevented.

Supporting this process, a meta-analysis by Premack and Wanous (1985) revealed that RJPs deflate initial expectations, and a meta-analysis by Wanous, Poland, Premack, and Davis (1992) affirmed that met expectations (whether manipulated or measured) enhance satisfaction and job survival. Notwithstanding such impressive evidence, empirical support primarily comes from testing the impact of RJPs on initial expectations (Hom, Griffeth, Palich, & Bracker, 1998; Rynes, 1990). Existing research may overstate the validity of this mediating process because pre-employment and met expectations represent different constructs (Louis, 1980). The few studies of met expectations report an inconsistent impact by RJPs on the construct (Colarelli, 1984; Horner, Mobley, & Meglino, 1979; Ilgen & Dugoni, 1977; Reilly, Brown, Blood, & Malatesta, 1981).

Perceived Employer Concern and Honesty

RJPs may also promote beliefs that the employer is trustworthy and concerned about the newcomer's welfare (Dugoni & Ilgen, 1981; Earnest et al., 2011). This perception of benevolence may foster feelings of obligations to reciprocate with continued affiliation (Cialdini, Petrova, & Goldstein, 2004; Meglino, DeNisi, Ravlin, Tomes, & Lee, 1990; Meglino, DeNisi, Youngblood, & Williams, 1988). Some studies relate that RJPs do foster perceptions that the company is candid and supportive (Meglino et al., 1988; Suszko & Breaugh, 1986) and enhance the impressions made by representatives of the firm (Colarelli, 1984; Ilgen &

Dugoni, 1977), while others (Dean & Wanous, 1984; Dugoni & Ilgen, 1981; Horner et al., 1979; Premack & Wanous, 1985) dispute this mechanism. Most recently, Earnest et al.'s (2011) meta-analytic path analysis approach concluded that honesty was the primary mechanism by which RJPs reduce voluntary turnover.

Commitment to Choice of Organization

According to another theory, RJPs strengthen job incumbency by reinforcing commitment to the original choice of organization (Ilgen & Seely, 1974; Meglino et al., 1988). New employees who are fully informed while choosing the job feel that they have more freedom in making their choices (Meglino & DeNisi, 1987; Wanous, 1977, 1980) and thus they feel more responsible personally and committed to the decision (O'Reilly & Caldwell, 1981; Salancik, 1977). Job candidates who accept the job despite warnings in RJPs about its drawbacks feel more bound to their choice, if only to reduce cognitive dissonance (Ilgen & Seely, 1974): employees who did receive RJPs feel cognitive dissonance about their initial decision when, later, they confront disagreeable work conditions. To resolve that dissonance, they rationalize their decision by overemphasizing the positive qualities of the job they have chosen, while de-emphasizing its negative qualities (Vroom & Deci, 1971). In a similar vein, individuals who select an organization after receiving an RJP are thought to be more likely to perceive the organization as attractive and as a good fit, and thus to be less likely to quit (Allen, Mahto, & Otondo, 2007; Earnest et al., 2011).

Self-Selection and Job Acceptance

According to the self-selection rationale, RJPs allow prospective employees to make better decisions about whether or not the job satisfies their personal needs (Bretz & Judge, 1998; Rynes, 1990; Wanous, 1980). Poorer fitting candidates self-select out of the process, leaving only those who are a better fit for the job and organization (Breaugh & Starke, 2000). Meta-analyses by Phillips (1998) and Premack and Wanous (1985) disclosed that applicants given previews are more likely to refuse job offers. Job refusal rates indirectly test the hypothesis of self-selection, which implies that samples of candidates who received RJPs are made up of different kinds of people from control samples of candidates who did not (Zaharia & Baumeister, 1981). The former should experience a higher congruency between their personal needs and the organizational climate than the latter, but will not necessarily turn down job offers (Wanous, 1973). Varying rates of refusal may mirror a different process, by which it is the RJPs that drive away qualified candidates but leave the less employable (and hence more loyal) to take the job (Rynes, 1990).

Coping Efficacy

RJPs may help newcomers cope with their new work roles because warnings of potential stress will allay disquiet (Ilgen & Dugoni, 1977; Wanous & Colella, 1989) and permits rehearsals of methods for handling it (Breaugh, 1983). Suszko and Breaugh (1986) found that recipients of RJPs managed stress better and felt less distress than did non-recipients, and Meglino et al. (1988, 1990) discerned that RJP recipients worried more about stressful events. Another way RJPs may enable coping is by reducing role ambiguity and increasing role clarity (Saks & Cronshaw, 1990).

Comprehensive Assessments of Mechanisms

Hom et al. (1998) revisited five principal reasons for how RJPs given after an employee is hired will strengthen job incumbency—namely, met expectations, commitment to the choice of job, value orientation, perceptions of the company's concern, and coping efficacy (Horner et al., 1979; Ilgen & Dugoni, 1977; Ilgen & Seely, 1974; Meglino & DeNisi, 1987). Post-hire previews, by experimentally controlling self-selection and post-decisional dissonance reduction, may better clarify how these mediators operate (Horner et al., 1979). Hom and colleagues extended structural equation modeling (SEM) to validate a theoretical framework encompassing all mediating processes. Their conceptualization further elucidated RJP translation by positing job satisfaction and withdrawal cognitions between RJP mediators and exits. This extended mediation reflected the view of many that RJP mediators activate a withdrawal sequence culminating in job separations (Horner et al., 1979; Vandenberg & Scarpello, 1990; Wanous, 1980, 1992). The model further proposed a causal flow: satisfaction → termination cognitions → quits (Hom, Caranikas-Walker, Prussia, & Griffeth, 1992; Hom & Griffeth, 1991; Price & Mueller, 1986; Williams & Hazer, 1986).

After showing that RJPs impact quits, Hom et al. (1998) tested their model with SEM analysis. Confirmatory methodology assessed the mediators' pathways to the RJP treatment and termination process, and they introduced direct linkages between RJP and withdrawal to this mediation model to verify the hypothesized *absence* of any direct effects of RJPs (Bollen, 1989). Their SEM application also addressed the question of whether or not RJP mediators indirectly affect quits by way of satisfaction and turnover cognitions. Sustaining the hypotheses about mediating processes, Hom et al. (1998) validated this structural model with a sample of registered nurses. The sample of accountants did not provide supporting evidence.

More recently, Earnest et al. (2011) conducted a meta-analysis of 52 studies including 75 unique effects. The meta-analytic effect size between RJPs and voluntary turnover was −.07, consistent with prior evidence. Effects of RJPs on mechanisms ranged from .02 on job acceptance to −.12 on initial expectations (consistent with the notion that RJPs reduce overly optimistic initial expectations). Earnest et al. (2011) went further and conducted a meta-analytic SEM assessing the role of met expectations, role clarity, perceptions of honesty, and organizational attraction in translating RJP effects on voluntary turnover. Interestingly, in the full model, only perceptions of organizational honesty translated the effects of RJPs to voluntary turnover (with RJPs-honesty $r = .11$ and honesty-turnover $r = -.48$).

Practical Design and Implementation

RJP Timing

Job candidates can receive RJPs while they are being recruited—before they decide whether or not to accept the job—or during orientation—after they have chosen the job (Wanous & Colella, 1989). Presumably, job previews are most effective in reducing turnover when they are delivered *before* the choice is made (Breaugh, 1983), when there is still time for self-selection and post-decisional dissonance to operate (Ilgen & Seely, 1974; Wanous & Colella, 1989). Even so, many studies find that post-hire RJPs can reduce quits (Dugoni & Ilgen, 1981; Hom et al., 1998; Horner et al., 1979; Meglino et al., 1988). The Earnest et al. (2011) meta-analysis actually found the effect size for voluntary turnover *larger* for post-hire ($-.10$) than pre-hire ($-.06$) RJPs.

Communication Modes

RJPs have been presented in various modes of communication, including booklets, audiovisual media, work samples, and interviews (Wanous & Colella, 1989). For example, Premack and Wanous (1985) found that booklet RJPs decreased exits as effectively as audiovisual RJPs. In a rare test, Colarelli (1984) compared two modes of delivering realistic previews, booklets and presentations by employees, and contended that the latter are more effective. Face-to-face interactions make the applicants pay attention and improve their comprehension. Employees, in addressing each applicant's particular concerns, communicate more relevant information. Employees are also more candid and are more credible sources because they occupy positions sought by applicants. Predictably, Colarelli (1984) found that RJPs given by employers reduced resignations among new bank tellers (three-month quit rate 14.6%) more than did booklet previews (44.9% quit rate).

Developmental Procedures

The construction of RJPs increasingly follows content validation methods to insure that they accurately and completely reflect the job content. For example, the development of an RJP requires a survey of many current employees and their superiors, who will independently verify the accuracy of statements about the job that were drawn from preliminary interviews (Dean & Wanous, 1984; Reilly, Tenopyr, & Sperling, 1979). Majority opinion (a 70% consensus) determines which statements are included.

RJP Content

Uncertainty over which dimension of job content—specificity, favorability, occupational focus, or subjective reality—should be emphasized in RJPs persists. Addressing one dimension, Dean and Wanous (1984) compared an RJP containing specific information about bank tellers with a more general RJP. Surprisingly, the specific RJP did *not* reduce turnover any more than did the generic preview. Comparing another dimension, Meglino et al. (1988) exposed army trainees to one of three audiovisual RJPs differing in favorability. One of these audiovisual RJPs, like most, consisted of a "reduction" preview, primarily portraying problems in the workplace. Another was an "enhancement" preview, emphasizing the positive attributes of the job. The third was a comprehensive RJP combining the other two. The combined RJP most lowered attrition among military trainees. The enhancement RJP reduced exits more than the reduction RJP did, leading one to speculate that enhancement RJPs may help new entrants in demanding jobs (such as military training) by modifying their overly pessimistic expectations (Wanous & Colella, 1989).

Considering another dimension of content, Hom et al. (1998) designed a preview about an occupation rather than a specific job in a particular company. They initially interviewed supervisors and accountants from several public accounting firms about accounting work and compiled their statements into a survey. Then they surveyed accountants in other firms, who confirmed the veracity of each statement. Comprising statements that 70% (or more) of the survey participants deemed valid, the RJP thus described standard features of the accounting *profession* across 27 firms. A later field experiment established that this occupational preview reduced voluntary exits among new accountants.

Job Complexity as a Moderator of RJP Efficacy

Early reports about the uneven effectiveness of RJPs stimulated conceptualizations of situational and personal moderators of their impact. In particular, RJPs may work best if newcomers are naive about the job and can freely choose to select themselves out of jobs they have previewed, that is, if they have other options (Breaugh, 1983). Yet traditional RJPs primarily portray "simplistic and highly visible" service jobs, suggesting that many samples of RJP recipients already have relatively accurate expectations (Wanous & Colella,

1989). Such visibility might explain why some tests report that RJPs fail to deter quits for some jobs, such as those of bank tellers (Reilly et al., 1981). Theorists have long maintained that RJPs most assist new entrants to complex roles (McEvoy & Cascio, 1985; Reilly et al., 1981). They presume that complex jobs comprise more varied, enriched tasks than do simple jobs. Because intrinsic work content is inherently abstract (Wanous, 1980), the nature of complex work is thus less visible to outsiders (Wanous & Colella, 1989). So, realistic portrayals would prove more informative and reduce turnover better than previews of simple work do. McEvoy and Cascio (1985) and Reilly et al. (1981) found RJPs did benefit employees in complex work roles most, but Premack and Wanous (1985) did not.

Notwithstanding such conflicting evidence, Hom et al. (1998) argued that the predominance of simple jobs in past studies of RJPs understated the moderating effects, restricting variance in job complexity (Rynes, 1990; Wanous & Colella, 1989): range restriction attenuates not only predictor strength, but also moderator effects (Hunter & Schmidt, 1990). In prior meta-analytical comparisons of the effects of RJPs across jobs of varying complexity, the jobs were categorized subjectively (McEvoy & Cascio, 1985; Premack & Wanous, 1985; Reilly et al., 1981). Without precise definitions of job complexity, such arbitrary classifications conceivably underlaid contradictory findings about the usefulness of RJPs for complex work (Wood, Mento, & Locke, 1987).

Going beyond traditional hourly jobs (Rynes, 1990), Hom et al. (1998) developed RJPs for accountants and registered nurses (RNs), whose occupations are more complex than those formerly examined and which may more readily disclose the superiority of RJPs for complex jobs. These professional RJPs reduced voluntary turnover among nurses, 8.5% of whom quit as compared with 17.1% of a control group (χ^2 [1, N = 158] = 2.62, p < .10) and certified public accountants (CPAs), 5% of whom quit as compared with 23% of a control group (χ^2 [1, N = 109] = 4.03, p < .05). Just the same, the mean effect size for professional previews (r = .15) did not significantly differ from previous (.09, McEvoy & Cascio, 1985; .06; Premack & Wanous, 1985). Hom et al. (1998) assigned professional jobs and those from earlier RJP studies into groups of complex and simple jobs using *Dictionary of Occupational Titles* (DOT) ratings (Avolio & Waldman, 1990; Schaubroeck & Ganster, 1993). Despite the objective job classification, the new meta-analysis did not generate larger correlations between RJPs and retention for complex jobs. However, Earnest et al. (2011) found that RJPs were more strongly related to voluntary turnover for white-collar (−.06) as opposed to blue-collar (−.02) jobs.

Recruitment Source: Employee Referrals

Substantial research has investigated the impact of the source from which applicants are attracted on post-hire outcomes such as turnover (for a review, see

Breaugh & Starke, 2000). Examples of the most commonly studied recruitment sources include newspaper ads, employee referrals, direct applications, school recruiting, state employment agencies, and job fairs, with only limited scholarly attention to technology and social media enabled sources such as online job boards and LinkedIn. There are two primary theoretical explanations offered for why outcomes such as turnover might be related to recruitment source: realistic information and individual differences (Barber, 1998; Breaugh & Starke, 2000). The former explanation suggests individuals recruited from different sources are likely to have more or less complete, accurate, and realistic information about job and organizational characteristics (Rynes, 1990). Those entering with better information are more likely to fit and find an easier time adapting to their new role, and thus be more likely to remain. The latter suggests that different sources reach different types of individual in ways that are then related to adjustment and success (Rynes, 1990).

For our purposes, the most relevant finding from this body of literature is that individuals hired through employee referrals tend to stay with the organization longer than those hired through other sources (Allen, 2008; Breaugh & Starke, 2000). From a theoretical perspective, referrals may receive more realistic information from the current employee providing the referral, and referrals may tap more qualified applicants because current employees are likely to pre-screen individuals for likely success because their own reputations are linked with the referred recruit.

Referral hiring remains popular, and may fill as many as 30% to 50% of openings in many organizations (Schlachter & Pieper, 2019). Schlachter and Pieper also incorporate a social enrichment perspective to thinking about employee referrals that suggests referrals are given additional support in the workplace and have easier access to social capital from relationships based on their preexisting relationship with the referrer. They also present an expanded model of referral hiring that considers important questions for future research across phases of the application and hiring process and incorporating important contextual considerations such as the referral medium and role of technology, the effects of job type, especially in a "gig" economy, and the possibility of differences by country and culture.

Biographical Predictors: Biodata

To insure a more stable, satisfied workforce (Kinicki, Lockwood, Hom, & Griffeth, 1990), employers typically screen out job applicants when they evince job instability—popularly known as "hobo syndrome" (Ghiselli, 1974; Hulin, 1991)—or the likelihood that they will not find satisfaction on the job (Judge, 1992; Woo, 2011). One way to identify biographical predictors (often referred to as biodata) of turnover is with weighted application blanks (WABs): using "the answers of current and former employees to application questions to empirically determine whether some items differentiate those who stay from those who leave" (Allen, 2008, p. 22). Items that differentiate can then be weighted according to how strongly they differentiate stayers from leavers, and used during selection of future applicants. Research suggests that well-developed WABs are among the best predictors of turnover, although they are not widely used by organizations (Allen et al., 2010; Griffeth & Hom, 2001).

Fear of charges of discrimination may be one reason for the limited use of WABs in practice (Gatewood & Fields, 1987). Inquiries about some demographic traits violate fair employment statutes, and screening based on certain background attributes (such as residence) may disproportionately reject minority or female applicants. Additionally, the apparent irrelevance of certain questions and potential invasion of privacy may prompt discrimination lawsuits (Breaugh & Dossett, 1989). Companies may face impaired public relations and sizeable litigation costs to defend so-called unfair questions. In spite of evidence that the questions are related to the job, some federal courts have even overturned WABs because firms failed to defend WABs as the best selection device by proving that alternative selection methods with less adverse impact do not exist (Arvey & Faley, 1988; Breaugh & Dossett, 1989).

To expand the use of WABs, Breaugh and Dossett (1989) advanced a more rational basis for choosing biographical data. Traditional empirical approaches provide little understanding about the reasons that biodata items predict turnover and they require large samples from which scoring keys may be developed. Breaugh and Dossett recommended that WABs include only biodata items that are verifiable (to encourage honesty among applicants) *and* that are known, according to accepted psychological theories, to underlie turnover. The selection of such items would improve the face validity of WABs, making them less objectionable to applicants.

Following these criteria, Breaugh and Dossett designed a WAB to predict turnover among bank tellers. They chose tenure on the previous job as a predictor, a choice that accords with the maxim "Past behavior is the best predictor of future behavior." They also selected employee referrals (a recruitment source) and relevance of prior work experience to index the realism of expectations, an underpinning, according to met-expectation theory (Wanous, 1980), of job survival. Last, they added educational attainment, presuming that educated applicants are more likely to quit because they have better job opportunities elsewhere (Cotton & Tuttle, 1986). Altogether, these biodata items moderately predicted turnover ($R = .44$); the Breaugh–Dossett method represents a practical (because it avoids the large sample requirements of empirical scoring keys) and defensible (because it uses theory-based item selection) way to design WABs and may overcome resistance from job applicants.

Personality

In contrast to the efficacy of WABs, early research reported disappointing predictive validity for personality measures and interest inventories (Griffeth & Hom, 1988; Mobley, 1982; Mowday, Porter, & Stone, 1978; Muchinsky & Tuttle, 1979; Porter & Steers, 1973). Generally speaking, early studies showed that personality tests provided modest or insignificant predictions of turnover. Such findings thus motivated Muchinsky and Tuttle (1979) to conclude that personality has a "very marginal impact on turnover" (p. 48).

Pessimistic conclusions about personality predictions of quits were nevertheless premature. For one, those traditional narrative reviews underestimated the predictive validity (and overestimated inconsistency in predictors) because they did not take into account statistical artifacts, such as unreliability, range restriction, and sampling error (Hunter & Schmidt, 1990). Early critiques also misinterpreted the utility of so-called modest predictive validities (Premack & Wanous, 1985). After all, a predictor's true usefulness depends not only on its predictive validity, but also on selection ratio (proportion of applicants hired to those applying), base rate (proportion of employees who quit), and correlations with other predictors (which tend to be relatively low for personality; Arvey & Faley, 1988).

Early critics also condemned personality inventories as susceptible to falsification by job applicants, who present themselves in a favorable light to obtain employment (Bernardin, 1987). Subsequent investigations dispute this claim, documenting that job applicants do not usually distort descriptions of themselves any more than incumbents do (Hough, Eaton, Dunnette, Kamp, & McCloy, 1990). Tett, Jackson, and Rothstein's (1991) meta-analysis concluded that personality scales do *not* predict recruits' performance less validly than that of current employees, contradicting conventional wisdom that recruits tend to falsify self-descriptions to obtain employment and thus undermine the validity of personality scales. Hough et al. (1990) found that a measure of social desirability (or the deliberate self-inflation of personal qualities) barely moderated the predictive validity of personality inventories. That is, the criterion-related validity of personality scales was only slightly lower for employees given to inflated self-descriptions than for employees who accurately describe themselves.

Research has established that personality scales, given methodological and theoretical advancements, can predict terminations. Early on, Barrick and Mount (1991) validated conscientiousness, openness to experience, and agreeableness as robust predictors; employers may best increase the predictive validity of personality tests by identifying the personality requirements of a given job by analyzing the job and then choosing or developing valid measures of *relevant* personality constructs (Tett et al., 1991). Employers might safeguard themselves against applicant distortions of self-descriptions by including social desirability scales, even though research refutes the persistent myth that the falsification of personality scales is pervasive or that it automatically threatens predictive validity (Hough et al., 1990). Such scales may identify dishonest job candidates (motivating a closer scrutiny of other hiring criteria) and may statistically adjust personality scores for intentional falsifications (Bannister, Kinicki, DeNisi, & Hom, 1987). Employers might develop forced-choice personality inventories to control for social desirability bias (Bernardin, 1987).

Meta-analytic work has found a range of modest effect sizes with a mixed dependent variable including tenure (Barrick & Mount, 1991), and some stronger relationships with a small number of effect sizes (Salgado, 2002). Zimmerman (2008) conducted a meta-analytic path model to estimate correlations between personality and turnover and to assess a model of how personality directly and indirectly affects turnover. This research focused on the five-factor model (FFM) of personality traits (Costa & McCrae, 1985), including conscientiousness, extraversion, agreeableness, openness to experience, and emotional stability. Based on results from 86 studies including 246 unique effects, Zimmerman (2008) found corrected correlations with turnover of −.20 for conscientiousness, −.04 for extraversion, −.25 for agreeableness, .10 for openness to experience, and −.18 for emotional stability. Meta-analytic path analysis showed that many of these relationships are partially mediated through traditional turnover antecedents such as job satisfaction, performance, and intent to quit; however, conscientiousness, agreeableness, and openness maintained their direct relationships with turnover.

Zimmerman, Swider, Woo, and Allen (2016) provided a novel theoretical perspective on how individual psychological differences such as personality influence withdrawal behaviors in work settings. They used the cognitive-affective processing system (CAPS) framework (Mischel & Shoda, 1995) to provide a theoretical foundation for a model of how individual differences operate in conjunction with situational features to influence work withdrawal. In their example, knowing that less agreeable individuals are more likely to quit is less useful than understanding why the less agreeable individual is more likely to quit (e.g., after being reprimanded in public; Zimmerman et al., 2016). Their model shows how, upon encountering particular work-related situations, personality affects how individuals encode or interpret the stimuli, affective responses, expectancies and beliefs, fit with goals and values, and self-regulatory plans. By organizing and advancing understanding of the role of personality in turnover, this model and the examples provided in Zimmerman et al. (2016) facilitate managers and future researchers to more systematically consider the role of personality.

Fit

The research stream on selecting for the fit between person and environment is an additional perspective on the relationship of individual differences and quits (Chatman, 1991). Kristof-Brown et al. (2005) define person–environment fit as "the compatibility between an individual and a work environment that occurs when their characteristics are well matched" (p. 281). Fit with the environment, job, organization, work group, and other referents have all emerged as important in understanding a range of organizational phenomena, including turnover.

As an early example of applying fit theory, following interactional psychology (Schneider, 1985), O'Reilly, Chatman, and Caldwell (1991) reasoned that shared and deeply held values of the members of an organization embody the organizational culture, and that employees' adherence to those cultural values fosters commitment to the company (O'Reilly & Chatman, 1986). To assess the fit between a person and a company, O'Reilly et al. (1991) introduced the organizational culture profile (OCP). The OCP compares people and organizations according to values (enduring preferences for a specific mode of conduct or end-state of existence; Rokeach, 1973) that are relevant and commensurate descriptors of *both* individuals and companies. Chatman (1991) and O'Reilly et al. (1991) validated the OCP, showing that person–culture fit among new accountants predicted retention ($r = .16$).

Turning to selection and operationalizing person–job fit differently, Bernardin (1987) designed a forced-choice personality inventory to screen out job applicants ill-suited for work as customer service representatives. Using a concurrent validation design, employees completed the personality inventory, and those selecting several valid discomforting descriptions resigned more often ($r = .31$). In essence, this personality scale identifies people who would fit the job poorly because they would be distressed by stressful events that actually occur on the job, and would more readily withdraw from the occupation.

Kristof-Brown et al. (2005) conducted a meta-analysis with 172 studies including 836 effects. Their results indicated corrected correlations between person–job fit and turnover of $r = -.08$, and between person–organization fit and turnover of $r = -.14$. Without enough empirical studies to incorporate other types of fit, they found corrected correlations between person–group fit and tenure of $r = .06$, and between person–supervisor fit and tenure of $r = .09$. Thus, assessing for fit during selection is likely to improve subsequent retention (Allen et al., 2010).

Socializing Newcomers

Turnover is often most pronounced among new employees (Griffeth & Hom, 2001; Mobley, 1982; Murnane, Singer, & Willet, 1988; Wanous, 1980), whose morale and commitment fall precipitously during early tenure (Hom & Griffeth, 1991; Wanous, 1980). Excessive premature quits implicate inadequate or incomplete organizational socialization as a fundamental cause (Feldman, 1988; Fisher, 1986). According to socialization scholars, entering a new organization is a time of uncertainty and ambiguity as newcomers must define the work role, win collegial acceptance, resolve conflicting demands, and develop proficiency in the job to become established (Feldman, 1988; Jones, 1986). Also, approximately 25% of U.S.

workers are undergoing socialization at any point in time (Bauer, Bodner, Erdogan, Truxillo, & Tucker, 2007; Rollag, Parise, & Cross, 2005).

Examples of early work studying how organizations can help newcomers adapt include Louis, Posner, and Powell (1983) surveying new business graduates, who reported on the availability and helpfulness of various socialization practices and their own attitudes to work. Peers, supervisors, and senior coworkers offered newcomers the most assistance. Surprisingly, business graduates regarded formal programs, such as on-site orientation and off-site residential training, as less helpful, and despite popular writings, mentors or sponsors were neither available nor helpful to new graduates (see Kantor, 1977). Although not widely endorsed by graduates, favorable off-site residential training and business trips most improved morale and intentions of staying. Several studies evaluated special orientation programs to help nursing graduates adjust to hospital life. Kramer and Schmalenberg's (1977) "bicultural training" is the most acclaimed program, serving as a model for others. Once a week during the first six weeks of employment, nursing graduates attend 90-minute "rap sessions," at which they share problems and ways to cope with them (and develop a "same boat consciousness"; Van Maanen & Schein 1979, p. 233). During the fourth week, new nurses read Kramer and Schmalenberg's workbook descriptions of common forms of reality shock, such as infrequent feedback and feelings of incompetence. Between four and five months after entry, the nurses also attend conflict-resolution workshops—first separately and later with their head nurses—at which they role-play ways to deal with routine conflicts, a common developmental hurdle for newcomers (Feldman, 1976, 1988). Kramer (1977) first evaluated bicultural training by recruiting 260 new RNs from eight medical centers. Half these RNs received bicultural training, while others received a traditional orientation. After a year, 90.2% of the biculturally trained nurses remained employed, whereas 60.2% of the control group nurses had quit. Similarly, Holloran, Mishkin, and Hanson (1980) found that only 3% of the nurses who completed the bicultural training resigned; the quit rate before the program began had been 42%.

Bauer et al. (2007) summarized research on socialization into a conceptual model in which newcomer information-seeking and organizational socialization tactics influence outcomes such as turnover through role clarity, self-efficacy, and social acceptance. That is, newcomers desire to understand what is expected of them, develop confidence in being able to meet these expectations, and in most cases feel accepted by others in the work environment. We focus particularly on the significant body of research that has arisen on the socialization tactics organizations use to help newcomers make sense of their new environment, deal with the uncertainty and potential reality shock associated with entering an unfamiliar context, and adapt to their new role, colleagues, and context (Allen, 2006).

Much of this research draws from Van Maanen and Schein's (1979) framework that identifies six dimensions describing socialization tactics: collective or individual (whether newcomers have common socialization experiences in groups or experience individualized socialization); formal or informal (whether newcomers are socialized in specific targeted activities just for them or with little separation from current employees, as in on-the-job training); sequential or random (whether the socialization process proceeds in clear steps to be completed or whether progress is more ambiguous); fixed or variable (whether there is a specific schedule for when socialization is complete or not); serial or disjunctive (whether experienced insiders are involved and serve as role models or not); and investiture or divestiture (whether newcomers are encouraged to affirm their own identity or to adopt a new identity aligned with the organization). Jones (1986) subsequently proposed that these tactics could be further categorized as focusing on the content, context, and social aspects of socialization, and arranged them on a continuum from most institutionalized (more collective, formal, sequential, fixed, serial, and investiture) to most individualized (more individual, informal, random, variable, disjunctive, and divestiture). In general, the more institutionalized tactics are thought to reduce newcomer turnover (Griffeth & Hom, 2001).

Allen (2006) proposed a model in which these socialization tactics would be negatively related to turnover in part by increasing perceptions of being embedded in the organizational context (Mitchell, Holtom, Lee, Sablynski, & Erez, 2001), and tested this model in a sample of 259 employees of a large financial services organization who had been employed less than a year. Hierarchical logistic regression results predicting turnover indicated that providing more social support (investiture socialization tactics) and providing positive role models (serial socialization tactics) significantly reduced the odds of quitting. When job embeddedness was added, serial tactics continued to demonstrate a direct effect, reducing the odds of quitting, whereas the effects of investiture tactics were primarily mediated through increased job embeddedness. Given that investiture and serial tactics are both classified by Jones (1986) as social, these results emphasize the importance of the social context in newcomer adjustment and adaptation (Allen, 2006; Cooper-Thomas, van Vianen, & Anderson, 2004). Allen (2006) recommends that involving experienced organizational insiders in newcomer socialization as trainers, mentors, or role models should directly improve retention, while providing positive feedback and social support to help newcomers adapt can retain them by embedding them in the organization.

Bauer et al. (2007) conducted a comprehensive meta-analysis of newcomer socialization research incorporating 70 unique samples. Their results indicated that socialization tactics classified as more institutionalized in Jones' (1986) framework demonstrated an inverse relationship with turnover (i.e., −.14 corrected correlation). Bauer et al. (2007) also conducted a meta-analytic path analysis showing that the effects of organizational socialization tactics on turnover were largely mediated by self-efficacy and social acceptance. Similarly to Allen (2006), they concluded that social tactics deserve additional research attention, and that organizations should consider providing newcomers with experienced insiders as guides and positive affirming feedback during socialization. Reviewing the literature as a whole, Allen et al. (2010) recommended four evidence-based conclusions for organizations concerned about socializing newcomers to manage retention: (1) involve experienced organizational insiders as role models, trainers, and mentors; (2) provide new hires with positive feedback as they adapt; (3) structure orientation activities so that groups of new hires experience them together; and (4) provide clear information about the timing, order, and completion of stages of the organizational socialization process.

Work Design

Another perspective on managing turnover involves the design of work. According to classic models of task design, employees find work motivating and attractive to the extent that they learn (by *knowing the results*) that they themselves (being *personally responsible*) performed well on a job they care about as *meaningful* (Hackman & Oldham, 1976, 1980). These "critical psychological states" derive from certain characteristics of a job: variety of skill (using various skills and talents); task identity (doing a whole and identifiable piece of work); task significance (doing work that substantially affects the work or lives of others); autonomy (freedom to schedule work and work procedures); and job feedback (obtaining direct and clear information about performance; Hackman & Oldham, 1980).

Several research streams indicate that job enrichment can curb turnover. Correlational studies find that employees holding complex jobs are less likely to quit (Katerberg, Hom, & Hulin, 1979; Price & Mueller, 1981, 1986). McEvoy and Cascio's (1985) meta-analysis revealed that field experiments enriching jobs reduced turnover more effectively than did RJPs (i.e., the effect of job enrichment [$r = .17$] exceeded the effect of RJPs [$r = .09$]). Griffeth (1985) randomly assigned part-time university desk receptionists to enriched or unenriched work conditions. Following Hackman and Oldham's (1980) implementing principles, he enriched the job—upgrading skill variety, task significance, and job feedback—and found that enriched work indeed reduced turnover.

Humphrey, Nahrgang, and Morgeson (2007) provided theoretical extensions and a meta-analytic summary of work design research. They extended prior work in two primary ways. One is expanding the conceptualization of the motivational characteristics of jobs beyond the well-established job characteristics in Hackman and Oldham's (1976) model, including, for example, job complexity and information-processing and problem-solving requirements. Their model also expanded the perspective on the types of autonomy different jobs might entail. The other is expanding beyond these motivational job characteristics to also consider characteristics of the work context, such as physical demands and ergonomics, as well as social characteristics, such as interdependence, social support, and even interactions with others outside of organizational boundaries.

Humphrey et al. (2007) conducted a meta-analytic review incorporating 259 articles with 6,333 unique correlations. Because of the small number of studies assessing actual turnover behavior, they report results for relationships with turnover intentions. The strongest corrected correlations with turnover intentions were interdependence (−.17), feedback from others (−.34), and social support (−.34). The set of social characteristics explained substantial variance in turnover intentions beyond the set of motivational characteristics. We note that, similarly to the socialization research considered above, each of these are characterized by Humphrey et al. (2007) as elements of the social context of work, emphasizing the important role of relationships in understanding turnover. Still, this research focused on turnover intentions; substantial future work assessing an expanded view of work design and turnover behavior is sorely needed.

Grant and Parker (2009) attempted to redesign work design theories to account for dramatic changes in the nature of work. They emphasize two perspectives: a relational view highlighting interdependence and interpersonal interaction, and a proactive view highlighting how individuals shape their own jobs and work contexts. The relational view draws from Grant's (2007) relational architecture of jobs, which focuses on the structural properties of jobs that connect employees to the impact of their actions on others. In this framework, jobs that provide more contact with others and have more impact on others are more motivating. Although focused on the effect on motivation to make a pro-social difference, the underlying arguments, in conjunction with what we know from prior work about social context, suggest more relational jobs would generally be associated with lower turnover. The proactive view considers research studying how individuals craft and negotiate their own job roles, consistent with the long understood role of autonomy (Parker, 1998; Parker, Williams, & Turner, 2006; Wrzesniewski & Dutton, 2001). The focus of this research has been on job performance, creativity, and other work behaviors; however, the emphasis on motivation and commitment suggests these processes may also influence turnover. As Allen et al. (2010) summarize, to manage retention, design jobs to increase meaningfulness, autonomy, variety, and social support.

Compensation and Reward Practices

Employers universally regard low or uncompetitive wages as a leading cause of turnover. To illustrate, partners in public accounting firms recounted in a statewide survey that dissatisfaction about pay is one of the principal reasons that their staff quits (Hom, Bracker, & Julian, 1988). Indeed, the widespread presumption that pay induces loyalty to a firm underlies the customary salary surveys which insure that current wages are competitive (Milkovich & Newman, 1993). Sharing this view, employees often mention pay as being central to their quit decisions. Many exit surveys find that former employees often blame their resignations on poor salaries or fringe benefits (Donovan, 1980; Huey & Hartley, 1988; Sigardson, 1982).

Notwithstanding such testimonials, scholars of turnover have, for several reasons, generally downplayed its impact. Indeed, Allen et al. (2010) identified "people quit because of pay" as one of the primary myths and misconceptions managers hold about employee turnover. Their review indicated that pay levels are only modestly related to turnover decisions ($r = -.11$), considerably weaker than job attitudes such as organizational commitment ($r = -.27$) or job satisfaction ($r = -.22$) or weighted application blanks ($r = .31$). They reasoned that perhaps instead of pay levels, individual perceptions of how satisfied they are with their pay might be more important; however, their review demonstrated an even weaker relationship between pay satisfaction and turnover ($r = -.08$).

Nevertheless, pay is complicated and certainly plays some role in employee turnover decisions, even if not as straightforward as a simple linear relationship between pay levels and quitting. For example, Brief and Aldag (1989) reviewed studies showing that pay can satisfy higher-order needs, such as achievement needs, a contradiction of the myth that pay meets only lower-order needs. In the wake of economic challenges and relentless global competition, compensation has become increasingly valued by Americans as their standard of living steadily declines (O'Reilly, 1992; Smith, 1992). Previous findings that people rank pay lower than they rank other attributes of a job understate the extrinsic motivation created by social desirability (Lawler, 1971). Policy-capturing studies that lessen respondent tendency to present a favorable impression to investigators as one not driven by greed reveal stronger pay preferences (Brief & Aldag, 1989). Research on satisfaction with life and subjective well-being denotes income as a prime basis for happiness (Brief & Aldag, 1989; Diener, 1984; Judge, 1992). Though not primarily underpinning happiness, work nonetheless renders economic benefits that enable people to enjoy more valued pursuits outside work, such as family activities and hobbies.

Methodological artifacts may have also underestimated correlations between pay (and pay satisfaction) and individual quits (Mobley, 1982; Mobley, Griffeth, Hand, & Meglino, 1979; Motowidlo, 1984; Weiner, 1980). Turnover research generally examines one job or organization, restricting pay variance and hence correlations between pay and quitting (Steel & Griffeth, 1989). Labor-economic studies on nationwide samples drawn from diverse firms and communities reveal that pay has larger effects (Blakemore, Low, & Ormiston, 1987; Shaw, 1987). The routine measurement of base salary (Price & Mueller, 1981, 1986) overlooks fringe benefits and incentive pay, rising expenditures in pay packages, and growing concerns to employees (Fernandez, 1986; Lewin, 1991; Milkovich & Newman, 1993). Turnover research often sampled secondary wage earners and young employees who have fewer financial needs (Donovan, 1980; Hom & Kinicki, 2001). It is the family breadwinners and mid-career adults—those bearing sizeable financial obligations—who may most value pay and more readily quit over poor incomes (Brief & Aldag, 1989). The most recent meta-analytic summary suggests somewhat stronger relationships when corrected for statistical artifacts: Rubenstein, Eberly, Lee, and Mitchell (2018) found corrected correlations with turnover of −.17 for pay, −.20 for linking rewards to pay, and −.28 for rewards beyond pay such as benefits, growth opportunities, and training.

Reviewing the existing research literature on rewards and turnover, Allen et al. (2010) recommended four evidence-based strategies: (1) lead the market for some types of rewards and some positions in ways that fit with business and HR strategy; (2) tailor rewards to individual needs and preferences; (3) promote justice and fairness in pay and reward decisions; and (4) explicitly link rewards to retention. Bryant and Allen (2013) considered compensation and benefits in terms of five elements: compensation structure; compensation procedures; types of compensation; fairness and equity; and vesting schedules. For example, one important element of compensation structure is the amount of pay dispersion across organizational levels. Research shows that wide gaps between an organization's lowest- and highest-paid employees may increase voluntary turnover (Bloom & Michel, 2002). Other research suggests that the fairness of procedures through which pay decisions are made influences turnover decisions through satisfaction and perceptions of organizational support (Fay & Thompson, 2001; Heshizer, 1994; Williams, Brower, Ford, Williams, & Carraher, 2008). Also, vesting schedules that are linked to tenure requirements also have an impact on employee retention (Heneman, 2007).

Pay dispersion may be particularly interesting as it relates to turnover because of potential sorting effects, or differential patterns of retention based on job performance levels (Gerhart & Rynes, 2003; Shaw & Gupta, 2007). Shaw and Gupta (2007) emphasize that it is important to determine whether pay dispersion resembles a tournament in which better performers are retained by the promise of higher rewards while poorer performers leave, or is more seniority-based in which long-tenured employees are rewarded highly, requiring only adequate performance. In a study of 226 organizations in the trucking industry, they found that pay dispersion with strong performance-based pay is negatively related to good performer turnover (dysfunctional turnover), whereas pay dispersion when performance-based pay is de-emphasized is positively related to good performer turnover (although only when pay system communication is high; results for poor performer turnover were not significant). The results suggest the importance of targeting compensation strategies at particular groups of employees and ensuring strong communication about pay systems.

Hom and Griffeth (1995) proposed a model, illustrated in Figure 9.1, summarizing prior conceptualizations (Heneman, 1985; Lawler, 1981; Miceli & Lane, 1991). This framework explicates the ways in which pay (and pay practices) can affect turnover, and suggests ways to promote retention. This model differentiates between attitudes toward variable and base pay and specifies common antecedents, although their effects on those attitudes are likely to vary (Heneman, Greenberger, & Strasser, 1988; Miceli & Lane, 1991; Scarpello, Huber, & Vandenburg, 1988). For example, job responsibilities may influence expectations about salary, whereas effectiveness in performing those duties may affect expectation about pay increases (Milkovich & Newman, 1993).

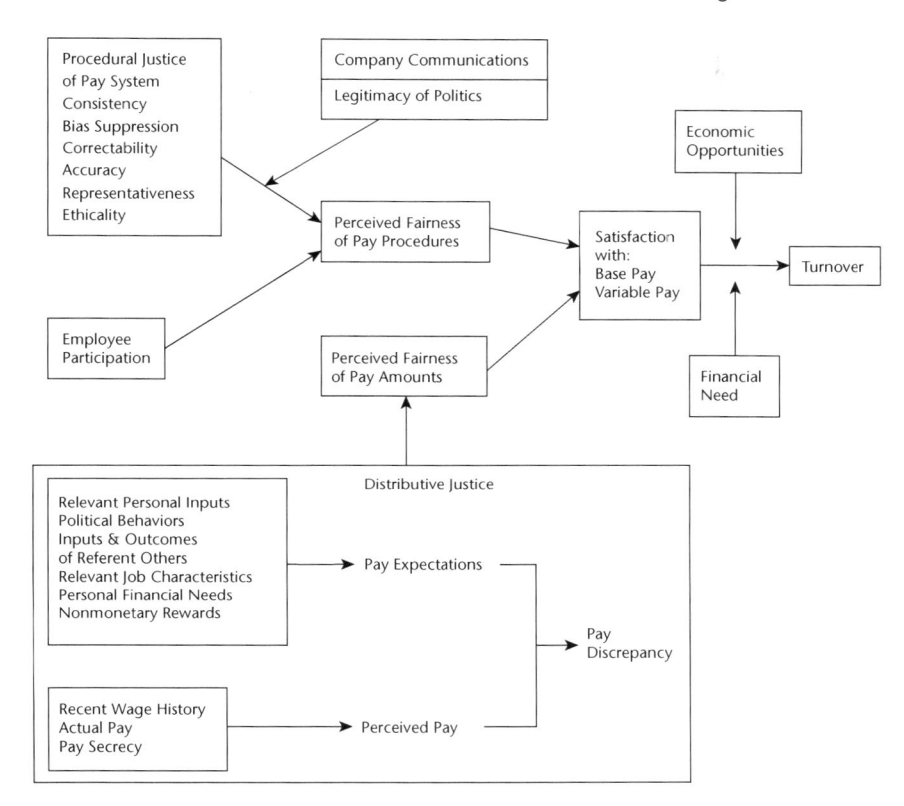

FIGURE 9.1 Hom and Griffeth's (1995) Model of How Pay Satisfaction and Its Antecedents May Affect Turnover

We theorize that discrepancy between expected (base or variable) pay and the amount received determines the perception of distributive justice (Lawler, 1971, 1981) because pay equity occurs when one gets what one deserves (Berkowitz, Fraser, Treasure, & Cochran, 1987). In line with Miceli, Jung, Near, and Greenberger (1991), this model contends that overpayment evokes satisfaction, not guilt (Miceli & Lane, 1991). Pay expectations depend, in turn, on personal job inputs (such as job performance) and the job characteristics (such as working conditions) that employees deem *relevant* contributions to the firm. Heneman et al. (1988) and Miceli et al. (1991) found that the belief that pay is based on personal accomplishments enhances pay satisfaction and fairness. Organizations may base pay on different criteria (or weight them differently; Greenberg & McCarty, 1990) from those that are important to employees, thereby confounding the employees' pay expectations.

This model recognizes political behaviors as potential pay bases, conforming to Gould and Penley's (1984) research showing that salaries increased most for managers who openly agreed with their superiors' opinions or who flattered them.

Employees' own comparisons of the contributions of and inducements offered to others shape pay expectations (Heneman, 1985; Lawler, 1971; Miceli & Lane, 1991). Countless studies revealed that the belief that others doing similar work (in or outside the firm) earn higher pay is demoralizing, as are perceptions that friends and relatives are getting higher wages (Miceli & Lane, 1991; Miceli et al., 1991; Scholl, Cooper, & McKenna, 1987; Sweeney, McFarlin, & Inderrieden, 1990).

This framework also suggests that expectations about pay stem from financial needs, such as family size and mortgage, which economic misery (e.g., inflation) exacerbates (Miceli & Lane, 1991; Scholl et al., 1987). Three national surveys disclosed, after controlling pay, greater pay dissatisfaction when earnings do not meet current expenses (Sweeney et al., 1990). Men adhering to the traditional role of the breadwinning sex may feel more financial need (and expect higher pay) if their wives work or earn higher wages than they do themselves (Mirowsky, 1987; Staines, Pottick, & Fudge, 1986). Non-monetary rewards (status symbols) may partially substitute for compensation and thus lower pay expectations (Lawler, 1971). An opinion survey found that intrinsic rewards promote satisfaction about pay (Berkowitz et al., 1987), and a laboratory experiment showed that high-status job titles may compensate for extra job duties—in lieu of more pay—and thereby ensure feelings of equity (Greenberg & Ornstein, 1983).

This model further identifies sources of perceived earnings, pinpointing real wages as a prime cause (Lawler, 1971; Miceli & Lane, 1991). Actual base pay dictates the meaningfulness of a pay hike (Lawler, 1981). Prior wage history—especially in recent jobs—also modifies perceptions of pay amounts because previous salaries set a standard for judging the value of current wages ("frame of reference"; Hulin, 1991; Smith, Kendall, & Hulin, 1969). Two national surveys showed that higher prior income made current pay seem small in comparison (Sweeney et al., 1990). Earlier salaries may also inflate expected pay because formerly well-paid people become accustomed to costly lifestyles or internalize inflated views of their self-worth (Lawler, 1971; Miceli & Lane, 1991).

Secrecy about pay policies may color pay perceptions (Lawler, 1971), though this influence hinges on whether employees over- or underestimate others' pay. Underestimating others' earnings raises one's own perceived pay (and pay satisfaction); overestimating lowers one's perceived pay (Miceli & Lane, 1991). Economic troubles, such as spiraling inflation, shrink pay perceptions by eroding the employee's purchasing power (Heneman, 1990).

Beyond distributive-justice bases, our conceptualization specifies that the rules of procedural justice underpin perceptions of fairness in pay practices (Folger & Greenberg, 1985; Miceli & Lane, 1991). Folger and Konovsky (1989) found that fair appraisal procedures, among them feedback and planning, improved satisfaction about pay raises, as did the perceived fairness of the raise. Miceli et al. (1991) found that federal managers regard their merit-pay plan as fair if their superiors follow formal performance-appraisal standards. Employee participation in pay design also fosters perceptions of procedural fairness (Miceli & Lane, 1991), an observation that is consistent with a "fair process effect," wherein people feel committed to outcomes they chose (Greenberg & McCarty, 1990). Laboratory experiments affirm this phenomenon, showing that subjects view reward outcomes—even bad outcomes—as more fair and satisfying whenever they believe that they have a say in allocation decisions (even though their influence is, experimentally, held immaterial) (Folger & Greenberg, 1985). Field studies reveal that when workers participate in pay designs, pay satisfaction is increased, and when subordinates are given the opportunity to share their opinions about performance during appraisal interviews, their satisfaction with merit-pay decisions is enhanced (Folger & Konovsky, 1989; Jenkins & Lawler, 1981).

The present perspective further posits communications about pay practices and the legitimacy of politicking as moderating procedural justice. Without widespread communication, even fair practices cannot induce impressions of fairness (Miceli & Lane, 1991), an observation that is borne out by studies from which it was found that open policies elicit satisfaction about pay (Greenberg & McCarty, 1990; Miceli & Lane, 1991). Explanations, or excuses, about wage-setting may soften employees' hostility toward unpopular pay decisions (Greenberg & McCarty, 1990). Besides this, personal values about the legitimacy of politics may decide whether or not violations of just allocation rules are offensive (Miceli & Lane, 1991). If politics dominate pay decisions, employees morally opposed to political bases may regard procedural infractions (uneven standards, rating biases) as unfair.

Alternative economic opportunities and financial needs may moderate the effects pay attitudes have on turnover. Employees dissatisfied with earning quit more readily if they can obtain better pay elsewhere (Motowidlo, 1983) or if they have urgent financial obligations (Brief & Aldag, 1989). Lawler (1971) argued that dissatisfaction about pay most induces quits if pay is personally important. Using this framework, we describe in the following section methods for improving redundant attitudes toward pay, and ultimately retention and how they work.

The model suggests that pay structures affect turnover through base pay satisfaction (Milkovich & Newman, 1993). Companies usually set the base pay for jobs through job evaluation and salary surveys (Henderson, 1989; Milkovich & Newman, 1993). An internal compensation committee or a consulting firm designing and applying a job evaluation plan may differ from employees in rating and weighting compensable factors. Nurses have long complained that prevailing job evaluation plans, such as the Hay Plan, undervalue nursing work because they neglect responsibility for human life (Brett, 1983). Given discrepant pay bases, job evaluation procedures might place a lower value on jobs than would the incumbents and set base salaries that fall below the incumbents' pay expectations. Pay dissatisfaction thus results because the pay is not commensurate with employee perceptions of the requirements and demands of the job.

Pay structure may induce exits if pay differentials between grades do not correspond to the incumbents' views of the relative differences in job worth

(Miceli & Lane, 1991). As Scholl et al. (1987) found, employees' comparisons with inputs and outcomes of others shape their pay satisfaction. Incumbents doing more demanding work may feel underpaid if their pay is not *sufficiently* higher than that of those holding simpler jobs. Despite a similar (or lesser) internal job worth, pay for male-dominated jobs is often more than for female-dominated jobs, thereby inducing women's advocacy for comparable worth (Milkovich & Newman, 1993). Similarly, labor shortages for some jobs may drive up hiring rates for new hires faster than the pay for seasoned employees in higher pay grade increases, compressing pay differentials (Milkovich & Newman, 1993). To illustrate, Gomez-Mejia and Balkin (1987) found that senior business faculty became dissatisfied with their pay when incoming new PhDs earned similar salaries because of a faculty shortage. Turbin and Rosse (1990) attributed the exodus of young engineers in high-technology firms (who lose a third of their recent graduates) to pay compression created by higher wages offered to new hires.

Common salary-survey practices may also disconfirm pay expectations. Often organizations survey other companies competing in their product, service, or labor market (Belcher, Ferris, & O'Neill, 1985; Milkovich & Newman, 1993). This sampling design may omit firms considered by employees as pay referents and thus produce market wages that fall below employees' estimates. Employees may not use surveyed (benchmark) jobs for their external pay comparisons. For example, Sweeney et al. (1990) found that employees compare their incomes to those earned by incumbents in *different* jobs. Given discrepant market estimates, wage surveys may set wages that violate the employees' pay expectations. Customary means to develop pay structures may not yield entirely fair wages, thwarting employees' pay expectations and weakening loyalty to the company.

Skill-based or knowledge-based pay plans may improve procedural and distributive justice (Lawler, 1990; Ledford, 1990). Unlike traditional job-based plans, these alternative pay structures base pay on what employees know rather than what they do (Milkovich & Newman, 1993). These programs distribute pay for *depth* of knowledge in one professional or technical job (Northern Telecom; Leblanc, 1990) or for *breadth* of knowledge of several production jobs, corresponding to different stages in a continuous process technology (General Mills; Ledford & Bergel, 1990) or manufacturing assembly (Honeywell; Ledford, Tyler, & Dixey, 1990). Studies (Lawler, 1990; Ledford, 1990; Milkovich & Newman, 1993) suggest higher distributive justice in knowledge-based pay plans because employees earn bigger paychecks (a more flexible, leaner workforce also permits higher earnings per employee). These programs accelerate salary growth because employees can progress as fast as they can master new skills or receive additional training. Traditional plans usually reserve major pay hikes for promotions, which hinge on available job openings over which the employees lack control. Skill-based pay also enhances perception of procedural fairness because salary increases follow clear and possibly more acceptable criteria: the acquisition of skills as judged by supervisors, colleagues, or special committees (Ledford, 1990). Job-based pay assigns salaries on criteria (compensation factors) and evaluations (judgments by anonymous compensation committees) that are usually obscure to employees (Miceli & Lane, 1991). Skill-based pay plans provide significant training resources to employees and require experienced members to train others (Lawler, 1990; Ledford et al., 1990). The intrinsic rewards derived from peer training and job rotation may further promote pay satisfaction (Berkowitz et al., 1987). Some plans pay production workers to learn administrative tasks, thus providing opportunities for autonomy and self-management (Lawler, 1990). Many skill-based plans pay competitive market wages and may offer merit pay (Ledford, 1990).

Skill-based pay may also directly increase the loyalty of the workforce. By broadening their skills, workers can transfer to other jobs in which there is more work rather than face layoffs during business downturns (Milkovich & Newman, 1993). Such greater job security reinforces inclinations to stay (Davy, Kinicki, & Scheck, 1991). Multiskilled employees may stay in the jobs they have because they cannot find comparable pay in other firms that offer separate, and lower, wages for distinct jobs (Lawler, 1990). Though sparse, empirical studies do suggest that pay-for-knowledge systems can enhance morale and retention. Ledford and Bergel (1990) found more satisfaction with pay and pay administration in the General Mills plan, and Leblanc (1990) reported that the Northern Telecom plan halved voluntary turnover. A study of 20 skill-based plans found higher levels of commitment and satisfaction among workers (Milkovich & Newman, 1993).

Variable pay, tying financial rewards to performance of the job or of the firm, can potentially reduce quits by effective performers (Dalton, Todor, & Krackhardt, 1982; Lawler, 1990; Mobley, 1982). Research studies established that contingency pay schemes bolster functional quits, motivating marginal performers to quit more readily (Bishop, 1990; Williams & Livingstone, 1994; Zenger, 1992). Other research finds that group incentives, delivering higher pay to most employees, can reduce overall quit rates (Blakemore et al., 1987; Wilson & Peel, 1991).

Nonetheless, merit-pay programs—the most common form of allocating variable pay—often do not increase productivity, and hence may not deter dysfunctional quits (Gomez-Mejia & Balkin, 1992; Lawler, 1990; Meyer, 1991; Schwab, 1991). Heneman's (1990) review of 22 field studies found that merit-pay programs produce few or inconsistent gains in performance. The chief reason behind their general ineffectiveness is a reliance on performance judgments, which are often biased or defective (DeVries, Morrison, Shullman, & Geriach, 1981; Lawler, 1990). As a result, employees do not hold "line of sight" beliefs that effort translates into monetary reward (Lawler, 1981). When so-called merit pay programs fail to foster beliefs among employees that higher performance can earn them greater financial rewards, they may fail to discourage effective performers from leaving (i.e., dysfunctional turnover). After all, why would superior performers stay when their accomplishments go unrewarded (Lawler, 1971)? Illustrating this weakness, the Wyatt Company found, in a broad survey, that only 27% of the workforce felt rewarded for doing a better job (Bleakley, 1993).

Aguinis, Joo, and Gottfredson (2011) summarized research-based principles for how to effectively apply monetary rewards in organizations: focus on defining and measuring performance accurately (Viswesvaran & Ones, 2000); align performance goals with organizational strategy (Aguinis et al., 2011); make rewards explicitly contingent on performance (Trevor, Reilly, & Gerhart, 2012); provide these contingent rewards in a timely manner (Aguinis, 2013); maintain justice principles, including distributive, procedural, and interactional (Ambrose & Schminke, 2009); and utilize a strategic mix of monetary and non-monetary rewards (Long & Shields, 2010).

Sarkar (2018) explicitly summarized the extant literature linking compensation and turnover, reviewing 81 articles linking compensation and turnover. She identified the evolution of research in the area into three time periods: pay as motivation (pre-1985); strategic pay design and administration (1985–2000); and high-commitment compensation practice (2000–2018). Focusing on this most recent time period, research in the HR domain began to emphasize high-performance work practices, incorporating elements of compensation within this higher-order construct (Guthrie, 2001). For example, Kehoe and Wright (2013) identified high-performance compensation practices as the availability of bonuses based on group and individual performance outcomes, merit-based pay raises, and high pay levels. Their study in 56 business units of a large food service organization found that high-performance HR practices, including compensation, were positively related to affective commitment and intent to remain with the organization. In a similar vein, Jiang, Lepak, Hu, and Baer (2012) classified HR practices into skills-enhancing, motivation-enhancing, and opportunity-enhancing, an extension of the ability-motivation-opportunity (AMO) model of HRM (Appelbaum, Bailey, Berg, & Kallenberg, 2000). They classified compensation practices as motivation-enhancing, and conducted a meta-analysis with 120 independent samples, and found a corrected correlation between motivation-enhancing practices (including compensation) and voluntary turnover of −.17, partially mediated by relationships with human capital and employee motivation. These studies reflect current trends toward considering compensation and reward practices as part of a larger HR bundle or system.

Promising Avenues for Future Research

There are several perspectives on controlling turnover that have received very limited scholarly research to date, yet are promising and worthy of additional attention. In particular, turnover researchers might seek to identify employees who are most quit-prone.

Gardner, Van Iddekinge, and Hom (2018) introduced the concept of pre-quitting behaviors: employees in the process of quitting may "leak" behaviors that others are able to observe and interpret, possibly leading to the early identification of individuals at risk of turnover. They began by identifying 116 pre-quitting behaviors (PQBs), and then sorting these into 58 prototypical PQBs. Ultimately, in a sample of 196 managers who had identified the presence of PQBs and estimated the likelihood of turnover, Gardner et al. (2018) found a positive relationship between manager identification of PQBs and employee turnover behavior. Future research replicating these results and considering others in the workplace, such as coworkers, subordinates, and possibly even customers, is needed. There may also be opportunities to capture PQBs using unobtrusive methods such as tracking social media or other types of trace data (e.g., email usage; Groysberg & Baden, 2018).

An approach grounded in job embeddedness theory and actively used by practitioners, but lacking scholarly data, is the use of stay interviews. Most organizational turnover analysis relies on attitudinal data such as engagement or satisfaction correlated with turnover rates to retrospectively interpret those rates and/or exit interviews with leavers to identify reasons for leaving (Griffeth & Hom, 2001). Stay interviews instead draw from a key insight of job embeddedness theory that reasons for staying may not always be the same as reasons for leaving (Mitchell et al., 2001). Stay interviews involve structured interviews with current employees to assess reasons for staying as well as issues that could initiate leaving. In addition to being theoretically grounded, stay interviews have the additional advantage of potentially enabling the identification of individual flight risks or issues that could lead to turnover early enough that undesirable turnover could perhaps be prevented. Stay interviews are ripe for rigorous scholarly research to assess whether managers are effectively able to identify individuals at risk of leaving from stay interviews. They also lend themselves to quasi-experimental designs to determine the effectiveness of interventions in reducing the likelihood of turnover among valued employees identified as potential flight risks.

Finally, practitioners are racing ahead to use predictive analytics to identify employees who are most at risk of quitting. Boudreau (2014) pointed out that a decade ago, Google was already using an algorithm analyzing data from employee performance reviews, promotion history, and pay history to identify flight risks, and is more recently using "big data" to more accurately predict who is likely to leave. In addition to personnel record data, organizations and consulting firms are also incorporating passive data such as communication patterns (tracked through company email and intranet systems; Groysberg & Baden, 2018), social media postings (scraped from websites), physical movements (tracked through employee identification card swipes), and even the emotional tone of interpersonal interactions (tracked through socio-emotional badges). Other firms are using publicly available databases and machine learning algorithms to identify employees who are susceptible to poaching by rival firms. One example relies on automated scraping of the internet for indicators of job-related shocks drawn from the unfolding model (Lee & Mitchell, 1994) such as stock price variation, analyst ratings, Glassdoor ratings, news articles, and regulatory or legal actions against a firm to identify employees who may be open to moving.

Research is needed on a variety of fronts. One is that unbiased research is needed to assess the effectiveness of predictive analytics models relative to traditional approaches, because the bulk of the research to date arises from proprietary data and methods from consulting firms with a vested interest in the outcomes. Another is the need to reconcile these data-driven approaches with turnover theory so as to avoid the pitfalls of sampling bias and capitalizing on chance relationships. Questions also remain as to how to effectively use the information provided by such data. Employees may feel as if their privacy has been violated if brought to their attention, or they could learn to game the system if individuals identified as flight risks routinely receive inducements to stay. Rigorous research is needed to explore the effectiveness of strategies for intervening with individuals or populations identified by algorithms as flight risks.

References

Aguinis, H. (2013). *Performance Management* (3rd ed.). Upper Saddle River, NJ: Pearson Prentice Hall.

Aguinis, H., Joo, H., & Gottfredson, R. K. (2011). What monetary rewards can and cannot do: How to show employees the money. *Business Horizons*, 54(6), 503–507.

Allen, D. G. (2006). Do organizational socialization tactics influence new-comer embeddedness and turnover? *Journal of Management*, 32, 237–256.

Allen, D. G. (2008). *Retaining Talent: A Guide to Analyzing and Managing Employee Turnover.* SHKM Foundation Effective Practice Guidelines Series, 1–43.

Allen, D. G., Bryant, P., & Vardaman, J. (2010). Retaining talent: Replacing misconceptions with evidence-based strategies. *Academy of Management Perspective*, 24, 48–64.

Allen, D. G., Mahto, R. V., & Otondo, R. F. (2007). Web-based recruitment: Effects of information, organizational brand, and attitudes toward a web site on applicant attraction. *Journal of Applied Psychology*, 92(6), 1696–1708.

Ambrose, M. L., & Schminke, M. (2009). The role of overall justice judgments in organizational justice research: A test of mediation. *Journal of Applied Psychology*, 94(2), 491–500.

Appelbaum, E., Bailey, T., Berg, P., & Kalleberg, A. (2000). *Manufacturing Advantage*. Ithaca, NY: Cornell University Press.

Aquino, K., Griffeth, R. W., Allen, D. G., & Hom, P. W. (1997). Integrating justice constructs into the turnover process: A test of a referent cognitions model. *Academy of Management Journal*, 40(5), 1208–1227.

Arvey, R. D., & Faley, R. H. (1988). *Fairness in Selecting Employees*. Reading, MA: Addison-Wesley.

Avolio, B. J., & Waldman, D. A. (1990). An examination of age and cognitive test performance across job complexity and occupational types. *Journal of Applied Psychology*, 75(1), 43–50.

Bannister, B., Kinicki, A., DeNisi, A., & Hom, P. W. (1987). A new method for the statistical control of rating error in performance ratings. *Educational and Psychological Measurement*, 47, 583–596.

Barber, A. E. (1998). *Recruiting Employees: Individual and Organizational Perspectives.* Thousand Oaks, CA: Sage.

Barrick, M. R., & Mount, M. K. (1991). The Big Five personality dimensions and job performance: A meta-analysis. *Personnel Psychology*, 44, 1–26.

Bauer, T. N., Bodner, T., Erdogan, B., Truxillo, D. M., & Tucker, J. S. (2007). Newcomer adjustment during organizational socialization: A meta-analytic review of antecedents, outcomes, and methods. *Journal of Applied Psychology*, 92(3), 707–721.

Belcher, D. W., Ferris, N. B., & O'Neill, J. (1985). How wage surveys are being used. *Compensation and Benefits Review*, 17(4), 34–51.

Berkowitz, L., Fraser, C., Treasure, F. P., & Cochran, S. (1987). Pay, equity, job gratifications, and comparisons in pay satisfaction. *Journal of Applied Psychology*, 72(4), 544–551.

Bernardin, H. J. (1987). Development and validation of a forced choice scale to measure job-related discomfort among customer service representatives. *Academy of Management Journal*, 30, 162–173.

Bishop, J. H. (1990). Job performance, turnover, and wage growth. *Journal of Labor Economics*, 8, 363–386.

Blakemore, A., Low, S., & Ormiston, M. (1987). Employment bonuses and labor turnover. *Journal of Labor Economics*, 5, 124–135.

Bleakley, F. R. (1993, July 6). Many companies try management fads, only to see them flop. *Wall Street Journal*, 1.

Bloom, M., & Michel, J. G. (2002). The relationships among organizational context, pay dispersion, and among managerial turnover. *Academy of Management Journal*, 45(1), 33–42.

Bollen, K. A. (1989). *Structural Equations with Latent Variables.* New York: Wiley.

Boudreau, J. (2014, September 5). Predict what employees will do without freaking them out. *Harvard Business Review*. Retrieved from https://hbr.org/2014/09/predict-what-employees-will-do-without-freaking-them-out

Breaugh, J. A. (1983). Realistic job previews: A critical appraisal and future research directions. *Academy of Management Review*, 8(4), 612–619.

Breaugh, J. A., & Dossett, D. L. (1989). Rethinking the use of personal history information: The value of theory-based biodata for predicting turnover. *Journal of Business and Psychology*, 3, 371–385.

Breaugh, J. A., & Starke, M. (2000). Research on employee recruitment: So many studies, so many remaining questions. *Journal of Management*, 26, 405–434.

Brett, J. (1983). How much is a nurse's job really worth? *American Journal of Nursing*, 83(6), 877–881.

Bretz, Jr., R. D., & Judge, T. A. (1998). Realistic job previews: A test of the adverse self-selection hypothesis. *Journal of Applied Psychology*, 83(2), 330–337.

Brief, A. P., & Aldag, R. J. (1989). The economic functions of work. In G. Ferris & K. Rowland (Eds.), *Research in Personnel and Human Resources Management* (vol. 7, pp. 1–23). Greenwich, CT: JAI Press.

Bryant, P. C., & Allen, D. G. (2013). Compensation, benefits and employee turnover: HR strategies for retaining top talent. *Compensation & Benefits Review*, 45(3), 171–175.

Chatman, J. A. (1991). Matching people and organizations: Selection and socialization in public accounting firms. *Administrative Science Quarterly*, 36, 459–484.

Cialdini, R. B., Petrova, P. K., & Goldstein, N. J. (2004). The hidden costs of organizational dishonesty. *MIT Sloan Management Review*, 45(3), 67–73.

Colarelli, S. M. (1984). Methods of communication and mediating processes in realistic job previews. *Journal of Applied Psychology*, 69, 633–642.

Cooper-Thomas, H. D., van Vianen, A., & Anderson, N. (2004). Changes in person–organization fit: The impact of socialization tactics on perceived and actual P–O fit. *European Journal of Work and Organizational Psychology*, 13, 52–78.

Costa, Jr., P. T., & McCrae, R. R. (1985). *The NEO Personality Inventory Manual*. Odessa, FL: Psychological Assessment Resources.

Cotton, J. L., & Tuttle, J. M. (1986). Employee turnover: A meta-analysis and review with implications for research. *Academy of Management Review*, 11, 55–70.

Dalton, D. R., Todor, W. D., & Krackhardt, D. M. (1982). Turnover overstated: A functional taxonomy. *Academy of Management Review*, 7, 117–123.

Davy, J. A., Kinicki, A. J., & Scheck, C. L. (1991). Developing and testing a model of survivor responses to layoffs. *Journal of Vocational Behavior*, 38, 302–317.

Dean, R. A., Ferris, K. R., & Konstans, C. (1988). Occupational reality shock and organizational commitment: Evidence from the accounting profession. *Accounting, Organizations and Society*, 13, 235–250.

Dean, R. A., & Wanous, J. P. (1984). Effects of realistic job previews on hiring bank tellers. *Journal of Applied Psychology*, 69, 61–68.

DeVries, D. L., Morrison, A. M., Shullman, S. L., & Geriach, M. L. (1981). *Performance Sppraisal on the Line*. New York: Wiley.

Diener, E. (1984). Subjective well-being. *Psychological Bulletin*, 95(3), 542–575.

Donovan, L. (1980). What nurses want. *RN*, 43, 22–30.

Dugoni, B. L., & Ilgen, D. R. (1981). Realistic job previews and the adjustment of new employees. *Academy of Management Journal*, 24, 579–591.

Earnest, D. R., Allen, D. G., & Landis, R. S. (2011). Mechanisms linking realistic job previews with turnover: A meta-analytic path analysis. *Personnel Psychology*, 64(4), 865–897.

Fay, C. H., & Thompson, M. A. (2001). Contextual determinants of reward systems' success: An exploratory study. *Human Resource Management*, 40(3), 213–226.

Fedor, D. B., Buckley, M. R., & Davis, W. D. (1997). A model of the effects of realistic job previews. *International Journal of Management*, 14, 211–221.

Feldman, D. C. (1976). A contingency theory of socialization. *Administrative Science Quarterly*, 21, 433–452.

Feldman, D. C. (1988). *Managing Careers in Organizations*. Glenview, IL: Scott, Foresman.

Fernandez, J. P. (1986). *Child Care and Corporate Productivity*. Lexington, MA: Lexington Books.

Fisher, C. D. (1986). Organizational socialization: An integrative review. In K. Rowland & G. Ferris (Eds.), *Research in Personnel and Human Resources Management* (pp. 101–146). Greenwich, CT: JAI Press.

Folger, R., & Greenberg, J. (1985). Procedural justice: An interpretive analysis of personnel systems. In K. M. Rowland & G. R. Ferris (Eds.), *Research in Personnel and Human Resources Management* (vol. 3, pp. 141–183). Greenwich, CT: JAI Press.

Folger, R., & Konovsky, M. A. (1989). Effects of procedural and distributive justice on reactions to pay-raise decisions. *Academy of Management Journal*, 32, 115–130.

Gardner, T. M., Van Iddekinge, C. H., & Hom, P. W. (2018). If you've got leavin' on your mind: The identification and validation of pre-quitting behaviors. *Journal of Management*, 44(8), 3231–3257.

Gatewood, R. D., & Fields, H. S. (1987). *Human Resource Selection*. Hinsdale, IL: The Dryden Press.

Gerhart, B., & Rynes, S. L. (2003). *Compensation: Theory, Evidence, and Strategic Implications*. Thousand Oaks, CA: Sage.

Ghiselli, E. E. (1974). Some perspectives for industrial psychology. *American Psychologist*, 80, 80–87.

Gomez-Mejia, L. R., & Balkin, D. B. (1987). The determinants of managerial satisfaction with the expatriation and repatriation process. *Journal of Management Development*, 6(1), 7–17.

Gomez-Mejia, L. R., & Balkin, D. B. (1992). *Compensation, Organizational Strategy, and Firm Performance*. Cincinnati, OH: South/Western.

Gould, S., & Penley, L. E. (1984). Career strategies and salary progression: A study of their relationships in a municipal bureaucracy. *Organizational Behavior and Human Performance*, 34(2), 244–265.

Grant, A. M. (2007). Relational job design and the motivation to make a prosocial difference. *Academy of Management Review*, 32, 393–417.

Grant, A. M., & Parker, S. K. (2009). Redesigning work design theories: The rise of relational and proactive perspectives. *Academy of Management Annals*, 3, 317–375.

Greenberg, J., & McCarty, C. L. (1990). Comparable worth: A matter of justice. In G. R. Ferris & K. M. Rowland (Eds.), *Research in Personnel and Human Resources Management* (vol. 8, pp. 265–301). Greenwich, CT: JAI Press.

Greenberg, J., & Ornstein, S. (1983). High status job title compensation for underpayment: A test of equity theory. *Journal of Applied Psychology*, 68(2), 285–297.

Griffeth, R. W. (1985). Moderation of the effects of job enrichment by participation: A longitudinal field experiment. *Organizational Behavior and Human Decision Processes*, 35, 73–93.

Griffeth, R. W., & Hom, P. W. (1988). Locus of control and delay of gratification as moderators of employee turnover. *Journal of Applied Social Psychology*, 18, 1318–1333.

Griffeth, R. W., & Hom, P. W. (2001). *Retaining Valued Employees*. Thousand Oaks, CA: Sage.

Griffeth, R. W., Hom, P. W., & Gaertner, S. (2000). A meta-analysis of antecedents and correlates of employee turnover: Update, moderator tests, and research implications for the next millennium. *Journal of Management*, 26(3), 463–488.

Groysberg, B., & Baden, K. C. (2018). *Trustsphere: Building a Market for Relationship Analytics*. Harvard Business School Case 9-418-070. Cambridge, MA: Harvard Business School.

Guthrie, J. P. (2001). High-involvement work practices, turnover, and productivity: Evidence from New Zealand. *Academy of Management Journal*, 44(1), 180–190.

Hackman, J. R., & Oldham, G. R. (1976). Motivation through the design of work: Test of a theory. *Organizational Behavior and Human Performance*, 16(2), 250–259.

Hackman, J. R., & Oldham, G. R. (1980). *Work Redesign*. Reading, MA: Addison-Wesley.

Henderson, R. (1989). *Compensation Management*. Englewood Cliffs, NJ: Prentice Hall.

Heneman, H. G. (1985). Pay satisfaction. In K. M. Rowland & G. R. Ferris (Eds.), *Research in Personnel and Human Resources Management* (vol. 3, pp. 115–139). Greenwich, CT: JAI Press.

Heneman, H. G., & Judge, T. A. (2006). *Staffing Organizations* (5th ed.). Burr Ridge, IL: Irwin/McGraw-Hill.

Heneman, R. L. (1990). Merit pay research. In G. R. Ferris & K. M. Rowland (Eds.), *Research in Personnel and Human Resources Management* (vol. 8, pp. 203–263). Greenwich, CT: JAI Press.

Heneman, R. L. (2007). *Implementing Total Rewards Strategies: A Guide to Successfully Planning and Implementing a Total Rewards System*. Alexandria, VA: SHRM Foundation.

Heneman, R. L., Greenberger, D. B., & Strasser, S. (1988). The relationship between pay-for-performance perceptions and pay satisfaction. *Personnel Psychology*, 41(4), 745–759.

Heshizer, B. (1994). The impact of flexible benefits plans on job satisfaction, organizational commitment and turnover intentions. *Benefits Quarterly*, 10(4), 84–90.

Holloran, S. D., Mishkin, B. H., & Hanson, B. L. (1980). Bicultural training for new graduates. *Journal of Nursing Administration*, 10, 17–24.

Hom, P. W., Bracker, J. S., & Julian, G. (1988, October). In pursuit of greener pastures. *New Accountant*, 4, 24.

Hom, P. W., Caranikas-Walker, F., Prussia, G. E., & Griffeth, R. W. (1992). A meta-analytical structural equations analysis of a model of employee turnover. *Journal of Applied Psychology*, 77(6), 890–909.

Hom, P. W., & Griffeth, R. W. (1991). Structural equations modeling test of a turnover theory: Cross-sectional and longitudinal analyses. *Journal of Applied Psychology*, 76, 350–366.

Hom, P. W., & Griffeth, R. W. (1995). *Employee Turnover*. Cincinnati, OH: South/Western.

Hom, P. W., Griffeth, R. W., Palich, L. E., & Bracker, J. S. (1998). An exploratory investigation into theoretical mechanisms underlying realistic job previews. *Personnel Psychology*, 51(2), 421–451.

Hom, P. W., & Kinicki, A. J. (2001). Toward a greater understanding of how dissatisfaction drives employee turnover. *Academy of Management Journal*, 44, 975–987.

Horner, S. O., Mobley, W. H., & Meglino, B. M. (1979). *An Experimental Evaluation of the Effects of a Realistic Job Preview on Marine Recruit Affect, Intentions, and Behavior* (Technical Report 9). Columbia, SC: Center for Management and Organizational Research.

Hough, L. M., Eaton, N. K., Dunnette, M. D., Kamp, J. D., & McCloy, R. A. (1990). Criterion-related validities of personality constructs and the effect of response distortion on those validities. *Journal of Applied Psychology*, 75, 581–595.

Huey, F. L., & Hartley, S. (1988). What keeps nurses in nursing. *American Journal of Nursing*, 88, 181–188.

Hulin, C. L. (1991). Adaptation, persistence, and commitment in organizations. In M. D. Dunnette & L. M. Hough (Eds.), *Handbook of Industrial and Organizational Psychology* (2nd ed., pp. 445–505). Palo Alto, CA: Consulting Psychologists Press.

Humphrey, S. E., Nahrgang, J. D., & Morgeson, F. P. (2007). Integrating motivational, social, and contextual work design features: A meta-analytic summary and theoretical extension of the work design literature. *Journal of Applied Psychology*, 92(5), 1332–1356.

Hunter, J. E., & Hunter, R. F. (1984). Validity and utility of alternative predictors of job performance. *Psychological Bulletin*, 96(1), 72–98.

Hunter, J. E., & Schmidt, F. L. (1990). *Methods of Meta-Analysis*. Newbury Park, CA: Sage.

Ilgen, D. R., & Dugoni, B. L. (1977). *Initial Orientation to the Organization*. Paper presented at the Annual Meeting of the Academy of Management, Kissimmee, Florida (August).

Ilgen, D. R., & Seely, W. (1974). Realistic expectations as an aid in reducing voluntary resignations. *Journal of Applied Psychology*, 59, 452–455.

Jenkins, G. D., & Lawler, E. E. (1981). Impact of employee participation on pay plan development. *Organizational Behavior and Human Performance*, 28(1), 111–128.

Jiang, K., Lepak, D. P., Hu, J., & Baer, J. C. (2012). How does human resource management influence organizational outcomes? A meta-analytic investigation of mediating mechanisms. *Academy of Management Journal*, 55(6), 1264–1294.

Jones, G. R. (1986). Socialization tactics, self-efficacy, and newcomers' adjustments to organizations. *Academy of Management Journal*, 29(2), 262–279.

Judge, T. A. (1992). The dispositional perspective in human resources research. In G. R. Ferris & K. M Rowland (Eds.), *Research in Personnel and Human Resources Management* (vol. 10, pp. 31–72). Greenwich, CT: JAI Press.

Kammeyer-Mueller, J. D., & Wanberg, C. R. (2003). Unwrapping the organizational entry process: Disentangling multiple antecedents and their pathways to adjustment. *Journal of Applied Psychology*, 88(5), 779–794.

Kantor, R. M. (1977). *Men and Women of the Corporation*. New York: Basic Books.

Katerberg, R., Hom, P.W., & Hulin, C. L. (1979). Effects of job complexity on the reactions of part-time workers. *Organizational Behavior and Human Performance*, 24, 317–332.

Kehoe, R. R., & Wright, P. M. (2013). The impact of high-performance human resource practices on employees' attitudes and behaviors. *Journal of Management*, 39(2), 366–391.

Kinicki, A. J., Lockwood, C. A., Hom, P.W., & Griffeth, R.W. (1990). Interviewer predictions of applicant qualifications and interviewer validity: Aggregate and individual analyses. *Journal of Applied Psychology*, 75, 477–486.

Kramer, M. (1977). Reality shock can be handled on the job. *RN*, 63, 11.

Kramer, M., & Schmalenberg, C. (1977). *Paths to Biculturalism*. Wakefield, MA: Contemporary Publishing.

Kristof-Brown, A. L., Zimmerman, R. D., & Johnson, E. C. (2005). Consequences of individuals' fit at work: A meta-analysis of person–job, person–organization, person–group, and person–supervisor fit. *Personnel Psychology*, 58(2), 281–342.

Lawler, E. E. (1971). *Pay and Organizational Effectiveness: A Psychological View*. New York: McGraw-Hill.

Lawler, E. E. (1981). *Pay and Organizational Development*. Reading, MA: Addison-Wesley.

Lawler, E. E. (1990). *Strategic Pay*. San Francisco, CA: Jossey-Bass.

Leblanc, P.V. (1990). Skill-based pay case number 2: Northern Telecom. *Compensation and Benefits Review*, 23, 39–56.

Ledford, G. E. (1990). Three case studies on skill-based pay: An overview. *Compensation and Benefits Review*, 23, 11–23.

Ledford, G. E., & Bergel, G. (1990). Skill-based pay case number 1: General Mills. *Compensation and Benefits Review*, 23, 24–38.

Ledford, G. E., Tyler, W. R., & Dixey, W. B. (1990). Skill-based pay case number 3: Honeywell Ammunition Assembly Plant. *Compensation and Benefits Review*, 23, 57–77.

Lee, T. W., Hom, P. W., Eberly, M. B., & Li, J. (2017). On the next decade of research in voluntary employee turnover. *Academy of Management Perspectives*, 31(3), 201–221.

Lee, T. W., & Mitchell, T. R. (1994). An alternative approach: The unfolding model of voluntary employee turnover. *Academy of Management Review*, 19(1), 51–89.

Lewin, T. (1991, April 28). High medical costs hurt growing numbers in U.S. *New York Times*, 1.

Long, R. J., & Shields, J. L. (2010). From pay to praise? Non-cash employee recognition in Canadian and Australian firms. *International Journal of Human Resource Management*, 21(8), 1145–1172.

Louis, M. R. (1980). Surprise and sense making: What newcomers experience in entering unfamiliar organizational settings. *Administrative Science Quarterly*, 25, 226–251.

Louis, M. R., Posner, B. Z., & Powell, G. N. (1983). The availability and helpfulness of socialization practices. *Personnel Psychology*, 36, 857–866.

McEvoy, G. M., & Cascio, W. F. (1985). Strategies for reducing employee turnover: A meta-analysis. *Journal of Applied Psychology*, 70, 342–353.

Meglino, B. M., & DeNisi, A. S. (1987). Realistic job previews: Some thoughts on their more effective use in managing the flow of human resources. *Human Resource Planning*, 10, 157–167.

Meglino, B. M., DeNisi, A. S., Ravlin, E. C., Tomes, W. E., & Lee, J. (1990). *The Effects of Realistic Job Preview and Prior Job Experience on the Retention of Correctional Officers.* Paper presented at the 50th Annual Convention of the Academy of Management, San Francisco, California.

Meglino, B. M., DeNisi, A. S., Youngblood, S. A., & Williams, K. J. (1988). Effects of realistic job previews: A comparison using an enhancement and a reduction preview. *Journal of Applied Psychology,* 73(2), 259–266.

Meyer, H. H. (1991). A solution to the performance appraisal feedback enigma. *Academy of Management Executive,* 5, 68–76.

Miceli, M., & Lane, M. C. (1991). Antecedents of pay satisfaction: A review and extension. In G. R. Ferris & K. M. Rowland (Eds.), *Research in Personnel and Human Resources Management* (vol. 9, pp. 235–309). Greenwich, CT: JAI Press.

Miceli, M. P., Jung, I., Near, J. P., & Greenberger, D. B. (1991). Predictors and outcomes of reactions to pay-for-performance plans. *Journal of Applied Psychology,* 76, 508–521.

Milkovich, G. T., & Newman, J. M. (1993). *Compensation (4th ed.).* Homewood, IL: BPI/Irwin.

Mirowsky, J. (1987). The psycho-economics of feeling underpaid: Distributive justice and the earnings of husbands and wives. *American Journal of Sociology,* 92(6), 1404–1434.

Mischel, W., & Shoda, Y. (1995). A cognitive-affective system theory of personality: Reconceptualizing situations, dispositions, dynamics, and invariance in personality structure. *Psychological Review,* 102(2), 246–268.

Mitchell, T. R., Holtom, B. C., Lee, T. W., Sablynski, C. J., & Erez, M. (2001). Why people stay: Using job embeddedness to predict voluntary turnover. *Academy of Management Journal,* 44, 1102–1121.

Mobley, W. H. (1982). *Employee Turnover: Causes, Consequences, and Control.* Reading, MA: Addison-Wesley.

Mobley, W. H., Griffeth, R. W., Hand, H. H., & Meglino, B. M. (1979). Review and conceptual analysis of the employee turnover process. *Psychological Bulletin,* 86, 493–522.

Motowidlo, S. J. (1983). Predicting sales turnover from pay satisfaction and expectation. *Journal of Applied Psychology,* 68, 484–489.

Motowidlo, S. J. (1984). Does job satisfaction lead to consideration and personal sensitivity? *Academy of Management Journal,* 27(4), 910–915.

Mowday, R. T., Porter, L. W., & Stone, E. F. (1978). Employees characteristics as predictors of turnover among female clerical employees in two organizations. *Journal of Vocational Behavior,* 12, 321–332.

Muchinsky, P. M., & Tuttle, M. L. (1979). Employee turnover: An empirical and methodological assessment. *Journal of Vocational Behavior,* 14, 43–77.

Murnane, R. J., Singer, J. D., & Willet, J. B. (1988). The career paths of teachers. *Educational Researcher,* 17, 22–30.

O'Reilly, B. (1992, August 24). The job drought. *Fortune,* 62.

O'Reilly, C. A., & Caldwell, D. F. (1981). The commitment and job tenure of new employees: Some evidence of postdecisional justification. *Administrative Science Quarterly,* 26(4), 597–616.

O'Reilly, C. A., & Chatman, J. (1986). Organizational commitment and psychological attachment: The effects of compliance, identification, and internalization. *Journal of Applied Psychology,* 71, 492–499.

O'Reilly, C. A., Chatman, J., & Caldwell, D. F. (1991). People and organizational culture: A profile comparison approach to assessing person–organization fit. *Academy of Management Journal,* 34, 487–516.

Parker, S. K. (1998). Enhancing role breadth self-efficacy: The roles of job enrichment and other organizational interventions. *Journal of Applied Psychology,* 83(6), 835–852.

Parker, S. K., Williams, H. M., & Turner, N. (2006). Modeling the antecedents of proactive behavior at work. *Journal of Applied Psychology*, 91(3), 636–652.
Phillips, J. M. (1998). Effects of realistic job previews on multiple organizational outcomes: A meta-analysis. *Academy of Management Journal*, 41(6), 673–690.
Porter, L. W., & Steers, R. M. (1973). Organizational, work, and personal factors in employee turnover and absenteeism. *Psychological Bulletin*, 80, 151–176.
Premack, S. L., & Wanous, J. P. (1985). A meta-analysis of realistic job preview experiments. *Journal of Applied Psychology*, 70, 706–719.
Premack, S. L., & Wanous, J. P. (1987). *Evaluating the Met Expectations Hypothesis*. Paper presented at the National Meeting of the Academy of Management, New Orleans, Louisiana (August).
Price, J. L., & Mueller, C. W. (1981). A causal model of turnover for nurses. *Academy of Management Journal*, 24, 543–565.
Price, J. L., & Mueller, C. W. (1986). *Absenteeism and Turnover of Hospital Employees*. Greenwich, CT: JAI Press.
Ramsay, C. S. (2006). *Engagement at Intuit: It's the People*. Society of Organizational and Industrial Psychology 21st Annual Conference, Dallas, Texas.
Reilly, R. R., Brown, B., Blood, M. R., & Malatesta, C. Z. (1981). The effects of realistic previews: A study and discussion of the literature. *Personnel Psychology*, 34(4), 823–834.
Reilly, R. R., Tenopyr, M. L., & Sperling, S. M. (1979). Effects of job previews on job acceptance and survival of telephone operator candidates. *Journal of Applied Psychology*, 64(2), 218–220.
Rokeach, M. (1973). *The Nature of Human Values*. New York: Free Press.
Rollag, K., Parise, S., & Cross, R. (2005). Getting new hires up to speed quickly. *MIT Sloan Management Review*, 46(2), 35–41.
Rubenstein, A. L., Eberly, M. B., Lee, T. W., & Mitchell, T. R. (2018). Surveying the forest: A meta-analysis, moderator investigation, and future-oriented discussion of the antecedents of voluntary employee turnover. *Personnel Psychology*, 71(1), 23–65.
Rynes, S. L. (1990). Recruitment, job choice, and post-hire consequences: A call for new research directions. In M. D. Dunnette & L. Hough (Eds.), *Handbook of Industrial and Organizational Psychology* (2nd ed., pp. 399–444). Palo Alto, CA: Consulting Psychologists Press.
Saks, A. M., & Cronshaw, S. F. (1990). A process investigation of realistic job previews: Mediating variables and channels of communication. *Journal of Organizational Behavior*, 11(3), 221–236.
Salancik, G. R. (1977). Commitment and the control of organizational behavior and belief. In B. M. Staw & G. Salancik (Eds.), *New Directions in Organizational Behavior* (pp. 1–54). Chicago, IL: St. Clair Press.
Salgado, J. F. (2002). The Big Five personality dimensions and counterproductive behaviors. *International Journal of Selection & Assessment*, 10(1/2), 117–125.
Sarkar, J. (2018). Linking compensation and turnover: Retrospection and future directions. *IUP Journal of Organizational Behavior*, 17, 43–75.
Scarpello, V., Huber, V., & Vandenburg, R. J. (1988). Compensation satisfaction: Its measurement and dimensionality. *Journal of Applied Psychology*, 73(2), 163–171.
Schaubroeck, J., & Ganster, D. C. (1993). Chronic demands and responsivity to challenge. *Journal of Applied Psychology*, 78, 73–85.
Schlachter, S. D., & Pieper, J. R. (2019). Employee referral hiring in organizations: An integrative conceptual review, model, and agenda for future research. *Journal of Applied Psychology*, in press.

Schneider, B. (1985). Organizational behavior. *Annual Review of Psychology*, 36, 573–611.

Scholl, R. W., Cooper, E. A., & McKenna, J. F. (1987). Referent selection in determining equity perceptions: Differential effects on behavioral and attitudinal outcomes. *Personnel Psychology*, 40(1), 113–124.

Schwab, D. P. (1991). Contextual variables in employee performance–turnover relationships. *Academy of Management Journal*, 34, 966–975.

Shaw, J. D., & Gupta, N. (2007). Pay system characteristics and quit patterns of good, average, and poor performers. *Personnel Psychology*, 60(4), 903–928.

Shaw, K. (1987). The quit propensity of married men. *Journal of Labor Economics*, 5, 533–560.

Sigardson, K. M. (1982). Why nurses leave nursing: A survey of former nurses. *Nursing Administration Quarterly*, 7, 20–24.

Smith, D. (1992, February 24). Are you better off? *Fortune*, 46, 38–42.

Smith, P. C., Kendall, L. M., & Hulin, C. L. (1969). *The Measurement of Satisfaction in Work and Retirement*. Chicago, IL: Rand McNally.

Staines, G. L., Pottick, K. J., & Fudge, D. A. (1986). Wives' employment and husbands' attitudes toward work and life. *Journal of Applied Psychology*, 71(1), 118–128.

Steel, R. P., & Griffeth, R. W. (1989). The elusive relationship between perceived employment opportunity and turnover behavior: A methodological or conceptual artifact? *Journal of Applied Psychology*, 74, 846–854.

Suszko, M., & Breaugh, J. A. (1986). The effects of RJPs on applicant self-selection and employee turnover, satisfaction, and coping ability. *Journal of Management*, 12, 513–523.

Sweeney, P. D., McFarlin, D. B., & Inderrieden, E. J. (1990). Using relative deprivation theory to explain satisfaction with income and pay level: A multistudy examination. *Academy of Management Journal*, 33(2), 423–436.

Tepper, B. J. (2000). Consequences of abusive supervision. *Academy of Management Journal*, 43(2), 178–190.

Tett, R. P., Jackson, D. N., & Rothstein, M. (1991). Personality measures as predictors of job performance: A meta-analytic review. *Personnel Psychology*, 44, 703–742.

Trevor, C. O., Reilly, G., & Gerhart, B. (2012). Reconsidering pay dispersion's effect on the performance of interdependent work: Reconciling sorting and pay inequality. *Academy of Management Journal*, 55(3), 585–610.

Turbin, M. S., & Rosse, J. G. (1990). Staffing issues in the high technology industry. In L. Gomez-Mejia & M. Lawless (Eds.), *Organizational Issues in High Technology Management* (pp. 227–241). Greenwich, CT: JAI Press.

Vance, R. J. (2006). *Employee Engagement and Commitment*. Retrieved from www.talentmap.com/knowledgecentre/pages/case%20studies/shrm_employeeengagementonlinereport.pdf

Van Maanen, J., & Schein, E. H. (1979). Toward a theory of organizational socialization. In B. M. Staw (Ed.), *Organizational Behavior* (vol. 1, pp. 209–264). Greenwich, CT: JAI Press. Vandenberg, R. J., & Scarpello, V. (1990). The matching model: An examination of the processes underlying realistic job previews. *Journal of Applied Psychology*, 75, 60–67.

Viswesvaran, C., & Ones, D. S. (2000). Perspectives on models of job performance. *International Journal of Selection & Assessment*, 8(4), 216–227.

Vroom, V. H., & Deci, E. L. (1971). The stability of post decisional dissonance: A follow-up study of the job attitudes of business school graduates. *Organizational Behavior and Human Performance*, 6, 36–49.

Wanous, J. P. (1973). Effects of realistic job preview on job acceptance, job attitudes, and job survival. *Journal of Applied Psychology*, 58, 327–332.

Wanous, J. P. (1977). Organizational entry: Newcomers moving from outside to inside. *Psychological Bulletin*, 84(4), 601–618.

Wanous, J. P. (1980). *Organizational Entry: Recruitment, Selection and Socialization of Newcomers*. Reading, MA: Addison-Wesley.

Wanous, J. P. (1992). *Organizational Entry* (2nd ed.). New York: Addison-Wesley.

Wanous, J. P., & Colella, A. (1989). Organizational entry research: Current status and future directions. In G. Ferris & K. Rowland (Eds.), *Research in Personnel and Human Resources Management* (pp. 59–120). Greenwich, CT: JAI Press.

Wanous, J. P., Poland, T. D., Premack, S. L., & Davis, K. S. (1992). The effects of met expectations on newcomer attitudes and behaviors: A review and meta-analysis. *Journal of Applied Psychology*, 77, 288–297.

Weiner, N. (1980). Determinants and behavioral consequences of pay satisfaction: A comparison of two models. *Personnel Psychology*, 33, 741–757.

Williams, C. R., & Livingstone, L. P. (1994). A second look at the relationship between performance and voluntary turnover. *Academy of Management Journal*, 37, 269–298.

Williams, L. J., & Hazer, J. T. (1986). Antecedents and consequences of satisfaction and commitment in turnover models: A reanalysis using latent variable structural equation methods. *Journal of Applied Psychology*, 71, 219–231.

Williams, M. L., Brower, H. H., Ford, L. R., Williams, L. J., & Carraher, S. M. (2008). A comprehensive model and measure of compensation satisfaction. *Journal of Occupational & Organizational Psychology*, 81(4), 639–668.

Wilson, N., & Peel, M. J. (1991). The impact on absenteeism and quits of profit-sharing and other forms of employee participation. *Industrial and Labor Relations Review*, 44, 454–468.

Woo, S. E. (2011). A study of Ghiselli's hobo syndrome. *Journal of Vocational Behavior*, 79(2), 461–469.

Wood, R. E., Mento, A. J., & Locke, E. A. (1987). Task complexity as a moderator of goal effects: A meta-analysis. *Journal of Applied Psychology*, 72(3), 416–425.

Wrzesniewski, A., & Dutton, J. E. (2001). Crafting a job: Revisioning employees as active crafters of their work. *Academy of Management Review*, 26(2), 179–201.

Zaharia, E. S., & Baumeister, A. A. (1981). Job preview effects during the critical initial employment period. *Journal of Applied Psychology*, 66(1), 19–22.

Zenger, T. R. (1992). Why do employers only reward extreme performance? Examining the relationships among performance, pay, and turnover. *Administrative Science Quarterly*, 37, 198–219.

Zimmerman, R. D. (2008). Understanding the impact of personality traits on individuals' turnover decisions: A meta-analytic path model. *Personnel Psychology*, 61(2), 309–348.

Zimmerman, R. D., Swider, B. W., Woo, S. E., & Allen, D. G. (2016). Who withdraws? Psychological individual differences and employee withdrawal behaviors. *Journal of Applied Psychology*, 101(4), 498–519.

10

DIVERSITY AND GLOBAL RESEARCH ON TURNOVER

Since the earliest turnover studies (Hom, Lee, Shaw, & Hausknecht, 2017), researchers have examined demographic characteristics as potential turnover predictors, often deriving selection tests from weighted application blanks. Since the passage of the civil rights legislation and the advent of diversity management, researchers increasingly investigated voluntary quits among women and people of color (Kalev, Kelly, & Dobbin, 2006; Leslie, Manchester, & Dahm, 2016). Presumably, higher turnover among these demographic subgroups may signal underlying workplace discrimination, while impeding corporate progress toward more diversified workforces (Hom, Roberson, & Ellis, 2008). Apart from this focus, American firms increasingly have globalized and employed more foreign nationals, while economic liberalization in command economies (notably, China) has prompted greater job mobility as employees and employers are free to dissolve employment relationships (Hom & Griffeth, 1995). Given that turnover can represent a significant and costly phenomenon in other societal cultures, scholars are investigating their etiology and ways to predict and curb excessive attrition (Allen & Vardaman, 2017; Maertz, Stevens, & Campion, 2003; Qin, Hom, & Xu, 2019). This chapter highlights the different research streams on turnover among demographic (U.S.) subpopulations as well as different nationalities.

Domestic Workforce Diversity and Turnover

Voluntary Turnover among Women in Male-Dominated Fields

Citing a corporate report, Schwartz (1989) first attracted widespread concern about the corporate exodus of women managers, declaring that "the rate of turnover in management positions is 2½ times higher among top-performing women than it is among men" (p. 65). Although meta-analyses (Griffeth, Hom, & Gartner, 2000; Rubenstein, Eberly, Lee, & Mitchell, 2018) report little or no sex differences in turnover, widespread descriptive and journalistic accounts suggest otherwise (Hom & Griffeth, 1995). Indeed, diversity studies of the greater plight of women in traditionally male-dominated occupations offering more prestige, power, or pay suggest their greater flight from such jobs. In such workplaces, gender inequity—and thus gender differences in turnover—is worse (Hewlett & Luce, 2005; Hom et al., 2008). Diversity scholars have long documented how women in male-dominated jobs (e.g., corporate managers, lawyers, auditors) are particularly disadvantaged, including more career obstacles (e.g., fewer mentors or exclusion from information networks), inequitable work outcomes (e.g., lower pay or fewer promotions), poor accommodations for family duties (e.g., "up-or-out" promotion systems in public accounting or law firms, stereotypes that mothers are less ambitious due to their supposedly higher family duties; Hoobler, Wayne, & Lemmon, 2009), and outright gender and sexual harassment (cf. Brett & Stroh, 1999; Dalton, Hill, & Ramsay, 1997; Elvira & Cohen, 2001; Lyness & Thompson, 1997; Riordan, Schaffer, & Stewart, 2005; Tsui & Gutek, 1999).

Despite such persuasive and broad findings for gender inequities, how such gender disadvantages translate in higher voluntary turnover among women in male-dominated occupational fields is equivocal. In line with turnover meta-analyses, Hom et al. (2008) concluded that existing research fail to consistently establish that women in non-traditional fields quit at higher rates than their male counterparts. What is more, empirical studies often assess other proxies than voluntary turnover, such as quit intentions, labor market exits, occupational attrition, reasons for leaving (collected from former employees), or terminations. After all, gender differences in such proxies may not necessarily correspond to gender differences in actual turnover (Allen, Weeks, & Moffitt, 2005), while exit interviews with only leavers may overstate discriminatory causes (Griffeth & Hom, 2001). Addressing the above shortcomings, Hom et al. (2008) conclude that women managers and professionals voluntarily leave at higher rates than their male counterparts based on a sample of over 400,000 employees from 16 national firms (where women constituted 28% of the exempt workforce). Despite this large-scale demonstration (which remains an outlier; Rubenstein et al., 2018), Hom et al. (2008) did not assess causal antecedents that might be responsible for gender differences in attrition, such as gender disparities in work outcomes, opportunities for social capital accumulation, or family structure (Stroh, Brett & Reilly, 1996). We thus might confidently assert that women in non-traditional fields suffer greater disadvantages or discrimination and that they are more liable to quit. Existing evidence, however, does not conclusively show that gender inequities are the causal mechanism underlying women's propensity to exit male-dominated occupations.

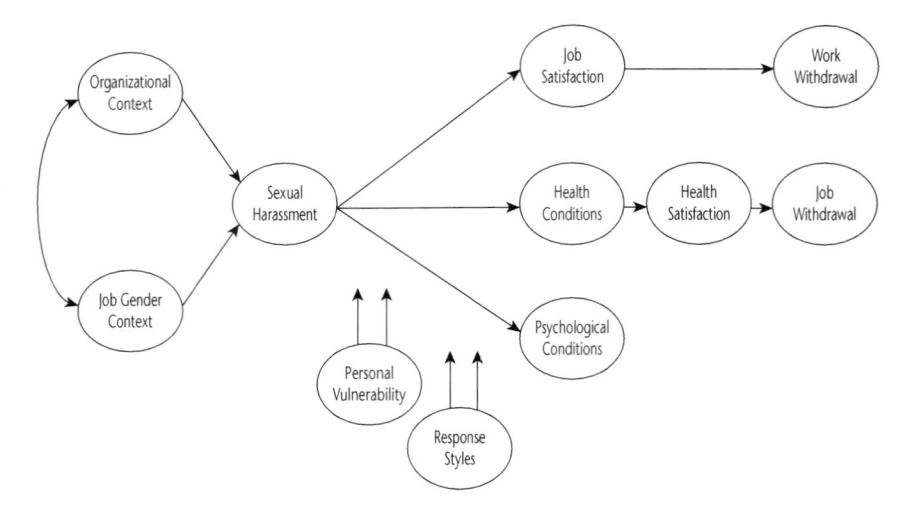

FIGURE 10.1 Fitzgerald, Drasgow, Hulin, Gelfand, and Magley's (1997) Model of Sexual Harassment

Sexual Harassment as Causal Antecedent

Louis Fitzgerald and her colleagues at the University of Illinois (Fitzgerald, Drasgow, Hulin, Gelfand, & Magley, 1997) formulated the most elaborate theory about how workplace discrimination—namely, sexual harassment—affects turnover among women employees (see Figure 10.1). Sexual harassment comprises: (a) gender harassment (crude verbal or physical actions that convey offensive misogynist attitudes); (b) unwanted sexual attention; and (c) sexual coercion (efforts to make job rewards contingent on sexual cooperation). They theorize that the prevalence of sexual harassment in an organization hinges on an organizational climate tolerating sexual harassment and "job gender context" (e.g., male-dominated work group, male sex-typed job). Harassment in turn negatively influences job (e.g., job satisfaction), health-related (e.g., physical symptoms, such as headaches and felt exhaustion), and psychological (e.g., depression) outcomes. As a form of occupational stress, they deduced that sexual harassment also increases "work withdrawal" (avoid work tasks by taking long breaks or leaving work early while remaining employed) and "job withdrawal" (complete withdrawal from a job in a particular organization by leaving or retiring) via those intermediate outcomes (e.g., job satisfaction, poor health). Further, they envisioned that the impact of harassment on any woman depends on her personal vulnerability and her response to the harassment. As predicted, sexual harassment reduced job satisfaction and increased psychological conditions (e.g., anxiety). While not directly affecting health conditions, they did find that diminished psychological conditions create more health symptoms. Their test also noted that health satisfaction (an outcome of health conditions) decreased work and job withdrawal. Finally, job satisfaction reduced job withdrawal (e.g., turnover), though not work withdrawal. In sum, this theory demonstrates how sexual harassment can boost quit propensity via its negative effects on job satisfaction, psychological distress, and poor physical health.

Bergman and Henning (2008) generalized this model for soldiers, showing that sexual harassment can increase job withdrawal (thoughts of leaving the military) by increasing job dissatisfaction and mental and physical health distress. Testing female sex as a marker of personal vulnerability, they also found that women soldiers confront more sexual harassment than do men in organizational climates tolerating sexual harassment as they are seen as diverging from masculine cultural ideal extolled in the U.S. military. Lacking membership in the hegemonic male group, these "interlopers" are vulnerable to harassment given weaker power and low status.

Racial Minority Turnover

Reviewing the turnover literature, several authors note that diversity scholars assume that members of racioethnic minorities are more quit-prone given massive empirical evidence about their exposure to workplace discrimination (Hom & Griffeth, 1995; Roberson, 2004). Undergirding such beliefs are striking journalistic or descriptive (e.g., case studies) accounts about elevated rates of quitting by minority incumbents (cf. Hom & Griffeth, 1995). Given worse employment conditions (e.g., lower pay, fewer promotions) and apparently exorbitant attrition, diversity scholars often conclude that minorities are leaving at higher rates because of greater workplace disadvantages or discrimination (Roberson, 2004).

Conceptual literature reviews summarizing empirical findings, however, challenge this pervasive assumption (Hom & Griffeth, 1995; Roberson, 2004). As Roberson (2004) observed, much "evidence" for higher minority attrition comes from corporate studies (e.g., Corning Glass report; Cox & Blake, 1991) or journalistic accounts based on informal observations by corporate informants (often justifying diversity programs). Besides qualitative descriptions, empirical studies claiming higher minority quits may rely on quit intentions as a proxy for turnover (McKay et al., 2007; Valentine, 2001). While the strongest turnover antecedent, quit intentions, however, rarely explain more than 25% of the variance in turnover (Allen et al., 2005). Further disputing apparent minority flight from workplaces are meta-analyses finding tenuous relationships between racial minority status and actual turnover. To illustrate, Griffeth et al. (2000) estimated a .01 correlation, while Rubenstein et al. (2018) estimated this correlation to be .02. Based on her critique, Roberson (2004) concluded that available evidence has "failed to consistently support" the commonly held view that people of color quit at higher rates (p. 223).

To account for such weak and often conflicting race–turnover relationships, Roberson (2004) formulated a framework identifying how moderator variables affect the race–turnover relationship, building on diversity research on racial discrimination (Hom & Griffeth, 1995). She further elaborated Hom and Griffeth's provisional model by introducing mediators—namely, race → workplace discrimination → job attitudes → turnover. Reviewing the diversity literature, Hom and Griffeth (1995) had argued that supervisory bias, poor leader–member exchange, pay inequity, impoverished job duties, performance pressures (reflecting stereotype threat), career immobility, indifferent or hostile peers, and tokenism may prompt higher minority attrition. Claiming that racial minorities do not always confront such workplace disadvantages, Roberson proposed that ethnicity, racial identity, career stage, diversity climate, and work group composition determine whether or not racial minorities encounter workplace discrimination. Although turnover researchers often combine different ethnic minorities given their limited representation in most firms, Roberson noted that such routine practices attenuate correlations between minority status and turnover because some minorities may not exit at higher rates than do Whites (e.g., Asian Americans; Hom et al., 2008). Importantly, different racial minorities experience different types and levels of discrimination (Berdahl & Min, 2012; Bergman, Palmieri, Drasgow, & Ormerod, 2007; Fiske, Cuddy, Glick, & Xu, 2002; Sidanius & Pratto, 2001). Many examinations find more negative attitudes toward Blacks and Hispanics than other racial minorities (Greenwald & Banaji, 1995; Hosoda, Stone, & Stone-Romero, 2003; Taylor, 1998; Ziegert & Hanges, 2005). For example, Whites view Blacks and Hispanic Americans as threats to their safety or property, while seeing Asians as threatening their values or access to valued resources (e.g., Ivy League college entry; Berdahl & Min, 2012; Cottrell & Neuberg, 2005; Fiske et al., 2002; Golden, 2007; Unz, 2012). Besides this, Bergman et al. (2007) found that Blacks and Hispanics (and Native Americans) *perceive* more racial harassment (e.g., derogatory remarks) and discrimination (e.g., fewer promotions) than do Asians or Whites. Even so, Asian Americans are outgroups to Whites and other minorities (Cottrell & Neuberg, 2005; Fiske et al., 2002). Seen as competent but cold, they arouse envy and dislike (Berdahl & Min, 2012; Cuddy, Fiske, & Glick, 2004; Lin, Kwan, Cheung, & Fiske, 2005) and face more ethnic harassment than Whites in the military (Bergman et al., 2007). Given such findings, Roberson's theory envisions racial disparities in workplace discrimination, whereby racioethnic group membership moderates the effects of race on workplace discrimination (posited mediators). Moreover, minorities identifying with their race (i.e., racial/ethnic identity) more readily notice discrimination toward their group and attribute negative actions by the dominant group as representing discrimination (Roberson, 2004). Even if one is not personally mistreated, perceived discrimination toward members of one's race may signal that one too is vulnerable to similar mistreatment in the future (e.g., bamboo ceiling for Asian Americans).

According to Roberson (2004), diversity climate is another prime moderator of the race → discrimination path. Organizational climates that see diversity efforts as ways to improve organizational functioning by incorporating minorities' perspectives rather than promoting fairness (by recruiting more minorities and assimilating them) or accessing broader clienteles (by recruiting minorities to serve niche markets) may most enhance minorities' career and work lives. Conceivably, positive diversity climates attenuate racial discrimination, thus lowering racial effects on turnover (and its immediate antecedents). In support, McKay et al. (2007) found that pro-diversity climates (where organizations value diversity) diminish quit intentions for both Whites and non-Whites, insuring against unfair group treatment. Moreover, Roberson (2004) envisioned career stage as another moderator of the race–turnover link, citing Thomas's (Thomas, 2001; Thomas & Gabarro, 1999) research that minority executives in corporations experience slower promotional rates during the first five years relative to Whites. After this early career stage, minority executives advance more rapidly and they "catch up" to Whites after ten years. Because minorities face career blocks during their early career but not later, career stage may also influence the race–turnover link.

Further, Roberson introduced work group demographic composition as another moderator of how race influences workplace inequities or mistreatment. Citing demographic studies (Cordero, DiTomaso, & Farris, 1996; Riordan & Shore, 1997; Tsui, Egan, & O'Reilly, 1992), she observed that increasing racioethnic diversity in work groups boosts Whites' quit propensity (as they feel outnumbered and disadvantaged). Yet rising White membership in work groups does not invoke higher quit propensity among minorities. Rather, they are more quit-prone if they are tokens or extremely underrepresented (less than 15%) as tokenism or solo status can bolster felt stereotype threat and their exclusion from social networks (Kanter, 1977; Roberson, Deitch, Brief & Block, 2003).

Roberson (2004) further proposed that race and racial identity moderates how workplace discrimination evokes dissatisfaction (i.e., discrimination → job attitudes). Because Blacks and Native Americans have been involuntarily incorporated into U.S. society, such "caste" minorities distrust the inherent fairness of the dominant culture. By contrast, Asians and Hispanics voluntarily come to the United States ("immigrant" minorities), optimistically believing that they can improve their lot through their personal efforts. Because caste minorities reject system fairness, they feel greater dissatisfaction (and more readily exit) when perceiving workplace discrimination or disadvantage compared to immigrant minorities. Racial/ethnic identity exhibits similar moderating effects for minorities identifying with their racial group may likely detect or interpret unfairness more negatively and thus feel more quit-prone. Finally, Roberson conceptualized that job level influences how job attitudes drive leaving (job attitudes → quit) because minorities in higher job levels (e.g., managers or professionals) have higher mobility aspirations than those in low-level jobs (where career ladders are short or nonexistent). When they encounter career obstacles, they may respond to such dissatisfying conditions by leaving (which is facilitated by affirmative action recruiting by other firms).

Despite Roberson's (2004) pioneering framework, few turnover researchers—to our knowledge—have investigated how workplace disadvantages or discrimination mediate the effects of race on turnover. The few "mediation" tests yield conflicting evidence for minority flight (aka "ethnic prominence), rarely assess discriminatory mediators, and apply deficient statistical tests of mediation (Mynatt, Omundson, Schroeder, & Stevens, 1997; Raver & Nishii, 2010; Rosser, 2004; Valentine, 2001). Given its import, we recommend more turnover research on the extent of minority flight and the reasons underlying such flight, using the Standard Research Design (Steel, 2002) at a minimum, and carrying out more rigorous mediating studies.

Double Jeopardy: Minority Female Flight

While race and gender dynamics each attract greater scrutiny, turnover researchers have long neglected the *intersection* of race and gender—or how racism and sexism operate in tandem to impel quits. Across academic disciplines (e.g., psychology, sociology), diversity theorists argue that race and gender discrimination cannot be understood independently of each other (Brown & Misra, 2003). After all, "women of color experience racism in ways not always the same as those experienced by men of color and sexism in ways not always parallel to experiences of white women" (Crenshaw, 1991, p. 1252). When both demographic attributes are examined together, diversity scholars conclude that women who are also racial minorities experience "double jeopardy"—that is, they are doubly disadvantaged by two stigmatized social identities (Beal, 1970; Berdahl & Moore, 2006)—which impels them to leave (Kulis & Miller, 1988). Descriptive and empirical research indicate that minority women face more career obstacles and discrimination than do minority men and Whites (Berdahl & Moore, 2006; Crenshaw, 1991; Williams, 2014). Organizational studies research thus finds that minority women earn low wages and hold marginal jobs (Barnum, Liden, & Ditomaso, 1995), while faring worse than Whites and minority men on occupational status and job authority (Kalev et al., 2006; Reskin & Padavic, 1994; Valentine, 2001). Besides this, Berdahl and Moore (2006) affirmed that minority women confront more gender and racial harassment than other demographic subgroups in ethnically diverse workplaces. Further, an audit experiment revealed more hiring discrimination toward Black women than Black men or Whites of either sex (Bendick, Jackson, & Reinoso, 1994), while an executive of a failing enterprise who is a Black woman is judged more harshly than a Black man or a White woman (Rosette & Livingston, 2012).

Based on such findings, Hom et al. (2008) derived a double jeopardy (DJ) attrition model positing that dual marginalization underlies minority female flight (MFF). In support, three studies have noted elevated quits among ethnic minority women (Hom et al., 2008; Kulis & Miller, 1988; Noonan & Corcoran, 2004). All the same, many attrition studies of joint sex and race effects reveal other turnover patterns, such as more quits among ethnic minorities (men and women alike) than ethnic majorities (Leonard & Levine, 2006; McKay et al., 2007; Raver & Nishii, 2010; Rosser, 2004).

Subordinate Male Target Hypothesis (SMTH)

Aside from an MFF pattern, intersectional studies noted that minority men exhibit the most turnover (Kaplan, Wiley, & Maertz, 2011; Leonard & Levine, 2006). Such findings dispute the double jeopardy thesis and fit with SMTH, an evolutionary psychology theory posting that minority males, not females, are most oppressed (Sidanius & Pratto, 2001; Sidanius & Veniegas, 2000). SMTH presumes that all societies are structured hierarchically, with dominant groups amassing resources by exploiting subordinate groups. Given intergroup competition, dominant males gain resources by aggressively behaving toward outgroups to preserve their group's status, power, and privilege. Subordinate males bear the brunt of persecution as they are deemed *more threatening* than subordinate females. By contrast, subordinate women incur milder aggression as they are indirectly targeted (due to affiliation or dependency on subordinate men) and constitute reproductive resources for dominant men. Affirming SMTH, stereotyping studies report that Black and Hispanic men rather than women are stigmatized as criminal, violent, or incompetent (Goff, Eberhardt, Williams, & Jackson, 2008a; Spohn & Holleran, 2000; Wilson, 1996). As Fiske et al.'s (2002) stereotype content model notes, minority men face "contemptuous prejudice" as they are seen as having low warmth and competence, whereas minority women face "paternalistic prejudice" where greater warmth toward their sex offsets their perceived incompetence.

According to Sidanius and Pratto (2001), a broad body of findings attest to heightened minority male discrimination in the criminal justice system, education, and employment. Summarizing 19 employment audits (where equally qualified dominant and subordinate applicants apply for jobs), Sidanius and Pratto (2001) concluded that "subordinate men were discriminated at higher rates than subordinate women" (p. 168). More recently, Milkman, Akinola, and Chugh (2015) observed that college professors more often reject email requests for research internships from prospective PhD students who are minority men than minority women or Whites. Similarly, Derous, Ryan, and Serlie (2015) demonstrated that Dutch recruiters judge résumés from Arab male job candidates as least suitable for jobs compared with those from Arab female or Dutch candidates. Apart from hiring discrimination, other research finds that minority men are less likely to attain management or leadership posts than minority women, while receiving lower performance ratings than the latter (Hosoda et al., 2003; Livingston & Pearce, 2009).

Ethnic Prominence

Turnover research on compound demographic effects also reports a third turnover pattern—namely, higher quit propensity for both minority men and women (McKay et al., 2007; Raver & Nishii, 2010; Rosser, 2004). Such findings are compatible with a third discrimination model that claims that minority women are oppressed as much as minority men (Levin, Sinclair, Veniegas, &

Taylor, 2002). Minority women confront more racism than sexism because their race is a more salient cue than their sex as minorities are numerically rare compared to numerically majority women (Kulik, Roberson, & Perry, 2007). Sustaining this theory, Goff, Thomas, and Jackson (2008b) found that Black male and female faces more than White faces are judged more race-stereotypical, while Bertrand and Mullainathan (2004) documented that fictitious résumés with White-sounding names received more callbacks from employers posting job openings than those with "Black" names, regardless of applicant sex. Further, Raver and Nishii (2010) found that minority women and men perceive more ethnic harassment than do Whites of either sex.

Intersectional Invisibility

Finally, studies of joint race and sex effects also reveal a fourth turnover pattern—minority women quitting least compared to minority men and Whites (Farber, 1994; Light & Ureta, 1992; Saporta & Farjoun, 2003; Sicherman, 1996). This pattern fits with "intersectional invisibility" theory, which claims that minority women suffer least discrimination because they are neither prototypical of their race nor sex (Sesko & Biernat, 2010). As Livingston, Rosette, and Washington (2012) explain, "because the prototypical Black is male ... and the prototypical woman is White, Black women tend to be defined as nonprototypical ... members of both their racial and gender groups," rendering them "invisible" (p. 355). Minority women thus confront less hostility than do minority men or White women, although such invisibility can marginalize them (Sesko & Biernat, 2010).

Sustaining this theory, Sesko and Biernat (2010) observed that White undergraduates poorly recognize photos of Black women compared to those of Black men and Whites, and misattribute statements made by a Black woman in a group discussion compared to those by other demographic subgroups. Livingston et al. (2012) also established that laboratory participants regard White female and Black male leaders as less effective compared to Black female leaders when acting dominantly. Because agentic behaviors are proscribed for Black men and White women, Black women suffer *less* backlash for being assertive as they marginally represent their race and sex. Further, Powell and Butterfield (2002) reported that minority women advance more quickly in a federal agency than minority men or Whites, while Williams' (2014) qualitative research discerned that Black women feel greater freedom to use an assertive, non-deferential style at work.

Methodological Limitations

Methodological problems plague empirical evidence for these four attrition-discrimination models. While not definitive, findings of direct (additive) effects of sex and race on voluntary turnover can be used to substantiate these models (e.g., MMF pattern evidencing dual discrimination; Hom et al., 2008). Yet many demographic studies on attrition often controlled potential proxies reflecting discriminatory treatment (e.g., low pay; Leonard & Levine, 2006) or outcomes (e.g., job dissatisfaction; Bergman, Palmieri, Drasgow, & Ormerod, 2012). Such controls underestimate joint race and sex effects by removing their indirect effects on turnover (Carlson & Wu, 2011).

Most of all, most scholarly inquiries into compound demographic effects fail to assess purported mechanisms behind their effects, despite widespread claims that harassment or discrimination underlies greater flight among minority men or women (Kulis & Miller, 1988; Raver & Nishii, 2010). To our knowledge, four studies investigated mediating mechanisms for compound demographic effects on quit propensity, with two suggesting support for ethnic prominence (Mynatt et al., 1997; Raver & Nishii, 2010; Rosser, 2004; Valentine, 2001). All the same, all but one (Raver & Nishii, 2010) directly assessed experienced discrimination, while most assessed indirect proxies for discriminatory treatment or experience (e.g., job satisfaction; Mynatt et al., 1997; Rosser, 2004). Moreover, these studies failed to use more powerful statistical tests of mediation, using instead discredited Baron–Kenny causal steps or the Sobel test (MacKinnon, Fairchild, & Fritz, 2007; Zhao, Lynch, & Chen, 2010).

We suggest future research testing these discrimination models because effective retention of minority male or female employees requires "accurate understanding of the organizational mechanisms that produce inequity" (Fernandez & Campero, 2017, p. 73). After all, diversity programs targeted at sexism or racism separately may not help women of color—or help them as much (Dobbins & Kalev, 2016; Hirsh & Cha, 2017). In particular, future tests should directly assess discriminatory mechanisms, while using more powerful statistical tests to verify their mediating role (i.e., assessing indirect effects with bootstrapped confidence intervals; Hayes, 2013). If possible, these attrition-discrimination models should be validated separately for different ethnic minorities whose quit rates likely differ if they are sufficiently represented in workforces (cf. Hom et al., 2008).

Following Kulik et al. (2007), we suggest theoretical refinements in these attrition-discrimination models specifying contextual moderators (Hernandez et al., 2016). Conceivably, different employment contexts (e.g., male-dominated occupations, Asian-dominated technical fields) may determine what demographic subgroups are viewed as good occupational fits and thus the level of discrimination they may encounter (Kulik et al., 2007). For example, Blacks may be perceived as poor fits to STEM occupations given negative stereotypes about their intellect, whereas Asian men may be regarded as poor fits to military roles, failing to meet masculine ideals or threatening Caucasian or Black men's hegemonic dominance in the U.S. military (Bergman & Henning, 2008). For example, in Williams' (2014) interviews, a Black woman who became a doctor after previously working as an engineer noted that people are reluctant to take her seriously because of her race. "In medicine, women are common but black people are rare," she claims (Williams, 2014, p. 196). When the interviewee was an engineer, where women are rare, she felt disrespected because she was a woman.

International Diversity and Turnover

As several authors had long forewarned (Hom & Griffeth, 1995; Maertz & Campion, 1998), the globalization of American business will surely inspire more turnover research on its growing international workforce (including expatriates working abroad) and increased dependency on foreign contract-labor suppliers for its global supply chain (Miller, Hom, & Gomez-Mejia, 2001). Increasingly, scholars have adopted turnover and embeddedness models to explain why expatriates withdraw from overseas assignments (Shaffer & Harrison, 1998; Tharenou & Caulfield, 2010) or tested their generalizability for predicting employee turnover in different countries or cultures (Allen & Vardaman, 2017). Although expatriate research scrutinizes withdrawal from offshore assignments, this work may offer insight into expatriates quitting their parent corporation as 38% of repatriated employees leave within a year of returning home (Allen & Vardaman, 2017). Because premature termination of expatriate assignments may culminate in organizational turnover, it is conceivable that what causes the former may also prompt the latter (e.g., failure abroad may impede career advancement in the parent corporation). Building on Allen and Vardaman's (2017) recent critique, we briefly discuss these two separate streams of withdrawal research.

Expatriate Withdrawal

Allen and Vardaman (2017) concluded that prevailing research investigates how expatriates' adjustment (including that of their family) can influence their decision to terminate offshore assignments prematurely (which can cost as much as $1 million; Shaffer & Harrison, 1998). Over the years, expatriate researchers have integrated explanatory constructs from traditional turnover theories (e.g., attitudes toward job and firm) to enrich accounts of expatriate withdrawal. Illustrative of this approach, Shaffer and Harrison (1998) found that job satisfaction and affective organizational commitment decreased expatriates' withdrawal cognitions, beyond the effects of cross-cultural adjustment (i.e., satisfaction living in local community, spousal adjustment abroad). Combining contemporary views on the unfolding model and job embeddedness, Tharenou and Caulfield (2010) sought to more fully explain expatriates' decision to return home (though their expatriates self-initiated work abroad). As path analysis of their model shows (Figure 10.2), various shocks (e.g., illness, elderly parent, wedding back home) can prompt expatriates to contemplate returning home. Yet they are less likely to decide to repatriate when they are embedded in the foreign community (e.g., they have

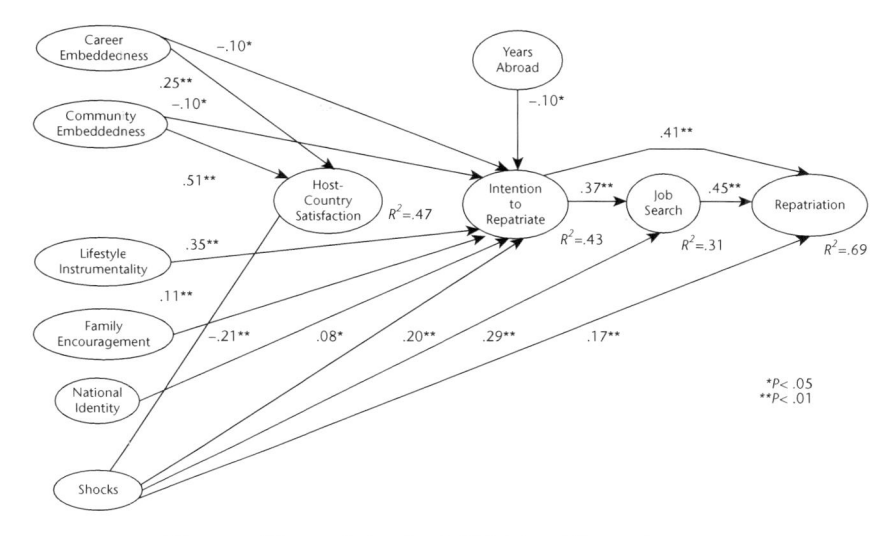

FIGURE 10.2 Theory of Repatriation by Self-Initiated Expatriates

"gone native" or develop intimate ties with local citizens) or offshore assignment (feeling "career embeddedness" because they can most advance their career goals by working abroad). Going beyond the unfolding model and job embeddedness theory, Tharenou and Caulfield (2010) also documented that lifestyle instrumentality (e.g., repatriation benefits, such as "better place to raise children") and encouragement to return home from home-country family (e.g., parents) also increased intentions to return home.

Allen and Vardaman (2017) identified a few studies investigating why repatriates decide to leave their employment, noting that perceived instrumentality of expatriate assignments for career advancement and satisfaction with the repatriation process (e.g., training after repatriation) improve repatriate retention. Extending this work, Kraimer, Shaffer, Harrison, and Ren (2012) used identity theory to explain why repatriates may quit their employment. Specifically, they demonstrated that repatriates when living abroad develop an international employee identity, where their former role as an expatriate has become central to their self-identity. This identity is strengthened when they were strongly embedded abroad (e.g., enjoyed living in their foreign post, formed many host-country friendships, and experienced sizeable sacrifices when leaving the host-country community). Upon returning home, this international employee identity may continue as repatriates may "incorporate the characteristics of past roles into their own identity" as they transition from expatriate to repatriate (Kraimer et al., 2012, p. 401). Kraimer et al. further theorized that repatriates may experience "identity strain" (i.e., threats to their identity) if the organization does not affirm or verify their international employee identity. Specifically, if they believe that their firm does not provide them with appreciable benefits relative to peers who did not complete expatriate assignments (e.g., more responsibilities, higher pay, promotions; aka *perceived job deprivation*), they would feel distressed as their identity would be threatened. Consequently, repatriates experiencing identity strain would exit the firm that is not valuing their international employee identity. In support, Kraimer et al. (2012) demonstrated an interaction between international employee identity and perceived job deprivation such that repatriates who continue to identify as international employees but perceived greater job deprivation felt greater identity strain, which in turn prompted them to quit.

In summary, Allen and Vardaman (2017) conclude that prevailing research on expatriate terminations and repatriate retention became overly dependent on traditional March–Simon formulations of turnover (e.g., Mobley, 1977; Mobley, Griffeth, Hand, & Meglino, 1979; Steers & Mowday, 1981). Moreover, they criticize existing studies for merely applying established theories and processes to the expatriate context. Excepting cultural novelty or cultural distance, they also note that cultural variables are rarely considered in expatriate studies. Encouragingly, recent studies are capitalizing on contemporary views on withdrawal since the March–Simon formulations, such as recognizing shocks and expatriate embeddedness as withdrawal influences (Kraimer et al., 2012; Tharenou & Caulfield, 2010). Moreover, these tests often "contextualize" explanatory constructs (e.g., job embeddedness) to better explain expatriate retention, such as specifying analogous specific forces embedding expatriates, such as career benefits of working abroad (aka host-country career embeddedness) and advantages of living overseas (aka host-country community embeddedness; Tharenou & Caulfield, 2010). Further, contemporary expatriate scholarship is no longer borrowing domestic turnover models but also generating new constructs that might have broader validity for accounting for other forms of turnover (e.g., identity strain; Qin et al., 2019).

Employee Turnover in Other Cultures or Societies

Given its historical roots in Anglo-American scholarship, it is not surprising that early international research on turnover by foreign nationals primarily tested theories developed and validated in the United States, Canada, England, and Australia (or UCEA; Maertz et al., 2003). Nevertheless, international investigations demonstrated broad cross-cultural generalizability for predominant theories of leaving or staying, such as traditional March–Simon models emphasizing workplace conditions (or attitudes toward them) and job opportunities (Chen, Wang, & Tang, 2016; Jiang, Baker, & Frazier, 2009; Linnehan & Blau, 2003; Miller et al., 2001; Posthuma, Joplin, & Maertz, 2005), the unfolding model (cf. Holtom, Mitchell, Lee, & Eberly, 2008), and job embeddedness (Hom et al., 2009; Jiang, Liu, McKay, Lee, & Mitchell, 2012; Ramesh & Gelfand, 2010). Indeed, Allen and Vardaman (2017) conclude international inquiries suggest that "turnover models and processes actually generalize quite well across cultural contexts" (p. 169).

While heartening, early and subsequent critiques of the emerging international turnover literature continue to complain that applying UCEA theories or constructs is misguided, presuming their universal validity (Maertz et al., 2003; Ramesh & Gelfand, 2010). When UCEA constructs and their operationalizations are applied without any contextualization (aka direct context-free transferability; Tsui, Nifadkar, & Ou, 2007), explanatory accounts of employee turnover in different cultures can be deficient. In light of these critiques, recent scholarship has begun contextualizing operationalizations of constructs. For example, Hom et al. (2009) adapted Mitchell and Lee's (2001) measures of job embeddedness for Chinese respondents by incorporating embedding forces salient in their society, such as loss of *guanxi* connections as a job sacrifice. More systematically, Peltokorpi (2013) interviewed 110 Japanese managers, employees, and recruiters to generate a comprehensive indigenous embeddedness measure, which revealed that intra-firm social capital, ingroup ties, and normative pressures are stronger on-the-job embedding forces in Japan than Western societies. Contextualizing the embeddedness construct, Ramesh and Gelfand (2010) also introduced family embeddedness as Mitchell and Lee's (2001) original construct ignores or understates how family influences can most shape Asian Indians' decisions to stay or leave.

Although international studies historically focused on one foreign society (speculating about how culture affects turnover models or predictors; Hom et al., 2009; Hom & Xiao, 2011), recent international studies are increasingly comparing multiple nationalities and testing cultural dimensions as moderators (cf. Allen & Vardaman, 2017). To illustrate, Sturman, Shao, and Katz (2012) examined the performance–turnover relationship across 24 foreign subsidiaries of a U.S. multinational firm. Using House, Hanges, Javidan, Dorfman, and Gupta's (2004) GLOBE measures of cultural dimensions (e.g., power distance, collectivism), they found that cultural dimensions affect the level of turnover across subsidiaries (e.g., turnover is lower in collectivist societies) as well as moderate the (nonlinear) performance–turnover relationship (where low and top performers quit more than satisfactory performers). We welcome more research of this type (cultural comparisons of multiple nationalities), as well as echo Allen and Vardaman's (2017) call for greater integration of cross-cultural perspectives into existing turnover and embeddedness models.

Chinese and Mexican Assembly-Line Workers

Because the United States increasingly depends on Chinese and Mexican labor for manufacturing its goods ("Emergence of a Trade Leviathan", 2018), turnover researchers seek to explain the high turnover rates by Chinese and Mexican workers in assembly plants in export-oriented processing zones (EPZs; Qin et al., 2019; West, 2004). Leaving behind the countryside where employment is limited to subsistence farming (Qin, Hom, Xu, & Ju, 2014), rural migrants seek a higher standard of living by emigrating to urban centers (e.g., coastal China, U.S.–Mexico border towns) where factory jobs are plentiful (as multinationals or their contractors open factories to capitalize on low-cost labor). There, EPZ workers staff physically demanding assembly lines for long hours. Although earning low pay, assemblers receive other benefits, such as subsidized meals and factory housing, while they can save enough income to send home remittances to families. Factory turnover rates are high (e.g., 60% in China; Fallows, 2012) because assembly workers can readily find alternative factory work and better their lot—if only slightly—by leaving lower-paid or disagreeable jobs (e.g., noisy work environment, unfair pay, unstable payroll; Daming & Sun Xiaoyun, 2010).

Early research initially examining Mexicans (working maquiladora factories) and then China (when its economy liberalized) tested traditional turnover theories that emphasize movement desirability and ease (March & Simon, 1958). These empirical studies find that assemblers *desire* to leave when feeling negative job attitudes (Chen et al., 2016; Liu & Peng, 2007; Smyth, Zhai, & Li, 2009; Tiano, 1994; West, 2000) or perceiving inferior job conditions (Miller et al., 2001; Tello, Greene, & Garcia, 2002; Williams & Passe-Smith, 1992). They are also quit-prone when they *can* readily find other factory work (Linnehan & Blau, 2003). Other studies reveal that turnover determinants identified by contemporary theories since the March–Simon (MS) models (Felps et al., 2009; Lee & Mitchell, 1994), such as "shocks" (Jiang et al., 2009; West, 2004) and turnover contagion (Maertz et al., 2003), also prompt EPZ workers to quit.

In short, this research on the EPZ workforce suffers from the same limitations as international studies of turnover among other workforces (Allen & Vardaman, 2017). That is, EPZ scholars often apply standard UCEA theory and research to this particular workforce, yet developing-world rural migrants materially differ from UCEA workforces not only culturally, but also in their "precarious employment" (working low-paid factory jobs lacking job security and fringe benefits, such as pension and health coverage; Lee, 2016) and rural-to-urban migration (requiring adaptation to new living circumstances; Qin et al., 2014, 2018). Moreover, this line of inquiry has yet to integrate newer perspectives on leaving and staying, such as job embeddedness (Allen & Vardaman, 2017).

Departing from this trend, Maertz et al. (2003) carried out a qualitative study using grounded theory by interviewing 147 Mexican assemblers to inductively derive an indigenous theory of maquiladora turnover. They identified five work values salient for impoverished Mexicans: (1) adequacy of pay for meeting family financial needs; (2) flexible work schedule allowing participation in valued non-work activity (e.g., family duties) given cultural norm of "working to live" rather than "living to work"; (3) developmental opportunities (prized among poorly educated peasants); (4) harmonious environment (as Mexicans value friendly relationships at work); and (5) avoidance of aversive tasks and working conditions (as assemblers prefer comfort and less exhausting work, such as air conditioning and attainable production goals).

Maertz et al. (2003) further identified three main workplace constituents that workers view as responsible for fulfilling these work values. To illustrate, workers hold organizations accountable for setting their pay and offering flexible schedules, while they perceive leaders as having control over their developmental opportunities and work assignments. To the extent that a particular constituent helps them satisfy their work values, workers will develop greater attachment to that constituent. The number and strength of attachment to these key constituents in turn determine voluntary quits. Akin to shocks (Lee & Mitchell, 1994), they also noted that certain triggers can reduce constituent attachments. Conflicts with peers may represent an internal trigger, whereas increased family duties may represent an external trigger. The former trigger reduces fulfillment of (valued) harmonious environment, whereas the latter reduces ability to participate in non-work roles (given that rigid work schedules cannot accommodate greater family duties). Given that peers and the firm fail to fulfill these values, workers blame them and thus reduce their attachment to them, and thus more likely quit. Finally, Maertz et al. (2003) identified an industry-wide turnover norm (beliefs that quitting maquila jobs is acceptable behavior and that many equivalent jobs are available) directly increasing turnover, while envisioning how perceived costs of leaving (e.g., senior-based promotions, search costs) can reduce quits by increasing organizational attachment.

This contextualized model identifies explanatory constructs that are neglected or understated in prevailing UCEA models (notably, traditional March–Simon formulations). Thus, this theory suggests that constituent commitment may be as important as (if not more so) than organizational commitment in this culture, whereas UCEA models typically regard the latter as a more central commitment form. Unlike UCEA models, this model recognizes the importance of family influences in this culture, such as Mexicans valuing work schedules allowing them to participate in family functions. Further, this model suggests contextualizing UCEA models to expand their focus beyond attitudes as turnover drivers to encompass normative pressures to quit (such as emanating from turnover norms).

Going beyond UCEA models, Qin et al. (2019) extended Kraimer et al.'s (2012) identity-strain perspective on repatriate retention to explain Chinese precariat quits, recognizing that Chinese migrants undergo an analogous stressful transition like repatriates when they abandon subsistence farming to become wage workers in distant urban factories. Qin et al. (2019) noted that predominant turnover models ignore transition stress experienced by Chinese migrants who "endure cultural shock when adapting to urban society, while being separated from their family in remote villages" (p. 3). They claim that Chinese rural migrants may harbor a provincial identity ("I am a farmer") because of their deep ancestral ties to farming and ongoing residential and farming rights to "their land" where they maintain a homestead.

When leaving rural homelands for better-paid employment, Chinese peasants must adapt to unfamiliar factory regimes and urban lifestyles. As Qin et al. (2019) explain, those harboring strong provincial identities endure *identity strain* during this rural-to-urban transition. That is, they confront negative stereotypes from urban dwellers who see them as country bumpkins, while factories treat them as menial laborers. Such stereotypes clash with migrants' identity as versatile and respected farmers. They are further stigmatized as second-class citizens who are denied amenities (e.g., affordable housing and schooling) available to urban residents. Because migrants' self-concepts are neither affirmed nor verified, they feel identity strain (especially if they cling onto their provincial identity), which hampers their ability to adapt to urban life. By contrast, those with weaker rural identity experience less identity strain and thus more readily assimilate to the urban environment by forging a new situational identity as urban citizen by adopting urban habits and developing social ties with local residents.

Qin et al. (2019) further argued that urban maladjustment (resulting in part from identity strain) initiates greater turnover among Chinese migrants. Migrants who have greater difficulty adjusting to the city (e.g., finding affordable housing, befriending residents speaking another dialect) or factory regimes (e.g., "endless assembly line toil, punishing work schedules, harsh factory disciplines"; Chan, 2013, p. 91) likely quit—to accept other factory jobs (where hometown natives are ample), relocate to other cities (closer to home villages), or return home (e.g., care for dependents). Finally, Qin et al. (2019) theorized that supervisory supportive climate—or whether or not a supervisor supports the entire collective of subordinates—can mitigate identity-strain effects (e.g., disrupting the identity strain → urban adjustment path). In China, supervisors are expected to behave paternalistically toward *all* subordinates (avoiding differential treatment) and promote harmonious relationships and team solidarity (Seo, Nahrgang, Carter, & Hom, 2018). As the dominant authority in EZP workplaces, supervisors can provide resources that help migrants collectively cope with identity strain (e.g., encourage expression of authentic selves, insure fair treatment regardless of hometown background or dialect). All told, supervisory support climates should buffer against the deleterious effects of identity strain. Their longitudinal study of 173 Chinese construction workers upheld a path model in which rural identity → identity strain → urban adjustment → turnover, while verifying that supervisory supportive climate attenuates the effects of identity strain on urban adjustment.

All told, we reiterate the above suggestions for future research on developing-world precariat turnover. That is, further scholarship might apply contemporary perspectives on leaving and staying (rather than the March–Simon models), while contextualizing their constructs and operationalizations for the EPZ context. Our understanding of the EPZ workforce would also advance if further inquiry sampled workers from multiple countries or cultures as nearly all studies have thus far examined one nationality. As much of U.S. manufacturing has been outsourced, it is less possible to compare the plight of American assemblers to that of foreign assemblers (Slocum, 1971). Thus, scholars might compare nationalities from various parts of the developing world (where EPZ factories flourish), including countries other than Mexico and China (e.g., Vietnam, Central America). Such multi-sample comparisons can allow scholars to investigate how cultural dimensions affect the EPZ withdrawal process (Allen & Vardaman, 2017).

References

Allen, D. G., & Vardaman, J. M. (2017). Recruitment and retention across cultures. *Annual Review of Organizational Psychology and Organizational Behavior*, 4, 153–181.

Allen, D. G., Weeks, K. P., & Moffitt, K. R. (2005). Turnover intentions and voluntary turnover: The moderating roles of self-monitoring, locus of control, proactive personality, and risk aversion. *Journal of Applied Psychology*, 90, 980–990.

Barnum, P., Liden, R. C., & Ditomaso, N. (1995). Double jeopardy for women and minorities: Pay differences with age. *Academy of Management Journal*, 38, 863–880.

Beal, F. M. (1970). *Double Jeopardy: To Be Black and Female*. Detroit, MI: Radical Education Project.

Bendick, M., Jackson, C.W., & Reinoso,V.A. (1994). Measuring employment discrimination through controlled experiments. *The Review of Black Political Economy*, 23(1), 25–48.

Berdahl, J. L., & Min, J.-A. (2012). Prescriptive stereotypes and workplace consequences for East Asians in North America. *Cultural Diversity and Ethnic Minority Psychology*, 18, 141–152.

Berdahl, J. L., & Moore, C. (2006). Workplace harassment: Double jeopardy for minority women. *Journal of Applied Psychology*, 91, 426–436.

Bergman, M. E., & Henning, J. B. (2008). Sex and ethnicity as moderators in the sexual harassment phenomenon: A revision and test of Fitzgerald et al. (1994). *Journal of Occupational Health Psychology*, 13, 152–167.

Bergman, M. E., Palmieri, P. A., Drasgow, F., & Ormerod, A. J. (2007). Racial/ethnic harassment and discrimination: In the eye of the beholder? *Journal of Occupational Health Psychology*, 12, 144–160.

Bergman, M. E., Palmieri, P. A., Drasgow, F., & Ormerod, A. J. (2012). Racial/ethnic harassment and discrimination, its antecedents, and its effect on job-related outcomes. *Journal of Occupational Health Psychology*, 17(1), 65–78.

Bertrand, M., & Mullainathan, S. (2004). Are Emily and Greg more employable than Lakisha and Jamal? A field experiment on labor market discrimination. *The American Economic Review*, 94, 991–1013.

Brett, J. M., & Stroh, L. K. (1999). Women in management: How far have we come and what needs to be done as we approach 2000? *Journal of Management Inquiry*, 8(4), 392–398.

Browne, I., & Misra, J. (2003). The intersection of gender and race in the labor market. *Annual Review of Sociology*, 29, 487–513.

Carlson, K., & Wu, J. (2011). The illusion of statistical control: Control variable practice in management research. *Organizational Research Methods*, 15, 413–435.

Chan, J. (2013). A suicide survivor: The life of a Chinese worker. *New Technology, Work and Employment*, 28, 84–99.

Chen, J., Wang, L., & Tang, N. (2016). Half the sky: The moderating role of cultural collectivism in job turnover among Chinese female workers. *Journal of Business Ethics*, 133, 487–498.

China: Emergence of a Trade Leviathan. (2018, December 17). *Wall Street Journal*. Retrieved from www.wsj.com/graphics/china-emergence-of-a-trade-leviathan/?mod=searchresults&page=1&pos=1

Cordero, R., DiTomaso, N., & Farris, G. F. (1996). Gender and race/ethnic composition of technical work groups: Relationship to creative productivity and morale. *Journal of Engineering and Technological Management*, 13, 205–221.

Cottrell, C. A., & Neuberg, S. L. (2005). Different emotional reactions to different groups: A sociofunctional threat-based approach to "prejudice." *Journal of Personality and Social Psychology*, 88(5), 770–789.

Cox, T. H., & Blake, S. (1991). Managing cultural diversity: Implications for organizational competitiveness. *Academy of Management Executive*, 5, 45–56.

Crenshaw, K. (1991). Mapping the margins: Intersectionality, identity politics, and violence against women of color. *Stanford Law Review*, 43(6), 1241–1299.

Cuddy, A. J. C., Fiske, S. T., & Glick, P. (2004). When professionals become mothers, warmth doesn't cut the ice. *Journal of Social Issues*, 60(4), 701–718.

Dalton, D., Hill, J., & Ramsay, R. (1997). Women as managers and partners: Context specific predictors of turnover in international public accounting firms. *Auditing: A Journal of Practice & Theory*, 16(2), 29–50.

Daming, Z., & Sun Xiaoyun, S. (2010). Research on "job hopping" by migrant workers from the countryside. *Chinese Sociology & Anthropology*, 43(2), 51–69.

Derous, E., Ryan, A. M., & Serlie, A. W. (2015). Double jeopardy upon résumé screening: When Achmed is less employable than Aïsha. *Personnel Psychology*, 68, 659–696.

Dobbins, F., & Kalev, A. (2016). Why diversity programs fail. *Harvard Business Review*, July–August, 52–60.

Elvira, M. M., & Cohen, L. E. (2001). Location matters: A cross-level analysis of the effects of organizational sex composition on turnover. *Academy of Management Journal*, 44, 591–605.

Fallows, J. (2012). Mr. China comes to America. *Atlantic Monthly*. Retrieved from www.theatlantic.com/magazine/archive/2012/12/mr-china-comes-to-america/309160

Farber, H. (1994). The analysis of interfirm worker mobility. *Journal of Labor Economics*, 12, 554–593.

Felps, W., Mitchell, T. R., Hekman, D., Lee, T. W., Holtom, B. C., & Harman, W. S. (2009). Turnover contagion: How coworkers' job embeddedness and coworkers' job search behaviors influence quitting. *Academy of Management Journal*, 52, 545–561.

Fernandez, R. M., & Campero, S. (2017). Gender sorting and the glass ceiling in high-tech firms. *ILR Review*, 70, 73–104.

Fiske, S. T., Cuddy, A. J. C., Glick, P., & Xu, J. (2002). A model of (often mixed) stereotype content: Competence and warmth respectively follow from perceived status and competition. *Journal of Personality and Social Psychology*, 82, 878–902.

Fitzgerald, L. F., Drasgow, F., Hulin, C. L., Gelfand, M. J., & Magley, V. J. (1997). Antecedents and consequences of sexual harassment in organizations: A test of an integrated model. *Journal of Applied Psychology*, 82(4), 578–589.

Goff, P. A., Eberhardt, J., Williams, M., & Jackson, M. C. (2008a). Not yet human: Implicit knowledge, historical dehumanization, and contemporary consequences. *Journal of Personality and Social Psychology*, 94, 292–306.

Goff, P. A., Thomas, M. A., & Jackson, M. C. (2008b). "Ain't I a woman?" Towards an intersectional approach to person perception and group-based harms. *Sex Roles*, 59, 392–403.

Golden, A. (2007). Fathers' frames for childrearing: Evidence toward a "masculine concept of caregiving." *Journal of Family Communication*, 7(4), 265–285.

Greenwald, A. G., & Banaji, M. R. (1995). Implicit social cognition: Attitudes, self-esteem, and stereotypes. *Psychological Review*, 102(1), 4–27.

Griffeth, R. W., & Hom, P. W. (2001). *Retaining Valued Employees*. Thousand Oaks, CA: Sage.

Griffeth, R. W., Hom, P. W., & Gartner, S. (2000). A meta-analysis of antecedents and correlates of employee turnover: Update, moderator tests, and research implications for the next millennium. *Journal of Management*, 26, 463–488.

Hayes, A. F. (2013). *Introduction to Mediation, Moderation, and Conditional Process Analysis*. New York: Guilford Press.

Hernandez, M., Avery, D., Tonidandel, S., Hebl, M., Smith, A., & McKay, P. (2016). The role of proximal social contexts: Assessing stigma-by-association effects on leader appraisals. *Journal of Applied Psychology*, 101, 68–85.

Hewlett, S. A., & Luce, C. B. (2005). Off-ramps and on-ramps. *Harvard Business Review*, 83, 17–26.

Hirsh, E., & Cha, Y. (2017). Mandating change: The impact of court-ordered policy changes on managerial diversity. *ILR Review*, 70, 42–72.

Holtom, B. C., Mitchell, T. R., Lee, T. W., & Eberly, M. B. (2008). Turnover and retention research: A glance at the past, a closer review of the present, and a venture into the future. *Academy of Management Annals*, 2, 231–274.

Hom, P. W., & Griffeth, R. W. (1995). *Employee Turnover*. Cincinnati, OH: South/Western.

Hom, P. W., Lee, T. W., Shaw, J. D., & Hausknecht, J. P. (2017). One hundred years of employee turnover theory and research. *Journal of Applied Psychology*, 102, 530–545.

Hom, P. W., Roberson, L., & Ellis, A. (2008). Challenging conventional wisdom about who quits: Revelations from corporate America. *Journal of Applied Psychology*, 93, 1–34.

Hom, P. W., Tsui, A. S., Wu, J. B., Lee, T. W., Zhang, A. Y., Fu, P. P., & Li, L. (2009). Explaining employment relationships with social exchange and job embeddedness. *Journal of Applied Psychology*, 94, 277–297.

Hom, P. W., & Xiao, Z. (2011). Embedding social capital: How *guanxi* ties reinforce Chinese employees' retention. *Organizational Behavior and Human Decision Processes*, 116, 188–202.

Hoobler, J. M., Wayne, S. J., & Lemmon, G. (2009). Bosses' perceptions of family-work conflict and women's promotability: Glass ceiling effects. *Academy of Management Journal*, 52, 939–957.

Hosoda, M., Stone, D. L., & Stone Romero, E. F. (2003). The interactive effects of race, gender, and job type on job suitability ratings and selection decisions. *Journal of Applied Social Psychology*, 33, 145–178.

House, R. J., Hanges, P. J., Javidan, M., Dorfman, P. W., & Gupta, V. (Eds.). (2004). *Culture, Leadership, and Organizations: The GLOBE Study of 62 Societies*. Thousand Oaks, CA: Sage.

Jiang, B., Baker, R. C., & Frazier, G. V. (2009). An analysis of job dissatisfaction and turnover to reduce global supply chain risk: Evidence from China. *Journal of Operations Management*, 27(2), 169–184.

Jiang, K., Liu, D., McKay, P. F., Lee, T. W., & Mitchell, T. R. (2012). When and how is job embeddedness predictive of turnover? A meta-analytic investigation. *Journal of Applied Psychology*, 97(5), 1077–1096.

Kalev, A., Kelly, E., & Dobbin, F. (2006). Best practices or best guesses? Assessing the efficacy of corporate affirmative action and diversity policies. *American Sociological Review*, 71, 589–617.

Kanter, R. M. (1977). *Men and Women of the Corporation*. New York: Basic Books.

Kaplan, D. M., Wiley, J. W., & Maertz, C. P., Jr. (2011). The role of calculative attachment in the relationship between diversity climate and retention. *Human Resource Management*, 50(2), 271–287.

Kraimer, M. L., Shaffer, M. A., Harrison, D. A., & Ren, H. (2012). No place like home? An identity strain perspective on repatriate turnover. *Academy of Management Journal*, 55(2), 399–420.

Kulik, C. T., Roberson, L., & Perry, E. L. (2007). The multiple category problem: Lateral inhibition in the hiring process. *Academy of Management Review*, 32, 529–548.

Kulis, S., & Miller, K. A. (1988). Are minority women sociologists in double jeopardy? *The American Sociologist*, 19, 323–339.

Lee, C. K. (2016). Precarization or empowerment? Reflections on recent labor unrest in China. *Journal of Asian Studies*, 75, 317–333.

Lee, T. W., & Mitchell, T. R. (1994). An alternative approach: The unfolding model of voluntary employee turnover. *Academy of Management Review*, 19, 51–89.

Leonard, J., & Levine, D. (2006). The effect of diversity on turnover: A very large case study. *Industrial and Labor Relations Review*, 59, 547–572.

Leslie, L. M., Manchester, C., & Dahm, P. (2016). Why and when does the gender gap reverse? Diversity goals and the pay premium for high potential women. *Academy of Management Journal*, 60(2), 402–432.

Levin, S., Sinclair, S., Veniegas, R. C., & Taylor, P. L. (2002). Perceived discrimination in the context of multiple group memberships. *Psychological Science*, 13, 557–560.

Light, L., & Ureta, M. (1992). Panel estimates of male and female job turnover behavior: Can female nonquitters be identified? *Journal of Labor Economics*, 10, 156–181.

Lin, M. H., Kwan, V. S. Y., Cheung, A., & Fiske, S. T. (2005). Stereotype content model explains prejudice for an envied outgroup: Scale of anti-Asian American stereotypes. *Personality and Social Psychology Bulletin*, 31(1), 34–47.

Linnehan, F., & Blau, G. (2003). Testing the impact of job search and recruitment source on new hire turnover in a maquiladora. *Applied Psychology: An International Review*, 52(2), 253–271.

Liu, B., & Peng, L. (2007). Exploration and test of a model of employees' voluntary turnover in China. *Frontiers of Business Research in China*, 1(3), 378–384.

Livingston, R. W., & Pearce, N. (2009). The teddy-bear effect: Does having a baby face benefit Black chief executive officers? *Psychological Science*, 20, 1229–1236.

Livingston, R. W., Rosette, A. S., & Washington, E. F. (2012). Can an agentic Black woman get ahead? The impact of race and interpersonal dominance on perceptions of female leaders. *Psychological Science*, 23, 354–358.

Lyness, K. S., & Thompson, D. E. (1997). Above the glass ceiling? A comparison of matched samples of female and male executives. *Journal of Applied Psychology*, 82(3), 359–375.

MacKinnon, D. P., Fairchild, A. J., & Fritz, M. S. (2007). Mediation analysis. *Annual Review of Psychology*, 58, 593–614.

Maertz, C. P., & Campion, M. A. (1998). 25 years of voluntary turnover research: A review and critique In C. L. Cooper & I. T. Robertson (Eds.), *International Review of Industrial and Organizational Psychology* (vol. 13, pp. 49–81). New York: Wiley.

Maertz, C. P., Stevens, M. J., & Campion, M. A. (2003). A turnover model for the Mexican maquiladoras. *Journal of Vocational Behavior*, 63, 111–135.

March, J. G., & Simon, H. A. (1958). *Organizations*. New York: Wiley.

McKay, P. F., Avery, D. R., Tonidandel, S., Morris, M. A., Hernandez, M., & Hebl, M. R. (2007). Racial differences in employee retention: Are diversity climate perceptions the key? *Personnel Psychology*, 60, 35–62.

Milkman, K. L., Akinola, M., & Chugh, D. (2015). What happens before? A field experiment exploring how pay and representation differentially shape bias on the pathway into organizations. *Journal of Applied Psychology*, 100(6), 1678–1712.

Miller, J. S., Hom, P. W., & Gomez-Mejia, L. (2001). The high cost of low wages: Does maquiladora compensation reduce turnover? *Journal of International Business Studies*, 32(3), 585–595.

Mitchell, T. R., & Lee, T. W. (2001). The unfolding model of voluntary turnover and job embeddedness: Foundations for a comprehensive theory of attachment. *Research in Organizational Behavior*, 23, 189–246.

Mobley, W. H. (1977). Intermediate linkages in the relationship between job satisfaction and employee turnover. *Journal of Applied Psychology*, 62, 237–240.

Mobley, W. H., Griffeth, R. W., Hand, H. H., & Meglino, B. M. (1979). Review and conceptual analysis of the employee turnover process. *Psychological Bulletin*, 86, 493–522.

Mynatt, P., Omundson, J., Schroeder, R., & Stevens, M. (1997). The impact of Anglo and Hispanic ethnicity, gender, position, personality and job satisfaction on turnover intentions: A path analytic investigation. *Critical Perspectives on Accounting*, 8, 657–683.

Noonan, M. C., & Corcoran, M. E. (2004). The mommy track and partnership: Temporary delay or dead end? *The Annals of the American Academy of Political and Social Science*, 596, 130–150.

Peltokorpi, V. (2013). Job embeddedness in Japanese organizations. *International Journal of Human Resource Management*, 24(8), 1551–1569.

Posthuma, R. A., Joplin, J. R. W., & Maertz, Jr., C. P. (2005). Comparing the validity of turnover predictors in the United States and Mexico. *International Journal of Cross Cultural Management: CCM*, 5(2), 165–180.

Powell, G. N., & Butterfield, D. A. (2002). Exploring the influence of decision makers' race and gender on actual promotions to top management. *Personnel Psychology*, 55, 397–428.

Qin, X., Hom, P. W., & Xu, M. (2019). Am I a peasant or a worker? An identity strain perspective on turnover among developing-world migrants. *Human Relations*, 72(4), 801–833.

Qin, X., Hom, P. W., Xu, M., & Ju, D. (2014). Applying the job demands-resources model to migrant workers: Exploring how and when geographical distance increases quit propensity. *Journal of Occupational & Organizational Psychology*, 87(2), 303–328.

Ramesh, A., & Gelfand, M. J. (2010). Will they stay or will they go? The role of job embeddedness in predicting turnover in individualistic and collectivistic cultures. *Journal of Applied Psychology*, 95(5), 807–823.

Raver, J. L., & Nishii, L. H. (2010). Once, twice, or three times as harmful? Ethnic harassment, gender harassment, and generalized workplace harassment. *Journal of Applied Psychology*, 95, 236–254.

Reskin, B., & Padavic, I. (1994). *Women and Men at Work*. Thousand Oaks, CA: Pine Forge Press.

Riordan, C. M., Schaffer, B. S., & Stewart, M. M. (2005). Relational demography within groups: Through the lens of discrimination. In R. Dipboye & A. Colella Hillsdale (Eds.), *Discrimination at Work: The Psychological and Organizational Bases* (pp. 37–62). Hillsdale, NJ: Lawrence Erlbaum Associates.

Riordan, C. M., & Shore, L. M. (1997). Demographic diversity and employee attitudes: An empirical examination of relational demography within work units. *Journal of Applied Psychology*, 82(3), 342–358.

Roberson, L. (2004). On the relationship between race and turnover. In R. W. Griffeth, & P. W. Hom (Eds.), *Innovative Theory and Empirical Research on Employee Turnover* (pp. 211–229). Greenwich, CT: Information Age.

Roberson, L., Deitch, E. A., Brief, A. P., & Block, C. J. (2003). Stereotype threat and feedback seeking in the workplace. *Journal of Vocational Behavior*, 62(1), 176–188.

Rosette, A. S., & Livingston, R. W. (2012). Failure is not an option for Black women: Effects of organizational performance on leaders with single versus dual-subordinate identities. *Journal of Experimental Social Psychology*, 48, 1162–1167.

Rosser, V. (2004). Faculty members' intentions to leave: A national study on their worklife and satisfaction. *Research in Higher Education*, 45, 285–309.

Rubenstein, A. L., Eberly, M. B., Lee, T. W., & Mitchell, T. R. (2018). Surveying the forest: Moderator investigation, and future-oriented discussion of the antecedents of voluntary employee turnover. *Personnel Psychology*, 71(1), 23–65.

Saporta, I., & Farjoun, M. (2003). The relationship between actual promotion and turnover among professional and managerial-administrative occupational groups. *Work and Occupations*, 30, 255–280.

Schwartz, B. (1989). *Psychology of Learning and Behavior* (3rd ed.). New York: W. W. Norton.

Seo, J. J., Nahrgang, J. D., Carter, M. Z., & Hom, P. W. (2018). Not all differentiation is the same: Examining the moderating effects of leader-member exchange (LMX) configurations. *Journal of Applied Psychology*, 103(5), 478–495.

Sesko, A. K., & Biernat, M. (2010). Prototypes of race and gender: The invisibility of Black women. *Journal of Experimental Social Psychology*, 46, 356–360.

Shaffer, M. A., & Harrison, D. A. (1998). Expatriates' psychological withdrawal from international assignments: Work, nonwork. and family influences. *Personnel Psychology*, 51(1), 87–118.

Sicherman, N. (1996). Gender differences in departures from a large firm. *Industrial and Labor Relations Review*, 49, 484–505.

Sidanius, J., & Pratto, F. (2001). *Social Dominance: An Intergroup Theory of Social Hierarchy and Oppression*. New York: Cambridge University Press.

Sidanius, J., & Veniegas, R. C. (2000). Gender and race discrimination: The interactive nature of disadvantage. In S. Oskamp (Ed.), *Reducing Prejudice and Discrimination* (pp. 47–69). East Sussex: Psychology Press.

Slocum, Jr., J. W. (1971). A comparative study of the satisfaction of American and Mexican operations. *Academy of Management Journal*, 14(1), 89–97.

Smyth, R., Zhai, Q., & Li, X. (2009). Determinants of turnover intentions among Chinese off farm migrants. *Economic Change & Restructuring*, 42(3), 189–209.

Spohn, C., & Holleran, D. (2000). The imprisonment penalty paid by young, unemployed black and hispanic male offenders. *Criminology*, 38, 281–306.

Steel, R. P. (2002). Turnover theory at the empirical interface: Problems of fit and function. *Academy of Management Review*, 27, 346–360.

Steers, R. M., & Mowday, R. T. (1981). Employee turnover and postdecision accommodation processes. In L. L. Cummings, & B. M. Staw (Eds.), *Research in Organizational Behavior* (vol. 3, pp. 235–282). Greenwich, CT: JAI Press.

Stroh, L. K., Brett, J. M., & Reilly, A. H. (1996). Family structure, glass ceiling, and traditional explanations for the differential rates of turnover of female and male managers. *Journal of Vocational Behavior*, 49, 99–118.

Sturman, M. C., Shao, L., & Katz, J. (2012). The effect of culture on the curvilinear relationship between performance and turnover. *Journal of Applied Psychology*, 97, 46–62.

Taylor, M. C. (1998). How White attitudes vary with the racial composition of local populations: Numbers count. *American Sociological Review*, 63(4), 512–535.

Tello, M. P., Greene, W. E., & Garcia, M. D. (2002). An integral model for forecasting of voluntary personnel turnover in the mexican maquiladora industry. *Journal of Business and Entrepreneurship*, 14(1), 37–51.

Tharenou, P., & Caulfield, N. (2010). Will I stay or will I go? Explaining repatriation by self-initiated expatriates. *Academy of Management Journal*, 53(5), 1009–1028.

Thomas, D. A. (2001). The truth about mentoring minorities race matters. *Harvard Business Review*, 79(4), 98–107.

Thomas, D. A., & Gabarro, J. J. (1999). *Breaking Through: The Making of Minority Executives in Corporate America*. Boston, MA: Harvard Business School Press.

Tiano, S. (1994). *Patriarchy on the Line: Labor, Gender, and Ideology in the Mexican Maquila Industry*. Philadelphia, PA: Temple University Press.

Tsui, A. S., Egan, T. D., & O'Reilly, C. A. (1992). Being different: Relational demography and organizational attachment. *Administrative Science Quarterly*, 37, 549–579.

Tsui, A. S., & Gutek, B. A. (1999). *Demographic Differences in Organizations: Current Research and Future Directions*. Lanham, MD: Lexington Books.

Tsui, A. S., Nifadkar, S. S., & Ou, A. Y. (2007). Cross-national, cross-cultural organizational behavior research: Advances, gaps, and recommendations. *Journal of Management*, 33(3), 426–478.

Unz, R. (2012). The myth of American meritocracy: How corrupt are Ivy League admissions? *The American Conservative*, 11(12), 14–51.

Valentine, S. R. (2001). A path analysis of gender, race, and job complexity as determinants of intention to look for work. *Employee Relations*, 23, 130–146.

West, M. (2000). *Employee Turnover in Mexico: A Cultural Investigation of Causes*. Unpublished doctoral dissertation, Arizona State University.

West, M. (2004). Investigating turnover in the international context. In R. W. Griffeth, & P. W. Hom (Eds.), *Innovative Theory and Empirical Research on Employee Turnover* (pp. 231–256). Greenwich, CT: Information Age.

Williams, E., & Passe-Smith, J. (1992). *The Unionization of the Maquiladora Industry: The Tamaulipan Case in National Context*. San Diego, CA: Institute for Regional Studies of the Californias.

Williams, J. C. (2014). Double jeopardy? An empirical study with implications for the debates over implicit bias and intersectionality. *Harvard Journal of Law & Gender*, 37, 185–242.

Wilson, T. C. (1996). Compliments will get you nowhere: Benign stereotypes, prejudice and anti-Semitism. *The Sociological Quarterly*, 37, 465–479.

Zhao, X., Lynch, J. G., & Chen, Q. (2010). Reconsidering Baron and Kenny: Myths and truths about mediation analysis. *Journal of Consumer Research*, 37, 197–206.

Ziegert, J. C., & Hanges, P. J. (2005). Employment discrimination: The role of implicit attitudes, motivation, and a climate for racial bias. *Journal of Applied Psychology*, 90(3), 553–562.

11
FUTURE RESEARCH DIRECTIONS

Since our first edition (Hom & Griffeth, 1995), there has been tremendous progress in theory and research on employee turnover. We conclude with a review of what has been accomplished since that date as well as what remains "unfinished business" and suggestions for future research directions.

Methodological Recommendations for Turnover Research

Investigating Change Trajectories

Our first edition 25 years ago recommended greater use of SEM techniques in conjunction with panel data and meta-analyses to validate turnover theories (cf. Hom, Caranikas-Walker, Prussia, & Griffeth, 1992; Hom & Griffeth, 1991). Since that 1995 critique, turnover researchers increasingly adopted such hybrid methodologies for theory testing, while favoring LGM or RCM methods over cross-lagged panel tests for analyzing longitudinal repeated-measures data (Bentein, Vandenberghe, Vandenberg, & Stinglhamber, 2005; Chen, Ployhart, Thomas, Anderson, & Bliese, 2011; Kammeyer-Mueller, Wanberg, Glomb, & Ahlburg, 2005; Zimmerman, 2008). All the same, such laudable efforts remain scarce as predominant (and more complex) turnover models have yet to be fully tested with such approaches. In consonant with Ployhart and Vandenberg's (2010) assertion that cross-sectional tests (the dominant research design in turnover studies; Allen, Hancock, Vardaman, & McKee, 2014; Steel, 2002) cannot truly test theories, we recommend greater applications of LGM or RCM methods for validating extant formulations.

Yet we recognize that LGM (or RCM) tests may not necessarily validate turnover theories. It may be false reasoning ("ecological fallacy") to presume that dynamic relationships between model variables will closely correspond to static structural relationships estimated by pervasive cross-sectional tests. After all, Dalal, Lam, Weiss, Welch, and Hulin (2009) established that observed *within-person* relationships between moods and work behaviors do not match *between-person* relationships between those variables. Rather than simplified models comprising only dynamic relationships and effects, existing LGM tests disclose that turnover antecedents' static *and* dynamic scores (aka intercept and slope scores) can exert causal influence on their consequents (Bentein et al., 2005; Lance, Vandenberg, & Self, 2000).

Because prevailing theories fail to incorporate temporal parameters (Miller, Katerberg, & Hulin, 1979), panel investigators may fail to capture (or imprecisely trace) temporal change in model variables when administering survey measures (Mitchell & James, 2001). As some scholars have envisioned (Hom & Griffeth, 1991) or observed (Lee, Mitchell, Holtom, McDaniel, & Hill, 1999), different model variables may change at different times or rates. If true, we cannot simply survey employees on the same *calendar dates* (Bentein et al., 2005; Chen et al., 2011; Hom & Griffeth, 1991) as not every component in a turnover model may change during the *same* time interval. After all, most theories specify stages in withdrawal processes, implying that distal antecedents of turnover must change *prior to* changes in downstream proximal antecedents. To illustrate, Rusbult and Farrell (1983) conceptualized that job satisfaction must first deteriorate before job commitment begins to increase. Moreover, changes for some variables (e.g., withdrawal cognitions; Hom & Griffeth, 1991) may be so instantaneous that their changes should be tracked over shorter time periods (ranging from hours or days rather than weeks or months apart) using experience sampling methods (Dalal et al., 2009). In short, we might best exploit modern panel data analytical techniques by further refining existing theories to specify when (and why) turnover determinants change and the duration of their change (besides specifying time-lags for causal impact; Mitchell & James, 2001). Apart from theory testing, we echo Hom, Lee, Shaw, and Hausknecht's (2017) call for more inquiry into change trajectories by turnover predictors, which can boost turnover predictions (cf. Call, Nyberg, Ployhart, & Weekley, 2015; Liu, Mitchell, Lee, Holtom, & Hinkin, 2012; Ng & Feldman, 2012, 2013)

Person-Centered Analyses

Commitment and embeddedness theorists are recently advocating an alternative "person-centered" (e.g., cluster analysis, latent profile analysis) rather than variable-centered analyses (e.g., regression, SEM) to examine commitment mindsets (Meyer & Herscovitch, 2001; Meyer, Morin, & Vandenberghe, 2015; Meyer, Stanley, & Parfyonova, 2012; Stanley, Vandenberghe, Vandenberg, & Bentein, 2013) or proximal withdrawal states (Hom, Mitchell, Lee, & Griffeth, 2012; Woo & Allen, 2014). Traditional variable-centered analyses examine relationships among variables, presuming that they generalize for the entire population when they may differ across various subgroups (Meyer, Stanley, & Vandenberg, 2013). By contrast, person-centered techniques recognize that "variables can combine differently for some types of individuals than they do for others" by identifying distinct profiles of "subgroups of individuals sharing similar patterns of variables within a population" (Meyer et al., 2012, p. 191). These subgroups may "share similar levels of, and/or relationships among, a system of variables" (Meyer et al., 2012, p. 195). Person-centered approaches can thus accommodate more complex combinations of multiple variables, while treating individuals more holistically.

Our first edition neglected person-centered approaches as theories about commitment mindsets or proximal withdrawal states had yet to be developed. These recent theoretical perspectives on commitment or withdrawal states of minds enhance understanding of turnover and warrant person-centered approaches to verify their existence (including discovery of other mindsets) and assess their differential effects on work attitudes and behaviors. While most progress has been made explicating and studying commitment profiles, we welcome more research on proximal withdrawal states (Hom et al., 2012). Preliminary research has differentiated among the four prime states (i.e., reluctant and enthusiastic staying and leaving mindsets) by documenting their behavioral differences (Li, Lee, Mitchell, Hom, & Griffeth, 2016). Yet future inquiries must more firmly attest to their existence or prevalence (as well as their substates) with latent profile analysis (Kabins, Xu, Bergman, Berry, & Willson, 2016). Further, the etiology of PWS states and how they change over time warrant investigation to fully validate Hom et al.'s (2012) theory.

Construct Validation

Our 1995 edition had prescribed more construct validation, which can not only improve validation of turnover theories, but also establish whether explanatory constructs are truly distinctive (given that successive waves of new theories may proliferate redundant constructs; Hom & Griffeth, 1995). Unfortunately, such mundane work remains undone, according to Allen et al.'s (2014) review, where only 25% of studies cite any corroborating evidence for their measures' construct validity. We thus recommend more efforts validating measures of theoretically central constructs such as perceived job alternatives (Griffeth, Steel, Allen, & Bryan, 2005) as well as new constructs (e.g., employee guarding; Gardner, Munyon, Hom, & Griffeth, 2018).

Expanded Research on Shocks, Link Defections, and Turnover Destinations

Shocks

Because the unfolding model has become the predominant theory of turnover (Hom et al., 2017) that ushered a paradigm shift (Hom, 2011) and identified potent turnover drivers (i.e., "shocks"; Holtom, Mitchell, Lee, & Inderriden, 2005), shocks warrant greater scrutiny. Lee and Mitchell (1994) originally classified them according to the different turnover paths they initiate, which Holtom et al. (2005) later termed "personal shocks" (triggering path 1 leaving), "negative work shocks" (triggering path 2 leaving), or "job offer shocks" (triggering path 3 leaving). Recently, Lee, Hom, Eberly, Li, and Mitchell (2017) suggested expanding this tripartite taxonomy by adopting Morgeson, Mitchell, and Liu's (2015) event attributes of novelty, disruptiveness, and criticality. Besides these dimensions, negative job shocks can be further decomposed into "impending negative events" (e.g., anticipated layoffs) and accumulated minor hassles (Purl, Hall, & Griffeth, 2016).

To explain why employees interpret events as "shocking," Lee and Mitchell (1994) identified image violation or activation of matching scripts as underlying those interpretations. Lee et al. (2017) further recommend consideration of other mechanisms that can clarify how employees appraise events, such as crisis decision-making theory (Shapiro, Hom, Shen & Agarwal, 2016). Further, embeddedness scholars have demonstrated that embedding forces can attenuate the negative effects of shocks on leaving (Lee, Burch, & Mitchell, 2014). Conceivably, positive events experienced at work ("positive shocks") may have a similar (moderating) impact. By the same token, turnover-inducing events may interact synergistically, exacerbating their negative impact. For example, an employee who was passed over for promotion (negative job shock; Burton, Holtom, Sablynski, Mitchell, & Lee, 2010) and also received an unsolicited job offer (path 3 shock) may feel doubly motivated to quit and thus exit quickly (Lee et al., 1999). All told, greater inquiry in the meaning of shocks and how different dimensions or types of shocks affect the withdrawal process will advance the unfolding model and understanding of turnover.

Link Defections

As noted in other chapters, embeddedness and social network scholars have increasingly demonstrated the explanatory and predictive value of workplace (and extra-work) relationships in deterring leaving (Ballinger, Cross, & Holtom, 2016; Lee et al., 2014). Considerably less scrutiny has been paid to how workplace links can engender leaving (Felps et al., 2009), though turnover scholars have long recognized that family pressures or spousal relocations can impel leaving (e.g., spousal relocation, parental leave; Lee, Mitchell, Wise, & Fireman, 1996; Maertz & Campion, 2004). In particular, future research needs to better identify the mechanisms underlying turnover contagion, such as how departing colleagues influence others to leave (by communicating job leads or undermining job attitudes by disparaging the current job or praising alternatives; Hulin, Roznowski, & Hachiya, 1985; Lee et al., 2017). Moreover, we welcome more direct assessments of turnover climates or norms (that may undergird turnover contagion), which pervade certain occupations (e.g., public accounting; Lee et al., 2017) or industries (e.g., maquila factories; Maertz, Stevens, & Campion, 2003). While often noted in qualitative research (Bartunek, Huang, & Walsh, 2008; Maertz et al., 2003), we have yet to empirically establish how turnover climates underlie collective turnover and promote turnover contagion.

Besides departing colleagues, we suggest more investigations into how departing leaders (whether immediate superiors or higher authorities) encourage more employee turnover, which theory (Shapiro et al., 2016) and incipient research (Li, Hausknecht, & Dugoni, 2018) suggest. While Chapter 7 suggests more research on theoretical mechanisms underlying leader departure effects (Shapiro et al., 2016), we suggest additional consideration of leader attributes because high-performing, charismatic, or humble departing leaders may invoke greater identity or social capital losses for subordinates left behind. We also recommend greater inquiry into "lift-outs," exploring why a group of subordinates may follow departing leaders to a *common* destination (Groysberg & Abrahams, 2006). Are they offered more attractive jobs or perks? Do they closely identify with the leader (Shapiro et al., 2016)? Are their colleagues also following the departing leader?

Turnover Destinations

Over the years, turnover theorists increasingly prescribed scrutinizing turnover destinations—where leavers end up after leaving, especially when they exit the labor market (Hom et al., 2012; Hulin et al., 1985; Lee et al., 1999). While the unfolding model identifies how different destination preferences invoke different turnover paths (e.g., extra-work roles may prompt path 1, while unsolicited jobs may prompt path 3; Lee & Mitchell, 1994), we have yet to understand the etiology of such destination preferences (Lee et al., 2017). Lee et al. (2017) suggest drawing from vocational models of career or life stages (Hom, Leong, & Golubovich, 2010) because quit decisions may represent "critical points marking the beginning or end of certain career or life stages" (Lee et al., 2017, p. 211). To illustrate, employees of childbearing age may leave the workforce temporarily to raise children, while employees nearing retirement may quit for more meaningful avocations. Moreover, what decision processes underlie employees' choice of extra-work roles over current work roles? Do they evaluate extra-work pursuits as having higher subjective expected utilities or better-fitting career goals or trajectories (Lee et al., 2017)? Complementing strategic management research (Somaya, Williamson, & Lorinkova, 2008; Wezel, Cattani, & Pennings, 2006), identifying which employing organizations leavers join may furnish more accurate estimates of turnover functionality (including the costs of collective turnover; Nyberg & Ployhart, 2013). Former employees joining competing firms may represent dysfunctional quits, whereas those joining employers' clients (e.g., accountants exiting public accounting for private industry) may represent functional quits.

Further, we seek greater insight into how spontaneous job opportunities or job offers invoke leaving (aka turnover path 3; Lee & Mitchell, 1994). While we welcome more in-depth knowledge of how dissatisfied employees find and evaluate alternatives (Steel, 2002), we lack understanding of how satisfied employees can be tempted away by prospering job markets or aggressive recruiters. We must expand the set of attributes that make employees marketable (attracting recruiters) by increasing their "movement capital" (Trevor, 2001), such as external visibility or objectivity of worker productivity (e.g., professional baseball players' batting average, academicians' publications; Allen & Griffeth, 2001). Moreover, prevailing turnover theory and research on job search have not kept up with technological developments in how the internet is facilitating job search, enabling employees to readily find alternative employment and thus quit. Indeed, turnover scholars have yet to fully appreciate how the internet can allow outside firms to more effectively poach employees who publicize their talent or capabilities (cf. Huang & Zhang, 2016). Further, we know that occupational labor markets vary in job opportunities (Steel, 1996), but how do they vary in amount or quality about information about job vacancies (Steel, 2002)?

Generalization vs. Contextualization

Hom and Griffeth (1995) prescribed more investigations into the generality of turnover models. They noted that "most theorists of turnover presume that their models hold universally, overlooking the possibility that formulations may falter in some subpopulations or settings" (p. 260). While evermore studies generalize withdrawal or embeddedness theories (Holtom, Mitchell, Lee, & Eberly, 2008; Jiang, Liu, McKay, Lee, & Mitchell, 2012; Lee et al., 2014), such efforts must continue to explore more diverse samples as Allen et al.'s (2014) review concluded that the "modal turnover study is conducted with 33-year-old college-educated Caucasians working full time in the United States" (p. 81). Focusing on overlooked but significant populations, we suggest more withdrawal research on gig economy workers, immigrants (documented and undocumented), LBQT persons, the disabled, ex-convicts, and dual-career couples. Following Allen and Vardaman's (2017) critique, we also suggest greater cross-cultural examinations of contemporary turnover and embeddedness models sampling multiple nationalities (especially understudied cultures) and assessing cultural moderators (Sturman, Shao, & Katz, 2012).

While generalizability is a worthy effort, we should not overlook contextualization of models for particular contexts (Lee et al., 2017). International scholars have long recognized that they must contextualize constructs or operationalizations to enhance a model's explanatory power in particular cultures (Tsui, Nifadkar, & Ou, 2007). Indeed, contemporary investigations already implicitly contextualize job embeddedness by assessing salient embedding forces for different organizations or cultures (Hom et al., 2009; Mitchell, Holtom, Lee, Sablynski, & Erez, 2001). Specifically, Hom et al. (2017) suggest refining theories to specify boundary conditions for withdrawal constructs because moderating effects are often overlooked by the prevailing preoccupation with direct effects (Allen et al., 2014). Moreover, contextualization may even identify explanatory constructs that may have greater generality beyond that context (Lee et al., 2017). To illustrate, Ramesh and Gelfand (2010) introduced family embeddedness to more precisely account for turnover among citizens in collectivist societies but discovered that this embedding force can also explain turnover among those in individualist societies.

Collective Turnover

As we noted earlier, turnover scholars are increasingly investigating collective turnover (Heavey, Holwerda, & Hausknecht, 2013; Park & Shaw, 2013). Theory and empirical research on its consequences have most evolved (Hausknecht & Holwerda, 2013; Nyberg & Ployhart, 2013). Going beyond conventional focus on HRM practices or systems (Batt & Colvin, 2011; Hom et al., 2009), we prescribe more attention devoted to formulating theoretical perspectives about the etiology of collective turnover (Hom et al., 2017), especially "process-oriented models that open up the black box of the collective turnover process" (Lee et al., 2017, p. 213). We further suggest developing different theories for organizational and team (or unit-level) turnover as their causes and effects likely differ. We have long recognized that generalizing from individual-level to collective turnover research may prove fallacious (Hulin et al., 1985). So might generalizing across different organizational levels (cf. Lee et al., 2017).

Empirical Research on Turnover Control or Prediction

Despite longstanding calls for evidence-based strategies for reducing turnover (Allen, Bryant, & Vardaman, 2010), validating interventions (other than job previews) using quasi-experimental or experimental tests is scant. Although Hom and Griffeth (1995) had long prescribed such tests to justify prescriptions for turnover control, evaluation research remains rare. Indeed, Hom et al. (2017) observed that "practitioner articles have mostly vanished from leading journals" (p. 540). Conceivably, turnover researchers are reluctant to carry out field experiments because they must be performed in organizational settings where they have limited control, must involve interventions that can meaningfully affect turnover, and must assess experimental effects over a protracted period. These requirements make field experiments more challenging than survey methodology or laboratory experiments, discouraging their implementation (Allen, Lee, & Reiche, 2015).

All the same, empirical support for practical suggestions may still be garnered from correlational designs (the most popular methodology in turnover research; Allen et al., 2015), which Hom and Griffeth (1995) termed "less robust methods." After all, medical scientists often derive practical prescriptions from longitudinal *correlational* designs (not just double-blinded experiments with placebo controls), though their studies are often based on large (more representative) samples, narrowly focused on particular causes (e.g., egg consumption as predictor of cardiovascular disease), and included statistical controls for an extensive set of extraneous influences (Zhong et al., 2019). That said, correlational designs might identify potential turnover remedies, though turnover researchers must focus on specific practices or retention inducements (e.g., certain fringe benefits; Miller, Hom, & Gomez-Mejia, 2001) rather than abstract turnover antecedents (e.g., affective commitment). Of course, academic outlets must welcome more practitioner-oriented rather than solely theory-testing studies.

More promising practical research investigates selection tests that forecast prospective unstable employees (Barrick & Zimmerman, 2005; Griffeth & Hom, 2001). While turnover scholars historically downplayed or neglected individual differences (and thus selection techniques), there is little doubt that past employment history (Woo, 2011), biodata (Russell, 2013), and personality tests (Villanova, Bernardin, Johnson, & Dahmus, 1994) can help screen out quit-prone job candidates. Given their bias toward academic theory, leading journals, however, are reluctant to publish validation studies about selection tests. This bias is further compounded by consultants' reluctance to share proprietary information about selection devices, let alone their attempts (if any) to validate them. Encouragingly, corporations are increasingly relying on internal workforce analytics data to analyze "big data" (e.g., personnel records and other non-traditional biodata, such as online searches, corporate emails, or badge swipes about workplace entry and exit; "Why people quit," 2016) to predict turnover risks (Hausknecht & Li, 2015). Such efforts seem promising, though they are unlikely to appear in journal publications given their proprietary (and confidential) nature.

References

Allen, D. G., Bryant, P. C., & Vardaman, J. M. (2010). Retaining talent: Replacing misconceptions with evidence-based strategies. *The Academy of Management Perspectives*, 24(2), 48–64.

Allen, D. G., & Griffeth, R. W. (2001). Test of a mediated performance–turnover relationship highlighting the moderating roles of visibility and reward contingency. *Journal of Applied Psychology*, 86(5), 1014–1021.

Allen, D. G., Hancock, J., Vardaman, J., & McKee, D. (2014). Analytical mindsets in turnover research. *Journal of Organizational Behavior*, 35, S61–S86.

Allen, D. G., Lee, Y., & Reiche, S. (2015). Global work in the multinational enterprise: New avenues and challenges for strategically managing human capital across borders. *Journal of Management*, 41(7), 2032–2035.

Allen, D. G., & Vardaman, J. M. (2017). Recruitment and retention across cultures. *Annual Review of Organizational Psychology and Organizational Behavior*, 4(1), 153–181.

Ballinger, G. A., Cross, R., & Holtom, B. C. (2016). The right friends in the right places: Understanding network structure as a predictor of voluntary turnover. *Journal of Applied Psychology*, 101(4), 535–548.

Barrick, M. R., & Zimmerman, R. D. (2005). Reducing voluntary, avoidable turnover through selection. *Journal of Applied Psychology*, 90(1), 159–166.

Bartunek, J. M., Huang, Z., & Walsh, I. J. (2008). The development of a process model of collective turnover. *Human Relations*, 61(1), 5–38.

Batt, R., & Colvin, A. (2011). An employment systems approach to turnover: Human resources practices, quits, dismissals, and performance. *The Academy of Management Journal*, 54(4), 695–717.

Bentein, K., Vandenberghe, C., Vandenberg, R., & Stinglhamber, F. (2005). The role of change in the relationship between commitment and turnover: A latent growth modeling approach. *Journal of Applied Psychology*, 90(3), 468–482.

Burton, J. P., Holtom, B. C., Sablynski, C. J., Mitchell, T. R., & Lee, T. W. (2010). The buffering effects of job embeddedness on negative shocks. *Journal of Vocational Behavior*, 76(1), 42–51.

Call, M. L., Nyberg, A. J., Ployhart, R. E., & Weekley, J. (2015). The dynamic nature of collective turnover and unit performance: The impact of time, quality, and replacements. *Academy of Management Journal*, 58(4), 1208–1232.

Chen, G., Ployhart, R., Thomas, H., Anderson, N., & Bliese, P. (2011). The power of momentum: A new model of dynamic relationships between job satisfaction and turnover intentions. *Academy of Management Journal*, 54, 159–181.

Dalal, R., Lam, H., Weiss, H., Welch, E., & Hulin, C. (2009). A within-person approach to work behavior and performance: Concurrent and lagged citizenship-counterproductivity associations, and dynamic relationships with affect and overall job performance. *Academy of Management Journal*, 52, 1051–1066.

Felps, W., Mitchell, T. R., Hekman, D. R., Lee, T. W., Holtom, B. C., & Harman, W. S. (2009). Turnover contagion: How coworkers' job embeddedness and job search behaviors influence quitting. *Academy of Management Journal*, 52(3), 545–561.

Gardner, T. M., Munyon, T. P., Hom, P. W., & Griffeth, R. W. (2018). When territoriality meets agency: An examination of employee guarding as a territorial strategy. *Journal of Management*, 44(7), 2580–2610.

Griffeth, R. W., & Hom, P. W. (2001). *Retaining Valued Employees*. Thousand Oaks, CA: Sage.

Griffeth, R. W., Steel, R. P., Allen, D. G., & Bryan, N. (2005). The development of a multidimensional measure of job market cognitions: The Employment Opportunity Index (EOI). *Journal of Applied Psychology*, 90(2), 335–349.

Groysberg, B., & Abrahams, R. (2006). Lift outs: How to acquire a high-functioning team. *Harvard Business Review*, 84(12), 133–140.

Hausknecht, J. P., & Holwerda, J. A. (2013). When does employee turnover matter? Dynamic member configurations, productive capacity, and collective performance. *Organization Science*, 24(1), 210–225.

Hausknecht, J. P., & Li, H. J. (2015). Big data in turnover and retention. In S. Tonidandel, E. B. King, & J. M. Cortina (Eds.), *SIOP Organizational Frontier Series. Big Data at Work: The Data Science Revolution and Organizational Psychology* (pp. 250–271). New York: Routledge.

Heavey, A. L., Holwerda, J. A., & Hausknecht, J. P. (2013). Causes and consequences of collective turnover: A meta-analytic review. *Journal of Applied Psychology*, 98(3), 412–453.

Holtom, B. C., Mitchell, T. R., Lee, T. W., & Eberly, M. B. (2008). Turnover and retention research: A glance at the past, a closer review of the present, and a venture into the future. *The Academy of Management Annals*, 2(1), 231–274.

Holtom, B. C., Mitchell, T. R., Lee, T. W., & Inderrieden, E. J. (2005). Shocks as causes of turnover: What they are and how organizations can manage them. *Human Resource Management*, 44, 337–352.

Hom, P. W. (2011). Organizational exit. In S. Zedeck (Ed.), *APA Handbooks in Psychology. APA Handbook of Industrial and Organizational Psychology, Vol. 2. Selecting and Developing Members for the Organization* (pp. 325–375). Washington, DC: American Psychological Association.

Hom, P. W., Caranikas-Walker, F., Prussia, G. E., & Griffeth, R. W. (1992). A meta-analytical structural equations analysis of a model of employee turnover. *Journal of Applied Psychology*, 77, 890–909.

Hom, P. W., & Griffeth, R. W. (1991). Structural equations modeling test of a turnover theory: Cross-sectional and longitudinal analyses. *Journal of Applied Psychology*, 76, 350–366.

Hom, P. W., & Griffeth, R. W. (1995). *Employee Turnover*. Cincinnati, OH: South/Western.

Hom, P. W., Lee, T. W., Shaw, J. D., & Hausknecht, J. P. (2017). One hundred years of employee turnover theory and research. *Journal of Applied Psychology*, 102(3), 530–545.

Hom, P. W., Leong, F. T., & Golubovich, J. (2010). Insights from vocational and career developmental theories: Their potential contributions for advancing the understanding of employee turnover. *Research in Personnel and Human Resources Management*, 29, 115–165.

Hom, P. W., Mitchell, T. R., Lee, T. W., & Griffeth, R. W. (2012). Reviewing employee turnover: Focusing on proximal withdrawal states and an expanded criterion. *Psychological Bulletin*, 138, 831–858.

Hom, P. W., Tsui, A. S., Wu, J. B., Lee, T. W., Zhang, A. Y., Fu, P. P., & Li, L. (2009). Explaining employment relationships with social exchange and job embeddedness. *Journal of Applied Psychology*, 94(2), 277–297.

Huang, P., & Zhang, Z. (2016). Participation in open knowledge communities and job-hopping: Evidence from enterprise software. *MIS Quarterly*, 40(3), 785–806.

Hulin, C. L., Roznowski, M., & Hachiya, D. (1985). Alternative opportunities and withdrawal decisions: Empirical and theoretical discrepancies and an integration. *Psychological Bulletin*, 97(2), 233–250.

Jiang, K., Liu, D., McKay, P. F., Lee, T. W., & Mitchell, T. R. (2012). When and how is job embeddedness predictive of turnover? A meta-analytic investigation. *Journal of Applied Psychology*, 97(5), 1077–1096.

Kabins, A. H., Xu, X., Bergman, M. E., Berry, C. M., & Willson, V. L. (2016). A profile of profiles: A meta-analysis of the nomological net of commitment profiles. *Journal of Applied Psychology*, 101(6), 881–904.

Kammeyer-Mueller, J., Wanberg, C., Glomb, T., & Ahlburg, D. (2005). Turnover processes in a temporal context: It's about time. *Journal of Applied Psychology*, 90, 644–658.

Lance, C. E., Vandenberg, R. J., & Self, R. M. (2000). Latent growth models of individual change: The case of new-comer adjustment. *Organizational Behavior and Human Decision Processes*, 83, 107–140.

Lee, T. W., Burch, T. C., & Mitchell, T. R. (2014). The story of why we stay: A review of job embeddedness. *Annual Review of Organizational Psychology and Organizational Behavior*, 1, 199–216.

Lee, T. W., Hom, P. W., Eberly, M. B., Li, J. J., & Mitchell, T. R. (2017). On the next decade of research in voluntary employee turnover. *Academy of Management Perspectives*, 31, 201–221.

Lee, T. W., & Mitchell, T. R. (1994). An alternative approach: The unfolding model of voluntary employee turnover. *Academy of Management Review*, 19(1), 51–89.

Lee, T. W., Mitchell, T. R., Holtom, B. C., McDaniel, L., & Hill, J. (1999). The unfolding model of voluntary turnover: A replication and extension. *Academy of Management Journal*, 42, 450–462.

Lee, T. W., Mitchell, T. R., Wise, L., & Fireman, S. (1996). An unfolding model of voluntary employee turnover. *Academy of Management Journal*, 39, 5–36.

Li, H. J., Hausknecht, J. P., & Dugoni, L. (2018). Initial and long-term change in unit-level turnover following leader succession: Contingent effects of outgoing and incoming leader characteristics. *Organizational Science*, in press.

Li, J., Lee, T. W., Mitchell, T. R., Hom, P. W., & Griffeth, R. W. (2016). The effects of proximal withdrawal states on job attitudes, job searching, intent to leave, and employee turnover. *Journal of Applied Psychology*, 101(10), 1436–1456.

Liu, D., Mitchell, T. R., Lee, T. W., Holtom, B. C., & Hinkin, T. (2012). When employees are out of step with coworkers: How job satisfaction trajectory and dispersion influence individual- and unit-level voluntary turnover. *Academy of Management Journal*, 55, 1360–1380.

Maertz, C. P., & Campion, M. A. (2004). Profiles in quitting: Integrating content and process turnover theory. *Academy of Management Journal*, 47, 566–582.

Maertz, C. P., Stevens, M. J., & Campion, M. A. (2003). A turnover model for the Mexican maquiladoras. *Journal of Vocational Behavior*, 63, 111–135.

Meyer, J. P., & Herscovitch, L. (2001). Commitment in the workplace: Toward a general model. *Human Resource Management Review*, 11(3), 299–326.

Meyer, J. P., Morin, A. J., & Vandenberghe, C. (2015). Dual commitment to organization and supervisor: A person-centered approach. *Journal of Vocational Behavior*, 88, 56–72.

Meyer, J. P., Stanley, L. J., & Parfyonova, N. M. (2012). Employee commitment in context: The nature and implication of commitment profiles. *Journal of Vocational Behavior*, 80(1), 1–16.

Meyer, J. P., Stanley, L. J., & Vandenberg, R. J. (2013). A person-centered approach to the study of commitment. *Human Resource Management Review*, 23(2), 190–202.

Miller, H. E., Katerberg, R., & Hulin, C. L. (1979). Evaluation of the Mobley, Horner, and Hollingsworth model of employee turnover. *Journal of Applied Psychology*, 64(5), 509–517.

Miller, J., Hom, P. W., & Gomez-Mejia, L. (2001). The high cost of low wages: Does maquiladora compensation reduce turnover? *Journal of International Business Studies*, 32(3), 585–595.

Mitchell, T. R., Holtom, B. C., Lee, T. W., Sablynski, C. J., & Erez, M. (2001). Why people stay: Using job embeddedness to predict voluntary turnover. *Academy of Management Journal*, 44(6), 1102–1121.

Mitchell, T. R., & James, L. R. (2001). Building better theory: Time and the specification of when things happen. *Academy of Management Review*, 26, 530–547.

Morgeson, F. P., Mitchell, T. R., & Liu, D. (2015). Event system theory: An event-oriented approach to the organizational sciences. *Academy of Management Review*, 40(4), 515–537.

Ng, T. W. H., & Feldman, D. C. (2012). The effects of organizational and community embeddedness on work-to-family and family-to-work conflict. *Journal of Applied Psychology*, 97(6), 1233–1251.

Ng, T. W. H., & Feldman, D. C. (2013). Changes in perceived supervisor embeddedness: Effects on employees' embeddedness, organizational trust, and voice behavior. *Personnel Psychology*, 663, 645–685.

Nyberg, A. J., & Ployhart, R. E. (2013). Context-emergent turnover (CET) theory: A theory of collective turnover. *Academy of Management Review*, 38(1), 109–131.

Park, T.-Y., & Shaw, J. D. (2013). Turnover rates and organizational performance: A meta-analysis. *Journal of Applied Psychology*, 98(2), 268–309.

Ployhart, R., & Vandenberg, R. (2010). Longitudinal research: The theory, design, and analysis of change. *Journal of Management*, 36, 94–120.

Purl, J., Hall, K. E., & Griffeth, R. W. (2016). A diagnostic methodology for discovering the reasons for employee turnover using shocks and events. In G. Saridakis & C. Cooper (Eds.), *Research Handbook on Employee Turnover* (pp. 213–246). Northampton, MA: Edward Elgar.

Ramesh, A., & Gelfand, M. J. (2010). Will they stay or will they go? The role of job embeddedness in predicting turnover in individualistic and collectivistic cultures. *Journal of Applied Psychology*, 95(5), 807–823.

Rusbult, C., & Farrell, D. (1983). A longitudinal test of the investment model: The development (and deterioration) of satisfaction and commitment in heterosexual involvements. *Journal of Applied Psychology*, 68, 429–438.

Russell, C. J. (2013). Is it time to voluntarily turn over theories of voluntary turnover? *Industrial and Organizational Psychology: Perspectives on Science and Practice*, 6(2), 156–173.

Shapiro, D. L., Hom, P. W., Shen, W., & Agarwal, R. (2016). How do leader departures affect subordinates' organizational attachment? A 360-degree relational perspective. *Academy of Management Review*, 41(3), 479–502.

Somaya, D., Williamson, I., & Lorinkova, N. (2008). Gone but not lost: The different performance impacts of employee mobility between cooperators versus competitors. *Academy of Management Journal*, 51, 936–953.

Stanley, L., Vandenberghe, C., Vandenberg, R., & Bentein, K. (2013). Commitment profiles and employee turnover. *Journal of Vocational Behavior*, 82(3), 176–187.

Steel, R. P. (1996). Labor market dimensions as predictors of the reenlistment decisions of military personnel. *Journal of Applied Psychology*, 81(4), 421–428.

Steel, R. P. (2002). Turnover theory at the empirical interface: Problems of fit and function. *Academy of Management Review*, 27, 346–360.

Sturman, M. C., Shao, L., & Katz, J. H. (2012). The effect of culture on the curvilinear relationship between performance and turnover. *Journal of Applied Psychology*, 97(1), 46–62.

Trevor, C. O. (2001). Interactions among actual ease-of-movement determinants and job satisfaction in the prediction of voluntary turnover. *Academy of Management Journal*, 44(4), 621–638.

Tsui, A. S., Nifadkar, S. S., & Ou, A. Y. (2007). Cross-national, cross-cultural organizational behavior research: Advances, gaps, and recommendations. *Journal of Management*, 33(3), 426–478.

Villanova, P., Bernardin, H. J., Johnson, D. L., & Dahmus, S. A. (1994). The validity of a measure of job compatibility in the prediction of job performance and turnover of motion picture theater personnel. *Personnel Psychology*, 47(1), 73–90.

Wezel, F. C., Cattani, G., & Pennings, J. M. (2006). Competitive implications of interfirm mobility. *Organization Science*, 17(6), 691–709.

Why people quit their jobs. (2016). *Harvard Business Review*, August, F1609A-PDF-ENG. Cambridge, MA: Harvard Business School Publishing.

Woo, S. E. (2011). A study of Ghiselli's hobo syndrome. *Journal of Vocational Behavior*, 79(2), 461–469.

Woo, S. E., & Allen, D. G. (2014). Toward an inductive theory of stayers and seekers in the organization. *Journal of Business and Psychology*, 29(4), 683–703.

Zhong, V. W., Van Horn, L., Cornelius, M. C., Wilkins, J. T., Ning, H., Carnethon, M. R., Greenland, P., Mentz, R. J., Tucker, K. L., Zhao, L., Norwood, A. F., Lloyd-Jones, D. M., & Allen, N. B. (2019). Associations of dietary cholesterol or egg consumption with incident cardiovascular disease and mortality. *JAMA*, 321(11), 1081–1095.

Zimmerman, R. D. (2008). Understanding the impact of personality traits on individuals' turnover decisions: A meta-analytic path model. *Personnel Psychology*, 61(2), 309–348.

INDEX

Abelson, M. A. 3, 7, 94–97
ability-motivation-opportunity (ABO) model 114, 264
absenteeism 30, 65, 66, 199; cusp catastrophe model 96; dynamic trajectories 159; Mobley et al. expanded model 85; Muchinsky-Morrow model 86; Steers-Mowday multi-route model 91; structural equation modeling 223
affective forces 134–135, 138, 139, 141
affective responses 90, 91, 198, 199
age: collective turnover 114; Mobley et al. expanded model 83; older employees 50; Steers-Mowday multi-route model 90; young employees 18, 73
agency theory 37
agreeableness 48, 49, 197, 199, 250, 251
Aguinis, H. 264
Ahlburg, D. 107
Ajzen, I. 228–230
Akinola, M. 283
Aldag, R. J. 257
Allen, D. G.: collective turnover 32–34; construct validation 302; costs of turnover 24; cross-cultural perspectives 288, 289, 305; culture 166; dominant analytical mindset 39, 156, 170, 171, 207–208; evidence-based HRM strategies 240, 241; expatriates 286, 287, 288; functional and dysfunctional turnover 17; job embeddedness 144; job satisfaction 156, 159; justice 159–160; model studies 305; pay 54; perceived alternatives 62, 171; performance-turnover relationship 163–165, 166; person-centered approach 155; personality 197–198, 251; post-acquisition turnover 37–38; proximal withdrawal state theory 143; research methods 235; rewards 257, 258; socialization 254, 255; Turnover Events and Shocks Scale 107–113; weighted application blanks 249; work design 256
Allen, N. 152
Allied-Signal 31
Allison, P. D. 65
alternative employment opportunities 60–65; collective turnover 114, 115; ease of movement 168–173; Farrell-Rusbult investment model 89; future research 304–305; Hom-Griffeth intermediate linkages model 78–79; Hulin et al. model of labor market effects 97–101; Lee-Mitchell unfolding model 105; Mobley et al. expanded model 83, 84–85, 86; Muchinsky-Morrow model 86–87; pay attitudes 261; Price model 81; Steers-Mowday multi-route model 90, 91–92, 93, 94; Turnover Events and Shocks Scale 112; *see also* job search; perceived alternatives
alternative forces 134, 135, 136, 138, 139, 140

alumni networks 20, 40
analytics 265–266, 301
Anderson, J. C. 224
Anderson, N. 157–158
Anderson, S. E. 226
Antel, J. J. 18
Aquino, K. 54
Arnold, H. J. 85
Ashforth, B. E. 187
assembly-line workers 2, 289–293
attachment bonds 152–153, 154, 291
attitudes 5, 7, 150; collective turnover 114, 115; cultural influences 166; performance-turnover relationship 163; pre-quitting behaviors 191; proximal withdrawal state theory 133, 135, 138–140, 143; racial minorities 281; Steers-Mowday multi-route model 91, 92, 93
Automatic Data Processing 28
autonomy 241, 255, 256, 263
avoidable turnover 7

baby boomers 7
Baer, J. C. 264
Balkin, D. B. 262
Ballinger, G. A. 192, 196–197
Barnett, G. A. 194–195
Barrick, M. R. 197, 250
Batt, R. 5–6
Bauer, T. N. 253, 254–255
Baysinger, B. 173
Beach, L. R. 101
Becker, H. S. 151, 152
Becker, T. E. 130
Becker, W. J. 166
Bedeian, A. G. 161
behavioral forces 135, 136, 141
benefits 53, 256, 257; collective turnover 114; Hulin et al. model of labor market effects 98; loss of 19; proximal withdrawal state theory 136; resistant leavers 143; Turnover Events and Shocks Scale 112
Bentein, K. 153–154
Bergel, G. 263
Bergman, M. E. 279, 280
Bernardin, H. J. 252
Bertrand, M. 284
Beyer, J. M. 21
bicultural training 253
Biernat, M. 284
big data 265, 307

Big Five personality traits 182, 197, 251
Bilgili, T. V. 37–38, 39
Billings, R. 170
biodata 241, 248–249, 307
Bliese, P. D. 157–158
Bolino, M. C. 21
bonuses 24, 25, 165, 264
boomerang employees 20, 21, 38
Bosco, F. A. 159–160
Boswell, W. R. 183
Boudreau, J. W. 162, 183, 265
Bozeman, D. P. 152
Bracker, J. S. 213
Breaugh, J. A. 244, 249
Breckenridge, B. G. 161
Brett, J. M. 19
Brewer, M. B. 195
Brief, A. P. 257
Brinsfield, C. 152–153
"brokers" 197
Bryan, N. 62, 171
Bryant, P. C. 17, 156, 258
Bryk, A. 219
burnout 30
Burt, R. S. 195, 196
Burton, J. 127
business opportunities 29
Butterfield, D. A. 284

calculative forces 134, 135, 138, 139, 141
Calderon, C. J. 37–38
Caldwell, D. F. 56, 252
Call, M. L. 27, 34, 39
Campero, S. 285
Campion, M. A. 3, 4–5
capacity index 11
CAPS see cognitive-affective processing system theory
Caranikas-Walker, F. 63
career advancement 23, 287
Carson, K. D. 56
Carson, P. P. 56
Carsten, J. M. 86, 173, 209
Carter, M. Z. 187
Cascio, W. F. 65, 160–161, 247, 255
casual workers 100
Caulfield, N. 126, 286–287
causation 224–227
CC see continuance commitment
centralization 52, 55, 81
CEOs see chief executive officers
CET see context-emergent turnover
CFA see confirmatory factor analysis

change trajectories 157–160, 217–221, 227–230, 231, 300–301; *see also* time/temporality
Chatman, J. A. 56, 152, 252
Chen, G. 157–158
Chen, Y.-R. 195
chief executive officers (CEOs) 30–31, 37–38, 39
children 18, 20, 48, 143, 304; *see also* family
China: *guanxi* networks 195–196, 289; job mobility 276; leader humility 188–189; leader-member exchange 187; migrant assembly-line workers 2, 289–290, 291–292; transformational leadership 188
Choi, D. 188–189
Chugh, D. 283
coerced leavers 137, 140, 142–143
cognitive ability 48, 49, 174
cognitive-affective processing system theory (CAPS) 198–200, 251
cognitive dissonance 75, 243, 245
cohesion 51, 54–55, 96, 97, 151
Colarelli, S. M. 245
collective turnover 10–11, 31–34, 38, 39–40; contagion 193–194; future research 306; leadership 187, 188, 191–192; theories of 113–115
collectivism 35, 167, 195, 289, 306
Colquitt, J. A. 159
Colvin, A. 5–6
commitment 50, 51, 53, 150–155, 156, 257; collective turnover 114; commitment profiles 153–155, 159; constituent 291; cusp catastrophe model 94–96, 97; expatriates 286; Farrell-Rusbult investment model 87–88, 89; Hulin et al. model of labor market effects 101; impact on performance 127; leader-member exchange 187; Lee-Mitchell unfolding model 105; mindsets 3, 301, 302; Price-Mueller models 82; proximal withdrawal state theory 131, 132, 133; realistic job previews 243, 244; role states 55; Steers-Mowday multi-route model 90, 91, 93; structural equation modeling 224–227; trajectories 159, 219–221, 301
communication: cultural influences 166; direct and indirect 21; instrumental 51, 54, 81; leader 51, 54; network centrality 195; pay practices 259, 261; Price-Mueller models 81; realistic job previews 245
community embeddedness 122, 123, 129, 130, 144, 286–287
compensation *see* pay
competition 9–10, 24, 29
confirmatory factor analysis (CFA) 150, 221, 228, 230
conscientiousness 48, 49, 197, 200, 250, 251
conservation of resources (COR) theory 126–127, 129–130
constituent forces 134, 135, 138, 139, 141
constraints 135
construct validation 302
contagion 22, 23, 24, 124; future research 303–304; leader departures 192, 193–194; migrant assembly-line workers 290; performance-turnover relationship 161
context-emergent turnover (CET) 32, 38
contextualization 305–306
continuance commitment (CC) 132
contractual stayers 137, 138, 141
Cooper-Thomas, H. 157–158
coping 57, 60, 244
COR *see* conservation of resources theory
correlational designs 207, 208, 224, 306–307
Coser, R. L. 28
costs: Farrell-Rusbult investment model 88, 89; Hulin et al. model of labor market effects 98; job search 182; opportunity 26–27, 169; relocation 20–21; savings 31; of turnover 1, 24–25
Cotton, J. L. 47
counterproductive work behaviors (CWBs) 125, 132, 133, 135, 138–140, 141–143
coworker embeddedness 124
coworker satisfaction 51, 54–55, 156
Cox regression model 165, 215–217
Crampon, W. J. 151
Crenshaw, K. 282
Cropanzano, R. 166
cross-cultural generalizability 288–289, 305
culture 166–167, 196, 288–289, 291, 293
Cummings, L. L. 84
Curry, J. P. 224
cusp catastrophe model 3, 94–97

customer service 28, 33, 34
CWBs *see* counterproductive work behaviors

Dalal, R. 301
Dalton, D. R. 6, 17, 29
data analytics 265–266, 301
Davis, K. S. 242
Day, N. E. 208
Dean, R. A. 246
Deci, E. L. 133
decision paths 102–107
demographic characteristics 48–50, 276; *see also* diversity
demoralization 22–23, 260
Derous, E. 283
desirability of movement 2, 174; commitment profiles 153; Employment Opportunity Index 171, 172; March-Simon model 73, 74, 155; migrant assembly-line workers 290; performance-turnover relationship 161, 162, 163
developing countries 2
developmental climates 193
discrimination 276; intersectionality 282; methodological issues 284–285; racial minorities 279–282, 283; weighted application blanks 249; women 277, 278
dissatisfaction 2, 50; avoidable turnover 7; cusp catastrophe model 94; demoralization 22; desirability of movement 73, 74; Hom-Griffeth intermediate linkages model 78, 80; Hulin et al. model of labor market effects 98–99, 100–101; indirect communication 21; job search 183; leadership 186; Lee-Mitchell unfolding model 103, 105; March-Simon model 155–156, 168; Mobley et al. expanded model 85; Mobley turnover process model 76–77, 78; Muchinsky-Morrow model 86; pay 27, 53, 256, 260, 261; performance-turnover relationship 161–162; personality 198; Price-Mueller models 82–83; promotions 56; proximal withdrawal subtypes 137, 139; racial minorities 281; self-image 73; Steers-Mowday multi-route model 92, 93; structural equation modeling 222; transition stress 19; unemployment 173; unmet expectations 74, 75, 242; withdrawal behaviors 8, 65; *see also* job satisfaction

dissonance 75, 243, 245
distributive justice: pay and rewards 51, 53–54, 259, 262, 264; Price-Mueller models 81, 82
diversity 6, 276–293; collective turnover 114; enhancement of 25; international 286–293; loss of 24; minority female flight 282–286; racial minorities 279–282; women 276–279, 282–286
divorce 20
dominant analytical mindset (DAM) 39, 156, 170, 171, 207–208
Dorfman, P. W. 289
Dossett, D. L. 249
double jeopardy 282–286
Dougherty, T. W. 173
Dreher, G. F. 173
dual-career couples 18, 21
Dunford, B. B. 183
Dutton, J. E. 21
dysfunctional turnover 6, 7–8, 9, 17, 38–39, 304

Earnest, D. R. 243, 244–245
ease of movement 2, 167–174; commitment profiles 153; March-Simon model 73–74, 155, 167–168; migrant assembly-line workers 290; performance-turnover relationship 162, 163
Eberly, M. B. 32, 47, 257–258, 303
economic opportunities 169, 173; *see also* alternative employment opportunities
education 18, 48, 49, 174; March-Simon model 73, 156; Mobley et al. expanded model 83; weighted application blanks 249
eigenvector centrality 196–197
electronic monitoring 114, 115
embeddedness 3, 5, 57, 60, 122–129; additional embedding forces 123–125; collective turnover 114, 115; contextualization 305; cultural context 289; dark side of 143–144; dynamic trajectories 159; embedded stayers 137, 138; expatriates 286–287, 288; forms 125–126; leadership 186, 187, 191; multifocal model 127–130; person-centered analyses 301; proximal withdrawal subtypes 135–136, 143; relocation costs 20; shocks 303; socialization 254; stay interviews 265
emotional stability 48, 49, 251

employability 137, 162, 183–184, 243
employee guarding 3, 181, 190
employee referrals 241, 248, 249
Employment Opportunity Index (EOI) 171–173
empowerment 30, 54, 134–135
engaged stayers 137–141
engagement 57, 60, 241
EOI *see* Employment Opportunity Index
EPZs *see* export-oriented processing zones
equity 51, 53, 259, 260; *see also* fairness; justice
equity theory 2, 77
Erez, M. 3, 74, 122
erosion model 194–195
ethnic prominence 283–284, 285
ethnicity 48, 49, 279–286
evidence-based strategies 240, 241
evolutionary job search 183–186
executives: brokerage 197; humility 189; minority 281; positive effects of turnover 30–31; post-acquisition turnover 37–38
exhaustion 55, 57, 58, 144, 174
exit interviews 5, 8, 24, 106, 277
expanded turnover model 83–86
expatriates 20, 126, 286–288
expectancy theory 2, 85, 106
expectations 51, 53, 57, 60; collective turnover 114, 115; cultural influences 166; met-expectations model 74–76, 91, 242, 249; Mobley et al. expanded model 83, 84; pay 258–259, 260, 261, 262; realistic job previews 242, 244, 245; Steers-Mowday multi-route model 90, 91, 92, 93; weighted application blanks 249
expected utility 10, 63–64, 83, 84–86, 105, 223; *see also* subjective expected utility
exploratory path analysis 221, 222
export-oriented processing zones (EPZs) 2, 289–293
extraversion 48, 49, 197, 199, 251

fairness 54, 81, 241, 258, 259, 260–261
family: Chinese culture 196; cultural influences 166; family embeddedness 123–124, 129, 130, 196, 289, 306; family programs 7; family separation 20; future research 303; kinship responsibilities 48, 49, 81, 82, 83, 90; migrant assembly-line workers 291; normative forces 136; resistant leavers 143; structural equation modeling 223; work-family conflict 5, 7, 10, 144, 159
Farrell, D. 3, 87–90, 170, 217, 301
feedback: appraisals 260; engagement 241; low performance 164; socialization 241, 254–255; work design 255, 256
Feeley, T. H. 194–195
Feldman, D. C. 19, 85, 124–125, 143–144, 191, 194
Felps, W. 124
Fernandez, R. M. 285
Ferris, K. R. 161
Festinger, L. 75
field experiments 306
Field, H. S. 161
Finkelstein, S. 30–31
first-order factor (FOF) latent growth modeling 228–230
Fiske, S. T. 283
fit 57, 60, 251–252; assessing during selection 241; job embeddedness 122, 123, 125, 128–129; March-Simon model 73; proximal withdrawal subtypes 138
Fitzgerald, L. F. 278
Fitzgerald, M. P. 58
Folger, R. 54, 260
Forrest, C. R. 84
fringe benefits 19, 53, 98, 256, 257; *see also* benefits
functional turnover 6, 17, 29–30, 304

Gaertner, S. 47, 81, 209
Gardner, T. M. 190–191, 265
Gelfand, M. J. 123–124, 196, 289, 306
gender 48, 49, 276–279; minority female flight 282–286; pay differences 262; *see also* women
General Mills 263
generalization 288–289, 305, 306
Gerbing, D. W. 224
Gerhart, B. 162, 173
Giles, W. F. 161
glass ceiling 10
global supply chains 2, 286
Glomb, T. M. 107
goals: cognitive-affective processing system theory 198, 199; commitment to company 150, 151, 152; engagement 241; leader-member exchange 193; Mobley et al. expanded model 83
Goff, P. A. 284
Gomez-Mejia, L. R. 262

Gottfredson, R. K. 264
Gould, S. 259
Grant, A. M. 256
Greenberger, D. B. 259
Griffeth, R. W.: commitment 151; demographic characteristics 48, 49; Employment Opportunity Index 171–172; expanded turnover model 83–86; generalizability 305; intermediate linkages model 78–81; job content, motivation, and new constructs 57; job satisfaction 51–52, 156; met-expectations model 75; meta-analyses 47; minority turnover 279–280; Mobley et al. expanded model 85; Mobley turnover process model 78; pay 54, 258–259; perceived alternatives 60–62, 101, 168, 170–171; performance-turnover relationship 160–161, 163–165, 166, 209; Price-Mueller models 82; promotions 56; proximal withdrawal state theory 130–133, 135–136; research on turnover control 306; survival analysis 213; turnover destinations 21; Turnover Events and Shocks Scale 107–113; voluntary, dysfunctional and avoidable turnover 7–8; withdrawal behaviors 66; withdrawal cognitions 63, 64; withdrawal process 105
growth needs 58
guanxi networks 195–196, 289
Gupta, N. 65, 258
Gupta, V. 289

habituation 74, 168
Hachiya, D. 74, 97–101, 168–169
Hackman, J. R. 58, 255
Halbrook, R. 26
Hall, K. E. 108
Hambrick, D. C. 30–31
Hancock, J. I. 32–34, 37, 39, 156
Hand, H. H. 78, 83–86, 151
Hanges, P. J. 289
Hanisch, K. A. 9
Hanna, M. 48
Hanson, B. L. 253
Harrison, D. A. 8–9, 126, 165, 286, 287–288
Hausknecht, J. P. 11, 31–32, 38–40, 159, 301
hazard function 210–217
healthcare benefits 19, 53
Heavey, A. L. 113–114, 115

Heneman, R. L. 259, 263
Henning, J. B. 279
hierarchical linear modeling (HLM) 165–166, 219–220
high-performance work practices (HPWPs) 3, 128
Hill, J. W. 105
Hinkin, T. R. 158
HLM *see* hierarchical linear modeling
Hobfoll, S. E. 130
Hollenbeck, J. R. 6
Hollingsworth, A. T. 78, 170, 206
Holloran, S. D. 253
Holtom, B. C.: influence of March and Simon 74; job embeddedness 3, 122, 127; job satisfaction 158; shocks 303; surveys 108; unfolding model 105, 106
Holwerda, J. A. 11
Hom, P. W.: change trajectories 301; commitment 151–152; context-emergent turnover 32; contextualization 305; demographic characteristics 48, 49; generalizability 305; intermediate linkages model 78–81, 103; job content, motivation, and new constructs 57; job embeddedness 123, 289; job satisfaction 51–52, 159; leader humility 188–189; leader-member exchange 187; meta-analyses 47; minority female flight 282; minority turnover 279–280; networks 195–196; opportunity costs 26; pay 54, 258–259; perceived alternatives 60–62, 101, 170; performance-turnover relationship 165, 166–167, 209; pre-quitting behaviors 265; Price-Mueller models 82; proximal withdrawal state theory 10, 130–133, 134–136, 141–143, 302; realistic job previews 244, 246, 247; research on turnover control 306; shocks 303; structural equation modeling 222; survival analysis 213; turnover destinations 9, 10, 21; Turnover Events and Shocks Scale 107–113; unemployment 173; voluntary, dysfunctional and avoidable turnover 7–8; withdrawal behaviors 66; withdrawal cognitions 63, 64; withdrawal process 105; women 277
honesty 242–243, 245
honeymoon-hangover effect 3, 19, 21, 38, 159
Horner, S. O. 78, 170, 206

318 Index

Hough, L. M. 250
House, R. J. 289
HPWPs *see* high-performance work practices
HRM *see* human resource management
Hu, J. 264
Hulin, C. L.: alternative employment opportunities 168–169; commitment 151–152; contagion 194; dissatisfaction 80; influence of March and Simon 74; labor market effects 97–101; moods and work behaviors 301; standard research practice 206; temporal shifts in turnover 217; withdrawal behaviors 8, 9; withdrawal cognitions 92
human capital 11, 32, 37, 114, 174
human resource management (HRM) 115, 134–135; ability-motivation-opportunity model 114, 264; evidence-based strategies 240, 241; performance-enhancing 6, 135, 137, 142
humility 188–189
Humphrey, S. E. 255–256
Hunter, E. J. 21
Huselid, M. A. 208

IBM 31
identity: identity strain 126, 287–288, 292; leader departures 304; racial/ethnic 280, 281; relational identities 23; socialization 254
image theory 101–102, 106
incentive pay 53, 161, 165, 257
Inderrieden, E. J. 106
individual characteristics 48–50, 90
influence 2, 57, 59
instrumental communications 51, 54, 81
integration 51, 54–55, 81, 82
intentions to quit 50, 63, 64; alternative employment opportunities 169; commitment 151; Hulin et al. model of labor market effects 98–99; job satisfaction 157–158, 159; Mobley et al. expanded model 83, 84; Muchinsky-Morrow model 86–87; network centrality 196; perceived alternatives 170; person-centered approach 155; personality 197–198, 251; Price-Mueller models 81, 82; proximal withdrawal state theory 133–134, 143; Steers-Mowday multi-route model 90, 91, 94; transformational leadership 188;
Turnover Events and Shocks Scale 109, 110–112, 113; unemployment 173–174; work design 256
inter-role conflict 80, 81, 223
intermediate linkages model 78–81, 103
internal motivation 48, 49, 57, 58, 153
international diversity 286–293
internet 266, 305
"intersectional invisibility" 284
intersectionality 282
interviews 5, 8, 106, 235, 265
investment model 3, 87–90
involuntary turnover 3–6, 35, 39, 132–133; collective turnover 10; performance 161; proximal withdrawal subtypes 137, 140, 142; survival analysis 210

Jackofsky, E. F. 74, 161, 162
Jackson, D. N. 250
Jackson, M. C. 284
Japan 289
Jaros, S. J. 80
Javidan, M. 289
Jenkins, G. D. 65
Jiang, K. 113, 114, 264
job avoidance 65, 80–81, 96, 100–101, 223; *see also* work avoidance behaviors
job-based pay plans 262–263
job characteristics 2, 58, 73, 151, 255
job complexity 58, 246–247, 255
job content 56–59, 83, 245–246
job design 241
job embeddedness 3, 5, 57, 60, 122–129; additional embedding forces 123–125; collective turnover 114, 115; contextualization 305; cultural context 289; dark side of 143–144; dynamic trajectories 159; embedded stayers 137, 138; expatriates 286–287, 288; forms 125–126; leadership 186, 187, 191; multifocal model 127–130; person-centered analyses 301; proximal withdrawal subtypes 135–136, 143; relocation costs 20; shocks 303; socialization 254; stay interviews 265; *see also* proximal withdrawal state theory
job enrichment 255
job evaluation plans 261
job involvement 57, 58–59, 90, 91, 93
job offers 164, 183, 185; cognitive-affective processing system theory 198; contagion 194; future research

304–305; job offer leavers 137, 139; refusal of 243
job protection forces 135, 136, 137
job satisfaction 50, 51, 155–160, 257; commitment 150; contagion 194; desirability of movement 174; ease of movement 174; economic opportunity 173; employment levels 169; expatriates 286; expectations 53; Farrell-Rusbult investment model 88, 89; growth needs 58; Hom-Griffeth intermediate linkages model 79; honeymoon-hangover effect 19; Hulin et al. model of labor market effects 97, 98–99, 100; leader humility 188, 189; Lee-Mitchell unfolding model 103; March-Simon model 73, 74, 155–156, 168; measurement window 209; met-expectations model 75; Mobley et al. expanded model 83, 84, 85; Mobley turnover process model 76–77, 78; Muchinsky-Morrow model 86–87; peer-group relations 54–55; performance-turnover relationship 161–162, 163, 164; personality 198, 251; Price model 81; proximal withdrawal state theory 131, 133, 135–136; realistic job previews 244; reward contingency 65–67; sexual harassment 278–279; stayers 22, 23, 38; Steers-Mowday multi-route model 90, 91; structural equation modeling 223, 224–227; trajectories 157–160, 217–219, 301; withdrawal behaviors 9; *see also* dissatisfaction
job scope 57, 58
job search 63–65, 181, 182–186, 305; coworker embeddedness 124; dynamic trajectories 159; Employment Opportunity Index 173; Farrell-Rusbult investment model 89, 90; Hom-Griffeth intermediate linkages model 78–79; Hulin et al. model of labor market effects 100, 101; Lee-Mitchell unfolding model 104; March-Simon model 168; Mobley turnover process model 77; networking 172; performance-turnover relationship 163; pre-quitting behaviors 191; proximal withdrawal state theory 135, 138–140; stayer profiles 155; Steers-Mowday multi-route model 90, 91–92; structural equation modeling 223

job security 91, 125, 263
job tension 94–95, 96, 97
Johnson, A. C. 84
Johnson, M. D. 188
Jones, G. R. 254
Joo, H. 264
Jung, I. 259
justice: dynamic trajectories 159–160; pay and rewards 51, 53–54, 241, 258, 259, 260–261, 262, 264; Price-Mueller models 81, 82

Kabins, A. H. 153, 154
Kacmar, K. M. 191
Kammeyer-Mueller, J. D. 107–108, 157, 160
Kanfer, R. 185
Katz, J. 289
Kedia, B. L. 37–38
Kehoe, R. R. 264
Kiazad, K. 127–130
Kinicki, A. J. 80, 222
kinship responsibilities 48, 49; Mobley et al. expanded model 83; Price-Mueller models 81, 82; Steers-Mowday multi-route model 90; *see also* family
Klein, H. 152–153
Klotz, A. C. 21
knowledge 30–31, 37
knowledge-based pay plans 262, 263
knowledge management 40
Konovsky, M. A. 54, 260
Koopman, J. 159
Krackhardt, D. M. 17, 23, 181, 194
Kraimer, M. L. 126, 287–288, 291
Kramer, M. 253
Kristof-Brown, A. L. 251–252
Kulik, C. T. 21, 285

labor market 173, 174, 305; Hulin et al. model of labor market effects 97–101; job search 183–184; Mobley et al. expanded model 83, 85; Muchinsky-Morrow model 87
Lam 29
Lam, H. 301
Lance, C. E. 161–162, 230–231
lateness 65, 66, 199
latent growth modeling (LGM) 227–234, 300–301
latent variable (LV) structural models 222–227
Lawler, E. E. 261

Lawton, G. W. 85
leader-member exchange (LMX) 51, 54, 186–187, 192–193
leadership 2, 51, 54, 181, 186–194; humility 188–189; leader departures 191–194, 304; motivational behaviors 187–188; prevention of turnover 190–191
Leblanc, P. V. 263
Ledford, G. E. 263
Lee, T. W.: change trajectories 301; collective turnover 306; context-emergent turnover 32; influence of March and Simon 74; interactive processes 38; job embeddedness 3, 122–123, 126, 127, 289; job satisfaction 158; meta-analyses 47; non-work influences 92; organizational interventions 40; Price-Mueller models 82; proximal withdrawal state theory 130–133, 135–136; qualitative research 106, 235; rewards 257–258; shocks 102–105, 106–107, 108, 142, 303; Steers-Mowday multi-route model 93; turnover destinations 21, 304; unfolding model 101–107, 141
legal forces 135, 136, 138, 140, 141
Lepak, D. P. 264
Li, H. J. 191
Li, J. J. 5, 32, 135–136, 143, 303
"lift-outs" 304
links: job embeddedness 122, 123, 125, 126, 128–129; link defections 303–304; networks 195
Liu, D. 158, 303
Livingston, R. W. 284
Livingstone, L. P. 65, 67, 161
LMX *see* leader-member exchange
Locke, E. A. 76, 84
locus of control 48, 49, 198
logistic regression 207, 208, 254
logit hazard function 213–215
Loher, B. T. 58
Louis, M. R. 75–76, 253
loyalty 56, 187; *guanxi* networks 195; pay expectations 262; skill-based pay 263; women 48

Madden, T. J. 228–230
Maertz, C. P. 4–5, 290–291
management, participative 54
managerial motivation 57, 59
manufacturing 2, 65, 289–293

March, J. G. 2, 72–74, 77, 84; ease of movement 167–168, 169, 170, 171, 174; expatriates 288; intentions to quit 91; job satisfaction 155–156; job search 182; perceived alternatives 76; performance 161; personality 197; structural relationships 221; unavoidable turnover 7
marital status 48, 49
marital strain 20, 21
Marriott Corporation 28
mate guarding 181, 190
Mathieu, J. E. 151, 152
Matta, F. K. 159
McDaniel, L. S. 105
McEvoy, G. M. 65, 160–161, 247, 255
McKay, P. F. 281
McKee, D. N. 39, 156
Meder, D. 26
MEF *see* multifocal embeddedness framework
Meglino, B. M. 76, 78, 83–86, 151, 246
men: ease of movement 73; pay satisfaction 260, 262; subordinate male target hypothesis 283
mentors 24, 193, 241, 253, 254, 255
merit pay 27, 91, 165, 260, 263–264
Merluzzi, J. 196
met-expectations model 74–76, 91, 242, 249
meta-analyses 47–67; collective turnover 32–34, 113–114; commitment 151; ease of movement 168; job satisfaction 156; performance moderators 35–36, 38; performance-turnover relationship 160, 161; person-job fit 252; personality 250, 251; post-acquisition turnover 37; realistic job previews 242, 243, 244–245, 247; rewards 257; socialization 254–255; unemployment 174; work design 255, 256
methodological approaches 82, 170, 206–235; attrition-discrimination models 284–285; Cox regression model 165, 215–217; dominant analytical mindset 39, 156, 170, 171, 207–208; empirical research 306–307; latent growth modeling 227–234, 300–301; logistic regression 207, 208, 254; qualitative research 106–107, 235; random coefficient modeling 217–221, 227, 300; recommendations 300–302; standard research practice 206–207,

209; structural equation modeling 37, 79–81, 114, 164, 207, 222–227, 244, 300; survival analysis 80–81, 154–155, 209–215, 217; testing causal models 221
Methot, J. R. 23
Mexico 2, 289–291
Meyer, J. P. 130, 152, 153, 302
MFF *see* minority female flight
Miceli, M. P. 259, 260
Michaels, C. E. 85, 99
middle managers (MMs) 188–189
migrant workers 289–292
Milkman, K. L. 283
millennials 7
Milliken, F. 21
minorities 1, 6, 48, 249, 279–286
minority female flight (MFF) 282–286
Mischel, W. 198
Mishkin, B. H. 253
Mitchell, T. R.: influence of March and Simon 74; job embeddedness 3, 122–123, 125, 127, 289; job satisfaction 158; leader humility 188; meta-analyses 47; Price-Mueller models 82; proximal withdrawal state theory 130–133, 135–136; rewards 257–258; shocks 102–105, 106–107, 108, 142, 303; turnover destinations 21; unfolding model 101–107, 141
Mitra, A. 65
MMs *see* middle managers
Mobil Corporation 18
mobility 163, 171–172, 185, 276, 281; *see also* ease of movement
Mobley, W. H. 2, 47, 76–78; assessment of motives 5; commitment 151; consequences of turnover 17; dissatisfaction 80; ease of movement 170; expanded turnover model 83–86; influence of March and Simon 74; intermediate linkages 103; job satisfaction 173; job search 182; personality 197; Price-Mueller models 82; reasons for attrition 4; standard research practice 206; Steers-Mowday multi-route model 92; withdrawal process 105
Moeller, N. L. 58
Molloy, J. 152–153
monitoring 114, 115
moral forces 134, 135
morale 22–23, 31, 111, 253, 263
Morgeson, F. P. 255–256, 303

Morita, J. G. 217
Morrow, P. C. 85, 86–87
Morse, B. 107–113
Mossholder, K. W. 161, 195
motivation: collective turnover 114; extrinsic 133, 257; internal 48, 49, 57, 58, 153; job search 185; leader motivational behaviors 187–188; managerial 57, 59; pay 264; proximal withdrawal state theory 130; theories of 2; work design 256
Motowidlo, S. J. 85
Mount, M. K. 197, 250
"movement capital" 305
Mowday, R. T. 74, 80, 82, 90–94, 170
Muchinsky, P. M. 85, 86–87, 250
Mueller, C. W. 22, 23, 81–83, 170, 222
Mullainathan, S. 284
multifocal embeddedness framework (MEF) 127–130
multilevel modeling 235
multiple regression 207
Murnane, R. J. 28–29
"mutual separations" 5

Nahrgang, J. D. 187, 255–256
National Longitudinal Survey of Youth (NLSY) 174
Near, J. P. 259
negative job shock leavers 137, 139, 141–142
network centrality 181–182, 194–195, 196–197
network closure 2
networking 171–172
neuroticism 197, 198, 200
new business ventures 31
Ng, T. W. H. 124–125, 143–144, 191, 194
Nishii, L. H. 284
Noe, R. A. 58
normative forces 135, 136, 138, 140, 291
Norris, D. R. 161
Northern Telecom 263
Nyberg, A. J. 27, 32, 39–40, 193

OCBs *see* organizational citizenship behaviors
occupational embeddedness 125, 128
Occupational Outlook Quarterly 173
OCP *see* organizational culture profile
OCQ *see* organizational commitment questionnaire
older employees 50

Oldham, G. R. 58, 255
Olive Garden 28
OLS *see* ordinary least squares regression analysis
on-the-job (OTJ) embeddedness 125, 127, 128
openness to experience 48, 49, 197, 198, 199, 250, 251
opportunity costs 26–27, 169
ordinary least squares (OLS) regression analysis 207, 208, 209, 217
O'Reilly, C. A. 56, 152, 252
organizational citizenship behaviors (OCBs) 8–9, 66, 67; collective turnover 114; commitment 152; engaged stayers 137–141; job embeddedness 126, 127, 129–130; leader-member exchange 193; proximal withdrawal state theory 132, 133, 134, 135, 138–140
organizational climate 27, 40, 52, 55–56; developmental 193; diversity 280–281; future research 303–304; Mobley et al. expanded model 83
organizational commitment questionnaire (OCQ) 151–152
organizational culture profile (OCP) 252
organizational equilibrium 72–73, 155, 171
organizational identification 192–193
organizational memory 24
organizational prestige 57, 59, 60, 168
organizational size 57, 73, 83, 168
orientation 25, 241, 253, 255
Ou, A. Y. 188–189
Ovalle, II, N. K. 63
Owens, B. P. 188

Palich, L. E. 213
Parfyonova, N. M. 153
Park, T. Y. 114
Parker, S. K. 256
participation: commitment 127; job satisfaction 51; March-Simon model 73, 156; participative management 54; pay design 260–261; Price-Mueller models 81
Passantino, L. G. 159
pay 256–264; collective turnover 114; evidence-based HRM strategies 241; pay dispersion 258; pay satisfaction 51, 53–54, 156, 256, 259–263; performance relationship 161; structural model 81; Turnover Events and Shocks Scale 112; *see also* rewards; wages
Payne, S. C. 154–155
peer-group relations 54–55, 57, 60
Peltokorpi, V. 144, 289
Penley, L. E. 259
pensions 19, 53
perceived alternatives (PA) 10, 60–65, 76, 101; construct validation 302; ease of movement 168–173; Hom-Griffeth intermediate linkages model 78–79; Hulin et al. model of labor market effects 100; March-Simon model 73–74; Mobley et al. expanded model 84–85; Mobley turnover process model 77, 78; Muchinsky-Morrow model 87; performance-turnover relationship 164; proximal withdrawal state theory 131; *see also* alternative employment opportunities
perceived behavioral control 228–230
perceived volitional control 5, 136–137, 143
Perera, S. 21
performance 3, 31, 160–167; collective turnover 11, 31–34, 38, 114; commitment 151; cultural context 289; cusp catastrophe model 96; functional turnover 6, 29–30; job embeddedness 126–127, 129; measurement window 209; Mobley et al. expanded model 85; optimal level of turnover 37; pay related to 263–264; performance-enhancing HRM 134–135, 137, 142; performance orientation cultures 167; personality 251; post-acquisition turnover 37–38; proximal withdrawal state theory 135, 138–140; quality of leavers and replacements 27; slackers 141; Steers-Mowday multi-route model 90, 91, 92, 93; withdrawal behaviors 8–9, 65–67; *see also* productivity
Perrewé, P. L. 152
person-centered analyses 155, 301–302
person-job fit 252
personal characteristics 48–50, 90, 151
personality 48, 49, 182, 197–200, 250–251, 252, 307
Pettman, B. O. 74
Phillips, J. M. 243
Pieper, J. R. 248
planned leavers 137, 139

Ployhart, R. E. 27, 32, 39–40, 157–158, 300
Podsakoff, P. 224, 227
Poland, T. D. 242
politics 259, 261
Porter, L. W. 23, 74–76, 93, 151, 152, 181, 194, 217
Posner, B. Z. 253
post-acquisition turnover 37–38, 39
Powell, G. N. 253, 284
power distance 167, 289
Pratto, F. 283
pre-quitting behaviors (PQBs) 190–191, 265
precarious employment 290–293
predictive analytics 265–266
preferences 134–135
pregnancy 4, 7
Premack, S. L. 242, 243, 245, 247
prestige 57, 59, 60, 168
Price, J. L. 2, 22, 23, 81–83, 170, 222
productivity 1, 114, 305; collective turnover 32–34; improvements in 29–30; leader-member exchange 193; loss of 24, 25, 26–27; Muchinsky-Morrow model 86; *see also* performance
professional services 28
professionalism 57, 59, 81, 82, 83
profit 34
promotions 22, 52, 56; gender inequity 277; job embeddedness 144; pay plans 262; performance-turnover relationship 162, 163, 165; Steers-Mowday multi-route model 91; structural model 81; Turnover Events and Shocks Scale 111
proximal withdrawal state theory (PWST) 10, 130–143; perceived volitional control 136–137; person-centered analyses 301, 302; staying/leaving preferences 132–134, 137–143; subtypes 132–134, 137–143
Prussia, G. E. 63
psychological contract 57, 166
psychological withdrawal 98, 100
Purl, J. 108, 109, 113
PWST *see* proximal withdrawal state theory

Qin, X. 291–292
qualitative research 106–107, 235
quality of service 27–29, 33, 34

R&D 30
race 48, 49, 279–286
racism 282, 284, 285
Rae, B. 21
Ramesh, A. 123–124, 196, 289, 306
random coefficient modeling (RCM) 217–221, 227, 300
Raudenbush, S. 219
Raver, J. L. 284
realistic job previews (RJPs) 75, 76, 213–215, 216–217, 240–247, 255
recruitment 24, 25, 27, 241, 247–248
referrals 24, 25, 241, 248, 249
Reichers, A. E. 152
Reilly, R. R. 247
Reina, C. 188
relational identification theory 187, 193
relational identities 23
relocation 18, 20–21, 136; *see also* spousal relocation
Ren, H. 126, 287–288
repatriates 126, 286–288
resignation styles 3
resistant leavers 140, 142–143
resource-based view 37
resources: conservation of resources theory 126–127, 129–130; Farrell-Rusbult investment model 88; job embeddedness 127–128, 129, 144; job search 184; networks 195–196
retirement: proximal withdrawal subtypes 137, 140, 142; voluntary and involuntary turnover 4
rewards 256–264; evidence-based HRM strategies 241; Farrell-Rusbult investment model 88, 89; Mobley et al. expanded model 83; reward contingency 51, 53–54, 65–67, 161–162, 164–165, 264
risk aversion 198
RJPs *see* realistic job previews
Roberson, L. 279–281
Roberson, Q. M. 159
role ambiguity 51, 55, 244
role clarity 51, 55, 244, 245, 253
role conflict 51, 55, 80, 81, 223
role overload 51, 55, 81
Rosette, A. S. 284
Rosse, J. G. 262
Rothstein, M. 250
routinization 57, 58, 81, 114
Roznowski, M. 74, 97–101, 168–169

Rubenstein, A. L.: demographic characteristics 48, 49; dynamic trajectories 159–160; job content, motivation, and new constructs 57, 58; job embeddedness 144; job satisfaction 50, 51–52, 156–157; meta-analyses 47–48; minority turnover 279; perceived alternatives 61, 168; performance-turnover relationship 161; promotions 56; rewards 53–54, 257–258; unemployment 174; withdrawal behaviors 66; withdrawal cognitions 63, 64
rural-urban migration 289–290, 291–292
Rusbult, C. E. 3, 87–90, 170, 217, 301
Ryan, A. M. 283
Ryan, R. M. 133

Sablynski, C. J. 3, 74, 122, 127
sacrifice: behavioral forces 136; job embeddedness 122, 123, 125, 126, 128–129, 144; proximal withdrawal subtypes 138, 140
Sager, J. 80
Salamin, A. 165, 166–167
salaries 51, 53–54, 98, 162, 256–263; *see also* pay; rewards; wages
Sanfey, A. G. 166
Sardeshmukh, S. R. 21
Sarkar, J. 264
Schein, E. H. 253–254
Schlachter, S. D. 248
Schmalenberg, C. 253
Schneider, J. 84
Scholl, R. W. 262
Schwab, D. P. 65, 163
Schwartz, B. 276–277
Scott, B. A. 159
second-order factor (SOF) latent growth modeling 230–234
selection 24, 27; costs 25; evidence-based HRM strategies 241; fit 252; selection process performance 66, 67; selection tests 307; self-selection 243, 245
self-determination theory 153
self-image 73, 156
self-regulation 185, 186, 199–200
self-selection 243, 245
Sellaro, C. L. 79
SEM *see* structural equation modeling
seniority benefits, loss of 19
Seo, J. J. 187, 188–189
Serlie, A. W. 283

service quality 27–29, 33, 34
Sesko, A. K. 284
SEU *see* subjective expected utility
sexism 282, 284, 285
sexual harassment 277, 278–279, 282
Shaffer, M. A. 126, 286, 287–288
Shao, L. 289
Shapiro, D. L. 192–194
Shaw, J. D. 114, 258, 301
Sheridan, J. E. 3, 26, 27, 55–56, 94–97
shocks: expatriates 287, 288; future research 302–303; identification with leaders 181; job embeddedness 127; leader departures 192, 193; migrant assembly-line workers 290; negative job shock leavers 137, 139, 141–142; neglect of leadership antecedents 186; neurotics 200; performance-turnover relationship 164, 166; predictive analytics 266; Turnover Events and Shocks Scale 107–113; unfolding model 102–105, 106–107, 164, 183, 302–303
Shoda, Y. 198
Sidanius, J. 283
"side bets" 151, 152
Simon, H. A. 2, 72–74, 77, 84; ease of movement 167–168, 169, 170, 171, 174; expatriates 288; intentions to quit 91; job satisfaction 155–156; job search 182; perceived alternatives 76; performance 161; personality 197; structural relationships 221; unavoidable turnover 7
Singer, J. D. 28–29, 212
skill-based pay plans 262–263
slackers 137, 138, 141
Sluss, D. M. 187
Smith, F. J. 151
SMTH *see* subordinate male target hypothesis
social capital 37, 128, 143–144; employee referrals 248; gender differences 277; Japan 289; leader departures 304; network centrality 196
social cues 194
social desirability 250–251, 257
social information processing theory 124
social networks 3, 20, 22, 23, 144, 181–182, 194–197
social support 20, 40, 254, 255, 256
socialization 19, 25, 38, 159, 241, 252–255
Soelberg, C. 32–34

Solectron 29
Spector, P. E. 85, 86, 99, 173, 209
Spector, W. D. 28
spousal relocation 5, 7, 18, 21; future research 303; job search 185; proximal withdrawal state theory 136; Steers-Mowday multi-route model 91
standard research practice (SRP) 206–207, 209
Stanley, L. J. 153–154
State Farm 28
Staw, B. M. 23, 27, 200
stay interviews 265
stayers: consequences of turnover 17–18, 22–23, 39; Lee-Mitchell unfolding model 106–107; methodological approaches 209; person-centered approach 155; psychology of staying 122–144; Turnover Events and Shocks Scale 110–112, 113
Steel, R. P.: dominant analytical mindset 207, 208; job search 168–169, 183–185; perceived alternatives 62, 170–171; promotions 56; standard research practice 206; withdrawal cognitions 63
Steers, R. M. 74–76, 80, 82, 90–94, 151, 170
STEM jobs 1, 285
stress 19, 57, 58, 108; Chinese migrants 291; cusp catastrophe model 94–95; job embeddedness 144; realistic job previews 244; role states 55; stressful jobs 30; unemployment rates 174
structural equation modeling (SEM) 37, 79–81, 114, 164, 207, 222–227, 244, 300
Stuchlik, M. 26
Sturman, M. C. 159, 165–166, 167, 289
subjective expected utility (SEU) 10, 63, 182, 185
subordinate male target hypothesis (SMTH) 283
supervision 51, 54; abusive 144; Chinese migrant workers 292; evidence-based HRM strategies 241; March-Simon model 73, 156; Mobley et al. expanded model 83; structural model 81; supervisory relationship quality 114, 115
supportiveness 52, 55
surveys 5, 18, 108, 207–208
survival analysis 80–81, 154–155, 209–215, 217

Suszko, M. 244
Sweeney, P. D. 262
Swider, B. W. 251
Switzerland 166–167

Takada, H. A. 28
teamwork 24, 27, 187
technology 30–31, 305
tenure: collective turnover 114; commitment profiles 154; demographic characteristics 50; March-Simon model 73, 74; Mobley et al. expanded model 83; Steers-Mowday multi-route model 90
termination practices 135, 136, 137
TESS *see* Turnover Events and Shocks Scale
Tett, R. P. 250
Tharenou, P. 126, 286–287
theory of planned behavior (TPB) 2, 228–230
theory of reasoned action 2
Thomas, D. A. 281
Thomas, M. A. 284
Thorpe, S. 26
time/temporality 39, 156–160, 208–209, 301; commitment profiles 154–155; Cox regression model 215–217; Farrell-Rusbult investment model 89; latent growth modeling 227–228, 230–234; random coefficient modeling 217–221; survival analysis 209–215; *see also* change trajectories
Todor, W. D. 17
top management: humility 189; positive effects of turnover 30–31; post-acquisition turnover 37–38, 39; social capital 144; *see also* leadership
TPB *see* theory of planned behavior
training 48, 49; costs 24, 25; evidence-based HRM strategies 241; Farrell-Rusbult investment model 88; movement capital 174; Price-Mueller models 81; socialization 253; Turnover Events and Shocks Scale 109, 112
transformational leadership 187–188
transition stress 19
trapped stayers 137, 138, 141
Trevor, C. O. 31–32, 38–40, 162, 163, 165–166, 174, 193
Turban, D. B. 20–21
Turbin, M. S. 262

turnover: avoidable and unavoidable 7–8; causes and correlates of 47–67; classic antecedents 150–174; consequences for leavers 17, 18–21, 38; consequences for organizations 24–38, 40; consequences for stayers 17–18, 22–23, 39; controlling 240–266, 306–307; cultural context 288–289; destinations 9–10, 21, 38–39, 132, 138–140, 304–305; functional and dysfunctional 6, 17, 304; future research directions 300–307; methodological approaches 206–235; migrant assembly-line workers 289–293; positive effects of 29–31, 40; racial minorities 279–286; significance of 1–3; theories of 72–115; understudied antecedents 181–200; voluntary and involuntary 3–6; women 276–279, 282–286; *see also* collective turnover; intentions to quit; withdrawal behaviors

Turnover Events and Shocks Scale (TESS) 107–113

Tuttle, M. L. 47, 250

Ulrich, D. 26
unavoidable turnover 7–8, 34
uncertainty avoidance 167
unemployment 168–169, 173–174; Hulin et al. model of labor market effects 97, 98–99; job search 185–186; Mobley et al. expanded model 83; Muchinsky-Morrow model 86–87; perceived alternatives 171; proximal withdrawal state theory 136; structural equation modeling 223
unfolding model 101–107, 141, 164, 166, 183, 266, 286, 302–303, 304
United States: assembly-line workers 289, 292–293; diversity 276; *Occupational Outlook Quarterly* 173; performance-turnover relationship 166–167; racial minorities 281, 285; socialization 252–253; UCEA models 123, 288, 289, 291
unmet expectations 74–76, 242

values: cognitive-affective processing system theory 198, 199; commitment to company 150, 151; job embeddedness 125; migrant assembly-line workers 291; Mobley et al. expanded model 83, 84, 85; organizational culture 252; personal 56; professional 59; realistic job previews 244; Steers-Mowday multi-route model 90, 91, 93
van Hooft, E. A. J. 185
Van Iddekinge, C. H. 265
Van Maanen, J. 253–254
Vandenberg, R. 153–154, 230–231, 300
Vandenberghe, C. 130, 153–154
Vardaman, J. M.: cross-cultural perspectives 288, 289, 305; culture 166; dominant analytical mindset 39; expatriates 286, 287, 288; functional and dysfunctional turnover 17; job satisfaction 156; network centrality 196
visibility 73–74, 163, 164–165, 168, 305
Vogel, R. 124
voluntary turnover 3–6, 7–8, 35; collective turnover 10; cost savings 31; ease of movement 174; methodological approaches 207; performance-turnover relationship 161, 162, 166; realistic job previews 244–245, 247; survival analysis 210; women 276–279

WABs *see* weighted application blanks; work avoidance behaviors
wages 18, 73, 98, 156, 256–263; *see also* pay; rewards
Waldman, D. A. 187, 188
Wanberg, C. R. 107, 185, 186
Wang, D. 159
Wanous, J. P. 242, 243, 245, 246, 247
Washington, E. F. 284
Weekley, J. 27
weighted application blanks (WABs) 48, 50, 182, 241, 248–249, 257, 276
Weinhardt, J. 107–113
Weiss, H. 301
Welch, E. 301
Wemmerus, V. 170
Wheeler, A. R. 126–127
Willett, J. B. 28–29, 212
Williams, C. R. 6, 65, 67, 161
Williams, J. C. 284, 285–286
Williams, L. J. 224, 226, 227
withdrawal behaviors 8–9, 47–48, 65–67; cusp catastrophe model 94–96; Hulin et al. model of labor market effects 98, 100, 101; Mobley et al. expanded model 83, 85; Muchinsky-Morrow model 86; proximal withdrawal state theory 135; sexual harassment 278–279; Steers-Mowday multi-route model 91–92

withdrawal cognitions 47, 50, 63; change trajectories 301; commitment 150; expatriates 286; Farrell-Rusbult investment model 89; Hom-Griffeth intermediate linkages model 79, 80–81; latent growth modeling 232–234; proximal withdrawal state theory 133–134; realistic job previews 244; Steers-Mowday multi-route model 92; structural equation modeling 223; unemployment 173

withdrawal intentions 78

women 1, 6, 48, 276–279; child-bearing 18; family programs 7; Mexican 143; minority female flight 282–286; pay differences 262; weighted application blanks 249

Woo, S. E. 143, 155, 251

work avoidance behaviors (WABs) 132, 133, 134, 138–140, 141–143; *see also* job avoidance

work design 255–256

work-family conflict 5, 7, 10, 144, 159

work satisfaction 57, 58; *see also* job satisfaction

working conditions 8, 50, 90, 92; cultural influences 166; Hulin et al. model of labor market effects 98; migrant assembly-line workers 290–291; transformational leadership 187

Wright, P. M. 264

Wyatt Company 264

Xiao, Z. 195–196
Xu, X. 154–155

young employees 18, 73
Youngblood, S. A. 85, 173

Zajac, D. 151, 152
Zhang, Z. 185
Zhu, J. 185
Zimmerman, R. D. 197, 198–200, 251

Made in the USA
Coppell, TX
01 June 2021